CHAMBERS

School

SCIENCE
DICTIONARY

CHAMBERS

CHAMBERS

An imprint of Chambers Harrap Publishers Ltd
7 Hopetoun Crescent
Edinburgh, EH7 4AY

First published in UK by Chambers Harrap Publishers Ltd 2003

Based on the hardcover edition of The American Heritage® Student Science Dictionary by the Editors of the American Heritage® dictionaries.

Copyright 2002 by Houghton Mifflin Company. Adapted by arrangement with Houghton Mifflin Company.

Study Supplement © Chambers Harrap Publishers Ltd 2003

ISBN 0550 10070 9

Cover artwork © Alfred Pasieka, supplied by Science Photo Library

Designed and typeset by Chambers Harrap Publishers Ltd, Edinburgh
Printed in Italy by Rotolito Lombarda SpA

Chambers Contributors

Project Editor and Publishing Manager
Patrick White

Assistant Editor
Susanna Flett

Editorial Assistance
Susan Donaldson
Amanda Jones

UK Educational Consultants
Ann and Patrick Fullick

Prepress Manager
Sharon McTeir

Prepress Controllers
Vienna Leigh
Paula McCulloch

CHAMBERS

SCIENCE
DICTIONARY

Did You Know?

acceleration
acid rain
adaptation
aerodynamics
alchemy
allergy
amber
antibody
artificial intelligence
aspirin
atmospheric pressure
bat
battery
benzene
bicarbonate of soda
big bang
biomass
bird
black hole
blood group
brain
Burgess Shale
cactus
cancer
capillary action
carbon
cathode-ray tube
Celsius
centripetal force
charge
circadian rhythm
compound eye
conduction
current
cyclone
desert
DNA
Dolly the sheep
Doppler effect
dwarf star
earthquake
eclipse
electromagnetic radiation
endorphin
enzyme

evolution
fat
fault
fibre optics
fluorescence
force
fungus
gene
glass
Gondwanaland
gravity
grey water
heavy water
hologram
hormone
infrared
Internet
iridium
keratin
laser
lightning
magnetism
mimicry
mirror
moon
neutrino
nuclear reactor
oxidation
ozone
pixel
plate tectonics
program
pulsar
quasar
radioactivity
radiocarbon dating
rainforest
red blood cell
relativity
sickle cell anaemia
sleep
solar cell
solar system
solution
sound
space-time

stem cell
subatomic particle
sublimation
symbiosis
tail
thermodynamics
transpiration
transplant
turbojet
ultrasound
vaccine
vitamin
wetland
whale
worm
zero

Usage

bacterium
berry
bug
byte
data
deduction
electronic
endemic
fruit
germ
heritable
hypothesis
infectious
light year
megabyte
metal
meteor
mitosis
nuclear
refraction
revolution
stalactite
temperature
tidal wave
vapour
velocity
weight

Word History

algebra
amphibian
brontosaurus
calculus
chlorophyll
element
entomology
gastropod
helium
humour
hydrophobia
influenza
mercury
noble gas
oxygen
pahoehoe
planet
rhinoceros
Rigel

Biography

Archimedes
Bohr, Neils
Copernicus, Nicolaus
Darwin, Charles
Einstein, Albert
Franklin, Benjamin
Galileo Galilei
Harvey, William
Herschel, William and
  Caroline
Hutton, James
Jenner, Edward
Lavoisier, Antoine
Leeuwenhoek, Anton
  van
Mendel, Gregor
Newton, Isaac
Pasteur, Louis
Pauling, Linus
Priestley, Joseph
Tesla, Nikola
Vesalius, Andreas

Understanding basic science means understanding its vocabulary. Each field of science is distinguished by a group of important concepts that scientists use to look at and explain what happens in the natural world. The *Chambers School Science Dictionary* is designed to help you understand these concepts through an understanding of the language that describes them. The dictionary explains the meanings of scientific terms in a straightforward way, but at the same time encourages the reader to learn more complex vocabulary.

Even basic science raises large questions that defy simple explanations. For this reason many of the entries in this book go beyond the usual one-sentence definition to include additional information of various kinds. For example, the entry for **glacier** tells you not only what a glacier is but also how it forms and how it moves. Other entries, such as **eclipse**, include extended definitions for related terms – in this case, **solar eclipse** and **lunar eclipse**. And entries for more than a hundred of the most interesting and important scientific terms, such as **big bang, DNA**, and **plate tectonics**, feature *Did You Know?* panels with lively, in-depth explanations of the scientific phenomena that make our world such a fascinating place.

This dictionary includes other kinds of explanatory notes as well. We often use scientific terms loosely in our everyday language, unaware of the exactness that scientists like to observe. For many of these words the dictionary includes *Usage* panels that discuss these differences. For example, would you call a tomato a *berry*? Do you think of a cucumber as a *fruit*? The notes at **berry** and **fruit** explain why botanists would answer "yes" to these questions, even though most other people would say "no." And the note at **infectious** tells you the distinction that scientists make between this word and the very similar words *contagious* and *communicable*.

Word History panels discuss the origins and often surprising history of scientific terms. Thus the note at **calculus** tells you how a simple Latin word meaning "pebble" came to be used for a sophisticated form of mathematics. And because the history of science is full of inspiring stories of people struggling to solve difficult problems, this book includes more than 300 entries for men and women from around the world who have developed the scientific knowledge we have today. Some of their most important discoveries, and some of their failures too, are described in the *Biography* panels at such entries as **Archimedes, Darwin** and **Pasteur**.

Because we learn not just from words but from images too, this dictionary includes more than 400 full-colour photographs and drawings to complement its definitions. Together with their captions, these images bring complicated ideas and structures to life in a way that a definition alone sometimes can't. The book also includes a number of full-page illustrated panels (what we call *A Closer Look*), as well as a number of tables and charts. See the Table of Contents for a list of these features.

This dictionary has been written to help students at GCSE and Higher level in their science studies. However, it is hoped that it will not only help its readers to pass exams, but also to encourage students to see how science affects all our daily lives. We hope that this book conveys the wonder and excitement of science, rendering it both infectious and contagious.

STRUCTURE OF ENTRIES

guideword

Compare cross-reference
use this to learn other words
that make important distinctions
in a subject area

art caption
provides
additional
explanation

derivative

nested entry
defines a closely
related term that is
derived from the
entry word

expanding universe

expanding universe A model of the universe in which the volume of the universe is expanding. It is based on the idea that the red shift in light from distant galaxies is evidence that all galaxies are moving away from one another. *See panels at* big bang, Doppler effect.

expansion 1. An increase in size, volume or quantity, usually due to heating. When substances are heated, their particles move faster, causing the substance to expand. 2. A number or other mathematical expression written in an extended form; for example, $a^2 + 2ab + b^2$ is the expansion of $(a + b)^2$.

experiment A test or procedure carried out under controlled conditions to determine the validity of a hypothesis or make a discovery. *See panel at* hypothesis.

explosion 1. A violent blowing apart or bursting caused by energy released from a very fast chemical reaction, a nuclear reaction or the escape of gases under pressure. 2. A sudden great increase: *a population explosion.*

exponent A number or symbol, placed above and to the right of the expression to which it applies, that indicates the number of times the expression is used as a factor. For example, the exponent 3 in 5^3 indicates $5 \times 5 \times 5$; the exponent 2 in $(a + b)^2$ indicates $(a + b) \times (a + b)$.

exponential Relating to a mathematical expression containing one or more exponents. ✦ Something is said to increase **exponentially** if its rate of change must be expressed using exponents. A graph of such a rate would appear not as a line, but as a curve that becomes steeper and steeper.

extensor A muscle that extends or straightens a limb or joint. *Compare* flexor.

■ **eye**
cross-section of a human eye

labels: vitreous humour, sclera, cornea, pupil, iris, lens, optic nerve, retina

exterior angle The angle formed between a side of a polygon and an extended adjacent side. *Compare* interior angle.

extinct 1. No longer existing or living. Plant and animal species become extinct for many reasons, including climate change, disease, destruction of habitat and local or worldwide natural disasters. The great majority of species that have ever lived are now extinct. 2. No longer active or burning: *an extinct volcano. —noun* extinction.

extrapolate To estimate the value of a quantity that falls outside the range in which its values are known.

extraterrestrial Originating, located or occurring outside the Earth or its atmosphere: *they are searching for evidence of extraterrestrial life.*

extrusion The emission of lava onto the surface of the Earth. ✦ Rocks that formed from the cooling of lava are called **extrusive rocks**. *Compare* intrusion.

eye 1. The organ of the body with which an animal is able to see or sense light. In vertebrate animals, the eye occurs as one of a pair, each consisting of a spherical structure that is filled with fluid. Incoming light is refracted by the cornea and transmitted through the pupil to the lens, which focuses the image onto the retina. *See more at* compound eye, eyespot. 2. *Botany.* A bud on a tuber, such as a potato. 3. The relatively calm area at the centre of a hurricane or similar storm. *See more at* hurricane.

eyepiece The lens or group of lenses closest to the eye in an optical instrument, such as a telescope.

■ **exterior angles**

Angles 1, 2, 7 and 8 are exterior angles. Angles 1 and 8 and angles 2 and 7 are alternate exterior angles.

122

See more cross-reference
use this to find additional
information at other entries

scientific field label

vi

See also cross-reference

use this to find related entries in a particular area

■ **lichen**

lightning

studies living organisms and their organization, life processes and relationships to each other and their environment. *Compare* physical science.

lift An upward force acting on an object. Lift can be caused because an object, such as an air balloon, displaces a weight of air greater than its own weight or because of a low-pressure area above an object, such as a wing, that is moving through a fluid. *Compare* drag. *See panel at* aerodynamics.

ligament A sheet or band of tough fibrous tissue that connects two bones or holds an organ of the body in place.

light 1. A form of electromagnetic energy that can be perceived by the human eye. It is made up of electromagnetic waves that travel at a speed of about 299,792 kilometres per second. 2. Electromagnetic energy that cannot be perceived by the human eye, as infrared light and ultraviolet light. *See panel at* electromagnetic radiation.

light-emitting diode *See* LED.

lightning A flash of light in the sky caused by an electrical discharge between clouds or between a cloud and the Earth's surface. The flash heats the air and usually causes thunder. Lightning may appear as a jagged streak ("forked lightning"), a bright sheet or, in rare cases, a glowing red ball.

entry word

vapour from the air. Lichens often live on rocks and tree bark and can thrive in extreme environments, such as mountain tops and the polar regions. *See also* fungus.

Liebig, Baron Justus von 1803–1873. German chemist who contributed to many areas of chemistry. He was one of the first to investigate organic compounds and to develop techniques for their analysis. Liebig also established one of the first teaching laboratories, where many 19th-century chemists were trained.

life 1. The property or quality that distinguishes living organisms from dead organisms and non-living matter. Life is shown in an organism that has the ability to grow, carry on metabolism, respond to stimuli and reproduce. 2. Living organisms considered as a group: *plant life; marine life.*

life cycle The series of changes in the growth and development of an organism from its beginning as an independent life form to its mature state in which offspring are produced. In simple organisms, such as bacteria, the life cycle begins when an organism is produced by fission and ends when that organism in turn divides into two new ones. In more complex organisms, the life cycle starts with the fusion of reproductive cells and ends when that organism produces its own reproductive cells, which then may go on to reproduce.

life science Any of several branches of science, such as biology, medicine or ecology, that

Did You Know?

lightning

The energy within a bolt of lightning is so great that it heats the air around it to temperatures up to five times greater than that of the surface of the sun, or 30,000°C. The rapid expansion of this superheated air is what creates the sounds we call thunder. The sounds travel to us more slowly than the light from lightning, so it is possible to estimate how far away a lightning strike is by timing the gap between when you see the lightning and when you hear the thunder it has produced. Count the seconds from when you see the flash until you hear the thunder, and divide this number by three. The result will be the number of kilometres you are from the point of the strike.

Did You Know? panel

Other panels include Usage, Biography, and Word History See list of panels on p. iv

biographical entry

a– A prefix meaning "without" or "not" when forming an adjective (such as *amorphous,* without form, or *atypical,* not typical), and "absence of" when forming a noun (such as *arrhythmia,* absence of rhythm). Before a vowel or *h* it becomes *an–* (as in *anhydrous, anoxia*).

aa A type of lava having a rough, jagged surface. It is relatively slow moving in its molten state, advancing in the form of massive blocks. *See panel at* **pahoehoe.**

aardvark A burrowing mammal of southern Africa, having a stocky body, large ears and a long tubular snout with a snake-like tongue which it uses for feeding on ants and termites.

abacus (*plural* **abacuses** *or* **abaci**) A computing device consisting of a frame holding parallel rods with sliding beads.

abalone Any of various edible molluscs that have a large, ear-shaped shell. The shell has a row of holes along the outer edge, and the interior is lined with mother-of-pearl.

abdomen 1. In humans and other mammals, the portion of the body that lies between the chest and the pelvis. The abdomen contains the stomach,

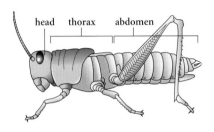

■ **abdomen**
a grasshopper, with wings removed in order to show the whole abdomen

intestines, liver, spleen and pancreas. **2.** A region similar to the abdomen in other vertebrates, such as a snake. **3.** In insects, arachnids and other arthropods, the abdomen forms the last section of the body. The abdomen has no legs attached to it. *—adjective* **abdominal.**

aberration 1. A deviation in the normal structure or number of chromosomes in an organism. **2.** The failure of a lens, mirror or telescope to bring rays of light coming from a source, such as a star, to a single focus, causing a distorted or blurred image.

ablation 1. The wearing away or destruction of the outer or forward surface of an object, such as a meteorite or a spacecraft, as it moves very rapidly through the atmosphere. The friction of the air striking the object heats and often melts or burns its outer layers. **2.** The process by which snow and ice are removed from a glacier or other mass of ice. Ablation typically occurs through melting, sublimation or wind erosion.

abomasum The fourth division of the stomach in ruminant animals, and the only one having glands that secrete acids and enzymes for digestion. It corresponds anatomically to the stomachs of other mammals. *See more at* **ruminant.**

■ **abacus**
On a Chinese abacus, the columns of beads go from right to left and represent ones, tens, hundreds, thousands and so on. The beads above the crossbar have a value of five; the beads below the crossbar have a value of one. The beads are totalled when moved down or up towards the crossbar.

abrasion

abrasion 1. The process of wearing away or rubbing down by means of friction. **2.** A scraped area on the skin.

abscess A collection of pus that forms at one place in the body and is surrounded by inflamed tissue.

abscissa The distance of a point from the y-axis on a graph in the Cartesian coordinate system. It is measured parallel to the x-axis. For example, a point having coordinates (2,3) has 2 as its abscissa. *Compare* **ordinate**.

absolute humidity The amount of water vapour present in a unit volume of air, usually expressed in kilograms per cubic metre. *Compare* **relative humidity**.

absolute scale A temperature scale having absolute zero as the lowest temperature. The Kelvin scale is an absolute scale.

absolute temperature Temperature measured or calculated on an absolute scale.

absolute value The value of a number without regard to its minus or plus sign. For example, the absolute value of +3 (written |+3|) and the absolute value of –3 (written |–3|) are both 3.

absolute zero The lowest possible temperature of matter, at which the particles of matter have the lowest amount of energy possible. Absolute zero is equal to –273.15°C.

absorption 1. *Biology.* The movement of a substance, such as a liquid or solute, across a cell membrane by means of diffusion or osmosis. **2.** *Chemistry.* The process of drawing a gas or liquid into a solid through the minute spaces between its parts. *Compare* **adsorption**. **3.** *Physics.* The

taking up and storing of energy, such as radiation, light or sound, without it being reflected or transmitted.

absorption spectrum The pattern of dark lines and colours made when light passes through an absorbing medium, such as a gas or liquid. The dark lines represent the colours that are absorbed. Because each type of atom absorbs a unique range of colours, the absorption spectrum can be used to identify the composition of distant substances, such as the gaseous outer layers of stars.

Ac The symbol for **actinium**.

AC Abbreviation of **alternating current**.

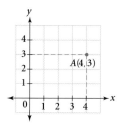

■ **abscissa**
The coordinates for A are (4,3); the abscissa is 4.

acceleration The rate of change of the velocity of a moving body with respect to time. *See more at* **gravity, relativity**.

Did You Know?

acid rain

We normally think of rain as something pure and natural, but in many parts of the world it is polluted with harmful acids from the moment it forms in the sky. How does this happen? When coal, petrol, and oil are burned as fuels, they give off the gases sulphur dioxide and nitrogen oxide. In the atmosphere, these compounds combine with water vapour to form highly corrosive sulphuric and nitric acids. Prevailing winds carry these acids away from the industrial areas where they originate, and they fall to Earth as acid rain. Acid rain is a serious environmental problem in parts of the world where there are many factories, power plants and cars close together, as in parts of the United States, Canada, Europe and Asia. It harms forests and soils and pollutes lakes and rivers, killing fish and other aquatic life. Acid rain can also damage buildings and monuments by eating away the stone and metal that they are made of.

the effect of acid rain on a statue

acceleration of gravity The acceleration of a body falling freely under the influence of the Earth's gravity. It is equal to approximately 9.8 metres per second per second.

accommodation The adjustment in the focal length of the lens of the eye. Accommodation permits images at different distances to be focused on the retina.

acellular Not made up of cells or not containing cells. The hyphae of some fungi are acellular.

–aceous A suffix used to form adjectives meaning "made of" or "resembling" a particular substance or material, such as *silicaceous,* containing silicon.

acetaldehyde *See* ethanal.

acetate *See* ethanoate.

acetic acid *See* ethanoic acid.

acetone *See* propanone.

acetylene *See* ethyne.

acetylsalicylic acid The chemical name for aspirin.

Achilles tendon A large tendon at the back of the leg connecting the calf muscles with the heel bone. The Achilles tendon is the strongest tendon in the body.

acid Any of a class of compounds that form hydrogen ions when dissolved in water. They also react, in solution, with bases and certain metals to form salts. Acids turn blue litmus paper red, have a sour taste and have a pH of less than 7. *Compare* **base.** *—adjective* **acidic.**

acid rain Rain, snow or other precipitation with a low pH, indicating a high amount of acidity.

acne A skin disease in which the oil glands become clogged and infected, often causing pimples to form, especially on the face. It is most common during adolescence.

acoustics **1.** *Used with a singular verb.* The scientific study of sound and its transmission. **2.** *Used with a plural verb.* The total effect of sound, especially as produced in an enclosed space: *a concert hall with excellent acoustics.*

acquired immune deficiency syndrome *See* **AIDS.**

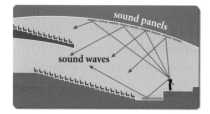

■ acoustics

Sound waves from a stage are reflected by sound panels and distributed throughout an auditorium.

---

acrylic acid *See* **propanoic acid.**

ACTH Short for *adrenocorticotropic hormone.* A hormone secreted by a lobe of the pituitary gland. It stimulates the adrenal glands to produce cortisone and related hormones.

actinide Any of a series of chemically similar metallic elements with atomic numbers ranging from 89 (actinium) to 103 (lawrencium). All of these elements are radioactive, and two of the elements, uranium and plutonium, are used to generate nuclear energy. *See* **Periodic Table,** pages 260–261.

actinium A silvery-white, highly radioactive metallic element of the actinide series that is found in uranium ores. It is used as a source of alpha rays. Its most stable isotope has a half-life of about 22 years. *Symbol* **Ac.** *Atomic number* 89. *See* **Periodic Table,** pages 260–261.

actinomorphic Relating to a flower that can be divided into equal halves along any diameter; radially symmetrical. The flowers of the rose and tulip, for example, are actinomorphic.

activation energy The least amount of energy that must be provided for a chemical reaction to occur. For example, striking a match on the side of a matchbox provides the activation energy, in the form of heat, necessary for the chemicals in the match to react together.

active site The part of an enzyme where the substance that the enzyme acts upon (called the substrate) is catalysed. *See more at* **enzyme.**

active transport The movement of ions or molecules across a cell membrane against a

Did You Know?

adaptation

The gazelle is extremely fast, and the cheetah is even faster. These traits are *adaptations* – characteristics or behaviors that give an organism an edge in the struggle for survival. Darwinian theory holds that adaptations are the result of a two-stage process: random variation and natural selection. Random variation results from slight genetic differences. For example, one cheetah in a group may be slightly faster than the others and thus have a better chance of catching a gazelle. The faster cheetah therefore has a better chance of being well-fed and living long enough to produce offspring. Since the cheetah's young have the same genes that made this parent fast, they are more likely to be fast than the young of slower cheetahs. The process is repeated in each generation, and thereby great speed becomes an adaptation common to cheetahs. This same process of natural selection also favours the fastest gazelles.

gradient, in other words from an area of lower concentration to an area of higher concentration. This involves an active carrier system. The energy needed for active transport is supplied by ATP.

acupuncture The practice of inserting thin needles into the body at specific points to relieve pain, treat a disease or anaesthetize a body part during surgery. Acupuncture has its origin in traditional Chinese medicine and has been in use for more than 5000 years.

acute angle An angle that is less than 90°. *Compare* **obtuse angle.**

adaptation 1. A change in an animal or plant

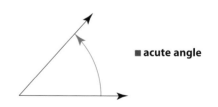

■ acute angle

that increases its chance of survival in a specific environment. Adaptations may involve changes in the body or in behaviour but they are the result of genetic differences between individuals: *Wings are an adaptation of the forelimbs of a bird for flight.* **2.** The change in the response of sensory receptors to a repeated stimulus. For example, a bad smell smells awful to begin with, but as the sensors become adapted, awareness of the smell is lost because the receptors stop responding.

addend A number that is added to another number.

addiction A physical or psychological need for a habit-forming substance, such as drugs or alcohol.

addition The act, process or operation of adding two or more numbers to compute their sum.

additive *noun.* A substance that is added in small amounts to something in order to improve its performance or quality, preserve its usefulness or make it more effective. —*adjective.* **1.** Being any of the primary colours red, green or blue, whose wavelengths may be mixed with one another to produce all other colours. *See more at* **colour. 2.** *Mathematics.* Marked by or involving addition.

adenine A base that is a component of DNA and RNA, forming a base pair with thymine in DNA

and a base pair with uracil in RNA during transcription.

adenoids Lymphatic tissue at the back of the throat which may be swollen due to infection. Adenoids can block breathing through the nose.

adenosine A compound, $C_{10}H_{13}N_5O_4$, that is found in living cells and is the main molecular component of DNA and RNA, as well as the energy-providing molecule ATP.

adenosine triphosphate *See* **ATP.**

adiabatic Occurring without gain or loss of heat. The passage of sound through air involves expansion and contraction of the air that is generally adiabatic.

adipose Relating to or consisting of animal fat; fatty.

adjacent angle Either of two angles having a common side and a common vertex.

adrenal gland Either of two endocrine glands, one located above each kidney, that produce several important hormones. ❖ The outer part of the adrenal gland, called the **adrenal cortex,** produces steroid hormones. ❖ The inner part of the adrenal gland, called the **adrenal medulla,** produces adrenaline.

adrenaline A hormone secreted by the adrenal gland in response to physical or mental stress, as from fear. The release of adrenaline causes the heart to beat faster and more strongly, the pupils to dilate, and the rate of breathing to increase. Adrenaline also causes an increase in the amount of sugar in the blood, which can be used by the body as fuel when more alertness or greater physical effort is needed.

adsorption The process by which molecules of a substance, such as a gas or a liquid, collect on the surface of another substance, such as a solid. The molecules are attracted to the surface but do not enter the solid's minute spaces, as in absorption. Some drinking-water filters consist of carbon cartridges that adsorb contaminants. *Compare* **absorption** (sense 2).

adult An animal or a plant that is fully grown and developed.

aerate 1. *Chemistry.* To add a gas, such as carbon dioxide, to a liquid. **2.** *Biology.* To supply with oxygen: *The lungs aerate the blood.*

■ adrenal gland
top: *cross-section of an adrenal gland*
bottom: *position of adrenal glands relative to kidneys*

adrenal cortex · adrenal medulla

right adrenal gland · left adrenal gland

kidney · kidney

Did You Know?

aerodynamics

The two primary forces in *aerodynamics* are lift and drag. *Lift* refers to forces perpendicular to the surface of an object (such as an aeroplane wing) that is travelling through the air. For example, aeroplane wings are designed so that when they move through the air, an area of low pressure is created above the wing; the low pressure produces a lift force that pulls the wing upwards (in a direction perpendicular to the wing's broad surface), and the wing pulls the aeroplane up with it. *Drag* forces, which are parallel to the object's surface, are usually caused by friction. Drag makes it more difficult for aeroplane wings to slice through the air, and so drag forces push against the forward motion of the plane. Large wings usually generate a lot of lift, but they also produce a lot of drag. In designing aeroplane wings, engineers need to take into account such factors as the speed and altitude at which the plane will fly, so that they can find a wing shape that balances lift and drag as well as possible.

passes over the aerofoil faster than it passes beneath it, resulting in greater pressure below than above. Propellers are aerofoils that are spun rapidly to provide propulsion.

aeronautics 1. The design and construction of aircraft. 2. The study of the piloting and navigation of aircraft.

aeroplane Any of various vehicles that are capable of flight, are held up by the force of air flowing around their wings and are driven by jet engines or propellers.

aerosol 1. A substance consisting of very fine particles of a liquid or solid suspended in a gas. Mist, which consists of very fine droplets of water in air, is an aerosol. *Compare* **emulsion, foam.** 2. A substance, such as paint, an insecticide or a hairspray, packaged under pressure for use in this form.

aerospace 1. Relating to the Earth's atmosphere and the space beyond. 2. Relating to the science and technology of flight.

aestivation *Zoology.* An inactive state resembling deep sleep, in which some animals living in hot climates, such as certain snails, pass the summer. Aestivation protects these animals against the heat and dryness of the summer. *Compare* **hibernation.**

aetiology The cause or origin of a disease.

aerobic Needing or using oxygen to live: *aerobic organisms.* ❖ Exercise that increases the activity of the heart and lungs improves the body's ability to use oxygen and is called **aerobic exercise.** ❖ **Aerobic respiration** is the process by which cells respire, constantly using oxygen to break down glucose. This releases as much energy as possible for the cells and also forms carbon dioxide and water as waste products. *Compare* **anaerobic.**

aerodynamic 1. Relating to objects, such as the wings of aeroplanes, that are designed to reduce wind drag. 2. Relating to aerodynamics.

aerodynamics The study of the movement of air and other gases and of the forces involved in their movements. It is also the study of the way objects, such as cars and aeroplanes, interact with air when they are moving through it.

aerofoil A part, such as an aircraft wing, designed to provide lift as air flows around its surface. Air

■ **aerodynamic**
top: *high wind drag on a less aerodynamic shape.* bottom: *low wind drag on a more aerodynamic shape*

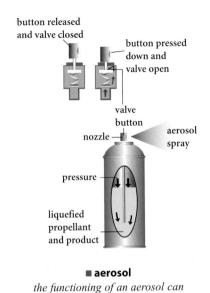

■ **aerosol**
the functioning of an aerosol can

afferent Relating to a nerve that carries sensory information towards the central nervous system. *Compare* **efferent**.

afforestation The planting of trees. —*verb* **afforest**.

aftershock A less powerful earthquake that follows a more forceful one. Aftershocks usually originate in the same place as the main earthquakes they follow.

Ag The symbol for **silver**.

agar A jelly-like material obtained from marine algae, especially seaweed. It is used as a medium for growing bacterial cultures in the laboratory and as a thickener and stabilizer in food products.

Agassiz, (Jean) **Louis** (Rodolphe) 1807–1873. Swiss-born American geologist and zoologist who in 1840 introduced the idea of the ice age. Agassiz carried out extensive fieldwork in Europe and the United States which led him to theorize that most of the Northern Hemisphere had once been covered by a vast sheet of ice. Earlier in his career, Agassiz published a groundbreaking study of fossil fish and was known as the greatest ichthyologist of his day.

agate A type of very fine-grained quartz found in various colours that are arranged in bands or in cloudy patterns. The bands form when water rich with silica enters empty spaces in rock, after which the silica comes out of solution and forms crystals, gradually filling the spaces from the outside inwards. The different colours are the result of various impurities in the water.

agent A substance that can cause a chemical reaction or a biological effect. *Compare* **reagent**.

agonist A muscle that actively contracts to produce a desired movement. *Compare* **antagonist**.

AIDS Short for *acquired immune deficiency syndrome*. A severe disease caused by HIV (human immunodeficiency virus), in which the immune system is attacked and weakened, making the body susceptible to other infections. The virus is transmitted through bodily fluids such as semen and blood. Because it is caused by a virus, it has been so far impossible to cure.

aileron A small section of the back edge of an aeroplane wing that can be moved up or down to control the plane's rolling and tilting movements.

air The colourless, odourless, tasteless mixture of gases that surrounds the Earth. Air contains about 78 per cent nitrogen and 21 per cent oxygen, with the remaining part being made up of argon, carbon dioxide, neon, helium and other gases.

air bladder 1. An air-filled sac in many fish that helps maintain buoyancy or, in some species, helps in respiration, sound production or hearing. Also called *swim bladder.* **2.** *See* **float**.

air sac 1. An air-filled space in the body of a bird that forms a connection between the lungs and bone cavities. **2.** *See* **alveolus**. **3.** A sac-like enlargement in the trachea of an insect. **4.** A bag-like piece of skin or tissue below the jaw of certain animals, such as the bullfrog and orang-utan, that can be inflated to increase sound production.

air vesicle *See* **float**.

airwaves Radio waves used to transmit radio and television signals.

Al The symbol for **aluminium**.

alanine A nonessential amino acid. *See more at* **amino acid**.

albino A person or animal born without normal colouring as a result of an inherited inability to

7

Did You Know?

alchemy

Because their goals were so unrealistic, and because they had so little success in achieving them, the practitioners of *alchemy* in the Middle Ages gained a reputation for being con artists. But this reputation is not fully deserved. While they never succeeded in turning lead into gold (one of their main goals), they did make discoveries which helped to shape modern chemistry. Alchemists discovered and purified a number of chemical elements, including mercury, sulphur and arsenic. They invented early forms of some of the laboratory equipment used today, including beakers, crucibles, filters and stirring rods. And they developed methods to separate mixtures and purify compounds by distillation and extraction that are still important.

produce melanin. Mammals that are albinos have white hair, pale skin and usually pinkish eyes.

albumen The white of the egg of certain animals, especially birds and reptiles, consisting mostly of the protein albumin. The albumen supplies water to the growing embryo and also cushions it.

albumin A class of proteins found in egg white, milk, blood and various other plant and animal tissues. Albumins dissolve in water and form solid or semi-solid masses when heated.

alchemy A medieval philosophy and early form of chemistry whose aims were the changing of common metals into gold, the discovery of a cure for all diseases and the preparation of a potion that gives eternal youth. The imagined substance capable of turning other metals into gold was called the philosopher's stone.

alcohol 1. A group of organic compounds that contain the hydroxyl group (–OH). Names of alcohols usually end in *–ol.* **2.** Ethanol.

alcoholism The excessive drinking of and dependence on alcoholic beverages.

Aldebaran The brightest star in the constellation Taurus. *See panel at* **Rigel.**

aldehyde A group of organic compounds containing the chemical group –CHO. Aldehydes are used in resins, dyes and organic acids.

alga (*plural* **algae**) Any of various green, red or brown organisms that grow mostly in water, ranging in size from single cells to large spreading seaweeds. Like plants, algae manufacture their own food through photosynthesis. They form a major component of marine plankton and are often visible as pond scum. Although they were once classified as plants, they do not have roots, stems or leaves, and are now viewed as protists.

algebra A branch of mathematics dealing with the relations and properties of quantities. It uses letters and other symbols to represent numbers, especially in equations to solve problems or to express general mathematical relationships.

algorithm A step-by-step procedure for solving a problem, especially a mathematical rule or procedure used to compute a desired result.

Word History

algebra

For much of the Middle Ages, the centre of scientific learning was not Europe, but the Islamic world of the Arabs. The Arabs studied the Greek classics of Plato and Aristotle while Europe nearly forgot about them. The Arabs were particularly interested in medicine and astronomy, and because astronomy requires making careful measurements and calculations, they became expert mathematicians. In the 800s, an Arabic mathematician named Muhammad al-Khwarizmi wrote a book called *The Book of Restoring and Balancing*, which explained the principles of algebra. Algebra had been developed earlier by mathematicians in Greece and India, but al-Khwarizmi's book, as the first comprehensive treatment of it, became a medieval bestseller. The Arabic word for "the restoring" in the book's title is *al-jabr*, which is the source of our word *algebra*. Al-Khwarizmi's own name is the source of another mathematical term in English, *algorithm*.

Alhazen *See* **Ibn al-Haytham.**

alien *Ecology.* Introduced to a region deliberately or accidentally by humans. Rhododendrons, grey squirrels and water voles are species that are alien to Britain but that have become widely naturalized throughout the country. *Compare* **endemic, indigenous.**

alimentary canal *See* **digestive tract.**

aliphatic Relating to organic compounds that do not contain a benzene ring; not aromatic. Alkanes are aliphatic compounds. *Compare* **aromatic.**

alkali (*plural* **alkalis** *or* **alkalies**) A chemical that acts like a base and dissolves in water, producing hydroxide ions.

alkali metal Any of a group of soft metals that form alkaline solutions when they react with water. They include lithium, sodium, potassium, rubidium, caesium and francium. Except for caesium, which has a gold sheen, alkali metals are white. The alkali metals have one electron in their outer shell, and therefore react easily with other elements and are found in nature only in compounds. *See* **Periodic Table,** pages 260–261.

alkaline 1. Capable of neutralizing an acid; basic. **2.** Relating to or containing an alkali. —*noun* **alkalinity.**

alkaline-earth metal Any of a group of metallic elements that includes beryllium, magnesium, calcium, strontium, barium and radium. Because the alkaline-earth metals have two electrons in their outer shell, they react easily with other elements and are found in nature only in compounds. *See* **Periodic Table,** pages 260–261.

alkaloid Any of a large class of complex organic compounds that contain nitrogen and mostly

■ **aliphatic**
the straight chain of carbon atoms of a propane molecule

occur in plants. Alkaloids have a wide range of physiological effects and many uses in medicine, but they can also be toxic. Morphine, quinine and nicotine are all alkaloids.

alkane Any of a group of hydrocarbons whose carbon atoms form chains linked by single bonds. Alkanes have the general formula C_nH_{2n+2} and include propane and butane.

alkene Any of a group of hydrocarbons whose carbon atoms form chains linked by one or more double bonds. Alkenes have the general formula C_nH_{2n} and include ethene and propene.

alkyne Any of a group of hydrocarbons whose carbon atoms form chains linked by one or more triple bonds. Alkynes have the general formula C_nH_{2n-2} and include ethyne and propyne.

allantois A membranous sac that grows out of the lower end of the alimentary canal in embryos of reptiles, birds and mammals. In mammals, the blood vessels of the allantois develop into the blood vessels of the umbilical cord.

allele Any of the possible forms in which a gene for a specific trait can occur. In almost all animal cells, two alleles for each trait are inherited, one from each parent. Alleles on each of a pair of chromosomes are called homozygous if they are the same as each other and heterozygous if they are different.

allergen A substance, such as pollen, that causes an allergy.

allergy A condition in which exposure to a particular substance or environmental influence, such as pollen, certain foods or sunlight, causes an abnormal physiological reaction. The reaction may include difficulty in breathing, sneezing, skin rashes and, in severe cases, shock or death. *See panel on* page 10.

alligator A large, meat-eating, aquatic reptile having sharp teeth and powerful jaws. Alligators have a broader, shorter snout than crocodiles, and their teeth do not show when the jaws are closed. Two species exist: one living in the southeast United States and one living in China.

allotrope Any of several crystalline forms of a chemical element. Charcoal, graphite and diamond are all allotropes of carbon.

alloy A metallic substance made by mixing and fusing two or more metals, or a metal and a non-

Did You Know?

allergies and allergens

Feeling miserable because of an allergic reaction? Perhaps you can find some comfort in the knowledge that the misery is an unhappy side effect of your immune system trying to protect you. The immune system recognizes that a particular substance, called an *allergen* (for example, dust, mould or pollen), might be dangerous. Antibodies, special molecules whose job is to round up the invaders, charge into action. The immune system, however, can overreact, causing some people to be so sensitive to these outside substances that they develop unpleasant symptoms, such as rashes, runny noses or even serious illness. People with severe symptoms can be given a series of special drug injections that prevent or lessen the allergic reaction by training the immune system to accept the allergen. Oddly enough, many people develop allergies after repeated exposures to an allergen. The difference is that controlled, small exposures through jabs prompt the immune system to grow accustomed to the allergen, while accidental, large exposures provoke the allergic reaction.

metal, to obtain desirable qualities such as hardness, lightness and strength. Brass, bronze and steel are all alloys.

alluvial fan A fan-shaped mass of alluvium, deposited by a river when its flow is suddenly slowed. Alluvial fans typically form where a river pours out from a steep valley through mountains onto a flat plain. Unlike deltas, they are not deposited into a body of standing water.

alluvium Sand, silt, mud or other matter deposited by flowing water, as in a riverbed, flood plain or delta.

Alpha Centauri A multiple star consisting of three stars in the constellation Centaurus. It is the star nearest Earth, at a distance of 4.4 light years, and it is the third brightest star in the night sky. ❖ **Proxima Centauri** is the individual star in

this system that is closest to Earth, but it is very faint and far from the system's centre of mass.

alpha particle A positively charged particle that consists of two protons and two neutrons bound together. It is emitted by the nucleus of some elements undergoing radioactive decay and is identical to the nucleus of a helium atom. Alpha particles are the slowest and least penetrating forms of nuclear radiation. ❖ The process by which a radioactive element emits an alpha particle is called **alpha decay**. Alpha decay results in the atomic number of the atom being decreased by two and the mass number being decreased by four. *See more at* **radiation, radioactive decay.**

alpha ray A stream of alpha particles.

Altair The brightest star in the constellation Aquila. *See panel at* **Rigel.**

alternate angles Two angles formed on opposite sides of a transversal that crosses two straight lines. The angles are both exterior or both interior, but not adjacent.

alternating current *or* **AC** An electric current that reverses its direction of flow at regular intervals. Because the voltage of alternating current can be easily controlled with transformers, this is the type of electricity generated by power stations. The transformers raise the voltage to make it more efficient to transmit over long distances, then lower the voltage for safer use in homes and buildings. *Compare* **direct current.** *See panels at* **current, Tesla.**

alternative medicine A health care practice that does not follow generally accepted medical methods and may not have a scientific explanation for its effectiveness. Examples of alternative medicines are homoeopathy and herbal medicine.

alternator An electric generator that produces alternating current. The generator consists of a coil of wire that rotates rapidly in a magnetic field, causing the current to flow first one way and then the other through the coil.

altimeter An instrument that measures and indicates the height above sea level at which an object, such as an aeroplane, is located.

altiplano A high mountain plateau, as in certain parts of the Andes Mountains.

altitude 1. The height of a thing above a reference level, usually above sea level or the Earth's surface. 2. *Astronomy.* The vertical angle between a celestial object and the horizon, as seen by the observer. Altitude and azimuth are the coordinates used to navigate with respect to the stars. 3. *Mathematics.* The perpendicular distance from the base of a geometric figure, such as a triangle, to the opposite vertex, side or surface.

altocumulus A fleecy white or grey cloud formation, usually occurring in wide patches or bands. Altocumulus clouds form at middle levels of the atmosphere.

altostratus A cloud formation that extends in flat, smooth sheets or layers of varying thickness. Altostratus clouds form at middle levels of the atmosphere.

alum Any of various crystalline salts in which a metal such as aluminium or chromium is combined with another metal such as potassium or sodium, especially aluminium potassium sulphate. Alum is widely used in industry as a hardener and purifier, and in medicine to induce vomiting and stop bleeding.

aluminium A lightweight, silvery-white metallic element that is easily shaped and a good conductor of electricity. It is the most abundant metal in the Earth's crust and is used to make a wide variety of products, ranging from drinks cans to aeroplane components. *Symbol* Al. *Atomic number* 13. *See* Periodic Table, pages 260–261.

Alvarez, Luis Walter 1911–1988. American physicist who studied subatomic particles. Alvarez built a device called a hydrogen bubble chamber that made it possible to analyse the reactions occurring between atomic nuclei inside it. His observations led to the theory that protons, neutrons and electrons are made of quarks. With his son, geologist **Walter Alvarez** (born 1940), he developed a theory that the extinction of dinosaurs was caused by climate changes resulting from a giant asteroid striking the Earth. *See panel at* iridium.

alveolus (*plural* alveoli) Any of the tiny air-filled sacs arranged in clusters in the lungs that allow oxygen to diffuse into the bloodstream and carbon dioxide to diffuse out of it. They are the site of gaseous exchange. Also called *air sac.*

Alzheimer's disease A disease that causes degeneration of parts of the brain. Symptoms include the gradual loss of memory and other mental abilities.

Am The symbol for americium.

AM Abbreviation of amplitude modulation.

amalgam An alloy of mercury and another metal, often silver, commonly used in fillings.

amber A hard, translucent, brownish-yellow

Did You Know?

amber

What is amber, and how does it preserve delicate tissues like the bodies of whole ants for millions of years? Certain trees, especially conifers, produce a sticky substance called resin to protect themselves against insects. Normally, it decays in oxygen through the action of bacteria. However, if the resin happens to fall into wet mud or sand containing little oxygen, it can harden and eventually fossilize, becoming the yellowish, translucent substance known as amber. If any insects or other organisms are trapped in the resin before it hardens, they can be preserved, often in amazing detail. While amber may sometimes preserve fragments of the DNA of the enclosed organisms, fossil mosquitoes would not contain enough dinosaur DNA to actually create clones.

fossilized ant

ambergris

substance that is the fossilized resin of ancient trees. It often contains fossil insects.

ambergris A greyish, waxy material formed in the intestines of sperm whales, often found floating at sea or washed ashore. It is used to make perfumes.

americium A synthetic, silvery-white, radioactive metallic element of the actinide series that is produced artificially by bombarding plutonium with neutrons. Americium is used as a source of alpha particles for smoke detectors and gamma rays for industrial gauges. Its most stable isotope has a half-life of 7950 years. *Symbol* **Am.** *Atomic number* 95. *See* **Periodic Table,** pages 260–261.

amethyst A purple or violet, transparent form of quartz used as a gemstone. The colour is caused by the presence of iron compounds in the crystal structure.

amide A compound containing the radical $CONH_2$.

amino acid Any of a large number of compounds that are found in living cells, contain carbon, oxygen, hydrogen and nitrogen, and join together to form proteins. ❖ About 20 amino acids are needed by animal cells to produce proteins, but only about half, called **non-essential amino acids,** can be produced by animal cells. The remaining half, called **essential amino acids,** must be obtained from food.

ammeter An instrument that measures an electric current and indicates its magnitude in amperes.

ammonia A colourless alkaline gas, NH_3, that is lighter than air and has a pungent odour. It is used

■ amoeba
amoeba Proteus extending its pseudopods

as a fertilizer and refrigerant, as well as in medicine, and in making dyes, textiles, plastics and explosives.

ammonite Any of the coiled fossil shells of a group of extinct molluscs related to the nautilus. Ammonites were especially abundant during the Mesozoic Era.

ammonium A positively charged ion, NH_4^+, derived from ammonia and found in a wide variety of organic and inorganic compounds.

amnesia A partial or total loss of memory, usually caused by shock or brain injury.

amnion A sac of thin, tough membrane containing a watery liquid in which the embryo of a reptile, bird or mammal is suspended. ❖ The watery fluid in the amnion is called **amniotic fluid.**

amoeba (*plural* **amoebas** *or* **amoebae**) A one-celled microscopic organism that constantly changes shape by forming pseudopods, temporary projections that are used for movement and for the ingestion of food. Amoebas are members of the group of organisms called protozoans.

amorphous 1. Not made of crystals. Glass is an amorphous substance. **2.** Lacking definite form or shape.

ampere A unit used to measure electric current. Electric current is a measure of how much electric charge passes a given point in a second. One ampere is equal to a flow of one coulomb per second.

■ ammonite

■ amphibian
top: *grey tree frog* bottom: *spring salamander*

Ampère, André Marie 1775–1836. French mathematician and physicist. He is best known for his analysis of the relationship between magnetic force and electric current, including the formulation of Ampère's law, a mathematical description of the strength of the magnetic field produced by the flow of electricity through a conductor. The ampere unit of electric current is named after him.

amphetamine Any of a group of drugs that stimulate the nervous system, causing heightened alertness and a faster heartbeat and metabolism. Amphetamines are highly addictive.

amphibian A cold-blooded vertebrate animal having moist skin without scales. Most amphibians lay eggs in water, and their young breathe with gills but develop lungs and breathe air as adults. Amphibians include frogs, toads and salamanders.

amphibole Any of a large group of minerals composed of a silicate joined to various metals, such as calcium, magnesium, iron or sodium. Asbestos is a mineral of the amphibole group.

amphioxus *See* **lancelet.**

amphoteric Capable of reacting chemically as either an acid or a base. Water, ammonia and the hydroxides of certain metals are amphoteric.

amplification An increase in the magnitude or strength of an electric current, a force or another physical quantity, such as a radio signal.

amplitude One half of the full extent of a vibration, oscillation or wave. The amplitude of an ocean wave, for example, is the maximum height of the wave crest above the level of calm water, or the maximum depth of the wave trough below the level of calm water. The amplitude of a pendulum swinging through an angle of 90° is 45°. *See more at* **wave.**

amplitude modulation A method of radio broadcasting in which the amplitude of the wave that carries the sound signal changes to reflect the various sounds that are to be reproduced, while the frequency of the wave remains the same. *Compare* **frequency modulation.**

amylase Any of various enzymes that break down starches into their component sugars, such as glucose. Amylase is present in fluid secreted by the pancreas, in saliva in some mammals and in plants.

anabolism The phase of metabolism in which complex molecules, such as the proteins and fats that make up body tissue, are formed from simpler ones. *Compare* **catabolism** — *adjective* **anabolic.**

Word History

amphibian

Amphibians are not quite fish and not quite reptiles. They spend part of their lives living in water, like fish, and breathing with gills; they usually spend another part of their lives breathing air with lungs and able to live on land, like reptiles. This double life is also at the root of their name, *amphibian*, which, like many scientific words, comes from Greek. It is made up of the Greek prefix amphi–, meaning "both" or "double", and the Greek word bios, meaning "life". Both these elements are widely used in other scientific words in English: bios, for example, is also seen in words like *biology*, *antibiotic* and *symbiotic*.

anaconda

anaconda A very large, mostly aquatic snake of tropical South America. It suffocates its prey by coiling around it or by drowning it and is the largest snake known.

anadromous Relating to fish that migrate up rivers from the sea to breed in fresh water. Salmon and shad are anadromous.

anaemia A condition in which the concentration of red blood cells or the amount of haemoglobin is too low to supply enough oxygen to the tissues of the body. A common cause of anaemia is a lack of iron in the diet, which limits the amount of haemoglobin that can be made. *See also* **sickle cell anaemia.** — *adjective* **anaemic.**

anaerobic Occurring or living in the absence of oxygen: *anaerobic bacteria.* ❖ **Anaerobic respiration** takes place in cells where there is a shortage or absence of oxygen. The glucose is not broken down completely and much less energy is released than in aerobic respiration. In mammals, lactic acid is formed as a waste product, while waste formed by plants and fungi is ethanol. *Compare* **aerobic.**

anaesthesia Loss of sensation to touch or pain, usually produced by nerve injury or by the administration of drugs, especially before surgery.

anaesthetic A drug used to induce anaesthesia.

analgesic A drug that deadens the sense of pain; a painkiller.

analogous Similar in function but having different evolutionary origins, as the wings of a butterfly and the wings of a bird. *Compare* **homologous.**

analogue Relating to a device that uses continuously changing physical quantities to represent data. For example, the position of the hands of a clock is an analogue representation of time.

analysis (*plural* **analyses**) The separation of a substance into its parts, usually by chemical means, for the study and identification of each component. ❖ **Qualitative analysis** determines what substances are present in a compound. ❖ **Quantitative analysis** determines how much of each substance is present in a compound.

analytic geometry The use of algebra to solve problems in geometry. In analytic geometry, geometric figures are represented by algebraic equations and plotted using coordinates.

anaphase The stage of cell division in which the doubled set of chromosomes separates into two identical groups that move to opposite ends of the cell. In mitosis, anaphase is preceded by metaphase and followed by telophase. *See more at* **meiosis, mitosis.**

anatomy 1. The structure of an animal or a plant or any of its parts. 2. The scientific study of the shape and structure of living things. —*adjective* **anatomical.**

Anaxagoras 500?–428 BC. Greek philosopher and astronomer who was the first to explain eclipses correctly. He also stated that the sun and stars were glowing stones and that the moon took its light from the sun.

androgen A male sex hormone. Any of several steroid hormones, such as testosterone, that control the development and maintenance of physical characteristics in males.

Andromeda A constellation in the Northern Hemisphere near Perseus and Cassiopeia. It contains a spiral-shaped galaxy visible to the naked eye.

–ane A suffix used to form the names of saturated hydrocarbons (hydrocarbons having only single bonds), such as *ethane. Compare* **–ene.**

pointer
spindle
lever
vacuum chamber

■ **aneroid barometer**
Expansion or contraction of the vacuum chamber, caused by a change in air pressure, forces the pointer to move.

anemometer An instrument that measures the speed of the wind. The most basic type of anemometer consists of a series of cups mounted at the end of arms that rotate in the wind. The speed with which the cups rotate is a measure of the wind speed.

anemone *See* **sea anemone.**

aneroid barometer A barometer made up of a vacuum chamber covered by a thin elastic disc. High atmospheric pressure pushes against the disc and causes it to bulge inwards, while low pressure does not push as hard, allowing the disc to bulge outwards.

aneurysm A swelling in the wall of an artery or vein caused by disease or injury.

angiosperm Any of a large group of plants that have flowers and produce seeds enclosed in an ovary or a fruit; a flowering plant. Most living plants are angiosperms. *Compare* **gymnosperm.**

angle 1. A geometric figure formed by two lines that begin at a common point or by two planes that begin at a common line. **2.** The space between such lines or planes, measured in degrees. *See also* **acute angle, obtuse angle, right angle.**

angle of incidence The angle formed by a ray or wave, as of light or sound, striking a surface and a line perpendicular to the surface at the point of impact. *See more at* **wave.**

angle of reflection The angle formed by a ray or wave reflected from a surface and a line perpendicular to the surface at the point of reflection. *See more at* **wave.**

angle of refraction The angle formed by the path of refracted light or other radiation and a line drawn perpendicular to the refracting surface at the point where the refraction occurred. *See more at* **wave.**

angstrom A unit of length equal to one hundred-millionth (10^{-8}) of a centimetre. It is used mainly to measure wavelengths of light and shorter electromagnetic radiation.

Ångström, Anders Jonas 1814–1874. Swedish physicist and astronomer who pioneered the use of the spectroscope in the analysis of radiation. By studying the spectrum of visible light given off by the sun, Ångström discovered that there is hydrogen in the sun's atmosphere. The angstrom unit of measurement is named after him.

angular momentum A quantity related to the motion of a body that is moving in a circle. The angular momentum depends on the mass and angular velocity of the body.

angular velocity The rate at which an object moving in a circular path changes its position, measured in radians per second.

anhydride A chemical compound formed from another, especially an acid, by the removal of water.

anhydrous Not containing water.

animal Any of a wide variety of multicellular organisms, most of which have a digestive tract, a nervous system, the ability to move voluntarily and specialized sensory organs for recognizing and responding to their environment. Animals cannot manufacture their own food and must feed on plants, other animals or other organic matter. Animals are grouped as a separate kingdom in taxonomy.

animal kingdom The category of living organisms that includes all animals. The scientific name of this kingdom is Animalia. *See table at* **taxonomy.**

anion An ion that has a negative charge. Hydroxide and chloride ions are anions. *Compare* **cation.**

ankylosaurus *or* **ankylosaur** A large, plant-eating dinosaur of the Cretaceous Period having a squat, heavily armoured body and a clubbed tail.

annelid Any of various worms or worm-like animals having soft, elongated bodies that are divided into ring-like segments. The earthworm and leech are annelids.

Anning, Mary 1799–1847. English fossil collector who supported her family by selling fossils she found in the rocks to wealthy collectors. In 1811, aged twelve, she discovered the fossil skeleton of an ichthyosaur which is now in the Natural History Museum in London. She also discovered the first plesiosaur (1821) and the first pterodactyl, Dimorphodon (1828). Mary Anning did a great deal to advance knowledge of prehistoric creatures with her sharp eyes and the care she took in preserving the specimens she found.

■ **annelid**

head of Thelepus crispus, the spaghetti worm

---

annual *Botany. adjective.* Completing a life cycle in one growing season. —*noun.* An annual plant. Tomatoes and sunflowers are examples of annuals. *Compare* **biennial, perennial.**

annual ring *See under* **growth ring.**

annular Forming or shaped like a ring.

anode **1.** The positive electrode in an electrolytic cell, towards which negatively charged particles are attracted. The anode has a positive charge because it is connected to the positively charged end of an external power supply. **2.** The positive electrode in a voltaic cell, such as a battery. The anode gets its positive charge from the chemical reaction that happens inside the battery, not from an external source. *Compare* **cathode.**

anomaly Something that is unusual, irregular or abnormal: *Flooding is an anomaly in desert regions of Africa.* —*adjective* **anomalous.**

anopheles Any of various mosquitoes that can transmit malaria to humans.

anorexia nervosa A disorder characterized by an abnormal fear of becoming obese and by persistent efforts to lose weight, leading to severe weight loss and malnourishment. It most commonly affects young women, who often stop menstruating, develop brittle bones and experience other physical changes as a result.

ant Any of various insects that live in large colonies composed of workers, soldiers and a queen. Ants often tunnel in the ground or in wood. Only the males and the queen have wings. *See also* **queen, soldier, worker.**

antagonist A muscle that resists or counteracts another muscle, as by relaxing while the opposite one contracts. *Compare* **agonist.**

Antarctic Circle The line of latitude approximately 66°33′ south. It forms the boundary between the South Temperate Zone and South Frigid Zone.

Antares A reddish, very bright binary star in the constellation Scorpio. It is a supergiant.

antenna (*plural* **antennae**) **1.** One of a pair of long, slender, segmented structures on the head of insects, centipedes, millipedes and crustaceans. Most antennae are organs of touch, but some are sensitive to odours and other stimuli. **2.** A metallic device for sending or receiving electromagnetic waves.

anther The pollen-bearing part at the upper end of the stamen of a flower. *See more at* **flower.**

anthracite A hard, shiny coal that has a high carbon content. It is valued as a fuel because it burns with a clean flame and without smoke or odour, but it is much less abundant than

■ **antenna**

paper wasp

Did You Know?

antibodies

Antibodies are complex, Y-shaped protein molecules that guard our bodies against diseases. The immune system's B lymphocytes, or B cells, develop into plasma cells, which can produce a huge variety of antibodies, each one capable of grabbing an invading molecule at the top ends of the Y. The molecules that antibodies recognize can be quite specific – they might exist only on a particular bacterium or virus. When that bacterium or virus enters the body, the antibodies quickly recognize its molecules, as if a sentry recognized an enemy soldier from his uniform. Once the invader is caught, the antibodies may make it inactive or lead it to cells that can destroy it. High numbers of a particular antibody may persist for months after an invasion. The numbers may then get quite small, but the experienced B cells can quickly make more of that specific antibody if necessary. Vaccines work by training B cells to do just that.

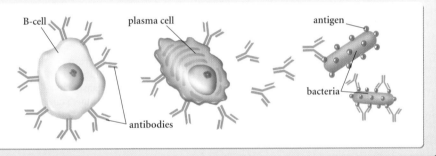

bituminous coal. *Compare* **bituminous coal, lignite.**

anthrax An infectious, usually fatal disease of mammals, especially cattle and sheep, caused by a bacterium. It can spread to people, causing symptoms ranging from blistering of the skin to potentially fatal infection of the lungs.

anthropology The scientific study of humans, especially of their origin, their behaviour, and their physical, social and cultural development.

anti– A prefix whose basic meaning is "against". It is used to form adjectives that mean "counteracting" (such as *antiseptic,* preventing infection). It is also used to form nouns referring to substances that counteract other substances (such as *antihistamine,* a substance counteracting histamine), and nouns meaning "something that displays opposite, reverse or inverse characteristics of something else" (such as *anticyclone,* a storm that circulates in the opposite direction from a cyclone).

antibiotic A substance, such as penicillin, that is capable of destroying or weakening certain microorganisms, especially disease-causing bacteria. Antibiotics are obtained from other microorganisms, especially moulds.

antibody A protein produced in the blood or tissues in response to the presence of a specific foreign antigen. Antibodies provide immunity against certain microorganisms and toxins by binding with them and often by deactivating them. Also called *immunoglobulin.*

anticline A fold of rock layers that slope downwards on both sides of a common crest. Anticlines form when rocks are compressed by plate-tectonic forces. They can be as small as a hill or as large as a mountain range. *Compare* **syncline.**

anticyclone A system of winds that spiral outwards around a region of high atmospheric pressure, circling clockwise in the Northern Hemisphere and anticlockwise in the Southern Hemisphere. *Compare* **cyclone.**

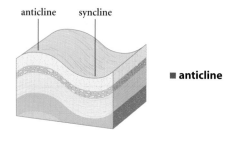

anticline   syncline

■ anticline

antidote 1. A substance that counteracts the effects of poison. 2. Something that relieves or counteracts something.

antigen A substance that stimulates the production of an antibody when introduced into the body. Antigens include toxins, bacteria, viruses and other foreign substances. *See panel at* **blood group.**

antihistamine Any of various drugs that relieve cold or allergy symptoms by blocking the action of histamine in the body.

antimatter A form of matter identical to ordinary matter except that its atoms have opposite electrical charges or magnetic characteristics.

antimony A metallic element having many forms, the most common of which is a hard, very brittle, shiny, blue-white crystal. It is used in a wide variety of alloys, especially with lead in car batteries, and in making flameproofing compounds. *Symbol* **Sb.** *Atomic number* 51. *See* **Periodic Table,** pages 260–261.

antinode In a standing wave, the region or point of maximum amplitude between two adjacent nodes. *Compare* **node** (sense 3).

antioxidant A chemical compound or substance that inhibits oxidation. Certain vitamins, such as vitamin E, are antioxidants and may protect body cells from damage due to oxidation.

antiparticle A particle of antimatter.

antipodes Two places on directly opposite sides of the Earth, such as the North Pole and the South Pole.

antiseptic A substance that prevents infection or rot by preventing the growth of micro-organisms.

antler A horny growth on the head of a deer, elk or other related animal, usually having one or more branches. Antlers typically grow only on males and are shed and grown again each year.

anus The opening at the lower end of the alimentary canal through which solid waste is excreted. —*adjective* **anal.**

aorta The main artery of the circulatory system in mammals. It carries blood with high levels of oxygen from the left ventricle of the heart to all the arteries of the body except those of the lungs.

apatite A usually green, transparent mineral consisting mainly of calcium phosphate. Apatite occurs as hexagonal crystals in igneous, metamorphic and sedimentary rocks, and is used as a source of phosphate for making fertilizers. It is the mineral used to represent a hardness of 5 on the Mohs scale.

apatosaurus *or* **apatosaur** A very large sauropod dinosaur of the late Jurassic Period, having a long neck and tail and a relatively small head. *See panel at* **brontosaurus.**

ape Any of various large, tailless primates having long arms and broad chests. Apes include the chimpanzee, gorilla and orang-utan. They live in the wild only in the Eastern Hemisphere. Generally they include the closest living relatives to human beings. *Compare* **monkey.**

apex The highest point, especially the vertex of a triangle, cone or pyramid.

aphelion The point farthest from the sun in the orbit of a body, such as a planet or a comet, that travels around the sun.

aphid Any of various small, soft-bodied insects that feed by sucking sap from plants. Aphids can be very destructive and can transmit plant diseases.

apogee 1. The point furthest from the Earth's centre in the orbit of the moon or an artificial satellite. 2. The point in the orbit of a body, such as a satellite, where it is farthest from the body around which it revolves, such as a planet. *Compare* **perigee.**

appendix (*plural* **appendixes** *or* **appendices**) A tubular projection attached to the caecum of the large intestine in humans and some other mammals. ❖ Inflammation of the appendix is called **appendicitis**. ❖ Surgical removal of the appendix is called an **appendectomy**.

Aquarius A constellation in the Southern Hemisphere near Pisces and Capricornus.

aquatic Relating to, living in or growing in water.

aqueous Relating to or dissolved in water.

aqueous humour The clear, watery fluid that fills the chamber of the eye between the cornea and the lens.

aquifer An underground layer of sand, gravel or porous rock that collects water and holds it like a sponge. Much of the water we use is obtained by drilling wells into aquifers.

Aquila A constellation in the Northern Hemisphere near Aquarius and Hercules.

Ar The symbol for **argon**.

Arabic numeral One of the numerical symbols 1, 2, 3, 4, 5, 6, 7, 8, 9 or 0. They are called Arabic numerals because they were introduced into western Europe from sources of Arabic scholarship.

arachnid Any of a group of arthropods having eight segmented legs, no wings or antennae and a body divided into two parts. One part consists of the head and thorax joined together, and the other part is the abdomen. Spiders, mites, scorpions and ticks are arachnids.

arc A part of the circumference of a circle.

Archaean The earlier of the two divisions of the Precambrian Eon, from about 3.8 to 2.5 billion years ago. During this time, the Earth had an atmosphere with little free oxygen, and the first

single-celled life appeared. *See chart at* **geological time**, pages 148–149.

archaebacterium *See* archaeon.

archaeology The scientific study of past human life and culture by the examination of physical remains, such as graves, tools and pottery.

archaeon (*plural* **archaea**) Any of a group of microorganisms that resemble bacteria but are different from them in certain aspects of their chemical structure, such as the composition of their cell walls. Archaea usually live in extreme environments, such as very hot or salty ones. The archaea are considered a separate kingdom in some classification systems, but a division of the prokaryotes in others. Also called *archaebacterium*.

archaeopteryx An extinct primitive bird of the Jurassic Period, having characteristics of both birds and dinosaurs. Like a dinosaur, it had a long, bony tail, claws at the end of its fingers and teeth. It also had wings and feathers, like a bird. Many scientists regard its discovery as evidence that birds evolved from small meat-eating dinosaurs. *See panel at* **bird**.

Archimedes 287?–212 BC. Greek mathematician, engineer and inventor. He made numerous mathematical discoveries, including the ratio of the radius of a circle to its circumference as well as formulae for the areas and volumes of various geometric figures. Archimedes created the science of mechanics, devising the first general theory of levers and finding methods for determining the centre of gravity of a variety of bodies. *See panel on* page 20.

Archimedes' Principle A law of physics that states that when a object is totally or partially immersed in a fluid, it experiences an upward force ("upthrust") equal to the weight of the fluid it displaces. The principle helps to explain why object float and sink, and why they seem lighter in water.

archosaur Any of a mostly extinct group of reptiles which includes the dinosaurs, pterosaurs and the modern crocodiles and other crocodilians.

Arctic Circle The line of latitude approximately 66°33′ north. It marks the southern boundary of the area in which the sun

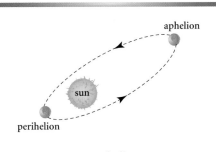

aphelion

sun

perihelion

■ **aphelion**

Biography

Archimedes

Archimedes would still be famous today even without the legend that he ran naked through the streets of his home in Sicily. One of his most important discoveries was that of buoyancy: an object placed in water displaces a volume of water equal to its own volume. The story goes that the king of Syracuse, Archimedes's home town, wanted Archimedes to test a golden crown to make sure it was made of pure gold (and not gold mixed with silver). According to the story, Archimedes puzzled over the problem until one day when he was taking a bath he saw how his body made the water overflow, and in a flash of insight discovered the principle of displacement. He ran out of his home yelling "Eureka!" (Greek for "I've found it!"), forgetting to dress first. He knew that gold was heavier than silver and now realized that a given weight of gold would have less volume – and therefore displace less water – than an equal weight of silver. He determined the volume of the crown from the volume of water it displaced, weighed the crown, and found that indeed it was too light to be made of pure gold.

does not rise on the winter solstice or set on the summer solstice.

Arcturus The brightest star in the Northern Hemisphere. It is in the constellation Boötes.

area The extent of a surface or plane figure as measured in square units.

arginine An essential amino acid. *See more at* **amino acid.**

argon A colourless, odourless element that is a noble gas and makes up about one per cent of the atmosphere. It is used in electric light bulbs, fluorescent tubes and welding. *Symbol* **Ar.** *Atomic number* 18. *See* **Periodic Table,** pages 260–261.

arid Very dry, especially having less rainfall than is needed to support most trees or woody plants: *an arid climate; an arid region.*

Aries A constellation in the Northern Hemisphere near Taurus and Pisces.

Aristotle 384–322 BC. Greek philosopher and scientist who profoundly influenced Western thought. Aristotle wrote about virtually every area of knowledge, including most of the sciences. Throughout his life he made careful observations, collected specimens and summarized all the existing knowledge of the natural world. He pioneered the study of zoology, developing a classification system for all animals and making extensive taxonomic studies. His systematic approach later evolved into the basic scientific method in the Western world.

arithmetic 1. The mathematical study of numbers and their properties under the operations of addition, subtraction, multiplication and division. **2.** Calculation using these operations.

arithmetic mean The value obtained by dividing the sum of a set of quantities by the number of quantities in the set. For example, if there are three test scores 70, 83 and 90, the arithmetic mean of the scores is their sum (243) divided by the number of scores (3), which is 81. *See more at* **mean.** *Compare* **average, median, mode.**

arithmetic progression A sequence of numbers such as 1, 3, 5, 7, 9 . . ., in which each

■ **aromatic**
The organic compound naphthalene is composed of two benzene rings.

term after the first is formed by adding a constant to the preceding number (in this case, 2). *Compare* **geometric progression.**

armadillo Any of several toothless, burrowing mammals of South America and southern North America. Armadillos have an armour-like covering of jointed bony plates and roll up into a ball when attacked.

armature 1. A rotating part of an electric motor or generator, consisting of wire wound around an iron core. The armature carries the electric current. **2.** A piece of soft iron connecting the poles of a magnet. **3.** The part of an electromagnetic device, such as a relay or loudspeaker, that moves or vibrates.

aromatic Relating to an organic compound containing at least one benzene ring or similar ring-shaped component. Naphthalene and TNT are aromatic compounds. *Compare* **aliphatic.**

array *Mathematics.* **1.** A rectangular arrangement of quantities in rows and columns. **2.** Numerical data ordered in a linear fashion, by magnitude.

Arrhenius, Svante August 1859–1927. Swedish physicist and chemist who first explained the process by which ions are formed or separated. He also investigated osmosis, toxins and antitoxins.

arrhythmia An abnormal rhythm of the heart.

arsenate A chemical compound containing the group AsO$_4$.

arsenic A nonmetallic element most commonly occurring as a grey crystal, but also found as a yellow crystal and in other forms. Arsenic and its compounds are highly poisonous and are used to make insecticides, weedkillers and various alloys. *Symbol* **As**. *Atomic number* 33. *See* **Periodic Table**, pages 260–261.

arteriole Any of the smaller branches of an artery, especially one that ends in the capillaries.

arteriosclerosis A thickening and hardening of the walls of the arteries that interferes with the circulation of the blood. It can be caused by disease and is also associated with high blood pressure and diets that are rich in cholesterol and saturated fats. *See also* **atherosclerosis.**

artery Any of the blood vessels that carry blood away from the heart. Arteries have muscular walls that expand and contract to help pump blood with high levels of oxygen to the tissues of the body. —*adjective* **arterial.**

artesian well A deep well that passes through hard, nonporous rock or sediment and reaches an aquifer in which the water is under enough pressure to rise to a height above the water table.
❖ In a **flowing artesian well** the water is under enough pressure to rise to the surface without being pumped.

arthritis Inflammation and stiffness of a joint

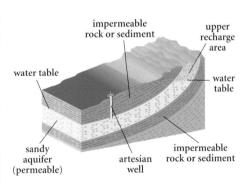

■ **artesian well**
If the water table in the recharge area is higher than the surface level of a well, then the water will flow from the well without being pumped.

Did You Know?

artificial intelligence

One laboratory devoted to research on *artificial intelligence* explains what they do: "Our goal is to understand the nature of intelligence and to engineer systems that exhibit intelligence". You may think of a computer as clever, but it is actually just following directions very fast. A truly intelligent device would be more flexible and would engage in the kind of "thinking" that people really do. An example of a system that artificial intelligence tries to reproduce is vision. A network of sensors combined with systems for interpreting the data may produce the kind of pattern recognition that we take for granted as seeing and understanding what we see. In fact, developing software that can recognize subtle differences in objects (such as those we perceive in the faces of two people) is very difficult. Differences that we can perceive without deliberate effort require massive amounts of data and careful guidelines for a system of artificial intelligence to recognize. Computers are necessary for artificial intelligence because they allow researchers to manage all the data needed to try to imitate true intelligence. The attempt to create artificial intelligence should lead to a better understanding of the human brain. After all, you can't copy it if you don't know how it works.

computer or other machine to perform actions thought to require intelligence. Among these actions are logical deduction and inference, creativity, the ability to make decisions based on past experience or insufficient or conflicting information and the ability to understand spoken language.

artiodactyl Any of various hoofed mammals having an even number of toes on each foot. Artiodactyls include the pig, sheep, ox, deer, giraffe and hippopotamus. Also called *even-toed ungulate.*

As The symbol for **arsenic.**

asbestos Any of several fibrous mineral forms of magnesium silicate. Asbestos is resistant to heat, flames and chemical action. Some forms have been shown to cause lung diseases. For this reason, asbestos is no longer used to make insulation, fireproofing material and brake linings.

ASCII *Computer Science.* A code that assigns numbers to the letters of the alphabet, the digits 0 to 9 and punctuation marks. For example, the capital letter A is coded as 65. (In the binary number system used by computers, 65 is written 1000001.) By standardizing the code used in representing written text, ASCII enables computers to exchange information.

ascorbic acid *See* **vitamin C.**

–ase A suffix used to form the names of enzymes. It is often added to the name of the compound that the enzyme breaks down, as in *lactase,* which breaks down lactose.

aseptic Free of microorganisms that cause

or joints. *See also* **osteoarthritis, rheumatoid arthritis.**

arthropod Any of numerous invertebrate animals having a segmented body, segmented appendages and an external skeleton. Crustaceans, insects and arachnids are all arthropods. Arthropods make up the largest phylum in the animal kingdom.

artificial Made by humans rather than occurring naturally: *artificial sweeteners; an artificial heart.*

artificial intelligence The ability of a

■ **artiodactyl**
left: *four-toed foot of a hippopotamus*
right: *two-toed foot of a giraffe*

disease: *she boiled the surgical instruments to make them aseptic.*

asexual reproduction *See under* reproduction.

asparagine A nonessential amino acid. *See more at* amino acid.

aspartic acid A nonessential amino acid. *See more at* amino acid.

asphalt A thick, sticky, dark-brown mixture of petroleum tars used in paving, roofing and waterproofing. Asphalt is produced as a by-product in refining petroleum and is also found in natural beds.

asphyxia Suffocation resulting from a severe drop in the level of oxygen in the body, leading to loss of consciousness and sometimes death.

aspirate To remove a liquid or gas from a body cavity by suction: *aspirate the lungs.*

Did You Know?

aspirin

The forest may not look like a chemist's. Nevertheless, plants have always provided humans with powerful medicines. For example, we no longer eat the bark of willow trees when we have headaches, but for thousands of years, people in pain did just that. About 100 years ago, scientists studying willow bark discovered that it could be used to make acetylsalicylic acid, better known as aspirin. *Aspirin* and willow bark are broken down in the stomach to supply us with the same powerful painkiller. Quinine, which people use to control the fevers of the disease malaria, originally came from the cinchona tree. Recently, researchers developed a new cancer drug, taxol, from the needles of yew trees. In fact, about 45 per cent of all cancer drugs are either natural products or slightly altered natural chemicals that scientists tinkered with to make more potent. Researchers still study traditional plant remedies in the hope of finding even more medicines from nature.

aspirin A white crystalline compound derived from salicylic acid and used as a drug to relieve fever and pain. Also called *acetylsalicylic acid.*

associative property The property of addition and multiplication which states that a difference in the grouping of numbers being added or multiplied will not change the result, as long as the order of the numbers stays the same. For example, 3 + (4 + 5) is equal to (3 + 4) + 5. *See also* commutative property, distributive property.

astatine A highly unstable, radioactive element that is the heaviest of the halogen elements. The most stable of its many isotopes has a half-life of only about eight hours. *Symbol* At. *Atomic number* 85. *See* Periodic Table, pages 260–261.

asteroid Any of numerous small, often irregularly shaped bodies that orbit the sun. Asteroids range from several hundred kilometres in diameter to the size of a speck of dust. ❖ Most are found in the region between the orbits of Mars and Jupiter known as the asteroid belt. *See panel at* solar system.

asthenosphere The upper part of the Earth's mantle. The asthenosphere lies beneath the lithosphere and consists of several hundred kilometres of partially molten rock. Because it is partially molten, seismic waves passing through this layer have slow velocities. *Compare* atmosphere, hydrosphere, lithosphere.

asthma A chronic disease characterized by a narrowing of the airways that is often caused by an allergy. It results in attacks of wheezing, coughing, difficulty in breathing and tightness of the chest.

astigmatism A defect of the eye in which the curvature of the cornea or lens is uneven. This prevents rays of light from being focused at a single point on the retina, resulting in indistinct or imperfect images.

Aston, Francis William 1877–1945. English physicist who is best known for his work on isotopes. He invented the mass spectrograph in 1919, with which he investigated the isotopic structures of elements and for which he won the Nobel Prize for chemistry in 1922. The Aston dark space, in electronic discharges, is named after him.

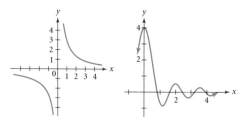

■ **asymptote**

left: *The x- and y-axes are both asymptotes of the curve (a hyperbola).*

right: *The x-axis is the asymptote of the wave.*

astral Relating to or coming from the stars; stellar: *astral distances.*

astringent A substance, such as alum, that checks the flow of bodily secretions by causing tissue contraction.

astro– A prefix that means "star" (as in *astrophysics*), "celestial body" (as in *astronomy*) or "outer space" (as in *astronaut*).

astronomical unit A unit of length equal to the average distance from Earth to the sun, approximately 150 million kilometres. It is used to measure distances within the solar system.

astronomy The scientific study of the universe and the objects in it, including stars, planets and nebulae. Astronomy deals with the position, size, motion, composition, energy and evolution of celestial objects. Astronomers

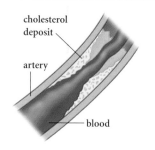

■ **atherosclerosis**

an artery narrowed by the build-up of cholesterol

analyse not only visible light but also radio waves, X-rays and other ranges of radiation that come from sources outside the Earth's atmosphere.

astrophysics The branch of astronomy that deals with the physical processes that occur in stars, galaxies and interstellar space.

asymmetry Lack of symmetry or balance.

asymptote A line whose distance to a given curve tends to zero. An asymptote may or may not intersect its associated curve.

At The symbol for **astatine**.

atavistic Reappearing after being absent from a strain of organism for several generations. Used of an inherited trait. —*noun* **atavism**.

ataxia Loss of muscular coordination as a result of damage to the central nervous system.

–ate A suffix used to form the name of a salt or an ester of an acid whose name ends in *–ic*, such as *ethanoate*, a salt or ester of ethanoic acid. Such salts or esters have one oxygen atom more than corresponding salts or esters with names ending in *–ite*. For example, a *sulphate* is a salt of sulphuric acid and contains the group SO_4, while a sulphite contains SO_3. *Compare* **–ite** (sense 2).

atherosclerosis Narrowing of the walls of the arteries caused by deposits of fatty substances (called plaques), especially cholesterol. It is the most common form of **arteriosclerosis**.

athlete's foot A contagious fungal infection of the feet that usually affects the skin between the toes, causing it to itch, blister and crack.

atmosphere 1. The mixture of gases that surrounds the Earth or some other celestial body. It is held by the force of gravity and forms various layers at different heights, including the troposphere, stratosphere, mesosphere, thermosphere and exosphere. The Earth's atmosphere, called air, is rich in nitrogen and oxygen; that of Venus is mainly carbon dioxide. *Compare* **asthenosphere, hydrosphere, lithosphere. 2.** A former unit of pressure equal to the pressure of the air at sea level, about 14.7 pounds per square inch or 1013 millibars. Now measured as 100,000 N/m^2.

atmospheric pressure Pressure caused by the weight of the air. At sea level it has a value of about 100,000 N/m^2 (which used to be known

exosphere

thermosphere

mesosphere

stratosphere

troposphere

■ **atmosphere**
The earth's atmosphere is divided into layers primarily according to differences in temperature. In the troposphere and mesosphere, air temperature drops with altitude, while in the stratosphere and thermosphere it rises. The exosphere extends indefinitely into space.

atomic bomb A very destructive bomb that derives its explosive power from the fission of atomic nuclei, usually plutonium or uranium 235 (an isotope of uranium). Also called *atom bomb.*

atomic clock An extremely precise clock whose rate is controlled by the vibration of particular atoms or molecules whose frequency does not change. The standard kind of atomic clock, which is based on the vibrations of caesium atoms, gains or loses less than one second in three million years. Atomic clocks are used to help track satellites, run navigation systems and study movements of the Earth's crust.

atomic energy *See* nuclear energy.

atomic mass *See* relative atomic mass.

atomic mass unit A unit of mass equal to $\frac{1}{12}$ the mass of an atom of the most common isotope of carbon (carbon-12), which is assigned a mass of 12. A hydrogen atom has a mass of 1 atomic mass unit since its mass is $\frac{1}{12}$ the mass of carbon-12.

atomic number The number of protons in the

as 1 atmosphere) and gradually decreases as the altitude increases.

atoll A coral island forming a ring that nearly or entirely encloses a shallow lagoon.

atom The smallest unit of an element, consisting of protons and neutrons in a dense central nucleus orbited by a number of electrons. Atoms are electrically neutral, so the number of protons always equals the number of electrons. During chemical reactions, atoms may lose, share or transfer some of their outer electrons when they become ions or join with other atoms to become compounds. *See panel at* **subatomic particle.** *See A Closer Look*, page 27.

atomic 1. Relating to an atom or atoms. **2.** Employing nuclear energy: *atomic weapons. See panel at* **nuclear.**

Did You Know?

atmospheric pressure

The atmosphere that blankets the Earth gently presses down on us, and the subtle variations in this *atmospheric pressure* greatly affect the weather. For example, forecasters often talk of low pressure bringing rain. In areas of low air pressure, the air is less dense and relatively warm, which causes it to rise. The expanding and rising air naturally cools and the water vapour in the air condenses, forming clouds and the drops that fall as rain. In high pressure regions, on the other hand, the air is dense and relatively cool, which causes it to sink. The water vapour in the sinking air does not condense, leaving the skies sunny and clear. So if you're trying to hit a six in cricket, would you prefer a beautiful, sunny day or one in which it looks like rain? On the overcast day, the ball has less air to push aside on its way out of the ground, making it easier to hit a six.

volcanic island

sea level

coral

lagoon

■ **atoll**

An atoll develops (from left to right) *when a volcanic island erodes and a ring of coral grows up around it. The depression left by the crater of an eroding volcano fills with water, forming a lagoon.*

nucleus of an atom. As atoms are electrically neutral, this number is also equal to the number of electrons orbiting about the atom's nucleus. The atomic number of an element determines its position in the Periodic Table.

ATP Short for *adenosine triphosphate.* An organic compound that is composed of adenosine and three phosphate groups. It serves as a source of energy for many metabolic processes. ATP releases energy as the phosphate groups are removed by hydolysis during cell metabolism.

atrioventricular Connecting or involving the atria and the ventricles of the heart.

atrium (*plural* **atria**) A chamber of the heart that receives blood from the veins and pumps it into a ventricle. Mammals, birds, reptiles and amphibians have two atria; fish have one. —*adjective* **atrial.**

atrophy The wasting away of a body part, most commonly caused by disease or nerve damage.

Au The symbol for **gold.**

AU Abbreviation of **astronomical unit.**

auditory Relating to hearing or the organs of hearing: *the auditory canal of the ear.*

auditory nerve The nerve that carries sensory information for sound and balance from the ear to the brain. The auditory nerve is a cranial nerve.

auricle 1. The visible part of the outer ear. **2.** An atrium of the heart.

Auriga A constellation in the Northern Hemisphere near Gemini and Perseus. It contains the bright star Capella.

aurora (*plural* **auroras** *or* **aurorae**) A brilliant display of bands of light in the sky at night, especially in polar regions. The light is caused by charged particles from the sun that are drawn into the atmosphere by the Earth's magnetic field.

aurora australis An aurora that occurs in southern regions of the Earth. Also called *southern lights.*

aurora borealis An aurora that occurs in northern regions of the Earth. Also called *northern lights.*

australopithecine Any of several early hominids of eastern and southern Africa, known from fossils to have lived from about four million to about one million years ago. The most complete australopithecine skeleton found so far, named Lucy by its discoverers, is estimated to be just over three million years old. While many scientists believe that australopithecines are ancestors of modern humans, not enough fossils have yet been found to establish any direct descent.

autism A disorder of development in which a person's ability to interact with others is severely limited. People with autism often have abnormal behaviour patterns, such as the repetition of specific movements or a tendency to focus on certain objects. —*adjective* **autistic.**

Atom

An atom consists of a nucleus, made up of protons and neutrons, surrounded by one or more energy levels, or electron shells, in which electrons orbit about the nucleus.

The lightest element, hydrogen, consists of one proton and one electron. The proton is located in the nucleus, and the electron orbits about it, in an electron shell (shown in red).

The next lightest element, helium, has two protons and two neutrons in its nucleus, and two electrons orbiting about it in the electron shell. Lithium, the next lightest element, has three protons, three neutrons and three electrons. Because the first electron shell can only hold two electrons, lithium's third electron is in a second electron shell (shown in green). This second shell can hold up to eight electrons.

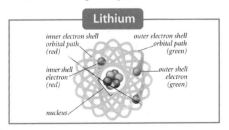

Larger atoms have as many as seven electron shells, each one successively larger than the one beneath it. The number of electrons orbiting in the outer shell determines how easily an element will react with other elements to form compounds. Elements whose outer shell is full are considered inert, and don't readily combine with other elements. Elements whose outermost shell has only one or two electrons will try to react with other elements to capture some of their electrons and fill their shell.

An oxygen atom, for example, has eight protons and eight neutrons in its nucleus, and eight electrons distributed throughout its two shells (shown in red and green). There are two electrons in the inner shell and six electrons in the outer shell. But because this outer shell has room for two more electrons, oxygen often reacts with other elements to gain two more electrons.

Water, one of the most common compounds on the Earth, forms in this way. An oxygen atom combines with two hydrogen atoms, thus filling its outermost shell by sharing one electron each with two atoms of hydrogen.

■ **aurora borealis**

auto– A prefix meaning "oneself", as in *autoimmune,* producing antibodies or immunity against oneself. It also means "by itself, automatic", as in *autonomic,* governing by itself.

autoimmune Relating to a reaction of the immune system in which antibodies are produced that attack the body's own cells and tissues, often causing illness.

autonomic nervous system The part of the nervous system of a vertebrate animal that regulates involuntary action, as of the intestines, heart or glands. It is divided into two parts, the sympathetic nervous system and the para-sympathetic nervous system.

autopsy A medical examination of a dead body to determine the cause of death.

autotrophic Relating to an organism that manufactures its own food from inorganic substances, such as carbon dioxide and nitrogen, using light or ATP for energy. All green plants and algae, and some bacteria and protists, are autotrophs. ❖ An organism capable of producing food from inorganic substances is called an **autotroph.** *Compare* **heterotrophic.**

autumn The season of the year occurring between summer and winter. In the Northern Hemisphere, it extends from the autumnal equinox to the winter solstice.

autumnal equinox The moment of the year when the sun crosses the celestial equator while moving from north to south. It occurs on 22 or 23 September, marking the beginning of autumn in the Northern Hemisphere. *Compare* **vernal equinox.**

auxin Any of various hormones or similar substances that promote and regulate the growth and development of plants. Auxins are produced in areas (called the meristem) in which new plant cells are formed. Auxins are also produced artificially in laboratories for purposes such as speeding growth and regulating how fast a fruit will ripen.

avalanche The fall or slide of a large mass, as of snow or rock, down the side of a mountain.

average A number, especially the arithmetic mean, that is derived from and considered typical or representative of a set of numbers. *Compare* **arithmetic mean, median, mode.**

Avery, Oswald Theodore 1877–1955. Canadian-born American bacteriologist who determined that DNA was the material that caused genetic changes in bacteria. His work was vital to scientists who later established that DNA is the carrier of genetic information in all living organisms.

avian Relating to birds.

aviary A large cage or enclosure for birds, as in a zoo.

Avicenna *See* **Ibn Sina, Hakim.**

Avogadro, Amedeo 1776–1856. Italian chemist and physicist who formulated the hypothesis known as Avogadro's law, which states that equal volumes of gases, under equal conditions of temperature and pressure, contain equal numbers of molecules.

Avogadro's number The number of atoms or molecules in a mole of a substance, approximately 6.022×10^{23}. *See more at* **mole³**.

avoirdupois weight A system of weights based on a pound of 16 ounces, used in many English-speaking countries to weigh everything except gems, precious metals and drugs.

axil The angle between the upper side of a leaf or stem and the stem or branch that supports it. A bud is usually found in the axil.

axiom A principle that is accepted as true without proof; a postulate.

axis (*plural* **axes**) **1.** An imaginary line around which an object rotates. In a rotating sphere, such as the Earth and other planets, the two ends of the axis are called poles. **2.** *Mathematics.* **a.** A line, ray or line segment with respect to which a figure or object is symmetrical. **b.** One of the straight lines of reference used to specify the position of points on a graph, eg. the horizontal x-axis and the vertical y-axis. **3.** *Anatomy.* The second cervical vertebra on which the head turns. **4.** *Botany.* The main stem or central part of a plant, about which plant parts, such as branches, are arranged. —*adjective* **axial.**

axon The long portion of a nerve cell that carries impulses away from the body of the cell. Also called *nerve fibre.*

azimuth The horizontal angle measured clockwise between a celestial object and the northern point of the horizon as seen by the observer. Azimuth and altitude are the coordinates used to navigate with respect to the stars.

azurite A dark-blue copper carbonate mineral having a glassy lustre and occurring in various forms. It is often found together with malachite. Azurite is used as a source of copper, as a gemstone and as a dye.

B The symbol for **boron**.

Ba The symbol for **barium**.

Babbage, Charles 1792–1871. British mathematician, inventor, and pioneer of machine computing. In the early 1820s, Babbage began to build a computer-like mechanical device called a difference engine, which was supposed to solve mathematical puzzles. Babbage never completed the construction of the difference engine, although a copy of it made in 1991 worked perfectly. In the 1830s, he designed a much larger machine, called an analytical engine, which could be programmed with punched cards. Although the analytical engine was never finished, it is recognized as the forerunner of the modern computer.

baboon Any of several large terrestrial monkeys of Africa and Asia. Baboons have a dog-like muzzle, a short tail and bare calluses on the buttocks.

bacillus (*plural* **bacilli**) Any of various bacteria that are shaped like a rod.

backbone *See* **vertebral column**.

Bacon, Roger 1214?–1292. English scientist and philosopher who is noted for the wide range of his knowledge and writing on scientific topics. Bacon asserted that mathematics is fundamental to science and that experimentation is essential to test scientific theories, ideas that were very advanced for his time. He did important work in the field of optics, explaining the principles of reflection and refraction and describing spectacles before they came into use.

bacteriology The scientific study of bacteria, especially in relation to disease.

bacterium (*plural* **bacteria**) Any of a large

■ **bacteria**
left to right: *the three main types of bacteria: cocci (spherical), bacilli (rod-shaped) and spirilla (spiral)*

■ badlands
badlands, South Dakota, USA

group of one-celled organisms that lack a cell nucleus, reproduce by fission or by forming spores, and in some cases cause disease. They are found in all living things and in all of the Earth's environments, and usually live off other organisms. Bacteria make up most of the kingdom of prokaryotes. —*adjective* **bacterial.**

badlands An area of heavily eroded land with numerous gullies or streambeds between ridges of variously coloured sand, silt and clay. Badlands usually form in dry regions where sudden, heavy rains wash away soil and keep most vegetation from becoming established.

Baekeland, Leo Hendrik 1863–1944. Belgian-born American chemist who developed Bakelite, the first plastic to harden permanently after heating (1907). His invention was a versatile and inexpensive material for manufacturing products such as telephones, cameras and furniture.

Baird, John Logie 1888–1946. Scottish electrical engineer and television pioneer. John Logie Baird was engineer to the Clyde Valley electric power company until he had to give up the job due to ill-health. Only then did he begin his research into the possibilities of television and managed to build a television apparatus almost entirely from scrap materials. In 1926 he gave the first demonstration of a television image and his system was taken on by the BBC in 1929. Other areas of Baird's research included radar, infrared television and systems for producing three-dimensional and coloured images, as well as projection onto a screen and stereophonic sound.

balance To adjust a chemical equation so that the number of each type of atom, and the total charge, on the reactant (left-hand) side of the equation matches the number and charge on the product (right-hand) side of the equation.

baleen A flexible horny substance hanging in plates from the upper jaw of certain whales. It is used by the whales to strain plankton from seawater when feeding. Also called *whalebone.*

ballistics The scientific study of the characteristics of projectiles, such as bullets or missiles, and the way they move in flight.

Baltimore, David Born 1938. American microbiologist who discovered the enzyme known as reverse transcriptase, which is capable of passing information from RNA to DNA. Prior to this discovery, it was assumed that information could flow only from DNA to RNA. Baltimore's work led to increased understanding of viruses that cause AIDS and certain forms of cancer.

bamboo Any of various tall grasses having jointed, woody, and often hollow stems. Some species of bamboo can reach heights of 30 metres or more. The young shoots of some types of bamboo are used as food.

band A specific range of electromagnetic wavelengths or frequencies, such as those used in radio broadcasting.

Banks, Sir Joseph 1743–1820. British botanist who took part in Captain James Cook's voyage around the world (1768–1771), during which he discovered and catalogued many species of plant and animal life.

Banting, Sir Frederick Grant 1891–1941. Canadian physiologist who isolated the hormone insulin, used in the treatment of diabetes. Banting conducted research into the secretions of the pancreas, including insulin. With Charles Best, he experimented with diabetic dogs, demonstrating that insulin lowered their blood sugar. Insulin was tested and proven effective on humans within months of the first experiments with dogs.

baobab An African tree having a large trunk, bulbous branches and hard-shelled fruit with an edible pulp. The baobab has spongy wood that holds large amounts of water, and the bark can be used to make rope, mats, paper and other items. Baobabs can live up to 3000 years.

bar A unit used to measure atmospheric pressure. It is equal to a force of 100,000 newtons per square metre of surface area, or 0.987 atmosphere.

barb 1. A sharp point projecting backwards, as on the sting of a bee. **2.** One of the hair-like branches on the shaft of a feather.

barbel 1. A slender, whisker-like feeler extending from the head of certain fish, such as the catfish. It is used for touch and taste. **2.** A large European freshwater fish of the carp family that has such feelers.

barbiturate Any of a group of drugs that reduce the activity of the nervous system and are used as sedatives. Barbiturates are highly addictive.

barbule A small barb or pointed projection, especially one that fringes the edges of the barbs of feathers.

bar chart A chart that shows values or amounts by means of vertical or horizontal bars separated by gaps. *See more at* **graph.**

Bardeen, John 1908–1991. American physicist who was one of the inventors of the transistor (1948) and later helped to develop the theory of superconductivity. Bardeen's research explained why the electrical resistance of certain materials disappears at temperatures close to absolute zero, thereby allowing a current to flow through them.

barite A usually white or clear mineral consisting of barium sulphate and occurring as flattened blades. Barite also occurs in a circular pattern of crystals that looks like a flower and, when coloured red by iron stains, is called a desert rose. Barite is used as a source of barium.

barium A soft, silvery-white metallic element that only occurs combined with other elements, especially in barite. Barium compounds are used in X-raying the stomach and intestines and in making fireworks and white pigments. *Symbol* **Ba.** *Atomic number* 56. *See* **Periodic Table,** pages 260–261.

barium sulphate A fine, white powder, $BaSO_4$. It is used in making textiles, rubber and plastic, and in taking X-rays of the digestive tract (when it is known as *barium meal*).

bark The protective outer covering of the trunk, branches, and roots of trees and other woody plants. Bark is usually divided into inner bark, consisting of phloem (tissue that distributes a watery mixture of sugars and growth hormones made in the leaves and buds), and outer bark, consisting of layers of dead cells from the inner bark. The outer bark protects the tree from heat, cold, insects and other dangers.

barnacle Any of various small, hard-shelled crustaceans that live in the sea and attach themselves to underwater objects, such as rocks and the bottoms of ships.

Barnard, Christiaan Neethling 1923–2001. South African surgeon who performed the first successful human heart transplant, in 1967.

barometer An instrument for measuring atmospheric pressure. Barometers are used to determine height above sea level and in weather forecasting. —*adjective* **barometric.**

barrier island A long, narrow sand island that is parallel to the mainland and serves to protect the coast from erosion.

barrier reef A long, narrow ridge of coral deposits parallel to the mainland and separated from it by a deep lagoon.

Bartlet, Neil Born 1932. British chemist famous for his discovery in 1962 of the first chemical compound of the noble gas xenon. This disproved a long held view that the noble gases do not form compounds. Since his discovery, several other compounds of noble gases have been discovered.

basalt A dark, fine-grained, igneous rock consisting mostly of feldspar, iron and magnesium. Basalt makes up most of the sea floor. It commonly forms when volcanic lava becomes solid. *See table at* **rock.**

■ **barnacle**

base 1. *Chemistry.* Any of a class of compounds that contain hydroxyl ions (OH⁻) and are capable of neutralizing acids in solution. They react with acids and certain metals to form water and salts. Bases turn red litmus paper blue, have a bitter taste, and have a pH of greater than 7. *Compare* **acid. 2.** *Mathematics.* **a.** The side or face of a geometric figure on which it is thought to stand. **b.** The number that is raised to various powers to generate the principal counting units of a number system. The base of the decimal system, for example, is 10. **c.** The number that is raised to a particular power in a given mathematical expression. In the expression a^n, a is the base. **3.** *Biology.* One of the purines (adenine or guanine) or pyrimidines (cytosine, thymine or uracil) found in DNA or RNA.

base pair The pair of nitrogen-containing bases, consisting of a purine linked by hydrogen bonds to a pyrimidine, that connects the complementary strands of a DNA molecule or of hybrid molecules joining DNA and RNA. The base pairs are adenine-thymine and guanine-cytosine in DNA, and adenine-uracil and guanine-cytosine in molecules joining DNA and RNA.

basic Having the chemical characteristics of a base; alkaline.

basin 1. An enclosed area filled with water. **2.** A region drained by a river and the streams that flow into it. **3.** A low-lying area on the Earth's surface in which thick layers of sediment have accumulated. Some basins are bowl-shaped, and

- carbon rod
- zinc casing
- ammonium chloride paste (electrolyte)
- carbon and manganese dioxide

■ **battery**
Electrons flow from the zinc casing through the light bulb to the carbon rod, making the bulb glow. The zinc casing acts as a negative electrode and the carbon rod acts as a positive electrode.

others are shaped like long valleys that have been filled in. Basins are important because they are often a source of valuable oil.

bat Any of various flying mammals that have thin wings consisting of skin that extends from the forelimbs to the hind limbs or tail. Bats are usually active at night and use echolocation to navigate.

bathyscaphe A free-diving vessel used to explore the deep sea. Bathyscaphes have a large floating hull attached to a round observation capsule that can hold one or more people.

bathysphere A spherical diving chamber in which people are lowered on a cable to explore the deep sea.

battery A device containing an electric cell or a series of electric cells that supplies a direct current by converting chemical, thermal, nuclear, or solar energy into electric energy. Common household batteries, such as those used in a torch, are usually made of dry cells (the chemicals producing the current are made into a paste). In other batteries, such as car batteries, these chemicals are in liquid form. *See panel on* page 34.

bauxite A soft, whitish to reddish-brown rock composed mainly of hydrous aluminium oxides. Bauxite forms from the breakdown of clays and is a major source of aluminium.

Did You Know?

bat

The well-known phrase "blind as a bat" is somewhat misleading. In fact, some bats have excellent eyesight, and bats on the whole are quite skilled in moving about and hunting prey in total darkness. Using a form of natural radar called *echolocation*, the bat emits a series of very high-pitched squeaks, inaudible to human ears, which reflect off objects in the bat's path. Relying on the pattern of echoes it hears, the bat can then avoid obstacles or home in on a specific target.

Did You Know?

battery

Where do *batteries* get the energy to make things work? From chemical reactions that go on inside them. The substances inside a battery are arranged in such a way that when they react with each other they pull electrons away from the battery's positive terminal and push them towards the negative terminal. If the battery is not connected to anything, the reaction doesn't go on very long; the electrons gathered at the negative terminal repel any additional ones that further reactions would carry there. But if you connect the two terminals with a wire, electrons will flow along the wire from negative to positive. On the way, they give up some of their energy to power whatever device you've connected, for example a light bulb or CD player. Eventually, the chemical reactions inside the battery change the nature of the positive and negative terminals and of the chemicals between them, making them unable to produce an electric current. In rechargeable batteries, you can restore the electricity-generating capacity of the terminals and the chemicals by passing electrical current through the battery backwards.

bay A body of water partially enclosed by land but having a wide outlet to the sea. A bay is usually smaller than a gulf.

B cell B cells are part of the immune system. They mature in the bone marrow before being released into the blood. In the presence of a specific antigen such as a bacterium or virus, a B cell divides. Some of the resulting cells form plasma cells which produce antibodies to inactivate or destroy the invading microbe. Others form memory cells which remember how to make the right antibodies for next time. *See panel at* **antibody.**

B complex *See* **vitamin B complex.**

Be The symbol for **beryllium.**

beach The area of accumulated sand, stone or gravel deposited along a shore by the action of waves and tides. Beaches usually slope gently towards the body of water they border and have a concave shape when viewed in cross section.

beak 1. The bill of a bird. **2.** A similar, often horny part forming the mouth of other animals, such as turtles and octopuses.

beaker A wide, cylindrical glass container with a pouring lip, used especially in laboratories.

bear 1. Any of various large mammals having a shaggy coat, a rounded head and a short tail. Bears eat plants and other animals, especially insects and small rodents. Bears walk with the entire lower surface of their foot touching the ground. **2.** Any of various other animals, such as the koala, that resemble a true bear.

Beaufort scale A scale for classifying the force of the wind, ranging from 0 (calm) to 12 (hurricane). The scale was devised in 1805 as a means of describing the effect of different wind speeds on ships at sea.

beaver A large aquatic rodent having thick brown fur, webbed hind feet and a broad flat tail. Beavers feed on bark and twigs. They have sharp front teeth adapted for gnawing and cutting down trees, which they use in constructing dams and lodges with underwater exits.

becquerel A unit used to measure the rate of radioactive decay. Radioactive decay is measured by the rate at which the atoms making up a radioactive substance are transformed into different atoms. One becquerel is equal to one of these atomic transformations per second.

Becquerel Family of French physicists, including **Antoine César** (1788–1878), one of the first investigators of electrochemistry; his son **Alexandre Edmond** (1820–1891), noted for his research on phosphorescence; and his grandson **Antoine Henri** (1852–1908), who discovered spontaneous radioactivity in uranium.

bed 1. A layer of sediment or rock that extends under a large area and has other layers below and sometimes above it: *a bed of coal.* **2.** The bottom of a body of water: *the bed of a stream.*

bedrock The solid rock that lies beneath the soil and other loose material on the Earth's surface.

bee Any of several winged, often stinging insects that have a hairy body and gather pollen and nectar from flowers. Most bees are solitary, but

■ **bee**

some bees, such as the honeybee, live in colonies with an organized social structure, consisting of workers, drones and a queen. Bees are important pollinators of flowering plants. *See also* **drone, queen, worker.**

beetle Any of numerous insects having biting mouthparts and hard forewings that cover the hind wings straight down the back when at rest. Beetles vary in size from nearly microscopic to several inches in length. *See panel at* **biomass.**

behaviour 1. The actions displayed by an organism in response to its environment. 2. One of these actions. Feeding and mating are examples of animal behaviours.

Bell, Alexander Graham 1847–1922. Scottish-born American scientist and inventor. Bell's lifelong interest in the education of deaf people led him to conceive the idea of transmitting speech by electric waves. In 1876 his experiments with a telegraph resulted in his invention of the telephone. He later produced the first successful

sound recorder, called a graphophone. Bell also invented the photophone (which transmitted speech by light rays), the audiometer (an early hearing aid) and many other devices.

belladonna Any of several alkaloids produced by the herb known as deadly nightshade. The alkaloids are poisonous but are also used in medicine, for example to increase the heart rate and treat Parkinson's disease.

Bell Burnell, Susan Jocelyn Born 1943. British astronomer. In 1967, working with astronomer Antony Hewish, she discovered the first pulsar.

bell curve A symmetrical bell-shaped curve that represents the typical distribution and frequency of the values of a set of random data. It slopes downward from a point in the middle corresponding to the mean.

benign Not likely to spread or get worse; not malignant: *a benign tumour.*

benthos 1. The bottom of a sea or lake. 2. The organisms living on sea or lake bottoms.

benzene A clear, colourless, flammable liquid, C_6H_6. It is derived from petroleum and used to make detergents, insecticides, motor fuels and many other chemical products. ❖ The six carbon atoms of benzene are arranged in a ring, called a **benzene ring**, having alternating single and double bonds, with a hydrogen atom attached to each carbon atom. This ring is a fundamental component of many other organic compounds. —*adjective* **benzyl.** *See panel on* page 36.

benzoic acid An aromatic, white, crystalline acid, $C_7H_6O_2$, used in preserving food, as a cosmetic, and in medicine.

beriberi A disease caused by a lack of the vitamin thiamine in the diet. It causes nerve damage and circulatory problems.

berkelium A synthetic, radioactive metallic element of the actinide series that is produced from americium, curium or plutonium. Its most stable isotope has a half-life of about 1400 years. *Symbol* **Bk.** *Atomic number* 97. *See* **Periodic Table,** pages 260–261.

Bernoulli Family of Swiss mathematicians. **Jacques** (or **Jakob**) (1654–1705) was a pioneer in the development of calculus and made an important contribution to probability theory. His brother **Jean** (or **Johann**) (1667–1748) also

■ **bell curve**
graph showing the distribution of a set of test scores where the average mark was a C

Did You Know?

benzene ring

According to some accounts, one of the key insights in the history of chemistry appeared in a dream. In 1865 chemists knew that a *benzene* molecule consisted of six carbon atoms and six hydrogen atoms. They also knew that carbon atoms have four bonds by which they can join with other atoms. But none of the chain-like structures that chemists knew about then worked with these numbers of atoms and bonds. The German chemist Friedrich August Kekulé had thought about this problem for a long time. One night he fell asleep and dreamed of snakes. One snake bit its own tail, forming a circle. Awakened by the image, Kekulé realized that the six carbon atoms in benzene formed a ring. Each carbon was bound once to one adjacent carbon and twice to the carbon on its other side. And each used its fourth bond to hold a hydrogen atom outside the ring. Modern chemistry owes much of its power to the understanding of ringed carbon compounds that started with Kekulé's dream.

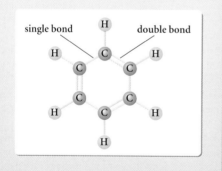

developed calculus and contributed to the study of complex numbers and trigonometry. Jean's son **Daniel** (1700–1782) was one of the first scientists to understand the concept of conservation of energy.

berry **1a.** A fruit that develops from a single ovary and has many seeds in fleshy pulp. Grapes, bananas, tomatoes and blueberries are true berries. **b.** Any small, juicy, fleshy fruit, such as a raspberry or strawberry, regardless of its botanical structure.

beryl A usually green or bluish-green mineral that is a silicate of beryllium and aluminium. Beryl occurs as transparent to translucent prisms in igneous and metamorphic rocks. Transparent varieties, such as emeralds, are valued as gems. Beryl is the main source of the element beryllium.

beryllium A hard, lightweight, steel-grey metallic element that is an alkaline-earth metal and is found in various minerals, especially beryl. It has a high melting point and resists corrosion. Beryllium is used to make sturdy, lightweight alloys and to control the speed of neutrons inside

Usage

berry

Most people think of a berry as a small, round fruit that grows on bushes and is eaten as a dessert or mixed with breakfast cereal. If the list of ingredients on a breakfast cereal packet includes "mixed dried berries", you wouldn't expect your cereal to contain pieces of cucumber or tomato. But to a botanist, cucumbers and tomatoes are in fact berries, while strawberries and raspberries are not. How can this be? Scientists have to be careful about the names they use for things, and sometimes the precise meaning that they give to a word is different from the general meaning that ordinary people understand. That is the case with the word *berry*. To a botanist, a berry is a fleshy fruit consisting of a single ovary that has multiple seeds. Other true berries besides cucumbers and tomatoes are bananas, oranges, grapes and blueberries. However, many fruits that are popularly called berries have a different structure and thus are not true berries. For example, strawberries and raspberries are aggregate fruits, developed from multiple ovaries of a single flower. The mulberry is not a true berry, either. It is a multiple fruit, like the pineapple, and is made up of the ovaries of several individual flowers.

the core of nuclear reactors. *Symbol* **Be**. *Atomic number* 4. *See* **Periodic Table,** pages 260–261.

Berzelius, Baron **Jöns Jakob** 1779–1848. Swedish chemist who is regarded as one of the founders of modern chemistry. Berzelius developed the concepts of the ion and of ionic compounds and made extensive determinations of atomic weights. In 1811 he introduced the classical system of chemical symbols, in which the names of elements are identified by one or two letters.

Bessemer process A method for making steel by forcing compressed air through molten iron to burn out carbon and other impurities.

Best, Charles Herbert 1899–1978. Canadian physiologist. When Charles Best was only a research student in 1921, he helped Frederick Banting to isolate the hormone insulin, used in the treatment of diabetes. They later shared a Nobel Prize for physiology or medicine. He discovered choline (a vitamin that prevents liver damage) and histaminase (the enzyme that breaks down histamine), introduced the use of the anti-coagulant heparin, and continued to work on insulin.

beta carotene A form of carotene widely found in plants and animals. Beta carotene is most efficiently converted to vitamin A in the liver.

beta particle A high-speed electron emitted by an atomic nucleus undergoing radioactive decay. A beta particle is created when a neutron becomes a proton. Beta particles have greater speed and penetrating power than alpha particles. ❖ The process by which a neutron becomes a proton and emits an electron is called **beta decay.** Beta decay results in the atomic number of an element being increased by one and its mass number staying the same. *See more at* **radiation, radioactive decay.**

beta ray A stream of beta particles.

Betelgeuse A reddish, very bright variable star in the constellation Orion. It is a supergiant. *See panel at* **Rigel.**

Bethe, Hans Albrecht Born 1906. German-born American physicist who was instrumental in the development of quantum physics. Bethe discovered that the sun and other stars derive their energy from a series of nuclear reactions, which came to be known as the carbon cycle, or Bethe cycle. Bethe also played an important role in the development of the atomic bomb, later working to educate the public about the threat of nuclear weapons.

Bh The symbol for **bohrium.**

Bhaskara 1114–1185. Indian mathematician who wrote the first work containing a systematic use of the decimal system.

Bi The symbol for **bismuth.**

bi– A prefix meaning "two." It is often used to form adjectives meaning "having two of" or "having double" something, such as in *bilateral,* having two sides.

bicarbonate of soda A white crystalline

Did You Know?

bicarbonate of soda

A white powder, *bicarbonate of soda* or *baking soda* is the common name for the chemical sodium hydrogen carbonate, $NaHCO_3$. Bicarbonate of soda is a base and reacts with acids in what is called *neutralization,* because both the acid and the base are converted into more neutral substances on the pH scale. Neutralization with bicarbonate of soda usually produces carbon dioxide gas, which you can observe bubbling away if you mix vinegar (an acid) and bicarbonate of soda. Such reactions are used in cooking to take advantage of the gas, as in getting a cake to rise. A small amount of bicarbonate of soda, about a half teaspoon, can even be mixed with water and swallowed to neutralize the acid that may cause indigestion. That neutralization reaction produces carbon dioxide gas in your stomach, which you expel – as a burp.

compound, $NaHCO_3$, chemically known as sodium hydrogen carbonate. It is used especially in beverages and as a leavening agent to make bread and cakes rise when baked. Also called *baking soda.*

biceps The muscle at the front of the upper arm that bends the elbow. The biceps has two points of attachment to bone at one end.

bicuspid *noun* A tooth having two points or cusps, especially a premolar. —*adjective* Of a heart valve, consisting of two flaps between the left atrium and the left ventricle. It prevents backflow of blood through the left side of the heart when the ventricles contract. *Compare* **tricuspid.**

biennial *adjective* Completing a life cycle normally in two growing seasons. —*noun* A biennial plant. Carrots, parsnips and sugar beet are some examples of biennials. *Compare* **annual, perennial.**

big bang The violent explosion of an extremely small, hot and dense body of matter between 12 and 18 billion years ago. It is viewed as the earliest event in a widely held model of the origin of the universe. *Compare* **steady state universe.**

bilateral symmetry Symmetrical arrangement of an organism or part of an organism along a central axis. A bilaterally symmetrical organism or part is divided into two equal halves. *Compare* **radial symmetry.**

bile A bitter, alkaline, greenish fluid produced in the liver from the breakdown of red blood cells and the metabolism of cholesterol. Much of it is stored in the gall bladder and released into the small intestine when food enters from the stomach. Bile is important because it neutralizes the acid mixture from the stomach, giving the enzymes of the small intestine ideal working conditions. It also helps in the digestion of fats.

bill The horny, projecting mouthparts of a bird. Bills have different sizes and shapes depending on how birds feed and what they eat.

binary *adjective* **1.** Having two parts. **2.** *Mathematics.* Based on the number 2 or the binary number system. —*noun Astronomy.* A binary star.

binary digit Either of the digits 0 or 1, used in the binary number system.

binary fission *See* **fission** (sense 2).

binary number system A method of representing numbers that has 2 as its base and uses only the digits 0 and 1. Each successive digit represents a power of 2. For example, 10011 represents $(1 \times 2^4) + (0 \times 2^3) + (0 \times 2^2) + (1 \times 2^1) + (1 \times 2^0)$, or $16 + 0 + 0 + 2 + 1$, or 19.

binary star A system of two stars that orbit a common centre of mass. The pair often appears as a single star to the naked eye.

binocular *adjective* Relating to or involving both eyes at once: *binocular vision.* —*noun* An optical device, such as a pair of field glasses, designed for use by both eyes at once and consisting of two small telescopes. Often used in the plural as *binoculars.*

Did You Know?

big bang

It's a chilling thought: in the 1920s, astronomers found that wherever they looked in space, distant galaxies were rapidly moving away from Earth. In other words, the universe was getting larger and larger. By calculating the speed of several galaxies and working back from there, astronomers learned that this expansion began between 12 and 18 billion years ago, when the entire universe was as small as a pea and almost infinitely dense. According to the widely accepted theory of the *big bang*, a massive explosion kicked off the expansion and was the origin of space and time. Now scientists must calculate how much mass the universe contains in order to see what lies ahead. If there is enough mass, the gravity attracting all the pieces to each other will eventually stop the expansion and pull all the pieces of the universe back together in a "big crunch". The universe would then be a closed universe. However, there may not be enough mass to support a universe that is closed. If that is the case, then an open universe would expand forever, and all the galaxies and stars would drift away from each other and become dark and cold.

binomial A mathematical expression having two terms, such as 3*a* + 2*b*.

binomial nomenclature The system used in science to name an organism, consisting of two terms, the first being the genus and the second the species. *Passer domesticus,* the scientific name of the common house sparrow, is an example of binomial nomenclature.

biochemistry The scientific study of the chemical composition of living matter and of the chemical processes that go on in living organisms.

biodegradable Capable of being decomposed by the action of biological agents, especially bacteria: *a biodegradable detergent.*

biodiversity The number and variety of different organisms found within a specified geographical region.

bioethics The study of the ethics surrounding biological and medical research and health-care practices.

biogenesis Generation of living organisms from other living organisms.

biogeography The scientific study of the geographical distribution of plant and animal life.

biological clock An internal system found in most living organisms that controls the cycle of various functions, such as sleep cycles in mammals and photosynthesis in plants. *See panel at* **circadian rhythm.**

biology The scientific study of life and of living organisms. Botany, zoology and ecology are all branches of biology.

bioluminescence Emission of light by living organisms, such as fireflies, glow-worms, and certain fish, jellyfish, plankton, fungi and bacteria. It occurs when chemical compounds react and give off light.

biomass 1. The total amount of living material in a given habitat. 2. Organic materials, such as plant matter and manure, that have not become fossilized and are used as a fuel or energy source. Biomass fuels produce less carbon dioxide than some fossil fuels, such as petroleum.

biome A large community of plants and animals that occupies a distinct region defined by its climate and dominant vegetation. Grassland, tundra, desert, tropical rainforest and deciduous

Did You Know?

biomass

The matter that makes up the Earth's living organisms is called biomass. Insects alone make up an amazing amount of *biomass.* The Scottish biologist JBS Haldane was once asked if the study of life on the Earth gave him any insights into God. Haldane replied jokingly that his research revealed that God must have "an inordinate fondness for beetles". Haldane made his comment because there are more beetle species – almost 400,000 now known – than species of any other animal. And beetles are only one kind of insect, of which there are almost one million species that are known and perhaps many millions more yet to be discovered. The number of individual insects is mind-boggling, about 10 quintillion (that's 10,000,000,000,000,000,000). Insects together probably have more biomass than any other type of land animal. And if we added up all the weights of all the people in the world, the biomass of all the insects would be 300 times as great.

and coniferous forests are all examples of biomes.

biomechanics The scientific study of the mechanics of motion in humans and other animals. Biomechanics is sometimes used by athletes to help analyse and improve their performance.

bionics The use of a system or design found in nature, such as the ability of plants to store solar energy, as a model for designing artificial systems, such as machines. —*adjective* **bionic.**

biophysics The science of using the laws of physics to understand biological processes. Biophysics involves the study of specific characteristics of living things, such as the ability of bats to navigate using echolocation.

biopsy A sample of tissue removed by a surgeon from a living body for examination and diagnosis.

biorhythm A recurring biological process, such

biosphere

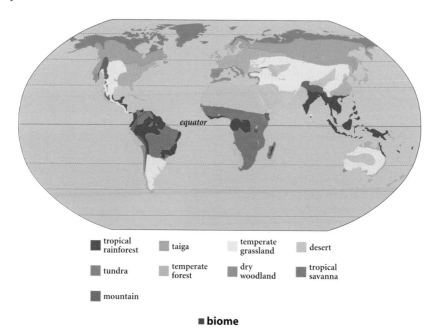

tropical rainforest

taiga

temperate grassland

desert

tundra

temperate forest

dry woodland

tropical savanna

mountain

■ **biome**

---

as sleep, that is controlled by the circadian rhythms of an organism.

biosphere The parts of the land, sea, and atmosphere in which organisms live.

biotechnology 1. The use of a living organism to solve an engineering problem or perform an industrial task. Using bacteria that feed on hydrocarbons to clean up an oil spill is one example of biotechnology. **2.** The use of biological substances to engineer or manufacture a product or substance, for example when genetically engineered bacteria are used to produce human insulin to be used by diabetics. *See more at* **genetic engineering.**

biotic Made up of living organisms; living: *the study of the effects of pollution on the biotic community of a marsh.*

biotin A vitamin belonging to the vitamin B complex that is important in the metabolism of carbohydrates and fats. It is found in liver, egg yolk, milk, yeast and some vegetables.

biotite A dark-brown to black mica found in igneous and metamorphic rocks.

biped An animal having two feet, such as a bird or human.

bipedal Standing or walking on two feet. ❖ The use of two feet for standing and walking is known as **bipedal locomotion.** The evolution of bipedal locomotion in humans was aided by the development of an upright head and backbone and of an arched foot.

bipinnate Relating to compound leaves that grow opposite each other on a larger stem; twice pinnate. Bipinnate leaves have a feathery appearance. The honey locust often has bipinnate leaves.

bird Any of numerous warm-blooded, egg-laying vertebrate animals that have wings for forelimbs, a body covered with feathers, a hard bill covering the jaw, and a four-chambered heart.

bismuth A brittle, pinkish-white, crystalline metallic element that occurs in nature as a free metal and in various ores. Bismuth has the greatest resistance to being magnetized of all metals and has the highest atomic number of all stable elements. It is used to make low-melting

Did You Know?

birds: modern-day dinosaurs?

Did birds evolve from dinosaurs? Most scientists who research the origin of birds think so, and they have lots of evidence to support this view. Small meat-eating dinosaurs and primitive birds share about 20 characteristics that neither group shares with other kinds of animals. Just a few of these include hollow bones, the position of the pelvis, the structure of their eggs, the shape of the shoulder blade, and a collarbone shaped into a wishbone. Dinosaurs had scales, and birds have modified scales – their feathers – and scaly feet. And it may be that at least some dinosaurs had feathers. Recently discovered fossils of a small dinosaur show that it had a feather-like covering. In fact, some primitive fossil birds and small meat-eating dinosaurs are so alike that it is difficult to tell them apart based on their skeletons alone.

alloys for fire-safety devices. *Symbol* **Bi.** *Atomic number* 83. *See* **Periodic Table,** pages 260–261.

bit The smallest unit of computer memory. A bit holds one of two possible values, either of the binary digits 0 or 1. *See panel at* **byte.**

bitmap *Computer Science.* A set of bits that represents a graphic image, with each bit or group of bits corresponding to a pixel in the image.

bitumen Any of various flammable mixtures of hydrocarbons and other substances found in asphalt and tar. Bitumens occur naturally or are produced from petroleum and coal.

bituminous coal A soft type of coal that burns with a smoky, yellow flame. Bituminous coal is the most abundant form of coal, but because of its high sulphur content its use can contribute to air pollution and acid rain. *Compare* **anthracite, lignite.**

bivalve A mollusc, such as a clam or oyster, whose shell consists of two halves hinged together. *Compare* **univalve.**

Bk The symbol for **berkelium.**

Black, Joseph 1728–1799. Scottish chemist. In 1756 he discovered carbon dioxide, which he called "fixed air." In addition to further studies of carbon dioxide, Black formulated the concepts of latent heat and specific heat.

Black Death A widespread epidemic of bubonic plague that occurred in several outbreaks between 1347 and 1400. It originated in Asia and then swept through Europe, where it killed about a third of the population.

black dwarf The celestial object that remains after a white dwarf has used up all of its energy and no longer gives off detectable radiation. *See panel at* **dwarf star.**

black hole An extremely dense celestial object that has a gravitational field so strong that nothing can escape, not even light. A black hole is formed by the collapse of a massive star's core in a supernova. *See more at* **star.**

Did You Know?

black hole

One of the strangest objects in the universe is the burnt-out remnant of a large star, known as a *black hole.* The name comes from the fact that the star collapses into itself, becoming infinitely dense so that its gravitational pull keeps even light from escaping. And if light can't get out, then nothing that ever enters the region near the black hole would ever escape. Rockets travelling to the moon or Mars need to achieve what is called escape velocity, the speed necessary to overcome the Earth's gravity. But since nothing can ever go faster than the speed of light, nothing could ever go fast enough to reach the escape velocity necessary to escape from a black hole.

black lung A lung disease of coal miners that is caused by the long-term inhalation of coal dust.

black water Waste water from flushed toilets. *See panel at* **grey water.**

black widow A very poisonous spider, the female of which has a black body, typically with a red, hourglass-shaped mark on the underside. The female often eats the male after mating.

bladder 1. A sac-shaped organ that stores the urine secreted by the kidneys, found in all vertebrates except birds and a few species of mammals known as monotremes. In mammals, the bladder is connected to each kidney by a ureter. **2.** An air bladder.

blade 1. The expanded part of a leaf or petal. *See more at* **leaf. 2.** The leaf of grasses and similar plants.

blastula (*plural* **blastulas** *or* **blastulae**) An embryo at the stage immediately following the division of the fertilized egg cell, consisting of a ball-shaped layer of cells around a fluid-filled cavity. This is the stage at which an embryo is replaced into the mother's uterus during infertility treatment using *in vitro* fertilization. *Compare* **gastrula.**

blight 1. Any of numerous plant diseases that cause leaves, stems, fruits and tissues to wither and die. Rust, mildew and smut are blights. Potato blight caused the failure of the potato crops that led to the terrible famines from 1845 to 1851. **2.** The bacterium, fungus or virus that causes such a disease.

blind spot The point on the retina where the optic nerve leaves the eye. There are no light-sensitive cells at this point, so there is a blind spot in the field of vision, but the brain 'fills in' the gap.

block and tackle A device consisting of a fixed pulley and a movable one, in which the rope attached to the load is passed over the fixed pulley, around the movable pulley, then back around the fixed one. Each pulley can have multiple grooves or wheels for the rope to pass over additional times. The more times the rope is passed around the two pulleys, the less effort is needed to raise a load.

blood 1. The fluid that circulates through the body of a mammal or other vertebrate animal by the action of the heart, carrying oxygen and nutrients to the body's cells and removing waste products from them. In humans and other vertebrates, blood consists of plasma containing red blood cells, white blood cells and platelets. **2.** A fluid that is similar in function in many invertebrate animals.

blood cell Any of the cells contained in blood; a red blood cell or white blood cell.

blood clot 1. A clot formed at the site of a wound, where bleeding is taking place. Platelets are involved in the formation of a network of protein threads. As red blood cells and more platelets pour out of the wound, they become entangled in the mesh, forming a jelly-like clot. This dries and hardens to form a scab to prevent the entry of bacteria and protect new skin as it grows. **2.** A blood clot may form within a closed blood vessel. If this happens, the blood clot can interfere with the circulation of the blood and can be fatal.

blood gas Any of the dissolved gases in blood plasma, especially oxygen and carbon dioxide.

blood group Any of the four main types into which human blood is divided: A, B, AB and O. Blood groups are based on the presence or absence of certain substances, called antigens, on red blood cells. Also called *blood type.*

blood plasma The clear, liquid part of the blood, composed mainly of water and proteins, in which the blood cells are suspended. The blood plasma of mammals also contains platelets.

■ **blood cell**
white blood cell surrounded by red blood cells

Did You Know?

blood groups

Blood transfusions used to be a doctor's treatment of last resort, since they often caused people to get sick and die. But in the 1890s, the American scientist Karl Landsteiner began to solve the transfusion puzzle. He found that all human red blood cells belonged to one of four groups, or *blood types*, which he named A, B, AB, and O. The types refer to substances, called *antigens*, found on the surface of these cells. Antibodies circulating in a person's blood normally recognize the antigens in that same person's blood cells and don't react with them. However, if a person with one blood group is given blood of another group, the antibodies bind to the foreign antigens, causing clumping of the blood and other serious reactions. So the key to the transfusion puzzle is to give a person blood that has matching antigens. Today, hospitals always test a blood sample before a transfusion to make sure there is a good match.

blood pressure The pressure of the blood in the vessels, especially the arteries, as it circulates through the body. Blood pressure varies with the strength of the heartbeat, the amount of blood being pumped, and the health of the blood vessels. *See more at* **high blood pressure.**

blood serum Blood plasma, especially blood plasma from which factors that cause clotting of the blood have been removed.

blood type *See* **blood group.**

blood vessel A tube or passage in the body through which blood circulates; an artery, a vein or a capillary.

blowhole 1. A hole or one of a pair of holes used for breathing and located on top of the head of whales, porpoises and dolphins. 2. A hole in ice to which aquatic mammals come to breathe.

blubber The thick layer of fat between the skin and the muscle layers of whales and other marine mammals. It insulates the animal from heat loss and serves as a food reserve.

blue-green alga *See* **cyanobacterium.**

blue shift A decrease in the wavelength of radiation emitted by an approaching celestial body as a result of the Doppler effect. Objects appear bluish because the shorter wavelengths of light are at the blue end of the visible spectrum. *Compare* **red shift.**

bog An area of wet, spongy ground consisting mainly of decayed or decaying moss and other vegetation. Bogs form as the dead vegetation sinks to the bottom of a lake or pond, where it decays to form peat.

Bohr, Niels Henrik David 1885–1962. Danish physicist who investigated atomic structure and radiation. Bohr developed a model of the atom in which electrons orbit the nucleus of an atom at set distances, changing levels only when energy is lost or gained, and emitting or absorbing radiation in the process. These ideas led to the development of quantum mechanics. *See panel on* page 44.

bohrium A synthetic, radioactive element that is produced by bombarding bismuth with chromium ions. Its most stable isotope has a half-life of 0.44 second. *Symbol* **Bh.** *Atomic number* 107. *See* **Periodic Table,** pages 260–261.

boil *verb* To change from a liquid to a gaseous state by heating or being heated to boiling point. —*noun* The act or condition of boiling: *bring the water to the boil.*

■ **blowhole**

Biography

Niels Bohr

At the beginning of the 20th century, scientists thought that atoms were organized a bit like a Christmas pudding, with a mixture of positive and negative charges loosely stuck together. Then Ernest Rutherford discovered the atomic nucleus and developed a model of the atom that was similar to the solar system, with negatively charged electrons orbiting a central nucleus the way planets revolve around the sun. Niels Bohr became interested in Rutherford's model, but it puzzled him because according to the laws of physics it should be very unstable. In trying to explain why it was not,

Bohr proposed that the electrons could travel only in specific, successively larger orbits around the nucleus. Any increase or decrease in an electron's energy meant that the electron changed place, jumping to a higher or lower orbit. Bohr assumed that when an electron jumps from an outer orbit to an inner one, it emits light. His theory explained the spectrum of light given off by hydrogen, the simplest atom, when its electron drops from a higher orbit to a lower one. Other scientists later modified and developed Bohr's theory into the area of science known as quantum mechanics.

boiling point The temperature at which a liquid changes to a vapour or gas. As the temperature of a liquid rises, the pressure of escaping vapour also rises, and at boiling point the pressure of the escaping vapour is equal to that exerted on the liquid by the surrounding air, causing bubbles to form. Typically, boiling points are measured at sea level. At higher altitudes, where atmospheric pressure is lower, boiling points are lower. The boiling point of water at sea level is 100°C; that of mercury is 356.58°C.

Boltzmann, Ludwig 1844–1906. Austrian physicist who developed statistical mechanics, the branch of physics that explains how the properties of atoms (such as mass and structure) determine the visible properties of matter (such as viscosity and heat conduction). Through his investigations of thermodynamics, Boltzmann developed numerous theories about the laws governing atomic motion and energy.

bond A force of attraction that holds atoms or ions together in a molecule or crystal. Bonds are usually created by a transfer or sharing of one or more electrons. There are single, double and triple bonds. *See also* **covalent bond, ionic bond, metallic bond.**

■ **bond**

In a water molecule (left), each hydrogen atom (H) shares an electron (yellow) with the oxygen atom (O), forming covalent bonds. In silver (centre), a metal, the negatively charged electrons (e) "float" around positively charged silver atoms (Ag), illustrating metallic bonding. In sodium chloride or salt (right), the sodium atom (Na) donates an electron to the chlorine atom (Cl), forming an ionic bond.

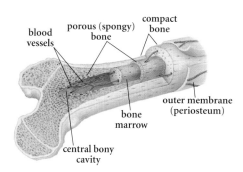

blood vessels
porous (spongy) bone
compact bone
outer membrane (periosteum)
bone marrow
central bony cavity

■ **bone**
cross-section of an adult human femur

bone 1. The hard, dense, calcified tissue that forms the skeleton of most vertebrates. Bone serves as a framework for the attachment of muscles and protects vital organs, such as the brain. It also contains large amounts of calcium, a mineral that is essential for proper cell function. Blood cells and platelets are produced in the marrow, the central cavity of bone. *See more at* **osteoblast, osteocyte.** 2. Any of the bones in a skeleton, such as the femur in the leg of a mammal.

bone marrow The spongy, red tissue that fills the bone cavities of mammals. Bone marrow is the source of red blood cells, platelets and most white blood cells.

Bonnet, Charles 1720–1793. Swiss naturalist who discovered parthenogenesis, by demonstrating that aphid eggs could develop without fertilization. Bonnet was also one of the first scientists to study photosynthesis.

bony fish A fish having a bony rather than cartilaginous skeleton. Most living species of fish are bony fish. *Compare* **cartilaginous fish, jawless fish.**

book lung The breathing organ of scorpions, spiders, and some other arachnids. It consists of membranes arranged in several parallel folds like the pages of a book.

Boole, George 1815–1864. British mathematician who wrote important works on many different areas of mathematics. He developed a method to describe reasoning using algebra that is now known as Boolean algebra.

Boolean algebra A mathematical system dealing with the relationship between sets, used to solve problems in logic and engineering. Variables consist of 0 and 1 and operations are expressed as *AND, OR* and *NOT*. Boolean algebra has been important in the development and programming of modern computers.

Boötes A constellation in the Northern Hemisphere near Virgo and Corona Borealis. It contains the bright star Arcturus.

borate A chemical compound containing the group BO_3.

borax A white, crystalline powder and mineral used as an antiseptic, as a cleansing agent, and in fusing metals and making heat-resistant glass. The mineral is an ore of boron.

boric acid A white or colourless crystalline compound, H_3BO_3, either naturally occurring or made from borax. It is used as an antiseptic and preservative, and in cements, enamels, and cosmetics.

boron A shiny, brittle, black nonmetallic element extracted chiefly from borax. It conducts electricity well at high temperatures but poorly at low temperatures. Boron is necessary for the growth of land plants and is used to make soaps, abrasives, and hard alloys. *Symbol* B. *Atomic number* 5. *See* **Periodic Table,** pages 260–261.

Bosch, Carl 1874–1940. German industrial chemist. Fritz Haber developed a new technique for making ammonia in the laboratory. However, it needed the skills of Carl Bosch (Haber's brother-in-law) to turn a laboratory technique into an industrial process, and by 1913 he had achieved this. The industrial production of ammonia involved converting nitrogen from the air and hydrogen from methane into ammonia at high temperatures and pressures. The process was enormously important as it allowed Germany – and later other countries – to produce nitrate fertilizers and explosives from the ammonia easily and relatively cheaply.

Bose, Satyendra Nath 1894–1974. Indian physicist known for his work in quantum mechanics, especially the development of theories describing the behaviour of subatomic particles.

botany 1. The scientific study of plants, including their growth, structure, and diseases. 2.

45

botulism

The plant life of a particular area: *the botany of southern Europe.*

botulism A severe, sometimes fatal food poisoning caused by eating food infected with a bacterium that produces a powerful nerve toxin. The bacterium grows in food that has been improperly preserved. ❖ The nerve toxin produced by this bacterium is called **botulin**.

boulder clay *See* **till**.

bovine *adjective* Relating to a cow or cattle. — *noun* An animal belonging to the genus *(Bos)* of ruminant mammals that includes the cow, wild ox and yak.

bovine spongiform encephalopathy *See* **mad cow disease**.

bowel The intestine, especially of a human. Often used in the plural as *bowels.*

Boyle, Robert 1627–1691. English physicist and chemist whose book, *The Sceptical Chemist* (1661), marked the beginning of modern chemistry. Boyle rejected the traditional theory that all matter was composed of four elements and defined an element as a substance that cannot be reduced to other, simpler substances or produced by combining simpler substances. Boyle also conducted important physics experiments with Robert Hooke that led to the development of Boyle's law.

Boyle's law The principle that the volume of a given mass of gas will increase as its pressure decreases, and will decrease as its pressure increases, as long as its temperature remains constant. *Compare* **Charles's law**.

Br The symbol for **bromine**.

brachial Relating to or resembling the arm or a similar part.

brachiopod Any of various invertebrate animals that live in the sea and resemble clams but are sedentary. Brachiopods have paired upper and lower shells attached to a stalk, and hollow tentacles covered with cilia that sweep food particles into the mouth.

brachiosaurus *or* brachiosaur (*plural* **brachiosauri** *or* brachiosaurs) A massive sauropod dinosaur of the Jurassic and Cretaceous Periods. It had forelegs that were longer than its hind legs, and nostrils on top of its head.

brackish Containing a mixture of seawater and fresh water; somewhat salty.

bract A small, leaf-like plant part growing just below a flower or flower stalk. Most bracts are thin and inconspicuous, but some are brightly coloured.

Bragg, Sir William Henry 1862–1942. British physicist who invented a device used to measure X-ray wavelengths. With his son, the physicist Sir William Lawrence Bragg (1890–1971), he developed the technique of X-ray crystallography, used to determine the atomic structure of crystals.

Brahe, Tycho 1546–1601. Danish astronomer who made the most accurate and extensive observations of the planets and stars in the age before the telescope. Brahe determined the position of stars and planets, demonstrated that comets follow regular paths, and made many systematic observations, without which Kepler could not have discovered that planets move in elliptical orbits.

brain 1. The part of the nervous system in vertebrates that is enclosed within the skull, is connected with the spinal cord, and is composed of grey matter and white matter. It receives and interprets impulses from sense organs, and it coordinates and controls body functions and activities, such as walking and talking. The brain is also the centre of memory, thought, and feeling. 2. A bundle of nerves in many invertebrate animals that is similar to the vertebrate brain in function and position.

brainstem The part of the vertebrate brain

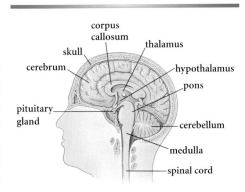

■ **brain**

located at the base of the brain and important in the control of many voluntary and involuntary body functions. In humans and other mammals, the brainstem is composed of the pons, medulla and midbrain.

brass A yellowish alloy of copper and zinc, usually 67 per cent copper and 33 per cent zinc. It sometimes includes small amounts of other metals. Brass is characterized by being strong and ductile, and by being resistant to many forms of corrosion.

breast An organ of female primates that contains milk-producing glands and usually occurs in pairs. It is present but undeveloped in the male.

breastbone *See* **sternum.**

breed *verb* 1. To produce or reproduce by giving birth or hatching: *mosquitoes breed in water.* 2. To raise animals or plants, often to produce new or improved types: *They are trying to breed a new type of corn.* —*noun* A group of organisms having common ancestors and sharing certain traits that

are not shared with other members of the same species. Breeds are usually produced by mating selected parents.

brine 1. Water saturated with or containing large amounts of a salt, especially sodium chloride. 2. The water of a sea or an ocean.

British thermal unit The amount of heat that is needed to raise the temperature of one pound of water by one degree Fahrenheit. This unit is used mainly to measure heat, but it can be applied to other forms of energy.

brittle Likely to break, snap or crack. *Compare* **ductile.**

broad-leaved, *also* **broad-leafed** Having broad leaves rather than needle-like or scale-like leaves. Azaleas, rhododendrons and holly are broad-leaved evergreens.

Broglie, Louis Victor De 1892–1987. French physicist who was the first to theorize that subatomic particles can behave as waves. Influenced by Albert Einstein's concept that waves can behave as particles, De Broglie proposed that the opposite was also true: that electrons, for example, can behave as waves. De Broglie's work developed the study of wave mechanics, which was important in the development of quantum physics.

bromate A chemical compound containing the ion BrO_3^-.

bromeliad Any of various tropical and subtropical plants found mainly in the Americas, usually having long, stiff leaves and colourful flowers. Many species of bromeliad grow on trees as epiphytes. The pineapple and Spanish moss are bromeliads.

bromide A compound, such as potassium bromide, containing bromine combined with another element or radical.

bromine A reddish-brown halogen element that can be found in combined form in seawater. The pure form is a nonmetallic liquid that gives off a highly irritating vapour. It is used to make dyes, sedatives and photographic film. *Symbol* **Br.** *Atomic number* 35. *See* **Periodic Table,** pages 260–261.

bronchial tube A bronchus or any of the tubes branching from a bronchus. The bronchial tubes decrease in size as they descend into the lungs.

bronchiole Any of the small, thin-walled tubes

Did You Know?

brain

At this very moment, these words are being scanned and interpreted by perhaps the most complex object in the world: the human brain. The bulbous organ that sits right behind your forehead is a collection of different parts that work together. For example, the two sides of the brain, called *hemispheres*, perform different tasks. The right hemisphere is responsible for musical and artistic ability and the ability to recognize faces. The left is where mathematical and logical analysis takes place, as well as most speech and language processing. Furthermore, each hemisphere is divided into four separate regions called *lobes*, which have their own jobs. Here's how specific the responsibilities of a particular brain area can be: in 2001 researchers discovered that there's an identifiable part of the brain (the medial ventral prefrontal cortex) where you make the connection that we call "getting" a joke.

that branch from a bronchus and end in the alveolar sacs of the lung.

bronchitis Inflammation of the bronchial tubes, often resulting from infection with a virus.

bronchus (*plural* **bronchi**) Either of the two main tubular structures branching from the trachea and leading to the lungs, where they divide into smaller branches.

Brønsted, Johannes Nicolaus 1879–1947. Danish physical chemist. Most of Brønsted's contributions to physical chemistry concerned the behaviour of solutions. He is best known for the new and very useful definition of acids and bases, which he developed at the same time as, but quite separate from, Thomas Lowry. The Brønsted-Lowry definition defines an acid as a substance with a tendency to lose a proton, and a base as a substance that tends to gain a proton. Brønsted's definition is still in use today.

brontosaurus *or* **brontosaur** One of the names given to a large vegetarian dinosaur discovered in the 1870s. The other name was **apatosaurus**.

bronze 1. An alloy of copper and tin, sometimes with small amounts of other metals. Bronze is harder than brass and is used both in industry and in art. 2. An alloy of copper and certain metals other than tin, such as aluminium.

Brown, Robert 1773–1858. Scottish botanist who brought back nearly 4000 species of plants for classification from Matthew Flinders' coastal survey of Australia in 1801–1805. He is well known for his investigation into the reproduction of plants and for being the first to note that, in general, living cells contain a nucleus. Then, in 1827, he first observed the movement of fine particles in a liquid. This movement is still called "Brownian motion" after the Scotsman who discovered it as he studied pollen grains under a microscope.

brown dwarf A celestial body that is similar to a star but does not emit light because it does not have enough mass to ignite internal nuclear fusion. *See panel at* **dwarf star.**

Brownian motion The random movement of microscopic particles suspended in a liquid or gas, caused by collisions between these particles and the molecules of the liquid or gas.

bryophyte A member of the Bryophyta, a large group of seedless green plants that live on land and lack tissues (known as vascular tissues) that circulate water and dissolved nutrients. Bryophytes include the mosses and liverworts.

bryozoan Any of various small aquatic animals that reproduce by budding and form moss-like or branching colonies attached to stones or seaweed.

BSE *See* **mad cow disease.**

Btu Abbreviation of **British thermal unit.**

bubble chamber A device used to observe the movements of charged subatomic particles. A bubble chamber consists of a container filled with liquid under pressure, kept at a temperature just below its boiling point. The pressure is reduced just before subatomic particles travel through the chamber. Although this reduction in pressure lowers the boiling point, the liquid does not boil until a disturbance is formed – and the subatomic

Word History

brontosaurus

Take a little deception, add a little excitement, stir them with a century-long mistake, and you have the mystery of the *brontosaurus*. Specifically, you have the mystery of its name. For 100 years this 70-foot-long, 30-ton vegetarian giant had two names. This case of double identity began in 1877, when bones of a large dinosaur were discovered. The creature was dubbed *apatosaurus*, a name that meant "deceptive lizard" or "unreal lizard". Two years later, bones of a larger dinosaur were found, and in all the excitement, scientists named it brontosaurus or "thunder lizard". This name stuck until scientists decided it was all a mistake – the two sets of bones actually belonged to the same type of dinosaur. Since it is a rule in taxonomy that the first name given to a newly discovered organism is the one that must be used, scientists have had to use the term *apatosaurus*. But "thunder lizard" had found a lot of popular appeal, and many people still prefer to call the beast *brontosaurus*.

particles form just such a disturbance. The paths of the subatomic particles are visible as trails of bubbles in the fluid. Bubble chambers are considered more useful than cloud chambers, because the bubbles remain visible longer than the condensation clouds of cloud chambers do. *Compare* **cloud chamber.**

bubo A swelling of a lymph node, especially of the armpit or groin. Buboes are characteristic of bubonic plague.

bubonic plague The most common form of plague, with symptoms including fever, vomiting, diarrhoea, and inflamed lymph nodes (called buboes). It is transmitted by fleas from infected rats or other rodents. The Black Death was an epidemic of bubonic plague. *See more at* **plague.**

Buchner, Eduard 1860–1917. German chemist whose great interest was in alcoholic fermentation. He showed that yeast itself is not actually necessary for fermentation to take place. His most important work was to discover the enzyme – zymase – which brings about the fermentation reaction even when isolated from the yeast organism. This was the first enzyme to be isolated and studied.

buckminsterfullerene An extremely stable, ball-shaped carbon molecule, C_{60}, whose structure looks like a geodesic dome. It is believed to occur naturally in soot. Also called *buckyball*. *See panel at* **carbon.**

buckyball *See* buckminsterfullerene.

bud *noun* 1. A small swelling on a branch or stem, containing an undeveloped flower, shoot or leaf. 2. A partly opened flower or leaf. 3. A small outgrowth on a simple organism, such as a yeast or hydra, that grows into a complete new organism of the same species. 4. A tiny part or organ, such as a taste bud, that is shaped like a bud. —*verb* To form or produce a bud or buds.

buffer 1. *Chemistry.* A substance that prevents change in the acidity of a solution when an acid or base is added to the solution. 2. *Computer Science.* A device or an area of a computer that temporarily stores data that is being transferred between two machines that process data at different rates, such as a computer and a printer.

Buffon, Comte Georges Louis Leclerc de 1707–1788. French naturalist who spent his life compiling the *Histoire naturelle*, in which he

---

Usage

bug

The word *bug* is often used to refer to tiny creatures that crawl along, such as insects and even small animals that are not insects, such as spiders and millipedes. But for scientists, the word has a much narrower meaning. Strictly speaking, bugs are those insects that have mouthparts adapted for piercing and sucking. The mouthparts of these bugs are contained in a beak-shaped structure. Thus scientists would classify an aphid, but not a beetle or a cockroach, as a bug. In fact, scientists often call aphids and their relatives true bugs, to distinguish them better from what everyone else calls "bugs".

---

attempted to discuss all of the facts about the natural world known at that time. It eventually reached 44 volumes and laid the foundation for later studies in biology, zoology and anatomy.

bug An insect, spider or similar small organism. In strict scientific usage, a bug is an insect belonging to the order of the true bugs. *See* **true bug.**

bulb 1. A round part of a stem that develops underground and contains the shoot of a new plant. A bulb is surrounded by leaf-like scales that provide nourishment to the new plant. Tulips, lilies and onions grow from bulbs. *Compare* **corm, rhizome, runner, tuber.** 2. The part of an incandescent or fluorescent lamp that gives off light. The bulb of an incandescent lamp contains a filament inside a usually rounded piece of glass. The bulb of a fluorescent lamp is a glass tube or chamber containing a mixture of gases without a filament.

bulimia An eating disorder in which episodes of binge eating are followed by fasting, self-induced vomiting, or other measures to prevent weight gain. It is most common among young women of normal or nearly normal weight.

Bunsen, Robert Wilhelm 1811–1899. German chemist who with Gustav Kirchhoff discovered the elements caesium and rubidium. Bunsen also

Did You Know?

Burgess Shale

Early animals on the Earth included many oddities. These animals had bizarre combinations of legs, spines, segments and heads found in no animals since, as if Nature were trying out different models to see what might work best. Many of these animals became extinct and left no descendants. Others may have evolved into groups that are well known today. We know a lot about these bizarre life forms thanks to the *Burgess Shale*, a 540-million-year-old formation of black shale in the Rocky Mountains of British Columbia in Canada. Unlike most rocks in which fossils are preserved, the Burgess Shale preserved the soft parts of organisms that normally would have rotted away (by reacting with oxygen) before the animals became fossils. This happened because the animals were killed instantly by a mudslide deep in the ocean, where there is very little oxygen. After the mud buried the animals, it hardened into shale. Thanks to this, we know a lot about the period of early animal evolution known as the Cambrian Explosion.

explained the action of geysers and invented various kinds of laboratory equipment, including the Bunsen burner.

Bunsen burner A small gas burner used in laboratories. It consists of a vertical metal tube connected to a gas fuel source, with adjustable holes at its base. These holes allow air to enter the tube and mix with the gas in order to make a very hot flame.

buoyancy The upward force that a fluid exerts on an object immersed in it. Buoyancy allows a boat to float on water.

burette A glass tube with fine gradations and with a tapered bottom that has a valve. It is used especially in laboratories to pour a measured amount of liquid from one container into another.

Burgess Shale A rock formation in the western

Canadian Rockies that contains numerous fossilized invertebrates from the early Cambrian Period.

burl A large, rounded outgrowth on the trunk or branch of a tree.

burn *verb* To be on fire; undergo combustion. A substance burns if it is heated up enough to react chemically with oxygen. *See panel at* **oxidation**. —*noun Medicine.* An injury produced by fire, heat, radiation, electricity or a caustic chemical agent. Burns are classified according to the degree of damage done to the tissues.

bursa (*plural* **bursae** *or* **bursas**) A flattened sac containing a lubricating fluid that reduces friction between a muscle or tendon and a bone. ❖ Inflammation of a bursa is called **bursitis**.

butane An organic compound, C_4H_{10}, found in natural gas and produced from petroleum. Butane is used as a fuel, refrigerant and propellant in aerosol cans. —*adjective* **butyl**.

butanoic acid A colourless fatty acid found in butter and certain plant oils. It has an unpleasant odour and is used in disinfectants and drugs.

butte A steep-sided hill with a flat top, often

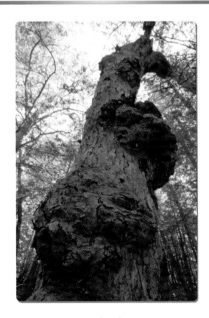

■ **burl**

Word History

byte/bit

The word *bit* is short for *bi*nary digi*t*. A bit consists of one of two values, usually 0 or 1. Computers use bits because their system of counting is based on two options: circuits in a microchip that are either *on* or *off*. Thus, a computer counts to seven in bits as follows: 0, 1, 10 [2], 11 [3], 100 [4], 101 [5], 110 [6], 111 [7]. Notice that the higher you count, the more adjacent bits you need to represent the number. For example, it requires two adjacent bits to count from 0 to 3, and it takes three adjacent bits to count from 0 to 7. A sequence of bits can represent not just numbers, but other kinds of data, such as the letters and symbols on a keyboard. The sequence of 0s and 1s that make up data are usually counted in groups of 8, and these groups of 8 bits are called *bytes*. The word *byte* is short for *b*inary digi*t* *e*ight. To transmit one keystroke on a typical keyboard requires one byte of information (or 8 bits). To transmit the three-letter word *the* requires three bytes of information (or 24 bits).

standing alone in an otherwise flat area. A butte is smaller than a mesa.

butterfly Any of various insects having slender bodies, knobbed antennae and four broad wings that are usually brightly coloured. Unlike moths, butterflies tend to hold their wings upright and together when at rest. *Compare* **moth.**

bypass An alternative pathway for the flow of blood or other body fluid, created by a surgeon as a detour around a blocked or diseased organ.

by-product Something produced in the process of making something else. For example, when plants produce carbohydrates by photosynthesis, oxygen is released as a by-product: *Asphalt and paraffin are by-products of the process of refining crude oil into gasoline.*

Byron, Augusta Ada. Countess of Lovelace. 1815–1852. British mathematician who collaborated with Charles Babbage in the development of the difference engine, an early computer. She compiled detailed notations about how the machine could be programmed.

byte A sequence of adjacent bits operated on as a unit by a computer. A byte usually consists of eight bits. Amounts of computer memory are often expressed in terms of megabytes (1,048,576 bytes) or gigabytes (1,073,741,824 bytes).

C c

c The symbol for the speed of light in a vacuum.

C 1. The symbol for **carbon**. 2. Abbreviation of **Celsius**.

Ca The symbol for **calcium**.

cactus (*plural* **cacti** *or* **cactuses**) Any of various plants that have thick, leafless, often spiny stems and grow in hot, dry places, chiefly in North and South America. Photosynthesis takes place in the stems of cacti, as the leaves have evolved into narrow spines to prevent water loss. Some kinds of cacti have brightly coloured flowers and edible fruit.

cadmium A rare, bluish-white metallic element that occurs mainly in small amounts in zinc ores. It is soft and easily cut with a knife. Cadmium is plated onto other metals and alloys to prevent corrosion, and it is used to make rechargeable batteries and nuclear reactors. *Symbol* **Cd**. *Atomic number* 48. *See* **Periodic Table**, pages 260–261.

caecum A large pouch forming the beginning of the large intestine. The caecum attaches to the ileum.

caesium A soft, easily shaped, silvery-white element that is an alkali metal. It melts at 28°C and is one of the most reactive metals. Caesium is used to make photoelectric cells, electron tubes and atomic clocks. *Symbol* **Cs**. *Atomic number* 55. *See* **Periodic Table**, pages 260–261.

caffeine A bitter white alkaloid found in tea, coffee and various plants. It is a mild stimulant.

Cainozoic The most recent era of geologic time, from about 65 million years ago to the present. The Cainozoic Era is characterized by the formation of modern continents and the diversification of mammals and plants. *See chart at* **geological time**, pages 148–149.

calcareous Composed of or containing calcium or calcium carbonate. Many carbonate rocks are calcareous.

calcification 1. *Medicine.* The accumulation of calcium or calcium salts in a body tissue.

Did You Know?

cactus

There are 2000 species of cacti, all specially adapted to survive in extremely dry climates, such as the desert areas of North and Central America. Cacti are excellent at conserving water. Their "leaves" are sharp spines, which have been known to cause great pain to animals interested in eating them. The spines also help the plant gather scarce water. Water vapour in the air condenses on the spines and then drips to the ground, where it is taken up by the roots. The roots are shallow and widely spread out to take advantage of this condensation and the rare desert rain showers. A cactus can be between 80 and 90 per cent water, and its thick walls keep its water from evaporating. In fact, a cactus can be a thousand times better at conserving water than a different kind of plant of the same weight.

Calcification normally occurs in the formation of bone. 2. *Geology.* **a.** The replacement of organic material, especially original hard material such as bone, with calcium carbonate during the process of fossilization. **b.** The accumulation of calcium in certain soils, especially soils of cool temperate regions where leaching takes place very slowly.

calcine To heat a substance to a high temperature without melting it, in order to turn it into a powder, oxidize it, or cause it to change in some other way.

calcite A usually white, clear, or pale-yellow mineral consisting of calcium carbonate. It occurs in many different forms and is the main component of chalk, limestone and marble. Calcite is the mineral used to represent a hardness of 3 on the Mohs scale.

calcium A silvery-white, moderately hard metallic element that is an alkaline-earth metal and occurs in minerals such as limestone and gypsum. It is a basic component of leaves, bones, teeth, and shells, and is essential for the normal growth and development of most animals and plants. Calcium is used to make plaster, cement and alloys. *Symbol* **Ca**. *Atomic number* 20. *See* **Periodic Table,** pages 260–261.

calcium carbonate A white or colourless crystalline compound, $CaCO_3$, occurring naturally in chalk, limestone and marble. It is used to make toothpaste, white paint and bleaching powder.

calcium chloride A white crystalline salt, $CaCl_2$. It attracts water very strongly, is used in refrigeration, and is spread on roads to melt ice and to control dust.

calculus The branch of mathematics concerned with maximum and minimum values of functions, rates of change, the area bounded by curves, and the volume bounded by surfaces. Calculus can be used to calculate such things as rates of change, the area bounded by curves, and the volume bounded by surfaces. *See more at* **differentiation, integration.**

calibrate 1. To check, adjust or standardize a measuring instrument, usually by comparing it with an accepted model: *calibrate an oven thermometer.* 2. To measure the diameter of the inside of a tube.

californium A synthetic, radioactive metallic element of the actinide series that is produced from curium or berkelium. Californium-252 has a very high rate of spontaneous fission and is used as a source of neutrons in medical research. Its most stable isotope has a half-life of about 900 years. *Symbol* **Cf.** *Atomic number* 98. *See* **Periodic Table,** pages 260–261.

calliper An instrument consisting of two curved, hinged legs, used to measure thickness and distance. Often used in the plural as *callipers.*

callus An area of the skin that has become hardened and thick, usually because of prolonged pressure or rubbing.

calorie 1. A unit of heat equal to the amount of heat needed to raise the temperature of one gram of water by one degree Celsius. 2a. A unit of heat equal to the amount of heat needed to raise the temperature of 1000 grams of water by one degree Celsius. Also called *kilocalorie* or *Calorie.* b. This unit used as a measure of the amount of heat energy released by food as it is digested by the body.

Calvin, Melvin 1911–1997. American chemist. In 1948 Calvin helped to work out the Thunberg-Wieland cycle by which some bacteria, unlike animals, can make glucose from ethanoate. This work led him on to investigate photosynthesis and he set up a team including many different types of scientists to determine exactly what went on as plants made their own food. The outcome was the Calvin cycle, the biological pathway by which plants fix carbon dioxide from the air and use it to make glucose.

calyx The sepals of a flower considered as a group.

cambium A tissue in the stems and roots of many seed-bearing plants, consisting of cells that

Word History

calculus

The branch of mathematics called *calculus* deals with problems that simple arithmetic or algebra cannot handle, such as finding areas and volumes of unusual shapes and solids, and measuring rates of change. The word *calculus* comes from the Latin word that means "little stone, pebble". How did a word meaning "little stone" come to refer to this branch of mathematics? The answer can be found in the counting methods used by the ancient Romans over 2000 years ago. They would add things up by using little pebbles or stones that represented particular numbers, as on an abacus. Later, the word *calculus* came to mean not just the pebble used in counting, but a counting system itself. Much more recently, it came to refer to the modern branch of mathematics, which was invented in the 17th century. The word *calculus,* incidentally, is also the source of the Latin word *calculare,* "to add up", which gives us our word *calculate.*

Cambrian Explosion The rapid diversification of multicellular animal life that took place around the beginning of the Cambrian Period. It resulted in the appearance of almost all modern animal phyla. *See panel at* **Burgess Shale.**

camouflage Protective colouring or other appearance that conceals an animal and enables it to blend into its surroundings.

camphor A white, gum-like, crystalline compound, $C_{10}H_{16}O$, having a strong odour and evaporating easily. It is used as an insect repellent and in making plastics and explosives.

cancer 1. A disease in which cells of a body part become abnormal and multiply without limit. Without treatment, the cells of some cancers may spread to and damage other tissues of the body. 2. A malignant tumour.

Cancer A constellation in the Northern Hemisphere near Leo and Gemini.

candela A unit used to measure the brightness

■ **camouflage**
this praying mantis is camouflaged against the leaves

divide rapidly to form new layers of tissue. The cambium is most active in woody plants, where it lies between the bark and wood of the stem. It is usually missing from monocotyledons, such as the grasses. ❖ The **vascular cambium** forms tissues that carry water and nutrients throughout the plant. On its outer surface the vascular cambium forms new layers of phloem, and on its inner surface, new layers of xylem. The growth of these new tissues causes the diameter of the stem to increase. ❖ The **cork cambium** creates cells that eventually become bark on the outside and cells that add to the cortex on the inside.

Cambrian The first period of the Palaeozoic Era, from about 545 to 495 million years ago, characterized by warm seas and desert land areas. During the Cambrian Period, animal life diversified rapidly and almost all modern animal phyla arose. *See chart at* **geological time,** pages 148–149.

Did You Know?

cancer

The word *cancer* refers to any of a number of illnesses caused by abnormal cells that multiply out of control. In some people, exposure to certain viruses, toxic chemicals, or abnormal amounts of radiation can cause changes in the parts of a cell's DNA that normally control and limit cell growth. These portions of DNA, called *oncogenes,* instruct cells to multiply abnormally. Large concentrations of cancer cells may produce lumps of cancerous tissue, called *tumours,* in a particular area of the body. Sometimes cancer cells break free from one area and travel through the bloodstream or lymph to other parts of the body, causing cancerous cells to grow there. Cancer treatments such as chemotherapy and radiation are designed to kill cancer cells, shrink tumours, and prevent the spread of the disease. With advances in the understanding of how genes work, scientists have begun using gene therapy to correct the faulty DNA that causes cancer cells to grow.

of a source of light. *See table at* **measurement.**

canine *adjective* **1.** Relating to a family of meat-eating mammals that includes dogs, wolves, foxes and coyotes. **2.** Relating to any of the four pointed teeth located behind the incisors in most mammals. In carnivores, the canine teeth are adapted for cutting and tearing meat. —*noun* **1.** An animal belonging to the canine family of mammals. **2.** A canine tooth.

Canis Major A constellation in the Southern Hemisphere near Orion. It contains Sirius, the brightest star in the night sky.

Canis Minor A constellation in the Northern Hemisphere near Hydra and the celestial equator. It contains the bright star Procyon.

canyon A long, deep, narrow valley with steep walls, cut into the ground by running water and often having a stream at the bottom.

capacitor A device used to store electric charge. Capacitors consist of two charged plates separated by an electrical insulator. The plates are charged by connecting them to a power supply. Charge then flows onto the plates so that positive charge is stored on one of the plates, and negative charge

---

battery

capacitor

charged plates

electrical insulator

■ **capacitor**

A capacitor is charged when electrons from a power source, such as a battery, flow to one of the two plates. Because the electrons cannot pass through the insulating layer, they build up on the first plate, giving it a negative charge. Electrons on the other plate are attracted to the positive terminal of the battery, causing that plate to become positively charged.

Did You Know?

capillary action

The paper towel industry owes its existence to *capillary action*. Towels easily absorb water because they consist of fibres containing tiny spaces into which liquids like water are drawn. This happens because the forces between the molecules in the liquid and the towel are larger than the forces between the molecules in the liquid. This effect can be seen very clearly if a narrow glass tube (sometimes called a *capillary tube*) is dipped into some water – the water rises up the tube. It is not only towels that rely on capillary action: the wax in a candle rises up the wick as a result of it, and the ink in a felt-tip pen reaches the tip of the pen in exactly the same way.

---

is stored on the other. Capacitors are used to regulate the flow of charge in electric circuits. ❖ The ability of a capacitor to store charge is called its **capacitance.** The capacitance depends on the area of the plates, the type of insulator, and the distance between the plates.

cape A point of land projecting into a body of water.

Capella A binary star in the constellation Auriga. It is one of the brightest stars in the night sky.

capillary Any of the tiny blood vessels that connect the smallest arteries to the smallest veins and form a network throughout the tissues of the body. The exchange of oxygen, nutrients, metabolic waste products and carbon dioxide between the tissues and the blood all takes place in the capillaries.

capillary action The movement of a liquid along the surface of a solid caused by the greater attraction of the liquid's molecules to the surface of the solid than to each other. The liquid's molecules adhere to the solid surface and also to each other, so that each molecule pulls the next one along. Water moves through the roots of trees or into the pores of a sponge or towel by capillary action.

Capricorn *or* **Capricornus** A constellation in

Did You Know?

carbon

Proteins, sugars, fats, and even DNA all contain many carbon atoms. The element *carbon* is also important, however, outside the chemistry of living things. The two most familiar forms of carbon – diamond and graphite – differ greatly because of the arrangement of their atoms. In diamond, each carbon atom bonds to four others in a dense network that makes the material the hardest substance known. But in graphite, each carbon atom bonds to only three others in a much looser arrangement of layers, each of which is weakly bonded to neighbouring layers. Because individual layers of carbon in graphite are so loosely connected, they are easily scraped away, which is why it is used as pencil "lead" for writing. In 1985 an entirely new form of carbon was discovered in which carbon atoms join to make a sphere called a *buckminsterfullerene* or *buckyball,* after the American architect Buckminster Fuller, who created buildings (*geodesic domes*) with a similar appearance. Scientists are currently looking for uses for buckyballs and tubes made from them.

the Southern Hemisphere near Aquarius and Sagittarius.

carapace A hard outer covering or shell made of bone or chitin on the back of animals such as turtles, armadillos and lobsters.

carbide A chemical compound consisting of carbon and a metal, such as calcium or tungsten. Many carbides are very hard and are used to make cutting tools and abrasives.

carbohydrate Any of a large class of organic compounds consisting of carbon, hydrogen and oxygen, usually with twice as many hydrogen atoms as carbon or oxygen atoms. Carbohydrates are produced in green plants by photosynthesis and serve as a major energy source in animal diets. Sugars, starches and cellulose are all carbohydrates.

carbon A naturally abundant, nonmetallic element that occurs in all organic compounds and can be found in all plants and animals. Diamonds and graphite are pure forms, and carbon is a major part of coal, petroleum and natural gas. Carbon can bond to itself and forms an enormous number of important molecules, many of which are essential for life. *Symbol* **C.** *Atomic number* 6. See **Periodic Table,** pages 260–261.

carbon-14 A naturally occurring radioactive isotope of carbon that is important in dating archaeological and biological remains by the technique known as radiocarbon dating. *See more at* **radiocarbon dating.**

carbonate *noun* A compound containing the group CO_3. Carbonates include minerals such as calcite and rocks such as limestone. —*verb* To add carbon dioxide to a substance, such as a drink.

carbon cycle The continuous process by which carbon is exchanged between organisms and the environment. Carbon dioxide is absorbed from the atmosphere by plants and algae and converted to carbohydrates by photosynthesis. Carbon is then passed into the food chain and returned to the atmosphere by the respiration and decay of animals, plants and other organisms. The burning of fossil fuels also releases carbon dioxide into the atmosphere.

carbon dating *See* **radiocarbon dating.**

carbon dioxide A colourless, odourless gas, CO_2, that is present in the atmosphere and is formed when any fuel containing carbon is burned in a plentiful supply of oxygen. It is produced by the respiration of animals and plants and by the decay of organic material. It is used by plants in photosynthesis to make carbohydrates. Carbon dioxide is also used in refrigeration, fire extinguishers and carbonated drinks.

carbon fixation The process by which carbon from the atmosphere is converted into carbon compounds, such as carbohydrates, in plants and algae, usually by photosynthesis.

Carboniferous The geological time from about 354 to 290 million years ago. The period is often divided into the Upper and Lower Carboniferous. The Carboniferous was the time when there were vast swamps. Plant remains accumulated in these swamps, eventually forming coal, an important

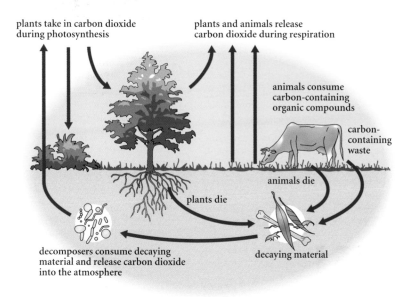

plants take in carbon dioxide during photosynthesis

plants and animals release carbon dioxide during respiration

animals consume carbon-containing organic compounds

carbon-containing waste

animals die

plants die

decomposers consume decaying material and release carbon dioxide into the atmosphere

decaying material

■ carbon cycle

fossil fuel. *See chart at* geological time, pages 148–149.

carbon monoxide A colourless, odourless gas, CO, formed when a compound containing carbon burns incompletely because there is not enough oxygen. It is present in the exhaust fumes of car engines and is very poisonous.

carcinogen A substance or agent that can cause cancer. Asbestos and tobacco products are examples of carcinogens.

carcinoma A cancerous growth on the surface of the skin, blood vessels or other organ or structure.

cardiac Relating to the heart: *a cardiac disorder.*

cardinal number A number, such as 3, 11 or 412, used in counting to indicate quantity but not order. *Compare* **ordinal number.**

cardinal point One of the four principal directions on a compass: north, south, east or west.

cardiology The branch of medicine that deals with the heart, its diseases and their treatment.

cardiopulmonary resuscitation *See* **CPR.**

cardiovascular Relating to the heart and blood vessels: *cardiovascular fitness.*

carnivore **1a.** An animal that feeds chiefly on the flesh of other animals. Carnivores include predators such as lions and alligators, and scavengers such as hyenas and vultures. *Compare* **herbivore. b.** Any of a taxonomic order of mammals of this kind, generally having large, sharp canine teeth. Dogs, cats, bears and weasels all belong to this order. **2.** A plant that eats insects, such as a Venus flytrap. —*adjective* **carnivorous.**

Carnot, Nicolas Léonard Sadi 1796–1832. French physicist and engineer who founded the science of thermodynamics. He was the first to analyse the working cycle and efficiency of the steam engine according to scientific principles. Carnot developed what would become the second law of thermodynamics and laid the foundation for work by Kelvin, Joule and others.

carotene An organic compound that occurs as an orange-yellow to red pigment in many plants and in animal tissue. In animals, it is converted to vitamin A by the liver. Carotenes give plants such as carrots, pumpkins and dandelions their characteristic colour.

Carothers, Wallace Hume 1896–1937. American chemist who developed the synthetic material nylon, patented in 1937.

carotid artery Either of the two large arteries in the neck that carry blood to the head.

carpal Any of the eight bones of the wrist lying between the forearm bones and the metacarpals. *See more at* **skeleton.**

carpal tunnel syndrome Pain, numbness or tingling in the hand, caused by compression of a nerve in the wrist. It is quite common and there are many causes, including arthritis, previous damage to the wrist and hormone problems. Recently, it has also been linked to excessive repetitive use of the fingers and wrist, as when using a computer keyboard.

carpel The female part of a flower. The carpel consists of the stigma, style, ovary and ovules. Like all the other parts of a flower, a carpel is a modified leaf. *See more at* **flower.**

carrier 1. A person or animal that serves as a host for a disease-causing organism and can transmit it to others, but does not have symptoms of the disease. Mosquitoes are carriers of malaria, for example. 2. An organism that carries a gene for a trait but does not show the trait itself, in other words it is heterozygous for a recessive gene. Carriers can produce offspring that express the trait by mating with another carrier of the same gene.

Carson, Rachel Louise 1907–1964. American marine biologist and writer whose best-known book, *Silent Spring* (1962), was an influential study of the dangerous effects of synthetic pesticides. Public reaction to the book resulted in stricter controls on pesticide use and shaped the ideas of the modern environmental movement.

Cartesian coordinate system A system in which the location of a point is given by coordinates that represent its distances from perpendicular lines that intersect at a point called the origin. A Cartesian coordinate system in a plane has two perpendicular lines (the x-axis and y-axis); in three-dimensional space, it has three (the x-axis, y-axis and z-axis).

cartilage A strong, flexible connective tissue that is found in various parts of the body, including the joints, the outer ear and the larynx. In the early development of most vertebrates, the skeleton forms as cartilage before most of it hardens into bone. —*adjective* **cartilaginous.**

cartilaginous fish A fish whose skeleton is made mainly of cartilage. Sharks, rays and skates are cartilaginous fish. *Compare* **bony fish, jawless fish.**

Cassiopeia A W-shaped constellation in the Northern Hemisphere near Andromeda and Cepheus.

Castor A bright multiple star in the constellation Gemini.

cat 1. Any of various meat-eating mammals including the lion, tiger, jaguar, lynx and cheetah. Most cats are solitary animals. All species except the cheetah have fully retractable claws. 2. The house cat, domesticated since ancient times and widely kept as a pet or a killer of rodents.

catabolism The phase of metabolism in which energy in the form of ATP is produced by the breakdown of complex molecules, such as proteins and fats, into simpler ones. *Compare* **anabolism.** —*adjective* **catabolic.**

catalyst A substance that speeds up the rate of a reaction but is not changed or used up itself. Catalysts work by lowering the activation energy of the reaction that they are catalysing. Catalysts in biological systems are known as enzymes. For example, finely divided iron is the catalyst in the Haber-Bosch process for making ammonia. —*verb* **catalyse.**

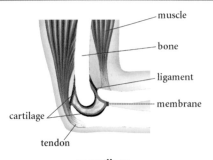

muscle
bone
ligament
membrane
cartilage
tendon

■ **cartilage**

catalytic converter A device containing catalysts such as platinum that is attached to modern car engines. It removes most of the unpleasant gases, such as sulphur dioxide and nitrogen oxides, produced by the engine of the car, making the exhaust gases far cleaner and reducing air pollution.

cataract 1. A cloudiness in the lens of an eye or the membrane that covers it, causing partial or total blindness. 2. A large, steep waterfall.

cat cracker A widely used term for a catalytic cracker, a system used in oil refineries to split the larger oil fractions into smaller useful ones. This is done by passing hot gases over hot catalysts to speed up thermal decomposition reactions.

caterpillar The worm-like larva of a butterfly or moth, often having fine hairs or brightly coloured patterns. Caterpillars feed on plants.

catfish Any of numerous scaleless, usually freshwater fish having whisker-like feelers on the upper jaw.

catheter A thin, flexible tube inserted into a duct of the body to remove a blockage or to drain fluid.

cathode 1. The negative electrode in an electrolytic cell, towards which positively charged particles are attracted. The cathode has a negative charge because it is connected to the negatively charged end of an external power supply. 2. The negative electrode in a voltaic cell, such as a battery. The cathode gets its negative charge from the chemical reaction that happens inside the battery, not from an external source. *Compare* **anode.**

cathode ray A beam of electrons streaming from the cathode (negatively charged end) of a vacuum tube. When cathode rays strike the anode (positively charged end) of the vacuum tube with sufficiently high energy, they produce X-rays.

cathode-ray tube A sealed tube in which electrons are made to escape from their atoms and move in a beam from the negatively charged end of the tube towards the positively charged end.

cation An ion that has a positive charge. Hydrogen and ammonium ions are cations. *Compare* **anion.**

catkin A long, thin cluster of tiny, petalless flowers growing on willows, birches, oaks,

Did You Know?

cathode-ray tube

Cathode-ray tubes (also called CRTs) are the visual display units (VDUs) in such items as conventional television sets, computer monitors, hospital heart-monitoring devices and laboratory oscilloscopes. CRTs are generally made up of sealed glass tubes that have had the air drawn out of them. At one end of the tube is a phosphor-coated screen, and at the other end is an electron "gun". The gun is a cathode (in this case a negative electrode). It directs a beam of electrons, also called a *cathode ray,* toward the screen. Coils outside the tube create magnetic fields that steer the beam on its way towards the screen. When the beam strikes the screen, it causes the phosphor to glow, producing an image.

poplars and certain other trees. The flowers on a catkin are either all male or all female. *See more at* **flower.**

CAT scan Short for *computerized axial tomography scan.* A cross-sectional view of an internal body part made by a computer that assembles a series of X-rays taken at different angles into a three-dimensional image. CAT scans are used in medicine to help diagnose a disease or disorder.

caudal Of or near the tail or hind parts of an animal: *a fish's caudal fin.*

cave A hollow or passage beneath the ground, or

■ CAT scan
a patient about to undergo a CAT scan

in the side of a hill or mountain with an opening to the surface. Caves can form in many ways, but especially from the dissolving of limestone.

Cavendish, Henry 1731–1810. British chemist and physicist who discovered hydrogen. He also showed that it was the lightest of all the gases and established that water is a compound of hydrogen and oxygen.

cavitation The sudden formation of bubbles in a liquid caused by mechanical forces, such as the moving blades of a ship's propeller.

Cd The symbol for **cadmium.**

CD Abbreviation of **compact disc.**

CD-ROM A compact disc containing permanently stored data that cannot be altered. *See more at* **compact disc.**

Ce The symbol for **cerium.**

celestial Relating to the sky or the heavens. Stars and planets are celestial bodies.

celestial equator A great circle on the celestial sphere in the same plane as the Earth's equator.

celestial pole Either of the points at which the extensions of the Earth's axis intersect the celestial sphere.

celestial sphere An imaginary sphere with the Earth at its centre. The stars, planets, sun, moon and other heavenly bodies appear to be located on this sphere.

cell 1. The basic unit of living matter in all organisms, consisting of protoplasm enclosed within a cell membrane. All cells except bacterial cells have a distinct nucleus that contains the cell's DNA as well as other structures like mitochondria and the endoplasmic reticulum. The main source of energy for all of the biological processes that take place within a cell is ATP. *See more at* **eukaryote, prokaryote. 2.** Any of various devices or units within such devices that are capable of converting some form of energy into electricity. Solar cells convert sunlight into electricity, and car batteries contain cells that convert chemical energy into electricity. —*adjective* **cellular.**

cell division The process by which a cell divides into two or more cells. Cell division is the means of reproduction in organisms that reproduce asexually, as by fission or spore formation. In organisms that reproduce sexually, cell division is the source of all tissue growth and repair. The two main types of cell division are mitosis and meiosis.

cell membrane The thin membrane that forms the outer surface of the protoplasm of a cell and regulates the passage of materials in and out of the cell. It is made up of proteins and lipids.

cellular respiration The process of metabolism by which cells obtain energy in the form of ATP. Glucose reacts with oxygen to

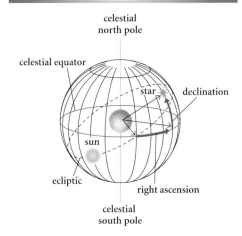

■ celestial sphere

Cell

The cell is the basic structural unit of all organisms. From the simplest single-celled animals to the most complex multicellular ones, cells perform all of the chemical processes needed to sustain life. The cells of eukaryotes – which include most organisms except bacteria – are made up of the same basic elements: a protective cell membrane, cytoplasm, a distinct nucleus that carries much of the organism's DNA, and small bodies called organelles. Cells vary in shape and form depending on the tasks they perform.

Typical Animal Cell

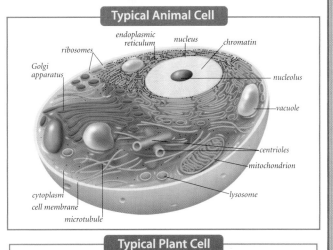

Typical Plant Cell

Specialized Cells

Nerve Cell (Neuron)

Nerve cells transmit electrical impulses within the nervous system.

Red Blood Cell

Red blood cells transport oxygen to and pick up carbon dioxide from the tissues of the body. They get their colour from an iron-containing compound called haemoglobin.

Guard Cell

Guard cells (shown in green-brown in the foreground) open and close pores (called stomata) in leaves, letting air in and water vapour out.

cellulose

provide energy, producing carbon dioxide and water as waste products.

cellulose A carbohydrate that is the main component of the cell walls of plants. It is insoluble in water and is used to make paper, cellophane, textiles, explosives and other products. ❖ An important compound derived from cellulose is **cellulose acetate**, forming a durable material that is used in making cinematographic film, magnetic tape, plastic film for wrapping and packaging, and textile fibres. It is often called *cellulose* or *acetate* for short.

cell wall The outermost layer of cells in plants, bacteria, fungi and many algae that gives shape to the cell and protects it from infection. In plants, it is made up mostly of cellulose. Animal cells do not have a cell wall.

Celsius Relating to a temperature scale on which the freezing point of water is 0° and the boiling point of water is 100° under normal atmospheric pressure. Abbreviation C.

Celsius, Anders 1701–1744. Swedish astronomer who invented the centigrade thermometer in 1742.

Centaurus A constellation in the Southern Hemisphere near the Southern Cross and Libra. It contains Alpha Centauri, the star nearest Earth.

centi– A prefix meaning "a hundredth", as in *centigram,* a hundredth of a gram.

centigrade *See* Celsius.

centigram A unit of weight in the metric system equal to 0.01 gram. *See table at* **measurement.**

centilitre A unit of volume in the metric system equal to 0.01 litre. *See table at* **measurement.**

Did You Know?

Celsius, Fahrenheit and Kelvin scales

In Europe and most of the world, a forecast of 37° would mean donning shorts and a T-shirt. In the United States, however, a temperature of 37° would see most people wrapping up warm. Why is this? Could it be that Americans feel the cold more? The reason, of course, is two different temperature scales. Americans favour the *Fahrenheit* scale, in which 37° means wintry conditions. Europeans, and most other nations, however, use the *Celsius* scale, in which 37° is equivalent to 98.6° Fahrenheit – body temperature! Scientists usually use Celsius, in which 0 is the freezing point of water (32°F) and 100 is its boiling point (212°F). (To convert between scales, see the table of measurements at the entry for *measurement.*) Scientists also use the *Kelvin* scale, where 0 is as cold as anything could ever get, which is about –273° Celsius (one Kelvin degree, or one kelvin, equals one Celsius degree). If it's going to be 37 kelvins, you'd better wear all the clothes you have, because your molecules will barely be moving at all.

centimetre A unit of length in the metric system equal to 0.01 metre. *See table at* measurement.

centipede Any of various worm-like arthropods

	human body	
freezing point of water	temperature (37°C, 98.6°F, 310K)	boiling point of water

Celsius	-20	-10	0	10	20	30	40	50	60	70	80	90	100
Fahrenheit	-4	14	32	50	68	86	104	122	140	158	176	194	212
Kelvin	253	263	273	283	293	303	313	323	333	343	353	363	373

■ **Celsius**

whose bodies are divided into many segments, each with a pair of legs. The front legs have venom glands and are used as pincers to catch prey. *Compare* millipede.

central angle An angle formed by two rays from the centre of a circle, with the centre forming the vertex.

central nervous system In vertebrate animals, the part of the nervous system that consists of the brain and spinal cord. *Compare* peripheral nervous system.

central processing unit The part of a computer that interprets and carries out instructions. It also transfers information to and from other components, such as a disc drive or the keyboard.

centre of gravity The point in a body through which the Earth's gravitational force acts, and around which the body's weight is evenly balanced.

centre of mass The point in a body that moves as though its entire mass were concentrated in it. It is usually in the same place as the centre of gravity.

centrifugal force The apparent force that seems to cause a body turning around a centre to move away from the centre. Centrifugal force is not a true force but is actually an example of inertia. *See panel at* centripetal force.

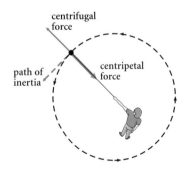

■ **centripetal force**
Centripetal force causes the ball being whirled at the end of a string to move in a circle about the person, and not to fly out and away along the path of inertia.

centrifuge A machine that separates substances of different densities by rotating them at very high speed. The denser substances are thrown further outwards than the less dense ones. A centrifuge can be used to separate cream from milk, or bacteria from a fluid.

centriole Either of a pair of cylinder-shaped bodies found in the centrosome of an animal cell. During mitosis, the centrioles move apart to help form the spindle, which then distributes the chromosomes in the dividing cell. *See more at* cell, meiosis, mitosis.

centripetal force The force that pulls an object moving in a circle towards the centre of the circle and causes the object to follow a curving path. The Earth's gravity acts as a centripetal force on the moon.

centromere The region of the chromosome to which the spindle fibre is attached during mitosis.

Did You Know?

centripetal force

In one popular fairground ride, people stand with their backs against the wall of a cylindrical chamber. The chamber spins rapidly and then the floor drops out, but the people on board remain pressed against the wall and don't fall down. Why? Most people would say that the reason people "stick" to the wall is because a *centrifugal,* or outward, force is pushing them against it. In fact, there is no outward force, no matter how strongly the people on the ride may think they feel one. It's actually just the opposite: the riders are really subject to an inward, or *centripetal,* force. As the ride spins, it forces the riders to travel in a circle. Objects (including people) in motion tend to travel in a straight line at constant speed unless they're acted on by some external force. To make an object travel along a curved path, you have to keep forcing it towards the "inside" of the curve. The walls of the ride do just that, pushing the riders towards the centre; the friction between the riders and the wall holds them up, so they seem to defy gravity.

centrosome

The centromere is where the chromatids join together in pairs before separating into individual chromosomes. *See more at* **meiosis, mitosis.**

centrosome A specialized region of the cytoplasm located next to the nucleus of a cell that in animal cells contains the centrioles.

cephalic Located on or near the head.

cephalochordate Any of various primitive chordate animals that lack a true vertebral column, having a notochord instead. The lancelets are cephalochordates.

cephalopod Any of various ocean molluscs, such as the octopus, squid and nautilus, having long tentacles around the mouth, a large head, a pair of large eyes and a sharp beak. If attacked, cephalopods squirt a cloud of dark inky liquid to confuse predators and make their escape.

cephalothorax The combined head and thorax of arachnids, such as spiders, and of many crustaceans, such as crabs.

Cepheus A constellation in the Northern Hemisphere near Cassiopeia and Draco.

ceratopsian Any of various medium-sized to large plant-eating dinosaurs of the late Jurassic and Cretaceous Periods. Ceratopsians walked on four legs and had a broad bony plate covering the neck, a beaked mouth and one or more horns on the head. Triceratops is an example of a ceratopsian.

cereal A grass, such as corn or wheat, whose starchy seeds are used as food.

cerebellum The part of the vertebrate brain that is located below the cerebrum at the rear of the skull and coordinates balance and muscle activity.

cerebral Relating to the brain or cerebrum.

cerebral cortex The outer layer of grey matter that covers the cerebral hemispheres in the brain of many vertebrate animals and is composed of folds of nerve cells and fibres. The cerebral cortex is responsible for higher functions of the nervous system including voluntary activity and the senses of hearing, vision, and touch. In humans, it is the centre of learning, language and memory.

cerebral hemisphere Either of the two symmetrical halves of the cerebrum. *See panel at* **brain.**

cerebral palsy A disorder caused by brain injury usually at or before birth, having symptoms that include poor muscle control and that often involve paralysis or abnormal stiffness of the muscles. Other forms of disability, such as mental retardation, may also be present.

cerebrospinal fluid The clear fluid that fills the cavities of the brain and spinal cord, serving to lubricate the tissues and to absorb shock.

cerebrum The largest part of the vertebrate brain, filling most of the skull and consisting of two cerebral hemispheres divided by a deep groove and joined by a mass of nerve fibres. The cerebrum processes complex sensory information and controls voluntary muscle activity. In humans it is the centre of thought, learning and memory.

Ceres The largest asteroid and the first to be discovered. It has a diameter of 1030 kilometres and orbits the sun between Mars and Jupiter.

cerium A shiny, grey metallic element of the lanthanide series. It is easily shaped and in pure form will ignite if scratched with a knife. It is used in glass polishing and as a catalyst in self-cleaning ovens. *Symbol* **Ce.** *Atomic number* 58. *See* **Periodic Table,** pages 260–261.

cervical 1. Relating to the cervix of the uterus. 2. Located at or near the part of the spine that forms the neck: *cervical vertebrae; a cervical disc.*

cervix The narrowed, lower end of the uterus, extending into the vagina.

cetacean Any of various, often very large marine mammals having an almost hairless body that resembles that of a fish. Cetaceans have a flat, horizontal tail and forelimbs modified into broad flippers. Whales, dolphins and porpoises are cetaceans.

Cf The symbol for **californium.**

CFC Abbreviation of **chlorofluorocarbon.** *See under* **fluorocarbon.**

Chadwick, Sir **James** 1891–1974. British physicist who discovered the neutron in 1932.

Chain, Sir **Ernst Boris** 1906–1979. German-born British biochemist who developed and purified penicillin with Howard Florey. Chain also helped to develop a way to manufacture the drug in large quantities and was involved in the first tests of its effects on humans.

chain reaction 1. *Physics.* A continuous series of nuclear fissions in which neutrons released from the splitting of one atomic nucleus collide with nearby nuclei, which in turn split and release more neutrons to collide with other nuclei, thus keeping the reaction going. *See more at* **fission.** *See panel at* **nuclear reactor.** 2. *Chemistry.* A reaction in which a change in one molecule causes changes in many other molecules until a stable compound is formed.

chalcedony A type of quartz that has a waxy lustre and varies from transparent to translucent. It is used as a gemstone. Agate and onyx are forms of chalcedony.

chalcopyrite A yellow metallic mineral consisting of iron, copper and sulphur. Chalcopyrite usually occurs as shapeless masses of grains and is an important ore of copper.

chalk A soft, white, grey or yellow limestone formed primarily from fossil seashells and consisting mainly of calcium carbonate. Chalk is used in making lime, cement and fertilizers, and as a whitening pigment in ceramics, paints and cosmetics. The chalk used for drawing or writing on blackboards, however, is usually artificial and not natural.

chameleon 1. Any of various small lizards of the Eastern Hemisphere, having the ability to change colour rapidly to blend in with their surroundings. They also have a long tail that helps them in climbing and large eyes that move independently of each other. 2. Any of various small lizards of the Western Hemisphere that can also change their colour.

chaos *Mathematics.* A system, such as the weather, that develops from a set of often simple initial conditions but behaves very differently if the initial conditions are changed even slightly. Chaotic systems often appear random and unpredictable, but in fact have regular patterns that are repeated at any scale of observation. *See more at* **fractal.**

charcoal A black porous form of carbon produced by heating wood or bone in little or no air. Charcoal is used as a fuel, for drawing, and in air and water filters.

charge A property of all particles of matter that determines whether they are attracted to or repelled by other particles. Charge is usually designated as positive or negative. Particles with like charges repel each other; particles with different or opposite charges attract each other.

Charles, Jacques Alexandre César 1746–1823. French physicist and inventor who formulated Charles's law in 1787. In 1783 he became the first person to use hydrogen in balloons for flight.

Charles's law The principle that the volume of a given mass of gas will increase as its temperature increases, and will decrease as its temperature decreases, as long as its pressure remains constant. *Compare* **Boyle's law.**

cheetah A long-legged, swift-running wild cat of Africa and southwest Asia, having spotted, light-brown fur and claws that do not fully retract. Cheetahs are the fastest land animals, able to sprint at up to 110 kilometres per hour.

chemical *adjective* Relating to or produced by means of chemistry: *a chemical discovery; a*

Did You Know?

charge

Electric *charge* is a basic property of elementary particles of matter. The protons in an atom have a positive charge, while its electrons have a negative charge. In an ordinary atom, the number of protons equals the number of electrons, so the atom is electrically neutral. If an atom gains some electrons, it becomes negatively charged. If it loses some electrons, it becomes positively charged. Atoms that become charged are called *ions.* Every charged particle is surrounded by an *electric field,* the region of space in which the charge exerts a force. Because of their electric fields, particles with unlike charges attract one another, and those with like charges repel one another. *Static electricity* consists of charged particles at rest. Electric *current* consists of moving charged particles, usually electrons or ions.

chemical change. —*noun* A substance obtained by or used in a chemical process; a chemical compound.

chemical engineering The branch of engineering that specializes in the development and manufacture of products involving chemicals.

chemical name The name of a chemical compound that shows the names of each of its elements or subcompounds. For example, the chemical name of bicarbonate of soda is sodium hydrogen carbonate.

chemistry 1. The scientific study of the structure, properties and reactions of the chemical elements and the compounds they form. 2. The composition, structure, properties and reactions of a substance.

chemosynthesis The formation of organic compounds using the energy released from chemical reactions instead of the energy of sunlight. Bacteria living in deep, dark areas of the sea are able to survive by chemosynthesis. They use energy derived from the oxidation of inorganic chemicals, such as sulphur from deep volcanic vents, to make their food. *Compare* **photosynthesis.**

chemotherapy The treatment of disease, especially cancer, with chemicals that have a specific poisonous effect on the cancerous or disease-causing cells.

chert A hard, brittle, reddish-brown to green sedimentary rock consisting of very small crystals of quartz.

chickenpox A highly contagious infection, usually occurring in young children, caused by a virus. Symptoms include an itchy skin rash and a high temperature. Also called *varicella.*

chimpanzee A dark-haired African ape that is somewhat smaller than a gorilla, lives mostly in trees, and has a high degree of intelligence. Chimpanzees, the closest living relatives of humans, live in close-knit groups and have elaborate social interactions.

chip *See* **integrated circuit.**

chiropractic A system for treating disorders of the body, especially disorders of the bones, muscles and joints, by manipulating the spine and other structures.

chitin A tough, semitransparent substance that is the main component of the exoskeletons of arthropods, such as the shells of crustaceans and the outer coverings of insects. Chitin is a carbohydrate and is also found in the cell walls of certain fungi and algae.

chlorate A chemical compound containing the ClO_3^- ion.

chloride A compound, such as ammonium chloride, containing chlorine combined with another element or radical.

chlorinate To add chlorine or one of its compounds to a substance. Water and sewage are chlorinated to be disinfected, and paper pulp is chlorinated to be bleached.

chlorine A greenish-yellow, gaseous halogen element that can combine with most other elements and is found chiefly in combination with sodium as common salt. Chlorine is very poisonous, being highly irritating to the nose, throat and lungs. It is used in purifying water, as a disinfectant and bleach, and in making many important compounds such as the plastic PVC. *Symbol* **Cl.** *Atomic number* 17. *See* **Periodic Table,** pages 260–261. *See panel at* **chlorophyll.**

chlorofluorocarbon *See under* **fluorocarbon.**

chloroform A colourless, toxic, sweet-tasting liquid, $CHCl_3$, used chiefly as a solvent. It was also once used as an anaesthetic.

chlorophyll Any of several green pigments found in photosynthetic organisms, such as green plants. Chlorophyll is composed of carbon, hydrogen, magnesium, nitrogen and oxygen. *See more at* **photosynthesis.**

chloroplast A tiny structure in the cells of green algae and green plants that contains chlorophyll. It is the site where light energy is trapped by the chlorophyll molecules and where photosynthesis takes place. *See more at* **cell, photosynthesis.**

cholera An infectious, sometimes fatal disease of the small intestine caused by a bacterium. It is contracted from contaminated water and food and causes severe diarrhoea, vomiting and dehydration.

cholesterol A fatty substance found in animals and plants that is a main component of cell membranes and is important in metabolism and

Word History

chlorophyll

From its name, we might think that chlorophyll has chlorine in it, but it doesn't. The *chloro–* of *chlorophyll* means "green"; chlorophyll in fact is the chemical compound that gives green plants their characteristic colour. The name of the chemical element *chlorine* comes from the same root as the prefix *chloro–*, and is so called because it is a greenish-coloured gas.

hormone production. In vertebrate animals, cholesterol is a major component of the blood. Higher than normal amounts of cholesterol in the blood, which can occur from eating too many fatty foods, may lead to diseases of the arteries such as atherosclerosis.

chordate Any of a large group of animals having at some stage of development a nerve cord and flexible spinal column (called a notochord) running along the back, and gill slits. Chordates include the vertebrates, lancelets and tunicates.

chorion The outer membrane that encloses the embryo of a reptile, bird or mammal. In mammals, the chorion contributes to the development of the placenta.

chromate A chemical compound containing the chromate ion CrO_4^{2-}.

chromatic Relating to colour or colours.

chromatid Either of the two strands formed when a chromosome duplicates itself during cell division. The chromatids are joined together by a single centromere and later separate to become individual chromosomes. *See more at* **meiosis, mitosis.**

chromatin The substance distributed in the nucleus of a cell that condenses to form chromosomes during mitosis. It consists mainly of DNA and proteins called histones.

chromatography A technique of chemical analysis used to separate substances in a mixture. The substances to be separated are placed on a stationary medium. A liquid or gas flows over this, carrying the substances at different rates depending on how strongly the molecules interact

with both the moving material and the stationary material.

chromium A hard, shiny, steel-grey metallic element that does not rust or become dull easily. It is used to plate other metals, to harden steel, and to make stainless steel and other alloys. *Symbol* **Cr.** *Atomic number* 24. *See* **Periodic Table,** pages 260–261.

chromosome A structure in all living cells that carries the genes that determine heredity. In all cells except bacterial cells, the chromosomes are thread-like strands of DNA and protein that are contained in the nucleus. In normal eukaryotic cells, the chromosomes occur in identical pairs, but in reproductive cells (the gametes) there is only a single set of chromosomes. In bacterial cells, which have no nucleus, the chromosome is a circular strand of DNA located in the cytoplasm.

chromosphere A glowing, transparent layer of gas surrounding the photosphere of a star, especially the sun. The sun's chromosphere is several thousand kilometres thick and is composed mainly of hydrogen.

chronometer An extremely accurate clock or other timepiece. Chronometers are used in scientific experiments, navigation and astronomical observations.

chrysalis 1. The pupa of certain kinds of insects, especially of moths and butterflies, that is

■ **chrysalis**
monarch butterfly chrysalis

inactive and enclosed in a firm case or cocoon from which the adult eventually emerges. **2.** The case or cocoon of a chrysalis.

cicada Any of various insects having a broad head and transparent wings. Male cicadas have a pair of sound-producing organs on the abdomen that produce a high-pitched buzz. Cicadas spend two or more years living underground as nymphs before emerging as adults that live for short periods in trees.

–cide A suffix that means "a killer of". It is used to form the names of chemicals that kill a specified organism, such as *pesticide,* a chemical that kills pests.

cilium (*plural* **cilia**) A hair-like projection capable of a whipping motion and found in certain

■ **circle**
The area of a circle is πr². The length of the circumference is 2πr.

vertebrate cells and microscopic organisms, especially protozoans. Some microorganisms, such as paramecia, use cilia for movement. Cilia lining the human respiratory tract act to remove foreign matter from air before it reaches the lungs.

cinchona Any of several evergreen trees and shrubs of South America whose bark is the source of quinine and certain other drugs used to treat malaria.

circadian rhythm A daily cycle of biological activity based on a 24-hour period and influenced by regular variations in the environment, such as the alternation of night and day.

circle A closed curve whose points are all in the same plane and at the same distance from a fixed point (the centre).

circuit **1.** A closed path through which an electric current flows or may flow. ❖ Circuits in

Did You Know?

circadian rhythm

Why do you sometimes wake up on time even if your alarm clock doesn't ring? How do nocturnal animals know when it is time to wake up? It's because you – and most other animals – have a kind of internal clock that controls the cycle of the day's biological activities, such as sleeping and waking. These daily biological activities are known as *circadian rhythms* because they are influenced by the regular intervals of light and dark in each 24-hour day. While the process underlying circadian rhythm is not completely understood, it is mainly controlled by the release of hormones. The brain regulates the amount of hormone released in response to the information it gets from light-sensitive cells in the eye, called *photoreceptors.* Circadian rhythms can be disrupted by changes in this daily schedule. For example, biologists have observed that birds exposed to artificial light for a long time sometimes build nests in the autumn instead of the spring. In humans who travel long distances by air, the local time of day no longer matches the body's internal clock, causing a condition known as *jet lag.*

■ **circuit**
Bulbs in a series circuit (left) *give off dim light since they each consume a portion of the power coming through a single circuit connected to the battery. In a parallel circuit* (right)*, bulbs shine brightly since each is directly connected in its own circuit to the power source.*

which a power source is connected to two or more components (such as light bulbs), one after the other, are called **series circuits**. If the circuit is broken, none of the components receives a current. Circuits in which a power source is directly connected to two or more components are called **parallel circuits**. If a break occurs in the circuit, only the component along whose path the break occurs stops receiving a current. **2.** A system of electrically connected parts or devices: *a microchip containing all the circuits of a computer.*

circuit board In a computer, an insulated board on which interconnected circuits and components such as microchips are mounted or etched.

circuit breaker A switch that automatically interrupts the flow of an electric current if the current becomes too strong.

circulation The flow of blood as it is pumped by the heart to all the tissues of the body and then back to the heart. Blood that is rich in oxygen is carried away from the heart by the arteries, and blood that is low in oxygen is returned to the heart by the veins. Nutrients and waste products are exchanged between the blood and the tissues of the body during circulation.

circulatory system The system that circulates blood through the body, consisting of the heart and blood vessels. In all vertebrates and certain invertebrates, the circulatory system is completely contained within a network of vessels. In vertebrates, the lymphatic system is also considered part of the circulatory system.

circum– A prefix meaning "around", as in *circumscribe*, to draw a figure around another figure.

circumference **1a.** The boundary line of a circle. **b.** The boundary line of a figure, area or object. **2.** The length of such a boundary, calculated as C=2πr or circumference of a circle = π × diameter.

circumscribe *Geometry.* To draw a figure around another figure so as to touch as many points as possible. A circle that circumscribes a triangle touches it at each of the triangle's three vertices.

cirrhosis A liver disease in which normal liver cells are gradually replaced by scar tissue, causing the organ to shrink, harden and lose its function.

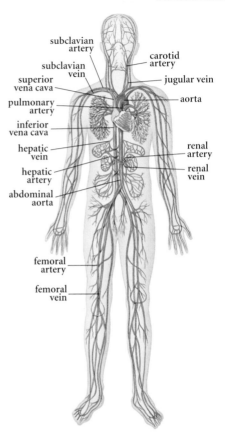

subclavian artery

carotid artery

subclavian vein

superior vena cava

jugular vein

pulmonary artery

aorta

inferior vena cava

hepatic vein

renal artery

hepatic artery

renal vein

abdominal aorta

femoral artery

femoral vein

■ **circulatory system**
In the diagram above, the blood vessels of the circulatory system are coloured according to whether they carry blood that is high in oxygen (red) or low in oxygen (blue). Most arteries, which carry blood away from the heart, are coloured red; most veins, which carry blood back towards the heart, are coloured blue.

Cirrhosis is most commonly caused by chronic alcohol abuse.

cirrocumulus A grainy or rippled cloud formation, usually occurring in sheets or bands. Cirrocumulus clouds form at upper levels of the atmosphere.

cirrostratus A thin, hazy cloud formation made up of ice crystals, often covering the sky in sheets

cirrus

and producing a halo effect around the sun. Cirrostratus clouds form at upper levels of the atmosphere.

cirrus A cloud formation made up of feathery white patches, bands or streamers of ice crystals. Cirrus clouds form at upper levels of the atmosphere.

citrate A salt or ester of citric acid, containing the citrate ion $C_6H_5O_7^{3-}$.

citric acid A white, odourless acid, $C_6H_8O_7$, having a sour taste and occurring widely in plants, especially in citrus fruit. It is used in medicine and as a flavouring.

citric acid cycle *See* **Krebs cycle.**

citronella The pale-yellow, lemon-scented oil obtained from the leaves of a tropical Asian grass, used in insect repellents and perfumes.

citrus 1. Any of various evergreen trees or shrubs bearing fruit with juicy flesh and a thick rind. Citrus trees are native to southern and southeast Asia but are grown in warm climates around the world. Many species have spines. The orange, lemon, lime and grapefruit are citrus trees. 2. The usually edible fruit of one of these trees or shrubs.

civil engineering The branch of engineering that specializes in the design and construction of projects such as bridges, roads, and dams.

Cl The symbol for **chlorine.**

clam Any of various bivalve molluscs having equal shells and a burrowing foot, some of which are edible. Clams include both marine and freshwater species.

class A group of organisms ranking above an order and below a phylum or division. *See table at* **taxonomy.**

classical physics Physics that is based on Newton's laws of motion and does not make use of quantum mechanics and the theory of relativity. ❖ **Classical mechanics** refers to Newton's laws of motion and other principles of mechanics based on them. Classical mechanics does not work when dealing with bodies moving at speeds close to that of light, or when making measurements of atoms and subatomic particles. These phenomena can only be described by quantum mechanics and the theory of relativity.

classification In biology, the systematic grouping of organisms according to the evolutionary or structural relationships between them. The traditional system of classification is called the Linnaean system. *See table at* **taxonomy.**

clavicle Either of two slender bones in humans and other primates that extend from the upper part of the sternum to the shoulder. Also called *collarbone. See more at* **skeleton.**

claw 1. A sharp, curved nail at the end of a toe of a mammal, reptile or bird. 2. A pincer, as of a lobster or crab, used for grasping.

clay A stiff, sticky, earthy material that is soft and flexible when wet and consists mainly of various silicates of aluminium. It is widely used to make bricks, pottery and tiles.

cleavage 1. *Geology.* The breaking of certain minerals along specific planes, making smooth surfaces. These surfaces are parallel to the faces of the molecular crystals that make up the minerals. A mineral that exhibits cleavage breaks into smooth pieces with the same pattern of parallel surfaces regardless of how many times it is broken. Some minerals, like quartz, do not have a cleavage and break into uneven pieces with rough surfaces. 2. *Biology.* In an embryo, the series of cell divisions by which a single fertilized egg cell becomes a many-celled blastula.

cleft palate Incomplete closure of the palate during development of an embryo, resulting in a split along part or all of the roof of the mouth. ❖ A vertical split or cleft in the upper lip that can occur with or without a cleft palate is called a **hare lip.**

climate The general or average weather conditions of a certain region, including temperature, rainfall and wind: *Caribbean islands have a year-round climate of warm breezes and sunshine.*

climatology The scientific study of climates, including the causes and long-term effects of variation in regional and global climates.

climax community An ecological community in which populations of plants or animals remain stable and exist in balance with each other and their environment. A climax community is the final stage of succession, remaining relatively unchanged until destroyed

70

by an event such as fire or human interference. *See more at* **succession.**

clitoris A sensitive external organ of the reproductive system in female mammals and some other animals that is capable of becoming erect. It is located above or in front of the urethra.

cloaca The body cavity into which the intestinal, urinary, and genital canals empty in birds, reptiles, amphibians, most fish and the primitive mammals known as monotremes. The cloaca has an opening for expelling its contents from the body.

clone *noun* **1.** A cell, group of cells, or organism that is produced asexually from a single ancestor. The cells of an individual plant or animal are clones because they all descend from a single fertilized cell. A clone may be produced by fission, in the case of single-celled organisms, or by budding, as in the hydra. Some plants can produce clones from horizontal stems, such as runners. Clones of cells and some plants and animals can also be produced in a laboratory. **2.** A copy of a sequence of DNA, as from a gene, that is produced by genetic engineering. The clone is then transplanted into the nucleus of a cell from which genetic material has been removed. —*verb*

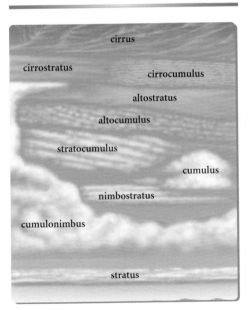

■ cloud

1. To produce or grow a cell, group of cells, or organism from a single original cell. **2.** To make identical copies of a DNA sequence. *See more at* **genetic engineering.**

closed 1. Relating to a curve, such as a circle, having no endpoints. **2.** Being a set with the property that the results produced by an operation (such as addition) on members of the set are also members of the set. The set of whole numbers is closed under addition (because whole numbers are the result of adding whole numbers), but not under division (because fractions may result from dividing one number by another).

closed circuit 1. An electric circuit through which current can flow in an uninterrupted path. **2.** A television system in which the signal is usually sent by cable to a limited number of receivers.

closed universe A model of the universe in which there is enough matter, and therefore enough gravitational force, to stop the expansion started by the big bang. *See panel at* **big bang.**

clot A thickened or solid mass formed from a liquid: *a blood clot.*

cloud 1. A visible mass of condensed water droplets or ice particles floating in the atmosphere. Clouds take various shapes depending on the conditions under which they form and their height in the atmosphere, ranging from ground or sea level to several kilometres above the Earth. **2.** A distinguishable mass of particles or gas, such as the collection of gases and dust in a nebula.

cloud chamber A device used to observe the movements of charged atomic particles and subatomic particles, such as ions and electrons. Cloud chambers consist of a closed container connected to a piston and filled with a gas. When the piston is suddenly moved outwards, the vapour expands and cools, forming a visible cloud of tiny droplets on any charged particles present. *Compare* **bubble chamber.**

cloud seeding A method of making a cloud give up its moisture as rain, especially by releasing particles of dry ice or silver iodide into the cloud.

club moss Any of various primitive plants that resemble mosses and reproduce by spores, but

■ **coelacanth**

have tissues (known as vascular tissues) that conduct fluids. Club mosses live in moist environments, have evergreen needle-like leaves, and often resemble miniature conifers. They live in tropical and temperate regions, with many tropical species growing in trees as epiphytes.

cm Abbreviation of **centimetre**.

Cm The symbol for **curium**.

cm³ Abbreviation of **centimetre cubed**, a measurement of volume.

cnidarian Any of various invertebrate animals that have a body with radial symmetry, tentacles and a sac-like internal cavity. They have a single opening for ingesting food and eliminating waste. Cnidarians include jellyfish, hydras, sea anemones and corals. Also called *coelenterate*.

Co The symbol for **cobalt**.

coagulate To change a liquid into a solid or nearly solid mass: *Exposure to air coagulates the blood.*

coal A dark-brown to black, natural solid substance formed from fossilized plants under conditions of great pressure, high humidity, and lack of air. Coal consists mainly of carbon and is widely used as a fuel and raw material. *See more at* **anthracite, bituminous coal, lignite**.

coal tar A thick, sticky, black liquid obtained by heating coal in the absence of air. It is used as a raw material for many dyes, drugs and paints.

cobalamin *See under* **vitamin B complex**.

cobalt A silvery-white, hard, brittle metallic element that occurs widely in ores containing other metals. It is used to make magnetic alloys, heat-resistant alloys and blue pigment for ceramics and glass. *Symbol* **Co**. *Atomic number* 27. *See* **Periodic Table**, pages 260–261.

cobra Any of several poisonous Asian or African snakes capable of spreading out the skin of the neck to form a flattened hood when excited.

coccus (*plural* **cocci**) Any of various bacteria that are shaped like a sphere and are usually linked together to form chains.

coccyx A small triangular bone at the base of the spine in humans and tailless apes. It is composed of several fused vertebrae. Also called *tailbone*. *See more at* **skeleton**.

cochlea A spiral tube of the inner ear that looks like a snail's shell and contains the nerve endings necessary for hearing.

Cockcroft, Sir John Douglas 1897–1967. British physicist. With the physicist Ernest Walton, he developed the particle accelerator. Their experiments with it led to the first successful splitting of an atom using artificially accelerated subatomic particles in 1932.

cockle Any of various bivalve molluscs having rounded or heart-shaped shells with radiating ridges.

cockroach Any of numerous brownish or black insects having a flat body and usually long antennae. Certain species are common household pests.

cocoon 1. A case or covering of silky strands spun by an insect larva and inhabited for protection during its pupal stage. 2. A similar protective structure, such as the egg cases made by spiders or earthworms.

coefficient A number or symbol multiplied with a variable or an unknown quantity in an algebraic term. For example, 4 is the coefficient in the term $4x$, and x is the coefficient in $x(a + b)$.

coelacanth Any of various fish having lobed, fleshy fins. They are the only living varieties of an ancient order of lobe-finned fish. Coelacanths were thought to be extinct until a living species was discovered in 1938.

coelenterate *See* **cnidarian**.

coevolution The evolution of two or more species that are dependent on one another, with each species adapting to changes in the other. The development of flowering plants and insects such as bees and butterflies that pollinate them is an example of coevolution.

cohesion The force of attraction that holds

molecules of a given substance together. It is strongest in solids, less strong in liquids, and least strong in gases. Cohesion allows the formation of drops in liquids, and clouds in the atmosphere.

cold-blooded Having a body temperature that changes according to the temperature of the surroundings. Fish, amphibians and reptiles are cold-blooded.

cold front The forward edge of an advancing mass of cold air that pushes under a mass of warm air. A cold front is often accompanied by heavy showers or thunderstorms. *See more at* **front.**

collagen The tough, fibrous protein found in bone, cartilage, skin, and other connective tissue. Collagen provides these body structures with the ability to withstand forces that stretch or lengthen them.

collarbone *See* **clavicle.**

collinear *Mathematics.* **1.** Sharing a common line, such as two intersecting planes. **2.** Lying on the same line, such as a set of points.

collision zone *See* **convergent plate boundary.**

■ **colony**
a penguin colony

■ **Colorado beetle**

colloid A mixture in which very small particles of one substance are distributed evenly throughout another substance. The particles are generally larger than those in a solution, and smaller than those in a suspension. Paints, milk and fog are examples of colloids. *Compare* **solution, suspension.**

colon The longest part of the large intestine, extending from the caecum to the rectum. Water is removed from the food waste received from the small intestine and is returned to the blood. The semi-solid material left at the end of the colon is passed out of the anus at intervals as faeces.

colonization *Ecology.* The spreading of a species into a new habitat.

colony A group of the same kind of animals, plants or one-celled organisms living or growing together: *a colony of ants; a colony of bacteria.*

Colorado beetle A yellow and black striped beetle that is a serious pest of potatoes. The beetle originated in the United States but is now found in Europe and elsewhere.

Colorado beetle A yellow and black striped beetle that is a serious pest of potatoes. The beetle originated in the United States but is now found in Europe and elsewhere.

colour The sensation produced by the effect of light waves striking the retina of the eye. The colour of something depends mainly on which wavelengths of light it emits, reflects or transmits. *See A Closer Look,* page 74.

colour-blind Unable to distinguish certain

Colour

A Closer Look

When beams of coloured light are mixed, or added, their wavelengths combine to form other colours. All colours can be formed by mixing wavelengths corresponding to the additive primaries red, green and blue. When two of the additive primaries are mixed in equal proportion, they form the complement of the third. Thus cyan (a mixture of green and blue) is the complement of red; magenta (a mixture of blue and red) is the complement of green; and yellow (a mixture of red and green) is the complement of blue. Mixing the three additive primaries in equal proportions produces white light.

When light passes through a colour filter, certain wavelengths are absorbed, or subtracted, while others are transmitted. The subtractive primaries cyan, magenta and yellow can be combined using overlapping filters to form all other colours. Thus overlapping filters of cyan (blue and green) and magenta (blue and red) filter out all wavelengths except blue; magenta (blue and red) and yellow (red and green) filter out all except red; and yellow (red and green) and cyan (blue and green) filter out all except green. Combining all three subtractive primaries in equal proportions filters out all wavelengths, producing black.

Colour Space

hue *value* *saturation*

We often describe different shades of colour as being dark, light, bright or pale. A particular colour can be described scientifically in terms of its *hue* (red, green, blue and so forth), its *value* (how light or dark it is), and its *saturation* (how intense or vivid it is). The diagram above organizes these aspects of colour into three dimensions: a central disc or ring displaying the range of hues, a vertical axis representing the values from light to dark, and a horizontal axis representing the degree of saturation from pale to intense.

Additive Primaries

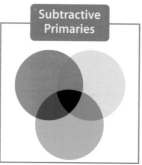

Subtractive Primaries

colours. Humans who are colour-blind usually cannot distinguish red from green. Many animals, including cats and dogs, are able to distinguish only a few colours.

coma[1] A state of deep unconsciousness resulting from disease or injury, from which a person cannot be roused. A person in a coma is usually unable to respond to events taking place outside the body.

coma[2] The brightly shining cloud of gas that encircles the nucleus and makes up the major portion of the head of a comet that is near the sun.

comb jelly Any of various invertebrate animals living in the sea and having transparent, jelly-like bodies. Comb jellies have eight rows of comb-like cilia used for swimming.

combustion 1. The process of burning. 2. A

■ **comet**

chemical change, especially through the rapid combination of a substance with oxygen, producing heat and, usually, light. *See also* **spontaneous combustion.**

comet A celestial object that orbits the sun along an elongated path. When close to the sun, a comet has a head made up of a gaseous coma surrounding a solid nucleus of ice, frozen gases and dust. A long, bright stream of gas and dust forms the tail of a comet. The comet's tail always points away from the sun, in the direction of the solar wind. *See panel at* **solar system.**

commensalism A symbiotic relationship between two organisms of different species in which one derives benefit without harming the other. *See panel at* **symbiosis.**

common cold An infection caused by a virus, in which the membranes lining the mouth, nose, and throat become inflamed. Its symptoms are a high temperature, sneezing and coughing.

common denominator A quantity into which all the denominators of a set of fractions may be divided without a remainder. For example, the fractions $\frac{1}{3}$ and $\frac{2}{5}$ have a common denominator of 15.

common divisor A number that is a factor of two or more numbers. For example, 3 is a common divisor of both 9 and 15. Also called *common factor.*

common factor A factor that two or more

numbers have in common. For exapmle, 5 is a common factor of 15 and 20.

common multiple A number divisible by each of two or more numbers without a remainder. For example, 12 is a common multiple of 2, 3, 4 and 6.

communicable Capable of being transmitted from person to person. Chickenpox is a communicable disease. *See panel at* **infectious.**

communications satellite An artificial space satellite used to transmit signals, such as television and telephone signals, from one ground station to another.

community A group of plants and animals living and interacting with one another in a particular place. A community can be small and local, as in a pond or city park, or it can be regional or global, as in a rainforest or the sea.

commutative property The property of addition and multiplication which states that a difference in the order in which numbers are added or multiplied will not change the result of the operation. For example, 2 + 3 gives the same sum as 3 + 2, and 2 × 3 gives the same product as 3 × 2. *See also* **associative property, distributive property.**

compact disc *or* **compact disk** *or* **CD** A small optical disc on which data such as music, text or graphic images are digitally encoded.

compass 1. A device used to determine geographical direction, usually consisting of a magnetic needle mounted so that it points to magnetic north. 2. A device used for drawing circles and arcs and for measuring distances, consisting of two legs hinged together at one end.

complement 1. A system of proteins found in the serum of the blood that helps antibodies destroy disease-causing bacteria or other foreign substances, especially antigens. 2. A complementary colour.

complementary angles Two angles whose sum is 90°.

complementary colour A secondary colour that, when combined with the primary colour whose wavelength it does not contain, produces white light. *See more at* **colour.**

complex number A number that can be expressed in terms of i (the square root of –1).

■ **complementary angles**
angles *AOC* +
BOC = 90°

Mathematically, such a number can be written a + bi, where a and b are real numbers. An example is 4 + 5i.

composite number An integer that can be divided by at least one other integer besides itself and 1 without leaving a remainder. 24 is a composite number since it can be divided by 2, 3, 4, 6, 8 and 12. No prime numbers are composite numbers. *Compare* **prime number.**

compost A mixture of decayed or decaying organic matter used to fertilize soil. Compost is usually made by gathering plant material, such as leaves, grass clippings and vegetable peel, into a pile or bin and letting it rot. Manure and other organic substances are often added to enrich the mixture or to speed up its decomposition.

composting toilet A toilet that uses little or no water and is connected to a tank in which waste material is decomposed by bacteria. Composting toilets are used especially to conserve water in areas where it is scarce.

compound *noun Chemistry.* A substance made up of two or more elements held together by chemical bonds into a molecule. The elements are combined in a definite ratio. Water, for example, is a compound having two hydrogen atoms and one oxygen atom in each molecule. —*adjective* Composed of more than one part, as in a compound eye or leaf.

compound eye An eye, as of an insect or crustacean, consisting of hundreds or thousands of tiny light-sensitive parts, with each part creating a portion of an image.

compound leaf A leaf that is composed of two or more leaflets on a common stalk. Clover, roses and rowan, ash and walnut trees have compound leaves.

compound lens *See* **lens** (sense 2b).

compression A force that tends to shorten or squeeze something, decreasing its volume.

Compton, Arthur Holly 1892–1962. American physicist who proved Albert Einstein's statement

Did You Know?

compound eye

The eyes have it – the important ability to see, that is. But not all eyes are the same. Insects and other arthropods (which include lobsters and other crustaceans) have *compound eyes,* which are quite different from the human eye. The compound eye, greatly magnified, looks like a fencer's mask. It consists of many repeating units, called *ommatidia,* each of which is a separate light receptor. Some species' eyes have many ommatidia while others have only a few – the more ommatidia an eye has, the better it can resolve images. But even with many ommatidia, the typical compound eye is poor compared with ours at creating a sharp image. A honey bee, for example, sees only

one-sixtieth as clearly as we do. However, the compound eye has other special talents. It is excellent at detecting motion, as the moving object passes from one ommatidium to the next. And some insects see ultraviolet light, which is invisible to us.

that a particle of light has momentum even though it has no mass. Compton's experiments showed that when particles of light (called photons) collide with other particles, such as electrons, they lose energy and momentum and the light's wavelength increases. This phenomenon became known as the Compton effect.

computer A device capable of processing information according to a set of instructions stored within the device. *See panel at* **program.**

computer science The study of the design and operation of computers and their application to science, business and the arts. *See A Timeline of Computing*, page 78.

concave Curved inwards, like the inside of a circle or sphere.

concentration The amount of a particular substance in a given amount of another substance, especially a solution.

conception The formation of a cell capable of developing into a new organism by the union of a sperm and an egg cell; fertilization.

conch Any of various tropical molluscs having a large spiral shell with a flared opening.

concussion An injury to the brain resulting from shaking or a blow to the head. Symptoms include temporary loss of consciousness and sometimes loss of memory.

condensation The change of a gas or vapour to a liquid, either by cooling or by being subjected to increased pressure. When water vapour cools in the atmosphere, for example, it condenses into tiny droplets of water, which form clouds.

conduction The flow of energy, such as heat or an electric charge, through a substance. In heat conduction, the energy flows by direct contact of the substance's molecules with each other. Although the molecules vibrate, they do not change position in the transfer of energy. In electrical conduction, energy flows by the movement of electrons or ions.

conductivity A measure of the ability of a material to allow heat or electricity to flow through it by conduction.

conductor A material or an object that conducts heat or electricity: *Copper is a good conductor of heat and electricity.*

condyle A rounded prominence at the end of a bone.

cone **1.** A three-dimensional surface or solid object in which the base is a circle and the sides narrow to form a point. The surface of a cone is formed mathematically by moving a line that passes through a fixed point (the vertex) along a circle. **2.** A rounded or elongated cluster of woody scales enclosing the reproductive structures of conifers such as pines, spruces and firs. Cones are either male, producing pollen, or female, bearing seeds. Male cones are much smaller than female cones. When the seeds become mature, the female cones expand to release them. **3.** One of the cone-shaped cells in the retina of the eye of many vertebrate animals. Cones are responsible for

Did You Know?

conduction, convection, and radiation

Heat is a form of energy connected with the movement of molecules. Heat travels by conduction, convection or radiation. In *conduction,* heat spreads through a solid by making its molecules vibrate faster. As faster molecules bump into slower ones, the slower ones are made to vibrate faster, and the solid becomes hotter. When liquids and gases are heated, their molecules, which are free to move about, move further apart. The hotter portions of the liquid or gas expand, become less dense, and rise, and cooler portions move down to take their place. This movement causes the liquid or gas to circulate in the process called *convection.* The currents of the sea are convection currents caused by the uneven heating of its waters by the sun. *Radiation* carries heat in the form of waves through space. A hot object, like the hot wire in a heat lamp, gives off energy waves called *infrared rays.* When these rays strike an object, its molecules absorb the rays' energy and vibrate or move faster, and so the object becomes hotter. The sunlight that warms your face has travelled through about 150 million kilometres of space by radiation.

Throughout recorded history, humans have used devices to help make calculations. Five thousand years ago, people manipulated abacuses with their fingers to add, subtract, multiply and divide numbers. Much later, mechanical devices were developed for these same tasks. During the twentieth century, the invention of electronics allowed for the development of computer science, making the computation of trillions of calculations per second possible and extending the use of computers into many aspects of people's daily lives. Current research in quantum physics should result in even more powerful computers in the decades to come. Below are some milestones in developing the hardware that has helped people perform calculations through the ages.

YEAR	MILESTONE
3000 BC	The abacus is invented in the Middle East.
1642 AD	Blaise Pascal invents the wheeled calculator.
1694	Wilhelm Leibniz invents the mechanical multiplier.
1820s	Charles Babbage designs the Difference Engine (never built) to use steam to perform computations.
1889	Herman Hollerith uses punch cards to tabulate the American census, reducing computation time from 10 years to six weeks.
1943	The British complete a secret code-breaking computer called Colossus to decode German war messages.
1944	Mark I, an electronic relay computer half the length of a football pitch with 500 miles of wiring, is used to create ballistics charts for the United States Navy.
1945	The ENIAC computer uses vacuum tubes and resistors to compute at speeds 1000 times faster than Mark I.
1951	The UNIVAC I computer becomes commercially available. It is the first computer that can store a program in memory.
1955	The first computer to use transistors (which are faster, more compact, and give off less heat than vacuum tubes) becomes available.
1971	Intel designs the first microprocessor. All the components of a central processor are now placed on one chip.
1975	The Altair 8800 personal computer is made available to the public. Within the next decade the electronic computer will become a tool used by millions of ordinary people in their homes.
1977	Apple Computer unveils the Apple II, the first personal computer to feature colour graphics.
1981	IBM introduces the IBM PC, which eventually becomes the standard for desktop computing. Popular applications include word processing and spreadsheets.
1990	Laptop computers become common. During the 1990s, they decrease in size and price.
1991	The World Wide Web offers researchers and students the ability to access electronic files. By the end of the decade, over one hundred million people seek and share information regularly on the Web.
1997	Handheld computers that are small enough to fit into a jacket pocket become widely available.

height
(*h*)

radius (*r*)

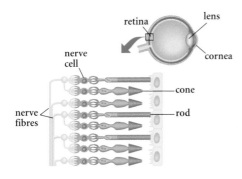

retina | lens

nerve cell

cornea

nerve fibres

cone

rod

■ **cone**

top: *The volume (V) of a cone can be calculated using the following equation:*
$$V = \frac{1}{3}\pi r^2 h.$$
bottom: *detail of the retina showing cones and rods*

daylight vision and, in some animals, for the ability to see colours. *Compare* **rod.**

congenital Existing at or before birth, as a defect or medical condition. *See panel at* **heritable.**

congestive heart failure Inability of the heart to circulate blood adequately to the lungs and outer body tissues, resulting in weakness and shortness of breath.

conglomerate A coarse-grained sedimentary rock that consists of pebbles, gravel or seashells cemented together by hardened silt, clay, calcium carbonate, or a similar material. *See table at* **rock.**

congruent *Geometry.* Having the same size and shape; matching exactly: *congruent triangles.*

conic projection A method of making a flat map of the Earth by projecting its surface features onto a cone, which is then flattened out so that parallels appear as arcs of circles. *Compare* **homolosine projection, Mercator projection, sinusoidal projection.**

conic section A curve formed by the intersection of a plane with a cone. Conic sections can appear as circles, ellipses, hyperbolas or parabolas, depending on the angle of the intersecting plane relative to the cone's base.

conifer Any of various trees or shrubs that bear cones. Conifers are dependent on the wind to blow pollen produced by the male cones to the female cones, where seeds develop. Conifers are usually evergreen, often have needle-shaped or scale-like leaves, and include the pine, fir, spruce, hemlock and yew.

conjugate angles Two angles whose sum is 360°.

conjugation A type of sexual reproduction in single-celled organisms, such as bacteria and some algae and fungi. In conjugation, two organisms or cells from the same species join together to exchange genetic material before undergoing cell division.

conjunctiva The mucous membrane that lines the inside of the eyelid and covers the surface of the eyeball. ❖ Inflammation of the conjunctiva is called **conjunctivitis.**

connective tissue Tissue that forms the framework and supporting structures of the body, including bone, cartilage, mucous membrane and fat.

■ **conic projection**

■ **constellation**
Diagram of the constellation Orion.
Betelgeuse, the large, reddish star, is the
coolest star in the constellation; Rigel, the
large, bluish-white star, is the hottest. Orion's
belt can be seen in the middle of the figure as
three stars in a straight line.

---

conservation 1. The protection, preservation, management, or restoration of wildlife and natural resources such as forests and water. 2. The continuance of a physical quantity, such as mass, in the same amount during a physical or chemical change.

constant 1. A quantity that is unknown but assumed to have a fixed value in a specified mathematical context. 2. A theoretical or experimental quantity, condition, or factor that does not vary in specified circumstances. Avogadro's number and Planck's constant are examples of constants.

constellation 1. A group of stars seen as forming a figure or design in the sky, especially one of 88 recognized groups. 2. An area of the celestial sphere occupied by one of the 88 recognized constellations.

constrictor Any of various snakes that tightly coil around and suffocate their prey. Boa constrictors, pythons and anacondas are constrictors.

consumer An organism that feeds on other organisms in a food chain. ❖ Herbivores that feed on green plants in a food chain are called **primary**

consumers, and carnivores that feed on herbivores are **secondary consumers.** Carnivores that feed on other carnivores are called **tertiary consumers.** *Compare* **producer.**

contact 1. *Electricity.* **a.** A connection between two conductors that allows an electric current to flow. **b.** A part or device that makes or breaks a connection in an electrical circuit. 2. *Geology.* The place where two different geological layers or rocks come together.

contagion 1. The transmission of disease resulting from contact between individuals: *Lack of sanitary conditions may lead to widespread contagion.* 2. A disease that is transmitted in this way: *The flu is a common contagion of the winter months.*

contagious Capable of being transmitted by direct or indirect contact; communicable: *a contagious disease. See panel at* **infectious.**

contaminate To make impure or unclean by mixture or contact.

continent One of the seven great landmasses of the Earth. The continents are Africa, Antarctica, Asia, Australia, Europe, North America and South America.

continental divide A region of high ground, from each side of which the river systems of a continent flow in opposite directions. ❖ In North America, the **Continental Divide** is a series of mountain ridges stretching from Alaska to Mexico.

continental drift The gradual movement of the Earth's continents towards or away from each

---

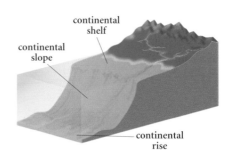

■ **continental shelf**

other. *See more at* **plate tectonics.** *See panel at* **Gondwanaland.**

continental rise A wide, gentle incline from the seafloor to the continental slope. The continental rise consists mainly of silt, mud and sand, and can be several hundreds of kilometres wide.

continental shelf The part of the edge of a continent covered by a shallow sea and extending to the steep slopes that descend into the deep part of the ocean.

continental slope The sloping region between the continental shelf and the continental rise. The continental slope is typically about 20 kilometres wide, consists of mud and silt, and is often intersected by underwater canyons.

contour line A line on a map joining points of the same elevation.

contour map A map that shows elevations above sea level and surface features of the land by means of contour lines.

contraceptive A substance or device capable of preventing pregnancy.

contraction The shortening and thickening of a muscle in action. Contraction of the biceps of the arm causes the elbow to bend.

control Something used as a standard of comparison in a scientific experiment. In an experiment to test the effectiveness of a new drug, for instance, the control is an inactive substance (such as a sugar pill) that is given to one group of people, so that their results can be compared with those of a group who actually took the drug. ❖ An experiment designed to test the effects of a single condition or factor on a system is called a **control experiment.** Only the condition being studied is allowed to vary, and all other conditions are kept constant.

convection The transfer of heat energy through a fluid (liquid or gas) by the movement of the fluid itself. When the fluid comes into contact with a source of heat, it expands and rises, and cooler fluid takes its place. Eventually, as the cooler fluid is heated, it moves as well, and a convection current forms, transferring the heat. *See panel at* **conduction.**

convection zone The outer part of the inside of a star, especially the sun, where energy travels outwards to the photosphere through convection. In this layer, hot gas rises, cools as it nears the surface and falls to be heated and rise again.

converge 1. To tend towards or approach an intersecting point. 2. In calculus, to approach a limit.

convergence 1. The act or process of converging; the tendency to meet in one point. 2. *Mathematics.* The property or manner of approaching a limit, such as a point, line, or value. 3. *Biology.* The evolution of superficially similar structures in unrelated species as they adapt to similar environments. An example of convergence is the development of fins independently in both fish and whales. Also called *convergent evolution.* *Compare* **divergence.**

convergent plate boundary A tectonic boundary where two plates are moving towards each other. If the two plates are of equal density, they usually push up against each other to form a mountain chain. If they are of unequal density, one plate usually sinks (subducts) beneath the other. Also called *collision zone.* *See more at* **tectonic boundary.** *Compare* **divergent plate boundary.**

convex Curving outwards, like the outer boundary of a circle or sphere.

warm air

cool air

■ **convection**

Air heated by a radiator rises, then cools and falls to be heated and rise again. This cycle creates a convection current that circulates hot air throughout a room.

Biography

Nicolaus Copernicus

The man who devised one of astronomy's most important theories wasn't even a trained astronomer: Nicolaus Copernicus studied medicine and law, and it was in his spare time that he wrote the book that made him famous. In the first, brief version of his theory, Copernicus set out his heliocentric system, stating that the sun is at the centre of the universe and that all the planets and stars revolve around it in circular orbits. In doing so, Copernicus was trying to explain the observed movements of the planets – those that, in the days before telescopes, were visible to the naked eye. These movements did not fit the older, Earth-centred (or geocentric) model of the universe devised by the Greek astronomer Ptolemy. Copernicus's sun-centred model offered a more accurate interpretation of planetary movement. He published a longer, more complete account of his theory in 1543, just before he died.

Almost all of his contemporaries doubted that his system could be true, and they kept working with the older, geocentric model. After Copernicus died, there were a few people who defended his model, including the astronomers Johannes Kepler and Galileo Galilei. But it took almost 150 years for Copernican theory to take hold, when Sir Isaac Newton published his theory of universal gravitation.

coordinate One of a set of numbers that determines the position of a point. Only one coordinate is needed if the point is on a line, two if the point is in a plane, and three if it is in space. When describing the position of a point on a graph, the coordinates for the x-axis and y-axis are written in brackets, separated by a comma, eg (2,3).

coordinate bond A type of covalent bond in which both the shared electrons are contributed by one of the two atoms. Also called *dative bond. See more at* **covalent bond.**

copepod Any of various very small crustaceans having an elongated body and a forked tail. Copepods are abundant in both salt and fresh water. They are an important food source for many water animals.

Copernicus, Nicolaus 1473–1543. Polish astronomer whose theory that Earth and other planets revolve around the sun provided the foundation for modern astronomy. He also proposed that the Earth turns once daily on its own axis.

copper A reddish-brown, easily shaped metallic element that is an excellent conductor of heat and electricity. It is widely used for electrical wiring, water piping, and rust-resistant parts, either in its pure form or in alloys such as brass and bronze. *Symbol* **Cu.** *Atomic number* 29. *See* **Periodic Table,** pages 260–261. *See panel at* **element.**

coquina A brittle limestone made of shells and shell fragments.

coral 1. Any of numerous small, sedentary animals that often form massive colonies in shallow sea water. They secrete a cup-shaped skeleton of calcium carbonate, which they can retreat into when in danger. Corals are cnidarians and have stinging tentacles radiating around their mouth opening. The tentacles are used in catching prey. **2.** A hard, stony substance consisting of the skeletons of these animals. It is typically white, pink, or reddish and can form large reefs that support an abundance of sea fish.

coral reef A mound or ridge of coral skeletons and calcium carbonate deposits. Coral reefs form in warm, shallow sea waters and provide food and shelter to a wide variety of fish and invertebrates. They also protect coastlines against erosion by causing large waves to break and lose some of their force before reaching land.

cordillera A long and wide chain of mountains, especially the main mountain range of a large landmass.

core 1. The hard or stringy central part of certain fruits, such as apples and pears, that contains the seeds. 2. The central or innermost portion of the Earth below the mantle, probably consisting of iron and nickel. It is divided into a liquid outer core, which begins at a depth of about 2900 kilometres, and a solid inner core, which begins at a depth of about 5000 kilometres. 3. A piece of magnetizable material, such as a rod of soft iron, that is placed inside an electrical coil or

■ **coral**
aerial and undersea views of coral reefs

transformer to intensify and provide a path for the magnetic field produced by the current running through the wire windings. 4. The central part of a nuclear reactor where atomic fission occurs. 5. A long, cylindrical sample of soil, rock or ice, collected with a drill to study the layers of material that are not visible from the surface.

cork 1. The outermost layer of tissue that becomes the bark of woody plants. Cork is formed on the outside of the tissue layer known as cork cambium. Once they mature, cork cells die. Also called *phellem.* 2. The lightweight, elastic outer bark of the cork oak, which grows near the Mediterranean Sea. Cork is used for bottle stoppers, insulation, and other products.

cork cambium A layer of cambium near the outer edge of the stems of woody plants that produces cork to the outside and cortex to the inside. Also called *phellogen. See more at* **cambium.**

corm A fleshy underground stem that is similar to a bulb but stores its food as stem tissue and has fewer and thinner leaf-like scales. Crocuses and gladioli produce new shoots from corms. *Compare* **bulb, rhizome, runner, tuber.**

cornea The tough transparent membrane of the outer layer of the eyeball that covers the iris and the pupil. *See more at* **eye.**

corolla The petals of a flower considered as a group or unit. *See more at* **flower.**

corollary A statement that follows with little or no proof required from an already proven statement.

corona 1. The irregular envelope of gas outside the chromosphere of a star, especially the sun. 2. A faintly coloured shining ring appearing around a celestial body, especially the moon or sun, when seen through a haze or thin cloud. 3. A crown-shaped structure on the inner side of the petals of some flowers, such as the daffodil.

Corona Borealis A constellation in the Northern Hemisphere between Hercules and Boötes.

coronary Relating to the heart. ❖ The two arteries that branch from the aorta to supply blood directly to the heart are called the **coronary arteries.**

■ **corona**

vascular tissue. In roots the cortex transfers water and minerals from the epidermis to the vascular tissue, which distributes them to other parts of the plant. The cortex also stores food manufactured in the leaves.

corundum An extremely hard mineral composed mainly of aluminium oxide. It occurs as gemstones such as ruby and sapphire and in a dark-coloured variety that is used for polishing and scraping. Corundum is the mineral used to represent a hardness of 9 on the Mohs scale.

corymb A flower cluster whose outer flowers have longer stalks than the inner flowers, so that together they form a round cluster that is rather flat on top. Yarrow and hawthorn have corymbs.

cos Abbreviation of **cosine.**

corpuscle Any of various cells or cell-shaped structures in the body, especially a blood cell.

corresponding angles Angles in similar positions on the same side of a transversal.

corrie A deep semicircular hollow high on a mountain slope, formed by glacial erosion.

corrosion The breaking down or destruction of a material, especially a metal, through chemical reactions. The most common form of corrosion is rusting, which occurs when iron combines with oxygen and water.

cortex 1. The outer layer of an organ or body part, such as the cerebrum or the adrenal glands. 2. The region of tissue next to the outermost layer of plant stems and roots. The cortex lies between the epidermis (the outermost layer) and the

cosecant The ratio of the length of the hypotenuse in a right-angled triangle to the length of the side opposite an acute angle; the inverse of the sine.

cosine The ratio of the length of the side adjacent to an acute angle of a right-angled triangle to the length of the hypotenuse.

cosmic Relating to the universe or the objects in it.

cosmology The branch of astronomy that deals with the origin, evolution and structure of the universe.

cosmos The universe, especially when considered as an orderly and harmonious whole.

cot Abbreviation of **cotangent.**

cotangent The ratio of the length of the adjacent side of an acute angle in a right-angled triangle to the length of the opposite side; the inverse of a tangent.

cotyledon A leaf of the embryo of a seed-bearing plant. Most cotyledons emerge, enlarge and become green after the seed has germinated. Cotyledons either store food for the growing embryo or absorb food that has been stored in the endosperm for eventual distribution to the growing parts of the embryo. Also called *seed leaf. See more at* **dicotyledon, monocotyledon.**

coulomb A unit used to measure electric charge. One coulomb is equal to the quantity of charge that passes a point in an electric circuit in one second when a current of one ampere is flowing through the circuit.

■ **corrosion**

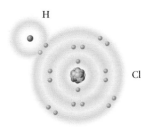

H

Cl

■ **covalent bond**
Covalent bonding as seen in a hydrogen chloride molecule. The hydrogen atom (H) shares an electron (yellow) with the chloride atom (Cl).

Coulomb, Charles Augustin de 1736–1806. French physicist who pioneered research on magnetism and electricity. He is best known for the formulation of Coulomb's law, which he developed as a result of his investigations of Joseph Priestley's work on electrical repulsion. Coulomb also established a law governing the attraction and repulsion of magnetic poles. The coulomb unit of electric charge is named after him.

Coulomb's law A law stating that the size of the force between two charged objects depends on the size of the charges of the objects and on the distance between them.

Cousteau, Jacques Yves 1910–1997. French underwater explorer, film producer and author. Cousteau invented scuba equipment, structures that permit humans to survive underwater for prolonged periods of time, and a small submarine known as a diving saucer. He made three feature films and several television series about marine life and later in his career became increasingly involved in biological research and marine conservation.

covalent bond A chemical bond formed when electrons are shared between two atoms. Usually each atom contributes one electron to form a pair of electrons that are shared by both atoms. *See more at* **bond, coordinate bond, double bond, ionic bond.**

cowrie Any of various tropical marine molluscs

having glossy, often brightly marked shells that are rounded on one side and relatively flat on the other. The shells have been used as currency in the South Pacific and Africa.

CPR Short for *cardiopulmonary resuscitation.* An emergency procedure in which the heart and lungs are made to work by compressing the chest overlying the heart and forcing air into the lungs. CPR is used to maintain circulation when the heart has stopped pumping on its own.

CPU Abbreviation of **central processing unit.**

Cr The symbol for **chromium.**

cranial Of or near the skull or cranium.

cranial nerve Any of the 12 pairs of nerves in humans and other mammals that connect the muscles and sensory organs of the head and upper chest directly to the brain. The cranial nerves include the optic nerve and the auditory nerve.

cranium The skull of a vertebrate animal. It encloses and protects the brain.

crater 1. A bowl-shaped depression at the top of a volcano or at the mouth of a geyser. Volcanic

■ **crater**
top: craters on the moon
bottom: meteorite crater in Death Valley, California, USA

85

craters can form because of magma explosions, in which a large amount of lava is thrown out from a volcano, leaving a hole, or because the roof of rock over an underground magma pool collapses after the magma has flowed away. **2.** A shallow, bowl-shaped hole in a surface, formed by an explosion or by the impact of a body, such as a meteorite.

creosote A yellow or brown oily liquid obtained from coal tar and used as a wood preservative and disinfectant.

crescent Partly but less than half illuminated. Used to describe the moon or a planet. *Compare* gibbous.

crest The highest part of a wave. *See more at* wave.

Cretaceous The third and last period of the Mesozoic Era, from about 142 to 65 million years ago, characterized by the development of flowering plants. The Cretaceous Period ended with the sudden mass extinction of dinosaurs and many other forms of life. *See chart at* geological time, pages 148–149.

Crick, Francis Henry Compton Born 1916. British biologist who with James D. Watson identified the structure of DNA. By analysing the patterns cast by X-rays striking DNA molecules, they discovered that DNA has the structure of a double helix, two spirals linked together by bases, forming ladder-like rungs. Their discovery formed the basis of molecular genetics. Crick continued to work on DNA, later working out how DNA carries its genetic information.

crinoid Any of various invertebrate sea animals having a cup-shaped body, feathery arms, and a stalk by which they attach themselves to a surface. Sea lilies and feather stars are types of crinoids.

crista (*plural* **cristae**) One of the folds of the inner membrane of a mitochondrion. *See more at* mitochondrion.

critical angle The angle at which a light ray leaving a dense medium is refracted so that its angle with the normal ray is 90°.

crocodile Any of various large, meat-eating, aquatic reptiles native to tropical and subtropical regions. Crocodiles have longer and slenderer jaws than alligators, and their teeth are visible when they close their jaws.

crocodilian Any of various large, lizard-like, meat-eating reptiles having long jaws with sharp teeth, flattened bodies and long tails, and mostly living in or near water. The crocodilians include crocodiles, alligators, caimans (from South America) and gavial (from India).

Crookes, Sir William 1832–1919. British chemist and physicist who discovered thallium in 1861 and invented the radiometer in 1875. He also investigated cathode rays, demonstrating that they consisted of charged particles.

cross *noun* A plant or animal produced by crossbreeding; a hybrid. —*verb* To crossbreed or cross-fertilize plants or animals.

crossbreed *verb* To produce a hybrid animal or plant by breeding two animals or two plants of different species or varieties. For example, crossbreeding a male donkey with a female horse will produce a mule. —*noun* An animal or a plant produced by breeding two animals or plants of different species or varieties; a hybrid.

cross-fertilization The fertilization that occurs when a male sex cell from one individual joins to a female sex cell from another individual of the same species. —*verb* **cross-fertilize.**

cross-pollination The transfer of pollen from the male reproductive organ (an anther or a male cone) of one plant to the female reproductive organ (a stigma or a female cone) of another plant. Insects and the wind are agents of cross-pollination. —*verb* **cross-pollinate.**

crow Any of various large birds having shiny black feathers and a raucous call. Crows are closely related to ravens, rooks, jackdaws and magpies.

crucible A heat-resistant container used to melt ores, metals, and other materials.

crust The solid, outermost layer of the Earth. ❖ The crust that lies underneath the continents is called **continental crust,** and is approximately 35 to 60 kilometres thick. It consists mostly of old rocks. ❖ The crust that lies underneath the seabed is called **oceanic crust,** and is approximately 5 kilometres thick. It consists of young basalt.

crustacean Any of various arthropods that live mostly in water and have a hard shell, a segmented body and jointed appendages. Crustaceans include crabs, lobsters, prawns and barnacles.

cryogenics The branch of physics that studies how matter behaves at very low temperatures.

crystal A solid composed of atoms, molecules, or ions arranged in regular patterns that are repeated throughout the structure to form a characteristic network. Crystals have straight edges and flat surfaces, and can occur in many sizes and shapes. ❖ The particular arrangement in space of these atoms, molecules or ions, and the way in which they are joined is called a **crystal lattice**. There are seven crystal groups or systems. Each is defined on the basis of the geometrical arrangement of the crystal lattice. —*adjective* **crystalline.**

crystallize To take on the form of crystals or cause to form crystals.

Cs The symbol for **caesium.**

csc Abbreviation of **cosecant.**

Cu The symbol for **copper.**

cube *verb* To multiply a number or a quantity by itself three times; to raise to the third power. For example, five cubed is $5 \times 5 \times 5$. —*noun* **1.** The product that results when a number or quantity is cubed. **2.** A solid having six equal square faces or sides.

cube number The product of any number multiplied by its square, ie the third power of a number, for example $2^3 (= 8)$.

cube root The number whose cube is equal to a given number. For example, the cube root of 125 is 5, since $5^3 = 125$.

cubic **1.** Referring to a volume unit of measurement: *cubic metre.* **2.** Involving a number or a variable that has been raised to the third power. **3.** Relating to a crystal having three axes of equal length intersecting at right angles. The mineral pyrite has cubic crystals. Also called *isometric. See more at* **crystal.**

cud Food that has been partly digested and brought up from the first stomach to the mouth again for further chewing by ruminants, such as cattle and sheep.

culm The stem of a grass or similar plant.

culture *noun* **1.** A medium for the growth of microorganisms or a batch of cells under specific conditions in a laboratory. **2.** Living material, such as a colony of cells or microorganisms, grown in a culture. —*verb* To grow microorganisms or a batch of cells in a culture.

cumulonimbus A very large cloud with a low, dark base and fluffy masses that billow upward to great heights. Cumulonimbus clouds usually produce heavy rain, thunderstorms or hailstorms.

cumulus A white, fluffy cloud often having a flat base. Cumulus clouds form at lower levels of the atmosphere and are generally associated with fair weather. However, large cumulus clouds that billow to higher levels can produce rain showers.

curie A unit used to measure the rate of radioactive decay. Radioactive decay is measured by the rate at which the atoms making up a radioactive substance are transformed into different atoms. One curie is equal to 37 billion (3.7×10^{10}) of these transformations per second. Many scientists now measure radioactive decay in becquerels rather than curies.

Curie, Marie 1867–1934. Polish-born French

| triclinic | orthorhombic | cubic (or isometric) | monoclinic | trigonal (or rhombohedral) | hexagonal | tetragonal |

■ **crystal**
Imaginary axes of symmetry in the seven main crystal systems are depicted using different colours. Within each crystal, axes having the same colour are of equal length.

chemist who pioneered research into radioactivity. Following Antoine Henri Becquerel's discovery of radioactivity, she investigated uranium with her husband, **Pierre Curie** (1859–1906). Together they discovered the elements radium and polonium. Marie Curie later isolated pure radium and developed the use of radioactivity in medicine.

curium A synthetic, silvery-white, radioactive metallic element of the actinide series that is produced artificially from plutonium or americium. Curium isotopes are used to provide electricity for orbiting satellites and space probes. Curium's most stable isotope has a half-life of 16.4 million years. *Symbol* **Cm**. *Atomic number* 96. *See* **Periodic Table**, pages 260–261.

current 1. A flowing movement in a liquid or gas, especially one that follows a recognizable course: *a current of cool air flowing through the room.* 2. A flow of electric charge. *See panel at* **charge**. 3. The amount of electric charge that passes a point in a unit of time, usually expressed in amperes.

curve 1. A line or surface that bends in a smooth, continuous way without sharp angles. 2. The graph of a function on a coordinate plane. In this technical sense, straight lines, circles and waves are all curves.

cutaneous Relating to the skin.

cuticle 1. The outer layer of skin; the epidermis. 2. The hard skin around the sides and base of a fingernail or toenail. 3. *Botany.* A waxy layer that covers the outermost tissue layer of a plant. The cuticle is secreted by the epidermis and helps prevent water loss and infection by parasites.

Cuvier, Baron **Georges Léopold Chrétien Frédéric Dagobert** 1769–1832. French anatomist who is considered the founder of comparative anatomy. He originated a system of zoological classification that grouped animals according to the structures of their skeletons and organs. Cuvier extended his system to fossils, and his reconstructions of the way extinct animals looked, based on their skeletal remains, greatly advanced the science of palaeontology.

cyanide Any of a large group of chemical compounds containing the radical CN, especially the very poisonous salts sodium cyanide and potassium cyanide. Cyanides are used to make plastics and to extract and treat metals.

cyanobacterium A type of bacterium that is capable of photosynthesis and was once thought to be a plant. Many cyanobacteria are able to convert nitrogen into chemical compounds used in cell metabolism. A combination of pigments, including chlorophyll, gives these bacteria their

Biography

current: direct and alternating

You listen to your portable CD player thanks to direct current, but you turn on the lights in your house thanks to alternating current. Direct current, or DC is electricity which flows in one direction only. Batteries are one source of direct current, while power packs like those used to run personal stereos or handheld computers from the mains are another. Transmitting electricity over long distances, for example from a power station to your home, would be impossible using DC. This is because the resistance of the wires used to carry the electricity would mean that most of the energy carried by the electric current would be wasted in heating up the wires. To get over this, electricity is generated in power stations as alternating current, or AC. The name "alternating current" tells you that the current flows first in one direction and then the other. In the UK, AC does this 50 times each second, and is said to have a frequency of 50 hertz. Using transformers, AC can be transmitted over large distances at very high voltages, reducing the energy losses in the wires. Before the electricity comes into your home or school, the voltage is reduced to around 240 volts.

characteristic blue-green colour. Also called *blue-green alga.*

cyber– A prefix that means "computer" or "computer network", as in *cyberspace,* the electronic medium in which online communication takes place.

cybernetics The study of communication and control processes in biological, mechanical and electronic systems. Research in cybernetics often involves the comparison of these processes in biological and artificial systems.

cycad Any of various cone-bearing evergreen plants that live in warm regions, have large feathery leaves, and resemble palm trees.

cyclone 1. A system of winds that spiral in towards a region of low atmospheric pressure, circling anticlockwise in the Northern Hemisphere and clockwise in the Southern Hemisphere. *Compare* **anticyclone. 2.** A violent rotating windstorm, such as a hurricane or tornado.

cyclotron A device that accelerates charged subatomic particles, such as protons and electrons,

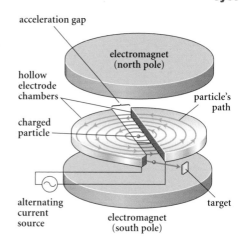

■ **cyclotron**
An alternating electric field attracts the particles from one side of the cyclotron to the other. The cyclotron's magnetic field, generated by the two electromagnets, bends each particle's path into a horizontal spiral, forcing it to accelerate in order to keep up with the alternating electric field. When the particle reaches its peak acceleration it is released to collide with the desired target.

Did You Know?

cyclone

Technically, a *cyclone* is nothing more than a region of low pressure around which air flows. In the Northern Hemisphere, the air moves anticlockwise around the low-pressure centre, while in the Southern Hemisphere, the air travels clockwise. Meteorologists also refer to *tropical cyclones,* which develop over warm water and can be huge, severe storms. Strong tropical cyclones are better known as hurricanes or typhoons, depending on where in the world they occur. Hurricanes occur in the Atlantic Ocean and Gulf of Mexico, while typhoons occur in the Pacific Ocean. Such storms can be devastating: two cyclones hit a coastal section of India within a few days of each other in 1999, killing an estimated 10,000 people. Because the word *cyclone* broadly defines a kind of air flow, cyclones are not confined to our planet. In 1999, the Hubble Space Telescope photographed a huge cyclone on Mars.

---

in an outwardly spiralling path, greatly increasing their energies. Cyclotrons are used to bring about high-speed particle collisions in order to study subatomic structures. *Compare* **linear accelerator.**

Cygnus A constellation in the Northern Hemisphere near Cepheus and Lyra.

cylinder A three-dimensional surface or solid object bounded by a curved surface and two parallel circles of equal size at the ends. The curved surface is formed by all the line segments joining corresponding points of the two parallel circles.

cyme A usually flat-topped or convex flower cluster in which the main stem and each branch end in a flower. Freesia and tomato plants have cymes.

cyst An abnormal sac in the body, composed of a membrane surrounding a fluid or a soft solid material.

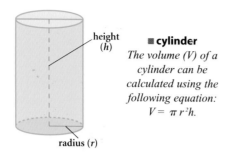

height (h)

radius (r)

■ **cylinder**
The volume (V) of a cylinder can be calculated using the following equation:
$$V = \pi r^2 h.$$

cysteine A nonessential amino acid. *See more at* amino acid. *See panel at* keratin.

cystic fibrosis An inherited disease affecting certain glands, causing them to produce abnormally large amounts of thick mucus. It mostly occurs in the pancreas and the mucus-secreting glands of the lungs, and results in problems with breathing and digestion.

cyto– A prefix meaning "cell", as in the word *cytoplasm.*

cytochrome Any of a class of proteins that are important in cell metabolism and respiration. By comparing different kinds of cytochromes, scientists can trace the evolutionary relationships of the organisms in which they occur.

cytology The scientific study of the formation, structure and function of cells.

cytoplasm The jelly-like material that makes up much of a cell inside the cell membrane, and, in eukaryotic cells, surrounds the nucleus. The organelles of the cell, such as mitochondria and (in green plants) chloroplasts, are contained in the cytoplasm. The cytoplasm together with the nucleus make up the cell's protoplasm. *See more at* cell.

cytosine A base that is a component of DNA and RNA, forming a base pair with guanine.

Dd

d Abbreviation of **diameter.**

Dalton, John 1766–1844. British chemist. His pioneering work on the properties of the Earth's atmosphere and gases led him to formulate the atomic theory. It stipulated that all matter is made up of combinations of atoms and that chemical reactions take place through the rearrangement of atoms.

Darwin, Charles Robert 1809–1882. British naturalist who proposed the theory of evolution based on natural selection (1859). Darwin's theory, that random variation of traits within an individual species can lead to the development of new species, revolutionized the study of biology.

data *Used with a singular or plural verb.* **1.** Information, especially when it is to be analysed or used as the basis for a decision. **2.** Information, usually in numerical form, suitable for processing by a computer. *See panel on* page 92.

dative bond *See* **coordinate bond.**

daughter cell Either of the two cells formed when a cell undergoes cell division. Daughter cells are genetically identical to the parent cell because they contain the same number and type of chromosomes.

Davy, Sir Humphry 1778–1829. British chemist who was a pioneer of electrochemistry, which is concerned with the interaction of electric and chemical phenomena. Davy used its methods to isolate sodium and potassium (1807), and barium,

Biography

Charles Darwin

During his years as a naturalist at sea on the HMS *Beagle* (1831–1836), Charles Darwin observed many new and wondrous things. But the part of the voyage that would change science forever took place in September 1835, when the *Beagle* reached the Galapagos Archipelago, a group of islands in the Pacific Ocean 650 miles west of Ecuador. Noting that the organisms there were isolated in a unique environment, Darwin wrote, "this archipelago . . . seems to be a little world within itself, the greater number of its inhabitants, both vegetable and animal, being found nowhere else". He observed 26 species of birds (only one of which was known to exist anywhere else), giant tortoises and other fascinating reptiles. What startled Darwin was the fact that each species was uniquely adapted to the particular island on which it lived. This observation prompted him to ask the questions that became the basis of his theory

of evolution, questions he would spend the rest of his life trying to answer. When he returned to Britain, Darwin refined his notes and continued to make scientific observations, this time of his own garden and the animals his family kept. After 23 years of sustained work, he published his theory in the work entitled *On the Origin of Species by Means of Natural Selection.*

Usage

data

In scientific writing, *data* is usually treated as a singular in much the same way as the word *information* is. We say *When the data comes in, we'll understand what happened.* But because the word is historically the plural of the Latin noun *datum,* it is sometimes used as a plural, as in *These data do not support your conclusions.* The plural use is less frequent than the singular.

boron, calcium and magnesium (1808). He also proved that diamonds are a form of carbon and invented a safety lamp for miners called the Davy lamp.

dB Abbreviation of **decibel.**

Db The symbol for **dubnium.**

DC Abbreviation of **direct current.**

DDT Short for *dichlorodiphenyltrichloroethane.* A powerful insecticide that is also poisonous to humans and animals. It remains active in the environment for many years and it accumulates in food chains so that the predators at the top of the chains are worst affected. The use of DDT has been banned in many places around the world. However, it is still sometimes used in places where its effectiveness as an insecticide is more important than the environmental damage that it causes, eg some areas badly affected by malaria.

deca– A prefix that means "ten", as in *decahedron,* a polygon having ten faces.

decagon A polygon having ten sides.

decapod **1.** A crustacean characteristically having ten legs, each joined to a segment of the thorax. Crabs, hermit crabs, lobsters and prawns are decapods. **2.** A cephalopod mollusc, such as a squid or cuttlefish, having ten arm-like tentacles.

decay *verb* **1.** *Biology.* To break down into component parts through the action of bacteria or fungi; decompose. **2.** *Physics.* To undergo radioactive decay. —*noun* **1.** *Biology.* The breaking down or rotting of organic matter through the action of bacteria or fungi; decomposition. **2.** *Physics.* Radioactive decay.

deci– A prefix that means "one tenth", as in *decilitre,* one tenth of a litre.

decibel A unit used to measure the loudness or intensity of a sound. The speaking voice of most people ranges from 45 to 75 decibels. *See panel at* **sound.**

deciduous **1.** Shedding leaves at the end of a growing season and regrowing them at the beginning of the next growing season. Most deciduous plants bear flowers and have woody stems and broad rather than needle-like leaves. Maples, oaks, elms, birches and cherry trees are deciduous. *Compare* **evergreen. 2.** Falling off or shed at a particular season or stage of growth: *Deer have deciduous antlers.*

decimal **1.** A representation of a real number using the base ten and decimal notation, such as 201.4, 3.89 or 0.0006. **2.** A decimal having no digits to the left of the decimal point except zero, such as 0.2 or 0.00354.

decimal fraction A number, such as 0.57, written in decimal notation and having only a zero to the left of the decimal point.

decimal notation A representation of a fraction or other real number using the base ten and consisting of any of the digits 0, 1, 2, 3, 4, 5, 6, 7, 8, 9 and a decimal point. Each digit to the left of the decimal point indicates a multiple of a positive power of ten, while each digit to the right indicates a multiple of a negative power of ten. For example, the number $26\frac{37}{100}$ can be written in decimal notation as 26.37, where 2 represents 2×10, 6 represents 6×1, 3 represents $3 \times \frac{1}{10}$ or $\frac{3}{10}$ and 7 represents $7 \times \frac{1}{100}$ or $\frac{7}{100}$.

decimal place The position of a digit to the right of the decimal point in a number written in decimal notation. In 0.079, for example, 0 is in the first decimal place, 7 is in the second decimal place and 9 is in the third decimal place. Abbreviated as **d.p.**

decimal point A full stop or dot used in decimal notation to separate whole numbers from fractions, as in the number 1.3, which represents $1 + \frac{3}{10}$.

decimal system A number system based on units of 10 and using decimal notation.

declination 1. The position of a celestial object above or below the celestial equator. It is measured as a vertical angle, from 0° at the celestial equator to 90° at one of the celestial poles. Declination and right ascension are the measurements used to map objects on the celestial sphere. *See more at* **celestial sphere. 2.** *See* **magnetic declination.**

decomposer An organism, often a bacterium or fungus, that feeds on and breaks down dead plant or animal matter. Decomposers make essential nutrients available to plants and other organisms in the ecosystem.

decomposition 1. The separation of a substance into simpler substances or basic elements. **2.** The process of decaying or rotting. Decomposition of dead organic matter is brought about by the activity of certain bacteria and fungi feeding on it.

deduction 1. The process of reasoning in which a conclusion follows necessarily from the premises; reasoning from the general to the specific. **2.** A conclusion reached by this process. —*verb* **deduce.**

deforestation The cutting down and removal of all or most of the trees in a forested area. Deforestation can damage the environment by causing erosion of soils, and it decreases biodiversity by destroying the habitats needed for different organisms. —*verb* **deforest.**

deglaciation The uncovering of land because of the melting of a glacier.

degree 1. A unit division of a temperature scale. *See panel at* **Celsius. 2a.** A unit for measuring an angle or an arc of a circle. One degree is $\frac{1}{360}$ of the circumference of a circle. **b.** This unit as used in measuring latitude or longitude on the Earth's surface. **3.** The degree of a polynomial equation, which has the form $bx + cx^2 + dx^3....zx^n = 0$, is the value of n.

dehydration 1. The process of losing or removing water or moisture. **2.** Excessive loss of water and often salts from the body, as from heavy sweating or illness.

Delbrück, Max 1906–1981. German-born American biologist who was a pioneer in the study of molecular genetics. He discovered that viruses can exchange genetic material to create new types of viruses.

delta A usually triangular mass of alluvium,

deposited at the mouth of a river. Deltas form when a river flows into a body of standing water, such as a sea or lake.

Democritus 460?–370? BC. Greek philosopher who developed one of the first atomist theories of the universe, which held that the world consists of an infinite number of very small particles.

dendrite 1. Any of several parts branching from the body of a nerve cell that receive and transmit nerve impulses. **2.** A mineral that has a branching crystal pattern. Dendrites often form within or on the surface of other minerals.

dendrochronology The study of annual rings in trees in order to analyse past climate conditions or to determine the date of past events. Trees grow more slowly in periods of drought or other environmental stress than they do under more favourable conditions, and thus the annual rings they produce are smaller. By observing the pattern

Usage

deduction/induction

The logical processes known as deduction and induction work in opposite ways. When you use *deduction,* you apply general principles to specific instances. So, using a mathematical formula to work out the volume of air that can be contained in a gymnasium is applying deduction. Similarly, you use deduction when applying a law of physics to predict the outcome of an experiment. By contrast, when you use *induction,* you examine a number of specific instances of something and make a generalization based on them. So, if you observe hundreds of examples in which a certain chemical kills plants, you might conclude by induction that the chemical is toxic to all plants. Inductive generalizations are often revised as more examples are studied and more facts are known. Certain plants that you have not tested, for instance, may turn out to be unaffected by the chemical, and you might have to revise your thinking. In this way, an inductive generalization is much like a hypothesis.

formed by a tree's rings, scientists can learn about the environmental changes that took place during the period in which it was growing. They can also match up the pattern in trees whose age is known to the pattern in a piece of wood found at an archaeological site, thereby establishing the approximate date of the site.

Deneb A bright star in the constellation Cygnus. It is a supergiant. *See panel at* **Rigel.**

denominator The number below the line in a fraction, indicating the number of equal parts into which one whole is divided. For example, in the fraction $\frac{2}{7}$, 7 is the denominator.

density A measure of the compactness of a substance. Density is equal to the amount of mass per unit of volume. In general, density increases as pressure increases and temperature decreases.

dentine The main bony part of a tooth beneath the enamel, surrounding the pulp chamber and root canals.

dentistry The branch of medicine that deals with the diagnosis, prevention and treatment of diseases of the teeth and gums.

dentition The type, number and arrangement of teeth in an animal species. In mammals, dentition consists of several different types of teeth, including incisors, canines and molars. The teeth of toothed fish and reptiles are usually of only one type.

deoxyribonucleic acid *See* DNA.

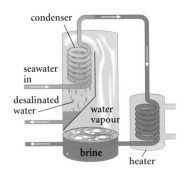

■ **desalination**
a diagram of a distillation process showing how seawater is desalinated

dependent variable In mathematics, a variable whose value is determined by the value of an independent variable. For example, in the function $y = x + 5$, y is the dependent variable because its value is determined by the value of x.

deposit Solid material left or laid down by a natural process. For example, deposits can include layers of sand and mud left by streams, an accumulation of stones and debris left by a melting glacier, or a layer of coal formed over many years as decomposing plant material became fossilized. —*noun* **deposition.**

depression An area of low pressure.

derivative In calculus, the slope of the tangent line to a curve at a particular point on the curve. Since a curve represents a function, its derivative can also be thought of as the rate of change of the corresponding function at the given point. Derivatives are computed using differentiation.

dermal Relating to the skin.

dermis The innermost layer of the skin in vertebrate animals, lying under the epidermis and containing nerve endings and blood and lymph vessels. In mammals, the dermis also contains hair follicles and sweat glands.

desalination The removal of salt from something, such as seawater or soil. —*verb* **desalinate.**

Descartes, René 1596–1650. French mathematician and philosopher. He determined that the position of a point can be defined by coordinates, a discovery that laid the foundation for analytical geometry.

desert A dry, barren region, usually having sandy or rocky soil and little or no vegetation. Most deserts receive less than 25 centimetres of precipitation each year, concentrated in short bursts. Deserts cover about one fifth of the Earth's surface and are mainly located along the Tropic of Cancer and the Tropic of Capricorn.

desertification The transformation into desert of land once suitable for agriculture. Desertification can result from climate change or from human practices such as cutting down forests or allowing too many animals to graze in a particular area.

desiccate To remove the moisture from something, or dry it thoroughly.

designer gene A gene that is created by manipulating the DNA in a cell so that a specific sequence of DNA molecules can be obtained. Designer genes can be used in genetic engineering to help scientists produce substances, such as proteins, needed for research.

detergent A cleaning agent that increases the ability of water to penetrate fabric and break down grease and dirt. Until the middle of the 20th century, soap was the only detergent available. However, the shortage of fats (from which soap is made) led to the development of synthetic detergents. Detergent molecules surround particles of grease and dirt, allowing them to be carried away. *Compare* **soap.**

detritus Loose fragments, such as sand or gravel, that have been worn away from rock.

deuterium An isotope of hydrogen whose nucleus has one proton and one neutron and whose atomic mass is 2. Deuterium is used widely as a tracer for analysing chemical reactions, and it combines with oxygen to form heavy water. Also called *heavy hydrogen. See more at* **hydrogen.** *See panel at* **heavy water.**

deviation *Mathematics.* The difference between one number in a set and the mean of the set.

Devonian The fourth period of the Palaeozoic Era, from about 417 to 354 million years ago, characterized by the appearance of forests, amphibians and insects. *See chart at* **geological time,** pages 148–149.

dew Water droplets that condense from the air onto cool surfaces. Dew usually forms at night, when air near the ground cools and cannot hold as much water vapour as warmer air.

dewclaw 1. A small, useless inner claw or toe in some dogs and other animals that does not reach the ground in walking. **2.** The false hoof of deer, pigs and other hoofed mammals, consisting of two toes.

dewlap A loose fold of skin hanging from the neck of certain animals, such as some dogs or cattle.

dew point The temperature at which air becomes saturated with water vapour and dew forms. The dew point varies depending on how much water vapour is in the air.

dextrose A sugar that is the most common form

Did You Know?

desert

A *desert* is defined by the water you won't find there. There's no official standard, but many people say that any place that gets less than about 25 centimetres of precipitation a year qualifies as a desert. Deserts do not have to be hot. Even the Sahara Desert in Africa, famous for heat, can get cold at night. And although many people think of the Sahara as the world's biggest desert, that distinction actually belongs to Antarctica, which is incredibly cold and amazingly dry, receiving the frozen equivalent of less than about 5 centimetres of water per year. In spite of this dryness, some animals and plants thrive in deserts. Each desert is therefore a unique ecosystem, a particular environment that includes organisms interacting with it and with each other.

Valley of Fire, Nevada, USA

of glucose, found in plant and animal tissues and also derived from starch.

di– A prefix that means "two", "twice" or "double". It is used commonly in chemistry, as in *dioxide,* a compound having two oxygen atoms.

dia– A prefix meaning "through" or "across", as in *diameter,* the length of a line going through a circle.

diabetes A disease caused by the body's inability to produce or use insulin properly. This causes abnormally high levels of sugar in the blood, giving rise to sugar being excreted in the urine, the best known symptom of the disease. Although it can cause serious problems if it is not treated, diabetes can be kept well under control by careful management of the diet and by taking insulin at regular intervals.

diagnosis (*plural* **diagnoses**) The identification by a doctor of a disease or injury, made by examining and taking the medical history of a patient.

diagonal A straight line connecting two nonadjacent corners in a polygon or two nonadjacent corners in a polyhedron that do not lie in the same face.

dialysis 1. The separation of the smaller molecules in a solution from the larger molecules by passing the solution through a semi-permeable or selectively permeable membrane that does not allow the large molecules through. 2. The removal of wastes from the bloodstream by a machine that performs dialysis when the kidneys do not function properly.

diameter 1. A straight line drawn across a circle through its centre. 2. The length of such a line.

diamond A form of pure carbon that occurs naturally as a clear crystal and is the hardest of all known minerals. It is used as a gemstone in its finer varieties. Poorly crystallized diamonds are used in abrasives and in industrial cutting tools. *See panel at* **carbon.**

diaphragm 1. A muscle that separates the chest cavity from the abdominal cavity. As the diaphragm contracts and relaxes, it changes the volume of the chest cavity (along with the movements of the ribs). This in turn affects the pressure in the chest and as a result air moves into and out of the lungs. 2. A thin, flexible disc, especially in a microphone or telephone receiver, that vibrates in response to sound waves to produce electrical signals, or that vibrates in response to electrical signals to produce sound waves.

diastole The period during the normal beating of the heart when the muscles of the heart relax and the chambers fill with blood. *Compare* **systole.**

diatom Any of various microscopic one-celled algae that live in water, have hard shells composed mostly of silica, and often live in colonies. Diatom shells are made of two symmetrical parts called valves. —*adjective* **diatomaceous.**

dicotyledon *or* **dicot** A flowering plant having two cotyledons that usually appear at germination of the seed. Dicotyledons have leaves with a network of veins radiating from a central main vein, flower parts in multiples of 4 or 5 and a tissue layer known as cambium. Most cultivated plants and many trees are dicotyledons. *See more at* **leaf.** *Compare* **monocotyledon.**

dielectric *adjective* Having little or no ability to conduct electricity. —*noun* A dielectric substance, such as glass or rubber.

diesel engine An internal-combustion engine in which the fuel oil is ignited by the heat of air that has been highly compressed in the cylinder.

difference 1. The amount by which one number or quantity is greater or less than another. The difference between 10 and 15, for example, is 5. 2. The amount remaining after one number or quantity is subtracted from another. In the equation $15 - 10 = 5$, the difference is 5.

differentiation 1. In calculus, the process of computing the derivative of a function. *Compare* **integration.** 2. The process by which cells or developing body or plant parts change in order to serve a specific function.

diffraction The spreading of a wave, such as a light wave, when it encounters an obstacle, such as an edge or a hole whose size is similar to the wavelength of the wave. The patterns made by the diffraction of waves can be useful for understanding the minute structures of objects. The diffraction patterns made by X-rays as they pass between the atoms of a molecule, for example, are studied in order to determine the molecule's overall structure. *See more at* **wave.**

diffusion 1. The movement of ions or molecules from an area of higher concentration to an area of lower concentration. Small molecules and ions can move across a cell membrane by diffusion. *Compare* **osmosis. 2a.** The reflection of light off an irregular surface in all directions. **b.** The process by which light passes through a transparent substance. 3. The spreading out of light or other radiation through an area so that its intensity becomes more or less uniform.

digestion 1. The process by which food is broken down into simple chemical compounds that can be absorbed and used as nutrients or

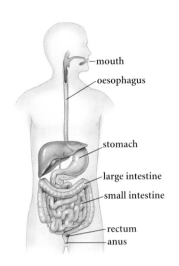

—mouth

oesophagus

stomach

large intestine

small intestine

rectum

anus

■ **digestive tract**

eliminated by the body. In most animals, nutrients are obtained from food by the action of digestive enzymes. In humans and other higher vertebrates, digestion takes place mainly in the small intestine. **2.** The decomposition of sewage by bacteria.

digestive tract The system of organs of the body that break down food into small molecules that can be absorbed and used by the cells. In higher vertebrates, it consists of the oesophagus, stomach and small and large intestines. Working with the digestive tract are associated organs and glands, such as the salivary glands, liver and pancreas, that produce substances necessary for digestion. Also called *alimentary canal, gastrointestinal tract.*

digit 1. A finger or toe. **2.** One of the ten Arabic numerals, from 0 to 9.

digital 1. *Anatomy.* Relating to or resembling a digit, especially a finger. **2.** Expressed in numerical form, especially for use by a computer: *they converted the image to a digital form.* **3.** *Computer Science.* Relating to a device that can read, write or store information represented in numerical form: *a digital camera.*

dihedral Formed by a pair of planes or sections of planes that intersect: *a dihedral angle.*

1,2-dihydroxyethane A poisonous, syrupy, colourless alcohol, $C_2H_6O_2$. It is used as an antifreeze in heating and cooling systems that use water. The old non-systematic name was **ethylene glycol** and, unlike many other older names, it is still often used.

dike A long mass of igneous rock that cuts across the structure of adjoining rock. It is often of a different composition than the rock it cuts across and can be useful in determining the age relationship between rocks.

dilate To widen or expand a body part: *The pupils of the eye dilate in the dark.*

dilute To make a substance less concentrated by adding a liquid such as water.

dimension 1a. *Mathematics.* Any one of the three physical or spatial properties of length, area and volume. In geometry, a point is said to have zero dimension; a figure having only length, such as a line, has one dimension; a plane or surface, two dimensions; and a figure having volume, three dimensions. The fourth dimension is often said to be time, as in the theory of general relativity. Higher dimensions can be dealt with mathematically but cannot be represented visually. **b.** The measurement of a length, width or thickness: *The dimensions of the window are 61 centimetres by 122 centimetres.* **2.** A unit, such as mass, time or charge, associated with a physical quantity and used as the basis for other measurements, such as acceleration.

dimer Any of various chemical compounds made of two smaller, identical molecules (called monomers) that are linked together.

dimetrodon An extinct, meat-eating reptile of the Permian Period having a body similar to an alligator's but with a tall, curved sail on its back. The sail had a thick network of blood vessels and may have been used to regulate the animal's body temperature. The dimetrodon belonged to the early group of reptiles that many scientists believe was ancestral to mammals.

dinoflagellate Any of numerous protozoans found mostly in the sea, usually having two flagella and an outer covering of cellulose. Dinoflagellates are one of the main components of plankton.

dinosaur Any of various extinct reptiles that

diode

lived mainly during the Mesozoic Era. Dinosaurs were meat-eating or plant-eating, dwelled mostly on land, and varied from the size of a small dog to the largest land animals that ever lived. *See more at* **ornithischian, saurischian.** *See panel at* **bird.**

diode An electron tube or a semiconductor that allows current to flow in one direction only. Diodes can be used to convert AC currents into DC currents.

dioecious Having male flowers on one plant and female flowers on another plant of the same species. The holly (only the female produces berries) and asparagus plants are dioecious. *Compare* **monoecious.**

dioxide A compound containing two oxygen atoms per molecule.

diphtheria A contagious disease caused by a bacterium and characterized by a high temperature, swollen glands and the formation of a membrane in the throat that prevents breathing. Diphtheria was once a leading cause of death in children, but children in many countries are now routinely immunized against it.

diplodocus A very large plant-eating dinosaur of the Jurassic Period. Diplodocus had a long, slender neck and tail and a small head with peg-like teeth,

and could grow to nearly 27 metres in length. It is one of the longest sauropod dinosaurs known.

diploid Having two sets of each chromosome in a cell or cell nucleus, one set from the female parent and one set from the male parent. In animals, all cells except reproductive cells are diploid. *Compare* **haploid.** *See panel at* **mitosis.**

dipole 1. A pair of equal and opposite electric charges or magnetic poles, separated by a small distance. 2. A molecule having two such charges.

Dirac, Paul Adrien Maurice 1902–1984. British mathematician and physicist. He developed a mathematical interpretation of quantum mechanics with which he was able to provide the first correct description of electron behaviour.

direct current *or* **DC** An electric current flowing in one direction only, as in a battery. *Compare* **alternating current.** *See panels at* **current, Tesla.**

directrix A straight line used in constructing a curve such as a parabola.

disaccharide Any of a class of sugars, including lactose and sucrose, that are composed of two monosaccharides.

disc 1. *Usually* **disk** *Computer Science.* A magnetic disc, such as a hard disc or an optical disc, such as a compact disc. 2. *Anatomy. See* **intervertebral disc.**

disk drive *Computer Science.* A device that reads data stored on a magnetic or optical disk and writes data onto the disk for storage.

dislocation Displacement of a bone from its normal position in a joint.

dispersion The separation of light or other radiation into individual components, usually according to frequency and wavelength. When a beam of white light (light that contains all colours) passes through a prism, for example, dispersion causes it to separate into the seven colours of the rainbow.

dissect —*verb* To cut apart or separate body tissues or parts for study. —*noun* **dissection.**

dissociation The separation of a substance into two or more simpler substances, or of a molecule into atoms or ions, by the action of heat or a chemical process. Dissociation is usually reversible.

■ **diode**
The heated cathode generates a cloud of electrons that are attracted by the anode, causing a current to flow from the cathode to the anode. Because the anode cannot generate electrons of its own, the current cannot flow in the opposite direction.

dissolve To pass or cause to pass into solution: *Salt dissolves in water, and water has the ability to dissolve salt.*

distillation A method of separating a substance that is in solution from its solvent or of separating a liquid from a mixture of liquids having different boiling points. The liquid to be separated is evaporated (as by boiling), and its vapour is then collected after it condenses. Distillation is used to separate fresh water from a salt solution and petrol from crude oil. ❖ The condensed vapour, which is the purified liquid, is called the **distillate**.

distributary A river that has branched off from the main river, especially at a delta.

distributive property The property which states that for certain mathematical operations, applying an operation (such as multiplication) to a set of quantities combined by another operation (such as addition) yields the same result as applying the first operation to each quantity individually and then combining those results by the second operation (in this case addition). Thus $2 \times (3 + 4)$ is equivalent to $(2 \times 3) + (2 \times 4)$, meaning that multiplication is distributive relative to addition. *See also* **associative property, distributive property.**

diurnal 1. Occurring in a 24-hour period; daily. **2.** Most active during the daytime. Many animals, including the apes, are diurnal. *Compare* **nocturnal. 3.** Having leaves or flowers that open in daylight and close at night. The flowering plants morning glory and crocus are diurnal.

divergence 1. *Mathematics.* The property of failing to approach a limit, such as a point, line or value. **2.** *Biology.* The evolution of different structures in related species as they adapt to different environments. An example of divergence is the development of wings in bats from the same bones that form the arm and hand or paw in most other mammals. Also called *divergent evolution. Compare* **convergence.**

divergent plate boundary A tectonic boundary where two plates are moving away from each other and new crust is forming from magma that rises to the Earth's surface between the two plates. Also called *spreading zone. See more at* **tectonic boundary.** *Compare* **convergent plate boundary.**

dividend A number divided by another. In the equation $15 \div 3 = 5$, the dividend is 15.

division 1. The act, process or operation of dividing one number or quantity by another; the process of finding out how many times one number or quantity is contained in the other. **2.** A group of plants ranking above a class and below a kingdom, corresponding to a phylum in other kingdoms. *See table at* **taxonomy.**

divisor A number used to divide another. In the equation $15 \div 3 = 5$, the divisor is 3.

DNA Short for *deoxyribonucleic acid.* The nucleic acid that is the genetic material determining the

Did You Know?

DNA

One of the wonders of nature is that the complexity and diversity of life can be contained in a molecule with a relatively simple structure. *Deoxyribonucleic acid,* commonly called *DNA,* exists mainly in the nucleus and mitochondria of each cell in an organism. DNA consists of two long strands linked together in a structure resembling a ladder twisted into a spiral, called a *double helix.* Each rung is made up of two chemical bases, called *nucleotides,* that are joined together by hydrogen bonds. There are four kinds of nucleotides in a DNA molecule: cytosine, guanine, adenine and thymine – C, G, A and T, for short. Specific sequences of these bases, known as *genes,* form codes that contain all of an organism's genetic information. When other components of a cell "read" this code, they produce proteins, the building blocks of life.

makeup of all living cells and many viruses. It consists of two strands of nucleotides linked together in a structure resembling a ladder twisted into a spiral that is known as a double helix. In eukaryotic cells, the DNA is contained mainly in the nucleus and mitochondria. DNA can replicate itself and synthesize RNA. *Compare* **RNA**. *See panel at* **gene**.

DNA fingerprinting The use of a sample of DNA to determine the identity of a person within a certain probability. DNA fingerprinting is done by analysing repeating patterns of base pairs in DNA sequences that are known to vary greatly among individuals.

Döbereiner, Johann Wolfgang 1780–1849. A German chemist who invented "Döbereiner's lamp", in which hydrogen, produced in the lamp by the action of sulphuric acid on zinc, burns on contact with a platinum sponge. He was also one of the first chemists to begin to see the patterns in the behaviour of the elements which led eventually to the development of the Periodic Table. In 1829 he showed that many of the elements known at the time could be arranged into groups of three, with all three showing similar properties. He called them triads. Other scientists took notice of his work and continued it.

dodecagon A polygon having 12 sides.

dodecahedron A three-dimensional geometric figure having 12 pentagonal surfaces.

dog 1. Any of various meat-eating mammals having a long muzzle and, in nearly all species, a four-toed foot. Many species hunt in packs that have complex social structures. Dogs include the wolf, fox, jackal and dingo. **2.** The domesticated dog, kept as a pet or work animal since ancient times and probably descended from the wolf. Domesticated dogs are bred in many varieties, though they all belong to the same species.

doldrums A region over the Atlantic Ocean near the equator, having weather characterized variously by calm air, light winds or squalls and thunderstorms. Hurricanes originate in this region.

Doll, Sir **Richard** Born 1912. British doctor and

Did You Know?

Dolly the sheep

A clone is a group of cells or organisms that are genetically identical and have all been produced from the same original cell. The most famous clone in the world is probably Dolly the sheep. In 1996 a team at the Roslin Institute near Edinburgh took the nucleus from an udder cell of one sheep. They put this nucleus into an egg taken from another sheep, having already removed the original nucleus from that egg. Finally, the newly created egg was placed in the uterus of yet another ewe. She successfully carried the lamb and so, after hundreds of failed attempts, Dolly was born and made scientific history.

The birth of Dolly was not announced until 1997, by which time scientists were sure that she was relatively normal. The team had tried hundreds of times to achieve one success. Dolly has gone on to give birth to several (uncloned) lambs of her own. However, there is now some concern that Dolly seems to be ageing faster than normal – at six years old she already had signs of arthritis.

Mice, cattle, goats and pigs have all been cloned since the arrival of Dolly, but cloning other species has not been successful. What is more, the success rate of any attempt at cloning seems to be very low. The arrival of Dolly led to fears that people would soon be cloning humans. So far that has not been the case, although some scientists claim to be trying. The hope behind cloning animals like sheep is to provide more genetically-engineered animals which could produce human medicines in their milk. As for cloning humans, no one is quite sure what benefits there could be, but there would certainly be lots of problems!

epidemiologist. In 1950 Richard Doll was the first person, with his colleague Austin Bradford Hill, to demonstrate the clear link between smoking and lung cancer at the end of an extensive study of people who had lung cancer. There was a huge increase in lung cancers in the 1940s and Doll and Hill showed that it was a direct result of the large increase in smoking that had begun 40 years before that. Richard Doll has developed the science of epidemiology – the study of the impact of disease on populations – throughout his working life. He has been involved in many studies looking at environmental and lifestyle influences on disease, particularly cancer, and his work has saved many lives through education programmes about the dangers of smoking.

Dolly the sheep In 1997 a team of scientists in Edinburgh managed to produce a cloned sheep which they called Dolly. Dolly was produced from a cell taken from the mammary gland of an adult ewe. Cloning plants is old technology, and even cloned frogs were relatively common but Dolly was the first mammal to be cloned. *See* **clone.**

dolomite 1. A grey, pink or white mineral consisting mainly of a carbonate of calcium and magnesium. Dolomite occurs as rhombohedral crystals with a pearly to glassy lustre. It is a common rock-forming mineral. **2.** A sedimentary rock containing more than 50 per cent of the mineral dolomite by weight.

dolphin Any of various, sea-dwelling mammals having a snout shaped like a beak, forelimbs shaped like flippers and horizontal tail flukes. Dolphins are related to, but smaller than, whales and are noted for their high intelligence. *Compare* **porpoise.**

Domagk, Gerhard Johannes Paul 1895–1964. German biochemist. Domagk did research into new dyes and drugs, and in particular he hoped to find a treatment against streptococci which caused widespread and generally lethal infections. He found a dye which would react with a substance called prontosil in the cells of a living animal to form a substance called sulfanilamide in the body. Domagk used it to cure his own small daughter who was dying of a streptococcal infection.

domain 1. *Mathematics.* The set of all values that an independent variable of a function can have. In the function $y = 2x$, the set of values that x (the independent variable) can have is the domain. *Compare* **range. 2.** *Biology.* A division of organisms that ranks above a kingdom in systems of classification that are based on shared similarities in DNA sequences rather than shared structural similarities. In these systems, there are three domains: the archaea, the bacteria and the eukaryotes.

dominant 1. Relating to the form of a gene that expresses a trait, such as hair colour, in an individual organism. The dominant form of a gene will show up in the appearance of the organism even if only one of the alleles is inherited. It overrides the information carried by other, recessive alleles. *See more at* **inheritance.** *Compare* **recessive. 2.** Being a species that has the greatest effect on other species within its ecological community. For example, in a forest where tall oaks are dominant, the shade they create and the acorns they produce help to determine what other species can thrive there.

Doppler effect The apparent change in the frequency of waves, as of sound or light, when the source of the waves is moving towards or away from an observer. *See panel on* page 102.

dormant 1. *Biology.* In an inactive state in which growth stops and metabolism is slowed. Many plants survive the winter as dormant seeds or bulbs. Hibernating animals are also in a dormant state. **2.** *Geology.* Not active but capable of renewed activity: *a dormant volcano.*

dorsal Of or on the back or upper surface of an animal: *the dorsal fin of a fish.*

double bond A type of covalent bond in which two electron pairs are shared between two atoms. Each atom contributes two electrons to the bond. *See more at* **covalent bond.**

down Fine, fluffy feathers that cover a young bird and underlie the outer feathers of certain adult birds. Down feathers are fluffy because they do not have interlocking barbules like adult outer feathers.

Down's syndrome A congenital disorder caused by the presence of an extra copy of chromosome 21. People with Down's syndrome all have some degree of mental retardation, which

Did You Know?

Doppler effect

When a fire engine rushes past you on the road with the siren on, you hear the siren change tone: the sound is higher pitched than normal as the fire engine approaches and lower pitched as it departs. That's because of the *Doppler effect*. Sound waves spread outward in all directions from the siren. The forward motion of the fire engine compresses the sound waves travelling ahead of it, making the wavelengths shorter. Sound having shorter wavelengths has higher frequency and therefore higher pitch – what you hear if the fire engine is moving towards you. Behind the fire engine, however, the sound waves are drawn apart. Longer wavelengths mean lower frequency and lower pitch, which is what you hear once the fire engine rushes past. The Doppler effect works on light waves, too; in fact, this was how scientists determined that the universe is expanding. The light from galaxies and other distant celestial objects is shifted toward the red end of the spectrum (a phenomenon called *red shift*). Red light has the longest wavelengths of visible light. The pioneering astronomer Edwin Hubble reasoned that the red shift was due to the Doppler effect: the galaxies are speeding away from us, drawing out the wavelengths of the light emitted behind them, and the universe as a whole is expanding.

high-frequency waves

low-frequency waves

can range from relatively mild to quite severe. They are also short and have a distinctive flattened face with fewer facial muscles, so that they lack subtlety of facial expressions. Heart defects are also often associated with Down's syndrome.

Draco A constellation in the polar region of the Northern Hemisphere between Ursa Minor and Ursa Major.

drag The force that opposes or slows a body's movement through a fluid medium such as air or water. Drag can be reduced by sleek designs that cause less turbulence. *Compare* **lift**. *See panel at* **aerodynamics**.

dragonfly Any of various insects having a long slender body and two pairs of many-veined wings that are held outstretched at rest.

drone A male bee, especially a honeybee whose only function is to fertilize the queen. Drones do not have a sting, do no work and do not produce honey.

drosophila Any of various small fruit flies, one species of which is used extensively in breeding experiments in genetic research to study patterns of inheritance.

drought A long period of abnormally low rainfall.

drug Any substance that is taken or administered to cause physiological changes, especially one

■ drought
Australian outback

prescribed by a doctor to treat or prevent a medical condition. Drugs that affect the central nervous system are often addictive.

drumlin An extended, oval hill or ridge formed and shaped by a glacier. Drumlins are longer than they are wide and have one steep and one gentle slope along their longest axis.

drupe A fleshy fruit, such as a peach, usually having a single hard stone that encloses a seed.

dry cell An electric cell, such as a torch battery, in which the chemicals producing the current are made into a paste so that they cannot spill from their container.

dry ice Solid carbon dioxide. Dry ice evaporates without first passing through a liquid state, by a process known as sublimation. It is used for refrigeration. *See panel at* **sublimation.**

dry measure A system of units for measuring dry commodities, such as grains, fruit and vegetables.

dubnium A synthetic, radioactive element that is produced from californium, americium or berkelium. Its most stable isotope has a half-life of 34 seconds. *Symbol* **Db**. *Atomic number* 105. *See* **Periodic Table,** pages 260–261.

duck-billed dinosaur *See* **hadrosaur.**

duct A tube or tube-like structure through which a secretion flows. An example is the bile duct which carries bile from where it is stored in the gall bladder to where it is needed in the duodenum.

ductile 1. Easily drawn out into a fine strand or wire. Gold and silver are ductile metals. *Compare*

brittle. **2.** Relating to rock or other materials that are capable of withstanding a certain amount of force by changing form before fracturing or breaking.

dune A hill or ridge of wind-blown sand. Dunes are capable of moving (by the motion of their individual grains) but usually keep the same shape.

duodecimal Relating to or based on the number 12; having 12 as the base. In the duodecimal number system, each digit represents a multiple of a power of 12 instead of 10. Thus the duodecimal number 24 represents $(2 \times 12^1) + (4 \times 12^0)$, or 28.

duodenum The first part of the small intestine, starting at the lower end of the stomach and extending to the jejunum.

dwarfism Abnormally short stature, usually caused by a hereditary disorder.

dwarf star A small star of low mass that

■ dune
top: *a large sand dune in Namib-Naukluft National Park, Namibia*
bottom: *sandstone cliffs formed from fossilized sand dunes in Monument Valley, Arizona, USA*

Did You Know?

dwarf star

Dwarf stars come in several varieties. The type of star known as a *white dwarf* is the remnant of a low- or medium-mass star (like our sun). When a low- or medium-mass star has burnt nearly all of its hydrogen, it begins to collapse under the influence of its own gravitational field. As it does so, it heats up, burning what little hydrogen remains. This burning provides the star with sufficient energy to expand again, cooling as it does so to become a *red giant*. The star then spends some time as a red giant, burning helium in its core, until it begins to collapse again. Once again, this provides enough energy for the star to expand, blowing off its outer layers as it does so. (Our sun will reach this stage in several billion years time, becoming big enough to swallow the Earth in its orbit!). Having blown off its outer layers, the core of the star remains as a *white dwarf.* A *black dwarf* is a burnt-out white dwarf that no longer gives off detectable radiation. Astronomers also refer to *brown dwarfs,* which are not stars. A brown dwarf is bigger than Jupiter, the biggest planet in our solar system, but too small to carry on the sustained nuclear reactions that are needed to become a true star.

gives off an average or below average amount of light.

Dy The symbol for **dysprosium.**

dynamic **1a.** Relating to energy or to objects in motion. **b.** Relating to the study of dynamics. **2.** Characterized by continuous change or activity.

dynamics The branch of physics that deals with the effects of forces on the motions of bodies. Also called *kinetics. Compare* **kinematics.**

dynamite A powerful explosive used in blasting and mining. It typically consists of nitroglycerin and a nitrate, combined with an absorbent material that makes it safer to handle.

dynamo An electric generator, especially one that produces direct current. *See more at* **generator.**

dyne A unit of force equal to the amount of force required to give a mass of one gram an acceleration of one centimetre per second for each second the force is applied.

dysentery A disease of the lower intestines characterized by severe diarrhoea, usually caused by infection with bacteria or parasites.

dyslexia A learning disorder that interferes with a person's ability to recognize and understand written words. *—adjective* **dyslexic.**

dysplasia Abnormal development or growth of tissues, organs or cells. *—adjective* **dysplastic.**

dysprosium A soft, silvery metallic element of the lanthanide series. Because it has a high melting point and absorbs neutrons well, dysprosium is used to help control nuclear reactions. *Symbol* **Dy.** *Atomic number* 66. *See* **Periodic Table,** pages 260–261.

E*e*

e An irrational number, with a numerical value of 2.718281828459. . . . It is mathematically defined as the limit of $(1+1/n)^n$ as n grows infinitely large. It has many applications in mathematics, especially as the base of natural logarithms.

E The symbol for **energy.**

eagle Any of various large birds of prey having a hooked bill, sharp claws and long broad wings. Eagles are related to hawks and falcons.

ear[1] The organ of hearing in humans and other vertebrate animals. The ear also plays an important role in maintaining balance. In many mammals, the ear is composed of three parts: the outer ear, the middle ear and the inner ear.

ear[2] The seed-bearing spike of a cereal plant, such as maize or wheat.

eardrum The thin, oval-shaped membrane that separates the middle ear from the outer ear. It vibrates in response to sound waves, which are then transmitted to the three small bones of the middle ear. Also called *tympanic membrane.*

Earth 1. The third planet from the sun and the fifth largest in the solar system. Earth is the only planet known to support life. It is also the only planet on which water in liquid form exists, covering more than 70 per cent of its surface. *See table at* **solar system,** pages 314–315. **2. earth** Dry land; the ground.

earthquake A sudden movement of the Earth's crust. Earthquakes are caused by the release of built-up stress within rocks along geological faults or by the movement of magma in volcanic areas. They are usually followed by aftershocks. *See panel at* **fault.**

earth science Any of several sciences, such as geology, oceanography or meteorology, that specialize in the origin, composition and physical features of the Earth.

earthworm Any of various segmented worms living in the ground that burrow into and enrich soil. Earthworms are annelids, related to the leeches, and vary in size from a few centimetres to around 3 metres in length. *See panel at* **worm.**

Eastern Hemisphere The half of the Earth that includes Europe, Africa, Asia and Australia.

ebb tide The period between high tide and low

■ earth
The inner core and outer core are made up mainly of iron and nickel, the lower and upper mantle mainly of iron and magnesium silicate minerals, and the crust mainly of silicate minerals.

Labels for the earth diagram: upper mantle (partially molten); lower mantle (solid); crust (solid); outer core (liquid); inner core (solid)

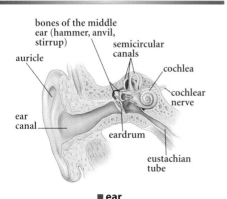

■ ear

Labels for the ear diagram: bones of the middle ear (hammer, anvil, stirrup); auricle; semicircular canals; cochlea; cochlear nerve; ear canal; eardrum; eustachian tube

Did You Know?

earthquake

If all the crockery falls out of your kitchen cupboard, you may honestly be able to say, "It's the Earth's fault"! Indeed, the Earth has faults – cracks where sections of its outer shell (the lithosphere) slip past each other, causing an *earthquake* when subjected to great forces. Three kinds of waves accompany earthquakes. Primary (P) waves have a push-pull type of vibration. Secondary (S) waves have a side-to-side type of vibration. Both P and S waves travel deep into the Earth, reflecting off the surfaces of its various layers. S waves cannot travel through the liquid outer core. By contrast, surface (L) waves – a third type of wave, named after the 19th-century British mathematician AEH Love – travel along the Earth's surface and do most of the damage associated with an earthquake. The total amount of energy released by an earthquake is measured on the Richter scale. On this scale, each increase by 1 corresponds to a tenfold increase in earthquake strength. So an earthquake measuring 5.0 on the Richter scale is 10 times stronger than one measuring 4.0. Earthquakes above 7 on the Richter scale are severe. The famous earthquake that flattened San Francisco in the United States in 1906 measured 7.8.

tide, during which water flows away from the shore. *Compare* **flood tide**. *See more at* **tide**.

Ebola virus A highly contagious virus that causes fever, bleeding, loss of consciousness and usually death.

ECG Abbreviation of **electrocardiogram**.

echidna Either of two burrowing, egg-laying mammals having a spiny coat, slender snout and long sticky tongue used for catching ants and termites. Echidnas are toothless and have claws used for digging. They are found in Australia, Tasmania and New Guinea.

echinoderm Any of various invertebrate sea animals having a hard spiny outer covering, an internal skeleton and a radially symmetrical body. Starfish, sea urchins and sea cucumbers are echinoderms.

echo 1. A repeated sound that is caused by the reflection of sound waves from a surface. The sound is heard more than once because of the time difference between the initial production of the sound waves and their return from the reflecting surface. **2.** A reflected radio wave. Echoes of radio waves are the basis for radar.

echolocation 1. A sensory system in certain animals, such as bats and dolphins, in which the animals send out high-pitched sounds and use their echoes to determine the position of objects. *See panel at* **bat. 2.** The use of reflected sound waves, as by radar or sonar, to determine the location and size of distant or underwater objects.

Eckert, John Presper 1919–1995. American engineer who contributed to the development of ENIAC (Electronic Numeral Integrator and Calculator), the first electronic computer (1946).

eclipse The partial or total blocking of light from one celestial body as it passes behind or through the shadow of another celestial body. ❖ In a **solar eclipse** the moon comes between the

Did You Know?

eclipse

Purely by chance, the sun is about 400 times wider than the moon but also 400 times further from the Earth. For this reason, the sun and the moon appear to be almost exactly the same size in the sky. Our unique vantage point makes for the spectacular phenomenon of a *total solar eclipse,* when the moon blocks out the sun. A total solar eclipse reveals the beautiful and delicate corona, wispy tendrils of charged gases that surround the sun but are invisible to the naked eye in normal sunlight. The orbits of the Earth around the sun and of the moon around the Earth are not perfect circles. Therefore the sun and moon may vary slightly in how big they appear to us, and the length of total solar eclipses can also vary. The maximum duration of a solar eclipse, however, when the Earth is furthest from the sun and the moon is nearest to the Earth, is only seven and a half minutes. Since looking at the sun can cause blindness, it is safest to view any solar eclipse indirectly. A good method is to project the image through a pinhole in a piece of paper onto another piece of paper.

sun and the Earth. ❖ In a **lunar eclipse** the moon enters the Earth's shadow.

eclipsing binary A variable binary star whose components pass in front of each other, thereby

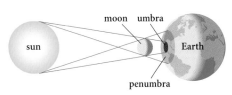

■ **eclipse**

A solar eclipse occurs when the moon passes between the sun and the Earth. An observer within the umbra will witness a total solar eclipse, while someone within the penumbra will observe a partial solar eclipse.

causing a regular eclipse of one of the stars and changes in brightness.

ecliptic The great circle on the celestial sphere that is made by the plane containing the Earth's orbit around the sun. The ecliptic traces the sun's apparent path in the sky in one year, as viewed from the Earth.

ecology 1. The scientific study of the relationships between living things and their environments. 2. A system of such relationships: *the fragile ecology of the desert.*

ecosystem An ecological community made up of plants, animals and microorganisms, together with their environment. A pond or a rain forest are each examples of complex ecosystems.

eczema Inflammation of the skin, often caused by an allergy to a particular substance. Symptoms include itching, scaling and blistering.

Eddington, Sir Arthur Stanley 1882–1944. British mathematician, astronomer and physicist who founded modern astrophysics. He conducted research on the evolution, structure and motion of stars and was one of the first scientists to provide evidence for the theory of relativity.

eddy A current, as of water or air, moving in a direction that is different from that of the main current. Eddies often move in a circular motion.

edentate *adjective* Lacking teeth. —*noun* Any of various mammals having few or no teeth. Sloths, armadillos and anteaters are edentates.

Ediacaran Relating to a group of fossilized organisms that are the earliest known remains of multicellular life. They are soft-bodied marine life forms that date from between 560 and 545 million years ago, during the late Precambrian Eon.

Edison, Thomas Alva 1847–1931. American inventor and physicist who took out more than 1000 patents in his lifetime. His inventions include the telegraph (1869), microphone (1877) and light bulb (1879). During World War I, Edison worked on a number of military devices, including flamethrowers, periscopes and torpedoes.

Edwards, Robert Geoffrey Born 1925. British physiologist. The focus of Robert Edwards' research was on human fertility and infertility, and the process of conception. Working with Patrick Steptoe, he played a major role in the successful development of the in vitro fertilization ("test-tube baby") programme. Edwards produced the conditions necessary for the egg and sperm to survive outside the womb. He discovered ways of encouraging immature eggs to ripen in a woman, and he provided the right artificial conditions to ensure successful fertilization and early development of the embryo outside the woman's body. In July 1978, Louise Brown, the first healthy "test-tube baby" was born as a result of the work of Edwards and Steptoe.

EEG Abbreviation of **electroencephalogram.**

eel 1. Any of various fish having long, snake-like bodies without scales. Eels typically migrate from fresh to salt water to spawn. **2.** Any of several similar fish, such as the lamprey.

efferent Relating to a nerve that carries motor impulses from the central nervous system to the muscles. *Compare* **afferent.**

effervescence The bubbling of a solution due to the escape of gas. The gas may form by a chemical reaction, as in a fermenting liquid, or by coming out of solution after having been under pressure, as in a carbonated drink.

efflorescence A whitish, powdery deposit on the surface of rocks or soil in dry regions. It is formed as mineral-rich water rises to the surface through capillary action and then evaporates. Efflorescence usually consists of gypsum, salt or calcite.

egg 1. The mature reproductive cell of female animals. The nucleus of an egg is capable of fusing with the nucleus of a sperm (the male reproductive cell) to form a new organism. In many species, eggs are produced by the ovaries. An egg carries half as many chromosomes as the other cells of the body. Also called *ovum.* **2.** In many animals, a structure consisting of this reproductive cell together with nourishment for the developing embryo and often a protective covering. It is laid outside the body of the female. **3.** In plants, algae and certain fungi, the reproductive cell whose nucleus is capable of fusing with the nucleus of a male reproductive cell to form a new organism. An egg has half as many chromosomes as the other cells of the organism. In gymnosperms and angiosperms, eggs are enclosed within ovules.

egg tooth A hard, tooth-like projection from the

beak of embryonic birds, or from the upper jaw of embryonic reptiles, that is used to cut the egg membrane and shell upon hatching and that later falls off.

Ehrlich, Paul 1854–1915. German bacteriologist who was a pioneer in the study of the blood and the immune system, and in the development of drugs to fight specific disease-causing agents. Ehrlich theorized that the interactions between cells, antibodies and antigens were chemical responses, and he developed systematic techniques to search for chemicals that would attack and destroy disease without harming human cells. In the process, he discovered a compound that was effective in combating sleepy sickness. He also discovered another drug, called salvarsan, that cured syphilis.

Einstein, Albert 1879–1955. German-born American physicist whose theories revolutionized scientific understanding of space and time. The special theory of relativity, published in 1905, established the equivalence of mass and energy. The general theory of relativity, published in 1915, stated that the force known as gravity is due to the curvature of space-time. Einstein also showed that light is composed of individual particles, later named photons. *See more at* **relativity.**

einsteinium A synthetic, radioactive metallic element of the actinide series that is usually produced from plutonium. The most stable isotope of einsteinium has a half-life of 1.3 years. *Symbol* **Es.** *Atomic number* 99. *See* **Periodic Table,** pages 260–261.

ejaculation The movement of semen out of the penis by waves of muscular contraction that occurs when a man reaches orgasm.

elasticity The ability of a solid to return to its original shape after being stretched or compressed by a force. Elasticity is a property of most solid materials, including rubber, steel and many body tissues. —*adjective* **elastic.**

Eldredge, Niles Born 1943. American palaeontologist who developed the theory of punctuated equilibrium with evolutionary biologist Stephen Jay Gould in 1972.

electric (*also* **electrical**) Relating to or operated by electricity: *electric power; an electrical appliance. See panel at* **electronic.**

Biography

Albert Einstein

Around 1900, the field of physics had fallen into confusion. The increased precision of new measuring devices had shown that the old laws of motion and gravity established by Galileo and Newton were unable to explain certain phenomena. For example, scientists now knew that the observed orbit of the planet Mercury differed slightly from that predicted by Newton's laws. And new laws describing the movement of electromagnetic waves were shown not to work under certain conditions. A way to solving these problems was opened in 1905 by an unknown 26-year-old office clerk named Albert Einstein. In that year, he published four path-breaking papers that revolutionized physics. Two of the papers introduced aspects of his theory of relativity, which broke away from the Newtonian reliance on space and time as unchangeable frames of reference. In one of these publications, Einstein argued that the speed of light is the same for all observers. A third paper showed that light consists of particles called photons. A fourth explained the random movement of particles suspended in a fluid (what is known as Brownian

motion). Later, in 1916, he showed that gravity is not just a force, but actually stretches or shrinks distances and even slows down time in relation to someone unaffected by the gravitational field. Einstein's new way of looking at gravity explained the variations in Mercury's orbit, and his theory that light consists not just of waves but of particles led to a more accurate description of electromagnetic radiation. For the next 50 years Einstein devoted himself to unveiling more of the mysteries of the physical world, and he also used his fame to promote peace and humanitarian causes.

electrical engineering The branch of engineering that specializes in the design, construction and practical uses of electrical systems.

electric cell A device that is capable of changing some form of energy, such as chemical or radiant energy, into electricity.

electricity 1. The collection of physical effects resulting from the existence of charged particles, especially electrons and protons, and their interactions. Particles with like charges repel each other. Particles with opposite charges attract each other. **2.** The electric current generated by the flow of electrons around a circuit and used as a source of power.

electrocardiogram A recording of the electrical activity of the heart. The electrocardiogram is used by doctors to analyse how well the heart is working and to diagnose abnormal heart rhythms. *Abbreviation* ECG. ❖ The machine used to record an electrocardiogram is called an **electrocardiograph.**

electrochemistry The scientific study of chemical reactions that produce an electric current and of the use of electricity to bring about chemical reactions.

electrode A piece of metal or carbon through which an electric current enters or leaves a liquid or gas, as in electrolysis.

electrodynamics The scientific study of electric charges, electric currents and the forces associated with them. Electrodynamics is a branch of physics.

electroencephalogram A recording of the electrical activity of the cerebral cortex of the brain. It is made by attaching electrodes to the scalp, then collecting, amplifying and recording the electrical impulses of the brain. Electroencephalograms are used to diagnose epilepsy, study sleep patterns and to check on the activity of the brain after injury. ❖ The machine used to record an electroencephalogram is called an **electroencephalograph**.

electrolysis A process in which a chemical change, especially decomposition, is brought about by passing an electric current through a solution of electrolytes so that the electrolyte's ions move towards the negative and positive electrodes and react with them.

electrolyte 1. A substance that when dissolved or melted becomes electrically conductive by breaking apart into ions. The movement of ions carries the current. 2. Any of these ions found in body fluids. Electrolytes are needed by cells to regulate the flow of water molecules across cell membranes.

electrolytic cell A device containing two electrodes immersed in a solution of electrolytes, used to bring about a chemical reaction. Electrolytic cells require an outside source of electricity to initiate the movement of ions between the two electrodes where the chemical change takes place. They have many practical uses including the recovery of pure metal from alloys and the plating of one metal with another. *Compare* **voltaic cell**.

electromagnet A device consisting of a coil of insulated wire wrapped around an iron core that becomes magnetized when an electric current flows through the wire. *See panel at* **magnetism**.

electromagnetic force The force arising from the attractions and repulsions associated with electric and magnetic fields. The electromagnetic force is one of the four basic forces in nature, being weaker than the strong nuclear force but stronger than the weak nuclear force and gravity.

electromagnetic induction The name given to the production of an electromotive force across the ends of a conductor, such as a wire, when it experiences a changing magnetic field.

electromagnetic radiation Energy that moves through space and matter both in the form of magnetic and electric waves and in the form of a stream of particles called photons.

electromagnetic spectrum The entire range of electromagnetic radiation. At one end of the spectrum are gamma rays, which have the shortest wavelengths and high frequencies. At the other end are radio waves, which have the longest wavelengths and low frequencies. Visible light, with intermediate wavelengths and frequencies, is near the centre of the spectrum.

electromagnetic wave A wave of energy consisting of oscillating electric and magnetic fields. Radio waves, light waves and X-rays are electromagnetic waves.

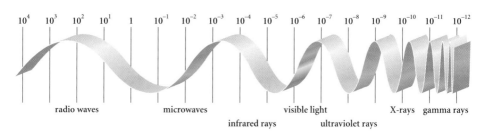

10^4 10^3 10^2 10^1 1 10^{-1} 10^{-2} 10^{-3} 10^{-4} 10^{-5} 10^{-6} 10^{-7} 10^{-8} 10^{-9} 10^{-10} 10^{-11} 10^{-12}

radio waves   microwaves   visible light   X-rays gamma rays

infrared rays   ultraviolet rays

■ **electromagnetic spectrum**

The electromagnetic spectrum can be measured in frequencies or in wavelengths. This diagram measures wavelengths in metres, ranging from the longest wavelengths (radio waves) to the shortest (gamma rays). Visible light, which is a band of colours from red to violet, is the only portion of the spectrum that can be seen by the human eye.

electromagnetic radiation

Many people have heard that light is made up of waves, but what does that mean? The answer seems very abstract: light and other forms of *electromagnetic radiation,* are made up of wave-shaped electric and magnetic fields that reinforce each other as they travel together. In the 19th century, physicists discovered that a changing electric field can create a magnetic field, and a changing magnetic field can create an electric field. So a wave-shaped electric field (for example, the field created when a charged particle such as an electron moves up and down) can create a wave-shaped magnetic field, which in turn reproduces the wave-shaped electric field. These mutually re-creating fields travel at the speed of light. Electromagnetic radiation can have a variety of properties, depending on its wavelength. Certain wavelengths make up the spectrum of visible light. Infrared light and radio waves have longer wavelengths, whereas ultraviolet light, X-rays and gamma rays have shorter wavelengths. These wave properties do not tell the full story of electromagnetic radiation, however. Some properties of visible light and other forms of electromagnetic radiation are better explained by thinking of them as streams of particles known as *photons.* The energy of the photons increases as the frequency of the waves gets higher.

electromagnetism 1. Magnetism produced by electric charge in motion. *See panel at* **magnetism. 2.** The scientific study of electricity and magnetism and the relationships between them.

electromotive Relating to or producing electric current.

electromotive force The potential difference between the terminals of an electric cell, battery or other electrical energy source when no current is being drawn from it. Electromotive force is a measure of the amount of energy that can be transferred to a given charge when it flows through a source of electrical energy. *Abbreviation* emf. *See also* **potential difference.**

electron A stable subatomic particle with a negative electric charge. Electrons surround the nucleus of an atom in orbits called shells or energy levels. Electrons behave both as particles and as waves, and their motion generates electric and magnetic fields. Though the electron has about 1/2000 of the mass of a proton, the magnitude of its charge is exactly the same as that of a proton. *See more at* **atom.**

electronegativity The electronegativity of an atom is a measure of its tendency to attract electrons in a bond. The more electronegative an atom, the more it tends to attract electrons towards itself.

electronic Relating to devices that work by the movement of electric charge carriers (such as electrons), especially across a vacuum or a semiconductor. ❖ The scientific study of this movement, along with the development of devices such as televisions and computer circuits that work by controlling this movement, is called **electronics.**

electron microscope An instrument that uses a beam of electrons to view objects that are too small to be seen with an ordinary microscope. As the electrons hit the object being viewed, other

electronic/electric

All electronic devices are electric, but not all electric devices are electronic. An *electric* device is simply one that is powered by electricity. An electric fan usually consists of an electric motor that moves fan blades in a circle. An *electronic* device usually has special components that control the movement of electrons across a vacuum (as in a vacuum tube) or a semiconductor. These components allow a great range of capabilities, from tuning in to radio and television channels, to performing complicated calculations on calculators, to reading the time from a digital watch.

electron tube

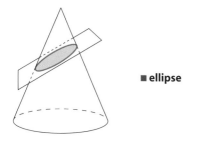

■ **ellipse**

---

electrons are knocked loose from its surface and are picked up by a detector that converts them into a black and white image. An electron microscope can give magnifications up to 500,000 times life size. An average person magnified this much would appear over 830km tall!

electron tube A sealed glass tube containing a small amount of gas, in which electrons move from a negatively charged electrode to a positively charged one. With the application and varying of an electric or magnetic field, the direction and number of electrons in the tube can be controlled. Electron tubes are used to amplify signals and change AC currents to DC currents. They have been mostly replaced by transistors but are still used in television screens and computer monitors and in microwave technology. *Compare* **vacuum tube.**

electron volt A unit used to measure the energy of subatomic particles. It is equal to the energy gained by an electron that is accelerated through a potential difference of one volt.

electrophoresis The migration of electrically charged particles through a fluid that is under the influence of an electric field. Electrophoresis is used especially to separate colloids for the purpose of studying their components.

electrostatic Relating to or caused by electric charges that do not move. *See more at* **static electricity.**

element 1. A substance that cannot be broken down into simpler substances by chemical means. An element is composed of atoms that have the same atomic number; that is, each atom has the same number of protons in its nucleus as all other atoms of that element. **2.** *Mathematics.* A member of a set.

elementary particle Any of the smallest known units of matter, such as quarks and neutrinos. Elementary particles are not made up of smaller units.

elephant 1. A large mammal having thick, nearly hairless skin, a long flexible trunk and long curved ivory tusks. There are two living species of elephants, the African and the Indian elephant. They can live over 60 years in the wild and display complex social behaviour. **2.** Any of various extinct animals, such as the mammoths, that are related to the living elephants.

elevation The vertical distance between a standard reference point, such as sea level, and the top of an object or point on the Earth, such as a mountain. The summit of Mount Everest is the highest elevation on Earth.

ellipse A closed, symmetrical curve shaped like an oval, which can be formed by intersecting a cone with a plane that is not parallel or perpendicular to the cone's base. The sum of the distances of any point on an ellipse from two fixed

Word History

element symbols

The symbols that scientists use for the chemical elements are usually abbreviations of the elements' names. Thus the symbol for hydrogen is H and the symbol for oxygen is O, both from the first letter of the name. But if you look at the Periodic Table (pages 260–261), you'll notice that some symbols are entirely different from the corresponding element names. The symbol for iron is Fe and the symbol for tin is Sn, for example. Why is this? It's because some elements were already known to the ancient Greeks and Romans, such as familiar metals like iron, copper, silver, gold, tin and lead. For these elements scientists use abbreviations of the Greek and Latin words for them. The Latin words for the six metals listed above are *ferrum, cuprum, argentum, aurum, stannum* and *plumbum*. From these names come, quite straightforwardly, the chemical symbols Fe, Cu, Ag, Au, Sn and Pb.

points (called the foci) remains constant no matter where the point is on the curve.

ellipsoid A three-dimensional geometric figure resembling a flattened sphere. Any cross section of an ellipsoid is an ellipse or circle.

El Niño A warming of the surface water of the eastern and central Pacific Ocean, occurring every 4 to 12 years and causing unusual weather patterns. The warmer water kills fish and plankton, brings heavy rains to western South America, and causes drought in eastern Australia and Indonesia. *Compare* **La Niña.**

Elton, Charles Sutherland 1900–1991. British ecologist. Charles Elton was the first biologist to develop the basic ideas of food chains and food webs that are now such an important part of any study of ecology. As a young man he spent several summers studying the relationships between the animals of Bear Island in the Arctic tundra and the scarce food resources available, and it was on this evidence that he based his ideas.

elytron (*plural* **elytra**) Either of the modified forewings of a beetle or related insect that encase the thin hind wings used in flight.

embryo 1. An animal in its earliest stages of development, especially in the uterus of female mammals or, in egg-laying animals, an animal developing in the egg until it is hatched. 2. A plant in its earliest stages of development, especially the miniature, partially developed plant contained within a seed. When conditions are right for germination, the embryo begins to grow and bursts through the seed coat. —*adjective* **embryonic.**

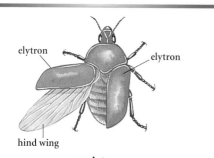

■ **elytron**

When closed, the elytron protects the hind wing. The elytra are opened for flight.

embryology The branch of biology that deals with embryos and their development.

embryo sac An oval structure within an ovule of a flowering plant that contains the egg cell. Together with the fertilized egg cell, it develops into a seed.

emerald A transparent, green form of the mineral beryl. It is valued as a gem.

emery A dark mineral that is very hard and is used in a crushed or powdered form for grinding and polishing.

emf Abbreviation of **electromotive force.**

emission 1. The act or process of emitting: *For environmental safety we must seek to reduce the factory's emission of fumes and smoke.* 2. Something that is emitted: *harmful emissions from traffic.*

emission spectrum The pattern of lines, colours or bands made when energy excites the atoms or molecules of a substance. The excited atoms may then give off energy in the form of light. Because each type of atom gives off light having a unique range of colours, the pattern of the emission spectrum can be used to determine the chemical properties of the substance.

emphysema A chronic disease in which the small air sacs of the lungs (called alveoli) become enlarged and eventually collapse, causing blockage to the flow of air. Symptoms include difficulty breathing and loss of physical endurance. Emphysema can be caused by the excessive smoking of cigarettes and other tobacco products.

empirical Relying on or derived from observation or experiment rather than theory: *empirical results prove the theory.*

empty set *Mathematics.* The set that has no members or elements.

emu A large, flightless Australian bird related to and resembling the ostrich but smaller in size.

emulsion A suspension of tiny droplets of one liquid in a second liquid. By making an emulsion, one can mix two liquids that ordinarily do not mix well, such as oil and water. *Compare* **aerosol, foam.** —*verb* **emulsify.**

enamel The hard substance covering the exposed portion of a tooth.

encephalitis Inflammation of the brain, usually caused by infection with a virus.

endangered species A plant or animal species existing in such small numbers that it is in danger of becoming extinct. An organism often becomes endangered because of destruction of its native habitat.

endemic 1. Found in or confined to a particular location, region, or people. Malaria, for example, is a disease endemic to tropical regions. **2.** *Ecology.* Native to a particular region or environment and not occurring naturally anywhere else. The kakapo parrot is endemic to New Zealand. *Compare* **alien, indigenous.**

endocrine gland Any gland of the body that produces hormones and secretes them directly into the bloodstream. In mammals, the thyroid gland, adrenal gland and pituitary gland, as well as the ovary, testis and pancreas, are all endocrine glands. ❖ The group of endocrine glands together with the hormones they secrete is known as the **endocrine system**. *See panel at* **hormone.**

endocrinology The branch of biology or medicine that deals with endocrine glands, their functions and their diseases.

endometrium The membrane that lines the uterus of a female mammal. A fertilized egg must attach itself to the endometrium to continue to develop.

endoplasmic reticulum A network of membranes within the cytoplasm of many cells that is important in protein synthesis and involved in the transport of cellular materials. All organisms except bacteria have at least one endoplasmic reticulum in their cells. *See more at* **cell.**

endorphin Any of a group of substances found in the nervous system, especially in the brain, that regulate the body's response to pain and other stimuli.

endoskeleton A supporting framework in an animal that is contained inside the body. Humans and many other vertebrate animals have bony endoskeletons. Certain invertebrate animals, such as sponges, have endoskeletons made up of needle-like structures called spicules. *Compare* **exoskeleton.**

endosperm The tissue that surrounds and provides nourishment to the embryo in plant seeds.

endothermic Causing or characterized by absorption of heat: *an endothermic chemical reaction. Compare* **exothermic.**

–ene A suffix used to form the names of

Usage

endemic/epidemic/pandemic

A disease that occurs regularly in a particular area, as malaria does in many tropical countries, is said to be *endemic.* The word *endemic,* built from the prefix *en–,* "in or within", and the Greek word *demos,* "people", means "within the people (of a region)". When a disease affects many more people than usual in a particular area, it is known as an *outbreak* of the disease, but if the increased incidence of the disease spreads across a large area or a whole country, it is known as an *epidemic.* This word, built from the prefix *epi–,* meaning "upon", and *demos,* means "upon the people". In order for a disease to become epidemic it must be highly contagious, that is, easily spread through a population. Epidemics of waterborne diseases such as cholera often occur after natural disasters such as earthquakes and severe storms that disrupt or destroy sanitation systems and supplies of fresh water. Influenza, better known as the flu, has been the cause not only of many epidemics throughout history, but also of a number of *pandemics.* A pandemic is when an epidemic spreads to affect many countries of the world at the same time. Only four diseases are known to have caused pandemics – flu, cholera, plague and AIDS.

endorphins

In the 1970s, scientists began to wonder why drugs like morphine could kill pain so effectively. Researchers knew that morphine attached to specific body molecules called receptors, so they deduced that these receptors probably existed because the body itself had natural painkilling compounds that also bonded to those receptors. They searched and finally found proteins called *endorphins,* a word that combines *endogenous,* meaning "naturally occurring within the body", and *morphine.* When your body is under stress, it can produce endorphins so that you can still function under what would otherwise be exceptionally painful conditions. Many long-distance runners, for example, claim that after they run for a while they start to feel exceptionally happy, a condition sometimes called a *runner's high.* High levels of endorphins in response to the strain of running seem to be responsible for this state of mind.

hydrocarbons having one or more double bonds, such as *ethene* and *propene. Compare –ane.*

energy The capacity or power to do work, such as the capacity to move an object (of a given mass) in a given direction by the application of force. Energy can exist in a variety of forms, such as electrical, mechanical, chemical, thermal or nuclear, and can be transferred from one form to another. It is measured by the amount of work done, usually in joules or watts. *See more at* **law of conservation of energy.**

engine A machine that turns energy into mechanical force or motion, especially one that gets its energy from a source of heat, such as the burning of a fuel. *See more at* **internal-combustion engine, jet engine, steam engine.**

engineering The application of science to practical uses such as the design of structures, machines and systems. *See more at* **chemical engineering, civil engineering, electrical engineering, mechanical engineering.**

enthalpy The amount of energy contained in a system.

entomology The scientific study of insects.

entropy A measure of the amount of disorder in a system. Entropy increases as the system's temperature increases. For example, when an ice cube melts and becomes liquid, the energy of the molecular bonds which formed the ice crystals is lost, and the arrangement of the water molecules is more random, or disordered, than it was in the ice cube.

environment All of the physical, chemical and biological conditions that together act on an organism or an ecological community and influence its growth and development. Soil, air, water, climate, plant and animal life, noise level and pollution are all components of an environ-

entomology

Scientists who study insects (there are more than a million species that can be studied!) are called entomologists. Why are they not called "insectologists"? Well, in a way they are. The word *insect* comes from the Latin word *insectum,* meaning "cut up or divided into segments". (The plural of *insectum,* namely *insecta,* is used by scientists as the name of the taxonomic class that insects belong to.) This Latin word was created in order to translate the Greek word for "insect", which is *entomon.* This Greek word also literally means "cut up or divided into segments", and it is the source of the word *entomology.* The Greeks had coined this term for insects because of the clear division of insect bodies into three segments, now called the head, thorax and abdomen.

ment. To survive, organisms must often adapt to changes in their environments.

enzyme Any of the proteins produced in living cells that act as catalysts in the metabolic processes of an organism. Enzymes are not affected by or broken down during the reactions they catalyse. For example, enzymes break down the large molecules found in food into smaller molecules which can be absorbed and used by the body during the process of digestion.

Eocene The second epoch of the Tertiary Period, from about 58 to 37 million years ago, characterized by warm climates and the rise of most modern families of mammals. *See chart at* **geological time,** pages 148–149.

eohippus *See* **hyracotherium.**

eon The longest division of geological time, containing two or more eras.

epicentre The point on the Earth's surface that is directly above the focus (the point of origin) of an earthquake.

epidemic A significantly increased incidence of a disease across a whole country. *See panel at* **endemic.**

epidemiology The branch of medicine that deals with the study of the causes, distribution and control of disease in populations.

epidermis 1. The protective outer layer of the skin of an animal. In invertebrate animals, the epidermis is made up of a single layer of cells. In vertebrates, the epidermis is made up of many layers of cells and overlies the dermis. Hair and feathers grow from the epidermis. **2.** The outer layer of cells of the stems, roots and leaves of plants. The cells of the epidermis are set close together to protect the plant from water loss, invasion by fungi and physical damage. *See more at* **photosynthesis.**

epiglottis A thin, triangular plate of cartilage at the base of the tongue that covers the glottis during swallowing to keep food from entering the trachea.

Did You Know?

enzymes

No matter how hard you find chemistry in school, you're still quite good at it: every day your body performs complex biochemistry. Many of the chemical reactions that take place inside you depend on the proteins known as enzymes. These large, globular proteins catalyse, or speed up, the reactions sometimes by as much as a million times. Enzymes are structured so that they bond to a second, specific molecule, called a substrate. When the enzyme and its substrate come together, at a place on the enzyme called the active site, the substrate is modified, for example by combining two different substrate molecules into a single molecule. The enzyme remains unchanged, breaks away, and is free to perform its chemical magic on a fresh substrate molecule. People have found uses for enzymes outside our bodies as well. For example, detergents may include enzymes that break down organic stains on clothing, and enzymes have long been used in making beer, wine and cheese.

■ **epiphyte**
epiphytic bromeliads growing on tree branches

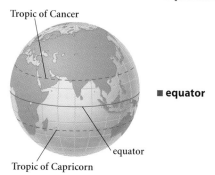

Tropic of Cancer

■ **equator**

equator

Tropic of Capricorn

epilepsy A disorder characterized by a tendency to have seizures. It is caused by an abnormal discharge of electrical activity in the brain.

epiphyte A plant that grows on another plant and depends on it for support but not food. Epiphytes get moisture and nutrients from the air or from small pools of water that collect on the host plant. Spanish moss and many orchids are epiphytes.

epithelium The thin, protective layer of cells that covers most of the outer surface of an animal body and lines the inner surface of many body parts. In vertebrate animals, the outer layer of the skin, called the epidermis, is composed of epithelium.

epoch The shortest division of geological time, being a subdivision of a period.

epoxide A ring-shaped chemical structure or compound consisting of an oxygen atom bonded to two other atoms, usually of carbon, that are already bonded to each other.

epoxy Any of various artificial resins that are tough, very adhesive and resistant to chemicals. Epoxies are used to make protective coatings and glues.

Epsom salts A bitter, colourless, crystalline salt, used in making textiles, in fertilizers, for medical purposes and as an additive to bath water to soothe the skin. It consists of hydrated magnesium sulphate.

equation 1. *Mathematics.* A written statement indicating the equality of two expressions. It consists of a sequence of symbols that is split into left and right sides joined by an equal sign. For example, $2 + 3 + 5 = 10$ is an equation. **2.** *Chemistry.* A written representation of a chemical reaction, in which the symbols and amounts of the reactants are separated from those of the products by an equal sign, an arrow or a set of opposing arrows. For example, $NaOH + HCl = NaCl + H_2O$ is an equation.

equator 1. The imaginary line forming a great circle around the Earth's surface halfway between the North and South poles. It divides the Earth into the Northern Hemisphere and the Southern Hemisphere. **2.** A similar circle on the surface of any celestial body.

equi– A prefix that means "equal" or "equally", as in *equidistant.*

equidistant Equally distant: *two points that are equidistant from a third point.*

equilateral Having all sides of equal length, as a square or as a triangle that is neither scalene nor isosceles.

equilibrium 1. *Physics.* The state of a body or physical system that is at rest or in constant and unchanging motion. The sum of all forces acting

■ **equilateral triangle**

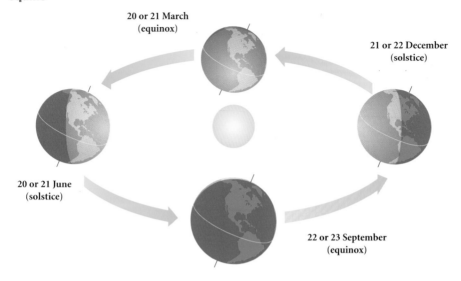

20 or 21 March
(equinox)

21 or 22 December
(solstice)

20 or 21 June
(solstice)

22 or 23 September
(equinox)

■ **equinox**

Changes in seasons occur as the position of the Earth in relation to the sun changes. Equinoxes and solstices mark the beginning of opposite seasons in the Northern and Southern Hemispheres. For example, the June solstice marks the beginning of summer in the Northern Hemisphere and of winter in the Southern Hemisphere. The September equinox marks the beginning of autumn in the Northern Hemisphere and of spring in the Southern Hemisphere.

on a body that is in equilibrium is zero (because opposing forces balance each other). A system that is in equilibrium shows no tendency to alter over time. **2.** *Chemistry.* The state of a reversible chemical reaction in which its forward and reverse reactions occur at equal rates so that the concentration of the reactants and products remains the same.

equine Relating to horses or similar animals, such as donkeys.

equinox 1. Either of the two moments of the year when the sun crosses the celestial equator. The vernal equinox occurs on 20 or 21 March, and the autumnal equinox occurs on 22 or 23 September. The days on which an equinox falls have about equal periods of sunlight and darkness. **2.** Either of the two points on the celestial sphere where the apparent path of the sun (known as the ecliptic) crosses the celestial equator. *Compare* **solstice.**

equivalent 1. Equal, as in value, meaning or force. **2.** Having a one-to-one correspondence, as between parts: *equivalent geometric figures.*

Er The symbol for **erbium.**

era A division of geological time, longer than a period and shorter than an eon.

Eratosthenes Third century BC. Greek mathematician and astronomer. He is best known for making an accurate estimate of the circumference of the Earth by measuring the angle of the sun's rays at two different locations at the same time. Eratosthenes also invented a method for listing the prime numbers that are less than any given number.

erbium A soft, silvery, easily shaped metallic element of the lanthanide series. It is used to make light signals stronger in long-distance telephone and computer cables that use fibre optics. *Symbol* **Er.** *Atomic number* 68. *See* **Periodic Table,** pages 260–261.

erection The hardening or enlargement of

certain tissues of the body, especially the penis, when filled with blood.

erg A unit used to measure energy or work, equal to the force of one dyne over a distance of one centimetre. This unit has been mostly replaced by the joule.

ergot A fungus that infects rye, wheat and other grain plants, forming black masses among the seeds. Grain infected with ergot is poisonous and can cause serious illness.

erosion The gradual wearing away of land surface materials, especially rocks, sediments and soils, by the action of water, wind or a glacier. Usually erosion also involves the transfer of eroded material from one place to another, as from the top of a mountain to an adjacent valley, or from the upstream portion of a river to the downstream portion. ❖ **coastal erosion** is where the coastline has been worn away by the sea. This erosion can be managed by the construction of gabions (cages containing rocks), groynes (fences) and sea walls.

erupt To release gas, ash, molten materials or hot water into the atmosphere or onto the Earth's surface.

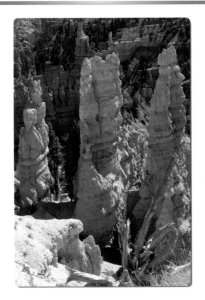

■ **erosion**

erythrocyte *See* **red blood cell.**

Es The symbol for **einsteinium.**

Esaki, Leo Born 1925. Japanese physicist who developed a very fast and very small type of diode that is now widely used in many electronic devices, especially computers.

escape velocity The velocity that a body, such as a rocket, must achieve to overcome the gravitational pull of the Earth or another celestial body.

escarpment A steep slope or long cliff formed by erosion or by vertical movement of the Earth's crust along a fault.

esker A long, narrow ridge of coarse sand and gravel deposited by a stream flowing in or under a melting sheet of glacial ice.

ester An organic compound formed when an acid and an alcohol combine and release water. Animal and vegetable fats and oils are esters.

estuary 1. The wide lower course of a river where it flows into the sea. The water in estuaries is a mixture of fresh water and salt water. 2. An arm of the sea that extends inland to meet the mouth of a river.

ethanal A colourless, flammable liquid, C_2H_4O, used to make ethanoic acid. A member of the aldehyde group. Old name *acetaldehyde.*

ethane A colourless, odourless, flammable gas, C_2H_6, occurring in natural gas. It is used as a fuel and in refrigeration.

ethanoate 1. A salt or ester of ethanoic acid. 2. Cellulose ethanoate or a product made from it, especially fibres or film. Old name *acetate. See more at* **cellulose.**

ethanoic acid A clear, pungent acid, $C_2H_4O_2$, occurring naturally in vinegar and also produced commercially. It is used as a solvent and in making rubber, cellulose acetate plastics, paints and dyes. A carboxylic acid. Old name *acetic acid.*

ethanol An alcohol, C_2H_6O, obtained from the fermentation of sugars and starches and also made artificially. It is the intoxicating ingredient of alcoholic beverages, and it is also used as a solvent. Also called *ethyl alcohol, grain alcohol.*

ethene A colourless, flammable gas, C_2H_4, obtained from petroleum and natural gas. It is used as a fuel, in making plastics and in ripening and colouring fruits. Also called *ethylene.*

ether

ether 1. An organic compound in which two hydrocarbon groups are linked by an oxygen atom. **2.** A colourless, flammable liquid, $C_4H_{10}O$. It is used as a solvent and was formerly used as an anaesthetic. **3.** A hypothetical medium formerly believed to permeate all space and to be the medium through which light and other electromagnetic radiation move. The existence of ether was disproved by the American physicists Albert Michelson and Edward Morley in 1887.

ethyl alcohol *See* **ethanol.**

ethylene *See* **ethene.**

ethylene glycol *See* **1,2-dihydroxyethane.**

ethyne A colourless, highly flammable and explosive gas, C_2H_2. It is used in gas lighting and in cutting and welding metal. An alkyne. Old name *acetylene.*

Eu The symbol for **europium.**

eucalyptus Any of numerous tall trees that are native to Australia. Eucalyptus trees have wood valued as timber and aromatic leaves containing an oil used in medicinal preparations.

Euclid Third century BC. Greek mathematician whose book, *Elements*, was used continuously until the 19th century. In it, he organized and systematized all that was known about geometry. Euclid's systematic use of deductions and axioms was widely regarded as a model working method and influenced mathematicians and scientists for over two thousand years.

euglena Any of various one-celled freshwater organisms that move with a long tail called a flagellum, have a reddish eyespot, and often

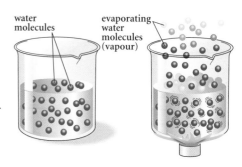

■ **evaporation**
On the left is a beaker filled with cool water. On the right, as the water is heated, molecules in the liquid move quickly apart. Molecules on the surface of the liquid will escape as vapour.

contain chlorophyll like plants. Euglenas are protozoans.

eukaryote An organism whose cells contain a nucleus surrounded by a membrane. All organisms except for bacteria, cyanobacteria and the bacteria-like organisms known as archaea are eukaryotes. *Compare* **prokaryote.**

Euler, Leonhard 1707–1783. Swiss mathematician who made many contributions to numerous areas of mathematics. He was one of the first to develop the methods used in calculus, and he introduced much of the basic mathematical notation still used today.

europium A very rare, silvery-white metallic element that is the softest member of the lanthanide series. It is used in making colour television tubes and lasers and in scientific research. *Symbol* **Eu.** *Atomic number* 63. *See* **Periodic Table,** pages 260–261.

eustachian tube A slender tube that connects the middle ear with the upper part of the throat (pharynx), serving to equalize air pressure on either side of the eardrum.

evaporation The change of a liquid into a vapour at a temperature below its boiling point.

evapotranspiration Loss of water from the Earth's surface through evaporation from soil, rocks and water and through transpiration from plants.

■ **euglena**
anatomy of a euglena

flagellum
eyespot
vacuole

nucleus
chloroplasts
cell membrane

even Divisible by 2 with a remainder of 0, such as 12 or 876.

even-toed ungulate *See* **artiodactyl.**

evergreen *adjective* Having green leaves or needles all year. *Compare* **deciduous.** —*noun* An evergreen tree, shrub or plant, such as the pine, holly or rhododendron.

evolution The process by which species of organisms undergo change over a long period of time through genetic variation and natural selection, resulting in the development of a new species. The evolutionary history of a species can be traced using fossils and recent advances in DNA technology to determine the relationships between it and earlier species to which it is related. *See also* **natural selection.** *See panel at* **Darwin.**

evolve **1.** To undergo evolution: *Birds may have evolved from reptiles.* **2.** To develop a characteristic through the process of evolution: *Cats have evolved an extraordinary sense of balance.* **3.** To undergo change or development: *Butterflies evolve from larvae.*

excitation **1.** *Biology.* The activity produced in an organ, tissue or cell of the body that is caused by stimulation, especially by a nerve or nerve cell. *Compare* **inhibition. 2.** *Chemistry, Physics.* The process of increasing the energy of a system.

excretion The removal of the waste products of metabolism by a living organism. These waste products include substances such as carbon dioxide produced during respiration, and urea produced by the breakdown of excess proteins. In plants and many relatively simple organisms, waste is eliminated by diffusion to the outside environment. More complex organisms, such as fish, amphibians, reptiles, birds and mammals, have special organs to deal with excretion of their waste products. For example, carbon dioxide is excreted by the lungs, while urea is removed by the kidneys. —*verb* **excrete.**

exo– A prefix that means "outside" or "external", as in *exoskeleton.*

exocrine gland Any gland of the body that produces secretions and discharges them into a cavity or through a duct to the surface of the body. In mammals, the sweat glands and mammary glands are exocrine glands.

exoskeleton A hard, protective outer body covering of an animal, such as an insect, crustacean or mollusc. The exoskeletons of insects and crustaceans are largely made of chitin. *Compare* **endoskeleton.**

exosphere The outermost region of the Earth's atmosphere, lying beyond the ionosphere and extending indefinitely into space. The air in the exosphere gets thinner and thinner until the lightest particles, such as hydrogen atoms, begin to escape the Earth's gravity.

exothermic Releasing heat: *an exothermic chemical reaction. Compare* **endothermic.**

expanding universe A model of the universe in which the volume of the universe is expanding. It is based on the idea that the red shift in light from distant galaxies is evidence that all galaxies are moving away from one another. *See panels at* **big bang, Doppler effect.**

Did You Know?

evolution

Darwin's theory of *evolution* by natural selection assumed that tiny adaptations occur in organisms constantly over exceptionally long periods of time. Gradually, a new species develops that is distinct from its ancestors. In the 1970s, however, biologists Niles Eldredge and Stephen Jay Gould proposed that evolution by natural selection was a far more bumpy road. Based on types of fossils that exist around the world, they said that evolution is better described through *punctuated equilibrium.* That is, for long periods of time, species in fact remain virtually unchanged, not even gradually adapting. They are in equilibrium, in a balance with the environment. But when confronted with environmental challenges – sudden climate change, for example – organisms adapt quite quickly, perhaps in only a few thousand years. These active periods are *punctuations,* after which a new equilibrium exists and species remain stable until the next punctuation.

expansion

expansion 1. An increase in size, volume or quantity, usually due to heating. When substances are heated, their particles move faster, causing the substance to expand. **2.** A number or other mathematical expression written in an extended form; for example, $a^2 + 2ab + b^2$ is the expansion of $(a + b)^2$.

experiment A test or procedure carried out under controlled conditions to determine the validity of a hypothesis or make a discovery. *See panel at* **hypothesis.**

explosion 1. A violent blowing apart or bursting caused by energy released from a very fast chemical reaction, a nuclear reaction or the escape of gases under pressure. **2.** A sudden great increase: *a population explosion.*

exponent A number or symbol, placed above and to the right of the expression to which it applies, that indicates the number of times the expression is used as a factor. For example, the exponent 3 in 5^3 indicates $5 \times 5 \times 5$; the exponent 2 in $(a + b)^2$ indicates $(a + b) \times (a + b)$.

exponential Relating to a mathematical expression containing one or more exponents. ❖ Something is said to increase **exponentially** if its rate of change must be expressed using exponents. A graph of such a rate would appear not as a line, but as a curve that becomes steeper and steeper.

extensor A muscle that extends or straightens a limb or joint. *Compare* **flexor.**

exterior angle The angle formed between a

■ **eye**
cross-section of a human eye

side of a polygon and an extended adjacent side. *Compare* **interior angle.**

extinct 1. No longer existing or living. Plant and animal species become extinct for many reasons, including climate change, disease, destruction of habitat and local or worldwide natural disasters. The great majority of species that have ever lived are now extinct. **2.** No longer active or burning: *an extinct volcano.* —*noun* **extinction.**

extrapolate To estimate the value of a quantity that falls outside the range in which its values are known.

extraterrestrial Originating, located or occurring outside the Earth or its atmosphere: *they are searching for evidence of extraterrestrial life.*

extrusion The emission of lava onto the surface of the Earth. ❖ Rocks that formed from the cooling of lava are called **extrusive rocks.** *Compare* **intrusion.**

eye 1. The organ of the body with which an animal is able to see or sense light. In vertebrate animals, the eye occurs as one of a pair, each consisting of a spherical structure that is filled with fluid. Incoming light is refracted by the cornea and transmitted through the pupil to the lens, which focuses the image onto the retina. *See more at* **compound eye, eyespot. 2.** *Botany.* A bud on a tuber, such as a potato. **3.** The relatively calm area at the centre of a hurricane or similar storm. *See more at* **hurricane.**

eyepiece The lens or group of lenses closest to the eye in an optical instrument such as a telescope.

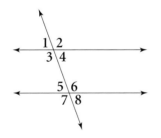

■ **exterior angles**
Angles 1, 2, 7 and 8 are exterior angles. Angles 1 and 8 and angles 2 and 7 are alternate exterior angles.

eyespot 1. An area that is sensitive to light and functions somewhat like an eye, found in certain single-celled organisms as well as many invertebrate animals. **2.** A round marking resembling an eye, as on the tail feather of a peacock.

eyestalk A movable stalk having a compound eye on its tip, found on crabs, lobsters and other crustaceans.

eyrie The nest of an eagle or other predatory bird, built on a cliff or other high place.

F f

F 1. The symbol for **fluorine. 2.** Abbreviation of **Fahrenheit.**

factor *noun* **1.** One of two or more numbers or expressions that are multiplied to obtain a given product. For example, 2 and 3 are factors of 6, and $a + b$ and $a - b$ are factors of $a^2 - b^2$. **2.** A substance found in the body, such as a protein, that is essential to a biological process. For example, growth factors are needed for proper cell growth and development. —*verb* To find the factors of a number or expression. For example, the number 12 can be factored into 2 and 6, or 3 and 4, or 1 and 12.

factorial The product of all of the positive integers from 1 to a given positive integer. It is written as the given integer followed by an exclamation mark. For example, the factorial of 4 (written 4!) is $1 \times 2 \times 3 \times 4$, or 24.

Fahrenheit Relating to or based on a temperature scale that indicates the freezing point of water as 32° and the boiling point of water as 212° under standard atmospheric pressure. *Abbreviation* F. *See panel at* **Celsius.**

Fahrenheit, Gabriel Daniel 1686–1736. German physicist. He invented the mercury thermometer in 1714 and devised the Fahrenheit temperature scale.

falcon Any of various birds of prey having a short curved beak, sharp claws and long pointed wings. Falcons often eat other birds and are usually smaller than hawks.

fallopian tube Either of a pair of tubes found in female mammals that carry egg cells from the ovaries to the uterus.

family A group of organisms ranking above a genus and below an order. *See table at* **taxonomy.**

fang A long, pointed tooth in vertebrate animals or a similar structure in spiders, used to seize prey and sometimes to inject venom. The fangs of a poisonous snake, for example, have a hollow groove through which venom flows.

farad A unit used to measure electric capacitance. A capacitor in which a charge of one coulomb can produce a difference of one volt between its two storage plates has a capacitance of one farad.

faraday A unit of electric charge, equal to about 96,494 coulombs, used to measure the electricity required to break down a compound by electrolysis.

Faraday, Michael 1791–1867. British physicist and chemist whose experiments into the connections between electricity, magnetism and light laid the foundation for modern physics. In 1831 he discovered electromagnetic induction when he produced electricity by moving a magnet inside a wire coil. Faraday invented the electric motor, generator and transformer, and discovered the carbon compound benzene.

farsightedness *See* **longsightedness.**

fat Any of a large number of oily compounds that are widely found in plant and animal tissues and serve mainly as a reserve source of energy. In mammals, fat is deposited beneath the skin and around the internal organs, where it also protects and insulates against heat loss. Fats are made up of a molecule of glycerol which has one, two or three long-chain fatty acids attached to it. The type of fatty acids determines the type of fat. *See more at* **saturated fat, unsaturated fat.**

fathom A unit of length equal to 1.8 metres, used to measure the depth of water.

fatty acid Any of a large group of organic acids, especially those found in animal and vegetable fats and oils. Fatty acids are made up of a long backbone of carbon atoms with hydrogen atoms attached and a carboxyl group (–COOH) at one end of the molecule. The length of the carbon chain varies, although in living organisms it is often between 15 and 17 carbon atoms long, and it may be *saturated* or *unsaturated*. In a saturated fatty acid each carbon atom is joined to the next

Did You Know?

fat

Fat is an important and necessary part of our diet. It contains more stored energy (calories) per gram than either protein or carbohydrate and so is an important energy source. It is used in the body to make important materials such as cell membranes and hormones. Fatty foods usually taste good because many of the chemicals which give food pleasant flavours are easily dissolved in fats, so the fattier a food is, the more flavoursome compounds it can carry. When more food is taken into the body than is needed, the extra energy is stored as fat. In a situation where the food supply is uncertain, this is a very good idea, storing extra fat when food is plentiful and using the fat stores up when food is scarce. The problem for many people in the developed world is that there is always plenty of food. Having some body fat is necessary as an energy store and as an insulator against the cold, but many people eat more than their body needs and so the fat stores build up. Obesity is becoming a major problem in countries such as the USA and the UK (as well as elsewhere in Europe) because high levels of body fat are linked to health problems including infertility, heart disease and certain types of cancers. Yet many of us find losing the fat stores, by eating less and exercising more, very difficult to do.

Some sea mammals, such as whales and seals, have enormous layers of fat under their skin. This fat is known as blubber and is vital for insulation against the cold water in which these animals swim. The blubber layer in a whale may be over 70cm thick – a serious layer of fat!

by a single bond, while in an unsaturated fatty acid the carbon chain contains at least one carbon-carbon double or triple bond.

fault A crack in a rock mass in the Earth's crust along which there has been movement. The rock on one side of the crack moves relative to the rock on the other side of the crack. Faults are caused by plate-tectonic forces. *See panel on* page 126 *and at* **earthquake**.

fauna The animals of a particular region or time period: *tropical fauna; prehistoric fauna.*

Fe The symbol for **iron**.

feather One of the light, flat structures that cover the skin of birds. A feather has a narrow, hollow shaft bearing flat vanes formed of many parallel

■ **fault**
left to right: *normal, reverse and strike-slip faults*

Did You Know?

faults

The Earth's crust is often cracked along surfaces known as planes. In some places the cracks extend only a tiny distance; in others they can run for hundreds of miles. When the rocks separated by a crack have moved past each other, the cracks are known as *faults*. The rocks move because they are pushed or pulled by the forces of plate tectonics. This movement often occurs in sudden jerks known as earthquakes. Geologists study faults to learn the history of the forces that have acted on rocks. *Normal* faults occur when rocks are being pulled apart. In this case, the rocks above the fault plane are moving down relative to the rocks below it. When rocks are pushed together, the opposite happens – the rocks above the plane move upward relative to the rocks below the plane; these types of faults are called *reverse faults*. *Strike-slip faults* occur when rocks slide past each other; rocks on either side of the crack slide parallel to the fault plane between them. *Transform faults* are a special category of strike-slip faults in which the crack is actually part of a boundary between two enormous tectonic plates. A famous example of this type of fault is the San Andreas Fault in California in the United States.

barbs. The barbs of outer feathers are formed of even smaller structures (called barbules) that interlock. The barbs of down feathers do not interlock.

feedback The return of a part of the output of a system or process to the input, especially when used to regulate an electrical system or an electronic process. Computers use feedback to regulate their operations. Feedback is also very important in biological systems, particularly in hormone systems such as in the control of blood sugar levels by insulin and the control of the female reproductive cycle by oestrogen and progesterone.

feeler A slender body part used for touching or sensing. The antennae of insects and the barbels of catfish are feelers.

feldspar Any of a group of abundant minerals consisting of silicates of aluminium with potassium, sodium and calcium. Feldspars range from white, pink or brown to greyish blue in colour. They occur in igneous, sedimentary and metamorphic rocks and make up more than 60 per cent of the Earth's crust.

feline *adjective* Of or belonging to the cat family, a group of meat-eating mammals that includes the lions, tigers, leopards and other cats. —*noun* An animal belonging to this family.

female *adjective* **1.** *Zoology.* **a.** Relating to a female reproductive cell (an egg or ovum). **b.** Being the sex that gives birth or produces offspring. **2.** *Botany.* **a.** Being a reproductive structure, especially a pistil or ovary, that produces a seed or seeds after fertilization. **b.** Bearing a pistil or pistils but not stamens: *female flowers.* —*noun* A female organism.

femur The long bone of the thigh or of the upper portion of the hind leg. *See more at* **skeleton.**

Fermat, Pierre de 1601–1665. French mathematician who is best known for his work on probability and on the properties of numbers. He formulated Fermat's last theorem, which remained unsolved for over three hundred years.

Fermat's last theorem A theorem stating that the equation $a^n + b^n = c^n$ has no solution if a, b, and c are positive integers and if n is an integer greater than 2. The theorem was first stated by the French mathematician Pierre de Fermat around 1630, but not proved until 1994.

fermentation Another name for anaerobic respiration. During fermentation, glucose and other sugars are broken down by enzyme action in the absence of oxygen into simpler compounds, and release small amounts of energy. Fermentation takes place in body cells when oxygen is in short supply, particularly in muscle cells, and lactic acid is produced. The process also occurs in bacteria and plant cells but is best known in yeast. When fermentation takes place in yeast cells, the waste products from the anaerobic breakdown of glucose are ethanol and carbon dioxide. The reaction is widely used in baking to make bread rise, and in the brewing and wine industries to make alcoholic drinks.

Fermi, Enrico 1901–1954. Italian-born American physicist who is best known for his work on nuclear physics. He discovered over 40 new isotopes and predicted the existence of the neutrino. In 1942, with Leo Szilard, Fermi built the world's first atomic reactor. Fermi also helped to develop the atomic bomb.

fermium A synthetic, radioactive metallic element of the actinide series that is produced from plutonium or uranium. Its most stable isotope has a half-life of about 100 days. *Symbol* **Fm.** *Atomic number* 100. *See* **Periodic Table,** pages 260–261.

fern Any of numerous seedless plants usually having feathery fronds divided into many leaflets. Ferns have vascular tissue-like plants that bear seeds but reproduce by means of spores.

ferric *See* iron (II).

ferrous *See* iron (II).

fertile 1. Capable of producing offspring, seeds or fruit; able to reproduce. 2. Capable of developing into a complete organism; fertilized: *a fertile egg.* 3. Capable of supporting plant life; favourable to the growth of crops and plants: *fertile soil.* —*noun* **fertility.**

fertilization 1. The joining of a female and male cell (gamete) to form a new individual cell which is genetically unique and has the potential to develop into a complete new organism. In many animals, such as mammals, fertilization occurs inside the body of the female. In fish, eggs are fertilized in the water. In plants, eggs are fertilized inside the parent plant. *See panel at* **pollination.** 2. The process of making soil more productive of plant growth, as by the addition of organic material or fertilizer. —*verb* **fertilize.**

fetus The unborn young of a mammal at the later stages of its development, especially a human embryo from its eighth week of development to its birth. —*adjective* **fetal.**

fever A body temperature higher than normal. Fever is usually a response by the body's immune system against infection, as by a virus.

Feynman, Richard Phillips 1918–1988.

American physicist who developed a method of using pictures to describe the processes in quantum theory.

Fibonacci, Leonardo 1170?–1250? Italian mathematician who popularized the modern decimal system and discovered the Fibonacci sequence of integers.

Fibonacci sequence The sequence of numbers, 1, 1, 2, 3, 5, 8, 13, . . ., in which each successive number is equal to the sum of the two preceding numbers. Many shapes occurring in nature, such as certain spirals, have proportions that can be described in terms of the Fibonacci sequence.

fibre 1. The parts of grains, fruits and vegetables that contain cellulose and are not digested by the body. Fibre helps the intestines function properly by stimulating the muscles of the intestinal walls. 2. One of the elongated, thick-walled cells that give strength and support to plant tissue. 3a. A single skeletal muscle cell; a muscle fibre. b. The axon of a nerve cell. —*adjective* **fibrous.**

fibreglass A material made up of very fine fibres of glass. Fibreglass is resistant to heat and fire and is used to make various products, such as building insulation and boat hulls. Because the fibres in fibreglass are capable of transmitting light around curves, fibreglass is an important component of fibre optics.

fibre optics The technology based on the use of fine glass or plastic fibres that are capable of transmitting light around curves. Fibre optics is used in medicine and for long-distance telephone and computer lines.

fibrillation A rapid twitching of muscle fibres, as of the heart, caused by the abnormal discharge of electrical nerve impulses.

fibrin A fibrous protein produced in response to bleeding that is the main component of blood clotting.

fibula The smaller of the two bones of the lower leg or lower portion of the hind leg. *See more at* **skeleton.**

field 1. A region of space in which a physical force, such as magnetism or gravity, operates. 2. The area in which an image is visible to the eye or to an optical instrument.

Did You Know?

fibre optics

In an optical fibre, a beam of light travels within a thin strand of glass or plastic. The light stays within the strand, even if the strand is curved or twisted. That's because the materials the optical fibre is made of – and the way in which the light is aimed into the fibre – are chosen so that when the light beam reaches the strand's outer edge it is reflected back into the strand, rather than escaping through the wall. Generally, when a beam of light travelling in one material strikes the boundary of another, some light travels through the boundary and some is reflected back into the original material. But if the speed of light in the material in which the beam starts out (the glass) is lower than the speed of light in the other material (the air or insulating material surrounding the fibre), and if the light strikes the boundary of the other material at a shallow enough angle, then all of the light is reflected and none escapes.

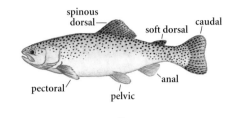

■ **fin**
fins on a typical bony fish

field magnet A magnet used to produce a magnetic field for the operation of an electrical device such as a motor or generator.

filament 1. A fine or slender thread, wire or fibre. **2.** The part of a stamen that supports the anther of a flower; the stalk of a stamen. *See more at* **flower. 3.** A fine wire that is enclosed in the bulb of an incandescent lamp and gives off light when an electric current is passed through it. **4.** A wire that acts as the cathode in some electron tubes when it is heated with an electric current.

filter 1. A material that has very tiny holes and is used to separate out solid particles contained in a liquid or gas that is passed through it. **2.** A device that allows certain frequencies of waves to pass while blocking the passage of others. For example, filters on photographic lenses allow only certain frequencies of light to enter the camera, and certain types of electronic circuits allow electrical signals to pass while blocking others with different frequencies.

filter feeder An aquatic animal, such as a clam or sponge, that feeds by filtering tiny organisms or fine particles of organic material from currents of water that pass through it.

filtration The act or process of filtering, especially the process of passing a liquid or gas, such as air, through a filter in order to remove solid particles.

fin One of the wing-like or paddle-like parts of a fish, dolphin or whale, used for propelling, steering and balancing in water.

finite Having a bound or limit; not infinite or unbounded: *a finite sum; a finite line segment.*

fir Any of various evergreen trees that bear cones and have flat needle-like leaves. Firs generally grow in northern regions or at higher altitudes.

fireball A meteor that is as bright or brighter than the brightest planets.

firefly Any of various beetles that are active at night and produce a flashing light in the abdomen. The flash is produced by a chemical reaction and enables males and females to find each other for mating.

firth A long narrow inlet of the sea. Firths are usually the lower part of an estuary, but are sometimes **fjords.**

fish (*plural* **fish** *or* **fishes**) Any of numerous cold-blooded vertebrate animals that live in water. Fish have gills for obtaining oxygen, a lateral line for sensing pressure changes in the water, and a vertical tail. Most fish are covered with scales and have limbs in the form of fins. *See more at* **bony fish, cartilaginous fish, jawless fish.**

fission 1. The splitting of the nucleus of an atom into two or more nuclei. The splitting occurs either spontaneously, because the nucleus has many neutrons and is unstable, or because the nucleus has collided with a free-moving neutron. The splitting of a nucleus releases one or more neutrons and energy in the form of radiation. *Compare* **fusion. 2.** A reproductive process in which a single cell splits to form two independent cells that later grow to full size. Bacteria and other single-celled organisms usually reproduce by means of fission. Also called *binary fission. See A Closer Look,* page 130.

fissure A long, narrow crack or opening in a rock face. Fissures are often filled with minerals of a different type from those in the surrounding rock.

fixed star A term sometimes used when referring to a star because the position of the stars in the sky relative to one another does not appear to change. Although the stars are in fact moving, this motion is so slow that their positions appear fixed and hardly alter during a person's lifetime.

fjord A long, narrow, winding inlet from the sea between steep slopes of a mountainous coast. Fjords usually occur where seawater flows into valleys formed near the coast by glaciers.

flagellate A protozoan that moves by means of a flagellum or flagella. Some flagellates, such as

the euglena, can make food by photosynthesis like plants, while others, such as the trypanosomes, are parasitic and cause disease.

flagellum (*plural* **flagella**) A slender tail-like structure extending from some single-celled organisms and many types of sperm. Flagella whip back and forth to produce movement.

flame The hot, glowing mixture of burning gases and tiny particles that arises from combustion.

flamingo Any of several large tropical wading birds having reddish or pinkish plumage, long legs, and a long flexible neck. Flamingos feed by scooping up water with their heads upside down and filtering the water through tissues in their large bills.

flash point The lowest temperature at which the vapour of a flammable liquid can be made to catch fire in air.

flask A rounded container with a long neck, used in laboratories.

flatfish Any of numerous saltwater fish, such as the flounder, halibut and sole, that have a flattened body and live on the seabed. During a flatfish's larval stage, the head twists and one eye migrates to the other side, so that both eyes in the adult are on one side of the body.

flatworm Any of various worms having a flat, unsegmented body that is bilaterally symmetrical. Many flatworms, such as the tapeworm, are parasites. Also called *platyhelminth.*

flea 1. Any of various small, wingless, bloodsucking insects that have legs adapted for jumping and live as parasites on warm-blooded animals. 2. Any of various small crustaceans, such as the water flea, that resemble or move like fleas.

fledgling A young bird that has just grown the feathers needed to fly and is capable of surviving outside the nest.

Fleming, Sir **Alexander** 1881–1955. Scottish bacteriologist who discovered penicillin in 1928. The drug was developed and purified 11 years later by Howard Florey and Ernst Chain. Fleming was also the first to administer typhoid vaccines to humans.

Fleming, Sir **John Ambrose** 1849–1945. British physicist and electrical engineer who

■ **fir**
Douglas firs can attain heights of more than 60 metres

Fission

Nuclear fission occurs when a heavy, unstable atomic nucleus splits into two or more lighter nuclei. For example, the nucleus of U-235 (an isotope of uranium) undergoes fission when it is struck by a free neutron. When this happens, the U-235 nucleus becomes so unstable that it splits into two or more fragments and releases two or three free neutrons. The combined mass of these fragments is less than that of the original nucleus and the neutron that produced them. The missing mass is transferred to the kinetic energy of the fragments and to gamma rays.

The free neutrons flying from the split nucleus may collide with other U-235 nuclei, causing them to break apart. This is the start of a chain reaction, where, within a few millionths of a second, the number of fission events multiplies rapidly. In nuclear reactors, the neutrons are slowed down or absorbed to control the reaction. In nuclear weapons, the chain reaction develops uncontrollably to produce the largest amount of energy possible.

Fusion

Nuclear fusion is basically the opposite of fission, but produces some similar results. Fusion occurs, for example, when two types of hydrogen atoms (deuterium and tritium) collide and turn into a single atom of helium and an extra neutron. As in fission, this process releases energy that is quickly multiplied as millions of these collisions occur in a fraction of a second. Nuclear fusion powers the sun and other stars, and it is the type of chain reaction that occurs in thermonuclear weapons.

invented the vacuum tube in 1904. His invention was essential to the development of radio. Fleming also helped develop electric devices designed for large-scale use, such as the electric lamp.

flexor A muscle that bends or flexes a joint. *Compare* extensor.

flint A very hard, grey to black sedimentary rock that makes sparks when it is struck with steel. Flint is a type of chert.

flipper A wide, flat limb adapted for swimming, found on aquatic animals such as whales, seals and sea turtles. Flippers evolved from legs.

float *verb* To remain suspended within or on the surface of a fluid without sinking. —*noun* An air-filled sac in certain aquatic organisms, such as kelp, that helps maintain buoyancy. Also called *air bladder, air vesicle*.

floe A mass or sheet of floating ice.

flood plain Flat land bordering a river and made up of sediments such as sand, silt and clay deposited during floods.

flood tide The period between low tide and high tide, during which water flows towards the shore. *Compare* ebb tide. *See more at* tide.

floppy disc *Computer Science.* A flexible plastic disc coated with magnetic material and covered by a protective jacket, used for storing data.

flora The plants of a particular region or time period: *desert flora; prehistoric flora.*

Florey, Sir **Howard Walter**. Baron Florey of Adelaide 1898–1968. Australian-born British pathologist who developed and purified penicillin, with Ernst Chain. Florey also helped to develop a way to manufacture the drug in large quantities and was involved in the first tests of its effects on humans.

flow chart 1. A diagram that shows the order of operations or sequence of tasks for solving a problem or managing a complex project. **2.** A schematic representation of a sequence of operations.

flower *noun* **1.** The reproductive structure of the seed-bearing plants known as angiosperms. The female reproductive part is known as the pistil, including the ovary, style and stigma, and the male reproductive part is the stamen, including

the filament and anther. The organs are enclosed in an outer envelope of petals and sepals. **2.** A flowering plant that is grown mainly for its brightly coloured petals. —*verb* To produce flowers; bloom. *See A Closer Look,* page 132.

flower head 1. A dense cluster of short flowers that together look like part of a single flower, as in the daisy or dandelion. **2.** A dense grouping of flower buds, as in broccoli and cauliflower.

flowering plant A plant that produces flowers and fruit; an angiosperm.

flu *See* influenza.

fluid A substance, such as air or water, in which the atoms or molecules can freely move past one another. Fluids flow easily and take on the shape of their containers. All liquids and gases are fluids. —*noun* **fluidity.**

fluke 1. Either of the two flattened fins of a whale's tail. **2.** A group of flatworms (the trematodes) that are parasites of other animals including humans, such as the blood fluke *Schistosoma* which causes bilharzia, a disease affecting 200 million people in the world.

fluorescence 1. The giving off of light by a substance when it is exposed to electromagnetic radiation, such as ultraviolet light or X-rays. Light

Did You Know?

fluorescence

Have you ever been in a room illuminated by an ultraviolet light and wondered why your white T-shirt, your shoelaces, and your teeth appear to glow? These objects appear so bright under ultraviolet light because they contain fluorescent materials that absorb energy from the ultraviolet rays (which are not visible to the human eye) and re-emit some of this energy as visible light. Therefore, these objects give off more visible light than is being shone on them, making them glow mysteriously. Many fabric whiteners leave fluorescent pigments behind in treated clothes; the clothes then look very bright because they absorb ultraviolet light from the environment and emit some of the absorbed energy as visible light.

Flower

Most flowers, like the Asiatic lily shown here, have both male and female organs. The anthers of the male organs release pollen that is transferred to the stigma, usually on a flower of another plant, by the wind or by pollinating animals such as insects and hummingbirds. Certain species, such as the birch tree, have flowers with only male organs and flowers with only female organs growing on the same plant. Some other species, such as holly, have flowers with male organs growing on one plant, and flowers with female organs growing on another.

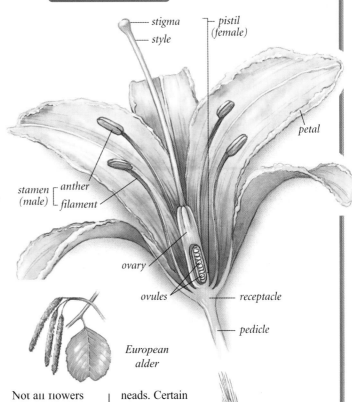

stigma

style

pistil (female)

petal

stamen (male) — *anther* — *filament*

ovary

ovules

receptacle

pedicle

European alder

Not all flowers occur as large individual blooms attached to a stem, as in the Asiatic lily and clematis. The flowers of rye grass, for example, are very small. Some plants, such as clover, have groups of flowers growing in clusters as flower heads. Certain trees, like the alder, produce blossoms in elongated clusters known as catkins. The sausage-like part of the bulrush is actually a head of densely packed female flowers. The bulrush's male flowers grow on the more slender tip that extends at the top.

clematis

wild rye

white clover

bulrush

is emitted only as long as the electromagnetic radiation continues to bombard the substance. *Compare* **phosphorescence** (sense 1). **2.** The light produced in this way.

fluorescent lamp A lamp that produces light by exciting the atoms of a mixture of argon gas and mercury vapour with electric current. Ultraviolet rays produced by the excited atoms strike a phosphor coating on the interior surface of the bulb, causing it to emit visible light. Fluorescent lamps are much more efficient than incandescent lamps because the excited atoms give off little of their energy as heat. *Compare* **incandescent lamp.**

fluoridate To add fluorine or a fluoride to something, especially to drinking water in order to prevent tooth decay.

fluoride A compound containing fluorine and another element or radical.

fluorine A pale-yellow, poisonous, gaseous halogen element that is highly corrosive. It is used to separate certain isotopes of uranium and to make refrigerants and high-temperature plastics. It is also added in fluoride form to some water supplies to prevent tooth decay. *Symbol* **F.** *Atomic number* 9. *See* **Periodic Table,** pages 260–261.

fluorite A mineral consisting of calcium fluoride. Fluorite occurs in many colours (especially yellow and purple), usually in crystals shaped like cubes or octahedrons, and is often fluorescent in ultraviolet light. It is the mineral used to represent a hardness of 4 on the Mohs scale.

fluorocarbon An inert, liquid or gaseous organic compound similar to a hydrocarbon but having fluorine atoms in the place of hydrogen atoms. Fluorocarbons are used in aerosol propellants and refrigerants. ❖ Fluorocarbons containing chlorine, which are known as **chlorofluorocarbons** (or CFCs), are destructive to the Earth's ozone layer. For this reason, the production and use of chlorofluorocarbons has been sharply reduced in recent years.

fluoroscopy A technique for viewing internal organs in which a continuous series of X-rays is taken, and the images are processed by a computer before being projected onto a display screen. Fluoroscopy makes it possible to see moving images of the body system being examined.

flux 1. A substance used in a smelting furnace to make metals melt more easily. **2.** The rate of flow of fluids, particles or energy across a given surface or area. **3.** *See* **magnetic flux.**

fly Any of numerous insects having one pair of wings and large compound eyes. Flies include the houseflies, horseflies and mosquitoes. Many species feed on other insects or as scavengers.

Fm The symbol for **fermium.**

FM Abbreviation of **frequency modulation.**

foam 1. A mass of small, frothy bubbles formed in or on the surface of a liquid, as from fermentation or shaking. **2.** A colloid in which particles of a gas are dispersed throughout a liquid. *Compare* **aerosol, emulsion.**

focal length The distance from the centre of a lens or mirror to the point where parallel rays of light converge to form an image (the point of focus).

focus (*plural* **focuses** *or* **foci**) **1.** A point at which rays of light come together or from which they appear to spread apart, after passing through a lens or being reflected from a mirror. **2.** The degree of clarity with which an eye or optical instrument produces an image: *a telescope with excellent focus.* **3.** A central point or region, such as the point at which an earthquake starts. **4.** *Mathematics.* A fixed point or one of a pair of fixed points used in constructing a curve such as an ellipse, a parabola or a hyperbola.

pin

cathode

phosphor coating

argon gas and mercury vapour mixture

■ **fluorescent lamp**

■ food chain
A typical food chain in a water community would include a plant that is eaten by tadpoles, a great diving beetle that eats tadpoles, a bullfrog that eats great diving beetles, and a river otter that consumes frogs.

fog A dense layer of cloud lying close to the surface of the ground or water.

fold A bend in a layer or in several layers of rock. Folds occur in rocks when they are compressed by plate-tectonic forces.

folic acid A vitamin belonging to the vitamin B complex that is important in cell growth and metabolism. It is found especially in green leafy vegetables and fresh fruit. Lack of folic acid can cause anaemia because it is necessary for the formation of red blood cells. It is also needed for healthy development of a fetus.

follicle 1. A small, protective sac in the body. In most vertebrate animals, fertilized eggs develop in follicles located in the ovaries. In mammals, hair develops and grows from follicles in the skin. 2. A dry fruit that has a single chamber and splits open along only one seam to release its seeds. Larkspur and monk's hood are follicles.

food chain The sequence of the transfer of food energy from one organism to another in an ecological community. In a typical food chain, plants are eaten by herbivores, which are then eaten by carnivores. These carnivores are in turn eaten by other carnivores. ❖ Many species of animals in an ecological community feed on both plants and animals, creating a complex system of interrelated food chains known as a **food web**. *See more at* **consumer, producer.**

food web A group of interrelated food chains in a particular ecological community.

fool's gold Any of several minerals, especially pyrite and chalcopyrite, sometimes mistaken for gold.

foot (*plural* **feet**) A unit of length equal to approximately 30.5 centimetres (12 inches). *See table at* **measurement.**

foot-and-mouth disease A highly contagious disease of cattle and other hoofed animals that is caused by a virus. Symptoms include fever and the presence of blisters around the mouth and hooves.

footwall The block of rock lying under an inclined fault. *See more at* **fault.** *Compare* **hanging wall.**

force *Physics.* Something that acts to change the speed or direction of movement of a body, or its shape. The SI unit of force is the neutron. *See more at* **fundamental forces.**

forebrain The front part of the brain in vertebrate animals. In humans, it consists of the thalamus, the hypothalamus and the cerebrum. *Compare* **hindbrain, midbrain.**

forensic medicine The branch of medicine involved in helping solve crimes. It is concerned with finding the causes of injury and death.

forensic science The area of science involved in helping solve crimes. The work uses a wide range of techniques including the identification of fingerprints, blood groups, DNA, fibres, paints and many other materials. It is also used in the analysis of the scenes of road accidents.

forest A dense growth of trees and usually bushes or other plants covering a large area.

Forests exist in all regions of the Earth except for regions of extreme cold or dryness. ❖ The science of cultivating and managing forests is called **forestry**.

formaldehyde *See* **methanal.**

formation A long layer of sediments or rocks that look alike and were formed at the same time. Formations are shown on geological maps, much as highways are shown on road maps.

formic acid *See* **methanoic acid.**

formula (*plural* **formulae**) **1.** A set of symbols showing the composition of a chemical compound. A formula lists the elements contained within it and indicates the number of atoms of each element with a subscript numeral if the number is more than 1. For example, H_2O is the formula for water, where H_2 indicates two atoms of hydrogen and O indicates one atom of oxygen. **2.** A set of symbols that expresses a mathematical rule or principle; for example, the formula for the area of a rectangle is $a = lw$,

■ **fossil**
fossils embedded in sandstone, found in Costa Rica

where a is the area, l the length, and w the width.

Forrester, Jay Wright Born 1918. American computer engineer who developed computer storage devices, including the first core memory for an electronic digital computer (1949).

Fossey, Dian 1932–1985. American zoologist who conducted extensive studies of mountain gorillas in the central African country of Rwanda. Her research brought about a new understanding of the gorilla's behaviour and habitat and supported conservation efforts in Africa.

fossil The hardened remains or imprint of a plant or animal that lived long ago. Fossils are often found in layers of sedimentary rock and along the beds of rivers that flow through them. Other sources of fossils include tar pits, ice and amber. ❖ Petroleum, coal and natural gas, which are derived from the accumulated remains of ancient plants and animals, are called **fossil fuels.** —*verb* **fossilize.**

Foucault, Jean Bernard Léon 1819–1868. French physicist who measured the velocity of light (1850) and proved that light moves more slowly in water than in air. In 1857 he constructed the first gyroscope.

fowl 1. A bird, such as a chicken, duck or turkey, that is raised or hunted for food. **2.** In scientific usage, any of various birds having large heavy bodies, short wings and legs built for running and scratching the ground. Most fowl nest on the

Did You Know?

force

The verb *force* might make you think of pushing really hard on a door that's jammed, or of banging the bottom of a stubborn ketchup bottle. The scientific meaning of the noun *force* also involves the movement of an object. Isaac Newton was the first person to explain what happens when one object exerts a force on another object. His third law of motion states that whenever two objects exert forces on each other, the forces are equal in size and opposite in direction. When forces cancel each other out, we say that they are *balanced*. If the forces acting on an object do not cancel each other out, the result is an *unbalanced* force acting on it. This unbalanced force will cause the object to accelerate in the same direction as the unbalanced force. The rate of this acceleration is given by Newton's second law of motion (force is equal to mass multiplied by acceleration, or $F = ma$).

ground. The pheasant, quail, grouse and partridge are all fowl.

Fr The symbol for **francium**.

fractal A geometric pattern repeated at ever smaller scales to produce irregular shapes and surfaces that cannot be represented by standard geometry. Even the most minute details of a fractal's pattern repeat elements of the overall geometric pattern. Fractals are widely used in computer modelling of irregular patterns and structures in nature, such as the patterns of seasonal weather. They are also considered to be a visual representation of chaos. *See more at* **chaos.**

fraction A number that compares part of an object or a set with the whole, especially the quotient of two whole numbers written in the form $\frac{a}{b}$. The fraction $\frac{1}{2}$, which means 1 divided by 2, can represent such things as 10 pencils out of a box of 20, or 50 pence out of a pound. *See also* **decimal fraction, improper fraction, proper fraction.**

fractionation The separation of a chemical compound into components, as by distillation or crystallization.

fracture 1. A break or crack in a solid object, such as rock. *See* **fault. 2.** A break or crack in a bone, usually also involving injury to surrounding structures. A fracture occurs when a force greater than the strength of the bone is applied, as in a fall.

francium An extremely unstable, radioactive

Biography

Benjamin Franklin

Scientist, inventor, statesman, printer, philosopher, musician and economist: Benjamin Franklin was all of these during his long life, but most of all he was curious. His curiosity about things led him to investigate the way they work, and sometimes to invent ways to make them work better. For example, he had poor vision and needed glasses to read. He got tired of constantly taking them off and putting them back on, so he worked out a way to make his glasses let him see both near and far. He had two pairs of spectacles cut in half and put half of each lens in a single frame. Today, we call glasses like these bifocals. In his role as a statesman, Franklin sailed to Europe many times. These voyages aroused his curiosity about ocean currents, and from the data he collected while at sea he created the first map of the Gulf Stream.

element that is the heaviest alkali metal. Francium occurs in nature, but less than about 30 grams are present in the Earth's crust at any time. The most stable of its several isotopes has a half-life of 21 minutes. *Symbol* **Fr.** *Atomic number* 87. *See* **Periodic Table,** pages 260–261.

Franklin, Benjamin 1706–1790. American public official, scientist, inventor and writer. He conducted experiments with electricity, established the direction of the prevailing storm track in North America, and determined the existence of the Gulf Stream. Franklin also invented bifocals and a type of stove that was widely used for indoor heating.

■ **fractal**
computer-generated fractal

Franklin, Rosalind 1920–1958. British chemist whose diffraction images, made by directing X-rays at DNA, provided crucial information that led to the discovery of its structure as a double helix. Franklin's work was never publicly acknowledged in her lifetime. She died from cancer at the young age of 38, before the importance of her work could be recognized by a Nobel Prize.

freeze To change from a liquid to a solid state by cooling or being cooled to the freezing point.

freeze-dry To preserve something by freezing it rapidly and then placing it in a vacuum chamber. The ice is then forced out, through sublimation, in the form of water vapour.

freezing point The temperature at which a liquid becomes a solid at a given pressure. For a given substance, the freezing point of its liquid form is the same as the melting point of its solid form. The freezing point of water is 0°C (32°F); that of liquid nitrogen is –209.89°C (–345.75°F).

frequency 1. *Physics.* The number of complete cycles of a wave, such as a radio wave, that occur per second. *See more at* **wave. 2.** *Mathematics.* The ratio of the number of occurrences of some event to the number of opportunities for its occurrence.

frequency modulation A method of radio broadcasting in which the frequency of the wave that carries the sound signal changes to reflect the signal that is to be reproduced, while the amplitude of the wave remains the same. Frequency modulation reduces noise and distortion in radio transmission. *Compare* **amplitude modulation.**

freshwater Consisting of or living in water that is not salty: *a freshwater pond; a freshwater fish.*

Fresnel, Augustin Jean 1788–1827. French physicist whose investigations of the properties of light were fundamental to the establishment of the theory that light moves in a wave-like motion. Fresnel also made great contributions to the field of optics, including the development of a compound lens for use in lighthouses.

friction The resistance to movement that occurs when two objects are in contact. It is friction, for example, that slows down a ball rolling on grass and causes the blade of a saw cutting wood to get hot. There is less friction between smooth surfaces than between rough surfaces. Friction can be reduced by using a lubricant such as oil or silicone.

Frigid Zone Either of two zones of the Earth of extreme latitude, the **North Frigid Zone,** extending north of the Arctic Circle, or the **South Frigid Zone,** extending south of the Antarctic Circle.

frog Any of numerous amphibians typically having smooth, moist skin, webbed feet, long hind legs used for leaping and no tail when fully grown. Frogs mostly live in or around water, and although some species, such as tree frogs, live on land, they all rely on water for reproduction. *Compare* **toad.**

frond 1. A leaf of a fern, usually consisting of multiple leaflets. **2.** A large, fan-like leaf of a palm tree. **3.** A large, leaf-like structure on seaweed.

front The boundary between two air masses that

■ **front**
cold front (left) *and warm front* (right)

have different temperatures. Fronts are often accompanied by rain or unsettled weather. *See more at* **cold front, warm front.**

frontal 1. *Anatomy.* Relating to the forehead. 2. *Meteorology.* Relating to a front.

frontal bone A bone of the skull, consisting of a part that corresponds to the forehead and a part that forms the roof of the eye sockets and cavities of the nose.

frontal lobe The largest and foremost part of each cerebral hemisphere. It controls voluntary muscle activity as well as reasoning, judgement and personality.

frost A deposit of tiny ice crystals on a surface. Frost is formed when water vapour in the air condenses at a temperature below freezing.

frostbite Damage to a part of the body as a result of exposure to freezing temperatures. It is caused by a loss of blood supply and the formation of ice crystals in the affected body part.

frost line The depth to which frost penetrates the earth.

fructose A simple sugar found in honey, many fruits and some vegetables. Fructose is similar to glucose, is sweeter than table sugar and is an important source of energy for cellular processes.

fruit The ripened ovary of a flowering plant that contains the seeds. Fruits can be dry or fleshy. Berries, nuts, grains, pods and drupes are fruits. *See panel at* **berry.** ❖ Fruits that consist of ripened ovaries alone, such as the tomato and pea pod, are called **true fruits.** ❖ Fruits that consist of ripened ovaries and other parts such as the receptacle or bracts, as in the apple and cucumber, are called **accessory fruits** or **false fruits.**

ft. Abbreviation of **foot.**

fuel A substance that produces useful energy when it undergoes a chemical or nuclear reaction. Fuel such as coal, wood, oil or gas provides energy when burned. Compounds in the body such as glucose are broken down into simpler compounds to provide energy for metabolic processes. Some radioactive substances, such as plutonium and tritium, provide energy by undergoing nuclear fission or fusion.

fuel cell A device that produces electricity by oxidizing a fuel. Fuel cells are used in space shuttles, where an electric current is produced by oxidizing hydrogen gas (the fuel) in an electrolyte cell.

fulcrum The point or support on which a lever turns.

full moon The phase of the moon in which it is visible as a fully illuminated disc. This phase occurs when the moon is on the opposite side of the Earth to the sun and is not in the Earth's shadow. *See more at* **moon.** *Compare* **new moon.**

fumarole A hole in the surface of the Earth from which hot smoke and gases escape. Fumaroles are found on or near volcanoes.

fume Smoke, vapour or gas, especially if irritating, harmful or smelly.

function 1. A relationship between two sets that matches each member of the first set with a unique member of the second set. Functions are often expressed as an equation, such as $y = x + 5$,

Usage

fruit/vegetable

To most of us, a *fruit* is the part of a plant that is eaten as a dessert or snack because it is sweet, but to someone who studies botany a fruit is a mature ovary of a plant, and as such it may or may not taste sweet. All species of flowering plants produce fruits that contain seeds. A peach, for example, contains a stone (or hard seed) that can grow into a new peach tree, while the seeds known as peas can grow into another pea plant. To a botanist, apples, peaches, peppers, tomatoes, pea pods, cucumbers and winged sycamore seeds are all fruits. A *vegetable* is simply part of a plant that is grown primarily for food. Thus, the leaf of spinach, the root of a carrot, the flower of broccoli, and the stalk of celery are all vegetables. In everyday, nonscientific talk we make the distinction between sweet plant parts (fruits) and non-sweet plant parts (vegetables). This is why we speak of peppers, cucumbers and courgettes – all fruits in the eyes of a botanist – as vegetables.

meaning that *y* is a function of *x* such that for any value of *x*, the value of *y* will be 5 greater than *x*. **2.** A quantity whose value depends on the value given to one or more related quantities. For example, the area of a square is a function of the length of its sides.

fundamental forces Four types of interaction that describe all forces acting between material objects. These are the gravitational and electromagnetic interactions, which act over large instances, and the strong and weak nuclear interactions, which operate only on a subatomic scale.

fungicide A chemical used to kill fungi which are causing diseases or damaging crops. *Compare* **herbicide, insecticide, pesticide.**

fungus (*plural* **fungi**) Any of a wide variety of organisms that reproduce by spores, including mushrooms, moulds, yeasts and mildews. The spores of most fungi grow a network of slender

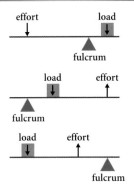

■ **fulcrum**

This diagram shows the relative position of the fulcrum in the three basic types of levers, with arrows indicating the direction of the effort and the downward force of the load.

Top: *The effort and load are on opposite sides of the fulcrum, as in a crowbar.*

Middle: *The load is between the fulcrum and effort, as in a wheelbarrow.*

Bottom: *The effort is between the fulcrum and load, as in a person's forearm, where the fulcrum is the elbow and the load is something held in the hand.*

Did You Know?

fungus

Fungi are everywhere. Most of us have eaten mushrooms, which are fungi. And you have probably eaten bread, made with yeast, another fungus. Old bread may grow mould, yet another fungus. Athlete's foot and a variety of other infections are caused by fungi, but, on the good side, a fungus also produces the medicine penicillin. A type of fungus is also used to make a new high-protein food called mycoprotein, which can be shaped and flavoured to resemble different kinds of meat, but which is very low in fat. About 100,000 different species of fungi exist. When you see a light-coloured irregular mass on a tree or rock, it is probably a lichen, which is a fungus and an alga living in a symbiotic relationship, benefiting each other. Fungi are neither plants nor animals; they are different enough to be classified by scientists into their own unique kingdom.

tubes called hyphae. These tubes are not made up of individual cells but consist of a cell wall containing cytoplasm and lots of nuclei. The hyphae spread into the tissue of dead or living organisms and feed off it. Food is digested using enzymes secreted by the hyphae, and the products of digestion are absorbed into the structure of the fungus. Fungi are grouped as a separate kingdom in taxonomy. They are very important to the ecosystem as decomposers, breaking down animal and plant material and returning it to the environment. *See table at* **taxonomy.** —*adjective* **fungal.**

funnel A utensil with a wide opening at one end and a tube at the other, used to pour liquids or other substances into a container with a small mouth.

fuse *noun* A safety device that protects an electric circuit from becoming overloaded. Fuses contain a length of thin wire that melts and breaks the circuit if too much current flows through it. Fuses have largely been replaced by circuit breakers. —*verb* **1.** To melt something, such as metal or glass, by heating. **2.** To blend two or more

fusion

substances by melting: *Bronze is made by fusing copper and tin.*

fusion 1. The joining together of light atomic nuclei, especially hydrogen nuclei, to form a heavier nucleus, especially a helium nucleus. Fusion occurs when light nuclei are heated to extremely high temperatures, forcing them to collide at great speed. The collision releases one or more neutrons and energy in the form of radiation. Fusion reactions power the sun and other stars. *See more at* **fission. 2.** A mixture or blend formed by fusing two or more things: *An alloy is a fusion of two or more metals.*

g 1. Abbreviation of **gram** or **gramme. 2.** The symbol for **acceleration of gravity. 3.** A symbol for **g-force.**

G 1. A symbol for **g-force. 2.** The symbol for **gravitational constant.**

Ga The symbol for **gallium.**

gabbro A usually dark, coarse-grained igneous rock composed mostly of plagioclase and pyroxene. It is mineralogically similar to basalt but has larger crystals. *See table at* **rock.**

Gabor, Dennis 1900–1979. Hungarian-born British physicist who invented the technique of holography in 1947.

gadolinium A silvery-white, easily shaped metallic element of the lanthanide series that occurs in nature as a mixture of seven isotopes. It is used to improve the heat and corrosion resistance of iron, chromium and various alloys. *Symbol* **Gd.** *Atomic number* 64. *See* **Periodic Table,** pages 260–261.

Gaia hypothesis This is a theory developed by English chemist James Lovelock in the 1970s, suggesting that the Earth is a vast, ancient living organism called Gaia. All the life forms of the planet are part of Gaia and so is all the inorganic material making up the planet. The different parts interact like cells in a smaller organism to maintain the balance of the atmosphere over millions of years for the benefit of Gaia.

galaxy Any of numerous large-scale collections of stars, gas and dust that make up the universe. A galaxy may range in diameter from 1500 to 300,000 light years.

Galen 130?–200? AD. Greek physician. He developed numerous theories about the structures and functions of the human body, many of which were based on information he gained from dissecting animals. Galen's theories formed the basis of European medicine until the Renaissance.

galena A grey, metallic mineral consisting of lead and sulphur. Galena usually occurs in cube-shaped crystals within veins of igneous rock or in sedimentary rocks. It is the main ore of lead.

Galileo Galilei 1564–1642. Italian astronomer, mathematician and physicist who was the first to use a telescope to study the stars and planets. He discovered that Jupiter has moons and that Venus has phases like those of the Earth's moon, suggesting that Venus orbits the sun. *See panel on page 142.*

gall An abnormal swelling of plant tissue, caused by insects, microorganisms or injury.

gall bladder A small, pear-shaped muscular sac in which bile is stored. The gall bladder is located beneath the liver and secretes bile into the small intestine through the bile duct.

gallium A rare, silvery metallic element that is found as a trace element in coal, bauxite and other minerals. It is liquid near room temperature and is used in thermometers and semiconductors. *Symbol* **Ga.** *Atomic number* 31. *See* **Periodic Table,** pages 260–261.

Galvani, Luigi 1737–1798. Italian physiologist

■ **galaxy**
the Andromeda galaxy

141

Biography

Galileo Galilei

In 1609 Galileo heard of the invention of the spyglass, a tube with a piece of glass at each end that made objects appear closer and larger when you looked through it. He set about making his own. One night Galileo used his telescope (as they began to be called) to look up at the moon. He was astonished to see its mountains and valleys, since the moon was believed to be perfectly smooth. Galileo continued to observe the heavens, and a few months later he discovered Jupiter's four largest moons. As he studied them, he realized that they were orbiting Jupiter, not Earth. Galileo's observations convinced him that Copernicus had been right when he stated that Earth and all the planets orbit the sun. Many people feared Copernicus's theory, which overthrew the long-held belief that the Earth was the centre of the universe. Because he openly supported Copernicus's theory, Galileo was called before the Church authorities and forced to declare that the theory was false. He was then put under house arrest, but he was nonetheless allowed to continue his scientific work until the end of his life.

famous for the discovery of animal electricity, inspired by his observation that dead frogs suffered convulsions when fixed to an iron fence to dry. He then showed that a frog would continue to twitch if it was part of a circuit involving metals, though he wrongly believed the current source to be in the material of muscle and nerve. Galvani's name lives on in the galvanometer, used from 1820 to detect electric current.

galvanic Relating to electricity that is produced by chemical reaction.

galvanometer An instrument that detects, measures and determines the direction of small electric currents.

gamete *See* **reproductive cell.**

gametophyte In plants, fungi and certain algae, the individual organism or generation of organisms that produces reproductive cells (called gametes). Each cell of a gametophyte has only one set of chromosomes, just as its gametes do. In nonvascular plants, such as mosses and liverworts, the gametophyte is the main plant form. In vascular plants, such as ferns, grasses, conifers and flowering plants, the gametophyte consists of only a few cells – the embryo sac and the pollen grain. *Compare* **sporophyte.**

gamma globulin A class of proteins in the blood plasma of humans and other mammals that function as part of the body's immune system. Antibodies are gamma globulins.

gamma ray A stream of electromagnetic radiation having wavelengths shorter than those of X-rays and therefore greater energy and penetrating power. Gamma rays are given off by unstable nuclei during radioactive decay. ❖ The emission of gamma rays by a nucleus is called **gamma decay.** Gamma decay does not change the atomic number or the mass number of an element. *See more at* **radiation, radioactive decay.**

ganglion (*plural* **ganglia**) A compact group of nerve cells having a specific function. In invertebrate animals, pairs of ganglia occur at intervals along the axis of the body, with the foremost pair functioning like a brain. In vertebrates, ganglia are usually located outside the brain or spinal cord and control the functioning of the body's internal organs.

gangrene The death of body cells or tissues in a living organism. Gangrene is usually found in the limbs, and is the result of the blood supply being cut off in some way. The affected part becomes cold, loses sensation, gets darker in colour and eventually starts to decompose. The bloodless tissue may become infected with bacteria, at which stage it can rapidly cause death. Gangrene can be treated with antibiotics in the early stages but often the only solution is to amputate the affected limb. Gangrene can set in as a result of frostbite, dirty wounds, diabetes where the blood flow is affected and illegal abortions.

garnet Any of several common red, brown, black, green or yellow minerals consisting of aluminium or calcium silicate. Garnets occur in igneous, metamorphic and sedimentary rocks, and are used as gemstones and industrial abrasives.

gas One of the three basic forms of matter, composed of atoms or molecules in constant random motion. Unlike a solid, a gas has no fixed shape and will take on the shape of the space available. Unlike a liquid, it has no fixed volume and will expand to fill the space available. — *adjective* **gaseous.**

gas exchange The movement of gases from an area of higher concentration to an area of lower concentration, especially the exchange of oxygen and carbon dioxide between an organism and its environment. In plants, gas exchange takes place in the leaves during photosynthesis. In small animals, gas exchange takes place through the whole body surface, but in larger animals, such as mammals, gas exchange between the air and the body takes place in specially adapted organs known as lungs.

gastric Relating to the stomach.

gastric juice A fluid secreted by glands lining the inside of the stomach. In adults, it contains hydrochloric acid and the enzyme pepsin, which is involved in the digestion of proteins.

gastrointestinal tract *See* **digestive tract.**

gastropod Any of various molluscs having a head with eyes and feelers, usually a coiled shell, and a muscular foot on the underside of its body with which it moves. Gastropods include both land-dwelling forms, like land snails and slugs, and aquatic species, like conches, cowries and whelks.

gastrula (*plural* **gastrulas** *or* **gastrulae**) An embryo at the stage following the blastula, in which the cells are distributed into layers that eventually develop into the organs of the body. *Compare* **blastula.**

Gauss, Karl Friedrich 1777–1855. German mathematician, astronomer and physicist. He brought about significant and rapid advances to mathematics with his contributions to algebra, geometry, statistics and theoretical mathematics.

Gay-Lussac, Joseph Louis 1778–1850. French chemist and physicist who developed a law governing the combination of gases. He discovered boron, with Louis Jacques Thénard, in 1808.

Gd The symbol for **gadolinium.**

Ge The symbol for **germanium.**

gear A wheel with teeth around its rim that mesh with the teeth of another wheel to transmit motion. Gears are used to transmit motion (as in a

Word History

gastropod

Snails, conches, whelks and many other similar animals with shells are all called gastropods by scientists. The word *gastropod* comes from Greek and means "stomach foot", a name that owes its existence to the unusual anatomy of snails. While they don't have feet like ours exactly, snails have a broad flat "foot" used for support and for forward movement. This foot runs along the underside of the animal – essentially along its belly. The Greek elements *gastro–*, "stomach", and *–pod*, "foot", are found in many other scientific names, such as *gastritis* (an inflammation of the stomach) and *sauropod* ("lizard foot", a type of dinosaur).

car transmission) or change the direction of motion in a mechanism (as in a differential axle). Speed in various parts of a machine is usually determined by the arrangement of gears.

Geiger, Hans Wilhelm 1882–1945. German physicist who was a pioneer in nuclear physics. He invented numerous instruments and techniques used to detect charged particles, including the Geiger counter (1908).

Geiger counter An electronic instrument that detects and measures nuclear radiation, such as X-rays or gamma rays. The Geiger counter consists of a gas-filled tube with an electrode connected to a counter. As radiation passes through the gas, ions are produced, making pulses of electric current that are registered by the counter.

gelatin An odourless, colourless protein substance obtained by boiling a mixture of water and the skin, bones and tendons of animals. The preparation forms a gel when allowed to cool. It is used in foods, drugs, glue and film.

Gell-Mann, Murray Born 1929. American physicist who studied the interactions of subatomic particles and helped develop a system for classifying them. He also introduced the concept of quarks.

Gemini A constellation in the Northern Hemisphere near Cancer and Auriga. It contains the bright stars Pollux and Castor.

gemma A bud-like outgrowth on certain organisms, such as the liverworts and mosses, that separates from the parent organism and develops into a new individual.

gene A segment of DNA, occupying a specific place on a chromosome, that is the basic unit of heredity. Genes act by directing the synthesis of proteins, which are the main components of cells and are the catalysts of all cellular processes. Physical traits, such as the shape of a plant leaf, the coloration of an animal's coat, and the texture of a person's hair, are all determined by genes. *See also* **dominant, recessive.** *See panels at* **DNA, Mendel.**

generator A machine that transfers kinetic energy to electrical energy. Generators create an electric current by means of a coiled electric wire that rotates between two magnets or a magnet rotating inside a stationary coil of wire.

■ **gear**

Gears can be used to reverse (1) or otherwise change (2,3) the direction of rotation. Gears of different size (1–4) change the speed of rotation.

gene therapy The treatment of disease, especially one caused by the inheritance of a defective gene, by replacing defective genes with healthy ones through genetic engineering.

genetic code The sequence of organic bases (called nucleotides) in DNA and RNA that determines the structure of each amino acid in a protein.

genetic engineering The science of artificially changing the genetic material of an organism. It usually involves taking a small piece of DNA (a gene) from one organism and transferring it to the genetic material of an entirely different organism (often a virus or bacterium). This technique can be used to produce a new trait in an organism or to enable one type of organism to make a biological substance, such as a protein or a hormone, usually made in a completely different type of organism. Genetic engineering has produced bacteria that can make human insulin, sheep that can produce human blood-clotting factors, and plants that can produce their own pesticides.

genetic map *or* **gene map** A graphic representation of the arrangement of genes on a chromosome. A genetic map is used to locate and

Did You Know?

genes

What makes a human different from a chimpanzee? Much of the answer lies in the *genes,* the basic units of heredity. Each gene is a specific segment of DNA, occupying a fixed place on a chromosome. Genes contain the chemical information needed to create different kinds of proteins. These proteins are used to repair cells and make new ones. The kinds of proteins, the amounts, and the order in which they are made all help determine how one type of cell differs from another and, ultimately, how one species of organism differs from another. Just how different are the genes making up different life forms? There are some genes that seem to be present in almost every known living organism from the simplest single-celled creature to human beings. These genes usually control the basic chemistry of the cell. Other genes can vary enormously, but not always as much as we might expect. In the case of human beings and chimpanzees, the difference is very small – about 98% of the DNA in a chimp cell is identical to the DNA in a human cell. This close similarity leads scientists to think that chimpanzees are our closest living relatives in the animal kingdom.

However, it is not only the type of genes that results in differences between species. Changes in the sequence of the genes on the chromosomes can also result in very different types of organisms. Studying the genomes of different species and working out the evolutionary relationships between them is a fascinating area of biology that is growing all the time as new information about genes and their sequencing becomes available.

identify the gene or genes that determine a particular inherited trait. ❖ Locating and identifying genes in a genetic map is called **genetic mapping.**

genetics The scientific study of the principles of heredity and the variation of inherited traits among related organisms. Genetics is a branch of biology.

genitals The organs of reproduction in animals, especially the external sex organs.

genome The total amount of genetic information in the chromosomes of an organism, including its genes and DNA sequences. The genome of eukaryotes is made up of a single, haploid set of chromosomes that is contained in the nucleus of every cell and exists in two copies in the chromosomes of all cells except reproductive cells. The human genome is made up of about 30,000 genes. ❖ The scientific study of genomes is called **genomics.**

genotype The genetic make-up of an organism as distinguished from its physical characteristics. *Compare* **phenotype.**

genus (*plural* **genera**) A group of organisms ranking above a species and below a family. *See table at* **taxonomy.**

geo– A prefix that means "earth", as in *geochemistry,* the study of the Earth's chemistry.

geocentric 1. Relating to or measured from the Earth's centre. **2.** Relating to a model of the solar system or universe having the Earth as the centre. *Compare* **heliocentric.**

geochemistry The study of the chemistry of the Earth, including its layers, waters and atmosphere.

geode A small, hollow, usually rounded rock lined on the inside with inward-pointing crystals. Geodes form when mineral-rich water entering a cavity in a rock undergoes a sudden change in pressure or temperature, causing crystals to form from the solution and line the cavity's walls.

geodesic dome A structure having the shape of a dome or partial sphere but made of flat triangular pieces that fit rigidly together.

geographic north The direction from any

■ geode

geometric progression A sequence of numbers in which each number is multiplied by the same factor to obtain the next number in the sequence; a sequence in which the ratio of any two adjacent numbers is the same. An example is 5, 25, 125, 625, . . ., where each number is multiplied by 5 to obtain the following number, and the ratio of any number to the next number is always 1 to 5. *Compare* **arithmetic progression.**

geometry The mathematical study of the properties, measurement and relationships of points, lines, planes, surfaces, angles and solids.

point on the Earth towards the North Pole. *Also called* true north. *Compare* **magnetic north.**

geography The scientific study of the Earth's surface and its various climates, countries, peoples and natural resources.

geological time The period of time covering the formation and development of the Earth, from about 4.6 billion years ago to the present day. *See chart,* pages 148–149.

geology 1. The scientific study of the origin of the Earth along with its rocks, minerals and land forms, and of the history of the changes these have undergone. 2. The structure of a specific region of the Earth, including its rocks, soils, mountains, fossils and other features.

geomagnetism The magnetic properties of the Earth. ❖ The magnetic field surrounding the Earth is called the **geomagnetic field.**

geophysics The application of physics to the scientific study of the Earth and its environment.

geothermal Relating to the internal heat of the Earth. The water of hot springs and geysers is heated by geothermal sources. ❖ Power that is generated using the Earth's internal heat is called **geothermal energy.**

geotropism The growth of an organism in response to gravity. The downward growth of plant roots is an example of positive geotropism. *—adjective* **geotropic.**

germ 1. A microscopic organism or substance, especially a bacterium or a virus, that causes disease. 2. The earliest living form of an organism; a seed, spore or bud.

Germain, Sophie 1776–1831. French mathematician who made significant advances in theoretical mathematics.

germanium A brittle, crystalline, greyish-white nonmetallic element that is found in zinc ores, coal and other minerals. It is widely used as a semiconductor and in wide-angle lenses. *Symbol* **Ge.** *Atomic number* 32. *See* **Periodic Table,** pages 260–261.

German measles A contagious disease caused by a virus in which symptoms, such as skin rash and a high temperature, are usually mild. German measles can cause congenital defects if contracted by a woman during early pregnancy. Also called *rubella.*

germ cell A reproductive cell of a plant or animal; a gamete. In mammals, germ cells are eggs or sperm.

germination The beginning of growth, as of a

■ **geothermal**
geothermal pool in Yellowstone National Park, USA

Usage

germ/microbe/pathogen

You've heard it many times. Some food falls on the floor, and someone (usually an adult) says, "Don't eat that now. It's got germs on it". The word *germ* has been used to refer to invisible agents of disease since the 19th century, when scientists were first learning about the nature of disease. Similarly, the term *microbe,* which comes from the Greek prefix *mikro–,* "small", and word *bios,* "life", is a term that arose in the late 19th century in reference to the microscopic organisms that caused disease. The terms *germ* and *microbe* thus became associated with an early era of scientific research in which knowledge was very limited, and they are no longer used much by scientists. Thanks to generations of research, scientists today can usually identify the specific agents of disease, such as individual species of bacteria or viruses. When they want to refer generally to agents of disease, they use the term *pathogen,* which comes from Greek *pathos,* "suffering", and the suffix *–gen,* "producer". The term *microorganism* is used to refer to any one-celled microscopic organism, whether it causes disease or is harmless.

seed, spore or bud. The germination of most seeds and spores occurs in response to warmth and water. —*verb* **germinate.**

gestation The period of time it takes a young animal to develop from conception to birth in the uterus of the mother. Gestation in human beings is about nine months.

geyser A natural hot spring that regularly ejects a spray of steam and boiling water into the air. The water is heated by coming into contact with hot rock or steam underground.

g-force The acceleration of a body in or as if it were in the Earth's gravitational field, expressed in multiples of the acceleration due to gravity on Earth (equal to 1 G). The acceleration due to

gravity on Jupiter, for example, is 2.5 Gs. Other accelerations, such as those of jet pilots making sharp turns, are also expressed in Gs.

giant star A very large star with a low density.

gibbous More than half but less than fully illuminated. Used to describe the moon or a planet. *Compare* **crescent.**

Gibbs, Josiah Willard 1839–1903. American mathematician and physicist known especially for his investigations of thermodynamics. He developed methods for analysing the thermodynamic properties of substances, and his findings established the basic theory for physical chemistry.

giga– A prefix that means: **1.** One billion (10^9), as in *gigahertz,* one billion hertz. **2.** 2^{30} (that is, 1,073,741,824), which is the power of 2 closest to a billion, as in *gigabyte. See table at* **measurement.**

gigabyte 1. A unit of computer memory or data storage capacity equal to 1024 megabytes (2^{30} bytes). **2.** One billion bytes. *See panel at* **megabyte.**

Gilbert, William 1544–1603. English court physician and physicist whose book *De Magnete* (1600) was the first comprehensive scientific work published in England. Gilbert demonstrated that the Earth itself is a magnet, with lines of force running between the North and South Poles. He theorized that magnetism and electricity were two types of a single force and was the first to use the words *electricity* and *magnetic pole.*

gill 1. The organ that enables most aquatic

■ **germination**
germination of a bean seed

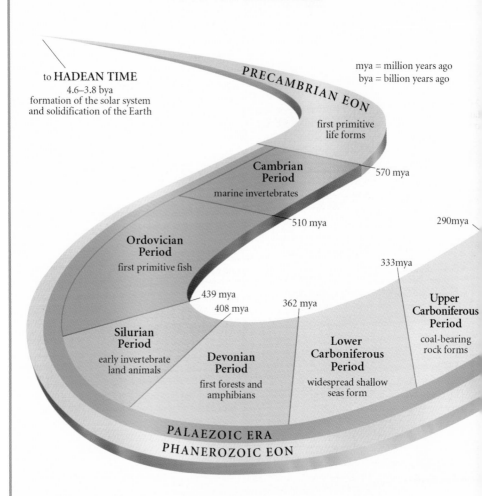

to **HADEAN TIME**
4.6–3.8 bya
formation of the solar system
and solidification of the Earth

PRECAMBRIAN EON

mya = million years ago
bya = billion years ago

first primitive
life forms

Cambrian Period
marine invertebrates

570 mya

510 mya

290mya

333mya

Ordovician Period
first primitive fish

439 mya

408 mya

362 mya

Upper Carboniferous Period
coal-bearing rock forms

Silurian Period
early invertebrate land animals

Devonian Period
first forests and amphibians

Lower Carboniferous Period
widespread shallow seas form

PALAEZOIC ERA
PHANEROZOIC EON

The Earth formed approximately 4.6 billion years ago. For the purpose of studying its history, scientists have separated these 4.6 billion years into a set of divisions, much as a year is divided into months, weeks, and days. The first 800 million years of the Earth's history are referred to as Hadean Time. During this time the solar system was forming and the Earth was solidifying. The 3.8 billion years after Hadean time are subdivided into eons, eras, periods, and epochs. Eons are the longest divisions of time, and epochs are the shortest. Most of the boundaries between the divisions correspond to visible changes in the types of life forms preserved as fossils in the corresponding rocks. Because our understanding of the Earth's history is based on what we learn by studying its rocks and the fossils within them, we know a lot more about the

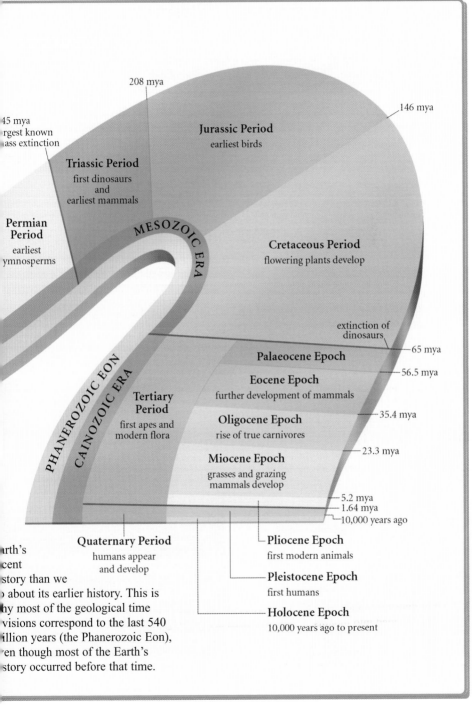

208 mya

146 mya

Jurassic Period
earliest birds

45 mya
rgest known
ass extinction

Triassic Period
first dinosaurs
and
earliest mammals

**Permian
Period**
earliest
ymnosperms

MESOZOIC ERA

Cretaceous Period
flowering plants develop

extinction of
dinosaurs

65 mya

Palaeocene Epoch

56.5 mya

PHANEROZOIC EON

CAINOZOIC ERA

Eocene Epoch
further development of mammals

**Tertiary
Period**
first apes and
modern flora

Oligocene Epoch
rise of true carnivores

35.4 mya

23.3 mya

Miocene Epoch
grasses and grazing
mammals develop

5.2 mya
1.64 mya
10,000 years ago

Quaternary Period
humans appear
and develop

└ **Pliocene Epoch**
first modern animals

arth's
cent
story than we
about its earlier history. This is
hy most of the geological time
visions correspond to the last 540
illion years (the Phanerozoic Eon),
en though most of the Earth's
story occurred before that time.

── **Pleistocene Epoch**
first humans

── **Holocene Epoch**
10,000 years ago to present

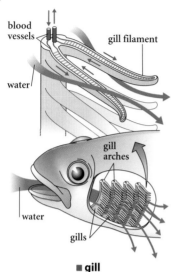

■ gill

Fish breathe by swallowing water and passing it through gill slits on each side of their head. Blood-filled filaments on the gills extract oxygen from the water as it flows through.

animals to take oxygen from the water. It consists of a series of membranes that have many small blood vessels. Oxygen passes into the bloodstream and carbon dioxide passes out of it as water passes across the membranes. **2.** One of the thin, plate-like structures on the underside of the cap of a mushroom or similar fungus.

gingiva The gums of the mouth. ❖ Inflammation of the gums is called **gingivitis.**

ginkgo A deciduous tree originally native to China, having fan-shaped leaves and fleshy yellow seeds. Ginkgoes are gymnosperms and do not have flowers.

gizzard A muscular pouch behind the stomach in birds. It has a thick lining and often contains swallowed sand or grit, which helps to break food into small pieces.

glacier A large mass of ice flowing very slowly through a valley or spreading outwards from a centre. Glaciers form over many years from packed snow in areas where snow accumulates faster than it melts. A glacier is always moving, but when its forward edge melts faster than the ice behind it

advances, the glacier as a whole shrinks backwards.

gland An organ in the body of an animal that produces and secretes a specific substance, such as a hormone. *See also* **endocrine gland, exocrine gland.**

glandular fever *See* **mononucleosis.**

glass A transparent or translucent material that has no crystalline structure and that usually breaks or shatters easily. It is made by melting a silicate, such as sand, with soda and lime. The soda causes the silicate particles to fuse, and the lime acts as a stabilizer.

glaucoma An eye disease in which the pressure of fluid inside the eyeball becomes abnormally high. The pressure can damage the optic nerve and lead to partial or complete loss of vision.

Global Positioning System A system that determines latitude and longitude of a particular location on the Earth by calculating the difference in the time it takes for signals sent from different satellites to reach a receiver at that location.

global warming An increase in the average temperature of the Earth's atmosphere, especially a sustained increase great enough to cause changes in the global climate. Many scientists believe that the Earth has been in a period of global warming for the past century or more, due in part to the increased production of greenhouse gases related to human activity (such as carbon dioxide from burning fossil fuels). *See more at* **greenhouse effect.**

■ glacier
Kenai Fjords, Alaska

Did You Know?

glass

Windows, television screens and spectacles all take advantage of the fact that we can see through *glass*. Like common sand, glass is made of silicon dioxide. But if they are made of the same chemical, why is it that sand is impossible to see through but glass is transparent? The startling see-through property of glass owes its existence to another amazing fact: although glass is hard, it is not truly a solid. Some scientists think of glass as a sort of frozen liquid, whereas others talk about glass as being a disordered kind of solid. Glass is thus different from what we usually think of as either a solid or a liquid. Rather than having the orderly

arrangement of most hard matter, the microscopic structure of glass resembles a liquid, stuck in time. The interiors of true solids have boundaries that scatter light, causing it to bounce off. Glass's liquid-like lack of these boundaries lets the light through. What happens when light strikes an atom in a substance is important too. When a light wave interacts with the electrons in an atom, its energy may be absorbed (and transferred to heat), it may be reflected or nothing may happen (and it continues on its path). The combination of these behaviours determines how much light is able to travel through the substance.

globular cluster A dense system of very old stars that has a more or less spherical structure. Globular clusters contain between 100,000 and 10 million stars, and have diameters of around 100 light years. *Compare* **open cluster.**

globulin A major class of proteins found in the seeds of plants and in the blood, muscle and milk of animals. *See also* **gamma globulin.**

glottis The area where the larynx opens out from the pharynx in the neck.

glucose A crystalline sugar having the formula $C_6H_{12}O_6$, found in plant and animal tissue. It is transported by blood and lymph to all the cells of the body, where it is broken down in the process of cellular respiration to provide energy for all cellular processes. The breakdown of glucose in the presence of oxygen produces energy in the form of ATP, and carbon dioxide and water are the waste products.

glutamic acid A nonessential amino acid. *See more at* **amino acid.**

glutamine A nonessential amino acid. *See more at* **amino acid.**

glycerine *See* **glycerol.**

glycerol The systematic name for glycerol is propane–1,2,3–triol. It is an alcohol that plays a

vital role in the structure of fats. When it is extracted, it is a sweet syrupy liquid which can be used as a solvent, sweetener or antifreeze. It is also used in making explosives (nitroglycerine) and soaps. Also called *glycerine.*

glycogen A carbohydrate stored in the liver and muscles of animals that is converted into glucose for energy when glucose levels in the blood are depleted.

glycolysis The process in cell metabolism by which carbohydrates and sugars, especially glucose, are broken down, producing ATP and pyruvic acid.

GMO Short for *genetically modified organism.* An organism that has had its genetic code altered to give it new and desirable properties. Increasing numbers of GMOs are being used all over the world in farming and biotechnology. Many people have expressed concerns about the use of GMOs, particularly in farming. There are worries about the effect of eating GMOs, both plants and animals, and also about the effects of these species on the environment. In the UK and some other countries, food containing GMOs is labelled to give people a choice about whether or not to eat it.

gnat Any of various small biting flies.

gneiss A type of metamorphic rock consisting of

Did You Know?

Gondwanaland

Sometimes a suggested solution to a scientific problem can raise more questions than it answers. So it was with Austrian geologist Eduard Suess's hypothesis explaining why identical groups of fossil plants occur in India, South America, southern Africa, Australia and Antarctica. The plants, known as the *Glossopteris flora,* had seeds that were too large to have blown across the vast expanses of water separating these land masses. In 1885 Suess proposed that the plant fossils were common to all of the land masses because the land masses were actually connected when the plants first developed, and only later broke apart into separate continents. Suess named this huge land mass *Gondwanaland,* after a region of central India called Gondwana. Few believed Suess's idea because most people could not see what would cause such a giant supercontinent to break apart.

In the early 1900s, Alfred Wegener, a German meteorologist, noticed other kinds of evidence for Gondwanaland, including similarities in animal fossils, rock types and marks left by glaciers across the continents of the Southern Hemisphere. Wegener used this evidence to propose the idea of *continental drift,* which says that the continents are always moving towards or away from one another. But it wasn't until the 1960s that Wegener's ideas or the concept of Gondwanaland were finally accepted, when the theory of *plate tectonics* was put forward to explain how the internal workings of the Earth could cause continents to move about.

---

light-coloured layers, usually of quartz and feldspar, alternating with dark-coloured layers of other minerals. The layers are often folded into curves. *See table at* **rock.**

Goddard, Robert Hutchings 1882–1945. American physicist who developed and launched the first successful liquid-fuelled rocket in 1926. He also invented numerous rocketry devices.

Goeppert-Mayer, Maria 1906–1972. German-born American physicist. She developed a model of the atomic nucleus that explained why certain nuclei were stable and had an unusual number of stable isotopes.

goitre An enlarged thyroid gland, visible as a swelling at the front of the neck. It is often associated with a diet that contains too little iodine.

gold A soft, shiny, yellow element that is the most easily shaped metal. It is very unreactive, so it occurs in veins and in alluvial deposits in its native state. Because it is very durable, resistant to corrosion, and a good conductor of heat and electricity, gold is used as a plating on electrical and mechanical components. It is also an international monetary standard and is used to make jewellery and decoration. *Symbol* **Au.** *Atomic number* 79. *See* **Periodic Table,** pages 260–261. *See panel at* **element.**

Goldberger, Joseph 1874–1924. Hungarian-born American physician. He investigated the cause and treatment of pellagra, a widespread and often fatal disease. Goldberger demonstrated that it was caused by a poor diet and introduced an effective method of prevention.

Golgi apparatus or **Golgi body** A structure within many cells that is composed of a series of sacs, called vesicles, and is thought to play a role in the synthesis and transport of proteins. All organisms except bacteria have at least one Golgi apparatus in their cells. *See more at* **cell.**

gonad An organ in animals that produces reproductive cells; an ovary or testis.

Gondwanaland A great southern super-continent that, according to the theory of plate tectonics, formed almost 300 million years ago. It subsequently broke up, forming the present continents of Africa, South America, Australia, Antarctica and the Indian subcontinent. *Compare* **Laurasia.**

■ **graft**

gonorrhoea A sexually transmitted disease caused by a bacterial infection that causes inflammation of the genitals and urinary tract.

Goodall, Jane Born 1934. British zoologist whose study of the behaviour and habitat of the chimpanzee has greatly increased understanding of primate behaviour. She established a research centre in the east African country of Tanzania and has been a leader in international conservation efforts.

googol The number 10 raised to the 100th power, written as 10^{100} or as 1 followed by 100 zeros.

gorge A deep, narrow passage with steep sides, often with a stream flowing through it.

gorilla The largest and most powerful of the apes, found in central African forests and mountains. Gorillas have a heavy, stocky body with dark hair, dwell on the ground, and feed mainly on leaves and stems. They live in close-knit groups and have elaborate social interactions.

Gould, Stephen Jay 1941–2002. American evolutionary biologist and historian of science. He developed the theory of punctuated equilibrium with Niles Eldredge in 1972.

gout A hereditary disorder caused by painful deposits of crystals in the joints, especially of the big toe, knee or elbow. It is caused by abnormally high levels of uric acid in the blood.

gradation *Geology.* The process by which the land is levelled off, as through the action of wind or water.

gradient 1. The slope of a line or the slope of a tangent to a curve at a particular point. A positive gradient slopes upwards and a negative one slopes downwards. The gradient is given by dividing the vertical distance by the horizontal distance. So a mountain road with a gradient of ten per cent rises 30 centimetres for every 300 centimetres of horizontal length. **2.** The rate at which a physical quantity, such as temperature or pressure, changes with another quantity, such as time.

gradualism The theory that new species evolve from existing species through gradual, often imperceptible, changes rather than through abrupt, major changes. The small changes are believed to result in perceptible changes over long periods of time. *Compare* **punctuated equilibrium.**

graduated Divided into or marked with intervals indicating measures, as of length, volume or temperature: *a graduated thermometer.*

graft *noun* **1.** A shoot or bud of one plant that is inserted into or joined to the stem, branch or root of another plant so that the two grow together as a single plant. Grafts are used to strengthen or repair plants, create dwarf trees, produce seedless fruit and increase fruit yields without requiring plants to mature from seeds. **2.** A transplant of body tissue, especially skin or bone, from one part to another. —*verb* **1.** To join a graft to another plant. **2.** To transplant tissue from one part of the body to another.

grain 1. A small, hard seed, especially of wheat, maize, rice or another cereal plant. **2.** A small particle of something, such as salt, pollen or sand.

grain alcohol *See* **ethanol.**

Gram, Hans Christian Joachim 1853–1938. Danish bacteriologist. He developed a method of staining bacteria with dyes, an important tool used to identify and classify bacteria and treat infections.

gram or **gramme** A unit of mass or weight in the metric system, equal to one thousandth of a kilogram. *See table at* **measurement.**

gram-negative Relating to a group of bacteria that generally are resistant to the effects of antibiotics or the actions of the body's immune cells. Gram-negative bacteria have relatively thin cell walls and, when subjected to a specialized laboratory staining method, do not change colour. *Compare* **gram-positive.**

gram-positive Relating to a group of bacteria that generally are sensitive to the destructive effects of antibiotics or the actions of the body's immune cells. Gram-positive bacteria have relatively thick cell walls and, when subjected to a specialized laboratory staining method, turn a dark-blue colour. *Compare* **gram-negative.**

grand unified theory *See* **unified field theory.**

granite A usually light-coloured, coarse-grained igneous rock composed mostly of quartz, feldspar and mica. It is one of the most common rocks in the crust of continents. *See table at* **rock.**

granulocyte Any of various white blood cells that contain granular material in the cytoplasm and are important in the body's defence against infection. Granulocytes are the most numerous of the white blood cells in humans. *See more at* **white blood cell.**

graph **1.** A diagram showing the relationship of quantities, especially such a diagram in which lines, bars or proportional areas represent how one quantity depends on or changes with another. **2.** A curve or line showing a mathematical function or equation, typically drawn in a Cartesian coordinate system.

graphical user interface *See* **GUI.**

graphics **1.** The representation of data in a way that includes images in addition to text. Computer-aided design, typesetting and video games, for example, involve the use of graphics. **2.** The process by which a computer displays information in the form of images.

graphite A naturally occurring steel-grey to black, crystalline form of carbon. The carbon atoms in graphite are strongly bonded together in sheets. Because the bonds between the sheets are weak, other atoms can easily fit between them, causing the graphite to be soft and slippery to the touch. Graphite is used in pencils and paints and as a lubricant and electrode. It is also used to control chain reactions in nuclear reactors because of its ability to absorb neutrons. *See panel at* **carbon.**

grass Any of various plants having narrow leaves, hollow stems and clusters of very small flowers. Grasses include many varieties of plants used for food and fodder and grown as lawns. Wheat, maize, sugar cane and bamboo are grasses. *See more at* **leaf.**

grasshopper Any of numerous large insects typically having two pairs of wings and long hind legs for jumping. Grasshoppers feed on plants and can be very destructive to plants. They are closely related to cockroaches, crickets and praying mantises.

grassland An area, such as a prairie or steppe, of grass or grass-like vegetation.

gravimeter **1.** An instrument used to measure

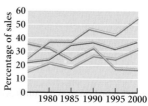

■ **graph**
top to bottom: *examples of a pie chart, bar chart and line graph*

specific gravity. **2.** An instrument used to measure variations in a gravitational field.

gravitation The force of attraction that tends to draw together any two objects in the universe. Gravitation increases as the mass of the objects increases and as their distance from each other decreases.

gravitational constant A number used to calculate the force of the gravitational attraction between two bodies in Newton's law of gravitation. The gravitational constant equals 6.67×10^{-11} cubic metres per kilogram per second squared. *See more at* **Newton's law of gravitation.**

gravity The attraction that objects have for each other merely because they have mass. Gravity is the weakest of the four basic forces in nature, being weaker than the strong nuclear force, the electromagnetic force and the weak nuclear force. *See more at* **acceleration, relativity, fundamental forces.**

gray A unit used to measure the energy absorbed from radiation (the "absorbed dose"). One gray is equal to one joule per kilogram. *See also* **sievert.**

great circle A circle on the surface of a sphere whose plane passes through the centre of the sphere. The Earth's equator is a great circle on the sphere of the globe.

greenhouse effect The trapping of the sun's radiation in the Earth's atmosphere due to the presence of greenhouse gases. *See A Closer Look,* page 156.

greenhouse gas Any of the atmospheric gases that contribute to the greenhouse effect. Greenhouse gases include carbon dioxide, water vapour, methane and nitrous oxide.

Greenwich Mean Time *See* **universal time.**

grey matter The brownish-grey tissue of the brain and spinal cord in vertebrate animals, made up chiefly of the cell bodies of neurons. *Compare* **white matter.**

grey water Waste water from household baths and washing machines that is recycled, especially for use in gardening or for flushing toilets. *See panel on* page 157.

Grimaldi, Francesco Maria 1618–1663. Italian physicist who confirmed Galileo's laws of falling bodies and produced a detailed map of the moon. Even more importantly, he discovered the diffraction of light, and carried out lots of research into interference and the effect of prisms on light.

Did You Know?

gravity

Isaac Newton described *gravity,* which he saw as the mutual attraction that two masses have for each other. Newton developed an equation that showed that any two objects in the universe, no matter how far apart or how small, exert an instantaneous gravitational effect on each other. These effects diminish, however, as the distance between the objects gets larger and as the masses of the objects get smaller, so that for many distant objects or objects with barely any mass, the effects of gravity are very small. Newton seemed to have the last word on gravity, until Albert Einstein came along. Einstein noted that gravity's effects could not be instantaneous, since they would have to travel at infinite velocities, violating his theory of relativity, which states that nothing can travel faster than light. He also showed that gravity and acceleration are related. Imagine, he said, that you are an astronaut standing in a stationary rocket on Earth: because of the Earth's gravity your feet are pressed against the rocket's floor with a force equal to your weight. Now imagine that you are in the same rocket, in outer space, in an area that has no gravitational pull. Even though you are weightless, if the rocket is accelerating and its floor is pushing against your feet, you feel as if you are being acted upon by a gravitational field. Unless you look out the window you have no idea whether the rocket is at rest on Earth or accelerating through space.

A Closer Look
Greenhouse Effect

A greenhouse is designed to trap the sun's energy. Sunlight can penetrate its glass roof to warm the soil, but the infrared waves emitted by the soil can't pass back through the glass, so it remains inside to warm the air.

sunlight (short-wave radiation)

atmosphere

greenhouse gases

heat (long-wave radiation)

A similar process takes place on the Earth as a whole. Sunlight penetrates the atmosphere to warm the Earth's surface, which then radiates heat into the lower level of the atmosphere. Although some of this heat passes out into space, much of it is absorbed by water vapour, carbon dioxide, and other gases in the air. These gases act like the glass roof of a greenhouse, trapping the infrared heat energy and warming the atmosphere.

ground 1. The solid surface of the Earth; land. 2. A connection between an electrical conductor and the Earth. 3. A point in an electrical system where the voltage is zero.

ground state The state of lowest possible energy, especially of subatomic particles. When subatomic particles, such as electrons and neutrons, are at a higher level of energy than their ground states, they emit radiation.

groundwater Water that flows or collects beneath the Earth's surface. Groundwater originates from rain and from melting snow and ice. It sinks into the ground, filling the small empty spaces in soil, sediment and porous rocks. Aquifers, springs and wells are supplied by the flow of groundwater.

group 1. Two or more atoms bound together that act as a unit in a number of chemical compounds: *a hydroxyl group*. 2. In the Periodic Table, a vertical column that contains elements having the same number of electrons in the outermost shell of their atoms. Elements in the same group have similar chemical properties. *See* **Periodic Table**, pages 260–261. 3. In mathematics, a set of elements and an operation. The operation takes two elements of the set and forms another element of the set, subject to certain conditions.

growth An increase in size, amount or volume, usually as a result of an increase in the number of cells. Growth of an organism may stop at maturity, as in the case of humans and other mammals, or it may continue throughout life, as in many plants.

growth ring A layer of wood formed in a plant

during a single period of growth. Growth rings are visible as concentric circles of varying width when a tree is cut crosswise. They represent layers of cells produced by the tissue known as vascular cambium. ❖ Most growth rings reflect a full year's growth and are called **annual rings.** But abrupt changes in the environment, especially in the availability of water, can cause a plant to produce more than one growth ring in a year. *See more at* **dendrochronology.**

guanine A base that is a component of DNA and RNA, forming a base pair with cytosine.

guano A substance composed chiefly of the partly decomposed dung of sea birds or bats. It is used as a fertilizer.

guard cell One of the paired cells that control the opening and closing of a stoma of a leaf. When water needs to be conserved, the guard cells close the stomata to prevent the loss of water by diffusion from the cells inside the leaf. *See more at* **cell.**

Did You Know?

grey water

White water is what you go rafting on. If you ever rafted on grey water, well, you'd need a good shower (in fresh water) at the end of the day to get rid of the smell. To understand grey water, it's best to first define something even smellier: *black water.* Black water is, quite simply, the water that gets flushed down the toilet, complete with the reasons *why* you flushed the toilet. Black water can also include water with other organic wastes – from the sink, for example. Grey water is still not drinkable, but it's less nasty than black water. Grey water is the stuff that goes down the drain from other uses, such as showering or laundry. Because it is relatively clean, grey water can be recycled in areas where water is scarce, to irrigate flowerbeds or to be fed into toilets to become black water. These uses conserve fresh water for drinking and bathing.

GUI Short for *graphical user interface.* An interface that is used to issue commands to a computer by means of a device such as a mouse that manipulates and activates on-screen images.

gulf A very large and deeply indented inlet of the sea extending far into the land.

Gulf Stream A warm ocean current of the northern Atlantic Ocean off eastern North America. It flows northwards and eastwards from the Gulf of Mexico, eventually dividing into several branches. A major branch continues eastwards to warm the coast and moderate the climate of northwest Europe.

gully A narrow, steep-sided channel formed in loose earth by running water. A gully is usually dry except after periods of heavy rainfall or after the melting of snow or ice.

gum[1] A sticky substance that is produced by certain plants and trees and dries into a brittle solid that dissolves in water.

gum[2] The firm connective tissue that surrounds and supports the bases of the teeth.

gut The digestive tract, especially of an invertebrate animal or an embryo of a vertebrate animal.

gymnosperm Any of a group of plants that produce seeds that are not enclosed in a fruit or ovary. Most gymnosperms are cone-bearing trees or shrubs. Seeds develop next to the inside surface of the scales of female cones. Gymnosperms include conifers, cycads and the ginkgo. *Compare* **angiosperm.**

gynaecology The branch of medicine that deals with the female reproductive system, its diseases and their treatment.

gypsum A colourless, white or pinkish mineral consisting of calcium phosphate. Gypsum occurs as individual blade-shaped crystals or as massive beds in sedimentary rocks. It is used in manufacturing plasterboard, cement and fertilizers. It is the mineral used to represent a hardness of 2 on the Mohs scale.

gyroscope An instrument consisting of a disc or wheel that spins rapidly about an axis like a top. The spinning motion keeps the axis fixed even if the base is turned in any direction, making the gyroscope an accurate navigational instrument and an effective stabilizing device in ships and aeroplanes.

H *h*

H The symbol for **hydrogen**.

Haber, Fritz 1868–1934. German chemist who was the first to produce ammonia synthetically, in 1908–1909.

habit 1. The characteristic shape of a crystal: *the cubic habit of pyrite.* **2.** The characteristic manner of growth of a plant: *a low plant with a creeping habit.*

habitat The area or natural environment in which an animal or plant normally lives, such as a desert, coral reef or freshwater lake. A habitat can often be home to many different organisms.

hackle 1. One of the long, slender, often glossy feathers on the neck of a bird, especially a rooster. **2. hackles** The hairs along the back of the neck of an animal, especially a dog, that can stand out and bristle in displaying aggression or fear.

Hadean Time The period of time within the Precambrian Eon between 4.6 and 3.8 billion years ago, when the solar system was forming and the Earth was solidifying. No rocks are known from this time, as they were probably eroded or drawn deep into the Earth and melted through the processes of plate tectonics. *See chart at* **geological time,** pages 148–149.

hadrosaur Any of various medium-sized to large plant-eating dinosaurs of the Cretaceous Period that had a duck-like bill and many series of rough grinding teeth. The hadrosaurs were the last group of ornithopod dinosaurs. Also called *duck-billed dinosaur.*

Haeckel, Ernst Heinrich 1834–1919. German biologist who was one of the first scientists to publicly support Darwin's theory of evolution. His own ideas about evolution attracted popular attention, and though they were later disproved, they helped to stimulate biological research.

haematite A reddish-brown to silver-grey mineral consisting of iron oxide. Haematite occurs in igneous, metamorphic and sedimentary rocks and is the most abundant iron ore.

haematoma The abnormal build-up of blood in an organ or other tissue of the body, caused by a break in a blood vessel. A bruise is a type of haematoma.

haemo– A prefix meaning "blood", as in *haemophilia,* a disorder in which blood fails to clot.

haemoglobin An iron-containing protein in the blood of many animals that, in vertebrates, carries oxygen from the lungs to the tissues of the body and carries carbon dioxide from the tissues to the lungs. Haemoglobin is contained in the red blood cells of vertebrates and gives these cells their characteristic colour. Haemoglobin is also found in many invertebrates, where it circulates freely in the blood. *See panel at* **red blood cell.**

haemophilia An inherited disease in which the blood does not clot properly, causing excessive bleeding. Haemophilia usually only affects males.

haemorrhage Bleeding, especially in excessive amounts.

hafnium A bright, silvery metallic element that occurs in zirconium ores. Because hafnium is very resistant to corrosion, it is used in nuclear reactors. *Symbol* **Hf.** *Atomic number* 72. *See* **Periodic Table,** pages 260–261.

hagfish Any of various jawless fish that resemble eels and may be related to the lampreys. Hagfish have several hearts, glands that produce slime, and tentacles around the mouth. They do not have eyes, a backbone or a stomach. Hagfish often feed on dead or dying fish by boring into them and eating them from the inside.

Hahn, Otto 1879–1968. German chemist who investigated radioactive elements and helped discover several new ones. His work on uranium and thorium led to the discovery of nuclear fission.

hahnium An earlier name for **dubnium.**

hail Precipitation in the form of rounded pellets of ice and hard snow that usually falls during

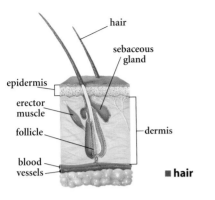

hair

sebaceous gland

epidermis

erector muscle

follicle

dermis

blood vessels

■ **hair**

1910. This comet is now named after him. Halley was also the first to catalogue the stars in the Southern Hemisphere (1679).

Halley's comet A comet that makes one complete orbit around the sun in approximately 76 years. It is visible to the unaided eye and last appeared in 1986.

hallucinogen A drug or chemical that causes a person to see, hear or otherwise sense something that is not real.

halo A hazy ring of coloured light in the sky around the sun, the moon or a similar bright object. It is caused by the reflection and refraction of light through ice crystals suspended in the upper atmosphere.

halogen Any of a group of five nonmetallic elements with similar properties. The halogens are fluorine, chlorine, bromine, iodine and astatine. Because they require only one further electron to acquire a full outermost shell, they react readily with most metals to form salts. The halogens are located in the column of the Periodic Table that is second from the right. *See* **Periodic Table**, pages 260–261.

halophyte A plant adapted to living in salty soil, as along the seashore. The mangrove and grasses that grow in salt marshes are halophytes.

hamstring A powerful group of muscles with strong tendons at the back of the thigh or hind leg.

hanging valley A small glaciated valley high above a main valley that has been deepened by glacial erosion.

hanging wall The block of rock lying above an inclined fault. *See more at* **fault**. *Compare* **footwall**.

haploid Relating to or having a single set of each chromosome in a cell or cell nucleus. In animals, only the reproductive cells are haploid. *Compare* **diploid**. *See panel at* **mitosis**.

hard disk A rigid magnetic disk fixed within a disk drive and used for storing computer data. Hard disks hold more data than floppy disks, and data on a hard disk can be accessed faster than data on a floppy disk.

hard drive A disk drive that reads data stored on hard disks.

thunderstorms. Hail forms when raindrops are blown up and down within a cloud, passing repeatedly through layers of warm and freezing air and collecting layers of ice until they are too heavy for the winds to keep them from falling.

hair 1. One of the fine strands that grow from the skin of humans and other mammals. Hair provides insulation against the cold in most mammals. Specialized hairs, such as porcupine quills, provide protection. **2.** A slender growth resembling a mammalian hair, found on insects and other animals. **3.** *Botany.* A fine, thread-like growth from the outer layer of plants.

half-life The average time needed for half the nuclei in a sample of a radioactive substance to undergo radioactive decay. For example, the half-life of radon 220 is 56 seconds. Starting with 100g of radon 220, after 56 seconds only 50g will remain. After 112 seconds, there will be 25g of radon 220, after 168 seconds, only 12.5g will remain, and so on.

halide A chemical compound consisting of a halogen and another element, especially one such as sodium or potassium that readily shares electrons. Salt is a halide.

halite A colourless or white mineral consisting of sodium chloride and occurring as cubic crystals. Halite is found in dried lakebeds in arid climates and is used as table salt.

Halley, Edmund 1656–1742. English astronomer who is best known for his study of comets. He accurately predicted that a comet observed in 1583 would return in 1758, 1835 and

hardness A measure of how easily a mineral can be scratched. Hardness is measured on the Mohs scale.

hard palate *See under* **palate.**

hardware A computer, its components and its related equipment. Hardware includes disc drives, integrated circuits, display screens, cables, modems, speakers and printers. *Compare* **software.**

hare Any of various mammals similar to rabbits but having longer ears and legs and giving birth to active, furred young. Most hares are burrowing animals but do not make extensive warrens the way rabbits do.

Harvey, William 1578–1657. English physician and physiologist who is remembered as the first person to demonstrate the function of the heart and the circulation of blood throughout the human body (1628).

hassium A synthetic, radioactive element that is produced by bombarding lead with iron ions. Its most stable isotope has a half-life of two milliseconds. *Symbol* **Hs**. *Atomic number* 108. *See* **Periodic Table**, pages 260–261.

hawk Any of various birds of prey having a short hooked bill, broad wings and strong claws for seizing prey. Hawks are usually smaller than eagles and larger than falcons.

Hawking, Stephen William Born 1942. British physicist noted for his study of black holes in

Biography

William Harvey

Two centuries before the birth of Christ, the ancient Chinese had developed a clear picture of the circulation of the blood through the heart but the knowledge did not spread beyond China itself. Then in the second century AD, the Greek physician Galen theorized that blood is created in the liver, passes once through the heart, and is then absorbed by bodily tissues. Galen's ideas went largely unchallenged for centuries in Europe, although in the intervening years several other people developed far more accurate models of the circulation of the blood. These include Ibn-Al-Nafis, an Arab doctor who in 1208 AD worked out exactly how blood flowed through the heart, and in the sixteenth century Michael Servetus also wrote a clear description of the circulation. However, it wasn't until 1628, when William Harvey published a book describing the circulation of blood throughout the body, that an accurate model became widely read and gradually accepted. Through his observations of human and animal dissections, Harvey saw that blood flows from one side of the heart to the other and that it flows through the lungs and returns to the heart to be pumped elsewhere. There was one missing part of the cycle: How did the blood pumped to distant body tissues get into the veins to be carried back to the heart? As an answer, Harvey offered his own, unproven theory, one that has since been shown to be true: blood passes from small, outlying arteries through tiny vessels called capillaries into the outlying veins. Harvey's views were so controversial at the time that many of his patients left his care, but his work became the basis for all modern research on the heart and blood vessels.

space and the origin of the universe, especially the big bang theory. His work has provided much of the mathematical basis for scientific explanations of the physical properties of black holes.

hay fever An allergic reaction to pollen that results in sneezing, itching and watery eyes. Hay fever occurs during the pollination season and can be caused by the pollens of many different plants, especially ragweed and certain trees and grasses.

hazardous waste A used or discarded material that can damage the environment and be harmful to health. Certain chemicals left over from industrial processes, and the radioactive remains of fuel used in nuclear power plants, are examples of hazardous waste.

He The symbol for **helium.**

headland An area of hard rock that projects into the sea. Erosion of headlands can cause arches, caves and stacks (pillars of rock), and wave-cut platforms at the base of retreating cliffs.

heart 1. The hollow, muscular organ that pumps blood through the body of a vertebrate animal by contracting and relaxing. In humans and other mammals, it has four chambers, consisting of two atria and two ventricles. The right side of the heart collects blood with low oxygen levels from the veins and pumps it to the lungs. The left side receives blood with high oxygen levels from the lungs and pumps it into the aorta, which carries it to all of the arteries of the body. The heart in other vertebrates functions similarly but often has fewer chambers. **2.** A similar but simpler organ in invertebrate animals.

heart attack A sudden interruption in the normal functioning of the heart that is often accompanied by severe pain. Heart attacks are usually caused by a blockage of one of the coronary arteries that supply the heart muscle itself with blood. Starved of glucose and oxygen, the tissue cannot work and the whole heart stops functioning properly.

heat 1. In physics, energy transferred from one place to another because of a temperature difference. *See panel at* **temperature. 2.** *See* **oestrus.**

heat exchanger A device used to transfer heat from one fluid to another without direct contact of the fluids. Heat exchangers contain a hot fluid that flows through one part of the exchanger and transfers its heat either to a cool fluid (water or air, for example) in another part or to the air outside of the exchanger. A car radiator is a heat exchanger, transferring the heat in a liquid that has circulated through the engine to the air.

heavy hydrogen *See* **deuterium.**

heavy water Water formed of oxygen and deuterium. Heavy water is much like ordinary water but has higher freezing and boiling points. It is used in certain nuclear reactors for cooling.

Heisenberg, Werner Karl 1901–1976. German physicist who was a founder of quantum mechanics. He described the uncertainty principle, which states that the more accurately one knows the position of a particle such as an electron, the less accurately one can know its velocity, and the more accurately one knows a particle's velocity, the less accurately one can know its position. *See more at* **uncertainty principle.**

heliocentric 1. In relation to the sun as seen from the sun's centre: *the heliocentric position of a planet.* **2.** Relating to a model of the solar system or universe having the sun as the centre. *Compare* **geocentric.** *See panel at* **Copernicus.**

heliotropism The growth or movement of a fixed organism, especially a plant, towards or away from sunlight. *—adjective* **heliotropic.**

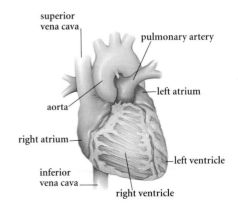

superior vena cava
pulmonary artery
left atrium
aorta
right atrium
inferior vena cava
left ventricle
right ventricle

■ **heart**
adult human heart

Did You Know?

heavy water

How can one drop of water be heavier than another? The answer lies at the atomic level. Normal hydrogen has a nucleus consisting entirely of one proton, around which whirls one electron. However, in a variety of hydrogen called *heavy hydrogen* or *deuterium,* a neutron accompanies the proton in the nucleus. Deuterium thus weighs about twice as much as standard hydrogen. The substance we call *heavy water* is D_2O in which many of the hydrogen atoms are replaced by deuterium. Heavy water played a part in the development of the atomic bomb during World War II. It is an excellent absorber of the neutrons that are produced in large quantities in a nuclear chain reaction. It therefore provided a means of regulating the reactions so that they could be studied safely. Once it was shown that a controlled chain reaction was possible, making a device that could create a powerful uncontrolled chain reaction – an atomic bomb – seemed within reach. Heavy water is still found today in nuclear power plants that use natural uranium fuel.

helium A colourless, odourless element that is a noble gas and occurs in natural gas, in radioactive ores, and in small amounts in the atmosphere. It has the lowest boiling point of any substance and is the second most abundant element in the universe. Helium is used to provide lift for balloons and blimps and to create chemically unreactive atmospheres, for example those used by deep-sea divers. *Symbol* **He**. *Atomic number* 2. *See* **Periodic Table,** pages 260–261.

helix 1. A three-dimensional spiral curve. In mathematical terms, a helix can be described as a curve turning about an axis on the surface of a cylinder or cone while rising at a constant upward angle from a base. **2.** Something, such as a strand of DNA, having a spiral shape.

Helmholtz, Hermann Ludwig Ferdinand von 1821–1894. German physicist and physiologist.

He was a founder of the law of conservation of energy. Helmholtz did pioneering research on vision and invented an instrument for examining the inside of the eye in 1851.

hemi– A prefix meaning "half", as in *hemisphere,* half a sphere.

hemiplegia Paralysis of one side of the body, usually resulting from injury to the brain.

hemisphere 1. One half of a sphere, formed by a plane that passes through the centre of the sphere. **2.** Either the northern or southern half of the Earth as divided by the equator, or the eastern or western half as divided by a meridian. **3.** One half of the celestial sphere. **4.** *See* **cerebral hemisphere.**

hemlock 1. Any of various coniferous evergreen trees of North America and eastern Asia, having small cones and short, flat leaves with two white bands underneath. **2.** Any of several poisonous European plants that have small, white flowers.

henry A unit used to measure electrical

Word History

helium

A lot of elements are named after the place they were first discovered, even if that place is 93 million miles away, as is the case with the element helium. In 1868 the French astronomer Pierre Janssen was studying a solar eclipse with a spectroscope, an instrument that breaks up light into a spectrum. When an element is heated hot enough to glow, the light emitted will produce a unique spectrum (pattern of lines) when refracted through a prism. Janssen noticed that the spectrum of the sun's corona, which is only visible during an eclipse, contained some lines produced by an unknown element. The element was then named *helium,* from *helios,* the Greek word for "sun". We now know that helium is produced abundantly by the nuclear fusion in all stars, and is also found in smaller amounts on Earth. The Greek word *helios* gives us many other words pertaining to the sun, such as *heliocentric* and *perihelion.*

inductance. When a current through a component in a circuit varies at the rate of one ampere per second and induces an electromotive force of one volt across the component, the component has an inductance of one henry.

Henry, Joseph 1797–1878. American physicist who studied electromagnetic phenomena. He constructed the first electromagnetic motor in 1829. The henry unit of inductance is named after him.

hepatic Relating to the liver.

hepatitis Inflammation of the liver, usually caused by infection with a virus. It is characterized by jaundice, a high temperature and weakness throughout the body.

heptagon A polygon having seven sides.

herbicide A chemical used to kill weeds. *Compare* **fungicide, insecticide, pesticide.**

herbivore An animal that feeds mainly or only on plants. *Compare* **carnivore.** *—adjective* **herbivorous.**

Hercules A constellation in the Northern Hemisphere near Lyra and Corona Borealis.

hereditary Passed or capable of being passed from parent to offspring by means of genes: *a hereditary trait.*

heredity The passage of biological traits or characteristics from parents to offspring through the inheritance of genes.

heritable Capable of being passed from one generation to the next through the genes; hereditary.

hermaphrodite An organism, such as an earthworm or flowering plant, having both male and female reproductive organs in a single individual.

hernia A condition in which an organ or other structure of the body protrudes through an abnormal opening in the body structure that normally contains it.

Hero First century AD. Greek mathematician who invented many water-driven and steam-driven machines and developed a formula for determining the area of a triangle.

herpes Any of several infections caused by a virus, characterized by the eruption of painful blisters on the skin or a mucous membrane.

herpetology The scientific study of reptiles and amphibians.

Herschel Family of British astronomers. Sir **William Herschel** (1738–1822) discovered Uranus (1781) and catalogued more than 800 binary stars and 2500 nebulae. His sister **Caroline Herschel** (1750–1848) discovered 8 comets and several nebulae and star clusters, and published a star catalogue in 1798. His son Sir **John Frederick William Herschel** (1792–1871) discovered 525 nebulae and pioneered celestial photography. *See panel on* page 164 *and at* **infrared.**

hertz A unit used to measure the frequency of vibrations and waves. One hertz is equal to one cycle per second. Radio waves are usually measured in megahertz, or millions of hertz.

Hertz, Gustav Ludwig 1887–1975. German physicist who, working with James Franck, showed that atoms will only absorb a fixed amount of energy. In this way he demonstrated the quantized nature of the atom's electron energy levels. Hertz's work was vital for the ideas of Niels Bohr (developing his theory of atomic structure), and for Max Planck (working with ideas on quantum theory).

Usage

heritable/congenital

The words *heritable* and *congenital* are often confused when used in describing medical conditions or diseases. A heritable disease is one that results from a variation or defect in the genetic make-up of an individual. Because of their genetic nature, heritable diseases, such as haemophilia, can be passed from one generation to the next. In this regard the diseases are no different from other genetic traits. A congenital disease is simply one that appears at birth (*congenital* comes from Latin *com–*, meaning "together", and *genitus,* meaning "born"). Congenital diseases may be heritable ones, but they may also result from some factor, such as a drug, infection or injury, that has upset the careful timing and balance of the developmental process in the uterus.

Biography

William and Caroline Herschel

Both William and Caroline Herschel began their professional careers as musicians. They were born in Germany and later moved to England, where Caroline became a soprano soloist in performances conducted by her brother. William's background in music theory spurred him to study mathematics and astronomy, and he taught his sister in turn. Both brother and sister produced a string of important discoveries. William was the first astronomer to study binary stars. His careful observations and his skill at mapping the stars led him to discover the planet Uranus in 1781. It was the first new planet to be discovered since ancient times. He further discovered two satellites of Uranus, Titania and Oberon (1787), and two of Saturn, Mimas and Enceladus (1789–1790). King George III appointed William his Astronomer Royal in 1787, and

Caroline was made his assistant. Caroline observed her first comet in 1786 and later discovered seven others, as well as nebulae and star clusters. After her brother's death in 1822, Caroline reorganized and published his catalogue of nebulae. She also continued her own observations up to the end of her life.

Hertzsprung-Russell diagram A graph of the natural brightness of stars plotted against their surface temperature or colour. It is used in the study of the life cycles of stars.

Hess, Harry Hammond 1906–1969. American geologist who studied the sea floor and developed the theory of sea-floor spreading. He theorized that sea floors were constantly renewed by the flow of magma from the Earth's mantle through the oceanic rifts. Hess's hypothesis became an important component of the theory of plate tectonics.

heterotrophic Relating to an organism that cannot manufacture its own food and instead obtains its food and energy by taking in organic substances, usually plant or animal matter. All animals, protozoans, fungi and most bacteria are heterotrophic. ❖ An organism that consumes organic matter or other organisms for food is called a **heterotroph**. *Compare* **autotrophic**.

heterozygous Having a contrasting pair of alleles for a particular gene on a chromosome, for

example, having one allele for tongue-rolling and one allele for non-rolling, or one allele for blue eyes and one allele for brown eyes. *Compare* **homozygous**.

Hewish, Antony Born 1924. British astronomer. In 1967, working with the astronomer Susan Bell Burnell, he discovered the first pulsar.

hexagon A polygon having six sides.

hexagonal 1. Having six sides. **2.** Relating to a crystal having three axes of equal length intersecting at angles of 60° in one plane, and a fourth axis of a different length that is

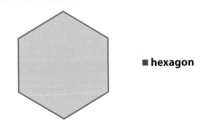

■ **hexagon**

perpendicular to this plane. The mineral calcite has hexagonal crystals. *See more at* **crystal.**

Hf The symbol for **hafnium.**

Hg The symbol for **mercury.**

hibernation An inactive state resembling deep sleep in which certain animals living in cold climates pass the winter. In hibernation, the body temperature is lowered and breathing and heart rates slow down. Hibernation protects the animal from cold and reduces the need for food during the season when food is scarce. *Compare* **aestivation.**

hiccough *or* **hiccup** A sudden and uncontrolled contraction of the diaphragm, causing the breath to be quickly drawn in and then immediately cut off by a closing of the throat.

high blood pressure A condition in which the pressure of the blood, especially in the arteries, is abnormally high. It is often caused because the blood vessels have become narrow or stiffened with age or as a result of fatty deposits. High blood pressure can increase the risk of heart attack or stroke. Also called *hypertension.*

high-tension Having a high voltage: *high-tension wires.*

high tide The time at which the tide reaches its highest level.

hilum A mark or scar on a seed, such as a bean, showing where it was formerly attached to the plant.

hindbrain The rearmost part of the brain in vertebrate animals. In humans, it consists of the pons and the medulla oblongata. *Compare* **forebrain, midbrain.**

hipbone Either of two large, flat bones, each forming one of the outer borders of the pelvis and consisting of the fused ilium, ischium and pubis.

Hipparchus Second century BC. Greek astronomer who mapped the position of 850 stars in the earliest known star chart. His observations of the heavens formed the basis of Ptolemy's Earth-centred model of the universe.

Hippocrates 460?–377? BC. Greek physician who is credited with establishing the foundations of scientific medicine. He and his followers worked to distinguish medicine from superstition

and magic beliefs by basing their treatment of illness on close observation and rational deduction.

hippopotamus A large, chiefly aquatic African mammal having a barrel-shaped body, thick skin, short legs and a wide-mouthed muzzle. Because its skin loses water quickly when exposed to the air, the hippopotamus must spend the day in water. It feeds at night on land grasses. *See panel at* **rhinoceros.**

histamine An organic compound found widely in animals and plants. In humans and other mammals, histamine is released as part of the body's immune response, causing a variety of changes in the body, including enlargement of the blood vessels, tightening of the airways and faster beating of the heart. The itchiness and sneezing typical of an allergic reaction are caused by the release of histamine.

histidine An essential amino acid. *See more at* **amino acid.**

histology The scientific study of the microscopic structure of plant and animal tissues.

histone Any of several proteins that, together with DNA, make up most of the chromatin in a cell nucleus. They are vital for the packing of the DNA into chromosomes before cell division can take place.

HIV Short for *human immunodeficiency virus.* The virus that causes AIDS by infecting the body's immune system.

hive 1. A structure for housing bees, especially honeybees. 2. A colony of bees living in such a structure.

hives Itchy welts on the skin that are redder or paler than the surrounding skin. Hives may result from an allergic reaction, but often the cause is unknown.

Ho The symbol for **holmium.**

Hodgkin, Dorothy Mary Crowfoot 1910–1994. British chemist. Using X-ray techniques, she determined the structure of several complex molecules, including penicillin and vitamin B_{12}.

Holmes, Arthur 1890–1965. British geologist who pioneered a method of determining the age of rocks by measuring their radioactive components.

holmium A soft, silvery, easily shaped metallic element of the lanthanide series. When exposed to a magnetic field, holmium becomes highly magnetic. It is mainly used in scientific research but has also been used to make electronic devices. *Symbol* **Ho**. *Atomic number* 67. *See* **Periodic Table**, pages 260–261.

Holocene The more recent of the two epochs of the Quaternary Period, beginning at the end of the last Ice Age, about 10,000 years ago. It is characterized by the development of human civilizations. Also called *Recent. See chart at* **geological time**, pages 148–149.

hologram A three-dimensional image of an object made by holography.

holography A method of making a three-dimensional image of an object by using a divided beam of light from a laser. The laser light is directed by mirrors so that one beam reflects off the object onto a photographic plate or film while the other beam is aimed directly at the plate or film. The two beams are combined to form a three-dimensional image of the object.

homeopathy A form of alternative medicine. The idea behind homeopathy is that "like cures like". Homeopathy differs from conventional medicine because it relies on giving patients very dilute solutions of drugs or natural extracts which, given in large amounts to a healthy person, would cause symptoms like those of the disease itself. Homeopathy aims to work with the body's natural defences and does not try to suppress symptoms, but to treat root causes.

homeostasis The maintenance of a steady internal state regardless of external conditions. Cells are very sensitive to changes in their environment. Whole organisms and individual cells regulate their chemical processes to keep their internal environment as stable as possible. This often involves complicated sensory systems and feedback mechanisms. The ability of mammals to maintain a steady internal body temperature regardless of the external temperature is an example of homeostasis.

hominid A member of the family of primates whose only living members are modern humans. All earlier hominids, such as australopithecines and members of the species *Homo erectus,* are now extinct.

Did You Know?

hologram

If you tear an ordinary photograph in two, each piece shows only a part of the original image. If you break a *hologram* in two, however, you end up with two holograms, each of which shows the entire original image, although from slightly different points of view. That's because each spot on a hologram contains enough information to show how the entire image would look if it were viewed from a particular vantage point. Imagine looking at a room through a peephole set in a solid door. What you see depends on where in the door the peephole is placed. Each piece of the hologram is a "peephole" view, and that's what makes the image look three-dimensional: as you move the hologram around or look at different parts of it, you see the original object from different angles, just as if it were a truly three-dimensional object and you were walking around it. The amount of information contained in holograms makes them very useful. They are much harder to copy than simple two-dimensional images, since to forge a hologram you'd have to know what the original object looked like from many angles. That's why credit cards, CDs, and other items include holographic stickers as indicators of authenticity.

Homo erectus An extinct species of humans that lived during the Pleistocene Epoch from about 1.6 million years ago to 200,000 years ago. Remains of *Homo erectus*, the first species of humans to master fire, have been found in Africa, Europe and Asia. It is widely thought to be the direct ancestor of modern humans.

Homo habilis An extinct species of humans considered to be an ancestor of modern humans and the earliest hominid to make tools. This species existed between about 2.2 and 1.5 million years ago.

homologous 1. Similar in structure and evolutionary origin but having different functions,

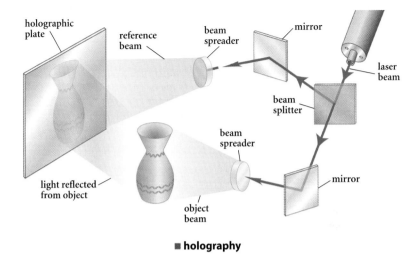

■ **holography**

as a human's arm and a seal's flipper. *Compare* **analogous. 2.** Being a set of two pairs of chromosomes, one pair from the female parent and one from the male parent, having genes for the same trait in the same positions. Genes on homologous chromosomes may not have the same form, however. For example, one set of homologous chromosomes may contain an allele for brown eyes and the other for blue eyes.

homolosine projection A method of making a flat map of the Earth's surface with interruptions in the oceans so that the continents appear with the most accurate area and shape possible. *Compare* **conic projection, Mercator projection, sinusoidal projection.**

Homo sapiens The modern species of humans. *Homo sapiens* evolved probably between 250,000 and 100,000 years ago in Africa. The closest living relative of *Homo sapiens* is the chimpanzee.

homozygous Having two of the same genes for a hereditary trait such as tallness at corresponding positions on the chromosomes. *Compare* **heterozygous.**

Hooke, Robert 1635–1703. English physicist, inventor, and mathematician. With Robert Boyle, Hooke demonstrated that both combustion and respiration require air and that sound will not travel in a vacuum. He studied numerous objects under microscopes and was the first to use the word *cell* to describe the patterns he observed.

Hooke's law In physics, a law describing the elastic behaviour of a material. Hooke's law states that the extension of an elastic material is directly proportional to the force required to produce the extension. If the material is stretched too far, Hooke's law no longer applies. The point beyond which Hooke's law no longer applies is called the limit of proportionality.

hookworm Any of numerous parasitic worms that have a hooked mouthpart by which they fasten themselves to the inside wall of the intestines of various animals, including humans.

Hopper, Grace Murray 1906–1992. American

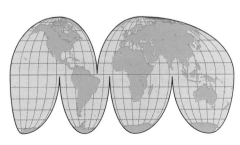

■ **homolosine projection**

Did You Know?

hormones

Most people are aware of the role of the nervous system in controlling the actions of the body. Less well know are the *hormones*, yet these chemical messengers control many of the processes going on in the human body at any one time. And hormones are just as important in other animals and even plants! In people, hormones are usually produced in special glands known as *endocrine glands*. They are secreted into the blood stream and carried around the body. The hormone molecules are picked up by special receptors on the cells of their target organ, where the message is received, understood and acted on.

Hormones carry out an amazing range of control functions in the body. Growth hormone, produced in a tiny gland in the brain, controls the growth of all the body tissues, including the bones, the muscles and the body organs. Oestrogen controls sexual development in girls and is involved in the monthly reproductive cycle, whilst testosterone controls sexual development in boys and stimulates sperm production throughout life. The level of glucose in the blood – and so the energy available to cells – is controlled largely by the hormone insulin, made in the pancreas. Thyroxine, made in the thyroid gland in the neck, controls the metabolic rate of the cells of the body.

The only time most people are aware of their hormones – apart from when they are going through puberty or suffering from premenstrual tension – is when something goes wrong. If too little or too much hormone is made by one of the endocrine glands, then serious health problems can arise. If the pancreas does not make enough insulin, the individual suffers from diabetes which can be fatal if not treated. Too much growth hormone results in giantism, whilst too little means a child fails to grow. Fortunately, hormonal diseases can usually be treated by either giving synthetic hormones or by operating to remove part of the gland. People have even learned to use certain human hormones for different purposes – the contraceptive pill uses a combination of female hormones to prevent pregnancy, whilst in fertility treatment different combinations of female hormones are used to help couples have children.

Plant hormones are also very important. They are involved in plant growth, responses to light and gravity and also in the setting and ripening of fruit. Farmers and commercial fruit-sellers make use of artificial versions of these hormones as weedkillers and also to control the ripening of fruit ready for sale.

mathematician and computer programmer who is noted for her development of programming languages.

horizon The circle on the celestial sphere along which the Earth and the sky appear to meet.

hormone A substance produced in one part of the body, especially in an endocrine gland, that has an effect on another part of the body, to which it is usually carried in the bloodstream. Hormones regulate many biological processes, including growth and metabolism.

hormone replacement therapy *or* HRT HRT is the name given to a form of treatment used to help women overcome the symptoms of the menopause. When the levels of natural female hormones drop as the ovaries become inactive, some women suffer uncomfortable symptoms. Also, once women have passed the menopause they are more likely to develop osteoporosis and heart disease. HRT involves giving women replacement hormones, which can help them to feel much better and look younger, and which help to prevent the thinning of the bones. However HRT does not suit all women. Many suffer unpleasant side effects, and recent research has suggested that HRT may increase the risk of women developing breast cancer and cardiovascular problems.

horn 1. Either of the bony growths projecting from the upper part of the head of certain hoofed mammals, such as cattle, sheep and goats. The horns of these animals are never shed, and they consist of bone covered by a hard substance called keratin. **2.** A hard growth that looks like a horn, such as an antler or a growth on the head of a giraffe or rhinoceros. Unlike true horns, antlers are shed yearly and have a velvety covering, and the horns of a rhinoceros are made not of bone but of hairy skin fused with keratin. **3.** The hard durable substance that forms the outer covering of true horns. It consists of keratin. *See panel at* **keratin.**

hornblende A common, green to black mineral found in many metamorphic and igneous rocks. It is composed of iron, calcium, magnesium and other metals.

horology The science of measuring time.

horse latitudes Either of two regions found over the Atlantic and Pacific Oceans about 30° north and south of the equator. Because winds are generally light and unsteady in the horse latitudes, sailing ships were often caught in them for days without enough wind to move.

horsepower A unit used to measure the power of engines and motors. One unit of horsepower is equal to the power needed to lift 550 pounds one foot in one second. This unit has been widely replaced by the *watt* in scientific usage. 1 horsepower is approximately equal to 750 watts.

horseshoe crab Any of various marine arthropods that have a large rounded shell covering the body, two large compound eyes on the shell and a stiff pointed tail. Horseshoe crabs are not in fact crabs, but belong to an ancient order of arthropods related to the spiders and extinct trilobites.

horticulture The science or art of raising and tending plants, especially flowers, fruits and vegetables.

host A cell or organism, such as a plant, animal or alga, on or in which another organism lives or feeds. For example, a cat may be a host to fleas that feed on its blood, or human skin cells may be a host to the athlete's foot fungus.

hot spot A volcanic area, usually 100 to 200 kilometres across, believed to lie above a rising plume of hot magma within the Earth. The source of the heat is thought to be the decay of radioactive elements deep within the Earth. The Hawaiian Islands are believed to have formed as the result of a tectonic plate moving over a hot spot. *See more at* **tectonic boundary.**

hot spring A spring of warm water, usually having a temperature greater than that of the human body.

HRT *See* **hormone replacement therapy.**

Hs The symbol for **hassium.**

Hubble, Edwin Powell 1889–1953. American astronomer. He demonstrated that there are galaxies beyond our own and that they are receding from ours, bolstering the theory that the universe is expanding. Hubble also established the first measurements for the age and radius of the known universe. His methods for determining them remain in use today. *See panel at* **Doppler effect.**

hue The property of colours by which they are seen as ranging from red through yellow, green and blue, as determined by the dominant wavelength of the light. *See more at* **colour.**

hull 1. The dry outer covering of a fruit, seed or nut; a husk. **2.** The enlarged calyx of a fruit, such as a strawberry, that is usually green and easily detached.

human 1. A member of the species *Homo sapiens*; a human being. **2.** A member of any of the extinct species of the genus *Homo,* such as *Homo erectus* or *Homo habilis,* that are considered ancestral or closely related to modern humans.

Human Genome Project A scientific research project designed to study and identify all of the genes in the human genome, to determine the base-pair sequences in human DNA, and to store this information in computer databases. The Human Genome Project is a collaboration between the scientists of a number of countries,

Word History

humour

Doctors in ancient times and in the Middle Ages thought the human body contained a mixture of four substances, called humours, that determined a person's health and character. The humours were fluids (*humor* means "fluid" in Latin), namely blood, phlegm, black bile and yellow bile. Illnesses were thought to be caused by an imbalance in the humours, as were defects in personality. Too much black bile, for example, was thought to make one gloomy, and too much yellow bile was thought to make one short-tempered. Modern English has words referring to these moods that come from the Greek words for the relevant humours. We call a gloomy person *melancholic,* from the Greek term for "black bile", and we call a short-tempered person *choleric,* from the Greek word for "yellow bile". Our word *humorous,* in fact, originally meant "having changeable moods due to the influence of different humours".

including the UK and the USA, the USA playing a major role in setting the project up in 1990. The first rough draft of the human genome was produced in the year 2000.

Humboldt, Baron (Friedrich Heinrich)

Alexander von 1769–1859. German naturalist and writer. He undertook scientific expeditions in South America, Asia and Europe and published works recording his observations. Humboldt made important contributions to the study of volcanoes, mountain ranges, ocean currents and the relation of climate to plant growth.

humerus The bone of the upper arm or the upper portion of the foreleg. *See more at* **skeleton.**

humidity *See* **absolute humidity, relative humidity.**

humour One of the four fluids of the body – blood, phlegm, black bile and yellow bile – whose relative proportions were thought in ancient and medieval medicine to determine general health and character.

humus A dark-brown or black organic substance made up of decayed plant or animal matter, which makes up an important component of the soil. Humus provides nutrients for plants and increases the ability of soil to retain water.

hurricane A severe, rotating tropical storm with heavy rains and cyclonic winds exceeding 119 kilometres per hour. Hurricanes originate in the tropical parts of the Atlantic Ocean or the Caribbean Sea and move generally northwards. They lose force when they move over land or colder seas. *See panel at* **cyclone.**

husbandry The application of scientific principles to agriculture, especially to animal breeding.

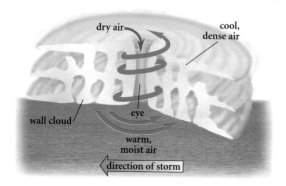

dry air
cool, dense air
wall cloud
eye
warm, moist air
direction of storm

■ **hurricane**
A hurricane forms when clusters of thunderstorms converge over warm water. Warm, moist air is drawn up into the clouds, creating tunnels as the air rises. The strongest winds and heaviest rains centre around the eye of the storm, while the eye itself remains calm.

Biography

James Hutton

As a gentleman farmer in late 18th-century Scotland, James Hutton noticed that the farmers' soil was carried away, ultimately out to sea, by the wind and rain. Hutton was a religious man, and he imagined that a God who was benevolent would create a way to recreate this lost soil. He theorized that the soil must be replaced when older rocks are pushed upward, forming new mountains, which are then eroded by the weather into soil. Hutton proposed heat as the source of this mountain-building: as it built up inside the Earth, it forced rocks to move upwards and created newer rocks from lava. He called this process Plutonism, in honour of Pluto, the Greek god of the underworld. Because the cycle of uplift and erosion had to take a very long time, Hutton concluded that the Earth must be very old. It was not until the 20th century that geologists, using a technique called radiometric dating, demonstrated that the Earth is in fact over four billion years old. Because of his groundbreaking insights, Hutton is known as the father of geology.

husk The dry outer covering of certain seeds or fruits, as of an ear of corn or a nut.

Hutton, James 1726–1797. Scottish geologist whose theories of rock and land formation laid the foundation for modern geology. He showed that, over long periods of time, the erosion of rocks produces sediments, which are transported by water, ice and air to locations at or near sea level. These sediments eventually become solidified into other rocks. He also showed that the Earth's heat causes igneous rocks to form and mountains to form through the upheaval of rock layers. Hutton demonstrated that the geological processes that created the landforms on the Earth are ongoing.

Huygens, Christiaan 1629–1695. Dutch physicist and astronomer. In 1655 he was the first person to describe accurately Saturn's rings, and discovered one of its satellites using a telescope he made himself. He made the first pendulum clock in 1657. Huygens also proposed that light consists of waves that vibrate up and down, perpendicular to the direction in which it travels. This theory, which explained light better than Newton's theory, was made public in 1690.

hybrid A plant or animal that has parents of different species or varieties. A mule, which is the offspring of a male donkey and a female horse, is an example of a hybrid. Hybrid animals are usually unable to reproduce.

hydra Any of several small freshwater polyps having a simple cylindrical body with a mouth-like opening surrounded by tentacles. The young develop from eggs or from buds.

hydrate *noun* A compound produced by combining a substance chemically with water. Many minerals and crystalline substances are

■ **hydra**
On the left, an immature hydra can be seen budding from the parent.

hydraulic

hydrates. —*verb* **1.** To combine a compound with water, especially to form a hydrate. **2.** To supply water to a person in order to restore or maintain a balance of fluids.

hydraulic 1. Operated by the pressure of water or other liquids in motion, especially when forced through an opening: *a hydraulic brake; a hydraulic jack.* **2.** Relating to hydraulics. **3.** Capable of hardening under water: *hydraulic cement.*

hydraulics The scientific study of water and other liquids, their uses in engineering, and the forces and pressures associated with them.

hydride A compound of hydrogen with another element or radical.

hydro– A prefix that means: **1.** Water, as in *hydroelectric.* **2.** Hydrogen, as in *hydrocarbon.*

hydrocarbon Any of numerous organic compounds, such as benzene, that contain only carbon and hydrogen.

hydrochloric acid A solution of hydrogen chloride in water. It is a very strong, poisonous and corrosive acid with a sharp odour and is used in food processing, metal cleaning and dyeing. Small amounts of hydrochloric acid are also secreted by the stomachs of animals for digestion.

hydrodynamics The scientific study of the forces exerted by fluids in motion.

hydroelectric Generating electricity through the use of the energy of running water: *a hydroelectric power station.*

hydrogen A colourless, odourless, highly flammable gaseous element that is the lightest and most abundant element in the universe. It occurs in water in combination with oxygen, in most organic compounds, and in small amounts in the atmosphere as a gaseous mixture of its three isotopes (protium, deuterium and tritium). In the sun and other stars, the conversion of hydrogen into helium by nuclear fusion produces heat and light. Hydrogen is used to make rocket fuel, synthetic ammonia and methanol, to hydrogenate fats and oils, and to refine petroleum. *Symbol* **H.** *Atomic number* 1. *See* **Periodic Table**, *pages* 260–261. *See panel at* **oxygen**.

hydrogenate To treat or combine chemically with hydrogen. Liquid vegetable oils are often hydrogenated to turn them into solids.

hydrogen bomb An extremely destructive bomb whose explosive power is derived from the energy released when hydrogen atoms are fused to form helium. A hydrogen bomb uses an atomic bomb to compress the hydrogen atoms and is much more powerful than an atomic bomb.

hydrogen bond A weak chemical bond in which a hydrogen atom that is already bonded to an atom in a molecule interacts weakly with another atom,

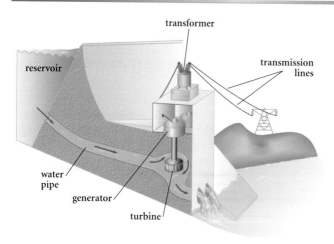

■ **hydroelectric**
Hydroelectric power uses the force of moving water to turn turbines. The turbines drive generators that convert the mechanical energy of moving water to electrical energy. Electricity is then changed by a transformer to the appropriate voltage and sent along transmission lines to consumers.

either in the same molecule or in a different one. The second atom is usually of a type that strongly attracts electrons, such as nitrogen or oxygen.

hydrogen carbonate The group HCO_3 or a compound containing it, such as sodium bicarbonate.

hydrogen chloride A colourless, corrosive, suffocating gas, HCl, used in making plastics and in many industrial processes. When mixed with water, it forms hydrochloric acid.

hydrogen cyanide A colourless, flammable, extremely poisonous liquid, HCN. It is used to make dyes, poisons and plastics. A solution of hydrogen cyanide in water forms a colourless acid that has a characteristic smell of bitter almonds.

hydrogen peroxide A colourless, dense liquid, H_2O_2, that is often used as a bleach or is diluted with water for use as an antiseptic.

hydrogen sulphide A colourless, poisonous gas, H_2S, that smells like rotten eggs. It is formed naturally by decaying organic matter and is found in volcanic gases. It has many industrial uses.

hydrologic cycle *See* **water cycle.**

hydrology The scientific study of the properties, distribution and effects of water on the Earth's surface, in the soil and underlying rocks, and in the atmosphere. —*adjective* **hydrologic.**

hydrolysis The splitting of a chemical compound into two or more new compounds by reacting with water. Hydrolysis plays a role in the breakdown of food in the body, as in the conversion of starch to glucose.

hydrometer An instrument used to measure the density of a liquid as compared to that of water. Hydrometers consist of a calibrated glass tube ending in a weighted glass sphere that makes the tube stand upright. The lower the density of the liquid, the deeper the tube sinks.

hydrophobia *See* **rabies.**

hydrophyte A plant that grows wholly or partly submerged in water. The lotus, water lily and bulrush are hydrophytes.

hydroponics The growing of plants in water supplied with nutrients rather than in soil.

hydrosphere All of the Earth's water, including surface water (water in seas, lakes and rivers), groundwater (water beneath the Earth's surface), ice, and water vapour in the atmosphere. *Compare* **asthenosphere, atmosphere, lithosphere.**

hydrostatics The branch of physics that deals with the study of fluids at rest and the forces and pressures associated with them.

hydrothermal 1. Relating to hot water, especially water heated by the Earth's internal heat. ❖ Power that is generated using the Earth's hot water is called **hydrothermal energy. 2.** *Geology.* Relating to the rocks, ore deposits and springs produced by hot water or magma.

hydrotropism The growth or movement of a fixed organism, especially a plant, towards or away from water. —*adjective* **hydrotropic.**

hydrous *Chemistry.* Containing water: *a hydrous salt.*

hydroxide An inorganic chemical compound containing a hydroxide ion, OH^-. Metal hydroxides are bases and nonmetal hydroxides are acids.

hydroxyl The group OH. It has a valency of 1 and is present in bases, certain acids, hydroxides and alcohols.

hyena Any of several meat-eating, dog-like mammals of Africa and Asia that feed mainly in groups as scavengers. Hyenas have very powerful jaws, a thick neck and relatively short hind limbs.

hygrometer An instrument that measures the humidity of the air.

Word History

hydrophobia

Hydrophobia is an older term for the disease rabies, and it means "fear of water". Because of this name, many people think that rabies makes one afraid of water. In fact, this is not the case (although rabies does cause mental confusion of other kinds). The name hydrophobia comes from the fact that animals and people with rabies get spasms in their throat muscles that are so painful that they cannot eat or drink, and so will refuse water in spite of being very thirsty.

hygroscope

hygroscope An instrument that records changes in the humidity of the air.

hymen A membrane that partly closes the opening of the vagina.

Hypatia 370?–415 AD. Greek philosopher, mathematician and astronomer whose writings on mathematics and astronomy were used as textbooks. She also invented instruments used to view the stars.

hyper– A prefix that means "more than normal",

■ **hyperbola**

Usage

hypothesis/law/theory

At its simplest, a law of science can be thought of as a summary of observations that scientists have made. A *law* is built on a limited number of observations, which makes it necessary for scientists to assume that it is possible to predict the behaviour of the world around us in the future based on observations made in the past. This is an assumption common to the whole of science, and the success of science in doing just this suggests that the assumption is a reasonable one.

A law supplies us with information about *how* the world may be expected to behave, based upon past experience, but it does not tell us anything about *why* the world behaves in this way. For example, the "gas laws" predict the behaviour of gases under given conditions, but they do not tell us very much about what a gas actually is or why it behaves in a particular way. It is the job of *theories* in science to tell us about the behaviour of things in rather more depth. Strangely, scientists and philosophers find it very hard to agree on the way in which scientific theories come about, although most would accept that they are best described as being "invented" (that is, made up by people) rather than simply "discovered".

One way in which theories are produced,

based on the ideas of the philosopher Sir Karl Popper, runs as follows: A scientist wishing to explain something about the behaviour of the world will formulate a tentative idea, called at this stage a *hypothesis*. This hypothesis must be based on existing scientific knowledge, but as long as it does not contradict this knowledge, it can be as bold and imaginative as the scientist wishes. The scientist then tests the hypothesis by carrying out a number of *experiments*. If it survives this testing, an account of the hypothesis and the tests it has survived is then published in a scientific journal so that other scientists can read about it and decide whether it is true or not, a process called *peer review*. Hypotheses that survive the process of peer review become accepted scientific knowledge, that is, they become theories.

It is important not to confuse use of the term "theory" in a scientific context with its use in everyday life, where it is often used to mean "guess". (For example, I may have a "theory" about why a particular football team is unlikely to win any competitions next year.) A theory in science is not a guess, but a very well-established framework that explains many observations and experimental results. A good theory will produce new hypotheses that can be tested, and so on.

eg *hyperactive*, more active than normal, or *hypertension*, blood pressure that is higher than normal.

hyperactivity **1.** A condition of greater than normal activity. **2.** An abnormally high level of activity or excitement shown by a person, especially a child, that interferes with the ability to concentrate or interact with others.

hyperbola A plane curve formed by a plane that cuts through both parts of a cone but does not pass through its vertex.

hyperopia *See* **longsightedness.**

hypertension *See* **high blood pressure.**

hypertext A computer-based text retrieval system that enables a user to access particular locations in web pages or other electronic documents by clicking on links within specific web pages or documents.

hypha (*plural* **hyphae**) One of the long slender tubes that form the structural parts of the body of a fungus. Masses of hyphae make up the mycelium.

hypnosis A trance-like state resembling sleep in which a person becomes very responsive to suggestions from another. A hypnotist can bring about a state of hypnosis in another individual where that person focuses exclusive attention on a particular object. It can also be self-induced through concentration and relaxation.

hypo– *or* **hyp–** A prefix that means "beneath" or "below", as in *hypodermic,* below the skin. It also means "less than normal", as in *hypoglycaemia,* having a level of sugar that is less than normal in the blood.

hypochondria A condition in which a person often believes that he or she is ill without actually being ill, or worries so much about becoming ill that it affects his or her life. ❖ A person with hypochondria is called a **hypochondriac.**

hypodermic needle A hollow needle used in medical syringes to inject a fluid beneath the skin.

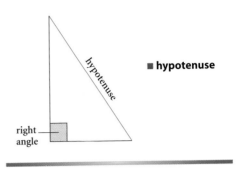
■ **hypotenuse**

hypoglycaemia An abnormally low level of sugar in the blood, usually caused by too much insulin and resulting in weakness and dizziness.

hypotenuse The side of a right-angled triangle opposite the right angle. It is the longest side, and the square of its length is equal to the sum of the squares of the lengths of the other two sides.

hypothalamus The part of the brain in vertebrate animals that lies below the thalamus. It regulates many biological processes, including body temperature, thirst, hunger and sleeping. The hypothalamus also controls hormone production of the pituitary gland.

hypothermia Abnormally low body temperature, often caused by prolonged exposure to cold.

hypothesis (*plural* **hypotheses**) A statement that explains a set of facts and can be tested to determine if it is false or inaccurate.

hypothesize To form a hypothesis.

hypothetical Relating to or based on a hypothesis: *a hypothetical state of matter that has not yet been shown to exist.*

hyracotherium (*plural* **hyracotheria**) A small primitive horse that lived about 60 million years ago during the early Eocene Epoch. It had three or four hoofed toes on each foot and is sometimes considered the ancestor of modern horses. It is sometimes called the "dawn horse", a translation of its earlier scientific name, *Eohippus.*

Hz Abbreviation of **hertz.**

I i

i The number whose square is equal to −1. Numbers expressed in terms of *i* are called imaginary or complex numbers. *See more at* **imaginary number, complex number.**

I The symbol for **iodine.**

Ibn al-Haytham *Latin name* **Alhazen** 965?–1040? Arab mathematician who is best known for his book on optics, which became very influential in Europe after it was translated in the 12th century. It contained a detailed description of the human eye and disproved the older Greek idea that vision is the result of the eye sending out rays to the object being looked at.

Ibn-Al-Nafis 1208–1288. Ibn-Al-Nafis was a physician, a linguist, a philosopher and a historian. He was the first chief of Al-Mansuri Hospital in Cairo and the dean of the School of Medicine in 1284 AD. He worked out the correct anatomy of the heart and the way the blood flowed through it. Ibn-Al-Nafis also worked out the correct anatomy of the lungs and was the first person known to record the coronary circulation – the vessels supplying blood to the heart itself. Shortly after his work had been translated into Latin in the 16th century, European scientists began to "discover" the same things.

Ibn Sina, Hakim *Also known as* **Avicenna**

■ **iceberg**
a "bergy bit" iceberg

980–1037. Persian physician and philosopher whose medical textbook, *Canons of Medicine,* greatly influenced European medical studies until the 17th century.

ibuprofen A medicine used to reduce fever, pain or inflammation.

ice Water frozen solid, normally at or below a temperature of 0°C (32°F).

ice age 1. Any of several cold periods during which glaciers covered much of the Earth. **2. Ice Age.** The most recent glacial period, which occurred during the Pleistocene Epoch and ended about 10,000 years ago. During the Pleistocene Ice Age, great sheets of ice which could be over a kilometre thick covered most of Greenland, Canada and the northern United States as well as northern Europe and Russia.

iceberg A massive body of floating ice that has broken away from a glacier. Most of an iceberg lies underwater, but because ice is not quite as dense as water, about one ninth of it remains above the surface. Icebergs are classified by their height above the waterline: "very large" = 75 metres or over; "large" = 46 to 75 metres; "medium" = 16 to 45 metres; "small" = 5 to 15 metres. Icebergs with a height between 1 and 4 metres above the waterline are known as "bergy bits", and less than 1 metre as "growlers".

icecap 1. A glacier spreading out from a centre and covering a large area. **2.** A polar cap.

ichthyology The scientific study of fish.

ichthyosaur Any of various extinct sea reptiles of the Mesozoic Era having a long beak, four flippers, a dolphin-like body and a tail with a large fin.

ideal gas A gas in which there is no force of attraction between the individual molecules, which occupy zero volume. Such a gas would obey the gas laws exactly. No known gas qualifies as an ideal gas, although a gas may behave approximately like an ideal gas under conditions in which it is at low pressure and at a temperature well above its boiling point.

igneous Relating to rocks formed by the cooling and hardening of magma or molten lava. Basalt and granite are examples of igneous rocks. *See table at* **rock.**

iguana Any of various large tropical American lizards, often having spiny projections along the back.

ileum The lower and largest part of the small intestine, connecting the jejunum to the caecum of the large intestine. It produces enzymes that complete the digestion of food. The lining is covered with microscopic projections, called villi, which give an increased surface area for the absorption of digested food molecules into the blood stream.

ilium The uppermost of the three bones that fuse together to form each of the hipbones in many vertebrate animals. *See more at* **skeleton.**

imaginary number A type of complex number in which the multiple of *i* (the square root of –1) is not equal to zero. Examples of imaginary numbers include 4*i* and 2 – 3*i*, but not 3 + 0*i* (which is just 3). *See more at* **complex number.**

imago An insect in its sexually mature adult stage after metamorphosis. *Compare* **larva, nymph, pupa.**

immiscible Incapable of being mixed or blended together. Immiscible liquids that are shaken together eventually separate into layers. Oil and water are immiscible. *Compare* **miscible.**

immune response A response of the body to a foreign substance, called an antigen, especially a microorganism or virus that causes disease. The immune response involves the action of white blood cells called lymphocytes, which work to deactivate foreign antigens, often by stimulating the production of antibodies.

immune system The system in humans and other animals that provides immunity by protecting against disease-causing agents, such as bacteria, viruses, parasites and fungi. The immune system is composed of the skin and mucous membranes, which provide an external barrier to infection, and the cells involved in the body's immune response, such as lymphocytes.

immunity Resistance of the body to infection by

■ **iguana**

a disease-causing agent, such as a bacterium or virus. Immunity is usually provided by the body's own immune system, which is determined by the action of one's genes. It may also be brought about by having had a disease or infection in the past and recovering from it. Immunity can also be induced artificially, especially by vaccination.

immunization 1. The production of immunity to an infectious disease in an individual through inoculation or vaccination. **2.** A specific inoculation or vaccination. —*verb* **immunize.**

immunodeficiency The inability to produce a normal immune response, usually as a result of a disease or inherited disorder.

immunoglobulin *See* **antibody.**

immunology The scientific study of the structure and function of the immune system.

impedance A measure of the opposition of an electric circuit to the flow of an alternating electric current through it. Impedance is measured in ohms.

impermeable Relating to a material through which substances, such as liquids or gases, cannot pass: *an impermeable cell wall.*

impetigo A contagious disease often affecting children, characterized by the formation of pimples and thick yellow crusts on the skin of the face.

improper fraction A fraction in which the numerator is greater than or equal to the denominator, such as $\frac{3}{2}$. *Compare* **proper fraction.**

impulse 1. A usually sudden flow of electrical current in one direction. Impulses typically occur as single events. 2. An electrical signal travelling along the axon of a nerve cell. Nerve impulses excite or inhibit activity in other nerve cells or in the tissues of the body, such as muscles and glands. 3. *Physics.* The magnitude of a force multiplied by the time for which the force acts.

In The symbol for **indium**.

inbreed To breed by continued mating of closely related individuals.

incandescent lamp A lamp that produces light by heating up a filament of wire inside a bulb with an electric current. Because the filament, usually made of tungsten, would oxidize quickly at high temperatures, the bulb is filled with a nonreactive gas, such as argon, which prevents this. *Compare* **fluorescent lamp.**

inch A unit of length equal to 2.54 centimetres ($\frac{1}{12}$ of a foot). *See table at* **measurement.**

incisor A tooth having a sharp edge adapted for cutting or gnawing, located in mammals in the front of the mouth between the canine teeth.

inclined plane A plane surface, such as a ramp, set at an acute angle to a horizontal surface. It is a simple machine because it requires less force to slide or roll a body up the plane than to raise the body vertically. Many tools are based on the principle of the inclined plane, such as the axe, screw, wedge and chisel.

incubate 1. To warm and hatch eggs by bodily heat; to brood. 2. To keep an organism, a cell or cell cultures in conditions favourable for growth and development. ❖ The incubation of a disease is the period between the time of infection and the time the first symptoms appear. ❖ An incubator is an insulated device in which organisms, cells or cell cultures are kept at a constant temperature and humidity.

incus One of the three small bones, called ossicles, in the middle ear. The incus is also called the anvil.

independent variable *Mathematics.* A variable whose value determines the value of other variables. For example, in the function $y = x - 4$, x is the independent variable because its value determines the value of y.

index of refraction The ratio of the speed of light in a vacuum to the speed of light in another medium, such as water or oil.

indicator A chemical compound that changes colour and structure when exposed to certain conditions and is therefore useful for chemical tests. Litmus, for example, becomes red in the presence of acids and blue in the presence of bases.

indicator species A species whose presence, absence or relative well-being in a given environment is a sign of the overall health of its ecosystem. By monitoring the condition and behaviour of an indicator species, scientists can determine how changes in the environment are likely to affect other species that are more difficult to study.

indigenous *Ecology.* Native to a particular region or environment but occurring naturally in other places as well. Red deer and badgers are indigenous to Britain. *Compare* **alien, endemic.**

indium A soft, easily shaped, silvery-white metallic element that occurs mainly in ores of zinc and lead. It is used in the manufacturing of semiconductors and bearings for aircraft engines and as a plating over silver in making mirrors. *Symbol* **In.** *Atomic number* 49. *See* **Periodic Table,** pages 260–261.

indricotherium (*plural* **indricotheria**) A very large, extinct land mammal of the Oligocene and Miocene Epochs, related to the rhinoceros. It stood 5.5 metres high at the shoulder and weighed 4 times as much as an elephant. The indricotherium is thought to have been the largest land mammal ever.

glass bulb

filament

inert gas

lead-in wires

base

■ **incandescent lamp**

conducting coil

magnet

current

current

■ **induction**

When a magnet moves through a conducting coil, it induces (generates) an electric current. The direction of the flow of the current depends on the direction in which the magnet moves. In the diagram on the left, the current runs from right to left. In the diagram on the right, the current runs from left to right.

Microorganisms that can cause infection include bacteria, fungi and protozoans.

infectious Capable of causing infection: *an infectious disease.*

infertile 1. Not capable of producing offspring, seeds or fruit; unable to reproduce. **2.** Not capable of developing into a complete organism: *infertile eggs.* **3.** Not capable of supporting plant life; unfavourable to the growth of crops and plants: *infertile soil. —noun* **infertility.**

infinity A space, extent of time or other quantity that has no limit.

inflammation The reaction of a part of the body to injury or infection, characterized by swelling, heat and pain. Inflammation increases the amount of blood flow to the injured area, bringing in more white blood cells and often healing the damaged tissue.

inductance The property of an electric circuit that makes it possible for an electromotive force to be created in a nearby circuit by a change of current in either circuit.

induction 1a. The process of deriving general principles from particular facts or instances. **b.** A conclusion reached by this process. *See panel at* **deduction. 2.** The generation of an electric current in a conductor, such as a copper wire, by moving the conductor through a magnetic field or by moving or varying a magnetic field that already affects the conductor. **3.** *See* **magnetic induction.**

induction coil A device that changes a low-voltage direct current in one circuit to a high-voltage alternating current in a second circuit. Induction coils are used for many purposes, such as firing spark plugs in car engines and starting oil burners.

inert Not chemically reactive.

inert gas *See* **noble gas.**

inertia The tendency of a mass at rest to remain at rest, or of a mass in motion to continue moving in a straight line at a constant speed unless a force is applied to it.

infection The invasion of the body by microorganisms or a virus that can cause disease.

Usage

infectious/communicable/ contagious

A *contagious* or *communicable* disease is one that can be transmitted from one living thing to another through direct or indirect contact. Thus the flu, which can be transmitted by coughing, as well as the tropical disease cholera, often acquired by drinking contaminated water, are contagious (or communicable) diseases. Modern medicine also uses the word *infectious* to refer to such diseases. *Infectious* has a slightly different meaning. It refers to diseases caused by *infectious agents* – agents such as viruses and bacteria that are not normally present in the body and can cause an infection. While the notion of contagiousness goes back to ancient times, the idea of infectious diseases is more modern, coming from the germ theory of disease, which was not proposed until the later 19th century. *Contagious* and *infectious* are also used to refer to people who have communicable diseases at a stage during which transmission to others is likely.

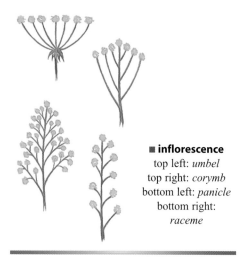

■ **inflorescence**
top left: *umbel*
top right: *corymb*
bottom left: *panicle*
bottom right:
raceme

inflorescence A group of flowers growing from a common stem, often in a characteristic arrangement.

influenza A contagious disease caused by a virus that is characterized by fever, inflammation of the airways and muscle pain. It often occurs in epidemics and pandemics, one of which killed 20

million people worldwide between 1917 and 1919.

information technology The development, installation and use of computer systems and applications. *Abbreviation* IT.

infrared Relating to the invisible part of the electromagnetic spectrum with wavelengths longer than those of visible red light but shorter than those of microwaves. *See more at* **electromagnetic spectrum.**

infrasound Sound whose wave frequency is too low (under 20 hertz) to be heard by humans.

inheritance The process by which traits or characteristics pass from parents to offspring through the genes.

inhibition The blocking or limiting of the action of an organ, tissue or cell of the body that is caused by the activity of certain nerves or by the release of a particular substance, such as a hormone or enzyme. *Compare* **excitation.**

ink A dark liquid ejected for protection by most cephalopods, including the octopus and squid.

inner ear The innermost part of the ear in many vertebrate animals, consisting of the cochlea and semicircular canals. It transmits sound vibrations to the brain and is also the organ of balance. *See more at* **ear.**

inoculation 1. The production of immunity in an individual through injection with a vaccine. 2. An injection of a specific vaccine. —*verb* **inoculate.**

inorganic 1. Not involving organisms or the products of their life processes. 2. Relating to chemical compounds that do not contain carbon (and especially hydrocarbons). Inorganic compounds occur mainly outside of living or once living organisms. Some inorganic compounds, such as carbon dioxide, contain carbon, but most do not. Salt (NaCl) and ammonia (NH_3) are typical inorganic compounds.

inorganic chemistry The branch of chemistry that deals with inorganic compounds.

input *noun* 1. The energy, power or work put into a system or device. 2. The data or programs put into a computer. —*verb* To enter data or a program into a computer.

insect Any of numerous small arthropods that have six segmented legs in the adult stage and a body divided into three parts. The three parts are the head, thorax and abdomen, and the thorax often has a pair of wings. Flies, bees, grasshoppers, beetles, butterflies and moths are all insects. More than 600,000 species are known, most of them beetles. *See panels at* **biomass, bug, entomology.**

insecticide A chemical used to kill insects. *Compare* **fungicide, herbicide, pesticide.**

insectivore 1. An animal or plant that feeds mainly on insects. 2. Any of an order of mammals that are small, eat insects and other invertebrate animals, and are usually active at night. The moles, shrews and hedgehogs are examples of insectivores. —*adjective* **insectivorous.**

insoluble Not capable of being fully dissolved; not soluble.

instinct An inherited tendency of an organism or species to behave in a certain way that is usually a reaction to something in the environment and that fulfils a basic need. Examples of behaviours that are the result of instinct include nest-building in birds, spawning in fish and food-gathering in insects.

insulate To cover or surround with a material that prevents the loss or transfer of heat, electricity or sound: *We insulated our attic to keep out the cold.* —*noun* **insulation.** —*noun* **insulator.**

insulin 1. A hormone produced in the pancreas that acts to regulate the amount of sugar in the blood by causing cells, especially liver and muscle cells, to absorb glucose from the bloodstream. 2. This hormone in a manufactured form, used to treat diabetes. It is usually injected because insulin is a protein and so would be digested in the gut if taken orally. Originally, it

■ **inheritance**
In this diagram, pink pea flowers are produced by dominant genes (P) and white pea flowers are produced by recessive genes (p). When flowers having two dominant genes are mated with flowers having two recessive genes (top row), the first generation of plants (middle row) all have one dominant and one recessive gene (Pp). Since dominant genes suppress recessive ones, all the flowers in the first generation will be pink. In the second generation (bottom row), one of the four plants will have two recessive genes. Therefore, three of the flowers in the second generation will be pink and one will be white.

was extracted from the pancreas of animals, but now most of the insulin used for treating diabetes is produced by genetically-engineered bacteria.

integer A positive or negative whole number or zero. The numbers 4, –876, and 5280 are all integers.

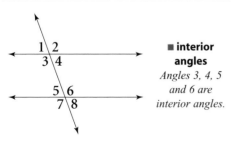

■ **interior angles**
Angles 3, 4, 5 and 6 are interior angles.

integral 1. Involving or expressed as an integer or integers. **2.** In calculus, the result of integration.

integrated circuit A device made of interconnected electronic components that are etched or imprinted onto a tiny slice of a semiconducting material, such as silicon or germanium. An integrated circuit smaller than a fingernail can hold millions of circuits. Also called *chip.*

integration In calculus, the inverse of differentiation. Integrating a given function results in a function whose derivative is the given function. Integration is used to compute such things as the areas and volumes of irregular shapes and solids. *Compare* **differentiation.**

integument A natural outer covering of an animal or a plant, such as skin, a seed coat or a shell.

inter– A prefix meaning "between" or "among", as in *interplanetary,* located between planets.

intercellular Located between or among cells: *intercellular fluid.*

intercept *Mathematics.* In a Cartesian coordinate system, the coordinate of a point at which a line, curve or surface intersects a coordinate axis. If a curve intersects the x-axis at (4,0), then 4 is the curve's x-intercept; if the curve intersects the y-axis at (0,2), then 2 is its y-intercept.

intercourse *See* **sexual intercourse.**

interference The result of two waves that meet or overlap. Waves interfering with each other produce a **resultant wave.** The amplitude of this resultant wave depends on the amplitude and phase of the original individual waves. ❖ **Constructive interference** occurs where two waves meet in phase (where their crests and troughs coincide), producing a resultant wave with an amplitude equal to the sum of those of the individual waves. ❖ **Destructive interference** occurs where two waves meet out of phase (where the crest of one wave meets the trough of another), cancelling each other out.

interferon Any of a group of proteins that are produced by animal cells in response to infection by a virus and that, in many cases, prevent replication of the virus. Some interferons trigger

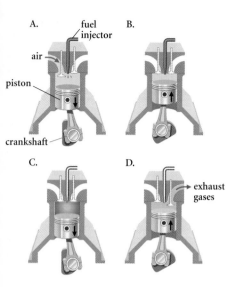

■ **internal-combustion engine**

cycles of a four-stroke diesel engine

A. intake stroke: *the piston moves down, drawing air and fuel into the cylinder*

B. compression stroke: *the piston moves up, compressing and heating the air and fuel mixture*

C. power stroke: *the hot air and fuel mixture ignites, forcing the piston down*

D. exhaust stroke: *the piston moves up, forcing the exhaust gases out of the cylinder*

that deals with the diagnosis and treatment of diseases affecting the internal organs of the body, especially in adults.

International Date Line An imaginary line through the Pacific Ocean roughly along the 180th meridian, agreed upon as the place where each new calendar day begins. The calendar day to the east of the line is one day earlier than it is to the west of the line.

International System A decimal system of units used mainly in scientific work, in which the basic quantities are length, mass, time, electric current, temperature, amount of matter and luminous intensity. *See table at* **measurement.**

international unit A unit for measuring a biologically active substance, such as a hormone or vitamin.

Internet A system connecting computers around the world using a common standard for transmitting and receiving data. This standard is known as TCP/IP, which stands for Transmission Control Protocol/Internet Protocol. *See also* **World Wide Web.**

interphase The stage of a cell cycle immediately following the completion of cell division (mitosis), during which complete development of the daughter cells takes place.

intersection 1. *Geometry.* The point or set of points where one line, surface or solid crosses another. **2.** *Mathematics.* The set that contains only those elements shared by two or more sets.

an immune response in the body. They have been investigated as treatment for many diseases, including certain cancers.

interior angle 1. Any of the four angles formed inside two straight lines when these lines are intersected by a third straight line. **2.** An angle formed by two adjacent sides of a polygon and included within the polygon. *Compare* **exterior angle.**

internal-combustion engine An engine whose fuel is burned inside the engine itself rather than in an outside furnace or burner. Petrol and diesel engines are internal-combustion engines; a steam engine is not.

internal medicine The branch of medicine

■ **International Date Line**

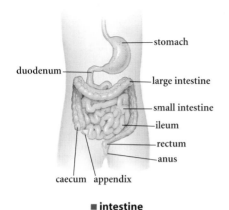

stomach

duodenum

large intestine

small intestine

ileum

rectum

anus

caecum   appendix

■ intestine

The intersection of the sets {3,4,5,6} and {4,6,8,10} is the set {4,6}.

intervertebral disc A broad disc of cartilage that separates adjacent vertebrae and acts as a shock absorber during movement.

intestine The part of the digestive tract that extends from the stomach to the anus, consisting of the small intestine and large intestine. The intestine is a muscular tube in which most of the processes of digestion take place.

intra– A prefix meaning "inside" or "within", as in *intravenous,* within a vein.

intravenous Within or into a vein: *an intravenous injection.*

intrusion The movement of magma through underground rocks within the Earth, usually in an upward direction. ❖ Rocks that formed from the underground cooling of magma are called **intrusive rocks.** *Compare* **extrusion.**

inverse *adjective* Relating to a mathematical operation whose nature or effect is the opposite of another operation. For example, addition and subtraction are inverse operations, as are multiplication and division. —*noun* **1.** An inverse operation. Subtraction is the inverse of addition. **2.** Either of two numbers or quantities that cancel each other out under a given mathematical operation. For example, the inverse of 5 under multiplication is $\frac{1}{5}$, since $5 \times \frac{1}{5} = 1$. The inverse of 5 under addition is –5, since $5 + -5 = 0$.

inverse-square law A principle in physics dealing with the phenomena that spread equally in all directions (such as sound, light and gravity) and describing how the intensity of these phenomena weakens over increasing distance. According to this principle, the intensity of the phenomenon changes by the inverse square of the distance from the source of the phenomenon. For example, an object placed three metres away from a light source will receive only one-ninth as much illumination as an object placed one metre from the light.

invertebrate *adjective* Having no backbone or spinal column. —*noun* An animal, such as a jellyfish, insect or worm, that has no backbone. Most animals are invertebrates.

in vitro Literally, in glass. This describes a process that would normally take place in a living organism taking place in an artificial environment such as a test tube, Petri dish or flask: *in vitro fertilization. Compare* **in vivo.**

in vivo Literally, in life. This describes a process taking place inside a living organism rather than in an artificial environment: *test a new drug in vivo. Compare* **in vitro.**

involuntary Not under conscious control. Most of the biological processes in animals that are vital to life, such as contraction of the heart, blood flow, breathing and digestion, are involuntary and controlled by the autonomic nervous system.

iodide A chemical compound consisting of iodine together with another element or radical.

iodine A shiny, greyish-black halogen element that is corrosive and poisonous. It occurs in very small amounts in nature but is abundant in seaweed. Iodine compounds are used in medicine, antiseptics and dyes. *Symbol* **I.** *Atomic number* 53. *See* **Periodic Table,** pages 260–261.

ion An atom or molecule that has an electric charge. Positive ions, or cations, are formed by the loss of electrons; negative ions, or anions, are formed by the gain of electrons. *See panel at* **charge.**

ionic bond A chemical bond formed between two ions with opposite charges. Ionic bonds form when one atom gives up one or more electrons to another atom. These bonds can form between a pair of atoms or between molecules and are the

Did You Know?

iridium

In 1978 geologist Walter Alvarez found an unusually high concentration of the element *iridium* in a layer of clay. This layer was formed at the time dinosaurs and many other organisms became extinct. The iridium deposits were a great surprise, since iridium is very rare at the Earth's surface. Most surface iridium is believed to come from outer space – from dust left over after meteors disintegrate in the atmosphere or smash into the Earth. Walter Alvarez's father, the physicist Luis Alvarez, suggested that the iridium came from the impact of a meteor about 10 kilometres across. He argued that such an impact would have caused an enormous explosion, sending huge clouds of dust into the atmosphere. The dust, blocking out the sun and causing acid rain for years, would have caused a worldwide ecological disaster. Many scientists think that such a disaster caused the extinction of dinosaurs and at least 70 per cent of all other species alive at the time, including most of the Earth's land plants. Geologists have since found iridium deposits in rocks of a similar date in over 100 places worldwide. In the early 1990s, a large impact crater of the same age as the iridium deposits was identified in the Yucatan peninsula of central Mexico. It is 200 kilometres wide and may well have been caused by the impact hypothesized by Luis Alvarez.

Radio waves, which normally travel in a straight line, can be transmitted long distances over the curved surface of the Earth because they bounce off certain layers of the ionosphere and return to Earth instead of continuing into space.

Ir The symbol for **iridium**.

iridium A rare, whitish-yellow element that is the most corrosion-resistant metal known. It is very dense, hard and brittle. Iridium is used to make hard alloys of platinum for jewellery, fountain-pen nibs and electrical contacts. *Symbol* **Ir**. *Atomic number 77. See* **Periodic Table**, pages 260–261.

iris The coloured part around the pupil of the eye in vertebrate animals, located between the cornea and lens. Contraction and expansion of the muscular iris controls the size of the pupil, thereby regulating the amount of light reaching the retina.

iron A silvery-white, hard, brittle metallic element that occurs abundantly in minerals such as haematite and magnetite. It can be magnetized and is used to make steel and other alloys important in construction and manufacturing. Iron is a component of haemoglobin, which allows red blood cells to carry oxygen and carbon dioxide through the body. *Symbol* **Fe**. *Atomic number 26. See* **Periodic Table**, pages 260–261. *See panel at* **element**.

iron (II) In a compound, iron with an oxidation number of +2 (old name *ferrous*).

iron (III) In a compound, iron with an oxidation number of +3 (old name *ferric*). Rust is a hydrated form of iron (III) oxide.

irradiate To expose to or treat with radiation so as to bring about a chemical or biological change. For example, meat sold as food is often irradiated to kill bacteria.

irrational number A real number that cannot be expressed as a ratio between two integers. If written in decimal notation, an irrational number would have an infinite number of digits to the right of the decimal point, without repetition. Pi and the square root of 2 are irrational numbers.

ischium The lowest or rearmost of the three bones that fuse together to form each of the hipbones in many vertebrate animals. *See more at* **skeleton**.

type of bond found in salts. *See more at* **bond, coordinate bond, covalent bond.**

ionize **1.** To add an electron to, or remove an electron from, an atom or group of atoms so as to give it an electric charge. **2.** To form ions in a substance. Lightning ionizes air, for example.

ionosphere A region of the Earth's atmosphere in which atoms are often ionized (electrically charged) by radiation from the sun. The ionosphere lies mostly in the lower thermosphere, from about 80 to 640 kilometres above the Earth.

island arc

■ **isosceles triangle**

● Carbon
○ Hydrogen

■ **isomer**

island arc A usually curved chain of volcanic islands occurring at a subduction zone. The chain occurs in the plate that rides over the subducting plate. It is curved because of the curvature of the Earth. Also called *volcanic arc.*

islets of Langerhans Irregular clusters of endocrine cells that are scattered throughout the tissue of the pancreas and secrete insulin.

iso– A prefix that means "equal", as in *isometric,* having equal measurements.

isobar A line drawn on a weather map connecting places having the same atmospheric pressure.

isoleucine An essential amino acid. *See more at* amino acid.

isomer One of two or more compounds composed of the same chemical elements in the same proportions but having a different arrangement of the atoms. Isomers differ from one another in at least one physical or chemical property. Lactose and sucrose are isomers.

isometric *See* cubic (sense 3).

isosceles Having at least two sides of equal length: *an isosceles triangle.*

isotherm A line drawn on a weather map connecting places having the same average temperature.

isotope One of two or more atoms that have the same number of protons but a different number of neutrons. Carbon-12, the most common form of carbon, has 6 protons and 6 neutrons, whereas carbon-14 has 6 protons and 8 neutrons.

IT Abbreviation of **information technology.**

-itis A suffix meaning "inflammation", as in bronchitis, inflammation of the bronchial tubes.

ivory The hard, smooth, yellowish-white substance forming the teeth and tusks of certain animals, such as the tusks of elephants and walruses and the teeth of certain whales.

186

Jacob, François Born 1920. French geneticist who studied how genes control cellular activity by directing the synthesis of proteins. With Jacques Monod, Jacob theorized that there are genes regulating the activity of other, neighbouring genes. Jacob and Monod also proposed the existence of messenger RNA.

jade A hard mineral that is pale green or white and is often used as a gemstone. Jade usually forms within metamorphic rocks.

jasper A reddish, brown or yellow variety of opaque quartz.

jaundice Yellowish discoloration, as of the skin and whites of the eyes. It is often a symptom of diseases like hepatitis that interfere with the normal processing of bile.

jaw 1. Either of two bony or cartilaginous structures that in most vertebrate animals form the framework of the mouth, hold the teeth and are used for biting and chewing food. The lower, movable part of the jaw is called the mandible. The upper, fixed part is called the maxilla. **2.** Any

of various structures of invertebrate animals, such as the pincers of spiders or mites, that function similarly to the jaws of vertebrates.

jawless fish Any of several primitive fish that lack a jaw and resemble the eels. Jawless fish include the lampreys and hagfish. *Compare* **bony fish, cartilaginous fish.**

jejunum The middle part of the small intestine, connecting the duodenum and the ileum.

jellyfish Any of numerous invertebrate marine animals having a soft, often umbrella-shaped body with stinging tentacles around a central mouth. Jellyfish are cnidarians and are related to the hydras and corals. *See also* **medusa, polyp.**

Jenner, Edward 1749–1823. British physician who pioneered the practice of vaccination. His experiments proved that people who had been inoculated with matter from cowpox, a mild skin disease of cattle, were immune to smallpox. Jenner's discovery laid the foundations for the science of immunology. *See panel on page 188.*

jet 1. A rapid stream of liquid or gas forced

■ **jellyfish**
moon jellyfish

Biography

Edward Jenner

In 1980 the World Health Organization declared that the deadly disease smallpox had been eradicated, thanks to the success of the smallpox vaccine. This triumph of medicine goes back more than 200 years, to the British physician Edward Jenner. Jenner based his work on a piece of folk wisdom from the countryside that few doctors had taken seriously: if a person got cowpox, a mild disease of cattle, the person never got smallpox. Jenner proved his theory scientifically in a famous experiment that he carried out on an eight-year-old boy, James Phipps, in 1796. He exposed the boy to a person with cowpox, then two months later exposed the boy to smallpox (something that would be considered unethical by today's standards). Luckily, and as Jenner expected, the boy warded off the smallpox with no problem. Before Jenner's experiments, a kind of vaccination against smallpox did exist in the form of exposing people to a mild form of the disease. While this often worked quite well, it was risky, and the exposed person sometimes died. Through further experiments Jenner refined his new method and soon set up the first successful vaccination programme in history. Because of his work, systematic vaccination as a way of preventing disease became a central part of medicine.

through a small opening or nozzle under pressure: *A jet of water shot out of the hose.* **2.** An aircraft or other vehicle propelled by a jet engine. **3.** A jet engine.

jet engine An engine that develops thrust by ejecting a jet of hot gases from fuel burned in a combustion chamber. *See more at* **turbojet.**

jet propulsion 1. The driving of an aircraft by the powerful thrust developed when a jet of gas is forced out of a jet engine. **2.** Propulsion by means of any fluid that is forced out in a stream in the opposite direction. Squids, octopuses and cuttlefish, for example, jet their way through the sea by taking in and then quickly expelling water.

jet stream A narrow current of strong wind circling the Earth in the upper atmosphere.

joint 1. A usually movable body part in which adjacent bones are held together by ligaments and other fibrous tissues. **2.** *Botany.* A point on a plant stem from which a leaf or branch grows.

Joliot-Curie, Irène 1897–1956. French physicist. With her husband, **Frédéric Joliot-Curie** (1900–1958), she made the first artificial radioactive isotope. The couple also contributed to the discovery of the neutron and the development of nuclear reactors.

■ **joint**
a human knee joint

■ **Jupiter**

joule A unit used to measure energy or work. One joule is equal to the work done when a force of one newton moves through a distance of one metre.

Joule, James Prescott 1818–1889. British physicist. His work established the law of conservation of energy, stating that energy is never destroyed but may be converted from one form into another. The joule unit of energy is named after him.

jugular vein Either of the two large veins on either side of the neck that drain blood from the head.

jungle An area of tropical, forested land having high humidity and a dense growth of trees, bushes and vines.

Jupiter The fifth planet from the sun and the largest, with a diameter about 11 times that of Earth. It turns on its axis faster than any other planet in the solar system, taking less than ten hours to complete one rotation. *See table at* **solar system,** pages 314–315. *See panel at* **planet.**

Jurassic The second and middle period of the Mesozoic Era, from about 205 to 142 million years ago, during which dinosaurs were the dominant form of land life and the earliest birds appeared. *See chart at* **geological time,** pages 148–149.

juvenile An animal or plant that is not fully grown or developed.

K

K 1. The symbol for **potassium. 2.** Abbreviation of **kelvin.**

kangaroo Any of various plant-eating marsupials of Australia and nearby islands, having short forelimbs, large hind limbs adapted for leaping and a long tapered tail. Female kangaroos have pouches in which their young, born tiny, blind and hairless, are suckled and grow.

kaolin A soft, fine, whitish sedimentary rock made of clay minerals, especially kaolinite. Kaolin forms from the weathering of other rocks that are rich in aluminium.

kaolinite An aluminium-rich silicate mineral that is the main component of kaolin.

karyotype The number and shape of chromosomes in the nucleus of a cell. Scientists prepare karyotypes by staining cell nuclei, placing them on slides and then photographing them through a microscope. Images of the chromosomes can then be grouped by size using a computer. Karyotypes are used to study the genetic makeup of an individual.

Kekulé von Stradonitz, Friedrich August 1829–1896. German chemist who was a founder of organic chemistry. His discovery of the structure of benzene, a basic unit of organic chemistry, was fundamental to understanding many other organic compounds. *See panel at* **benzene.**

kelp Any of various brown, often very large seaweeds that live in colder ocean regions. Kelp are varieties of brown algae. Some species grow over 60 metres long.

kelvin A unit of absolute temperature having the same value as one Celsius degree. It is used in the Kelvin scale. *See more at* **Celsius.** *See table at* **measurement.**

Kelvin, First Baron. *Title of* **William Thomson** 1824–1907. British mathematician and physicist known especially for his work on heat and electricity. In 1848 he proposed a scale of temperature independent of any physical substance, which became known as the Kelvin scale.

Kelvin scale A scale of temperature beginning at absolute zero (–273.15°C). Each degree, or kelvin, has the same value as one degree on the Celsius scale. On the Kelvin scale water freezes at 273.15 K and boils at 373.15 K. *See panel at* **Celsius.**

Kepler, Johannes 1571–1630. German astronomer and mathematician who was the first to accurately describe the elliptical orbits of the Earth and the planets around the sun. He also demonstrated that planets move fastest when they are closest to the sun and that a planet's distance from the sun can be calculated if its period of revolution is known.

keratin A tough, fibrous protein that is the main structural component of hair, nails, horns, feathers and hooves.

kernel 1. A grain or seed, especially of a cereal plant such as corn or wheat, that is enclosed in a husk. **2.** The inner, often edible part of a nut, or the stone of a fruit, such as a peach or plum.

kerosene A thin, light-coloured oil that is obtained from petroleum and used mainly as a fuel in domestic heating boilers and jet engines.

ketone Any of a class of organic compounds, such as acetone, having a group consisting of a carbon and an oxygen atom (–CO) joined on either side to a carbon atom of a hydrocarbon radical.

kettle A steep, bowl-shaped hollow in ground once covered by a glacier. Kettles are believed to form when a block of ice left by a glacier becomes covered by sediments and later melts, leaving a hollow.

kg Abbreviation of **kilogram.**

Khorana, Har Gobind Born 1922. Indian-born American biochemist. He developed one of the

keratin

Nature ingeniously uses the same chemicals to perform a wide variety of functions in living things. An example is the group of closely related proteins known as the *keratins*. When nature wants something hard and tough for an animal, it turns to keratins. Your nails and hair are made mostly of a kind of keratin, and so are a dog's claws, a bird's beak, and a goat's horns. Even the hard material called baleen that some whales have in their mouths to help them eat is made of a variety of keratin. All proteins are strings of amino acids, and the keratins' secret is the amino acid known as cysteine. This amino acid tends to form strong bonds with other cysteines in the protein. The different keratins vary in hardness, depending on how many cysteine bonds are present. The bonds are what make the keratins as hard as – well, nails!

first artificial genes and determined the sequence of nucleic acids for each of the amino acids in the body.

Khwarizmi, Muhammad ibn-Musa al- 780?–850? Arab mathematician and astronomer. His work was widely translated into Latin, introducing Arabic numerals and algebraic concepts to Western mathematics. The word *algorithm* is derived from his name. *See panel at* **algebra.**

kidney Either of a pair of organs that are located in the rear of the abdominal cavity of vertebrate animals and that regulate the amount of water in the body and filter out wastes from the bloodstream in the form of urine. Each kidney is connected to the bladder by a muscular tube called a ureter.

killer whale A large dolphin found in all the world's oceans, having a black body with a white underside and a tall, triangular dorsal fin. Killer whales grow up to 9 metres in length. Also called *orca.*

kilo– A prefix that means: **1.** One thousand, as in *kilowatt,* one thousand watts. **2.** 2^{10} (that is, 1024), which is the power of 2 closest to 1000, as in *kilobyte.*

kilobit *Computer Science.* **1.** One thousand bits. **2.** 1024 (that is, 2^{10}) bits. *See panel at* **megabyte.**

kilobyte 1. A unit of computer memory or data storage capacity equal to 1024 (that is, 2^{10}) bytes. **2.** One thousand bytes. *See panel at* **megabyte.**

kilocalorie *See* **calorie** (sense 2a).

kilogram The basic unit of mass in the metric system, equal to 1000 grams. *See table at* **measurement.** *See panel at* **weight.**

kilohertz A unit of frequency equal to 1000 cycles per second. It is used to express the frequency of radio waves.

kilometre A unit of length in the metric system, equal to 1000 metres. *See table at* **measurement.**

kilowatt A unit of power equal to 1000 watts.

kilowatt-hour A unit used to measure energy, especially electrical energy. One kilowatt-hour is equal to energy transferred at a rate of one kilowatt for a period of one hour.

kinematics The branch of physics that deals with the characteristics of motion without regard for the effects of forces or mass. *Compare* **dynamics.**

■ kidney
Blood that flows through a kidney is filtered to remove waste, such as urea and excess water. This process results in the by-product urine, which travels through the ureter to the bladder, where it is stored until emptied by urination.

■ **Klein bottle**

kinetic energy The energy possessed by a body as a result of being in motion. Kinetic energy is dependant upon the mass and velocity of the object. *Compare* **potential energy.**

kinetics *See* **dynamics.**

kingdom The highest classification into which living organisms are grouped, ranking above a phylum. One widely accepted system of classification divides life into five kingdoms: prokaryotes, protists, fungi, plants and animals. *See table at* **taxonomy.**

Kirchhoff, Gustav Robert 1824–1887. German chemist who with Robert Bunsen discovered the elements caesium and rubidium. He also investigated the solar spectrum and researched electrical circuits and the flow of currents.

Klebs, Edwin 1834–1913. German bacteriologist. With Friedrich Löffler, he isolated the bacillus that causes diphtheria (1884). Klebs also demonstrated the presence of bacteria in infected wounds and showed that tuberculosis can be transmitted through infected milk.

Klein bottle A theoretical surface in topology that has no inside or outside. It can be pictured in ordinary space as a tube that bends back upon itself, entering through the side and joining with the open end. A true Klein bottle would not actually intersect itself. *Compare* **Möbius strip.**

km Abbreviation of **kilometre.**

kneecap *See* **patella.**

koala A tree-dwelling Australian marsupial that resembles a small bear. Koalas have greyish fur, large ears and sharp claws, and they feed exclusively on leaves and shoots of the eucalyptus tree.

Koch, Robert 1843–1910. German bacteriologist who demonstrated that specific diseases are caused by specific microorganisms. He identified the bacilli that cause anthrax, tuberculosis and cholera, and he showed that fleas and rats are responsible for transmission of the bubonic plague and that the tsetse fly is responsible for transmitting the tropical disease sleeping sickness.

Köhler, Georges Jean Franz Born 1946. German scientist who investigated the immune system. With César Milstein he developed a method of producing antibodies that fight specific cells. The antibodies are used to diagnose and treat specific forms of cancer and other diseases.

Komodo dragon An Indonesian monitor lizard that is the largest living lizard. It can grow up to 3

■ **Komodo dragon**

metres long, has dark skin and feeds on eggs and small animals.

Kr The symbol for **krypton**.

Krebs, Sir **Hans Adolf** 1900–1981. German-born British biochemist who discovered the Krebs cycle in 1936.

Krebs cycle A series of chemical reactions in most aerobic organisms in which cells break down glucose and other molecules in the presence of oxygen to produce carbon dioxide and energy in the form of ATP. The Krebs cycle occurs in the mitochondria of all organisms except bacteria. Also called *citric acid cycle.*

krill Small crustaceans that float in the sea in huge numbers and are one of the most important parts of zooplankton. Krill are the main food of baleen whales and many other marine organisms. They form a vital part of many marine food webs.

Kroto, Harry Born 1939. English chemist noted for his work in detecting unstable molecules through the use of methods such as microwave and photoelectron spectroscopy, including the study of molecules which exist in space. However, he is best known for his 1985 discovery of the third allotrope of carbon C60, known as "buckminster-fullerene" (familiarly "buckyballs"). *See* **buckminsterfullerene.**

krypton A colourless, odourless element that is a noble gas. It is used in certain fluorescent lamps and photographic flash lamps. *Symbol* **Kr.** *Atomic number* 36. *See* **Periodic Table,** pages 260–261.

Kuiper belt A disc-shaped region in the outer solar system, containing thousands of small, icy celestial bodies. Comets that make one complete orbit of the sun in less than 200 years come from this area. The Kuiper belt lies beyond the orbit of Neptune and includes Pluto, which is traditionally classed with the planets, but is believed by some astronomers to simply be a large Kuiper belt object. *Compare* **Oort cloud.**

kwashiorkor A disease, usually seen in children, caused by lack of protein in the diet and resulting in swelling of the limbs, enlargement of the liver, pot belly, reduced growth and change in the colour of the skin and hair.

Kwolek, Stephanie Born 1923. American chemist who pioneered the use of polymers to make synthetic fibres. She developed the first liquid crystal polymer fibre, now used to make many products, including bulletproof vests.

L l

l Abbreviation of **litre.**

La The symbol for **lanthanum.**

laboratory A room or building equipped for scientific research and for conducting experiments, especially under controlled conditions.

labour The process by which the birth of a mammal occurs, beginning with contractions of the uterus and ending with the delivery of the fetus or infant and the placenta.

labyrinth The system of tubes and spaces that make up the inner ear of many vertebrate animals.

lacrimal Relating to or producing tears: *the lacrimal glands.*

lactase An enzyme that is found in the small intestine, liver and kidneys of mammals and catalyses the breakdown of lactose into simpler sugars, such as glucose.

lactation The secretion or production of milk by the mammary glands, occurring in female mammals after giving birth.

lactic acid An organic acid produced when milk sours or various fruits ferment. It is used as a flavouring and preservative for foods. Lactic acid is also produced by muscle tissue during exercise, especially when oxygen supply is limited, and can cause cramping pains. Also called 1-*hydroxypropanoic acid.*

lactose A white crystalline sugar that is found in milk. It is used in the manufacture of various foods. ❖ The inability to properly digest lactose is called **lactose intolerance.** This condition is caused by a lack of the enzyme lactase and can cause stomach cramps and other symptoms.

lagoon 1. A shallow body of salt water close to the sea but separated from it by a narrow strip of land, such as a barrier island, or by a coral reef. 2. A shallow pond or lake close to a larger lake or river but separated from it by a barrier.

Lagrange, Comte **Joseph Louis** 1736–1813. French mathematician and astronomer who made important contributions to algebra and calculus. His work on celestial mechanics extended scientific understanding of planetary and lunar motion.

lake A large inland body of standing fresh or salt water.

Lamarck, Jean-Baptiste Pierre Antoine de Monet Chevalier de 1744–1829. French naturalist and evolutionist who investigated the relations between species and the origins of different species, which he wrote about in his famous book *Philosophie zoologique.* Here he suggested that characteristics acquired during the lifetime of one organism can be inherited by its offspring and later generations. Although Lamarck's ideas were later shown to be wrong, his work was nevertheless very important. Lamarck broke with the old notion of unchanging species created by God. He recognized that species needed to adapt to survive environmental changes, and his ideas prepared the way for Darwin's now accepted theory of evolution.

lamina 1. *Botany.* The expanded area of a leaf or

■ lagoon
Efate Island, Vanuatu, South Pacific

petal; a blade. **2.** A thin layer of bone, membrane or other tissue. **3.** *Geology.* A thin layer of sediment.

laminar flow Movement of a fluid in which the motion of the particles of fluid is very orderly and all particles move along straight lines in the same direction. Laminar flow is common in viscous fluids, especially those moving at low velocities. *Compare* **turbulent flow.**

lamprey Any of various fish having a body like an eel, a skeleton made of cartilage and a jawless sucking mouth. Lampreys attach to other fish in order to feed on their blood.

lancelet Any of various small, transparent, fish-like animals that live in water and have a structure similar to that of vertebrates, but with a notochord instead of a true backbone. Lancelets are cephalochordates. Also called *amphioxus.*

land bridge A neck of land that connects two land masses; an isthmus.

landfill A disposal site where solid waste, such as paper, glass and metal, is buried between layers of dirt and other materials in such a way as to reduce contamination of the surrounding land. Modern landfills are often lined with layers of absorbent material and sheets of plastic to keep pollutants from leaking into the soil and water. Also called *sanitary landfill.*

landform Any recognizable, naturally formed feature on the Earth's surface. Landforms have a characteristic shape and can include such large

■ **larva**
larvae of the Japanese beetle

features as plains, plateaus, mountains and valleys, as well as smaller features such as hills and canyons.

land mass A large, continuous area of land, such as a continent or a very large island.

landslide 1. The downward sliding of a relatively dry mass of earth and rock. **2.** The mass of soil and rock that moves in this way.

Landsteiner, Karl 1868–1943. Austrian-born American pathologist who discovered human blood groups. *See panel at* **blood group.**

Langevin, Paul 1872–1946. French physicist who pioneered the use of sonar techniques to detect submarines. He also advanced the theory of magnetism and the study of the molecular structure of gases.

La Niña A cooling of the surface water of the eastern and central Pacific Ocean, occurring every 4 to 12 years and causing unusual weather patterns. The cooler water brings drought to western South America and heavy rains to eastern Australia and Indonesia. *Compare* **El Niño.**

lanolin A yellowish-white, fatty substance obtained from wool and used in soaps, cosmetics and ointments.

lanthanide Any of a series of 15 naturally occurring metallic elements. The lanthanides include elements having atomic numbers from 57 to 71. They are grouped apart from the rest of the elements in the Periodic Table because they all behave in a similar way in chemical reactions. Also called *rare-earth element. See* **Periodic Table,** pages 260–261.

lanthanum A soft, easily shaped, silvery-white metallic element of the lanthanide series. It is used to make glass for lenses and lighting for film and television studios. *Symbol* **La.** *Atomic number* 57. *See* **Periodic Table,** pages 260–261.

large intestine The wide lower section of the intestine that extends from the end of the small intestine to the anus. In most vertebrate animals, it includes the caecum, colon and rectum. In the large intestine, water is reabsorbed from undigested food into the blood, leaving faecal material which accumulates in the rectum.

larva (*plural* **larvae** *or* **larvas**) **1.** An animal in an early stage of development that differs greatly

Did You Know?

laser

A *laser* emits a thin, intense beam of light that can travel long distances without diffusing or spreading out very much. Almost any light beam consists of many waves travelling in roughly the same direction. In laser light, the waves are all precisely in step with each other. Such light is called *coherent.* Lasers produce coherent light through a process called *stimulated emission.* The laser contains a chamber in which atoms of a medium such as a synthetic ruby rod or a gas are excited to a high energy level. When a light wave of the correct frequency is sent through the chamber from an electronic flash tube, it makes the excited atoms emit light that is in step with the original wave. These waves then stimulate other atoms to emit more coherent light. The chamber has mirrors at both ends, so the light travels back and forth, repeatedly stimulating emission. One of the mirrors is partially transparent so that the laser beam can exit from that end.

in appearance from its adult stage. Larvae are adapted to a different environment and way of life than adults and go through a process of metamorphosis in changing to adults. Tadpoles are the larvae of frogs and toads. **2.** The immature, wingless and usually worm-like feeding form of those insects that undergo three stages of metamorphosis, such as butterflies, moths and beetles. Insect larvae hatch from eggs, later turn into pupae, and finally turn into adults. *Compare* **imago, nymph, pupa.**

laryngitis Inflammation of the larynx, usually caused by a virus.

larynx The upper part of the trachea in most vertebrate animals, containing the vocal cords. Air passes through the larynx on the way to the lungs. Also called *voice box.*

laser A device that emits a very narrow and intense beam of light or other radiation. The light is generated by exciting the atoms of a medium, which may be a crystal, gas or liquid. The colour of laser light depends on the difference in energy between the atoms in their excited state and their ground state. Lasers are used for many purposes, such as cutting hard substances and destroying diseased tissue, as well as in telecommunications.

latent heat The quantity of heat absorbed or released by a substance undergoing a change of state, such as ice changing to water or water changing to ice, at constant temperature and pressure.

latent period The incubation period of a disease; the time elapsing between an infection and the appearance of symptoms.

lateral line A series of tube-like canals along the head and sides of fish and some amphibians by which vibrations, as from water currents, and changes in pressure are detected.

latex 1. The colourless or milky sap of certain trees and plants, such as poppies, spurges and the rubber tree, that hardens when exposed to the air. Latex usually contains gum resins, waxes and oils. **2.** An emulsion of rubber or plastic droplets in water that looks like the latex of plants. It is used in paints, adhesives and synthetic rubber products.

latitude Distance north or south on the Earth's

surface, measured in degrees from the equator, which has a latitude of 0°. The distance of a degree of latitude is about 111 kilometres or 60 nautical miles. Latitude and longitude are the coordinates used to identify any point on the Earth's surface. *Compare* **longitude.**

lattice *See under* **crystal.**

laughing gas Nitrous oxide used as a mild anaesthetic.

Laurasia A supercontinent of the Northern Hemisphere made up of the land masses that currently correspond to North America, Greenland, Europe and Asia (except India). According to the theory of plate tectonics, Laurasia formed at the end of the Precambrian Eon and broke up in the middle of the Mesozoic Era. *Compare* **Gondwanaland.**

lava 1. Molten rock that flows from a volcano or from a crack in the Earth. *See more at* **magma. 2.** The igneous rock formed when this substance cools and hardens.

Lavoisier, Antoine Laurent 1743–1794.

French chemist who is regarded as one of the founders of modern chemistry. In 1778 he discovered that air consists of a mixture of two gases, which he called oxygen and nitrogen. Lavoisier also discovered the law of conservation of mass and devised the modern method of naming chemical compounds. His wife, **Marie** (1758–1836), assisted him with his laboratory work and translated a number of important chemistry texts. Unfortunately, his career was cut short when he was put to the guillotine during the French Revolution. *See panels at* **oxygen, Priestley.**

law A statement that describes what will happen in all cases under a specified set of conditions. Laws describe an invariable relationship among phenomena. Boyle's law, for instance, describes what will happen to the volume of a gas if its pressure changes and its temperature remains the same. *See panel at* **hypothesis.**

law of conservation of energy The principle that energy can neither be created nor be destroyed, now part of the first law of thermodynamics. The term is also used as a

Biography

Antoine Lavoisier

Although Antoine Lavoisier made many fundamental contributions to the science of chemistry, rather than being known for major experiments or discoveries, he is best known for being the first scientist to collect and publish everything that was known about chemistry in his time. His *Elementary Treatise of Chemistry,* published in 1789, is regarded as the first textbook on modern chemistry. In it, Lavoisier presented a systematic and unified view of new theories and established a system for naming chemical compounds. Lavoisier also put to rest an important and longstanding theory about combustion, a mysterious process that had baffled the greatest minds since antiquity. For centuries it was believed that a substance called *phlogiston,* thought to be a volatile part of all combustible substances,

was released during the process of combustion. By repeating the experiments of Joseph Priestley, Lavoisier demonstrated that combustion is a process in which the burning substance combines with a constituent of the air, the gas he named *oxygen.*

law of conservation of mass

synonym for the first law of thermodynamics. *See panel at* **thermodynamics.**

law of conservation of mass The principle that matter can neither be created nor be destroyed, now part of the first law of thermodynamics. *See panel at* **thermodynamics.**

law of gravitation *or* **law of universal gravitation** *See* **Newton's law of gravitation.**

Lawrence, Ernest Orlando 1901–1958. American physicist who built the first cyclotron, a type of particle accelerator, in 1929.

lawrencium A synthetic, radioactive metallic element of the actinide series that is produced by bombarding californium with boron ions. Its most stable isotope has a half-life of 3.6 hours. *Symbol* **Lr.** *Atomic number* 103. *See* **Periodic Table,** pages 260–261.

laws of motion *See* **Newton's laws of motion.**

laws of thermodynamics Three laws that state how energy is transformed from one form into another. *See panel at* **thermodynamics.**

LCD Short for *liquid-crystal display.* A low-power, flat-panel display used in many digital devices to display numbers or images. It is made up of a substance that is almost liquid, but also has a crystal structure like a solid, sandwiched between filtering layers of glass or plastic. When the device is turned on, the molecules of the "liquid crystal" twist so that they can either reflect or transmit light that falls on them to produce the number or image indicated by a computer.

leach To remove the soluble materials from a substance, such as ash or rock, by passing a liquid through or over it: *Heavy rains leached minerals from the soil.*

lead A soft, easily shaped, heavy, bluish-grey metallic element that is extracted chiefly from galena. It is very durable and resistant to corrosion and is a poor conductor of electricity. Lead is used to make radiation shielding and containers for corrosive substances. *Symbol* **Pb.** *Atomic number* 82. *See* **Periodic Table,** pages 260–261. *See panel at* **element.**

leaf *noun* A flat, usually green plant part that grows on the stem and takes in carbon dioxide and sunlight to manufacture food by photosynthesis. Leaves consist of an outer tissue layer (the epidermis) through which water and gases are exchanged, a spongy inner layer of cells that contain chloroplasts, and veins that supply water and minerals and transport food. Some leaves are simple, while others are compound, consisting of multiple leaflets. *—verb* To produce leaves.

leaflet A small leaf or leaf-like part, especially one of the blades or divisions of a compound leaf.

leafstalk The stalk by which the leaves of most plants are attached to a stem. Also called *petiole.*

Leakey Family of British scientists. **Louis** (1903–1972) is known for fossil discoveries of early humans made in close collaboration with his wife, **Mary** (1913–1996). In 1959, while working in the east African country of Tanzania, Mary Leakey uncovered skull and teeth fragments of a species called *Zinjanthropus,* now thought to be about 1.75 million years old. The next year the Leakeys discovered remains of a larger-brained species, called *Homo habilis.* Their discoveries provided powerful evidence that human ancestors were of greater age than was previously thought, and that they had evolved in Africa rather than in Asia. Their son **Richard** (born 1944) and his wife **Meave** (born 1942) have continued the family's research and discoveries. In 2001 Meave Leakey discovered a skull belonging to an entirely new genus, called *Kenyanthropus platyops* and believed to be 3.5 million years old.

learning disability Any of various disorders of attention, memory or reasoning that interfere with the ability to learn, especially the ability to learn mathematics or develop language skills.

Leavitt, Henrietta Swan 1868–1921. American astronomer who discovered four novae and over 2400 variable stars. She also developed a mathematical formula used to measure intergalactic distances.

lecithin A fatty substance containing phosphorus that is present in most plant and animal tissues and is an important structural part of cell membranes. Lecithin is used commercially in foods, cosmetics, paints and plastics for its ability to form emulsions.

LED Short for *light-emitting diode.* An electronic semiconductor device that emits light when an electric current passes through it. LEDs are used for indicator lights, such as those on the front of a disc drive.

leech Any of various worms that live in water

A Closer Look

Leaf

Flowering plants are classified as monocotyledons or dicotyledons. The leaves of monocotyledons have parallel veins and are often sessile (attached directly to the stem without a stalk). The leaves of dicotyledons have net veins and are usually attached to the plant by a leafstalk.

Leaves have a shape and structure adapted to the specific habitat of each kind of plant. Leaves that are narrow and needle-like are designed to limit water loss. Broad leaves are designed for wetter climates and make maximum use of sunlight for photosynthesis.

Monocotyledon sorghum

Dicotyledon sweetgum

blade — vein — midrib —

leafstalk —

stem —

— stem

Broad leaf oak

Grass bamboo

Needle Norway pine

Spine cactus

and suck blood from other animals, including humans. One species, the medicinal leech, has been used in bloodletting and in helping to heal wounds and surgical grafts. Leeches are annelids and are related to earthworms.

Leeuwenhoek, Anton van 1632–1723. Dutch naturalist and pioneer of microscopic research. He was the first to describe protozoa, bacteria and spermatozoa. He also made observations of yeasts, red blood cells and blood capillaries, and traced the life histories of such animals as the flea, ant and weevil. *See panel on* page 200.

legume 1. Any of a variety of plants having pods that contain seeds. Because of a symbiotic relationship with bacteria that live in nodules on their roots, legumes are able to take nitrogen from

Leibniz

Biography

Anton van Leeuwenhoek

As a young man, Anton van Leeuwenhoek worked in a draper's shop, where he used magnifying glasses to examine the quality of the cloth. This led him to begin building microscopes as a hobby, and he used them to examine hair, blood, insects and other things, keeping detailed records and drawings of his observations. Eventually, van Leeuwenhoek made hundreds of microscopes, each one for a different investigation, with specimens permanently mounted so he could study them as long as he wanted to. Some of the discoveries he made with his microscopes include protozoans (1674), bacteria (1676), blood cells (1674) and the structure of nerves (1717). Van Leeuwenhoek lived a very long life, and he remained active and curious throughout it. By the time of his death at the age of 90, he had made more than 400 microscopes.

the air and convert it into compounds that enrich soils. Beans, peas and clover are all legumes. **2.** The pod or seed of such a plant, used as food.

Leibniz, Baron **Gottfried Wilhelm von** 1646–1716. German philosopher and mathematician. He invented the mathematical processes of differentiation and integration, which greatly expanded the field of calculus. Leibniz also established the foundations of probability theory and designed a practical calculating machine.

lemur Any of several small nocturnal mammals found only on the island of Madagascar. Lemurs have large eyes, soft fur and a long tail, and live in trees. They are distantly related to monkeys.

Lenoir, Jean-Joseph-Étienne 1822–1900. French inventor who designed and assembled the first practical internal-combustion engine (1859).

lens 1. A transparent structure behind the iris of the eye that focuses light entering the eye on the retina. **2a.** A piece of glass or plastic shaped so as to focus or spread parallel light rays that pass

through it to form an image. **b.** A combination of two or more such lenses used to form an image, as in a camera or telescope. Also called *compound lens.*

Leo A constellation in the Northern Hemisphere near Cancer and Virgo.

Leonardo da Vinci 1452–1519. Italian artist, scientist, and inventor whose scientific insights were far ahead of their time. He investigated anatomy, geology, botany, hydraulics, optics, mathematics, meteorology and mechanics. Leonardo designed the first helicopter, parachute and bicycle, all of which were made centuries after his death, using modern materials and technology.

leprosy A disease caused by a bacterium that damages nerves, skin and mucous membranes. Leprosy progresses slowly, but if untreated it can destroy the affected body tissues.

leucine An essential amino acid. *See more at* **amino acid.**

leukaemia Any of several cancers of the blood in which abnormal white blood cells multiply uncontrollably, eventually crowding out normal cells in the bone marrow.

leukocyte *or* **leucocyte** *See* **white blood cell.**

lever A simple machine consisting of a bar that pivots on a fixed support, the fulcrum, and is used to transmit force. For example, a lever with the fulcrum positioned between the two ends can raise or move a heavy weight at one end as the bar is pushed down at the other. *See more at* **fulcrum.**

Leyden jar An early device for storing electric charge. It consists of a glass jar with conductive metal foil covering most of the inner and outer surfaces (all except the top parts). A metal rod or wire, used to transfer charge into and out of the jar, touches the inner foil and then exits through an insulating stopper in the neck.

Li The symbol for **lithium.**

Libra A constellation in the Southern Hemisphere near Scorpius and Virgo.

lichen An organism that consists of a fungus and an alga living together in a symbiotic relationship. The alga supplies nutrients by photosynthesis, while the fungus shades the alga from excessive sunlight and supplies water by absorbing water

■ **lichen**

vapour from the air. Lichens often live on rocks and tree bark and can thrive in extreme environments, such as mountain tops and the polar regions. *See also* **fungus.**

Liebig, Baron **Justus von** 1803–1873. German chemist who contributed to many areas of chemistry. He was one of the first to investigate organic compounds and to develop techniques for their analysis. Liebig also established one of the first teaching laboratories, where many 19th-century chemists were trained.

life 1. The property or quality that distinguishes living organisms from dead organisms and non-living matter. Life is shown in an organism that has the ability to grow, carry on metabolism, respond to stimuli and reproduce. **2.** Living organisms considered as a group: *plant life; marine life.*

life cycle The series of changes in the growth and development of an organism from its beginning as an independent life form to its mature state in which offspring are produced. In simple organisms, such as bacteria, the life cycle begins when an organism is produced by fission and ends when that organism in turn divides into two new ones. In more complex organisms, the life cycle starts with the fusion of reproductive cells and ends when that organism produces its own reproductive cells, which then may go on to reproduce.

life science Any of several branches of science, such as biology, medicine or ecology, that studies living organisms and their organization, life processes and relationships to each other and their environment. *Compare* **physical science.**

lift An upward force acting on an object. Lift can be caused because an object, such as an air balloon, displaces a weight of air greater than its own weight or because of a low-pressure area above an object, such as a wing, that is moving through a fluid. *Compare* **drag.** *See panel at* **aerodynamics.**

ligament A sheet or band of tough fibrous tissue that connects two bones or holds an organ of the body in place.

light 1. A form of electromagnetic energy that can be perceived by the human eye. It is made up of electromagnetic waves that travel at a speed of about 299,792 kilometres per second. **2.** Electromagnetic energy that cannot be perceived by the human eye, as infrared light and ultraviolet light. *See panel at* **electromagnetic radiation.**

light-emitting diode *See* **LED.**

lightning A flash of light in the sky caused by an electrical discharge between clouds or between a cloud and the Earth's surface. The flash heats the air and usually causes thunder. Lightning may

Did You Know?

lightning

The energy within a bolt of lightning is so great that it heats the air around it to temperatures up to five times greater than that of the surface of the sun, or 30,000°C. The rapid expansion of this superheated air is what creates the sounds we call thunder. The sounds travel to us more slowly than the light from lightning, so it is possible to estimate how far away a lightning strike is by timing the gap between when you see the lightning and when you hear the thunder it has produced. Count the seconds from when you see the flash until you hear the thunder, and divide this number by three. The result will be the number of kilometres you are from the point of the strike.

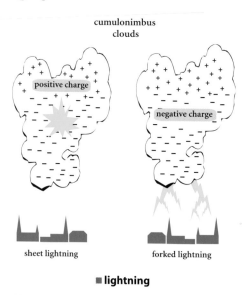

cumulonimbus
clouds

positive charge

negative charge

sheet lightning   forked lightning

■ **lightning**

appear as a jagged streak ("forked lightning"), a bright sheet or, in rare cases, a glowing red ball.

light year The distance that light travels in a vacuum in one year, equal to about 9.4 trillion kilometres.

lignin A complex organic compound that binds to cellulose fibres and hardens and strengthens the cell walls of plants. It is the chief noncarbohydrate constituent of wood.

lignite A soft, brownish-black form of coal having more carbon than peat but less carbon than bituminous coal. Lignite is easy to mine but does not burn as well as other forms of coal. *Compare* **anthracite, bituminous coal.**

lime A white, lumpy powder made of calcium oxide (CaO). It is made by heating limestone, bones or shells, and is used to make glass, paper, steel and building plaster. It is also added to soil to lower its acidity.

limestone A sedimentary rock consisting primarily of calcium carbonate, often in the form of the mineral calcite. Limestones can occur in many colours but are usually white, grey or black. They often contain fossil shells and other marine organisms. *See table at* **rock.**

line A geometric figure formed by a point moving in a fixed direction and in the reverse direction.

The intersection of two planes is a line. ❖ The part of a line that lies between two points on the line is called a **line segment**.

linear Of or resembling a line. ❖ A **linear equation** is an algebraic equation, such as $y = 4x + 3$, in which the variables are of the first degree (that is, raised only to the first power). The graph of such an equation is a straight line.

linear accelerator A device that accelerates charged subatomic particles, such as protons and electrons, in a straight line by means of alternating negative and positive impulses from electric fields. Linear accelerators are used to bring about high-speed particle collisions in order to study subatomic structures. *Compare* **cyclotron.**

line of force A line used to show the direction of force of an electric or magnetic field. *See panel at* **magnetism.**

Linnaeus 1707–1778. Swedish naturalist who founded the modern classification system for the naming of plants and animals. In 1749 he introduced the use of two names for each type of organism, the genus and the species names, known as the binomial system. *See more at* **binomial nomenclature.**

lipase An enzyme that speeds up the breakdown of fats to form glycerol and fatty acids.

lipid Any of a large group of organic compounds composed of fats and fatty compounds that are oily to the touch and insoluble in water. Lipids include fatty acids, oils, waxes, sterols and triglycerides. They are a source of stored energy and are a component of cell membranes.

liquefaction 1. *Chemistry.* The act or process of turning a gas into a liquid. **2.** *Geology.* The

Usage

light year

It is important to remember that a light year is a measure of distance, not time. A light year is the length of empty space that light can traverse in a year, close to ten trillion kilometres. When scientists calculate how many light years the stars are from Earth or from one another, they are calculating their distance, not their age.

process by which sediment that is very wet starts to behave like a liquid. Liquefaction is often caused by severe shaking, as in earthquakes.

liquid One of the three basic forms of matter. Unlike a solid, a liquid has no fixed shape, but instead has a characteristic readiness to flow and therefore takes on the shape of any container. Unlike a gas, a liquid usually has a volume that remains constant or changes only slightly under pressure.

liquid-crystal display *See* **LCD.**

Lister, Joseph. First Baron Lister 1827–1912. British surgeon who introduced strict standards of hygiene to hospitals to help combat infection. As a young doctor, Lister observed that patients with compound fractures (fractures with bone protruding through the skin) often died of infection. He became convinced that infection was spread by contact with the air and demonstrated that keeping wounds clean and covered decreased infection. In 1865 he read about Pasteur's germ theory of disease and established a system of antiseptic measures that dramatically decreased the number of deaths caused by infection. Lister's practices were gradually adopted by hospitals throughout Europe.

lithium A soft, silvery metallic element that is an alkali metal and occurs in small amounts in some minerals. It is the lightest of all metals and is highly reactive. Lithium is used to make alloys, batteries, glass for large telescopes and ceramics. *Symbol* **Li.** *Atomic number 3. See* **Periodic Table,** pages 260–261.

lithosphere The outer part of the Earth, consisting of the crust and upper mantle. Its thickness varies from about 1 to 2 kilometres at points where tectonic plates are moving apart, to between 250 and 500 kilometres under the continents. *Compare* **asthenosphere, atmosphere, hydrosphere.**

litmus A coloured powder, obtained from certain lichens, that changes to red in an acid solution and to blue in an alkaline solution. ❖ Litmus is typically added to paper to make **litmus paper,** which is used to determine whether a solution is basic or acidic.

litre A unit of volume equal to 1000 cm^3

represented by the symbol l or L. The lower case symbol is generally used, unless there is a danger that it may be confused with the numeral 1. The litre is not strictly a unit in the SI system – the SI unit of volume is the metre^3. In SI units, 1 litre is equivalent to 1 decimetre^3 (1 dm^3).

littoral *adjective* Of or on a shore, especially a seashore: *the littoral zone. —noun* The zone between the limits of high and low tides.

liver 1. A large glandular organ in the abdomen of vertebrate animals that is essential to many metabolic processes. The liver secretes bile, stores fat and sugar as reserve energy sources, converts harmful substances to less toxic forms and regulates the amount of blood in the body. **2.** A similar organ of invertebrate animals.

liverwort Any of numerous small, green plants that lack vascular tissue and do not bear seeds. Liverworts usually grow in moist soil and on damp rocks and tree trunks. They are related to the mosses.

lizard Any of numerous reptiles having a scaly, often slender body, a tapering tail and usually four legs. Lizards typically have movable eyelids, unlike most other reptiles. The iguana and chameleon are lizards.

load 1. The resistance that a machine must overcome in order to work. **2.** The power output of a generator or power plant.

loam Soil composed of approximately equal quantities of sand, silt and clay. It typically also contains decayed plant matter known as humus.

Lobachevski, Nikolai Ivanovich 1792–1856. Russian mathematician who developed two systems of geometry that were not based on Euclid's axioms.

lobe 1. A rounded projection, as on a leaf or body part. **2.** An anatomical division of an organ of the body, such as the liver or lungs, bounded by fissures and connective tissue.

lobe-finned fish Any of various bony fish with fins that are rounded and fleshy, suggesting limbs. The lobe-finned fish are thought by some to be ancestors of amphibians and other land-dwelling vertebrate animals. They first appeared in the Ordovician Period and are extinct except for the coelacanth and lungfish.

locomotion The ability of an animal to move

from place to place. In many animals, locomotion is produced by the action of limbs or other appendages, such as wings or flagella. Other organisms, such as snakes, propel themselves by thrusting the body sideways against a hard surface. Fish move through the water by means of wave-like muscle contractions that course through the body from head to tail.

lodestone *or* **loadstone** A piece of the mineral magnetite that acts like a magnet.

loess A very fine grained silt or clay, thought to be deposited as dust blown by the wind. Most loess is believed to have originated during the Pleistocene Epoch from areas of land covered by glaciers and from desert surfaces.

logarithm The power to which a base must be raised to produce a given number. For example, if the base is 10, then 3 is the logarithm of 1000 (written log 1000 = 3) because $10^3 = 1000$.

logic The study of the principles of reasoning.

longitude Distance east or west on the Earth's surface, measured in degrees from a certain meridian, usually the prime meridian at Greenwich in London, which has a longitude of 0°. The distance of a degree of longitude is about 111 kilometres or 60 nautical miles at the equator, narrowing to zero at the poles. Longitude and latitude are the coordinates used to identify any point on the Earth's surface. *Compare* **latitude**.

longitudinal wave A wave in which the particles of the medium through which the wave moves vibrate in the same direction as the wave travels. Sound waves are a type of longitudinal wave. *See more at* **wave**. *Compare* **transverse wave**.

longsightedness The ability to see distant objects better than objects at close range. It is caused by the eye focusing incoming light behind the retina rather than directly on it, usually because of a problem with the shape of the eyeball or because the lens does not change shape sufficiently. Also called *hyperopia* and *farsightedness*. *Compare* **shortsightedness**.

long ton *See* **ton** (sense 2).

Lonsdale, Dame Kathleen Yardley 1903–1971. Irish physicist. In 1929 her X-ray analysis showed that the carbon atoms in the benzene ring are arranged hexagonally and are in the same plane.

Lorenz, Konrad Zacharias 1903–1989. In the late 1930s, the Austrian Konrad Lorenz founded the science of ethology, the study of animal behaviour under natural conditions. Much of his work was carried out with Nikolaas Tinbergen. Rather than studying animal learning in laboratories, Lorenz and his colleagues made a point of investigating the behaviour of animals in the wild. They mainly studied the behaviour of birds, fish and some insects whose behaviour contains a relatively high proportion of instinctive patterns, and they made comparisons between the species. His studies led to a deeper understanding of behaviour patterns.

louse (*plural* **lice**) Any of numerous small, wingless insects that often live as parasites on the bodies of other animals, including humans. Lice have mouthparts adapted for biting or sucking, and they often feed on blood.

lowest common denominator The least common multiple of the denominators of a set of fractions. For example, the lowest common denominator of $\frac{1}{3}$ and $\frac{3}{4}$ is 12.

low tide The time at which the tide reaches its lowest level.

Lr The symbol for **lawrencium**.

Lu The symbol for **lutetium**.

lumbar Located at or near the part of the back

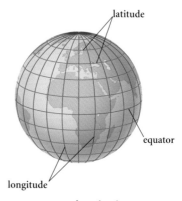

■ **longitude**

lying between the lowest ribs and the hips: *lumbar vertebrae*; *the lumbar spine.*

lumen 1. *Anatomy.* The central space in a tubular organ, such as a blood vessel or intestine. **2.** *Physics.* A unit used to measure the amount of light passing through a given area per second. One lumen is equal to the amount of light that passes through a given area (shaped like a cone) that is illuminated by a light with a brightness of one candela.

luminescence 1. The emission of light as a result of the excitation of atoms by a source of energy other than heat. *Bioluminescence, fluorescence* and *phosphorescence* are examples of luminescence that can be produced by biological or chemical processes. **2.** The light produced in this way.

lunar 1. Relating to the moon: *a lunar mountain.* **2.** Measured by the revolution of the moon: *a lunar month.*

lunar eclipse *See under* **eclipse.**

lung 1. Either of two spongy organs in the chest of air-breathing vertebrate animals that serve as the organs of gas exchange. Blood flowing through the lungs picks up oxygen from inhaled air and releases carbon dioxide, which is exhaled. Air enters and leaves the lungs through the bronchial tubes. **2.** A similar organ found in some invertebrates.

lungfish Any of several tropical freshwater fish that, in addition to having gills, have lung-like organs for breathing air. Lungfish have a long, narrow body, and certain species can survive periods of drought inside a mucus-lined cocoon in the mud. The lungfish and the coelacanth are the only living lobe-finned fishes.

Luria, Salvador Edward 1912–1991. Italian-born American biologist whose research on gene mutation and bacteria increased scientific understanding of the role of DNA in bacterial viruses.

lustre The shine from the surface of a mineral. Lustre is important in describing different kinds of minerals. It is usually characterized as metallic, glassy, pearly or dull.

lutetium A silvery-white metallic element of the lanthanide series that is used in nuclear technology. Its radioactive isotope is used to find the age of meteorites. *Symbol* **Lu.** *Atomic number* 71. *See* **Periodic Table,** pages 260–261.

lux A unit used to measure illumination. One lux is equal to one lumen per square metre.

L wave *See* **surface wave.** *See panel at* **earthquake.**

Lwoff, André Michel 1902–1994. French microbiologist who studied the genetics of bacterial viruses and explained how they reproduce. His findings have been important in cancer research and in understanding how viruses resist drugs.

lye A strong alkaline solution of potassium hydroxide or sodium hydroxide, made by allowing water to wash through wood ashes. It is used to make soap.

Lyell, Sir Charles 1797–1875. Scottish geologist who is considered one of the founders of modern geology. His *Principles of Geology* (1830–1833) had a powerful influence on the science of his day.

Lyme disease A disease caused by bacteria that is transmitted by a species of tick called a deer tick. It begins as a large red spot at the site of the tick bite that expands to a rash, and is usually followed by chills, a high temperature and fatigue, often lasting for several weeks. If untreated it can lead to serious and long-term complications.

lymph The clear fluid flowing through the lymphatic system that serves mainly to bathe and nourish the tissues of the body. It is composed of blood plasma that has leaked out through the capillaries into the tissues.

lymphatic system A network of vessels, tissues and organs in vertebrate animals that helps the body regulate fluid balance and fight against disease. The vessels of the lymphatic system drain excess fluid (called lymph) from the tissues and return it to the circulating blood. Lymphocytes circulate throughout the lymphatic system.

lymph node A bean-shaped mass of tissue found along the vessels of the lymphatic system. Lymph nodes act to filter foreign substances from the blood.

lymphocyte Any of various white blood cells that function in the body's immune system by recognizing and deactivating specific foreign substances called antigens. Certain lymphocytes (called *B cells*) act by stimulating the production of antibodies. Others (*T cells*) contain receptors on their cell surfaces that are capable of recognizing and binding to specific antigens. *See also* **white blood cell.**

Lyra A constellation in the Northern Hemisphere near Cygnus and Hercules.

lysine An essential amino acid. *See more at* **amino acid.**

lysis The disintegration of a cell that results from destruction of the cell membrane by a specific substance, especially an antibody or toxin.

lysosome A structure in the cytoplasm of many cells that is surrounded by a membrane and contains enzymes that digest food molecules. *See more at* **cell.**

M m

m 1. Abbreviation of **mass. 2.** Abbreviation of **metre.**

machine 1. A simple device that applies force or changes the direction of a force in order to perform a task. The lever, pulley, inclined plane, screw, wedge, and the wheel and axle are all simple machines. **2.** A device made of simple machines and used to perform a task: *a washing machine.*

Mach number The ratio of the speed of a body to the speed of sound in a particular medium. For example, an aeroplane flying through air at twice the speed of sound has a Mach number of 2.

macro– A prefix that means "large", as in *macronucleus,* a large kind of nucleus.

macroclimate The climate of a large geographical area. *Compare* **microclimate.**

macromolecule A large molecule, such as a protein, consisting of many smaller molecules linked together.

macrophage Any of the large white blood cells in many vertebrates that engulf and break down foreign particles and bacteria in blood or lymph. Macrophages are important in the body's defence against disease and are found mainly in the spleen, lymph nodes and liver.

macula An area near the centre of the retina in vertebrate animals where vision is sharpest.

mad cow disease A disease of cattle in which the tissues of the brain deteriorate and take on a spongy appearance, resulting in abnormal behaviour and loss of muscle control. Mad cow disease is thought to be caused by infection-carrying agents called prions. A form of the disease is thought to be transmitted to humans through eating meat. Also called *bovine spongiform encephalopathy (BSE).*

Magellanic Clouds Three small, irregular galaxies that lie relatively near the Milky Way galaxy. The Large Magellanic Cloud and the Small Magellanic Cloud are visible to the naked eye in the Southern Hemisphere. They were named after the Portuguese explorer Ferdinand Magellan, who was the first person to describe them clearly. In the early 1980s, another galaxy called the Mini Magellanic Cloud was found lying about 20,000 light years beyond the Small Magellanic Cloud.

magma The molten rock material that originates under the Earth's crust and forms igneous rock when it has cooled. When magma cools and solidifies beneath the Earth's surface, it forms what are known as intrusive rocks. When it reaches the Earth's surface, it flows out as lava and forms extrusive (or volcanic) rocks.

magnesium A lightweight, moderately hard, silvery-white metallic element that is an alkaline-earth metal and burns with an intense white flame. It is an essential component of chlorophyll and is used in lightweight alloys, flash photography and fireworks. *Symbol* **Mg.** *Atomic number* 12. *See* **Periodic Table,** pages 260–261.

magnesium oxide (also known as **magnesia**) A white powder, MgO, used in heat-resistant materials because of its very high melting point. It is also used in medicine as an antacid or laxative.

magnet 1. A rock, piece of metal or other solid that has the property of attracting iron or steel. A lodestone is a natural magnet, but most magnets today are made by inducing magnetism in a material such as steel or a metal alloy. Magnets have two magnetic poles, called north and south. **2.** An electromagnet.

magnetic Having the properties of a magnet; showing magnetism.

magnetic declination The horizontal angle between the true geographic North Pole and the magnetic north pole, at any given point on the Earth's surface.

magnetic disc A memory device, such as a floppy disc or a hard disc, that is covered with a magnetic coating. Digital information is stored on magnetic discs in the form of microscopically small, magnetized needles.

magnetic field The area around a magnet in which its magnetism can affect other objects. *See panel at* **magnetism.**

magnetic flux A measure of the strength of the magnetic field around a magnet or an electric current, based on the total number of magnetic lines of force that pass through a specific area. The unit of magnetic flux is the tesla (T).

magnetic force 1. The force that exists between two magnets, caused by the interaction of their magnetic fields. This force causes the magnets to attract or repel one another. 2. The force that exists between two moving, electrically charged particles, causing them to attract or repel one another.

magnetic north The direction towards which the north-seeking arrow of a compass points. ❖ The **magnetic north pole** is the northern pole of the Earth's magnetic field and changes slightly in response to variations in the Earth's magnetism. The current magnetic north pole is located in the Arctic Islands of Canada. *Compare* **geographic north.**

magnetic pole 1. Either of two areas of a magnet where the magnetic field is strongest. *See panel at* **magnetism.** 2. Either of two points on the Earth's surface towards which a compass needle points. One of these points is referred to as the North Pole and one as the South Pole. The location of the magnetic poles, which are found near to but not exactly at the geographic poles, changes gradually over time.

magnetic resonance imaging *or* **MRI** The use of nuclear magnetic resonance to produce images of the molecules that make up a substance, especially the soft tissues of the human body. Magnetic resonance imaging is used in medicine to diagnose disorders of body structures that do not show up well on X-rays. *See more at* **nuclear magnetic resonance.**

magnetic storm A disturbance or fluctuation in the Earth's magnetic field, caused by streams of charged particles given off by solar flares.

magnetism 1. The force produced by a magnetic field. 2. The properties or effects of magnets: *Magnetism causes a compass needle to point north.*

magnetite A usually brown to black, magnetic mineral composed of an iron oxide. Magnetite occurs in many different types of rocks, commonly as small octahedrons. It is an important source of iron.

magnetize To cause an object to become magnetic. For example, a steel bar may be magnetized by stroking it in one direction with one end of a bar magnet.

magnetometer An instrument for measuring the magnitude and direction of a magnetic field. Magnetometers are often used in archaeological and geological investigations to determine the intensity and direction of the Earth's magnetic field at various times in the past.

magnetron An electron tube that produces microwave radiation by applying magnetic and electric fields to a stream of electrons emitted by a heated filament. Magnetrons are used in radar and in microwave ovens.

Did You Know?

magnetism

The force known as *magnetism* is caused by the motion of electrons. As these tiny, negatively charged particles revolve around an atomic nucleus, they create an electric current that produces a *magnetic field.* This invisible field is made up of closed loops called *lines of force* that surround and run through the atom like tiny racetracks. The places where these lines of force come together are strongly magnetic and are called north and south *poles.* In some substances, these tiny magnetic fields naturally align, and the entire substance acts like a magnet – with north and south poles and a magnetic field. These naturally magnetic substances are called *permanent magnets.* Other things, such as a coil of wire, may be made to behave like a magnet by running electric current through them. These electrically produced magnets, called *electromagnets,* are used in many devices, such as the one that translates electrical signals into the voice you hear on the telephone.

magnitude 1. The brightness of a star or another celestial body as seen from the Earth, measured on a numerical scale in which lower numbers mean greater brightness. The dimmest stars visible to the unaided eye have magnitude 6, while the brightest star outside our solar system, Sirius, has magnitude −1.4. The moon has magnitude −12.7 and the sun has magnitude −26.8. **2.** A measure of the total amount of energy released by an earthquake, as indicated on the Richter scale.

maiasaura *or* **maiasaur** A duck-billed dinosaur of the late Cretaceous Period of North America. Its remains suggest that the adults lived in herds and cared for their young in large nesting sites.

Maiman, Theodore Harold Born 1927. American physicist who constructed the first working laser, in 1960.

mainframe A large, powerful computer, often serving many terminals. Mainframe computers have now largely been replaced by desktop computers joined together in networks.

malachite A bright-green copper carbonate mineral found in copper veins and used as a copper ore. Malachite often occurs together with the mineral azurite.

malaria An infectious disease found in tropical areas. It is caused by the *Plasmodium* parasite, which is transmitted by female *Anopheles* mosquitoes. The parasite is transmitted when the mosquito takes a blood meal from a human before laying her eggs, and the parasites then attack the red blood cells of their human hosts. Malaria causes repeated attacks of chills, fever and sweating. It results in weakness and eventually death. Around 267 million people in the world are infected with malaria and about 2 million people die each year as a result of the disease.

male *adjective* **1.** *Zoology.* **a.** Relating to a male reproductive cell (a sperm cell). **b.** Being the sex that can fertilize egg cells and father offspring: *a male kangaroo.* **2.** *Botany.* **a.** Being a structure, especially a stamen or anther, that produces reproductive cells or nuclei that are capable of fertilizing a female reproductive cell. **b.** Bearing stamens but not pistils: *male flowers.* —*noun* A male organism.

malignant Likely to spread or get worse: *a malignant tumour.*

malleable Capable of being shaped or formed in its solid state, especially by pressure or hammering. Gold is the most malleable substance known.

malleus The largest and outermost of the three small bones (called ossicles) in the middle ear. It is also called the hammer.

malnutrition Poor nourishment caused by lack of essential foods or by disease.

malocclusion A condition in which the upper and lower teeth do not meet properly; a faulty bite.

Malpighi, Marcello 1628–1694. Italian anatomist who was the first to use a microscope in the study of anatomy. He discovered the capillary system, extending the work of William Harvey.

maltose A sugar made by the action of various enzymes on starch. It is formed in the body during digestion.

mammal Any of various warm-blooded vertebrate animals whose young feed on milk that is produced by the mother's mammary glands. Mammals have sweat glands, and the mammary glands are a specially modified version of these. Unlike other vertebrates, mammals have a diaphragm that separates the heart and lungs from the other internal organs, red blood cells that lack a nucleus and usually hair or fur. All mammals except for the monotremes bear live young. Dogs, mice, whales and humans are mammals.

mammary gland One of the glands in female mammals that produces milk. It is present but undeveloped in the male. In most animals, the gland opens onto the surface by means of a nipple or teat.

mammogram An X-ray image of the human breast, used to detect tumours or other abnormalities.

mammoth Any of various extinct elephants of very large size that had long, upwardly curving tusks and thick hair. Mammoths lived throughout the Northern Hemisphere during the Ice Age.

manatee Any of various plant-eating water mammals living in rivers and bays along the tropical Atlantic Ocean. Manatees avoid contact

■ **mammoth**

with humans, have flippers shaped like paddles and are more closely related to elephants than they are to dolphins or whales.

mandible **1.** The lower part of the jaw in vertebrate animals. *See more at* **skeleton. 2.** One of the pincer-like mouthparts of insects and other arthropods.

manganese A greyish-white, hard, brittle metallic element that occurs in several different minerals. It is used to increase the hardness and strength of steel and other important alloys. *Symbol* **Mn.** *Atomic number* 25. *See* **Periodic Table,** pages 260–261.

manometer An instrument that measures the pressure exerted by liquids and gases.

mantle **1.** The layer of the Earth between the crust and the core. It consists mainly of silicate minerals and has an upper, partially molten part and a lower, solid part. The upper mantle is the source of magma and volcanic lava. **2.** The layer of soft tissue that covers the body of a clam, oyster

or other mollusc and secretes the material that forms the shell.

marble A metamorphic rock consisting primarily of calcite and dolomite. Marble is formed by the action of heat and pressure on limestone. Although it is usually white to grey in colour, it often has irregularly coloured marks due to impurities. *See table at* **rock.**

Marconi, Guglielmo 1874–1937. Italian physicist and inventor. In 1901 he used radio waves to transmit signals in Morse code across the Atlantic Ocean. Soon after his experiment, radio waves became established as a medium for communications.

mare (*pronounced* maray) (*plural* **maria**) Any of the large, dark areas on the moon or on Mars or other planets.

marine Relating to or living in the sea: *marine ecosystems; marine animals.*

marine biology The scientific study of organisms living in or dependent on the sea.

marrow *See* **bone marrow.**

Mars The fourth planet from the sun and the third smallest, with a diameter about half that of Earth. Mars has seasons similar to but much longer than Earth's. *See table at* **solar system,** pages 314–315. *See panel at* **planet.**

marsh An area of low-lying wet land, often having an abundance of reeds and rushes.

■ **manatee**

■ **manometer**

To calculate pressure in a U-tube manometer, add the sum of the readings above and below zero. The manometer on the left is at equilibrium. The manometer on the right shows readings of 2 above zero and 2 below zero, indicating a pressure of 4.

■ **Mars**

marsupial Any of various mammals whose young are very undeveloped when born and continue developing outside their mother's body attached to one of her nipples. Most marsupials have longer hindlegs than forelimbs, and the females usually have pouches in which they carry their young. Kangaroos, opossums and koalas are marsupials. Marsupials are only found in Australia, Tasmania and New Guinea, except for opossums and shrew opossums which are found in South America.

maser Any of several devices that amplify or generate microwaves. Masers are similar to lasers but emit microwaves instead of light.

mass A measure of the amount of matter contained in a physical body. Mass is independent of gravity and is therefore different from weight. *See panel at* **weight.**

mass-energy equivalence The principle that mass and energy can be converted into each other and that a particular quantity of mass is equivalent to a particular quantity of energy. The principle was stated mathematically by Albert Einstein as $E = mc^2$, where E is the energy in joules, m is the mass in kilograms and c is the speed of light in metres per second.

mass number The total number of neutrons and protons in the nucleus of an atom. For example, nitrogen has 7 protons and 7 neutrons in its nucleus, giving it a mass number of 14.

mass spectrometer A device that ionizes atoms and molecules and then uses electric or magnetic fields to determine the mass/charge ratio of these ions. The range of ions produced by a particular substance, whether an element or compound, is known as the **mass spectrum** of the substance.

mastication The chewing or grinding of food by the teeth.

mastodon Any of several extinct mammals similar to elephants and mammoths except in the shape of their molar teeth. Like elephants, mastodons had a pair of long, curved tusks growing from their upper jaw, but they also sometimes had a second pair from the lower jaw. They lived from the Oligocene Epoch to the end of the Ice Age.

mastoid A protruding area of bone in the lower part of the skull that is located behind the ear in humans and many other vertebrates.

mathematics The study of the measurement, relationships and properties of quantities and sets, using numbers and symbols. Arithmetic, algebra, geometry and calculus are branches of mathematics.

matrix 1. A substance within which something is contained or embedded. The mineral grains of a rock in which fossils are embedded make up a matrix. Bone cells are embedded in a matrix of collagen fibres and mineral salts. **2.** *Mathematics.* An array of numbers arranged in rows and columns and enclosed by brackets. An $m \times n$ matrix consists of mn numbers arranged in m rows and n columns.

matter Something that occupies space, has mass and can exist ordinarily as a solid, liquid or gas.

maturation The process of becoming fully developed or ripe, as when a reproductive cell, such as an egg or a sperm, becomes capable of fertilization.

Maury, Matthew Fontaine 1806–1873. American naval officer and oceanographer who charted the currents and winds of the Atlantic, Pacific and Indian Oceans and wrote the pioneering book *Physical Geography of the Sea* (1855).

maxilla The upper part of the jaw in vertebrate animals.

maximum (*plural* **maxima**) **1.** The greatest known or greatest possible number, measure, quantity or degree. **2.** *Mathematics.* The greatest value of a function, if it has such a value.

Maxwell, James Clerk 1831–1879. Scottish physicist who developed four laws of electromagnetism showing that light is composed of electromagnetic waves. He determined that Saturn's rings are composed of a large number of tiny particles and experimented with colour vision, producing the first colour photograph (1861).

Mayr, Ernst Walter Born 1904. US zoologist whose early work was on the birdlife of the Pacific Ocean. He led three scientific expeditions to New Guinea and the Solomon Islands (1928–1930), but in his later career he became one of the most important proponents of the neo-Darwinian concepts of evolution. Mayr was also the first person to propose the "founder effect", describing the genetic bottleneck of a population "founded" by a few individuals.

McClintock, Barbara 1902–1992. American geneticist who proved that genes can change position on chromosomes. By studying the chromosomes found in maize, McClintock discovered that the genes for specific traits, such as kernel colour, did not remain in the same place on the chromosomes. Her discoveries were not immediately accepted by other scientists, however. She spent decades completing more research before her work, which overturned one of Gregor Mendel's main theories about heredity, was finally recognized.

Md The symbol for **mendelevium**.

mean A number or quantity having a value that is intermediate between other numbers or quantities, especially an arithmetic mean or average. *See more at* **arithmetic mean.**

meander A sharp U-shaped bend in a river.

mean time Time measured with reference to an imaginary sun that lies in the same plane as the Earth's equator and that is orbited by the Earth at a constant speed. Using this convention results in equal, 24-hour days throughout the year. If days were measured by the actual movement of the sun, they would vary slightly in length at different times of the year.

measles A highly contagious disease that is caused by a virus and usually occurs in childhood. Symptoms include a high temperature, coughing and a rash that begins on the face and then spreads to other parts of the body. In some parts of the world, measles is still a disease that kills many children. However, there is a very effective vaccine against it, so the number of cases of measles in countries like the UK, most of Europe and the US is now very low.

measurement A system for determining quantity, capacity or dimension. All systems of measurement use units whose amounts have been arbitrarily set and agreed upon. Several systems of measurement are in common use, notably the metric system and the imperial system. The metric system has been officially adopted as the international standard for use in science, providing scientists all over the world with an efficient way of comparing the results of experiments conducted at different times and in different places.

mechanical engineering The branch of engineering that specializes in the design, production and uses of machines.

mechanics **1.** The branch of physics that focuses on motion and on the effects of forces and energy on solids, liquids and gases at rest or in motion. **2.** The functional aspect of a system: *the mechanics of blood circulation.* **3.** The development, production and use of machines or mechanical devices.

Medawar, Sir Peter Brian 1915–1987. British zoologist and pioneering immunologist. Peter Medawar began his pioneering work on burns victims during World War II. He studied skin grafting as a potentially life-saving treatment for badly burned patients, and he realized that rejection of a graft occurred by the same immunological mechanism as the response of the body to foreign bodies. He went on to investigate the problems of tissue rejection in transplant operations. With his colleague Sir Macfarlane Burnet he showed that prenatal injection of tissues from one individual to another resulted in the acceptance of the donor's tissues.

median **1.** In a sequence of numbers arranged from smallest to largest the median is: **a.** The middle number, when such a sequence has an odd

Measurement Table

THE INTERNATIONAL SYSTEM OF UNITS

The International System of Units is an expanded and modified version of the metric system made up of base units from which all others in the system are derived. Larger or smaller multiples of any base unit are formed by adding a prefix to the unit and multiplying it by the appropriate factor. For example, to get a kilometre (multiplying factor = 10^3), you would multiply one metre by 1000. Similarly, to get a centimetre (multiplying factor = 10^{-2}), you would multiply one metre by 0.01. The International System is commonly referred to throughout the World as SI, the abbreviation for Système International.

BASE UNITS

Unit	Quantity	Symbol
metre	length	m
kilogram	mass	kg
second	time	s
ampere	electric current	A
kelvin	temperature	K
mole	amount of matter	mol
candela	luminous intensity	cd

PREFIXES

Prefix	Symbol	Multiplying Factor	Prefix	Symbol	Multiplying Factor
tera-	T	10^{12} = 1,000,000,000,000	deci-	d	10^{-1} = 0.1
giga-	G	10^{9} = 1,000,000,000	centi-	c	10^{-2} = 0.01
mega-	M	10^{6} = 1,000,000	milli-	m	10^{-3} = 0.001
kilo-	k	10^{3} = 1000	micro-	m	10^{-6} = 0.000,001
hecto-	h	10^{2} = 100	nano-	n	10^{-9} = 0.000,000,001
deca-	da	10 = 10	pico-	p	10^{-12} = 0.000,000,000,001

THE METRIC SYSTEM

LENGTH

Unit	Relation to Other Metric Units
picometre	0.001 nanometres
nanometre	1000 picometres
micrometre	1000 nanometres
millimetre	1000 micrometres
centimetre	10 millimetres
decimetre	10 centimetres
metre	100 centimetres
hectometre	100 metres
kilometre	1000 metres
megametre	1000 kilometres

LIQUID VOLUME OR CAPACITY

Unit	Relation to Other Metric Units
millilitre	0.001 centilitres
centilitre	10 millilitres
decilitre	10 centilitres
litre	1000 millilitres
hectolitre	100 litres
kilolitre	1000 litres

WEIGHT

Unit	Relation to Other Metric Units
microgram	0.001 micrograms
milligram	1000 micrograms
gram	1000 milligrams
kilogram	1000 grams
tonne	1000 kilograms

Also:

cubic centimetre	1 millilitre	1000 cubic millimetres = 1 cubic centimetre
cubic decimetre	1 litre	1000 cubic centimetres = 1 cubic decimetre
cubic metre	1 kilolitre	1000 cubic decimetres = 1 cubic metre

CONVERSION BETWEEN METRIC AND IMPERIAL SYSTEMS

FROM IMPERIAL TO METRIC

When you know	multiply by	to find
inches	25.4	millimetres
	2.54	centimetres
feet	30.48	centimetres
yards	0.91	metres
miles	1.61	kilometres
fluid ounces	28.4	millilitres
pints	0.56	litres
quarts	1.14	litres
gallons	4.54	litres
ounces	28.35	grams
pounds	0.45	kilograms

FROM METRIC TO IMPERIAL

When you know	multiply by	to find
millimetres	0.04	inches
centimetres	0.39	inches
metres	3.28	feet
	1.09	yards
kilometres	0.62	miles
millilitres	0.03	fluid ounces
litres	0.88	quarts
	0.22	gallons
	1.76	pints
grams	0.035	ounces
kilograms	2.20	pounds

TEMPERATURE CONVERSION BETWEEN CELSIUS AND FAHRENHEIT

$$°C = (°F - 32) \div 1.8$$

$$°F = (°C \times 1.8) + 32$$

Condition	Celsius	Fahrenheit
Boiling point of water	100°	212°
Normal body temperature	37°	98.6°
Freezing point of water	0°	32°

Condition	Celsius	Fahrenheit
Lowest temperature Gabriel Fahrenheit could obtain mixing salt and ice	-17.8°	0°

number of values. For example, in the sequence 3, 4, 14, 35, 280, the median is 14. **b.** The average of the two middle numbers, when such a sequence has an even number of values. For example, in the sequence 4, 8, 10, 56, the median is 9 (the average of 8 and 10). *Compare* **arithmetic mean, average, mode. 2.** A line joining a vertex of a triangle to the midpoint of the opposite side.

medicine 1. The scientific study of diagnosing, treating or preventing disease and injury to the body or mind. **2.** A drug or other substance used to treat a disease or injury.

medium (*plural* **media**) **1.** A substance, such as agar, in which bacteria or other microorganisms are grown for scientific purposes. **2.** A substance through which energy, especially in waves, is transmitted. Sound waves, for example, can travel through the medium of a solid (such as wood or steel), a liquid (such as water) or a gas (such as air). In contrast, seismic waves can travel through the Earth's solid layers and in some cases its liquid layer (the outer core) as well, but they cannot travel through air. *See more at* **wave.**

medulla 1. *See* **medulla oblongata. 2.** The central core of an anatomical structure, such as the adrenal gland or the kidney.

medulla oblongata The lowermost portion of the brainstem in humans and other mammals. It regulates many involuntary functions, such as breathing and circulation.

medusa A cnidarian in its free-swimming stage. Medusas are bell-shaped, with tentacles hanging down around a central mouth. Jellyfish are medusas, while corals and sea anemones lack a medusa stage and exist only as polyps. *Compare* **polyp.**

mega– A prefix that means: **1.** Large, as in *megatherium,* large animal. **2.** One million, as in *megahertz,* one million hertz. **3.** 2^{20} (that is, 1,048,576), which is the power of 2 closest to a million, as in *megabyte.*

megabit *Computer Science.* **1.** One million bits. **2.** 1,048,576 (that is, 2^{20}) bits. *See panel at* **megabyte.**

megabyte 1. A unit of computer memory or data storage capacity equal to 1024 kilobytes (2^{20} bytes). **2.** One million bytes.

megadose An exceptionally large dose, as of a drug or vitamin. *See also* **megavitamin.**

megafauna Large or relatively large animals of a particular place or time period. Sabre-toothed tigers and mastodons belong to the extinct megafauna of the Oligocene and Pleistocene Epochs.

megahertz A unit of frequency equal to one million cycles per second, used to express the frequency of radio waves.

megaparsec One million parsecs.

megatherium A large, extinct ground sloth that

Usage

megabyte

Usually the prefix *kilo–* means "one thousand", and the prefix *mega–* means "one million". However, in the calculation of data storage these prefixes have a different meaning. Data storage capacity (measured in bytes) is based on powers of 2 because of the binary nature of bits (1 byte is 8, or 2^3, bits). Here, the prefix *mega–* refers to the power of 2 closest to 1,000,000, which is 2^{20}, or 1,048,576. Thus, a megabyte is 1,048,576 bytes, although it is also used less technically to refer to a million bytes. Similarly, the prefix *kilo–* refers either to 1000 or to 2^{10} (1024). Measuring the transmission of data is somewhat different from measuring its storage. Since a bit of transmitted data is considered as one signal pulse rather than an either/or unit, it is natural to count transmitted bits using ordinary numbers instead of the binary system. So a megabyte of transmitted data usually refers to a million (not 1,048,576) bits. Other prefixes for greater amounts, such as *giga–* and *tera–,* follow similar rules for data storage and transmission.

lived from the Miocene through the Pleistocene Epochs, primarily in South America. It was as large as an elephant, had long curved claws and ate plants.

megavitamin A dose of a vitamin that is much greater than the amount required to maintain health. *See also* **megadose**.

megavolt One million volts.

megawatt One million watts.

meiosis A type of cell division, occurring in two phases, that reduces the number of chromosomes in reproductive cells to half the original number. It results in the production of reproductive cells (called gametes) in animals and the formation of spores in plants, fungi and most algae. The starter cells in the sex organs are normal diploid cells. The first phase of meiosis involves duplication and then separation of the chromosomes, followed by division into two daughter cells that each contain half the number of chromosomes as the original cell. In the second phase, each of the new cells divides to give four haploid daughter cells, each carrying half the genetic information of the original cell. These are the sex cells. *See panel at* **mitosis.**

Meitner, Lise 1878–1968. Austrian-born Swedish physicist who was the first to describe the process of nuclear fission. Her contributions to the field of nuclear fission led to the development of the atomic bomb and nuclear energy.

meitnerium A synthetic, radioactive element that is produced by bombarding bismuth with iron ions. Its most stable isotope has a half-life of 70 milliseconds. *Symbol* **Mt.** *Atomic number* 109. *See* **Periodic Table,** pages 260–261.

melanin A dark pigment found in the skin, hair, scales, feathers and eyes of animals. It provides protection against the sun's rays by absorbing ultraviolet light.

melanism Dark coloration of the skin, hair, fur

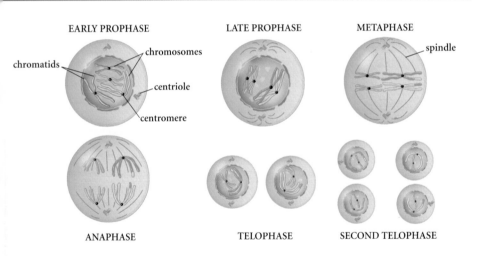

EARLY PROPHASE   LATE PROPHASE   METAPHASE

chromosomes

chromatids

centriole

centromere

spindle

ANAPHASE   TELOPHASE   SECOND TELOPHASE

■ **meiosis**

In early prophase, chromosomes line up to form pairs, centrioles move towards opposite ends of the cell, and the membrane surrounding the nucleus disappears. In late prophase, the chromatids line up along the centre of the cell. During metaphase, each member of a chromatid pair becomes attached to spindle fibres from opposite ends of the cell. In anaphase, the chromosomes from each chromatid pair separate and begin to move towards opposite ends of the cell. During telophase, the cell divides into two new daughter cells, each with half the original number of chromosomes. In second telophase, each of the two daughter cells from the first division divides again to produce a total of four daughter cells, each having just a single set of chromosomes.

215

or feathers because of a high concentration of melanin.

melanoma A type of skin cancer that arises from the cells that produce melanin, usually appearing as a dark-coloured spot or mole.

melt To change from a solid to a liquid state by heating or being heated to the melting point.

meltdown Severe overheating of a nuclear reactor core, resulting in melting of the core and escape of radioactive material.

melting point The temperature at which a solid becomes a liquid. For a given substance, the melting point of its solid form is the same as the freezing point of its liquid form. The melting point of ice is 0°C; that of iron is 1535°C. *See also* **freezing point**.

meltwater Water that comes from melting snow or ice, especially from a glacier.

member *Mathematics.* **1.** A quantity that belongs to a set; an element of a set. **2.** The expression on either side of an equality sign.

membrane 1. A thin, flexible layer of tissue that covers, lines, separates or connects cells or parts of an organism. **2.** *See* **cell membrane**. **3.**

Chemistry. A thin sheet of natural or synthetic material that is permeable to substances in solution.

membranous 1. Relating to, made of or similar to a membrane. **2.** Characterized by the formation of a membrane or a layer like a membrane.

memory 1. The ability to remember past experiences or learnt information. **2a.** A unit of a computer in which data is stored for later use. **b.** A computer's capacity for storing information: *How much memory does this computer have?*

menarche The first occurrence of a menstrual period in a woman or other female primates. *See also* **menstrual cycle, menstruation**.

Mendel, Gregor Johann 1822–1884. Austrian botanist and founder of the science of genetics. He formulated the important principles, known as Mendel's laws, that formed the basis of modern genetics.

Mendeleev, Dmitri Ivanovich 1834–1907. Russian chemist. He devised the Periodic Table, which shows the relationships between the chemical elements. It was first published in 1869.

mendelevium A synthetic, radioactive metallic

Biography

Gregor Mendel

Gregor Mendel entered a monastery at the age of 21, later becoming a priest. He was sent to a university to study mathematics and science. When he returned to the monastery, he combined his interests in maths and botany by carrying out experiments on pea plants. Mendel cross-pollinated plants of different sizes and shapes, as well as plants that produced different colours of flowers or peas. He analysed each generation of new plants that were produced by this cross-pollination. He observed that some characteristics remained constant in every generation, while others remained hidden, or recessive, and became apparent only in later generations. We now refer to the unit of inheritance which determines a particular

trait as a gene, and the different forms of that gene which it is possible to inherit as alleles. Mendel proved that two alleles exist for each trait and that each allele comes from a different parent. A recessive trait becomes visible only when both alleles for the trait are present, but a dominant trait is visible even when only one dominant allele is present. Mendel summarized his discoveries in 1865 in laws that became fundamental to the study of human heredity.

element of the actinide series that is produced by bombarding einsteinium with helium ions. Its most stable isotope has a half-life of about two months. *Symbol* **Md.** *Atomic number* 101. *See* **Periodic Table,** pages 260–261.

Mendel's law The principles first proposed by Gregor Mendel to describe the inheritance of traits as they are passed from one generation to the next. The first law is known as the **law of segregation.** It states that in a diploid organism, one unit (or allele) for each trait is inherited from each parent, to give a total of two alleles for each trait. The segregation (separation) of each pair of alleles takes place when the gametes are formed. Mendel's second law is the **law of independent assortment.** This states that different traits are inherited independently of each other. In other words, traits like height and eye colour have nothing to do with each other. Mendel's laws are still very relevant today, although we now know that there are a number of exceptions to his second law because some genes are linked and so inherited together. *See more at* **hereditary, heredity, inheritance.**

meninges The membranes enclosing the brain and spinal cord.

meningitis Inflammation of the membranes (meninges) that enclose the brain and spinal cord, usually resulting from a bacterial infection.

meniscus 1. A lens that is concave on one side and convex on the other. **2.** The curved upper

■ **Mercator projection**

surface of a column of liquid. The surface is concave if the molecules of the liquid are attracted to the container walls and convex if they are not. **3.** A piece of cartilage shaped like a crescent and located at the junction of two bones in a joint, such as the knee. *See more at* **joint.**

menopause The time at which female menstruation ceases, occurring usually between 45 and 55 years of age in humans. *Compare* **menarche.**

menses *See* **menstruation.**

menstrual cycle The series of bodily changes in women and other female primates in which the lining of the uterus thickens to allow for implantation of a fertilized egg. The cycle takes about a month to complete, with ovulation usually occurring around the midway point. If the egg produced is not fertilized, the lining of the uterus breaks down and is discharged during menstruation.

menstruation The monthly flow of blood from the uterus of a non-pregnant female that begins at puberty in girls and in the females of other primates. Also called *menses.*

mental illness Any of various disorders or diseases characterized by processes of thought and behaviour considered to be abnormal.

menthol A white, crystalline compound obtained from peppermint oil. It is used as a flavouring and as a mild anaesthetic.

Mercalli scale A 12-point scale for measuring the amount of ground movement during an earthquake. *Compare* **Richter scale.**

Mercator projection A method of making a

■ **meniscus**
The meniscus of water (left, dyed red) is concave and that of mercury (right) is convex.

flat map of the Earth's surface so that the meridians and parallels appear as straight lines that cross at right angles. In a Mercator projection, the areas furthest away from the equator appear larger, making the polar regions greatly distorted. *Compare* **conic projection, homolosine projection, sinusoidal projection.**

mercury A silvery-white, dense, poisonous metallic element that is a liquid at room temperature. It is used to make thermometers and pesticides. *Symbol* **Hg.** *Atomic number* 80. *See* **Periodic Table,** pages 260–261.

Mercury The planet closest to the sun and the second smallest, with a diameter about two-fifths that of Earth. Mercury's surface is covered with mountains, craters, ridges and valleys. It orbits the sun once every 88 days, the shortest amount of time for any planet. *See table at* **solar system,** pages 314–315. *See panel at* **planet.**

meridian 1a. An imaginary line forming a great circle that passes through the North and South Poles. **b.** Either half of such a circle from pole to pole. All the places on the same meridian have the same longitude. *See more at* **equator. 2.** *Astronomy.* A great circle passing through the poles of the celestial sphere and the point on the celestial sphere that is directly above the observer.

meristem Plant tissue whose cells actively divide to produce new tissues that cause the plant to grow. The cells of the meristem are not specialized but can become specialized to form the tissues of roots, leaves and other plant parts. The growing tips of roots and stems and the tissue layer known as cambium are part of a plant's meristem.

mesa An area of high land with a flat top and two or more steep, cliff-like sides. Mesas are larger than buttes and smaller than plateaus, and are common in the southwest United States and Mexico.

Mesolithic The cultural period of the Stone Age between the Palaeolithic and Neolithic, beginning at different times in different parts of the world, about 40,000 to 10,000 years ago. The Mesolithic is marked by the appearance of small-bladed stone tools and weapons and by the beginnings of settled communities. *Compare* **Neolithic, Palaeolithic.**

mesophyll The tissues of a leaf in which photosynthesis occurs. These mainly consist of the palisade layer and the loosely packed parenchyma tissue, known as the spongy mesophyll, which contains lots of air spaces.

mesosphere The layer of the Earth's atmosphere lying above the stratosphere and below the thermosphere, from about 50 to 80

Word History

mercury

Like a few other elements, mercury has a chemical symbol, Hg, that bears no resemblance to its name. This is because Hg is an abbreviation of the Latin name of the element, which was *hydrargium.* This word in turn was taken over from Greek, where it literally meant "water-silver". With this name the Greeks were referring to the fact that mercury is a silvery liquid at room temperature, rather than a solid like other metals. Similarly, an older English name for this element is *quicksilver,* which means "living silver", referring to its ability to move like a living thing. (The word *quick* used to mean "alive", as in the Biblical phrase "the quick and the dead".) The term *mercury* refers to the fact that the element flows about quickly: the name comes from the Roman god Mercury, who was the swift-footed messenger of the gods.

■ **mesa**
Northern Territory, Australia

Usage

metal

We think of metals as hard, shiny materials used to make things like paper clips and cars. But for chemists, a *metal* is a chemical element that loses electrons in a chemical reaction. Metal atoms do this because of the structure of their electron shells – the layers in which electrons are arranged around an atom's nucleus. If an element's outermost electron shell is filled, the element is stable and does not react easily. But if the shell contains only a few electrons, the atom will try to share them with another atom in a chemical reaction, thereby becoming stable. Elements having only one electron in their outermost shell are the most reactive; all they have to do to become stable is lose this electron. Such elements are *alkali metals* like sodium and potassium, and they are listed in the left-hand column of the Periodic Table, pages 260–261. The metals further towards the right-hand side of the Periodic Table, such as tin and lead, have more electrons in their outermost shell and are not as reactive because sharing or losing all these electrons would require more energy. The elements that fall between these extremes are somewhat reactive and are called *transition elements*. They include elements like iron, copper, tungsten and silver.

kilometres above the Earth's surface. In the mesosphere, temperatures decrease with increasing altitude.

Mesozoic The era of geological time from about 245 to 65 million years ago. The Mesozoic Era was characterized by the development of flowering plants and by the appearance and extinction of dinosaurs. *See chart at* **geological time**, pages 148–149.

messenger RNA *See under* RNA.

metabolism The chemical processes by which cells produce the substances and energy needed to sustain life. In metabolism, organic compounds are broken down to provide heat and energy, while simpler molecules are used to build complex compounds like proteins for growth and repair of tissues. Many metabolic processes are brought about by the action of enzymes. —*adjective* **metabolic.**

metacarpal Any of the bones of the hand lying between the carpal bones and the bones of the fingers or digits (phalanges). *See more at* **skeleton.**

metal 1. Any of a large group of elements, including iron, gold, copper, lead and magnesium, that are good conductors of heat and electricity. Metals can be hammered into thin sheets or drawn into wires. They are usually shiny and opaque. All metals except mercury are solid at room temperature. **2.** An alloy, such as steel or bronze, made of two or more metals.

metallic bond The chemical bonding that holds the atoms of a metal together. This bond is formed from the attraction between mobile electrons and fixed, positively charged metallic atom nuclei. Whereas most chemical bonds are localized between specific neighbouring atoms, metallic bonds extend over the entire molecular structure. *See more at* **bond.**

metalloid 1. An element that is not a metal but that has some properties of metals. Arsenic, for example, is a metalloid that looks like a metal, but is a poor conductor of electricity. **2.** A nonmetallic element, such as carbon, that can form alloys with metals. *See also* **metal.**

metallurgy The science and technology of extracting metals from their ores, refining them for use and creating alloys and useful objects from them.

metamorphic 1. *Zoology.* Relating to metamorphosis. *See* **metamorphosis. 2.** *Geology.* Relating to metamorphism. Metamorphic rocks are formed when igneous, sedimentary or other metamorphic rocks undergo a physical change due to extreme heat and pressure. These changes often produce folded layers and veins in the rocks, and they can also cause pockets of precious minerals to form. *See table at* **rock.**

metamorphism The process by which rocks are changed in composition, texture or structure by extreme heat and pressure.

metamorphosis Dramatic change in the form and often the habits of an animal during its development after birth or hatching. The transformation of a maggot into an adult fly and of a tadpole into an adult frog, are examples of metamorphosis. The young of such animals are called larvae.

metaphase The stage of cell division in which the spindle forms and chromosomes line up along the centre of the cell. In mitosis, metaphase is preceded by prophase and followed by anaphase. *See more at* **meiosis, mitosis.**

metastasis The spread of cancerous cells from one area of the body to other areas. —*verb* **metastasize.**

metatarsal Any of the bones of the foot lying between the tarsal bones and the bones of the toes or digits (phalanges). *See more at* **skeleton.**

metazoan A multicellular animal of the group

■ **metamorphosis**
development of a monarch butterfly from egg to larva (caterpillar) to pupa (chrysalis) to imago (adult)

Metazoa, especially one having a body made up of many cells arranged in tissues and organs.

meteor 1. A bright trail or streak of light that appears in the night sky when a meteoroid enters the Earth's atmosphere. The friction with the air causes the rock to glow with heat. 2. A rocky body that produces such light. Most meteors burn up before reaching the Earth's surface. *See panel at* **solar system.** ❖ A **meteor shower** occurs when a large number of meteors appear together and seem to come from the same area in the sky. *See also* **meteorite, meteoroid.**

meteor/meteorite/meteoroid

The streaks of light we sometimes see in the night sky and call *meteors* were not identified as interplanetary rocks until the 19th century. Before then, the streaks of light were considered only one of a variety of atmospheric phenomena, all of which were given the name *meteor.* Rain was an *aqueous meteor,* winds and storms were *airy meteors* and streaks of light in the sky were *fiery meteors.* This general use of *meteor* survives in our word *meteorology,* the study of the weather and atmospheric phenomena. Nowadays, astronomers use any of three words for rocks from interplanetary space, depending on their stage of descent to the Earth. A *meteoroid* is a rock in space that has the potential to collide with the Earth's atmosphere. Meteoroids range in size from a speck of dust to a chunk about 100 metres in diameter, though most are smaller than a pebble. So, if a small or tiny asteroid or fragment of a comet is floating in orbit near the Earth, it is called a meteoroid. When a meteoroid enters the atmosphere, it becomes a *meteor.* The light that it gives off when heated by friction with the atmosphere is also called a *meteor.* If the rock is not obliterated by the friction and lands on the ground, it is called a *meteorite.* For this term, scientists borrowed the *–ite* suffix used in the names of minerals like malachite and pyrite.

meteorite A meteor that reaches the Earth's surface without completely burning up. *See also* meteor, meteoroid. *See panel at* meteor.

meteoroid A rocky celestial body that travels through interplanetary space in an orbit that crosses the Earth's orbit. *See also* meteor, meteorite. *See panel at* meteor.

meteorology The scientific study of the atmosphere and of atmospheric conditions, especially as they relate to weather. *See panel at* meteor.

methanal A colourless gas, CH_2O, having a sharp, suffocating odour. It is used in making plastics and is mixed with water to form a solution to preserve biological specimens.

methane A colourless, odourless, flammable gas that is the simplest of the hydrocarbons, having the formula CH_4. It is the major constituent of natural gas and is released during the decomposition of plant or other organic compounds, as in marshes and coal mines.

methanoic acid A colourless, caustic, fuming liquid, CH_2O_2, that occurs naturally as the poison of ants and stinging nettles. It is used in making textiles and paper and in insecticides.

methanol A colourless, toxic, flammable liquid, CH_4O, used as an antifreeze, a general solvent and a fuel.

methionine An essential amino acid. *See more at* amino acid.

methyl The organic radical —CH_3, derived from methane. The methyl group occurs in many important chemical compounds such as methyl alcohol.

metre The basic unit of length in the metric system. *See table at* measurement.

metre-kilogram-second Relating to a system of measurement in which the metre, the kilogram and the second are the basic units of length, mass and time.

metric Relating to the metre or the metric system. *See table at* measurement.

metric system A decimal system of weights and measures based on the metre as a unit of length, the kilogram as a unit of mass and the litre as a unit of volume. *See table at* measurement.

metric ton A unit of mass or weight equal to 1000 kilograms. *See table at* measurement.

mg Abbreviation of milligram.

Mg The symbol for magnesium.

MHz Abbreviation of megahertz.

mica Any of a group of aluminium silicate minerals that can be split easily into thin, partly transparent sheets. Mica is common in igneous and metamorphic rocks. It is highly resistant to heat and is used in electric fuses and other electrical equipment.

Michelson, Albert Abraham 1852–1931. German-born American physicist. With Edward Morley he disproved the existence of ether, the hypothetical medium of electromagnetic waves.

micro– A prefix that means: **1.** Small, as in *microorganism,* a very small organism. **2.** One millionth, as in *microgram,* one millionth of a gram.

microbe A microorganism, especially a bacterium that causes disease. *See panel at* germ.

microbiology The scientific study of the structure and function of microorganisms.

microclimate The climate of a small, specific place within a larger area. An area as small as a garden or park can have several different microclimates depending on how much sunlight, shade or exposure to the wind there is at a particular spot. *Compare* macroclimate.

microcline A type of feldspar consisting of potassium aluminium silicate. Microcline is white, pink, red-brown or green.

micrograph A photograph of an object viewed through a microscope.

micrometer A device for measuring very small distances, angles or objects.

micrometre A unit of length in the metric system equal to one millionth of a metre. Also called *micron.*

micron *See* micrometre.

microorganism An organism that can be seen only with the aid of a microscope. Microorganisms include bacteria, protozoans, algae and fungi. *See panel at* germ.

microscope An instrument used to magnify objects that are hard to see or are invisible to the naked eye. Optical microscopes consist of a lens or combination of lenses. Others, such as the electron microscope, use different means of magnification, such as beams of electrons.

microsecond A unit of time equal to one millionth of a second.

microtubule Any of the tube-shaped structures that help cells maintain their shape and assist in forming the cell spindle during cell division. Microtubules are found in the cytoplasm of the cells of all organisms except bacteria.

microwave **1.** A high-frequency radio wave used in radio broadcasting and radar. *See more at* **electromagnetic spectrum. 2.** An oven in which food is cooked, warmed or thawed by means of microwaves.

midbrain The middle part of the brain in vertebrate animals. In most animals except mammals, the midbrain processes sensory information. In mammals, it serves mainly to connect the forebrain with the hindbrain. *Compare* **forebrain, hindbrain.**

middle ear The part of the ear in most mammals that contains the eardrum and three small bones, called ossicles, which transmit sound vibrations from the eardrum to the inner ear. *See more at* **ear.**

magnetron   microwave   rotating
              beam   reflector

■ **microwave**
A microwave oven is activated when an electric current causes a magnetron to emit a beam of microwaves. The beam is distributed throughout the unit by a rotating reflector. The microwaves agitate water molecules in the food, generating enough heat to cook it.

mid-ocean ridge A long mountain range on the seafloor, extending almost continuously through the North and South Atlantic Oceans, the Indian Ocean and the South Pacific Ocean. A deep rift valley is located at its centre, from which magma flows and forms new oceanic crust. As the magma cools and hardens it becomes part of the mountain range. *See more at* **tectonic boundary.**

midrib The central or main vein of a leaf. *See more at* **leaf.**

migraine A severe, throbbing headache, often accompanied by nausea, that usually affects only one side of the head and tends to recur.

migratory Travelling from one place to another at regular times of year, often over long distances. Salmon, whales and swallows are all migratory animals.

mildew Any of various fungi that form a white or greyish coating on surfaces, such as plant leaves, cloth or leather, especially under damp, warm conditions.

mile **1.** A unit of length equal to about 1609 metres (5280 feet or 1760 yards). Also called *statute mile.* **2.** *See* **nautical mile.** *See table at* **measurement.**

milk A white liquid produced by the mammary glands of female mammals for feeding their young. Milk contains protein, fat, vitamins, minerals and sugars, especially lactose.

Milky Way The galaxy containing the solar system. It is visible as a broad band of faint light in the night sky.

milli– A prefix that means "one thousandth", as in *millimetre,* one thousandth of a metre.

millibar A unit of atmospheric pressure equal to 0.001 bar.

milligram A unit of mass or weight in the metric system equal to 0.001 gram. *See table at* **measurement.**

millilitre A unit of fluid volume or capacity in the metric system equal to 0.001 litre. *See table at* **measurement.**

millimetre A unit of length in the metric system equal to 0.001 metre. *See table at* **measurement.**

millipede Any of various worm-like arthropods having a body composed of many narrow segments, most of which have two pairs of legs.

■ **Milky Way**
the summer Milky Way photographed from Mount Graham, Arizona, USA

Millipedes feed on plants and, unlike centipedes, do not have venomous pincers. *Compare* **centipede.**

Milstein, César Born 1927. British-born Argentinian immunologist. With Georges Köhler he developed a method of producing antibodies that fight specific cells. The antibodies are used to diagnose and treat specific forms of cancer and other diseases.

milt Fish sperm, together with the milky liquid that contains them.

mimicry The resemblance of one organism to another or to an object in its surroundings for concealment or protection from predators.

mineral 1. A naturally occurring, solid, inorganic element or compound having a uniform composition and a specific crystal structure. Minerals typically have a characteristic hardness and colour, or range of colours, by which they can be recognized. **2.** A natural substance of commercial value, such as iron ore, coal or crude oil, that is obtained by mining, quarrying or drilling.

mineralogy The scientific study of minerals, their composition and properties and the places where they are likely to occur.

mineral oil A colourless, odourless and tasteless oil distilled from petroleum. It is used as a lubricant and, in medicine, as a laxative.

minimum (*plural* **minima**) **1.** The lowest known or lowest possible number, measure,

---

Did You Know?

mimicry

For many organisms, the chances of survival are improved because they have evolved to imitate the looks, sounds, actions or other characteristics of a different organism. *Mimicry,* the name for this imitation of one species by another, is especially common among insects. In one classic example, the viceroy butterfly is protected from being eaten by birds because its wing markings resemble the striking orange and black markings of the monarch butterfly. The monarch is a dangerous dinner for birds; it contains chemicals that make them so sick that they vomit and their hearts beat dangerously fast. The viceroy, on the other hand, makes a tasty meal, but because it looks like the monarch, birds tend to avoid it. Mimicry can also help a predator catch prey: some ant-eating spiders, for example, look like the ants they eat. Disguised in this way, they have an easy time catching unsuspecting ants.

---

quantity or degree. **2.** *Mathematics.* The lowest value of a function, if it has such a value.

minuend A number from which another is subtracted. For example, in the numerical expression $100 - 23 = 77$, the minuend is 100.

minute 1. A unit of time equal to $\frac{1}{60}$ of an hour or 60 seconds. **2.** A unit of angular measurement that is equal to $\frac{1}{60}$ of a degree or 60 seconds.

■ **mimicry**
a treehopper disguised as a thorn

Miocene The fourth epoch of the Tertiary Period, from about 23 to 5 million years ago, characterized by the development of grasses and grazing mammals. *See chart at* **geological time,** pages 148–149.

mirage An optical illusion in which nonexistent bodies of water and upside-down reflections of objects appear in the distance. A mirage occurs when light is bent after entering a low layer of hot air at an angle.

mirror A surface that is able to reflect light, often used to form an image of an object placed in front of it.

miscible Relating to two or more substances, such as water and alcohol, that can be mixed together in any proportion without separating. *Compare* **immiscible.**

> ## Did You Know?
>
> ### mirrors
>
> The earliest mirrors, some dating to over 3000 years ago, were highly polished pieces of bronze or another metal. Later on, in the Middle Ages, the technique began of covering one side of a piece of glass with a sheet of reflective metal. Nowadays, mirrors are usually coated with an extremely thin layer of silver or aluminium. While you may use mirrors just to look at yourself in the bathroom each morning, in science they have many important uses. Mirrors are used in microscopes, telescopes and lasers, as well as in devices that collect light for solar power and the devices that make holograms. For instance, a common type of telescope called a *reflecting telescope* has a concave mirror (curved inwards) at one end. This mirror, unlike your bathroom mirror, is coated on the front side with the reflecting layer; if light were allowed to pass through the glass first, it could get distorted and interfere with accurate observation. Light waves hitting the curved surface are reflected so that they all come together at a single point, the *focus.* The larger the mirror, the more powerful the telescope; the largest ones are over 9 metres wide.

Mitchell, Maria 1818–1889. American astronomer and academic noted for her study of sunspots and nebulae and for the discovery of a comet (1847).

mite Any of various very small arachnids that often live as parasites on other animals or plants. Like ticks and unlike spiders, mites have no division between the cephalothorax and abdomen.

mitochondrion (*plural* **mitochondria**) A structure in the cytoplasm of all cells except bacteria in which food molecules are broken down in the presence of oxygen and converted to energy in the form of ATP. Mitochondria contain their own DNA. *See more at* **cell.**

mitosis The process in cell division in which the nucleus divides to produce two new nuclei, each having the same number and type of chromosomes as the original. Early in mitosis, each chromosome duplicates itself to form two identical strands (called chromatids), which then line up along the centre of the cell by attaching to the fibres of the cell spindle. The pairs of chromatids then separate, each strand of a pair moving to an opposite end of the cell. When a new membrane forms around each of the two groups of chromosomes, division of the nucleus is complete. The four main phases of mitosis are prophase, metaphase, anaphase and telophase.

mixed number A number, such as $7\frac{3}{8}$, consisting of a whole number and a vulgar fraction.

mixture A composition of two or more substances that are not chemically combined with each other and are capable of being separated.

ml *or* **mL** Abbreviation of **millilitre.**

inner membrane
outer membrane
cristae
ribosomes

■ **mitochondrion**

mitosis/meiosis

Mitosis and *meiosis* are easily confused, since both words refer to processes of cell division. Most cells have two full sets of chromosomes and are technically called *diploid* cells. When such a cell divides, it must first duplicate its chromosomes so as to produce two daughter cells that are also diploid. This type of cell division is called *mitosis,* and all somatic cells – that is, cells used for the maintenance, functioning and growth of an organism – reproduce in this way. By contrast, reproductive cells, or gametes, are created by another kind of cell division, called *meiosis.* Meiosis also starts out by duplicating the chromosomes, but there are two divisions instead of one, with the result that four daughter cells are produced rather than two. Since the number of chromosomes is halved with each division, each daughter cell has just a single set of chromosomes and is called a *haploid* cell. During reproduction, the union of a female gamete with a male gamete restores the two full sets of chromosomes in a new organism.

mm Abbreviation of **millimetre.**

MMR vaccine A triple vaccine that protects against three common childhood diseases – measles, mumps and rubella (German measles). It is used extensively all over the world, and in the UK it is given to children when they are around 15 months old. In the late 20th century some researchers in the UK claimed to have found evidence that the MMR vaccine was linked to the development of Crohn's disease and autism in some children. There was immense debate and many parents refused to have their children

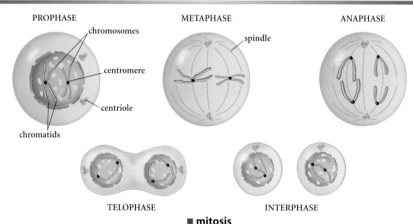

■ **mitosis**

During prophase, chromosomes thicken and shorten. They have been copied to form two chromatids held together by a centromere. The centrioles move to opposite ends of a cell, and the membrane around the nucleus disappears. In metaphase, a spindle is formed to which the centromeres attach, lining up the chromosomes at the centre. In anaphase, the chromatids split, and the chromosomes from each chromatid pair move to opposite ends of the spindle. In telophase, the spindle disappears, and a nuclear membrane forms around the chromosomes at each end of the cell. The cytoplasm of the dividing cell begins to separate during mitosis and ends after division of the nucleus is complete. During interphase, the daughter cells develop and the chromosomes duplicate.

vaccinated. As a result the number of deaths and of children left severely damaged from measles and mumps began to rise. The great majority of scientific evidence suggests that the MMR vaccine is safe to use and that the benefits outweigh any possible risks, but in the UK some people are still very concerned about the vaccine.

Mn The symbol for **manganese**.

Mo The symbol for **molybdenum**.

moa Any of various flightless, wingless, ostrich-like birds of New Zealand that have been extinct for over a century. One species grew to 4 metres in height, making it the largest bird of modern times.

Möbius strip A continuous one-sided surface formed from a rectangular strip by rotating one end 180° and attaching it to the other end. *Compare* **Klein bottle.**

mode The value that occurs most frequently in a data set. For example, in the set 125, 140, 172, 164, 140, 110, the mode is 140. *Compare* **arithmetic mean, average, median.**

model A description or concept of a system or set of observable events that accounts for all its known properties in a reasonable way.

modem A device for converting between analogue and digital signals. Modems are most often used to allow computers to communicate over telephone wires by converting the digital signals used by computers into analogue signals that travel through the telephone system, and then converting the analogue signal back into a digital signal at the other end.

moderator A substance, such as graphite or water, placed in a nuclear reactor to slow neutrons down to speeds at which they are likely to cause additional nuclear fission.

modification A change in an organism that results from external influences and is not inheritable.

modulate To vary the amplitude, frequency or some other characteristic of electromagnetic waves in a way that makes them correspond to a signal or to information that is to be transmitted.

Mohorovičić discontinuity *or* **Moho** The boundary between the Earth's crust and mantle. The Mohorovičić discontinuity is located at an average depth of 8 kilometres under the oceans and 32 kilometres under the continents. Scientists discovered this boundary because they noticed that the velocity of seismic waves increases sharply as the waves pass from the Earth's crust into the mantle.

Mohs scale A scale used to measure the relative hardness of a mineral by its resistance to scratching. There are ten standard minerals on this scale, ranging from talc, the softest (measuring 1 on the scale), to diamond, the hardest (measuring 10 on the scale).

molar[1] *Chemistry.* **1.** Relating to a mole. **2.** Containing one mole of solute per litre of solution. *See* **mole**[3].

molar[2] Any of the teeth located towards the back of the jaws, having broad crowns for grinding food. Adult humans have 12 molars.

mole[1] A small, usually dark growth on the skin.

mole[2] Any of various small mammals that have silky fur, strong forefeet for burrowing and poor vision. Moles usually live underground and eat insects and earthworms.

mole[3] The relative atomic or formula mass of any substance in grams. For example, the element sulphur has a relative atomic mass of 32, so 1 mole of sulphur has a mass of 32 grams. Carbon dioxide, CO_2, has a relative formula mass of 44, so one mole of carbon dioxide has a mass of 44 grams. The number of particles (atoms, molecules or ions) in a mole is equal to Avogadro's number, 6.02×10^{23}.

molecular formula A chemical formula that shows the total number and kinds of atoms in a molecule, but not their structural arrangement. For example, the molecular formula of aspirin is $C_9H_8O_4$. *Compare* **structural formula.**

■ **Möbius strip**

molecular weight *See* relative formula mass.

molecule A group of two or more atoms linked together by sharing electrons in a chemical bond.

mollusc Any of numerous soft-bodied invertebrate animals, usually living in water and frequently having a hard outer shell. Mollusc bodies have a muscular foot, a well-developed circulatory and nervous system and often complex eyes. Molluscs include gastropods (snails and shellfish), slugs, octopuses and squids.

molybdenum A hard, silvery-white metallic element that resists corrosion and remains strong at high temperatures. It is used to harden and toughen steel and to make wire that can withstand high temperatures. Molybdenum is an essential trace element in plant metabolism. *Symbol* **Mo**. *Atomic number* 42. *See* **Periodic Table**, pages 260–261.

momentum A quantity used to measure the motion of a body, equal to the product of its mass and velocity. Any change in the speed or direction of a body changes its momentum.

moneran *See* prokaryote.

mongoose Any of various mammals of Asia and Africa that resemble weasels and are noted for their ability to kill poisonous snakes such as cobras.

monitor 1. A device that accepts video signals from a computer and displays information on a screen. *See panel at* **pixel**. 2. Any of various meat-eating lizards living in tropical regions of Asia and Africa and in Australia and New Guinea. Monitors range in length from about 2.5 centimetres to 3 metres, the largest being the Komodo dragon of Indonesia.

monkey Any of various primates of medium size that have long tails. Most monkeys live in trees in tropical or subtropical regions. Baboons, macaques, mandrills and marmosets are monkeys. *Compare* **ape**.

mono– A prefix that means "one, only, single", as in *monochromatic,* having only one colour. It is often found in chemical names where it means "containing just one" of the specified atom or group, as in *carbon monoxide,* which is carbon attached to a single oxygen atom.

monochromatic 1. Having or appearing to have only one colour: *monochromatic light.* 2. Consisting of a single wavelength of light or other radiation: *monochromatic X-rays.*

monoclinic Relating to a crystal having three axes of different lengths. Two of the axes are at oblique angles to each other, and the third axis is perpendicular to the plane that is made by the other two. The mineral gypsum has monoclinic crystals. *See more at* **crystal.**

monocotyledon *or* monocot Any of various flowering plants having a single cotyledon in the seed. Monocotyledons have leaves with parallel veins and flower parts in multiples of 3. Grasses, palms, lilies and irises are monocotyledons. *See more at* **leaf.** *Compare* **dicotyledon.**

monocyte Any of various large white blood cells that circulate in the blood and mature into macrophages. Monocytes engulf and break down microorganisms capable of causing infection.

Monod, Jacques Lucien 1910–1976. French biochemist. With François Jacob, he proposed the existence of messenger RNA. They also studied how genes control cellular activity by directing the synthesis of proteins.

monodactyl An animal having only one toe, digit or claw on each limb.

monoecious Having separate male flowers and female flowers on the same plant. Maize and oaks are monoecious plants. *Compare* **dioecious.**

monomer A molecule that can combine with others of the same kind to form a polymer. Glucose molecules, for example, are monomers that can combine to form the polymer cellulose.

monomial An algebraic expression consisting of a single term, such as $4x$.

mononucleosis A contagious disease caused by a virus and characterized by a high temperature, sore throat, swollen lymph nodes and tiredness. The symptoms may last for several weeks. It is commonly known as **glandular fever.**

monosaccharide Any of a class of simple carbohydrates that cannot be broken down to simpler sugars by hydrolysis. Fructose is a monosaccharide.

monosodium glutamate A white, crystalline salt used to flavour food, especially in China and

Japan. It occurs naturally in tomatoes, Parmesan cheese and seaweed.

monotreme The most primitive type of living mammal. Monotremes lay eggs, and the females have no teats but provide milk directly through the modified sweat glands in their skin to their young. Monotremes include only the duck-billed platypus, found in Australia and New Guinea, and the echidnas, found only in New Guinea.

monounsaturated Relating to an organic compound, especially an oil or fatty acid, having only one double or triple bond per molecule. *See more at* **unsaturated.**

monoxide A compound consisting of two elements, one of which is a single oxygen atom. Carbon monoxide, for example, contains a carbon atom bound to a single oxygen atom.

monsoon 1. A system of winds that influences the climate of a large area and that reverses direction with the seasons. Monsoons are caused primarily by the seasonal changes in temperature over large areas of land and water. **2.** In southern Asia, a wind that blows from the southwest in summer and usually brings heavy rains.

moon 1. Often **Moon.** The natural satellite of Earth, visible by reflection of sunlight and travelling around Earth in a slightly elliptical orbit at an average distance of about 384,500 kilometres. The moon's average diameter is 3476 kilometres, and its mass is about $\frac{1}{80}$ that of Earth. **2.** A natural satellite revolving around a planet: *the moons of Jupiter.* **3.** The moon as it appears at a particular time in its cycle of phases: *a half moon.*

moraine A mass of boulders, pebbles, sand and mud deposited in the form of a long ridge along the front or sides of a glacier. Moraines typically form because of the ploughing effect of a moving glacier, which causes it to pick up rock fragments and sediments as it moves, and because of the periodic melting of the ice, which causes the glacier to deposit these materials during warmer intervals. ❖ A moraine that forms in front of a glacier is a **terminal moraine.** ❖ A moraine that forms along the side of a glacier is a **lateral moraine.**

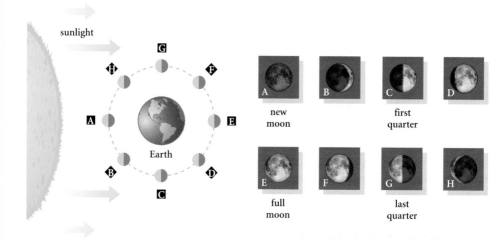

■ **moon**

Half of the moon is always in sunlight, as seen on the left. The relative positions of Earth, the moon and the sun determine how much of the lit half can be seen from Earth, as seen on the right. These forms in which the moon appears are known as phases.

Morley, Edward Williams 1838–1923. American chemist and physicist who with Albert Michelson disproved the existence of ether, the hypothetical medium of electromagnetic waves.

morphine A drug extracted from opium, used in medicine to relieve severe pain and for its sedative effects. It can be highly addictive.

morphology The size, shape and structure of an organism or one of its parts. Biologists usually describe the morphology of an organism separately from its physiology.

Moseley, Harry 1887–1915. English physicist who measured the X-ray spectra of over 30 different metals, and suggested that the regular variance from element to element was related to the nuclear charge, allowing the atomic numbers of elements to be calculated. Discontinuities in the spectral series made it clear that a number of elements were missing from the periodic table. Moseley's work made it possible to predict their properties; these elements were soon discovered and Moseley's ideas confirmed. Moseley's work

was an important step in advancing knowledge of the nature of the atom, firmly establishing that the properties of the elements are determined by atomic number rather than atomic weight.

mosquito Any of various winged insects, related to the flies, whose females suck blood through a tubular piercing organ called a proboscis. In tropical regions some kinds of mosquito can transmit diseases such as malaria and yellow fever.

moss 1. Any of numerous small, green plants that lack vascular tissue and do not bear seeds. Mosses usually live in moist, shady areas and grow in clusters or mats on the ground and on rocks and tree trunks. **2.** Any of a number of plants that look like mosses but are not related to them. For instance, reindeer moss is a lichen, Irish moss is an alga and Spanish moss is a flowering plant.

moth Any of various insects that resemble butterflies but are nocturnal and have smaller and less brightly coloured wings, stouter bodies and hair-like or feathery antennae. Unlike butterflies, moths tend to hold their wings out horizontally when at rest. *Compare* **butterfly.**

motherboard The main circuit board of a computer, usually containing the central processing unit and main system memory as well as circuitry that controls the disc drives, keyboard, monitor and other peripheral devices.

mother-of-pearl The hard, smooth, pearly layer on the inside of certain seashells, such as abalones and certain oysters. It is used to make buttons and jewellery. Also called *nacre. See also* **pearl.**

motile Moving or able to move by itself. Sperm and certain spores are motile. —*noun* **motility.**

motor *noun* A machine that uses a form of energy, such as electric energy or the explosive power of a fuel, to produce mechanical motion. —*adjective* Involving the nerves which carry information away from the central nervous system to the body, and the responses of the muscles to those nerves: *motor control; a motor nerve. Compare* **sensory.**

mould Any of various fungi that often form a fuzzy growth on the surface of organic matter. Some moulds cause food to go bad, but others are beneficial, such as those used to make certain

Did You Know?

moon

We earthlings usually think of our moon as *the* moon, but any planet's natural satellites are properly called moons. Jupiter has at least 28 moons, while Saturn has 30, and additional small ones around these and other planets may yet be discovered. Earth's moon is also not necessarily typical of other moons in the solar system. No water exists on our moon, but some scientists think that one of Jupiter's moons, Europa, may have liquid water under a thick layer of ice that might support life. Titan, a moon of Saturn, is also thought to have an environment that can support primitive life: a sea of ethane instead of water. Earth's moon is very quiet, geologically. By comparison, Io, another of Jupiter's moons, is a violent cauldron of geological activity. It is covered with huge volcanoes that emit plumes of sulphur so enormous that they can be seen by the Hubble Space Telescope orbiting Earth.

moult

cheeses and those from which drugs like penicillin were developed.

moult To shed an outer covering, such as skin or feathers, for replacement by a new growth. Many snakes, birds and arthropods moult.

mountain A generally massive and usually steep-sided raised portion of the Earth's surface. Mountains can occur as single peaks or as part of a long chain. They can form through volcanic activity, by erosion or by the collision of two tectonic plates. The Himalayas, which are the highest mountains in the world, formed when the plate carrying the landmass of India collided with the plate carrying the landmass of China.

mouse (*plural* **mice**) **1.** Any of numerous small rodents usually having a pointed snout, rounded ears and a long narrow tail. Some kinds live in or near human dwellings. **2.** A movable hand-held device that is connected to a computer and is moved about on a flat surface to direct the cursor on a screen. A mouse also has buttons for activating computer functions.

mouthpart Either of the appendages occurring in pairs in insects and other arthropods that extend from the head and are used for feeding.

MRI Abbreviation of **magnetic resonance imaging**.

Mt The symbol for **meitnerium**.

mucous membrane Any of the membranes lining the passages of the body that open onto the outside, such as the respiratory and digestive tracts. Cells in the mucous membranes secrete mucus, which lubricates the membranes and protects against infection.

mucus The slimy substance secreted by mucous membranes to lubricate and protect them. *See also* **phlegm.**

multi– A prefix that means "many" or "much", such as *multicellular,* having many cells.

multicellular Having or consisting of many cells: *multicellular organisms. Compare* **unicellular.**

multiple A number that may be divided by another number with no remainder. For example, 4, 10 and 32 are multiples of 2.

multiple sclerosis A disease of unknown cause in which the sheaths (myelin) around nerve

■ **moult**
A dragonfly nymph undergoes several moults during its development.

fibres become damaged. The nerves in the brain, spinal cord and eye are most commonly affected, causing weakness, loss of balance and coordination and visual disturbances. *Abbreviation* **MS.** *See also* **myelin.**

multiple star A system of three or more stars that usually orbit a common centre of mass. The group appears as a single star to the unaided eye. Alpha Centauri is a multiple star.

multiplicand A number that is multiplied by another number.

multiplication 1. The mathematical operation that consists of adding a number (the multiplicand) to itself a specified number of times. Thus multiplying 6 by 3 means adding 6 to itself three times. **2.** A mathematical operation performed on a pair of numbers in order to derive a third number called a product. It is sometimes convenient to consider multiplication as repeated addition in which one number indicates how many times the other is to be added together. For example, 3×4 equals $4 + 4 + 4$, which equals 4×3 and also equals $3 + 3 + 3 + 3$, in each case totalling 12.

multiplier The number by which another number is multiplied.

multiply To perform multiplication on a pair of quantities.

mumps A contagious disease, usually affecting children, that is caused by a virus. Symptoms include inflammation of the salivary glands, especially those at the back of the jaw. Mumps can lead to serious complications including brain damage and, in boys, sterility. Many children in the developed world are now vaccinated against mumps.

muscle A body tissue composed of elongated cells (called muscle fibres) that contract to produce movement. In vertebrate animals, voluntary movement is produced by the action of muscles on bone. Movement of the muscles of the heart and other organs is involuntary and controlled by the autonomic nervous system. —*adjective* **muscular.**

muscovite A usually colourless to pale-grey mineral composed mostly of a silicate of potassium and aluminium. Muscovite is one of the most common forms of mica.

muscular dystrophy Any of several hereditary diseases in which a person's muscles gradually deteriorate, causing progressive weakness.

mushroom Any of various fungi having a stalk topped by a fleshy, often umbrella-shaped cap. Some mushrooms are edible; others are poisonous.

mutation A change in the genes or chromosomes of an organism. Mutations occurring in the reproductive cells, such as an egg or sperm, can be passed from one generation to the next. Some mutations are harmful and some have no effect at all. Others can increase an organism's ability to survive. A mutation that benefits a species may evolve by means of natural selection into a trait shared by all members. *See panel at* **sickle cell anaemia.**

mutualism A symbiotic relationship between two organisms of different species in which each member benefits. *See panel at* **symbiosis.**

mycelium (*plural* **mycelia**) The mass of fine branching tubes (called hyphae) that forms the main growing structure of a fungus. Visible structures like mushrooms are reproductive structures produced by the mycelium.

mycology The scientific study of fungi.

myelin A whitish, fatty substance that forms a sheath around many nerve fibres. Myelin insulates the nerves and permits nerve impulses to travel more rapidly. The white matter of the brain is composed of nerve fibres covered in myelin.

myopia *See* **shortsightedness.**

N The symbol for **nitrogen**.

Na The symbol for **sodium**.

nacre *See* **mother-of-pearl.**

nadir The point on the celestial sphere that is directly below the observer and opposite the zenith.

nano– A prefix that means: **1.** One billionth, as in *nanosecond,* one billionth of a second. **2.** Very small or at a microscopic level, as in *nanotube.*

nanotube A type of carbon molecule in which the carbon atoms form a cylindrical or doughnut-like shape.

naphtha Any of several products made by refining petroleum or by breaking down coal tar. Naphtha is usually flammable, and is used as a solvent and as an ingredient in petrol. It is also used to make plastics.

naphthalene A white crystalline compound made from coal tar or petroleum and used to make dyes, moth repellents, explosives and solvents. Structurally, naphthalene consists of two benzene rings fused together with a common side.

narcotic Any of a group of drugs used to relieve pain and cause drowsiness. Narcotics are highly addictive.

nasal Relating to the nose: *the nasal passages.*

natural gas A mixture of hydrocarbon gases that occurs naturally beneath the Earth's surface, often with or near petroleum deposits. Natural gas contains mostly methane, but also has varying amounts of ethane, propane, butane and nitrogen. It is used as a fuel and in making organic compounds.

natural history The study and description of living things and natural objects, especially their origins, evolution and relationships to one another. Natural history includes the sciences of zoology, botany, geology and palaeontology.

naturalist A person who specializes in natural history, especially in the study of plants and animals in their natural surroundings.

naturalize To adapt or accustom a plant or animal to living in a region to which it is not native. Eucalyptus trees are native to Australia but have become naturalized in many other parts of the world.

natural logarithm A logarithm whose base is the irrational number *e*. Natural logarithms are frequently used in calculus. *See more at* **e.** *Compare* **common logarithm.**

natural number A positive integer.

natural resource Something, such as a forest, a mineral deposit or fresh water, that is found in nature and is necessary or useful to humans.

natural selection The principle that only organisms best suited to their environment survive long enough to pass on their genetic characteristics to their offspring. According to this principle, the proportion of the species having these characteristics increases with each generation. Natural selection results from random variation of genetic traits in a species and forms the basis of the process of evolution. *See panels at* **adaptation, evolution.**

nature 1. The world and its naturally occurring phenomena, together with all of the physical laws that govern them. **2.** Living organisms and their environments.

nautical mile A unit of length used in air and sea navigation, equal to about 1852 metres. *See table at* **measurement.**

nautilus A tropical sea mollusc having a spiral shell with alternating white and light-brown bands on the outside and many chambers on the inside. The nautilus is related to the squid and octopus.

Nb The symbol for **niobium**.

Nd The symbol for **neodymium**.

Ne The symbol for **neon**.

Neanderthal *or* **Neandertal** An extinct variety of human that lived throughout Europe and in parts of Asia and Africa during the late

■ **nebula**
planetary nebula, Milky Way

origin of the solar system according to which a rotating nebula cooled and contracted, flattening into a disc shape with a central bulge. The matter in the disc condensed into the planets, their moons, asteroids and comets, while the great mass at the centre became the sun.

nectar A sweet liquid secreted by certain flowers that is consumed by pollinating insects and birds and is gathered by bees to make honey.

needle 1. A narrow, stiff leaf, such as those of firs, pines and other conifers. The reduced surface area of needles minimizes water loss and allows needle-bearing plants to live in dry climates. *See more at* **leaf. 2.** *See* **hypodermic needle.**

negative 1. Less than zero, eg –3. **2.** Having the electric charge of an electron. The symbol for a negative charge is a minus sign. **3.** Having more electrons than protons. Negatively charged bodies, such as atoms or molecules, repel other negatively charged bodies but attract positively charged bodies. **4.** Not showing the presence of a suspected disease or microorganism, as in a blood test.

nematocyst One of the stinging cells in the tentacles of a jellyfish, hydra or related animal, used to capture prey and ward off attackers.

nematode Any of several slender cylindrical worms, usually of tiny size, that live in great numbers in water, soil, plants and animals. They have a simple structure, with a long hollow gut separated from the body wall by a fluid-filled space. Several nematodes are parasites on animals and humans and cause disease.

neodymium A shiny, silvery metallic element of the lanthanide series that exists in two forms. It is used to make glass for welders' goggles and purple glass for lasers. *Symbol* **Nd.** *Atomic number* 60. *See* **Periodic Table,** pages 260–261.

Neolithic The period of human culture that began around 10,000 years ago in the Middle East and later in other parts of the world. It is characterized by the beginning of farming, the domestication of animals, the development of crafts such as pottery and weaving, and the making of polished stone tools. *Compare* **Mesolithic, Palaeolithic.**

neon A rare element that is a noble gas and occurs naturally in extremely small amounts in

Pleistocene Epoch, until about 30,000 years ago. Neanderthals had a stocky build and large skulls with thick eyebrow ridges and big teeth. They usually lived in caves, made stone tools and were the earliest humans known to bury their dead. Neanderthals were either a subspecies of modern humans or a separate, closely related species. Also called *Neanderthal man.*

neap tide A tide in which the difference between high and low tide is the least. Neap tides occur twice a month when the sun and moon are at right angles to the Earth. When this is the case, their total gravitational pull on the Earth's water is weakened because it comes from two different directions. *Compare* **spring tide.** *See more at* **tide.**

nearsightedness *See* **shortsightedness.**

nebula (*plural* **nebulae** *or* **nebulas**) A thinly spread cloud of interstellar gas and dust. It will appear as a bright patch in the night sky if it reflects light from nearby stars, emits its own light, or re-emits ultraviolet radiation from nearby stars as visible light. If it absorbs light, the nebula appears as a dark patch. In dark nebulae, stars form from clumps of hydrogen gas. *See more at* **star.**

nebular hypothesis An explanation of the

■ neon
neon signs

the atmosphere. It is colourless but glows reddish orange when electricity passes through it, such as in a tube in an electric sign. Neon is also used for refrigeration. *Symbol* **Ne**. *Atomic number* 10. *See* **Periodic Table,** pages 260–261.

neoprene A tough synthetic rubber that is resistant to the effects of oils, solvents, heat and weather.

nephritis Inflammation of the kidneys.

nephron One of the units of the kidney that filter waste products from the blood and produce urine.

Neptune The eighth planet from the sun and the fourth largest, with a diameter almost four times that of Earth. Neptune has a very active weather system with extremely long and powerful storms. It is the second coldest planet in the solar system, with an average surface temperature of –225°C. *See table at* **solar system,** pages 314–315. *See panel at* **planet.**

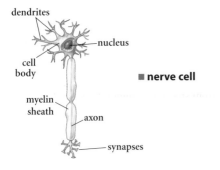

dendrites
nucleus
cell body
myelin sheath
axon
synapses

■ nerve cell

neptunium A silvery, radioactive metallic element of the actinide series. It occurs naturally in trace amounts in uranium ores and is produced artificially as a by-product of plutonium production. The most stable isotope of neptunium has a half-life of 2.1 million years. *Symbol* **Np**. *Atomic number* 93. *See* **Periodic Table,** pages 260–261.

nerve Any of the bundles of fibres made up of nerve cells that carry information in the form of electrical impulses throughout the body. Nerves send sensory information to the brain and spinal cord and carry impulses to the muscles, organs and glands.

nerve cell Any of the cells of the nervous system. Nerve cells typically consist of a cell body, which contains a nucleus and receives incoming nerve impulses through synapses, and an axon, which carries impulses away from the cell body. Also called *neuron. See more at* **cell.**

nerve fibre *See* **axon.**

nervous system The system of nerve cells and tissues that regulates the actions and responses of vertebrate and many invertebrate animals. The nervous system of vertebrates consists mainly of the brain, spinal cord and nerves. The nervous systems of invertebrates vary from a simple network of nerves to a complex nerve network under the control of a primitive brain. *See also* **autonomic nervous system, central nervous system, peripheral nervous system.**

net *Mathematics.* A flat shape that can be folded up into a solid shape.

neural Relating to the nerves or nervous system.

neurology The branch of medicine that deals with the diagnosis and treatment of disorders of nerves and the nervous system.

neuron *See* **nerve cell.**

neurotransmitter A chemical substance that helps transmit nerve impulses from one nerve cell to another by diffusing across the synapse.

neutral 1. Neither acid nor alkaline. **2.** Having positive electric charges exactly balanced by negative electric charges.

neutralize To make an acid or an alkaline solution neutral.

neutrino Any of three electrically neutral

■ newt
immature red-spotted newt

species have rough skin. They are amphibians, like frogs and toads.

newton A unit used to measure force. One newton is equal to the force needed to accelerate a mass of one kilogram one metre per second per second.

Newton, Sir Isaac 1642–1727. English mathematician and scientist. He invented a form of calculus and formulated the law of universal gravitation, a theory about the nature of light and three laws of motion. His treatise on gravitation, presented in *Principia Mathematica* (1687), was in his own account inspired by the sight of a falling apple. *See panel on* page 236.

Newton's law of gravitation The principle that two bodies exert a gravitational attraction for each other that increases as their masses increase and as the distance between them decreases. In mathematical terms, the force equals the product

subatomic particles that travel at the speed of light. Because they have no charge and negligible mass, neutrinos are very hard to detect

neutron An electrically neutral subatomic particle that is part of the nucleus of an atom and has a mass slightly greater than that of a proton. Beams of neutrons from nuclear reactors are used to bombard the atoms of various elements to produce fission and other nuclear reactions and to determine the atomic arrangements in molecules. *See more at* **atom.**

neutron star A celestial object consisting of an extremely dense mass of neutrons, formed by the forcing together of protons and electrons in the collapse of a massive star. Most neutron stars rotate very rapidly. Many have powerful magnetic fields that focus radio waves, light and other radiation into two beams that point outwards from the magnetic poles. *See more at* **star.**

Newcomen, Thomas 1663–1729. English inventor who developed an early steam engine (1711) that was used successfully to pump water.

new moon The phase of the moon that occurs when it passes between the Earth and the sun, making it either invisible or visible only as a thin crescent at sunset. *See more at* **moon.** *Compare* **full moon.**

newt Any of several small salamanders that live both on land and in the water. The water-dwelling species have smooth skin, while the land-dwelling

Did You Know?

neutrinos

Neutrinos were not observed until 1956, roughly a quarter of a century after the physicist Wolfgang Pauli first proposed, on theoretical grounds, that they might exist. Pauli was studying certain radioactive decay processes in which it seemed that energy somehow mysteriously disappeared. He suggested that the energy was carried away by a very small, electrically neutral particle that was not being detected. (He originally wanted to name the particle a neutron but didn't publish the suggestion, and a few years later the particle we now know as the neutron was discovered and named in print. The Italian physicist Enrico Fermi then coined the term neutrino, which means "little neutron" in Italian.) Neutrinos are hard to detect because they interact only very weakly with other forms of matter. Most of the neutrinos that reach the Earth from space pass right through and go out the other side. Even a chunk of iron a few light years thick would stop only about half of the neutrinos that struck it.

Biography

Isaac Newton

Isaac Newton was born prematurely, just after midnight on Christmas Day 1642 in Lincolnshire, and was not expected to survive his first day. Brought up on a farm, Newton did not go to school until he was twelve, where he became fluent in Latin but learnt no maths and no science. When he was seventeen his family stopped his schooling and tried to persuade him to take over his father's farm. Newton was a dreadful farmer, because he would read and study while the animals escaped and the fields were neglected! It was not long before Newton's uncle and schoolteacher persuaded his mother that university was the place for her son, and at 18 years of age he went to Cambridge. Once at university, Newton worked hard, teaching himself mathematics because he needed it to understand a book on astronomy he had bought. He quickly discovered both a great love for the subject and an enormous ability. Newton was a law unto himself. He kept large amounts of his work to himself for years because he was worried about publishing it and being criticized, attacking anyone who did not agree with him, and hiding many of his ideas away from other people. Probably his most famous work concerns gravity. In the summer of 1665, the University of Cambridge closed down due to an outbreak of the plague and

Newton went back home to Lincolnshire. One day, while sitting in his apple orchard, he heard an apple fall from a tree. He suddenly realized that the apple fell because the Earth had attracted it, and in that moment his theory of gravitation was born. From his work on gravity, Newton went on to define the nature of mass, weight, force, inertia and acceleration. He also worked on light and colour, developed whole areas of mathematics including calculus, and was an enthusiastic alchemist who among many other feats tasted almost all of the known heavy metals (which we now know are poisonous!). Alexander Pope, a poet who lived at the same time as Newton, wrote: *Nature and Nature's laws lay hid in night; God said, "Let Newton be!" and all was light.* Despite his strange behaviour, Newton's work still represents one of the greatest contributions to science ever made.

of the two masses multiplied by the gravitational constant and divided by the square of the distance between them. Also called *law of gravitation, law of universal gravitation. See panel at* **gravity.**

Newton's laws of motion The three laws proposed by Sir Isaac Newton to define the concept of force and describe motion, used as the basis of classical mechanics. The first law states that a body at rest tends to stay at rest, and a body in motion tends to stay in motion at a constant speed in a straight line, unless acted upon by a force. The second law states that the acceleration of a body is equal to the force acting upon it divided by the body's mass. The third law states that for every action there is an equal and opposite reaction.

Ni The symbol for **nickel.**

niacin A vitamin belonging to the B complex that is important in carbohydrate metabolism. It is found in liver, fish and whole-grain foods. *See also* **vitamin B complex.**

niche The function or position of a species within an ecological community. A species' niche includes the physical environment to which it has become adapted as well as its role as producer and consumer of food resources.

nickel A silvery, hard, easily shaped metallic element that occurs in ores along with iron or magnesium. It resists oxidation and corrosion and is used to make alloys such as stainless steel. It is also used as a coating for other metals. *Symbol* **Ni**. *Atomic number* 28. *See* **Periodic Table**, pages 260–261.

nicotine A poisonous compound occurring naturally in the tobacco plant. It is used in medicine and as an insecticide. In small doses nicotine has a stimulating effect on the nervous system, and it can be addictive.

nictitating membrane A transparent inner eyelid in birds, reptiles, amphibians and some mammals that protects and moistens the eye without blocking vision.

nimbostratus A low, grey, dark cloud formation often covering the entire sky. Nimbostratus clouds usually produce steady rain, sleet or snow.

nimbus A rain cloud.

niobium A soft, silvery, easily shaped metallic element that usually occurs in nature together with the element tantalum. It is used to build nuclear reactors, to make steel alloys and to allow magnets to conduct electricity with almost no resistance. *Symbol* **Nb**. *Atomic number* 41. *See* **Periodic Table**, pages 260–261.

nipple A small projection near the centre of the mammary gland, as of the human breast, containing in females the outlets of the milk ducts.

nitrate A salt or ester of nitric acid; a compound containing the group NO_3. Nitrates dissolve extremely easily in water and are an important component of the nitrogen cycle. *Compare* **nitrite**.

nitre A naturally occurring mineral form of potassium nitrate, used to make gunpowder.

nitric Containing nitrogen, especially with a valency of 5. *Compare* **nitrous**.

nitric acid A clear, colourless to yellow liquid, HNO_3. It is very corrosive and is used to make fertilizers, explosives, dyes and rocket fuels. Nitric acid can dissolve most metals.

nitrification The process by which bacteria in soil oxidize ammonia and form nitrates and nitrites. Because the nitrates and nitrites can be absorbed by the roots of green plants, nitrification is an important step in the nitrogen cycle.

nitrifying bacteria Any of various soil bacteria that change ammonium compounds into nitrites or change nitrites into nitrates as part of the nitrogen cycle.

nitrite A salt or ester of nitrous acid; a compound containing the group NO_2. Nitrites are an important component of the nitrogen cycle and are used as food preservatives. *Compare* **nitrate**.

nitrogen A nonmetallic element that makes up about 78 per cent of the atmosphere by volume, occurring as a colourless, odourless gas. It is a component of all proteins, making it essential for life, and it is also found in various minerals. Nitrogen is used to make ammonia, nitric acid, TNT and fertilizers. *Symbol* **N**. *Atomic number* 7. *See* **Periodic Table**, pages 260–261. *See panel at* **oxygen**.

nitrogen cycle The continuous process by which nitrogen is exchanged between organisms and the environment. Some of the atmosphere's free nitrogen combines with other elements to form compounds that are deposited in the soil. These are then converted by bacteria, in a process called nitrification, into nutrients that are absorbed by the roots of green plants. Nitrogen is then passed into the food chain and returned to the soil by the metabolism and decay of plants and animals.

nitrogen fixation The process by which free nitrogen from the air is combined with other elements to form organic compounds that plants can use as nutrients. Cyanobacteria and certain other forms of bacteria, especially those that live in the roots of legumes, convert gaseous nitrogen into organic compounds.

nitroglycerine A thick, pale-yellow, explosive liquid formed by treating glycerine with nitric and sulphuric acids. It is used to make dynamite, and in medicine to dilate blood vessels.

nitrous Containing nitrogen, especially with a valency of 3. *Compare* **nitric**.

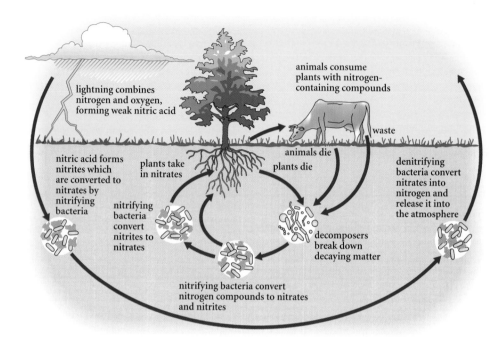

■ **nitrogen cycle**

nitrous oxide A colourless, sweet-smelling gas, N_2O. It is used as a mild anaesthetic, when it is often called *laughing gas*. Nitrous oxide occurs naturally in the atmosphere and is a greenhouse gas. Also called *dinitrogen monoxide.*

No The symbol for **nobelium.**

nobelium A synthetic, radioactive metallic element in the actinide series that is produced by bombarding curium with carbon ions. Its most stable isotope has a half-life of about three minutes. *Symbol* **No.** *Atomic number* 102. *See* **Periodic Table**, pages 260–261.

noble gas Any of the six gases helium, neon, argon, krypton, xenon and radon. Because the outermost electron shell of atoms of these gases is full, they do not react chemically with other substances except under certain special conditions. Also called *inert gas. See* **Periodic Table**, pages 260–261.

nocturnal 1. Occurring at night. **2.** Most active at night. Many animals, such as owls and bats, are

nocturnal. *Compare* **diurnal. 3.** Having flowers that open during the night and close at daylight. Nocturnal plants are often pollinated by moths.

Word History

noble gas

What makes a noble gas so noble? The noble gases are a group of six chemical elements, normally occurring in gaseous form, that do not react chemically with other elements or chemical compounds except very rarely. Helium and neon are two familiar examples. The fact that the noble gases do not mix with other elements became the basis for a comparison with nobility. The nobility – the class that rules many societies and includes royalty – usually keep to themselves and do not mix with common folk.

node 1. *Anatomy.* A small mass or lump of body tissue that either occurs naturally, as in the case of lymph nodes, or is a result of disease. **2.** *Botany.* **a.** A point on a stem where a leaf is attached or has been attached. **b.** A swelling or lump on a tree; a knob or knot. **3.** *Physics.* A point or region of a vibrating or oscillating system, such as the standing wave of a vibrating guitar string, at which the amplitude of the vibration or oscillation is zero. *Compare* **antinode. 4.** *Astronomy.* **a.** Either of the two points at which the orbit of a planet intersects the ecliptic. **b.** Either of the two points at which the orbit of a satellite intersects the plane of orbit of a planet.

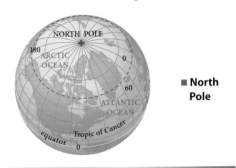

■ **North Pole**

nodule 1. *Anatomy.* A small, usually hard mass of tissue. **2.** *Botany.* A small knob-like outgrowth found on the roots of many plants that are legumes. *See more at* **legume.**

non-renewable Relating to a natural resource, such as oil or iron ore, that cannot be replaced once it has been used. *Compare* **renewable.**

normal fault A geological fault in which the hanging wall has moved downwards relative to the footwall. Normal faults occur where two blocks of rock are pulled apart, as by tension. *See more at* **fault.**

Northern Hemisphere 1. The half of the Earth north of the equator. **2.** *Astronomy.* The half of the celestial sphere north of the celestial equator.

northern lights *See* **aurora borealis.**

North Pole The northern end of the Earth's axis of rotation, a point in the Arctic Ocean.

North Star *See* **Polaris.**

notochord A flexible rod-like structure that forms the main support of the body in the embryos of vertebrate animals, later developing into a true backbone. Primitive relatives of the vertebrates, known as lancelets and tunicates, only have a notochord and never develop a backbone. Animals having a notochord during some stage of their development are called chordates.

nova (*plural* **novae** *or* **novas**) A white dwarf star that suddenly becomes extremely bright as a result of the explosion on its surface of material taken from a nearby star. It gradually returns to its original brightness over a period of weeks to years. *Compare* **supernova.**

Np The symbol for **neptunium.**

nuclear 1. Relating to or forming a cell nucleus. **2.** Relating to atomic nuclei. **3.** Using energy derived from the nuclei of atoms: *a nuclear power plant.*

nuclear energy 1. The energy released during a nuclear reaction. **2.** Electricity generated by a nuclear reactor.

nuclear magnetic resonance The absorption and emission of energy (as specific frequencies of radio waves) by the nuclei of atoms that are placed within a strong magnetic field. Because certain atoms absorb specific frequencies, nuclear magnetic resonance is used to analyse substances in spectroscopy and to

Usage

nuclear/atomic

The words nuclear and atomic mean the same thing when referring to generating electricity or to weapons: We talk about nuclear (or atomic) power stations and nuclear (or atomic) weapons. But in most scientific uses nuclear and atomic mean different things. Nuclear is used to refer to the nucleus of an atom, where the protons and neutrons are found. When a radioactive element gives off a neutron, for example, this can be described as a nuclear event. By contrast, the word atomic is used to refer to the atom as a whole. So when two or more atoms share electrons to form a covalent bond, this is called an atomic interaction.

examine soft body tissues in magnetic resonance imaging (MRI).

nuclear physics The scientific study of the properties of atomic nuclei, including their structure and reactions.

nuclear reaction A reaction, as in fission, fusion or radioactive decay, that changes the

energy or structure of an atomic nucleus. *See more at* **fission, fusion.**

nuclear reactor A device in which a nuclear chain reaction is started and controlled, producing heat which is usually used to generate electricity.

nuclear weapon A weapon whose destructive power comes from nuclear energy; an atomic

Did You Know?

nuclear reactor

The core of a nuclear reactor consists of fuel rods containing pellets of fissionable material, usually uranium-235 or plutonium-239. These isotopes are made up of unstable atoms that readily split apart and release free neutrons that strike other unstable atoms, causing them to split. The fuel rods contain enough fissionable material that is close enough together to start what is called a chain reaction. If left unaltered, the chain reaction would cause the fuel rods to overheat and melt. To prevent this, and to regulate the reaction, the fuel rods are interspersed with control rods made of a material (usually boron or cadmium) that absorbs some of the neutrons given off by the fuel. Inserting the control rods deeper into the reactor core slows down the reaction. If the control rods are fully inserted, the reaction will stop. The chain reaction releases enormous amounts of energy

which is used to heat a coolant as it circulates through the core in a closed loop. Some reactors use a gas (carbon dioxide) as the coolant, while others use water at high pressure. This coolant flows through a steam generator where steam is produced in a secondary loop. The steam is used to drive turbines which turn generators, producing electricity. Because the water in the secondary loop does not flow through the core, there is no danger of it becoming radioactive. Nuclear power is by far the most efficient means of generating electricity in the world today. It remains controversial, however, because much of the equipment needed to generate it, including the used-up fuel rods and the water inside the container vessels, remains radioactive for thousands of years. So far there is little agreement about how to store this material safely.

bomb or a hydrogen bomb. Also called *thermo-nuclear weapon.*

nucleic acid Any of a group of organic compounds found in living cells and viruses that control the hereditary material of a cell or virus by regulating the synthesis of proteins. The two main nucleic acids are DNA and RNA.

nucleolus (*plural* **nucleoli**) A usually round structure located in the nucleus of a cell and involved in the formation of ribosomes, the sites of protein synthesis in cells.

nucleon A proton or a neutron, especially as part of an atomic nucleus.

nucleotide Any of a group of organic compounds composed of one of several nitrogen bases linked to a sugar and a phosphate group. The nucleic acids DNA and RNA are made up of chains of nucleotides. *See panel at* **DNA.**

nucleus (*plural* **nuclei**) **1.** *Physics.* The positively charged central region of an atom, composed of protons and neutrons and containing most of the mass of the atom. *See more at* **atom. 2.** *Biology.* The structure in the cytoplasm of a living cell that contains the cell's DNA and controls its metabolism, growth and reproduction. A nucleus surrounded by a membrane is found in almost all the cells of eukaryotes and thus sets them apart from the cells of prokaryotes, such as bacteria, which do not contain nuclei. *See more at* **cell. 3.**

Astronomy. The solid central part of a comet, composed of ice, frozen gases and dust.

nudibranch *See* **sea slug.**

nuée ardente A cloud of hot gas and ash ejected from a volcano.

numeral A symbol or mark used to represent a number.

numerator A number written above the line in a vulgar fraction to indicate the number of parts of the whole. For example, 2 is the numerator in the fraction $\frac{2}{7}$.

nutrient A substance that provides nourishment. Plants absorb nutrients mainly from the soil in the form of minerals and other inorganic compounds. Animals obtain nutrients from the foods they eat or take in. The three most important nutrients for animals are protein, carbohydrate and fat.

nutrition The process by which an organism obtains the nutrients needed for growth and metabolism.

nylon Any of various very strong, elastic, artificial resins. Nylon can be formed into fibres, sheets or bristles, and is used to make fabrics and plastics.

nymph The immature form of those insects that do not pass through a pupal stage. Nymphs usually resemble the adults, but are smaller, lack fully developed wings and are sexually immature. *Compare* **imago, larva, pupa.**

O The symbol for oxygen.

oak Any of numerous trees that bear acorns and often have leaves that are irregularly notched or lobed.

oasis (*plural* **oases**) A small area in a desert that has a supply of water and is able to support vegetation. An oasis forms when groundwater lies close enough to the surface to form a spring or to be reached by wells.

objective The lens or group of lenses that first receives light from the object in an optical instrument such as a telescope.

observation 1. The act of perceiving and recording something with instruments. 2. The result or record of such notation: a meteorological observation.

obsidian A shiny, usually black, volcanic glass. Obsidian forms from lava that cools so quickly that minerals do not have a chance to form within it.

obstetrics The branch of medicine that deals with the care of women during pregnancy and childbirth.

obtuse angle An angle that is more than 90° and less than 180°. *Compare* **acute angle**.

occipital lobe The rearmost lobe of each cerebral hemisphere, containing the main visual centres of the brain.

occlusion 1. An obstruction in a passageway, especially of the body. 2. The manner in which the upper and lower sets of teeth fit together.

occultation The passage of a celestial object between an observer and another celestial object, blocking the second object from view. An occultation occurs when the moon moves between the Earth and the sun in a solar eclipse.

ocean Any of the principal divisions of the body of saltwater covering 72% of the Earth's surface, including the Atlantic, Pacific, Indian and Arctic Oceans. *See also* **sea**.

■ **octagon**

oceanography The scientific study of oceans, the life that inhabits them, and their physical characteristics, including the depth and extent of ocean waters, their movement and chemical make-up, and the topography and composition of the ocean floors. Oceanography also includes ocean exploration.

ocellus (*plural* **ocelli**) 1. A small, simple eye or eyespot, found in many invertebrates. 2. A marking that resembles an eye, as on the wings of some butterflies.

octagon A polygon having eight sides.

octahedron A three-dimensional geometric figure with eight triangular faces.

octane Any of several hydrocarbon compounds having the formula C_8H_{18}. Octane is commonly added to petrol to prevent uneven burning of fuel in internal-combustion engines.

octopus (*plural* **octopuses** or **octopi**) Any of numerous sea molluscs having a soft rounded body and eight tentacles, each having two rows of suckers used for grasping and holding. Octopuses have large and highly developed eyes and a sharp beak-like mouth. They are considered to be the most intelligent invertebrate animals.

ocular —*adjective* Of or having to do with the eye or the sense of vision. —*noun* The eyepiece of a microscope, telescope or other optical instrument.

odd Divisible by 2 with a remainder of 1, such as 17 or –103.

odd-toed ungulate *See* **perissodactyl.**

oedema An excessive accumulation of fluid in body tissue that results in swelling.

Oersted, Hans Christian 1777–1851. Danish physicist who founded the science of electromagnetism with his discovery (1820) of the magnetic effect produced by an electric current.

oesophagus The tube of the digestive tract through which food passes from the throat to the stomach.

oestrogen Any of a group of steroid hormones that primarily regulate the growth, development, and function of the female reproductive system. The main sources of oestrogen in the body are the ovaries and the placenta. Oestrogens are also formed by certain plants.

oestrous cycle The series of bodily changes that occur in the female of most mammals between one fertile period and another. The oestrous cycle usually takes place during a specific period known as the breeding season, which ensures that the young are born at a time when the chance of survival is greatest. The length of the cycle varies from species to species.

oestrus The period during which a female mammal is fertile and ready to mate. Also known as being *on heat* or *in season* when with reference to certain types of animal, eg dogs and horses.

ohm A unit used to measure the electrical resistance of a material. One ohm is equal to the resistance of a conductor through which a current of one ampere flows when a potential difference of one volt is applied to it.

Ohm, Georg Simon 1789–1854. German physicist who discovered the relationship between voltage, current and resistance in an electrical circuit. His discovery is now known as Ohm's law. The unit of electrical resistance is named after him.

Ohm's law A physical principle stating that the electric current through a conductor is directly proportional to the potential difference across it, as long as the temperature stays constant.

–oid A suffix meaning "like" or "resembling", as in *ellipsoid*, a geometric solid that resembles an ellipse.

oil 1. Any of a large class of liquid or easily melted substances that are typically very slippery and greasy. Oils are flammable, do not mix with water, and include animal and vegetable fats as well as substances of mineral or synthetic origin. They are used in food, soap and candles, and make good lubricants and fuels. **2.** Petroleum.

–ol A suffix used to form the names of chemical compounds in the alcohol group, eg *ethanol, propanol.*

olfactory Relating to the sense of smell or the organs of smell.

olfactory nerve The nerve that carries sensory information on smell from the nose to the brain. The olfactory nerve is a cranial nerve.

Oligocene The third epoch of the Tertiary Period, from about 35 to 23 million years ago, characterized by the continued development of modern mammalian groups and the rise of the first cats, dogs and related mammals. *See chart at* **geological time,** pages 148–149.

olivine An olive-green to brownish-green mineral consisting primarily of iron, magnesium and silica. Olivine is a common mineral in the igneous rocks, such as basalt and gabbro, that make up most of the Earth's crust beneath the sea.

omasum The third division of the stomach in ruminant animals. It removes excess water from food and further reduces the size of food particles

■ **octopus**
common octopus

before passing them to the abomasum for digestion by enzymes. *See more at* **ruminant.**

ommatidium (*plural* **ommatidia**) One of the tiny light-sensitive parts of the compound eye of insects and other arthropods. An ommatidium resembles a single simplified eye. *See more at* **compound eye.**

omnivore An organism that eats both plants and animals. —*adjective* **omnivorous.**

oncogene A gene containing a mutation in its DNA that causes normal cells to turn into cancerous ones. *See panel at* **cancer.**

oncology The branch of medicine that deals with the diagnosis and treatment of cancer.

–one A suffix used to form the names of chemical compounds in the ketone group, eg *propanone, butanone.*

onyx A type of quartz that occurs in bands of different colours, often black and white.

Oort cloud A vast, nearly spherical swarm of comets and icy bodies dating from the origin of the solar system, orbiting the sun in all directions. The cloud extends halfway to the nearest star but it has never been directly observed; its existence was proposed as the source of long-period comets by the Dutch astronomer Jan Hendrik Oort in 1950. There are estimated to be more than 100 billion comets in the Oort cloud. Any comets from the cloud that come into the solar system take about 200 years to complete an orbit. *Compare* **Kuiper belt.**

opacity The quality or condition of being opaque.

opal A usually transparent mineral consisting of hydrous silica. Opal can occur in almost any colour, but it is often pinkish white with a milky or pearly appearance. It typically forms within cracks in igneous rocks, in limestones and in mineral veins. It also occurs in the silica-rich shells of certain marine organisms.

opaque Not letting light pass through; neither transparent nor translucent. Metals and many minerals are opaque.

open circuit An electric circuit through which current cannot flow because the path is broken or interrupted by an opening.

open cluster A loose group of anything up to

several hundred young stars that formed from clouds of dust and gas in the arms of a spiral galaxy. The Pleiades is an open cluster. *Compare* **globular cluster.**

open universe A model of the universe in which there is not enough matter, and therefore not enough gravitational force, to stop the expansion started by the big bang. *See panel at* **big bang.**

operating system Software designed to control the hardware of a specific data-processing system in order to allow users and programs to make use of the system.

operculum A lid or flap covering an opening, such as the gill cover in some fish or the horny flap covering the opening of a snail.

ophthalmology The branch of medicine that deals with the eye, its diseases and their treatment.

opium A highly addictive, yellowish-brown drug obtained from the pods of a variety of poppy, from which other drugs, such as morphine, are prepared.

opossum Any of various rat-like mammals that mostly dwell in trees and have thick fur, a long snout and a long hairless tail. The tail is often used to hang from branches. Opossums are marsupials and carry their young in a pouch until they grow older, when they cling to their mother's back or tail with their tails. When attacked by predators, opossums "play dead" or "play possum" by collapsing and lying still.

Oppenheimer, J(ulius) Robert 1902–1967. American physicist who directed the laboratory at Los Alamos, New Mexico, during the development of the first atomic bomb (1942–1945).

opposable thumb A thumb that can be placed opposite the fingers of the same hand. Opposable thumbs allow the digits to grasp and handle objects, and are characteristic of primates.

optic Relating to the eye or vision.

optical 1. Relating to sight; visual. **2.** Relating to optics. **3.** Relating to or using visible light: *optical astronomy.*

optical disc A plastic-coated disc that stores digital data, such as music or text, as tiny pits etched into its surface. Optical discs are read by a laser scanning the surface.

optical fibre A flexible transparent fibre, usually made of glass or plastic, through which light can be reflected to transmit images or data from one end to the other. Unlike other communications cables, which are made of metal and transmit data as fluctuating electric currents, optical fibres transmit data as pulses of light. *See more at* **fibre optics**.

optic nerve The nerve that carries sensory information from the retina of the eye to the brain. The optic nerve is a cranial nerve.

optics The scientific study of light and vision.

oral Relating to the mouth.

orang-utan A large ape of the islands of Borneo and Sumatra, having long arms and a reddish-brown coat. Orang-utans are highly intelligent and usually solitary. The word orang-utan literally means "wild man".

orbit *noun* **1a.** The path of a celestial body or an artificial satellite as it revolves around another body. **b.** One complete revolution of such a body. *See panel at* **solar system**. **2.** The path of a body in a field of force surrounding another body; for example, the path of an electron in relation to the nucleus of an atom. **3.** Either of two bony hollows in the skull containing the eye and its associated structures. —*verb* **1.** To move in an orbit around another body. **2.** To put into an orbit: *orbit a satellite*.

orbital The region within the shell of an atom in which an electron is most likely to be found. One or more orbitals make up each electron shell.

orca *See* **killer whale**.

orchid Any of numerous tropical and subtropical plants that grow on the ground or in trees as epiphytes. Orchids have irregularly shaped flowers with one petal larger than the others.

order A group of organisms ranking above a family and below a class. *See table at* **taxonomy**.

ordinal number A number, such as 3rd, 11th or 412th, used in counting to indicate position in a series but not quantity. *Compare* **cardinal number**.

ordinate The distance of a point from the x-axis on a graph in the Cartesian coordinate system. It is measured parallel to the y-axis. For example, a point having coordinates (2,3) has 3 as its ordinate. *Compare* **abscissa**.

Ordovician The second period of the Palaeozoic Era, from about 510 to 439 million years ago, characterized by the appearance of primitive fish. *See chart at* **geological time**, pages 148–149.

ore A mineral or rock from which a valuable or useful substance, especially a metal, can be extracted at a reasonable cost.

organ A collection of different tissues working together to carry out one or more specialized functions for the whole body. Examples of organs are the eyes, kidneys and heart of an animal, and the roots and leaves of a plant.

organelle A structure or part that is enclosed within its own membrane inside a cell and has a particular function. Organelles are found only in eukaryotic cells and are absent from the cells of prokaryotes like bacteria. The nucleus, mitochondrion and chloroplast are examples of organelles.

organic **1.** Involving organisms or the products of their life processes. **2.** Relating to chemical compounds containing carbon, especially hydrocarbons. **3.** Of food and other materials, produced to strict criteria without the use of the majority of chemical fertilizers and pesticides available. Any fertilizers or pesticides used must be of animal or vegetable origin and be approved by bodies such as the Soil Association. *See table on* page 246.

organic chemistry The branch of chemistry that deals with carbon and carbon compounds. *See table on* page 246.

organism An individual form of life, such as a bacterium, fungus, plant or animal, that is capable of growing and reproducing. Organisms are composed of one or more cells.

orgasm The peak of sexual excitement for both men and women.

origin The point on a graph where the horizontal x-axis and vertical y-axis cross, having a value of zero on both sides.

Orion A constellation in the region of the celestial equator near Gemini and Taurus. It contains the bright stars Betelgeuse and Rigel.

ornithischian One of the two main types of

Organic Compounds

Chemical compounds containing one or more carbon atoms are called **organic compounds**. Hundreds of thousands of organic compounds are found in nature or have been artificially made. They range from the very simple, like methane, with its five atoms, to the very complex, like DNA, which has millions of atoms.

A very common class of organic compounds, called the **alkanes**, all have one or more carbon atoms arranged in a row, or chain. Atoms are attached to each other in a molecule by sharing

electrons; these attachments are called **covalent bonds**. Because of its particular structure, a carbon atom (C) must share a total of four electrons with other atoms. In an alkane, each carbon in the chain shares one electron with its neighbouring carbon, forming what are called **single bonds** (indicated by single lines between the element symbols in the diagrams below). The remaining electrons are shared with hydrogen atoms (H). Below are illustrated the first four compounds in the alkane series – methane, ethane, propane and butane:

methane
CH_4

ethane
C_2H_6

propane
C_3H_8

butane
C_4H_{10}

A large number of compounds can be created by modifying these basic alkanes. For example, replacing one of the hydrogen atoms at the end of an ethane molecule with a group containing an oxygen atom and a hydrogen atom (OH) produces ethanol, the most familiar form of alcohol:

A slightly more complicated modification of a basic alkane, shown below, produces ethanoic acid, the acid occurring in vinegar. The double line between the carbon and the upper oxygen atom indicates that two electrons (rather than one) are shared between the two atoms, forming what is called a **double bond**:

The carbon atoms in organic molecules can also be joined to each other by double bonds, or (more rarely) **triple bonds**, in which three electrons are shared. Two such molecules are ethene, with a double bond between the carbon atoms, and ethyne, with a triple bond:

ethanol
C_2H_6O

ethanoic acid
$C_2H_4O_2$

ethene
C_2H_4

ethyne
C_2H_2

Very often, chains of carbon atoms loop to form rings. The basic ring compound in organic chemistry is benzene, which has six carbon and six hydrogen atoms. The carbon atoms are joined to each other by alternating single and double bonds:

benzene
C_6H_6

■ oscillation
The time it takes the pendulum to swing from **a**
to **b** *and back to* **a** *is known as its period. The
dashed red line from the central point represents the pendulum at rest.*

orthorhombic Relating to a crystal having
three axes of different lengths intersecting at right
angles. The mineral topaz has orthorhombic
crystals. *See more at* **crystal.**

Os The symbol for **osmium.**

oscillation 1. A steady, uninterrupted,
backward and forward swinging about a central
point. *Compare* **vibration.** 2. A single cycle of
motion about a central position.

oscilloscope An electronic instrument used to
measure changing electric voltages. It displays the
waveforms of electric oscillations on a screen.

–osis A suffix that means: 1. Diseased condition,
as in *tuberculosis.* 2. Condition or process, as in
osmosis.

osmium A hard, brittle, bluish-white metallic
element. Osmium is the densest naturally
occurring element. It is used to make very hard
alloys for fountain pen nibs and electrical
contacts. *Symbol* **Os.** *Atomic number* 76. *See*
Periodic Table, pages 260–261.

osmosis The net movement of solvent

dinosaurs. Ornithischians have a pelvis similar to
that of modern birds, and include all the plant-
eating dinosaurs except the sauropods. They
include armour-plated, horned and duck-billed
varieties. *Compare* **saurischian.**

ornithology The scientific study of birds.

ornithopod One of the main types of
ornithischian dinosaurs, including the hadrosaurs.
Ornithopods walked on their hind legs and had
three blunt toes on each foot. They lived from the
late Triassic Period until the end of the Cretaceous
Period.

orthoclase A type of feldspar consisting of
potassium aluminium silicate. Orthoclase is
typically white, pink, yellow or brown, but it can
also be colourless. It is especially common in
igneous rocks.

orthopaedics The branch of medicine that
deals with the correction or treatment of disorders
or injuries of the bones, joints and associated
muscles.

■ osmosis
left: *The concentration of sugar molecules is
greater on the right side of the membrane than
on the left. The water molecules are small
enough to move across the membrane, but the
larger sugar molecules cannot pass through.*
right: *The water molecules move across the
membrane until the water and sugar molecules
are of equal concentration on both sides. This
lowers the water level on the left side and raises
it on the right side.*

molecules from a region where they are at a higher concentration to a region where they are at a lower concentration, through a partially permeable membrane. The movement of solvent will continue until the concentrations of the solutions on both sides of the membrane are equal, unless a build-up of pressure on one side prevents it.

ossicle A small bone, especially one of the three located in the middle ear (the incus, malleus and stapes) that transmit sound vibrations from the eardrum to the inner ear.

ossification The process of bone formation, brought about by the action of specialized bone cells called osteoblasts.

osteoarthritis A form of arthritis that is characterized by wearing down of the cartilage of the joints.

osteoblast A cell that produces the collagen needed for the development of new bone. As new bone grows and hardens, osteoblasts become embedded in the bone matrix. Once embedded, they are no longer able to secrete collagen and are called osteocytes.

osteocyte A cell with branching parts that is embedded in the matrix of bone. Osteocytes regulate the metabolism of bone tissue.

osteoporosis A condition in which the bones become porous and weak from loss of minerals, especially calcium. The risk of developing osteoporosis increases with age. Women are particularly at risk once they lose the protection of the female sex hormones after the menopause.

ostrich A very large African bird having a small head, a long neck and long, strong legs. Ostriches cannot fly but can run very fast, and are the largest living species of bird.

otter Any of various meat-eating mammals that live in or near water and have webbed feet and thick brown fur. Otters are related to the weasels.

ounce 1. A unit of weight equal to $\frac{1}{16}$ of a pound and containing 16 drams or 480 grains. *See table at* **measurement. 2.** A unit of volume or capacity used to measure liquids, equal to $\frac{1}{20}$ of a pint and containing 8 fluid drams or 1.8 cubic inches. *See table at* **measurement.**

outcrop An area of visible bedrock that is not covered with soil.

outer ear The part of the ear in many mammals that is made chiefly of cartilage and includes the passage leading to the eardrum. The outer ear gathers and focuses incoming sound waves and transmits them to the inner ear. *See more at* **ear.**

output 1. The energy, power or work produced by a system or device: *the output of an engine.* **2.** The information that a computer produces by processing a specific input.

ovary 1. The reproductive organ in female animals that produces eggs and the sex hormones oestrogen and progesterone. In most vertebrate animals, the ovaries occur in pairs. **2.** The part of a flower pistil that contains ovules. The ovary is located at the base of the pistil and ripens into a fruit after fertilization of one or more of the ovules. *See more at* **flower.** — *adjective* **ovarian.**

oviduct A tube through which eggs or egg cells are carried to the uterus in mammals or to the outside of the body in other animals. The fallopian tubes are oviducts.

oviparous Producing eggs that hatch outside the body. Amphibians, birds, and most insects, fish and reptiles are oviparous. *Compare* **ovoviviparous, viviparous.**

ovipositor A tube in many female insects that extends from the end of the abdomen and is used to lay eggs.

ovoviviparous Producing eggs that hatch within the female's body. Some fish and reptiles are ovoviviparous. *Compare* **oviparous, viviparous.**

ovulation The release of eggs or egg cells from the ovary in female animals, regulated in mammals by hormones of the pituitary gland. In humans and most other primates, ovulation usually occurs midway through the menstrual cycle.

ovule A small part in a plant ovary that becomes a seed after it has been fertilized by a male cell. *See more at* **flower.**

ovum (*plural* **ova**) *See* **egg** (sense 1).

owl Any of various birds of prey that are usually active at night and have a large head, large forward-facing eyes, a short hooked bill and a flat round face.

oxalic acid A poisonous, crystalline acid found in a number of plants. It is used for many industrial purposes, including rust removal and bleaching. Its systematic name is *ethanedioic acid.*

oxbow lake A shallow curved lake formed when a meander of a river is cut off as a result of erosion.

oxidation 1. The chemical combination of a substance with oxygen. 2. A chemical reaction in which an atom or ion loses electrons, thus undergoing an increase in its oxidation number. Removing an electron from an iron atom having a valency of +2 changes the valency to +3. *Compare* **reduction.**

oxidation number The oxidation number of an atom in a molecule is the charge that it would have if the electrons in each of its bonds belonged to the more electronegative element.

oxide A compound of oxygen and another element or radical. Water (H_2O) is an oxide.

oxidize To undergo or cause to undergo oxidation.

oxygen A nonmetallic element that exists in its free form as a colourless, odourless gas and makes up about 21 per cent of the Earth's atmosphere. It

---

Word History

oxygen, hydrogen and nitrogen

In 1786, the French chemist Antoine Lavoisier coined a term for the element *oxygen* (*oxygène* in French). He used Greek words for the coinage: *oxy–* means "sharp", and *–gen* means "producing". Oxygen was called the "sharp-producing" element because it was thought to be essential for making acids. Lavoisier also coined the name of the element *hydrogen,* the "water-producing" element, in 1788. Soon after, in 1791, another French chemist, J A Chaptal, introduced the word *nitrogen,* the "nitre-producing" element, referring to its discovery from an analysis of nitric acid.

---

is the most abundant element in the Earth's crust and occurs in many compounds, including water, carbon dioxide and iron ore. Oxygen combines with most elements, is required for combustion and is essential for life in most organisms. *Symbol* **O.** *Atomic number* 8. *See* **Periodic Table,** pages 260–261.

oxygenate To combine or mix with oxygen, as in a physical, chemical or biological system. Blood is oxygenated in the lungs.

oxyhaemoglobin The compound formed when a molecule of haemoglobin binds with a molecule of oxygen. In vertebrate animals, haemoglobin is carried in the red blood cells. In the lungs purplish-red haemoglobin combines with oxygen to form bright red oxyhaemoglobin as the blood becomes oxygenated.

oyster Any of several molluscs of shallow waters, having a rough, irregularly shaped, double-hinged shell. Many kinds of oysters are used as food, and some kinds produce pearls inside their shells.

ozone A poisonous, blue form of oxygen that has three atoms per molecule rather than the usual two and so has the chemical formula O_3. It is produced by electricity passing through air, as in a lightning strike, and also by the sun's radiation reacting with ordinary oxygen or with the pollutants in smog.

Did You Know?

oxidation

If you've ever seen rust or watched a candle burn, then you have seen oxidation. Oxidation involves electrons being removed from a substance and transferred to another substance. When iron rusts, it reacts with oxygen, and when a candle burns, the wax (which contains carbon, hydrogen and oxygen) also reacts with oxygen. But oxidation doesn't have to involve oxygen – there are many substances that can remove electrons from another substance other than oxygen. This is something that oxygen is very good at, which is why chemists use the term *oxidation.*

Did You Know?

ozone

For the Earth's organisms, including people, ozone can be a lifesaver or a threat to health, depending on how high it is found in the atmosphere. The ozone that lingers in the lower atmosphere is a pollutant and contributes to respiratory diseases like asthma. But in the upper atmosphere, ozone protects us from the more severe forms of the sun's radiation. The region of the atmosphere in which ozone is most concentrated is known as the ozone layer, which lies from about 20 to 50 kilometres above the Earth. Because ozone absorbs certain wavelengths of harmful ultraviolet radiation, this layer acts as an important protection for life on the Earth. In recent years the ozone has thinned or disappeared in parts of the ozone layer, creating an ozone hole that lets in dangerous amounts of ultraviolet radiation. Ozone holes are created in part by the presence of certain industrial or commercial chemicals released into the atmosphere, particularly compounds like chlorofluorocarbons (CFCs). The thinning of the ozone layer is leading to higher levels of UV radiation reaching the surface of the Earth. This in turn increases the risk of people developing skin cancers such as melanoma as the UV radiation damages the cells of the skin.

Ozone is used commercially in water purification, in air conditioning, and as a bleach.

ozone layer A region of the Earth's atmosphere with a high concentration of the gas ozone that shields the Earth from the sun's harmful ultraviolet radiation.

■ **ozone**

This image of the Southern Hemisphere was generated by a satellite instrument that measures infrared radiation from the Earth. The irregular circles of purple, red and grey over Antarctica indicate an ozone hole, where ozone levels are progressively thinner.

P

P The symbol for **phosphorus**.

Pa The symbol for **protactinium**.

pacemaker An electronic device that is surgically implanted to regulate the heartbeat.

pachycephalosaurus A medium-sized, plant-eating dinosaur of the late Cretaceous Period with a domed skull up to 25 centimetres thick.

pachyderm Any of various large, thick-skinned mammals, such as the elephant, rhinoceros or hippopotamus.

pack ice A large area of floating ice consisting of a mixture of ice fragments packed or squeezed together.

paediatrics The branch of medicine that deals with the medical treatment of infants and children.

Paget, Sir James 1814–1899. British surgeon and researcher who was a pioneer of modern pathology. He discovered the cause of trichinosis in 1834.

pahoehoe Lava with a smooth, swirled surface. It is highly fluid and spreads out in shiny sheets. *Compare* **aa**. *See table at* **rock**.

palaeo– A prefix that means: **1.** Prehistoric, as in *Palaeocene.* **2.** Early or primitive, as in *Palaeolithic.*

Palaeocene The earliest epoch of the Tertiary Period, from about 65 to 56.5 million years ago, characterized by the appearance of placental mammals and widespread volcanic activity, leading to the formation of the Rocky Mountains and the Himalayas. *See chart at* **geological time,** pages 148–149.

Palaeolithic The cultural period of the Stone Age that began about 2 million years ago, marked by the earliest use of tools made of chipped stone. The Palaeolithic Period ended at different times in different parts of the world, between about 40,000 and 10,000 years ago. *Compare* **Mesolithic, Neolithic.**

palaeontology The scientific study of extinct life forms by studying their fossil remains.

Palaeozoic The era of geological time from about 570 to 245 million years ago. The Palaeozoic Era is characterized by the appearance of marine invertebrate animals, primitive fish and reptiles, and land plants. *See chart at* **geological time,** pages 148–149.

palate The roof of the mouth in vertebrate animals, separating the mouth from the passages of the nose. ❖ The bony part of the palate is called the **hard palate.** ❖ A soft, flexible, rear portion of the palate, called the **soft palate,** is present in mammals only and serves to close off the mouth from the nose during swallowing.

palisade layer A layer of cells just below the upper surface of most leaves, consisting of cylindrical cells that contain many chloroplasts and stand at right angles to the leaf surface. The palisade layer is the main site of photosynthesis in the plant. Also called *palisade parenchyma. See more at* **photosynthesis.**

palladium An easily shaped, greyish-white metallic element that occurs naturally with platinum. Because it can absorb large amounts of hydrogen, it is used as a catalyst in reactions involving hydrogen. Palladium and its alloys are used to make electrical contacts and jewellery. *Symbol* **Pd.** *Atomic number* 46. *See* **Periodic Table,** pages 260–261.

palm Any of various evergreen trees of tropical and subtropical regions, usually having a branchless trunk with a group of large, feather-like or fan-shaped leaves at the top.

palmate 1. Having a shape similar to that of a hand with the fingers extended. Some kinds of coral and the antlers of elks and certain deer are palmate. **2.** *Botany.* Of a leaf, having three or more veins, leaflets or lobes radiating from one point. Maples have palmate leaves. **3.** *Zoology.* Having webbed toes, as the feet of many swimming and diving birds do.

palp A segmented organ extending from the mouthparts of arthropods, used for touch or taste.

pampas Large treeless grasslands in southern South America, particularly Argentina.

pancreas A long, irregularly shaped gland in vertebrate animals that is located behind the stomach. It secretes the hormone insulin and also produces some of the enzymes needed for digestion, which are secreted into the small intestine.

pandemic An outbreak of a disease that spreads over a very wide area, including more than one country. *See panel at* **endemic.**

Pangaea A supercontinent made up of all the world's present landmasses as they are thought to have been joined during the Permian and Triassic

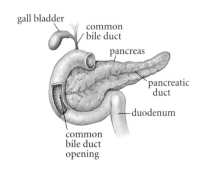

gall bladder

common bile duct

pancreas

pancreatic duct

duodenum

common bile duct opening

■ **pancreas**

Periods. According to the theory of plate tectonics, Pangaea later broke up into Laurasia and Gondwanaland, which eventually broke up into the continents we know today.

panicle A branched flower-head, common in grasses, in which the youngest flowers are at the tip of the flower stalk. Oats have panicles.

pantothenic acid A vitamin belonging to the B complex that is important in the metabolism of fats and carbohydrates. It is found in liver, yeast and many vegetables. *See also* **vitamin B complex.**

papilla (*plural* **papillae**) A small projection from a body surface, especially a taste bud on the tongue.

parabola A plane curve formed by the intersection of a cone with a plane parallel to a straight line on the slanting surface of the cone. Each point of the curve is equidistant from a fixed point, called the focus, and a fixed straight line, known as the directrix.

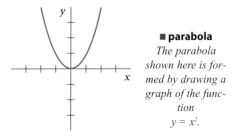

■ **parabola**
The parabola shown here is formed by drawing a graph of the function $y = x^2$.

paraffin 1. A waxy, white or colourless solid mixture made from petroleum and used to make candles, wax paper, lubricants and waterproof coatings. **2.** A fuel oil obtained from petroleum or coal and used in aircraft and domestic heaters.

parallax An apparent change in the position of an object, such as a star, relative to a distant background, when it is viewed from two different positions. The parallax of nearby stars caused by observing them from opposite points in the Earth's orbit around the sun is used in estimating the stars' distance from the Earth.

parallel *adjective* Relating to lines or surfaces that are the same distance apart at every point. Parallel lines are usually marked with arrows. —*noun* Any of the imaginary lines encircling the Earth's surface parallel to the plane of the equator, used to represent degrees of latitude. *See more at* **equator.**

parallel circuit *See under* **circuit.**

parallelogram A four-sided plane geometric figure in which each pair of opposite sides is parallel.

paramecium (*plural* **paramecia** *or* **parameciums**) Any of various freshwater protozoans that are usually oval in shape and that move by means of cilia.

■ **parallelogram**

parameter A quantity whose value can vary in general but is fixed when the quantity is used in a specific mathematical expression involving one or more other variables. For example, in finding the area of a circle, one needs to know the length of the circle's radius; that length is a parameter that will have different values for circles of different sizes.

paraplegia Paralysis of the lower part of the body, caused by injury to the spinal cord.

parasite An organism that lives in or on a different kind of organism (called the host) from which it gets some or all of its nourishment. Parasites are generally harmful to their hosts, and in some cases they may even destroy the other organism, although more often the damage they do is minor. Lice and tapeworms are parasites of humans.

parasitism A relationship between two organisms of different species in which one organism benefits and the other is generally harmed. *See panel at* **symbiosis.**

parasympathetic nervous system The part of the autonomic nervous system that tends to act in opposition to the sympathetic nervous system, for example by slowing down the heart and dilating the blood vessels. It also regulates the function of many glands, such as those that produce tears and saliva.

parathyroid gland Any of four kidney-shaped glands located behind or within the thyroid gland of many vertebrate animals. The parathyroid glands secrete a hormone (called parathyroid hormone) that regulates the amount of calcium in the blood.

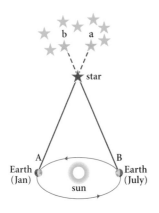

■ **parallax**

Viewed from point A, a nearby star appears to occupy position a *against a background of more distant stars. Six months later, from point B, the star appears to occupy position* b.

parenchyma The basic tissue of plants, consisting of thin-walled, nonspecialized cells that sometimes adapt to specialized functions. The internal layers of leaves, the cortex and pith of the

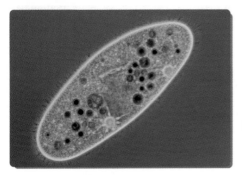

■ **paramecium**

stem, and the soft parts of fruits are made of parenchyma. In higher plants, parenchyma supports the plant body, roots and leaves; it also stores water and contains chloroplasts in which photosynthesis takes place.

parietal lobe The middle portion of each cerebral hemisphere, where sensory information from the body is processed.

Parkinson's disease A disease of the brain, usually in older people, that tends to become more severe over time. Symptoms include tremors, slowed movement and rigid muscles.

parsec A unit of astronomical length equal to 3.26 light years. It is based on the distance from the Earth at which a star would have a parallax of one second of arc.

parthenogenesis Reproduction in which an egg develops without fertilization, as in certain insects such as aphids, ants and bees. —*adjective* **parthenogenetic.**

partial product A product formed by multiplying the multiplicand by one digit of the multiplier when the multiplier has more than one digit. For example, the product of 67 multiplied by 12 is 134 (that is, 67×2) + 670 (that is, 67×10), or 804. In this example 134 and 670 are partial products.

particle 1. A very small piece of solid matter; a speck: *particles of dust.* 2. An elementary or subatomic particle.

particle accelerator Any of several machines, such as the cyclotron and linear

accelerator, that increase the speed and energy of protons, electrons or other atomic particles in order to collide them with other particles, producing new particles. Particle accelerators are used to study the atomic nucleus, to create radioactive isotopes, and to release elementary particles such as quarks. *See panel at* **subatomic particle.**

particulate *adjective* Formed of very small, separate particles. Dust and soot are forms of particulate matter. —*noun* A very small particle, as of dust or soot. Particulates that are given off by the burning of oil, petrol and other fuels can remain suspended in the atmosphere for long periods, where they are a major component of air pollution and smog.

pascal A unit used to measure pressure. One pascal is equal to one newton per square metre.

Pascal, Blaise 1623–1662. French mathematician, physicist and philosopher. He invented the mechanical calculator and the syringe. With Pierre de Fermat, he developed the mathematical theory of probability.

Pascal's law The principle that if a fluid is under pressure from the outside, the pressure is distributed evenly throughout the fluid.

passerine Belonging to the order of perching birds, including more than half of all living birds. Passerine birds are of small to medium size, have three toes pointing forward and one pointing back, and are often brightly coloured. The songbirds are passerines.

Pasteur, Louis 1822–1895. French chemist who founded modern microbiology. His early work with fermentation led him to invent the process of pasteurization. Pasteur established that germs cause communicable diseases and infections. He developed vaccines for anthrax, chicken cholera and rabies.

pasteurization A process in which an unfermented liquid, such as milk, or a partially fermented one, such as beer, is heated to a specific temperature for a certain amount of time in order to kill harmful germs or prevent further fermentation. During pasteurization, the liquid is not allowed to reach its boiling point so as to avoid changing its molecular structure.

patella The small, flat, movable bone at the front

Biography

Louis Pasteur

In the mid-19th century, there was little understanding of the causes of disease, and few effective ways of either curing or preventing the infectious diseases which took so many lives. People had many beliefs which to modern eyes seem very strange. For example, they believed in spontaneous generation – that living organisms such as the maggots in rotting meat, or frogs emerging from mud, had appeared spontaneously by the will of God.

Louis Pasteur began his scientific career as a chemist, and as part of his work he showed that fermentation was the result of the action of a microorganism – yeast – on sugar to form ethanol. Until then, it had been believed that the sugar simply disintegrated in a special way. Fascinated by what he had found, Pasteur went on to disprove the idea of spontaneous generation by demonstrating that the moulds and other organisms that develop in broth when it is left for several days are carried in the air – they do not simply appear from nowhere. His work rapidly led to the process we now know as pasteurization of milk.

Pasteur became convinced that microorganisms in the air and water might also be causing disease in people and animals. He spent the rest of his working life isolating the organisms which caused diseases such as anthrax and rabies. He didn't just isolate the microbes – he used them to develop vaccines to prevent the diseases. His successful work on a vaccine to prevent anthrax in farm animals was widely publicized. As a result of that, Pasteur's work with the rabies vaccine, and the studies of other scientists such as Robert Koch and Lister, the germ theory of disease became widely accepted, providing the foundation for modern medicine. As a result, millions of lives have been saved around the world in the years since Pasteur's death. He was a hero in his own lifetime and remains one of the great scientists of all time.

of the knee in most mammals. Also called *kneecap. See more at* **skeleton.**

pathogen An agent that causes infection or disease, especially a microorganism, such as a bacterium or protozoan, or a virus. *See panel at* **germ.**

pathology 1. The scientific study of disease and its causes, processes and effects. **2.** The physical changes in the body and its functioning as a result of illness or disease.

Pauli, Wolfgang 1900–1958. Austrian-born American physicist. He formulated a principle stating that no two electrons in an atom can have identical energy, masses and angular momentums at the same time. This principle is known as the Pauli Exclusion Principle.

Pauling, Linus Carl 1901–1994. American chemist noted for his work on the structure and nature of chemical bonding. After studying in Europe with Niels Bohr and other physicists, Pauling applied quantum physics to chemistry. He discovered the structure of many molecules found in living tissue, especially proteins and amino acids. While studying the structure of haemoglobin, Pauling discovered the genetic defect that causes sickle cell anaemia.

Pavlov, Ivan Petrovich 1849–1936. Russian physiologist who studied the digestive system of dogs. His experiments showed that if a bell is rung whenever food is presented to a dog, the dog will eventually salivate when it hears the bell, even if no food is presented. This demonstration of what is known as the conditioned response prompted later scientific studies of human and animal behaviour.

Pb The symbol for **lead.**

Pd The symbol for **palladium.**

pearl A smooth, slightly iridescent, white or greyish rounded growth inside the shells of some molluscs. A pearl, which forms as a reaction to the presence of a foreign particle, consists of thin layers of mother-of-pearl that are deposited around the particle. The pearls of oysters are often valued as gems. *See also* **mother-of-pearl.**

peat Partially decayed vegetable matter, especially mosses, found in bogs. Peat is burned as a fuel and is also used as a fertilizer.

pectin Any of a group of substances that are found in ripe fruit and can be made to form gels. Pectins are derived from carbohydrates. They are used in certain medicines and cosmetics and in making jellies.

pectoral Located in or attached to the chest: *a pectoral muscle; the pectoral fin.*

pedicel A small stalk supporting a single flower in a plant.

peduncle 1. *Botany.* The stalk of a single flower or flower cluster. *See more at* **flower. 2.** *Zoology.* A stalk supporting an animal organ, such as the eyestalk of a lobster.

Pegasus A constellation in the Northern Hemisphere near Aquarius and Andromeda.

pegmatite Any of various coarse-grained igneous rocks that often occur as wide veins cutting across other types of rock. Pegmatites form from magma or lava that is rich in water and cools slowly, allowing the crystals to grow to large sizes.

pelican Any of various large, web-footed water birds of warm regions, having a large expandable pouch under the lower bill. The pouch is used for scooping up water and fish.

pellagra A disease caused by a lack of niacin in the diet. It causes skin and digestive disorders and mental deterioration.

Biography

Linus Pauling

Linus Pauling is as well known for his efforts to make the world a better place as for advancing the frontiers of scientific knowledge. After devoting two decades to investigating chemical bonding, he made one of his most important discoveries one day while convalescing. Playing with pieces of paper, he imagined them as molecules, and in a few hours he had worked out how amino acids are arranged in proteins. For this and related work he won the Nobel Prize in Chemistry in 1954. Pauling also worked tirelessly on behalf of world peace. He studied the harmful effects of nuclear fallout from atomic weapons and concluded that they should be banned. His views made him many enemies; he was accused of being a Communist and was prevented from travelling abroad for a while, almost missing the award ceremony for his Nobel Prize. Pauling did not give in, however. He helped get a petition signed by thousands of scientists calling for an end to nuclear testing. In 1962 he won the Nobel Peace Prize for his efforts. He is the only person ever to receive two unshared Nobel Prizes. Pauling devoted much of his later life to researching the health benefits of large doses of vitamins and minerals, especially vitamin C.

pelvis The basin-shaped structure in vertebrate animals that joins the spine and lower or hind limbs. In primates, the pelvis is composed of the two hipbones joined to the sacrum. It contains and supports the intestines, bladder and internal reproductive organs.

pendulum A mass hung from a fixed support so that it is able to swing freely under the influence of gravity. Pendulums are often used to regulate the action of various devices, especially clocks.

penguin Any of various flightless sea birds having white feathers on their fronts and black feathers on their backs. They live mostly in or near Antarctica. With their webbed feet, narrow flipper-like wings and scale-like feathers, penguins are adapted for swimming underwater, where they feed on fish and other sea animals. On land, they have an upright posture.

penicillin Any of a group of antibiotics obtained from penicillium moulds or produced synthetically, used to treat or prevent infections caused by a wide variety of bacteria.

penicillium Any of various green and blue-green fungi that grow as moulds on citrus fruit, cheese and bread, including several species used to produce penicillin and certain other antibiotics.

peninsula A piece of land that projects into a body of water and is connected to a larger landmass.

penis 1. The male reproductive organ of mammals and some reptiles and birds. In mammals, the penis contains the urethra, which carries urine from the bladder and releases semen

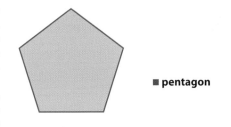
■ **pentagon**

containing sperm during reproduction. **2.** A similar organ found in the males of some invertebrate animals.

Penrose, Roger Born 1931. British mathematician and physicist. With Stephen Hawking he studied the physics of black holes.

pentagon A polygon having five sides.

penumbra 1. A partial shadow between regions of complete shadow and complete illumination, especially as cast by the Earth, the moon or another body during an eclipse. **2.** The greyish outer part of a sunspot. *Compare* **umbra.**

pepsin A powerful enzyme that breaks down proteins in the stomach of vertebrate animals.

peptide A chemical compound that is composed of a chain of two or more amino acids and is usually smaller than a protein. Some hormones and antibiotics are peptides.

per cent One part in a hundred. For example, 62 per cent (also written 62%) means 62 parts out of 100.

percentile Any of the 100 equal parts into which the range of the values of a set of data can be divided in order to show the distribution of those values. The percentile of a given value is determined by the percentage of the values that are smaller than that value. For example, a test score that is higher than 95 per cent of the other scores is in the 95th percentile.

perchloric acid A clear, colourless liquid, $HClO_4$, that is very corrosive and, under some conditions, extremely explosive. It is a powerful oxidant and is used as a catalyst and in explosives.

perennial *Botany. adjective* Living for several years. —*noun* A perennial plant. Asters, irises and peonies are some examples of perennials. *Compare* **annual, biennial.**

■ **peninsula**

perfect number A positive integer that equals the sum of all of its divisors other than itself. An example is 28, whose divisors (not counting itself) are 1, 2, 4, 7 and 14, which added together give 28.

peri– A prefix that means: **1.** Around, as in *pericardium,* the membrane around the heart. **2.** Near, as in *perihelion,* the point at which a planet is nearest the sun.

perianth The outer envelope of a flower, consisting of the sepals or the petals or both.

pericardium The membrane sac that encloses the heart in vertebrate animals.

periderm The outer, protective layers of tissue of woody roots and stems, consisting of the cork cambium and the tissues produced by it. *See more at* **cork cambium.**

perigee **1.** The point nearest the Earth in the orbit of the moon or an artificial satellite. **2.** The point in the orbit of a body, such as a satellite, where it is nearest the body around which it revolves, such as a planet. *Compare* **apogee.**

perihelion The point nearest the sun in the orbit of a body, such as a planet or comet, that travels around the sun.

perimeter **1.** The sum of the lengths of the segments that form the sides of a polygon. **2.** The total length of any closed curve, such as the circumference of a circle.

period **1.** A division of geological time, longer than an epoch and shorter than an era. **2.** The time it takes for a regularly recurring action or event to be repeated; a cycle. **3.** An instance or occurrence of menstruation. **4.** *Chemistry.* In the Periodic

Table, any of the seven horizontal rows that contain elements arranged in order of increasing atomic number. All the elements in a particular period have the same number of electron shells in their atoms. *See* **Periodic Table,** pages 260–261.

Periodic Table A table in which the chemical elements are arranged in order of increasing atomic number. Elements with similar properties are arranged in the same column (called a group), and elements with the same number of electron shells are arranged in the same row (called a period). *See table,* pages 260–261.

peripheral nervous system In vertebrate animals, the part of the nervous system that lies outside the brain and spinal cord. It includes the nerves that extend to the limbs. *Compare* **central nervous system.**

periscope An instrument that has angled mirrors or prisms and allows observation of objects not in the direct line of vision.

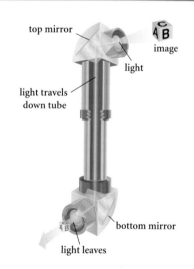

■ **periscope**
Light enters the top lens of the periscope, reflects off a mirror set at a 45° angle, travels down the periscope tube, and reflects off a second mirror, also set at a 45° angle. The light that reflects off the second mirror exits through the bottom lens and into the eye of the user.

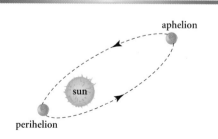

■ **perihelion**

perissodactyl Any of various hoofed mammals having an odd number of toes. Horses, tapirs and rhinoceroses are perissodactyls. Also called *odd-toed ungulate.*

peristalsis The wave-like muscle contractions in the organs of the digestive tract that push food into the stomach and then to the intestines. Peristalsis starts in the oesophagus and ends when digested food is eliminated as waste.

peritoneum The membrane that lines the inside of the abdomen and encloses the abdominal organs.

Perkin, Sir William Henry 1838–1907. English chemist. William Perkin made his first major discovery in a private laboratory he fitted out in his home. Here, in 1856, he attempted to synthesize quinine, much in demand for the treatment of malaria. He didn't succeed, but after conducting the same experiment with another compound he was able to extract a brilliant purple dye, subsequently named mauveine. With the encouragement of the dyeing firm J Pullar and Son, he built a factory to manufacture mauveine, which was a great commercial success, initiated the modern synthetic dyestuffs industry and introduced a new range of colours into human life. In 1874 Perkin sold his dyeworks in order to devote himself exclusively to his chemical research.

permafrost A layer of permanently frozen subsoil, reaching depths up to 1600 metres. Permafrost is found throughout most of the polar regions.

permeable Capable of being passed through or permeated, especially by liquids or gases: *a permeable membrane.*

Permian The seventh and last period of the Palaeozoic Era, from about 290 to 245 million years ago. The Permian Period was characterized by the formation of the supercontinent Pangaea, the rise of conifers, and the diversification of reptiles. It ended with the largest known mass extinction in the history of life. *See chart at* **geological time,** pages 148–149.

peroxide 1. A compound containing the group O_2. When any peroxide is combined with an acid, one of the products is hydrogen peroxide. 2. Hydrogen peroxide.

perpendicular *adjective.* Intersecting at or forming a right angle or right angles. —*noun* A line or plane that is perpendicular to a given line or plane.

Perseus A constellation in the Northern Hemisphere near Andromeda and Auriga.

pertussis *See* **whooping cough.**

Perutz, Max Ferdinand 1914–2002. Austrian-born British biochemist who determined the structure of haemoglobin, demonstrating that it is composed of four chains of molecules.

pesticide A chemical used to kill harmful animals or plants. *Compare* **fungicide, herbicide, insecticide.**

petal One of the often brightly coloured parts of a flower surrounding the reproductive organs. Petals may be separate or joined at their bases. As a group, the petals are called the corolla. *See more at* **flower.**

petiole *See* **leafstalk.**

Petri dish A shallow, circular dish with a loose cover, used to grow cultures of microorganisms.

petrifaction *also* petrification The process by which organic materials are turned into rock. Petrifaction occurs when water that is rich with inorganic minerals, such as calcium carbonate or silica, passes slowly through organic matter, such as wood, replacing its cellular structure with minerals.

petrochemical Any of a large number of chemicals made from petroleum or natural gas. Important petrochemicals include benzene, ammonia, ethene, and polystyrene. Petro-chemicals are used to produce a wide variety of

■ **Petri dish**
a researcher working with cultures in Petri dishes

Periodic Table of the Elements

The Periodic Table is a systematic arrangement of the chemical elements according to their atomic structure. The elements are arranged so that their **atomic numbers** – the number of protons in each element's nucleus – increase as you read across each row from left to right. So hydrogen (atomic number 1) comes first in the Table, helium (atomic number 2) comes second, lithium (atomic number 3) comes third, and so on.

The first Periodic Table to be widely accepted and used by other chemists was designed by Dmitri Mendeleev in 1869. At that time only 63 of the elements were known. Today we know a total of 112. When Mendeleev made the first table he knew that other elements would eventually be discovered, and he left empty spaces so that the new elements could be added as they were found.

Periods

The elements are placed into seven rows, or **periods**, according to the number of electron shells in their atoms. Each atom consists of a nucleus of neutrons and protons surrounded by one or more energy levels, or shells, in which electrons are continuously orbiting. The smallest atoms have only one electron shell. Larger atoms have as many as seven shells, each one successively larger than the one inside it. Hydrogen and helium have only one electron shell and are therefore placed in Period 1, while sodium and chlorine have three shells and are placed in Period 3. By noting the period in which an element is located, you can immediately know how many electron shells it has.

Lanthanides and Actinides

The elements of the **lanthanide series** (elements 57–71) and the **actinide series** (elements 89–103) all behave in a manner similar to that of the elements Sc and Y. But since they have different atomic numbers, they are separated from the main Periodic Table to make it easier to read.

Groups

The elements are organized into separate columns, or **groups**, according primarily to the number of electrons occupying their outermost shell. This number is important because it strongly affects the way an element will behave in a chemical reaction. Since the elements in each group have the same number of electrons in their outer shell, they share certain types of chemical behaviours, such as the ability to combine with other elements to form compounds. In the case of the larger elements in Periods 4 to 7, the number of electrons in some of the inner shells also affects their behaviour and thus determines where their groups are placed in the Table.

Group 3	Group 4	Group 5	Group 6	Group 7	Group 0
					2 **He** Helium 4.0026
5 **B** Boron 10.811	6 **C** Carbon 12.011	7 **N** Nitrogen 14.0067	8 **O** Oxygen 15.9994	9 **F** Fluorine 18.9984	10 **Ne** Neon 20.183
13 **Al** Aluminium 26.9815	14 **Si** Silicon 28.086	15 **P** Phosphorus 30.9738	16 **S** Sulphur 32.066	17 **Cl** Chlorine 35.453	18 **Ar** Argon 39.948

25 **Mn** Manganese 54.9380	26 **Fe** Iron 55.845	27 **Co** Cobalt 58.9332	28 **Ni** Nickel 58.69	29 **Cu** Copper 63.546	30 **Zn** Zinc 65.39	31 **Ga** Gallium 69.72	32 **Ge** Germanium 72.61	33 **As** Arsenic 74.9216	34 **Se** Selenium 78.96	35 **Br** Bromine 79.904	36 **Kr** Krypton 83.80
43 **Tc** Technetium (98)	44 **Ru** Ruthenium 101.07	45 **Rh** Rhodium 102.905	46 **Pd** Palladium 106.4	47 **Ag** Silver 107.868	48 **Cd** Cadmium 112.41	49 **In** Indium 114.82	50 **Sn** Tin 118.71	51 **Sb** Antimony 121.76	52 **Te** Tellurium 127.60	53 **I** Iodine 126.9045	54 **Xe** Xenon 131.29
75 **Re** Rhenium 186.2	76 **Os** Osmium 190.2	77 **Ir** Iridium 192.2	78 **Pt** Platinum 195.08	79 **Au** Gold 196.967	80 **Hg** Mercury 200.59	81 **Tl** Thallium 204.38	82 **Pb** Lead 207.2	83 **Bi** Bismuth 208.98	84 **Po** Polonium (210)	85 **At** Astatine (210)	86 **Rn** Radon (222)
107 **Bh** Bohrium (264)	108 **Hs** Hassium (265)	109 **Mt** Meitnerium (268)	110† (269)	111† (272)	112† (277)						

† Until official names are given to new elements, names based on a Latin translation of the atomic number are used: eg. *ununbium* (Latin *unus* '1' + *unus* '1' + *bi* '2') for element 112.

61 **Pm** Promethium (145)	62 **Sm** Samarium 150.36	63 **Eu** Europium 151.96	64 **Gd** Gadolinium 157.25	65 **Tb** Terbium 158.925	66 **Dy** Dysprosium 162.50	67 **Ho** Holmium 164.930	68 **Er** Erbium 167.26	69 **Tm** Thulium 168.934	70 **Yb** Ytterbium 173.04	71 **Lu** Lutetium 174.97
93 **Np** Neptunium (237)	94 **Pu** Plutonium (244)	95 **Am** Americium (243)	96 **Cm** Curium (247)	97 **Bk** Berkelium (247)	98 **Cf** Californium (251)	99 **Es** Einsteinium (252)	100 **Fm** Fermium (257)	101 **Md** Mendelevium (258)	102 **No** Nobelium (259)	103 **Lr** Lawrencium (262)

Alkali metals

Actinide series

Transition elements

Non-metals

Alkaline-earth metals

Other metals

Lanthanide series (rare-earth elements)

Noble gases

materials, such as plastics, explosives, fertilizers and synthetic fibres.

petrol A highly flammable mixture of liquid hydrocarbons that are derived from petroleum. Petrol is used as a fuel for internal-combustion engines in cars, motorcycles, and vans.

petroleum A thick, black to yellow, flammable liquid mixture of hydrocarbons. Petroleum occurs naturally, mainly below the Earth's surface, and is believed to originate from the accumulated remains of ancient plants and animals. It is the source of petrochemicals and is used to make petrol, lubricating oils, plastics and many other products. Also called *crude oil.*

petrology The scientific study of the origin, composition, and structure of rocks.

pH A numerical measure of the acidity or alkalinity of a solution, measured on a scale of 0 to 14. Neutral solutions have a pH of 7, acidic solutions have a pH lower than 7 and alkaline solutions have a pH higher than 7.

phagocyte An organism or specialized cell that engulfs and ingests other cells or particles. Phagocytes in vertebrate animals include white blood cells called macrophages, which help the body fight disease by breaking down foreign particles and bacteria. ❖ The process by which phagocytes engulf and break down bacteria or particles, as of food, is called **phagocytosis**. Single-celled organisms such as amoebas ingest food by the process of phagocytosis.

phalanges The small bones of the fingers or toes in humans or the digits in other primates. *See more at* **skeleton.**

Phanerozoic The period of geological time from about 570 million years ago to the present, including the Palaeozoic, Mesozoic and Cainozoic Eras. The Phanerozoic Eon is marked by an abundance of fossil evidence of life, especially more complex forms. *See chart at* **geological time,** pages 148–149.

pharmacology The scientific study of drugs and their effects, especially in the treatment of disease.

pharynx The passage that leads from the cavities of the nose and mouth to the larynx (voice box) and oesophagus.

phase 1. Any of the forms, recurring in cycles, in which the moon or a planet appears. **2.** *See* **state of matter. 3.** *Physics.* Any part of a repeated pattern of oscillatory motion relative to a fixed starting point or time. *See more at* **wave.**

phellem *See* **cork** (sense 1).

phelloderm The tissue produced on the inside of the cork cambium in woody plants. It forms a secondary cortex. *See more at* **cork cambium.**

phellogen *See* **cork cambium.**

phenol A poisonous, white crystalline compound used as a disinfectant and to make plastics and drugs. It used to be known as *carbolic acid.*

phenolphthalein A white or pale-yellow, crystalline powder used as an indicator for acid and basic solutions. It is also used as a laxative and in making dyes.

phenotype The physical appearance of an organism as distinguished from its genetic make-up. The phenotype of an organism depends on which genes are dominant and on the interaction between genes and environment. *Compare* **genotype.**

phenyl The organic radical C_6H_5, made by removing one hydrogen atom from benzene.

phenylalanine An essential amino acid. *See more at* **amino acid.**

pheromone A chemical that is secreted by an animal and influences the behaviour or development of other animals of the same species. For example, the male and female of many species establish territory and attract mates by means of pheromones. Queen bees give off a substance that prevents other females in the hive from becoming sexually mature, with the result that only the queen bee mates and lays eggs.

phlegm Mucus produced by the mucous membranes of the respiratory tract. *See also* **mucus.**

phloem A tissue in vascular plants that conducts food from the leaves to the other plant parts. Phloem consists primarily of tube-like cells that have porous openings. In mature woody plants it forms a sheath-like layer of tissue in the stem, just inside the bark. *See more at* **cambium, photosynthesis.** *Compare* **xylem.**

phlogiston A colourless, odourless and weightless substance once believed to be the combustible part of all flammable substances and to be given off as flame during burning. In the 18th century, Antoine Lavoisier proved that phlogiston does not exist. *See panel at* **Lavoisier.**

phosphate A compound containing the group PO₄. Phosphates are important in metabolism and are frequently used in fertilizers.

phosphor A substance that can emit light after absorbing some form of radiation. The insides of television screens and fluorescent lamp tubes are coated with phosphors. *See panel at* **cathode-ray tube.**

phosphorescence 1. The giving off of light by a substance as a result of having absorbed energy from a form of electromagnetic radiation, such as visible light or X-rays. Unlike fluorescence, phosphorescence continues for a short while after the source of radiation is removed. *Compare* **fluorescence** (sense 1). **2.** The light produced in this way.

phosphorus A highly reactive nonmetallic element important to living organisms, occurring naturally in phosphates and existing in white (or sometimes yellow), red and black forms. Phosphorus is used to make matches, fireworks and fertilizers and to protect metal surfaces from corrosion. *Symbol* **P.** *Atomic number* 15. *See* **Periodic Table,** pages 260–261. —*adjective* **phosphoric.**

photo– A prefix that means "light", as in *photoreceptor.*

photodegradable Capable of being chemically decomposed by light. For example, photodegradable plastic becomes brittle and breaks into smaller pieces when exposed to sunlight, helping reduce litter and environmental damage.

photoelectric Relating to the electrical effects of light. For example, exposure to light can bring about the emission of electrons from a material, the generation of an electric current, or a change in the electrical resistance of a material. ❖ The emission of electrons from a material, such as a metal, as a result of being struck by photons (light) is called the **photoelectric effect.**

photometry The measurement of the intensity, brightness or other properties of light.

photomicrograph A photograph made through a microscope.

photon The smallest unit of light or other electromagnetic energy, having no mass and no electric charge. *See panel at* **electromagnetic radiation.**

photoreceptor A specialized structure or cell that is sensitive to light. In vertebrate animals, the photoreceptors are the rods and cones of the eye's retina. *See panel at* **circadian rhythm.**

photosphere The thin, outer layer that forms the visible surface of a star, especially the sun.

photosynthesis The process by which green plants, algae and certain forms of bacteria make carbohydrates from carbon dioxide and water in the presence of chlorophyll, using light as energy. Photosynthesis normally releases oxygen as a by-product. *Compare* **chemosynthesis.** *See panel at* **transpiration.** *See A Closer Look,* page 264.

phototropism The growth or movement of a fixed organism, especially a plant, towards or away from light. —*adjective* **phototropic.**

photovoltaic cell *See* **solar cell.**

phrenology The study of the shape of the skull as a means of determining character and intelligence. Phrenology has been disproven as a science.

phylum (*plural* **phyla**) A group of organisms ranking above a class and below a kingdom. *See table at* **taxonomy.**

physical chemistry The branch of chemistry that is concerned with the physical structure of chemical compounds, the amount of energy they have, the way they react with other compounds, and the bonds that hold their atoms together.

physical science Any of several branches of science, such as physics, chemistry or geology, that studies the nature and properties of energy and non-living matter. *Compare* **life science.**

physics The scientific study of matter and energy and the relations between them.

physiology The scientific study of an organism's vital functions, such as circulation, respiration and digestion.

phytoplankton Plankton consisting of plants and plant-like organisms, such as algae. Phyto-plankton are a major source of food for aquatic

Photosynthesis

A leaf is a plant's food factory. It makes food by photosynthesis, a two-stage process that converts the energy of sunlight into chemical energy. In the first stage, light from the sun strikes leaf cells that contain special structures called chloroplasts. The chloroplasts contain chlorophyll, the green pigment that traps light energy and makes photosynthesis possible. Using water molecules brought up from the soil, the chloroplasts transfer the light energy into chemical energy in the form of ATP. The water is split into hydrogen and oxygen, with the oxygen being given off as a waste product. In the second stage, which does not require light, the chloroplasts use the chemical energy stored in the ATP to combine the hydrogen with carbon dioxide from the air to make glucose. The glucose is then distributed throughout the plant as food.

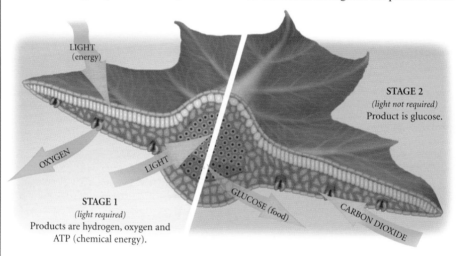

LIGHT (energy)

STAGE 2
(light not required)
Product is glucose.

OXYGEN

LIGHT

STAGE 1
(light required)
Products are hydrogen, oxygen and ATP (chemical energy).

GLUCOSE (food)

CARBON DIOXIDE

Photosynthesis takes place in the column-like cells of the palisade layer and in the irregularly shaped cells of the spongy mesophyll. Chloroplasts are present in both kinds of cells, but are especially numerous in the palisade layer. The cells receive carbon dioxide from air that enters the leaf through holes called stomata.

The stomata also allow oxygen produced by photosynthesis to escape. Water from the roots is supplied by the vascular tissue known as xylem. Glucose made by the leaf is distributed to the rest of the plant by the vascular tissue known as phloem.

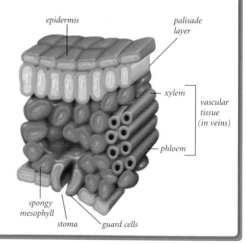

epidermis

palisade layer

xylem

vascular tissue *(in veins)*

phloem

spongy mesophyll

stoma

guard cells

spark plugs

fuel and air

compressed fuel and air

piston

shaft

■ piston

The fuel-air mixture in the left-hand chamber expands when ignited by the spark plug, pushing the pistons down and turning the shaft to which it is attached. The turning shaft drives the piston in the right-hand cylinder upwards. It will then be pushed down in the same way when the fuel-air mixture enters that chamber and is ignited. The alternating action of the two pistons keeps the shaft turning.

animals and fix large amounts of carbon, which would otherwise be released as carbon dioxide.

pi An irrational number that has a numerical value of 3.14159265359. . . and is represented by the symbol π. It expresses the ratio of the circumference of a circle to its diameter and appears as a constant in many mathematical expressions.

pictogram A representation of frequency using pictures, where one picture will usually stand for a specified value.

pie chart A circular diagram split into sectors, used to show the percentage proportions into which a whole is divided up. *See more at* **graph.**

piezoelectric effect The generation of an electric charge in certain non-conducting materials, such as quartz crystals and ceramics, when they are subjected to mechanical stress (such as pressure or vibration), or the generation of vibrations in such materials when they are subjected to an electric field.

pigment 1. An organic compound that gives a

characteristic colour to plant or animal tissues and is involved in vital processes. Chlorophyll and haemoglobin are examples of pigments. 2. A substance or material used as colouring.

pincers A jointed grasping claw of certain animals, such as lobsters or scorpions.

pine Any of various evergreen trees that bear cones and have clusters of needle-shaped leaves. Pines are found chiefly in cooler temperate regions in the Northern Hemisphere.

pineal gland A small gland that is located near the brain and is involved in the regulation of hormones. In many animals, the pineal gland controls metabolism, hibernation and sexual development.

pinnate Of a leaf, having parts or divisions arranged on each side of a common axis in the manner of a feather. Ash, oak and walnut trees have pinnate leaves.

pinniped Any of various carnivorous, aquatic mammals having long, smooth bodies and fin-like flippers for swimming. Pinnipeds include seals and walruses.

pint In the imperial system, a unit used to measure liquids equivalent to 0.568 litre (20 fluid ounces). *See table at* **measurement.**

pipette A narrow glass tube that is open at both ends and often marked to show volume. It is used for transferring liquids.

Pisces A constellation in the Northern Hemisphere near Aries and Pegasus.

pistil The female reproductive organ of a flower, consisting of the ovary, style and stigma. *See more at* **flower.**

pistillate 1. Having one or more pistils. 2. Having pistils but no stamens. Female flowers are pistillate.

piston A solid cylinder or disc that fits snugly into a hollow cylinder and moves back and forth under the pressure of a fluid, as in many engines, or moves or compresses a fluid, as in a pump or compressor.

pitch 1. A thick, tar-like substance used for roofing, waterproofing and paving. 2. Any of various natural bitumens, such as asphalt, having similar uses. 3. A resin derived from the sap of a cone-bearing tree, such as a pine.

pitchblende

pitchblende A brown to black, often crusty mineral that is a principal ore of uranium. It is highly radioactive.

pith 1. *Botany.* The soft, spongy tissue in the centre of the stems of most flowering plants. Composed of parenchyma cells, the pith is gradually compressed by the inward growth of the vascular tissue known as xylem. As the plant grows older, the pith dries out and often disintegrates, leaving the stem hollow. 2. The soft white tissue that lies beneath the rind of many citrus fruits, eg oranges.

pituitary gland A gland at the base of the brain in vertebrate animals that regulates the function of most of the body's hormone-producing glands and organs, including the thyroid and adrenal glands. The pituitary gland also controls overall body growth.

pit viper Any of various venomous snakes having a small pit below each eye that is used to sense heat. Their fangs are hollow and folded back in the mouth when the snake is not striking prey. Pit vipers are mostly found in the Western Hemisphere and include the cottonmouth and rattlesnakes.

pixel The most basic unit of an image on a computer or television screen. Pixels are arranged in rows and columns and are lit up in a specific pattern to create an image.

placebo A substance resembling a drug but containing only inactive ingredients, used especially in scientific experiments to test the effectiveness of a drug. Researchers give one group of people a real drug and another group a placebo and then determine whether the people taking the drug get better results than the people taking the placebo.

placenta 1. The disc-shaped organ which develops on the lining of the uterus during pregnancy. It contains tissue from both the mother and the developing fetus. In the placenta there is an exchange of materials – the fetus gets food and oxygen from the mother while carbon dioxide and other waste products pass out from the fetus into the maternal blood supply so that they can be excreted by the mother. The placenta is expelled from the mother's body in the final stage of the birth process. 2. *Botany.* The part of the ovary of

Did You Know?

pixels

If you look at a picture in a comic very closely, you will see that coloured or shaded areas are often made of very tiny dots. Images on computer screens are also composed of very tiny dots known as *pixels.* (Pixel is derived from *picture element.*) The computer controls each pixel individually. Most monitors have hundreds of thousands or millions of pixels that are illuminated or dimmed to create an image. The colours on a monitor consist of arrangements of red, blue and green pixels that adjust in intensity to create all of the colours that you see on a screen. Pixels vary in size according to the model of monitor. Monitors with the smallest pixels have the sharpest images, but they require more memory to store data about the colour and intensity of each pixel.

a flowering plant to which the ovules are attached. —*adjective* **placental.**

placer A deposit of minerals, such as gold or magnetite, left by a river. The minerals are usually concentrated in one area because they are relatively heavy and therefore settle out of the river's currents more quickly than lighter sediments such as silt and sand. When mineral prospectors pan for gold, they look for placer deposits.

plagioclase Any of a series of common feldspar minerals, consisting of mixtures of sodium and calcium aluminium silicates. Plagioclase is typically white, yellow or reddish-grey, but it can also be blue to black. It is especially common in igneous rocks.

plague 1. Any highly infectious, usually fatal epidemic disease. 2. An often fatal disease caused by a bacterium transmitted to humans usually by fleas that have bitten infected rats or other rodents. The most common form of plague is bubonic plague, though plague can also exist as a highly contagious form infecting the lungs and as an extremely severe form infecting the blood.

plain 1. A large, relatively flat, usually treeless area of land. **2.** A broad, level expanse, such as an area of the sea floor or a lunar mare.

plan *Mathematics*. A view of a three-dimensional object from directly above.

Planck, Max Karl Ernst Ludwig 1858–1947. German physicist who formulated quantum theory (1900), which explained and predicted certain phenomena that could not be accounted for in classical physics. Planck's theory was essential to the work of Albert Einstein, Niels Bohr and many other modern physicists.

plane *noun* A flat surface, such that a straight line joining any two points on the surface lies entirely on it. —*adjective* Lying in a plane: *a plane curve.* ❖ A solid shape has a **plane of symmetry** if it can be divided into two pieces which are mirror images of each other.

plane geometry The mathematical study of geometric figures whose parts lie in the same plane, such as polygons, circles and lines.

planet A celestial body that does not produce its own light, is larger than an asteroid, and is illuminated by light from a star, such as the sun, around which it revolves. In our solar system there are nine known planets: Mercury, Venus, Earth, Mars, Jupiter, Saturn, Uranus, Neptune and Pluto. —*adjective* **planetary.**

planetary nebula A nebula consisting of an expanding shell of gas, mostly hydrogen, that surrounds a hot, compact central star. *See more at* **star.**

plankton Small organisms that float or drift in great numbers in bodies of salt or fresh water. Plankton is a primary food source for many animals, and consists of bacteria, protozoans, certain algae, cnidarians, tiny crustaceans such as copepods, and many other organisms.

plant Any of a wide variety of multicellular organisms, most of which manufacture their own food by means of photosynthesis. Plants have cells with cell walls made of cellulose, are immobile, and have no nervous system. They range in size from a few millimetres to trees that stand over 90 metres tall. Plants are grouped as a separate kingdom in taxonomy.

plant kingdom The category of living

Word History

planet names

To learn the origins of the names of the planets is to learn something about Roman mythology. Mercury moves fastest through the sky and was named after the swift-footed messenger of the gods. Venus was named after the Roman goddess of love because of its striking brightness and beauty in the morning and evening sky. The reddish appearance of Mars reminded early astronomers of the colour of blood, so Mars was named after the Roman god of war. Jupiter is the largest of the planets and was named after the king of the gods. Jupiter's father was Saturn, the name given to the next planet after Jupiter. To continue that logic, the name of Saturn's own father, Uranus, was given to the next planet after Saturn. Viewed through a telescope, the planet Neptune appears sea-green in colour, and takes its name from the Roman god of the sea. Finally, the darkest reaches of the solar system are the home of the frozen planet Pluto, named after the god of the cold world of the dead, the underworld.

organisms that includes all plants. The scientific name of this kingdom is Plantae. Also called vegetable kingdom. *See table at* **taxonomy.**

plaque 1. A film of mucus and bacteria on the surface of the teeth. **2.** A deposit of fatty material on the inner lining of an artery wall, characteristic of atherosclerosis.

plasma 1. *See* **blood plasma. 2.** Protoplasm or cytoplasm. **3.** A state of matter similar to a gas but consisting of positively charged ions with most or all of their detached electrons moving freely about. Because the concentrations of free electrons and positively charged ions are nearly equal, a plasma is electrically neutral. Plasmas are produced by very high temperatures, as in the sun and other stars, and also by the ionization resulting from exposure to an electric current, as in a fluorescent light bulb or a neon sign.

plasma cell

plasma cell A cell that produces antibodies as part of an immune response. B cells develop into plasma cells. *See panel at* **antibody**.

plasmodium (*plural* **plasmodia**) **1.** A mass of protoplasm having many cell nuclei but not divided into separate cells. It is formed by the combination of many amoeba-like cells and is characteristic of the active, feeding phase of certain slime moulds. **2.** Any of various single-celled organisms (called protozoans) that exist as parasites in vertebrate animals, one of which causes malaria.

plaster of Paris A form of calcium phosphate derived from the mineral gypsum. It is mixed with water to make casts and moulds.

plastic *noun* Any of numerous artificial compounds formed by linking simple chemical units into giant molecules called polymers. They can be moulded into objects, pressed into thin layers, and drawn into fibres for use in textiles. Thermosoftening plastics are soft or liquid when heated, while thermosetting plastics cannot be melted or softened once they have been moulded into their original shape. —*adjective* Capable of being moulded or formed into a shape.

plastid A structure found in plant cells, green algae, and certain protozoans. Some plastids, such as the chloroplasts in plant leaves, contain pigments.

plate *noun* **1.** A thin, flat sheet of metal or other material, especially one used as an electrode in a storage battery or capacitor. **2.** In plate tectonics, one of the sections of the Earth's lithosphere (crust and upper mantle) that is in constant motion along with other sections. *See more at* **tectonic boundary**. —*verb* To coat or cover with a thin layer of metal.

plateau An elevated, comparatively flat expanse of land.

platelet Platelets are tiny fragments of much larger cells in the bone marrow and are found in large numbers in mammalian blood. When the tissue is damaged, and bleeding occurs, the platelets break open, releasing several chemicals that help to cut off the blood flow to the area and bring about the cascade of changes that lead to clots forming at the site of a wound.

plate tectonics In geology, a theory that the Earth's lithosphere (crust and upper mantle) is divided into a number of large, plate-like sections that move as distinct masses. *See panels at* **fault**, **Gondwanaland**. *See more at* **tectonic boundary**.

platform The basic technology of a computer system's hardware and software, defining how a computer is operated and determining what other kinds of software can be used. Additional software or hardware must be compatible with the platform.

platinum A soft, easily shaped, silver-white

Did You Know?

plate tectonics

Have you ever noticed that the Earth's continents seem to fit together like pieces of a jigsaw puzzle? This observation led the German meteorologist Alfred Wegener to propose his theory of continental drift in 1912. Since rocks and fossils were found to match up in parts of different continents, it seemed that they must have once been joined, but no one could explain how such large landmasses could move so far apart. This problem was not solved until the 1960s, when the theory of *plate tectonics* was proposed. According to this theory, the continents move apart by riding piggyback on plates – huge slabs of the Earth's lithosphere – that are much larger than the continents themselves. The plates move like parts of a conveyor belt powered by huge convection currents of molten rock that many geologists believe is heated by the decay of radioactive elements deep within the Earth. Although they only move a few centimetres per year, over hundreds of millions of years the continents are carried thousands of kilometres. Along their boundaries, the plates crumple, scrape or pull apart from one another, giving rise to volcanoes and earthquakes, and creating and destroying rock on the ever-changing surface of the planet.

metallic element that occurs worldwide with similar metals. It has a high melting point and does not corrode in air. Platinum is used as a catalyst and in the manufacture of jewellery, electrical contacts and dental crowns. *Symbol* **Pt**. *Atomic number* 78. *See* **Periodic Table**, pages 260–261.

platyhelminth *See* **flatworm**.

platypus An egg-laying mammal of Australia and Tasmania that spends much of its life in water. Platypuses have a broad flat tail, webbed feet and a snout resembling a duck's bill.

playa A dry lake bed at the bottom of a desert basin, sometimes temporarily covered with water. Playas have no vegetation and are among the flattest geographical features in the world.

Pleiades A loose collection of several hundred stars in the constellation Taurus, at least six of which are visible to the unaided eye.

Pleistocene The earlier of the two epochs of the Quaternary Period, from about 1.6 million to 10,000 years ago. The Pleistocene Epoch was characterized by the formation of widespread glaciers in the Northern Hemisphere and by the appearance of humans. *See chart at* **geological time**, pages 148–149.

pleura (*plural* **pleurae**) A membrane that encloses each lung and lines the chest cavity.

Pliocene The fifth and last epoch of the Tertiary Period, from about 5 to 1.6 million years ago,

characterized by the appearance of distinctly modern animals. *See chart at* **geological time**, pages 148–149.

Plough, the A group of seven stars forming the outline of an old-fashioned hand plough. The other name for this constellation is Ursa Major (the Great Bear).

plucking A process of glacial erosion by which a glacier freezes onto rocks and pulls them away when it moves.

plumage The covering of feathers on a bird.

plume 1. *Zoology.* A feather, especially a large one. **2.** *Geology.* A body of magma that rises from the Earth's mantle into the crust. ❖ If a plume rises to the Earth's surface, it erupts as **lava**. ❖ If it remains below the Earth's surface, it eventually solidifies into a body of rock known as a **pluton**. **3.** *Ecology.* An area in air, water, soil or rock containing pollutants released from a single source. A plume often spreads in the environment due to the action of wind, currents or gravity.

plumule The developing bud of a plant embryo, situated just below the cotyledons and often containing immature leaves. *See more at* **germination**.

Pluto The ninth and usually furthest planet from the sun and the smallest in size, with a diameter about one-sixth that of Earth's. Pluto orbits the sun once every 248 years, the longest amount of time for any planet. It is the coldest planet in the solar system, with an average surface temperature of –236°C. *See table at* **solar system**, pages 314–315. *See panel at* **planet**.

pluton A large body of igneous rock formed when a plume of magma cools underground. Although most plutons are deep within the Earth's crust, some become exposed at the surface due to plate-tectonic processes.

plutonium A silvery, radioactive metallic element of the actinide series that has the highest atomic number of all naturally occurring elements. It can be found in trace amounts in uranium ores and is produced artificially by bombarding uranium with neutrons. It is absorbed by bone marrow and is highly poisonous. Plutonium is used in nuclear weapons and as a fuel in nuclear reactors. Its most stable isotope has a half-life of 76 million years.

■ **platypus**

pluvial

Symbol **Pu.** *Atomic number* 94. *See* **Periodic Table**, pages 260–261.

pluvial 1. Relating to rain; rainy: *During the Pleistocene Epoch there were many pluvial periods.* 2. Caused by rain: *pluvial lakes.*

Pm The symbol for **promethium**.

pneumatic 1. Relating to air or another gas: *pneumatic pressure.* 2. Filled with or operated by compressed air: *a pneumatic drill.*

pneumonia Any of several infections resulting in inflammation of the lungs, caused by bacteria or viruses.

Po The symbol for **polonium**.

pod A fruit or seed case that splits along two seams to release its seeds when it matures. Legumes, such as peas and beans, produce pods.

–pod A suffix meaning "foot". It is used in the scientific names of the members of many groups of organisms, such as *arthropod,* an organism having "jointed feet", and *sauropod,* a dinosaur having "lizard feet".

point A geometric object having no dimensions and no property other than its location. The intersection of two lines is a point.

polar bond A type of covalent bond between two atoms in which electrons are shared unequally. Because of this, one end of the molecule has a slightly negative charge and the other a slightly positive charge. *See more at* **covalent bond.**

polar cap 1. The mass of permanent ice that covers either of the Earth's polar regions. 2. The mass of frozen carbon dioxide and water that covers either of the polar regions of the planet Mars.

polar circle The Arctic Circle or the Antarctic Circle.

polar coordinate system A system of coordinates in which the location of a point is determined by its distance from a fixed point at the centre of the coordinate space (called the pole), and by the measurement of the angle formed by a fixed line (the polar axis, corresponding to the x-axis in Cartesian coordinates) and a line from the pole through the given point. The polar coordinates of a point are given as (r, θ), where r is the distance of the point from the pole, and θ is the measure of the angle.

Polaris A very bright star in Ursa Minor. It is almost at the north celestial pole and so is also referred to as the North Star or Pole Star. However, eventually its position will change and Polaris will no longer be the Pole Star.

polarity 1. The state of having two opposite poles: *magnetic polarity.* 2. *Physics.* The status, whether negative or positive, of the poles of a magnet, the terminals of an electrode, etc.

polarize 1. To cause the positive and negative electric charges in an object, such as an atom or molecule, to become separated from each other. This is typically done by placing the object in an electric field. 2. To control the direction of the vibration of electromagnetic waves. Polarized light, for example, consists of electromagnetic waves that vibrate in a single plane, rather than in all directions as in ordinary light.

pole 1. *Mathematics.* **a.** Either of the points at which an axis that passes through the centre of a sphere intersects the surface of the sphere. **b.** The fixed point used as a reference in a system of polar coordinates. It corresponds to the origin in the Cartesian coordinate system. **2a.** *Geography.* Either of the points at which the Earth's axis of rotation intersects the Earth's surface; the North Pole or South Pole. **b.** Either of the two similar points on another planet. **3.** *Physics.* A magnetic pole. **4.** *Electricity.* Either of two oppositely charged terminals, such as the two electrodes of an electrolytic cell or the electric terminals of a battery. *—adjective* **polar.**

polio A contagious disease, caused by a virus, that mainly affects the nerve cells of the spinal cord and brain, often leading to muscle weakness and paralysis. Polio has been eradicated from most of the world by means of an effective vaccination programme. The name is a shortened form of **poliomyelitis.**

pollen Powdery grains that contain the male reproductive cells of most plants. In flowering plants, pollen is produced by the anthers of stamens.

pollen tube The slender tube formed by the pollen grain that penetrates an ovule after pollination and releases the male gametes.

■ pollen
a bee collecting pollen

pollination The process by which plant pollen is transferred from the male reproductive organs to the female reproductive organs. Once pollination has taken place, fertilization usually follows, leading to successful seed formation. In flowering plants, pollen is transferred from the anther to the stigma, often by the wind or by insects. In cone-bearing plants, male cones release pollen that is usually borne by the wind to the ovules of female cones. —*verb* **pollinate.**

pollutant A substance, especially a waste material, that contaminates air, water or soil.

pollution The contamination of air, water or soil by substances that are harmful to living things. ❖ Light from cities and towns at night that interferes with astronomical observations is known as **light pollution.** It can also disturb natural rhythms of growth in plants and other organisms. ❖ Continuous noise that is loud enough to be annoying or physically harmful is known as **noise pollution.** ❖ Heat from hot water that is discharged from a factory into a river or lake, where it can kill or endanger aquatic life, is known as **thermal pollution.**

Pollux One of two bright stars, called the heavenly twins, in the constellation Gemini, the other star being Castor.

Polly the sheep The first animal to be successfully cloned from an animal (Dolly the sheep) that itself is a clone.

polonium A very rare, naturally radioactive, silvery-grey or black metallic element. It is produced in extremely small amounts by the radioactive decay of radium or the bombardment of bismuth or lead with neutrons. *Symbol* **Po.** *Atomic number* 84. *See* **Periodic Table,** pages 260–261.

poly– A prefix meaning "many", as in *polygon,* a figure having many sides.

polychaete Any of various often brightly coloured, meat-eating worms that are related to earthworms and leeches and usually live in the sea. Each segment of a polychaete has a pair of

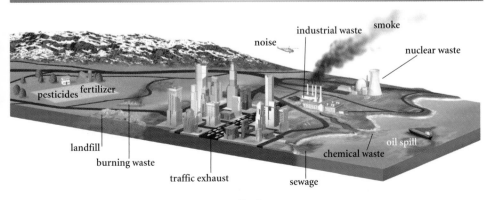

■ pollution
Pollution can affect air, water or land and can threaten the health of humans, wildlife and plants.

fleshy appendages that are tipped with bristles, used for swimming or burrowing.

polychromatic 1. Of or having many colours. **2.** Consisting of radiation of more than one wavelength.

polyester Any of various synthetic resins that are light, strong and resistant to weather. Polyesters are long chains of esters and are used to make plastics and artificial fibres, such as Terylene, widely used for clothing.

polyethene (old name **polyethylene**) A polymer made by joining many ethene monomers in an addition reaction. Polyethene is easily moulded and is resistant to other chemicals. It can be repeatedly softened and hardened by heating and cooling, and it is used for many purposes, such as making containers, tubes and packaging.

polygon A closed plane figure having three or more sides. Triangles, rectangles and octagons are all examples of polygons. ❖ A **regular polygon** has all sides and angles equal.

polyhedron A three-dimensional geometric figure whose faces are polygons. A tetrahedron, for example, is a polyhedron having four triangular faces.

polymer Any of various chemical compounds made of smaller, identical molecules (called monomers) linked together. Some polymers, like cellulose, occur naturally, while others, like nylon, are artificial. Polymers have extremely high molecular weights, make up many of the tissues of organisms, and are used to make such materials as plastics, concrete, glass and rubber. ❖ The process by which molecules are linked together to form polymers is called **polymerization.**

polymorphism 1. The existence of two or more different forms in an adult organism of the same species, as of an insect. In bees, the presence of queen, worker and drone is an example of polymorphism. Differences between the sexes and between breeds of domesticated animals are not considered examples of polymorphism. **2.** The crystallization of a compound in at least two distinct forms. Diamond and graphite, for example, are polymorphs of the element carbon. They both consist entirely of carbon but have different crystal structures and different physical properties.

polynomial An algebraic expression that is represented as the sum of two or more terms. The expressions $x^2 - 4$ and $5x^4 + 2x^3 - x + 7$ are both polynomials.

polyp A cnidarian in its sedentary stage. Polyps have hollow, tube-shaped bodies with a central mouth on top surrounded by tentacles. Some cnidarians, such as corals and sea anemones, only exist as polyps, while others turn into medusas as adults or lack a polyp stage completely. *Compare* **medusa.**

polysaccharide Any of a class of carbohydrates that are made of long chains of simple carbohydrates (called monosaccharides). Starch and cellulose are polysaccharides.

polystyrene A plastic polymer that is transparent, hard and rigid. It is used in a wide variety of manufactured products, ranging from kitchen utensils to solid-foam insulation.

polyunsaturated Relating to an organic compound, especially a fat, in which more than one pair of carbon atoms are joined by double or triple bonds. *See more at* **unsaturated.**

polyurethane Any of various resins used to make tough resistant coatings, adhesives and electrical insulation.

pond An inland body of standing water that is smaller than a lake.

pons A thick band of nerve fibres in the brainstem of mammals that links the brainstem to the cerebellum and upper portions of the brain. It is a major pathway for the transmission of nerve impulses among different portions of the brain.

population A group of individuals of the same species occupying a specific habitat, community or other defined area: *the population of turtles in a pond; the elk population in North America.*

pore 1. A tiny opening, as one in an animal's skin or on the surface of a plant leaf or stem, through which liquids or gases may pass. **2.** A space in soil, rock or loose sediment that is not occupied by mineral matter and allows the passage or absorption of fluids, such as water, petroleum or air.

poriferan *See* **sponge** (sense 1).

porous Having many pores or other small spaces that allow a gas or liquid to pass through. —*noun* **porosity.**

porphyry A fine-grained igneous rock containing some relatively large crystals, especially of feldspar.

porpoise Any of several small, toothed whales having a blunt snout and a triangular dorsal fin. *Compare* **dolphin**.

positive 1. Greater than zero, for example the number 12. 2. Having the electric charge of a proton. The symbol for a positive charge is a plus sign. 3. Showing the presence, as in a blood test, of a suspected disease or microorganism.

post– A prefix that means "after", as in *postoperative*, after an operation, or "behind", as in *postnasal,* behind the nose or nasal passages.

postulate A principle that is accepted as true without proof; an axiom.

potash Any of several chemical compounds that contain potassium, especially potassium carbonate (K_2CO_3), which is a strongly alkaline material obtained from the ash of burnt wood and used in fertilizers.

potassium A soft, highly reactive silvery-white metallic element that is an alkali metal and occurs in nature only in compounds. It is essential for the growth of plants and is used especially in fertilizers and soaps. *Symbol* **K**. *Atomic number* 19. *See* **Periodic Table**, pages 260–261.

potassium hydroxide A white, corrosive, solid compound, KOH, used in bleaches and to make soaps and detergents. It is soluble in water and very soluble in alcohol.

potassium nitrate A transparent, white, crystalline compound and strong oxidizing agent, KNO_3. It is used in gunpowder and fireworks, in making glass, and in fertilizer. Also called *saltpetre. See also* **nitre**.

potential 1. In an electric (or gravitational) field, the potential energy per unit charge (or mass in a gravitational field) at a point in the field. 2. The difference in voltage between two points in an electric circuit.

potential difference The energy transferred or work done per unit charge in moving a charge between two points in an electric field.

potential energy The energy possessed by a body as a result of its position or condition rather than its motion. A raised weight, coiled spring or charged battery has potential energy. *Compare* **kinetic energy.**

potentiometer 1. An adjustable resistor used to control the magnitude of the voltage that is applied to an electric circuit. Potentiometers are used in the volume controls of radios and televisions. 2. An instrument for measuring an unknown voltage by comparison with a known voltage, such as that of a generator.

pound A unit of weight equal to 16 ounces (about 453.6 grams). *See table at* **measurement**. *See panel at* **weight**.

power 1. *Physics.* The rate at which energy is transferred or work is done with respect to time, measured in watts (W). *Compare* **energy, work.** 2. *Mathematics.* The number of times a number or an expression is multiplied by itself, as shown by an exponent. Thus ten to the power of six, or 10^6, equals one million. 3. A number that represents the magnification of an optical instrument, such as a microscope or telescope. A 500-power microscope can magnify something 500 times.

Pr The symbol for **praseodymium.**

prairie An extensive area of flat or rolling grassland, especially the large plain of central North America.

praseodymium A soft, silvery, easily shaped metallic element of the lanthanide series that develops a green tarnish in air. It is used to colour glass and ceramics yellow and to make glass for welders' goggles. *Symbol* **Pr**. *Atomic number* 59. *See* **Periodic Table**, pages 260–261.

praying mantis Any of various predatory insects that are usually pale green and have two pairs of walking legs and a pair of strong grasping forelimbs. Praying mantises are related to cockroaches, and the female often eats her mate.

pre– A prefix that means "earlier, before", or "in advance", as in *prenatal,* before birth.

Precambrian The span of geological time from about 4600 to 570 million years ago. During the Precambrian Eon, which is divided into the Hadean, Archaean and Proterozoic, primitive forms of life first appeared on Earth. *See chart at* **geological time**, pages 148–149.

precession 1. The motion of the axis of a spinning body, such as the wobbling of a spinning top, that arises when an external force acts on the axis. 2. The motion of this kind made by Earth's axis, caused mainly by the gravitational pull of the sun, moon and other planets. ❖ The

precipitate

precession of the equinoxes is the slow westward shift of the autumnal and vernal equinoxes along the ecliptic, resulting from precession of the Earth's axis. A complete precession of the equinoxes takes 25,800 years.

precipitate *verb* **1.** To cause water vapour to condense from the atmosphere and fall as rain or snow. **2.** To separate chemically from a solution in the form of a solid. *—noun* A solid material separated from a solution by chemical means: *an insoluble precipitate.*

precipitation A form of water that falls from the atmosphere to the Earth's surface, such as rain, snow, sleet, hail and dew. There are three types of rainfall: convectional (high temperatures make warm air rise), cyclonic (warm air rises over cold air) and relief (air is forced to rise over a mountain).

predator An animal that lives by capturing and eating other animals.

pregnancy **1.** The condition of being pregnant. **2.** The time during which one is pregnant; gestation.

prehensile Adapted for seizing, grasping or holding, especially by wrapping around an object. The feet of many birds and the tails of monkeys are prehensile.

premolar Any of eight bicuspid teeth in mammals, arranged in pairs on both sides of the upper and lower jaws between the canines and molars. Premolars are used to tear and grind food.

pressure The force acting on a surface, divided by the area over which it acts. The unit of pressure is the pascal (Pa). $1 \text{ Pa} = 1 \text{N/m}^2$.

Priestley, Joseph 1733–1804. British chemist who discovered oxygen (1774) and ten other gases, including hydrogen chloride, sulphur dioxide and ammonia.

primary **1.** Relating to a primary colour. **2.** *Botany.* Relating to plant tissues in the tips of roots and shoots whose cells divide to cause the plant to grow lengthwise.

primary colour Any of a group of colours from which all other colours can be made by mixing. *See more at* **colour.**

primary wave An earthquake wave in which rock particles vibrate parallel to the direction of wave travel. Primary waves can travel through both solids and liquids. Also called *P wave. See panel at* **earthquake.**

primate Any of various mammals having a highly developed brain, eyes facing forward, a shortened nose and muzzle, and opposable thumbs. Primates usually live in groups with complex social systems, and their high intelligence allows them to adapt their behaviour successfully to different environments. Lemurs, monkeys, apes and humans are primates.

Biography

Joseph Priestley

When Joseph Priestley met Benjamin Franklin in 1766, it was the beginning of a friendship that would have an enormous impact on science. Franklin's enthusiasm about his experiments with electricity convinced Priestley to conduct his own experiments. Priestley developed an improved technique for isolating gases in a sealed glass vessel. Using a magnifying glass to focus the rays of the sun on a piece of mercuric oxide, he discovered a gas that made a candle burn more brightly, while all the other gases he tested extinguished its flame. Priestley did not appreciate the full implications of his discovery, however. When he told the French chemist Antoine Lavoisier about his discovery, Lavoisier repeated Priestley's experiments and was able to prove that air was not an element but was made up of various parts, and that combustion required the presence of Priestley's gas. Lavoisier gave the element its name, *oxygen.*

prime meridian The meridian with a longitude of 0°, used as a reference line from which longitude east and west is measured. It passes through Greenwich in London. Also called *Greenwich meridian.*

prime factor The prime factors of a number are the prime numbers that, when multiplied together, produce that number. For example, the prime factors of 12 are $2 \times 2 \times 3$, or $2^3 \times 3$.

prime number A positive integer that can only be divided by itself and 1 without leaving a remainder. Examples of prime numbers are 7, 23 and 67. The number 1 is not a prime number. *Compare* **composite number.**

primitive 1. Relating to an early or original stage: *a primitive form of life.* 2. Having evolved very little from an early type. Lampreys and sturgeon are primitive fish.

prion A particle composed of protein, similar to a virus but lacking DNA or RNA. Prions are thought to be the agent of infection of some diseases of the nervous system, such as BSE (bovine spongiform encephalopathy) in cattle.

prism 1. A geometric solid in which the two ends are matching parallel polygons and all other surfaces are parallelograms. 2. A solid of this type, often made of glass with triangular ends, used to disperse light and break it up into a spectrum.

probability A number expressing the likelihood of the occurrence of a given event, especially a fraction expressing how many times the event will happen in a given number of tests or experiments. For example, when rolling a six-sided true (ie not biased) dice, the probability of rolling a particular side is 1 in 6, or $\frac{1}{6}$.

proboscis 1. The long, flexible snout of an elephant or tapir. 2. The slender, tubular feeding and sucking organ of certain invertebrates, such as butterflies and mosquitoes.

Procyon The brightest star in the constellation Canis Minor, and the eighth brightest star in the sky at night.

producer An organism that serves as a source of food for other organisms in a food chain. Producers include green plants, which produce food through photosynthesis, and certain bacteria that are capable of converting inorganic

substances into food through chemosynthesis. *Compare* **consumer.**

product A number or quantity obtained by multiplication. For example, the product of 3 and 7 is 21.

progesterone A steroid hormone that prepares the uterus for pregnancy, maintains pregnancy, and promotes development of the mammary glands. The main sources of progesterone are the ovary and the placenta.

program *noun* 1. The set of steps, including the collection and processing of data and the presentation of results, that is necessary for a computer to solve a problem. 2. The set of instructions that a computer must execute in carrying out these steps. —*verb* To define the set of instructions used by a computer.

prokaryote Any of a wide variety of one-celled organisms that lack a distinct cell nucleus or other structures bound by a membrane and that have

Did You Know?
program
When you program a video cassette recorder, you are making a set of instructions that tell the video what to do. Similarly, when programmers write computer *programs,* they are creating a set of instructions that make a computer perform particular tasks or functions. Modern programs are typically created on a computer in a special program called an *application development environment.* This program includes a blank screen and various methods for adding words, pictures and buttons to the screen. Using an artificial language consisting of a set of words and grammatical rules for stringing them together, the programmer writes instructions describing what the program will do when the user enters a command or clicks on a button, for example. The application development environment stores the programmer's instructions and translates them into instructions that the computer can understand and perform.

DNA that is not organized into chromosomes. Prokaryotes reproduce asexually, are the most primitive and ancient of known forms of life, and include bacteria and blue-green algae. Prokaryotes are grouped as a separate kingdom in taxonomy. Also called *moneran. Compare* **eukaryote.** *See table at* **Taxonomy.**

proline A nonessential amino acid. *See more at* **amino acid.**

promethium A radioactive metallic element of the lanthanide series. Promethium does not occur in nature, but it can be found as a product of the fission of uranium. It has 17 isotopes, one of which can be used to make miniature batteries that work at extreme temperatures for up to five years. *Symbol* **Pm.** *Atomic number* 61. *See* **Periodic Table,** pages 260–261.

prominence A tongue-like cloud of flaming gas that erupts from the surface of the sun.

proof An argument used to show the truth of a mathematical assertion. The method of proving an assertion was first devised by the Greek mathematician Euclid in about 300 BC. A proof involves identifying the initial assumptions, then using the rules of logic to reason from these in order to produce the proof. This process uses results that have already been shown to be true (theorems), and statements that are self-evident (axioms).

propane A colourless, gaseous hydrocarbon, C_3H_8, found in petroleum and natural gas. It is widely used as a fuel.

propanoic acid A colourless, corrosive liquid, $C_3H_4O_2$, that readily forms polymers. It is used to make plastics, paints, synthetic rubbers and textiles. Old name *acrylic acid.*

propanone A colourless, extremely flammable liquid, C_3H_6O, that is widely used as a solvent, for example in nail-polish remover. A ketone. Old name *acetone.*

propeller A device consisting of a series of twisted blades mounted around a shaft and spun to force air or water in a specific direction and thereby move an aircraft or boat.

proper fraction A fraction in which the numerator is less than the denominator, such as $\frac{1}{2}$. Also called *vulgar fraction. Compare* **improper fraction.**

prophase The first stage of cell division. Before prophase begins, the chromosomes duplicate to form two long, thin strands called chromatids. During prophase itself, the chromatids condense and thicken and the membrane surrounding the nucleus disappears. In mitosis, prophase is followed by metaphase. *See more at* **meiosis, mitosis.**

prostaglandin Any of a group of substances that are derived from fatty acids and have a wide range of effects in the body. Prostaglandins influence the contraction of the muscles that line many internal organs and can lower or raise blood pressure.

prostate gland A gland in male mammals at the base of the bladder that opens into the urethra. It secretes a fluid that is a major component of semen.

protactinium A rare, extremely toxic, radioactive metallic element of the actinide series that occurs in uranium ores. Its most common isotope has a half-life of 32,500 years. *Symbol* **Pa.** *Atomic number* 91. *See* **Periodic Table,** pages 260–261.

protease Any of various enzymes that bring about the breakdown of proteins into peptides or amino acids by hydrolysis. Pepsin is an example of a protease.

protein One of a large class of complex organic chemical compounds that are essential for life. Proteins play a central role in biological processes and form the basis of living tissues. They consist of long, looping or folding chains of smaller compounds called amino acids. Enzymes, antibodies and haemoglobin are examples of proteins.

Proterozoic The later of the two divisions of the Precambrian Eon, from about 2.5 billion to 540 million years ago. The Proterozoic was characterized by the build-up of oxygen in the atmosphere and the appearance of the first multicellular eukaryotes. *See chart at* **geological time,** pages 148–149.

protist Any of a large variety of usually one-celled organisms, including the protozoans, most algae, and the slime moulds. Protists are eukaryotes (that is, they have cell nuclei) and live in water or in watery tissues of organisms. They are grouped as a separate kingdom in taxonomy. Also called *protoctist. See table at* **taxonomy.**

protium The most abundant isotope of hydrogen, having an atomic mass of 1. Its nucleus consists of a single proton. *See more at* **hydrogen.**

protoctist *See* **protist.**

proton A stable subatomic particle that has a positive electric charge and is part of the nucleus of an atom. Its charge is opposite to that of an electron but is equal in magnitude. A proton's mass is 1836 times that of an electron. *See more at* **atom.**

protoplasm A substance resembling jelly that forms the living matter in all plant and animal cells. Protoplasm is made up of proteins, fats and other substances suspended in water. It includes the nucleus and cytoplasm.

protozoan Any of a large group of one-celled organisms that have a cell nucleus and live in water or as parasites. Many protozoans move about by means of appendages known as cilia or flagella. Protozoans include the amoebas and paramecia and are classified as protists.

Proxima Centauri *See under* **Alpha Centauri.**

pseudopod *also* **pseudopodium** (*plural* **pseudopods** *or* **pseudopodia**) A temporary foot-like extension of the protoplasm of a one-celled organism, such as an amoeba, used for moving about and for surrounding and taking in food.

psychiatry The branch of medicine that deals with the study and treatment of mental illness.

psychology The scientific study of mental processes and behaviour.

psychosis (*plural* **psychoses**) A mental illness so severe that a person loses the ability to think logically, to communicate and to relate to others. A person with a psychosis loses contact with reality and often shows dramatic changes in behaviour. Psychoses can be caused by diseases affecting the brain. —*adjective* **psychotic.**

Pt The symbol for **platinum.**

pteranodon Any of several large, extinct, flying reptiles of the Cretaceous Period, having a long pointed head, no teeth and a wingspan of 6 metres or more.

pterodactyl Any of various small, extinct, flying reptiles of the late Jurassic and Cretaceous Periods. The pterodactyls were about the size of small to medium-sized birds.

pterosaur Any of various extinct, flying reptiles of the Jurassic and Cretaceous Periods with wings consisting of a flap of skin supported by an elongated fourth digit on each forelimb. Pterosaurs had wingspans ranging from less than about 30 centimetres to close to 15 metres.

Ptolemaic system The astronomical system of Ptolemy, in which the Earth is at the centre of the universe and all celestial bodies revolve around it. The sun, moon and planets revolve at different levels in circular orbits, and the stars lie in fixed locations on a sphere that revolves beyond these orbits.

Ptolemy Second century AD. Greek astronomer and mathematician who based his astronomy on the belief that all heavenly bodies revolve around the Earth. *See more at* **Copernicus.**

ptyalin An enzyme found in saliva that breaks down starches into sugars. Also known as *salivary amylase.*

Pu The symbol for **plutonium.**

puberty The stage in the development of humans and other primates marked by maturing of the reproductive organs and by the start of menstruation in females and sperm production in males. During puberty, the production of sex

■ **pterodactyl**
the skeleton of a pterodactyl

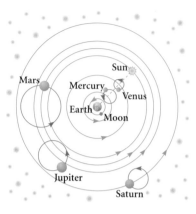

■ Ptolemaic system

Ptolemy believed that the Earth was at the centre of the universe and that the sun and planets orbited Earth (with the planets also moving in smaller circles called epicycles). In this system, the centres of Mercury's and Venus's epicycles always lie on the line shown in the diagram between Earth and the sun.

hormones causes other physical changes, including breast development in females and deepening of the voice in males.

pubis The forwardmost of the three bones that fuse together to form each of the hipbones. *See more at* **skeleton.** *—adjective* **pubic.**

pulley A simple machine consisting of a wheel over which a pulled rope or chain runs to change the direction of the pull used for lifting a load. Combinations of two or more pulleys working together reduce the force needed to lift a load. *See also* **block and tackle.**

pulmonary Relating to the lungs: *a pulmonary infection.*

pulmonary artery An artery that carries blood with low levels of oxygen from the right ventricle of the heart to the lungs.

pulmonary vein A vein that carries blood with high levels of oxygen from the lungs to the left atrium of the heart.

pulsar A spinning neutron star that emits radiation, usually radio waves, in very short and very regular pulses. Because a pulsar's magnetic poles do not align with the poles of its axis, its beams of radiation sweep around like the beacon of a lighthouse.

pulse The rhythmical expansion and contraction of the arteries as blood is pumped through them by the beating of the heart.

pumice A usually light-coloured, porous, lightweight rock of volcanic origin. The pores form when water vapour and gases escape from the lava during its quick solidification into rock.

pump A machine for raising or transferring fluids. Most pumps function either by compression or suction.

punctuated equilibrium The theory that new

> ## Did You Know?
>
> ### pulsar
>
> When a very large star goes off like a giant bomb, in a celestial explosion known as a supernova, the core of the star collapses into either a neutron star or a black hole. In 1054, one of these explosions could be seen in the sky during both day and night for 23 days. Chinese astronomers took note of this "guest star", and rock paintings and pottery found in Arizona and New Mexico suggest that Native Americans also recorded this phenomenon. In the 18th century, astronomers discovered the remains of this exploded star in a bright cloud of gas called the Crab Nebula, in the constellation Taurus. In the late 1960s, 900 years after the supernova, astronomers found a source of rapidly pulsing radio waves, with 30 flashes per second, near the centre of this nebula. The source of this pulsating radiation is an object that was named a *pulsar.* We now know that a pulsar is a rapidly rotating neutron star whose radiation is emitted like a fast-spinning flashing light. Over 1000 pulsars have now been detected, which suggests that there are likely to be around 200,000 in the whole of our galaxy.

■ pyrite

species evolve suddenly over relatively short periods of time, followed by longer periods in which little genetic change occurs. Punctuated equilibrium is a revision of Darwin's theory that evolution takes place at a slow, constant rate over millions of years. *Compare* **gradualism**. *See panel at* **evolution**.

pupa (*plural* **pupae**) An insect in the non-feeding stage of development between the larva and adult, during which it typically undergoes a complete transformation within a protective cocoon or hardened case. Only certain kinds of insects, such as moths, butterflies, ants and beetles, develop as larvae and pupae. *Compare* **imago, larva, nymph**. —*adjective* **pupal**.

pupil The opening in the centre of the iris of the eye through which light enters and reaches the retina.

purine Any of a group of organic compounds containing two rings of alternating carbon and nitrogen atoms. Purines include caffeine and uric acid, as well as the two bases adenine and guanine, which are components of DNA and RNA.

pus A thick, yellowish-white liquid that forms in infected body tissues. It consists mainly of dead white blood cells.

P wave *See* **primary wave**. *See panel at* **earthquake**.

pyramid A solid shape with a plane base and

---

python

sloping triangular sides meeting in a common vertex.

pyridoxine *See under* **vitamin B complex**.

pyrimidine Any of a group of organic compounds having a single ring with alternating carbon and nitrogen atoms. Pyrimidines include the bases cytosine, thymine and uracil, which are components of nucleic acids.

pyrite A silver to yellow, metallic mineral consisting of iron and sulphur. Pyrite often crystallizes in cubes or octahedrons but also occurs as shapeless masses of grains. It is used as a source of iron and in making sulphur dioxide. Because of its shiny look and often yellow colour, it is sometimes mistaken for gold and for this reason is also called *fool's gold*.

pyroxene Any of a series of rock-forming minerals consisting of mixtures of calcium, sodium, magnesium or iron silicates. Pyroxenes vary in colour from white to dark green or black and are characterized by a rectangular-shaped cross section. They occur in igneous and metamorphic rocks.

pyruvic acid A colourless organic liquid formed by the breakdown of carbohydrates and sugars during cell metabolism. It is the final product of the process known as glycolysis and has the formula $C_3H_4O_3$. Its systematic name is *2-oxopropanoic acid.*

Pythagoras Sixth century BC. Greek philosopher who theorized that numbers constitute the essence of all natural things. He developed Pythagoras' theorem and was one of the first to apply mathematical order to observations of the stars.

Pythagoras' theorem A theorem stating that the square of the length of the hypotenuse (the longest side) of a right-angled triangle is equal to the sum of the squares of the lengths of the other sides. It is mathematically stated as $c^2 = a^2 + b^2$, where c is the length of the hypotenuse and a and b the lengths of the other two sides.

python Any of various very large and colourful snakes of Africa, Asia and Australia. Pythons are not poisonous, but coil around and suffocate their prey, which can be as large as wild deer.

quadrant 1. An arc equal to one quarter of the circumference of a circle; an arc of 90°. **2.** Any of the four regions into which a plane is divided by the axes of a Cartesian coordinate system. The quadrants are numbered anticlockwise from one to four, beginning with the quadrant in which both the x- and y-coordinates are positive (usually the upper right quadrant). **3.** An instrument with an arc of 90°, used to measure the angle between a celestial object and the horizon.

quadratic Relating to a mathematical expression containing a term of the second degree, such as $x^2 + 2$. ❖ A **quadratic equation** is an equation involving the square, but no higher power, of an unknown quantity or variable. Its general form is $ax^2 + bx + c = 0$, where a, b and c are constants. ❖ The **quadratic formula** is

$$x = \frac{-b \pm \sqrt{b^2 - 4ac}}{2a}$$

The formula is important in algebra, where it is used to calculate the roots of quadratic equations.

quadriceps The large, four-part muscle at the front of the thigh that acts to extend the leg.

quadrilateral A polygon that has four sides, such as a rectangle or rhombus.

quadriplegia Paralysis of the body from the neck down, caused by injury to the spinal cord. *Compare* **paraplegia.**

quadrumanous Having four feet with opposable first digits and being able to use all of them as hands, as is characteristic of primates other than humans.

quadruped An animal having four feet, such as most reptiles and mammals.

qualitative analysis A test performed on a substance or mixture to identify its chemical components.

quantitative analysis A test performed on a substance or mixture to find out the amounts and proportions of its chemical components.

quantity *Mathematics.* Something, such as a number or symbol that represents a number, on which a mathematical operation is performed.

quantum (*plural* **quanta**) *Physics.* A discrete amount, or packet, of energy, charge, angular momentum or other physical property that is the smallest amount capable of existing on its own.

quantum mechanics *See* **quantum theory.**

quantum physics The branch of physics that uses quantum theory to describe and predict the properties of a physical system.

quantum theory A theory in physics based on the principle that matter and energy behave both as particles and as waves. According to this theory, matter and energy are composed of tiny units of electromagnetic energy called quanta. Quantum theory is used to explain such phenomena as the photoelectric effect and the uncertainty principle. ❖ Another term for quantum theory is **quantum mechanics,** which also refers specifically to the use of quantum theory in studying the structure and behaviour of atoms and molecules.

quark Any of a group of elementary particles that are the fundamental units that combine in

■ **quartz**

Did You Know?

quasar

"The universe is not only stranger than we imagine", Albert Einstein said, "It is stranger than we *can* imagine". In the 1960s, astronomers found some very strange objects that we now call quasars in the far reaches of the universe. A quasar is like a far-off floodlight. It appears to be an extremely distant star putting out huge amounts of energy. In fact, just one of these objects can be a trillion times brighter than the sun. All of the radiation that a quasar gives off comes from a small area at its centre, and many astronomers believe that the source of the energy is an enormous black hole rotating at the centre of a young galaxy. Quasars are among the most distant celestial objects known. Some are more than ten billion light years away, meaning their radiation has taken ten billion years to reach us. So when we look at quasars, we're observing these objects as they were billions of years ago, and we're able to see part of the early history of the universe.

threes to make up protons and neutrons. *See panel at* **subatomic particle.**

quart A unit of volume or capacity used in liquid measure, equal to 1.14 litres ($\frac{1}{4}$ gallon). *See table at* **measurement.**

quartz A hard, transparent mineral composed of silicon dioxide. Quartz is the most common of all minerals. It occurs as a component of rocks such as sandstone and granite, and separately in a variety of forms such as rock crystal, flint and agate. Some crystalline forms, such as amethyst, are valued as gemstones. Quartz is the mineral used to represent a hardness of 7 on the Mohs scale.

quartzite A metamorphic rock consisting entirely of quartz. Quartzite forms when quartz crystals in sandstone or chert grow into larger crystals during metamorphism.

quasar Short for *quasi-stellar radio source.* An extremely distant, compact and star-like celestial object. The power output of a quasar is several thousand times that of the Milky Way galaxy.

Quaternary The second and last period of the Cainozoic Era, from about 1.6 million years ago to the present, characterized by the appearance of humans. *See chart at* **geological time,** pages 148–149.

queen The fertile, fully developed female in a colony of social bees, ants or termites. The queen's sole function is to lay eggs.

quicksand A deep bed of loose sand mixed with water, forming a soft, shifting mass that yields easily to pressure and tends to swallow objects resting on its surface.

quill The hollow shaft of a feather, the bottom of which attaches to the bird's skin.

quinine A bitter-tasting, colourless drug derived from the bark of the cinchona tree, used to treat malaria. *See panel at* **aspirin.**

quotient The number that results when one number is divided by another. If 6 is divided by 3, the quotient can be represented as 2, or as 6 ÷ 3, or as the fraction $\frac{6}{3}$.

r 1. *Mathematics.* Abbreviation of **radius. 2.** or **R** *Electricity.* Abbreviation of **resistance.**

Ra The symbol for **radium.**

rabies A usually fatal viral disease of warm-blooded animals that causes inflammation of the brain and spinal cord. It is transmitted by the bite of an infected animal and can be prevented in humans by a vaccine. *See panel at* **hydrophobia.**

raceme A flower cluster in which each flower grows on its own stalk from a common stem. The lily of the valley and horse chestnut have racemes.

radar 1. A method of detecting distant objects and determining their position, speed or other characteristics by causing radio waves to be reflected from them and analysing the reflected waves. **2.** The equipment used in doing this.

radar gun A usually hand-held device that measures the velocity of a moving object by sending out a continuous radio wave and measuring the frequency of reflected waves.

radial symmetry The arrangement of similar forms or features around a central point. The bodies of echinoderms, such as starfish and sea urchins, are radially symmetrical. *Compare* **bilateral symmetry.**

radian A unit of angular measure equal to a little more than 57°. This is the measure of an angle whose vertex is the centre of a circle and whose two rays intersect the circle so as to form an arc

with the same length as the circle's radius. From this it follows that 2π radians = 360°.

radiant 1. Sending forth light, heat or other radiation: *a radiant star.* **2.** Consisting of or transmitted as radiation.

radiant energy Energy in the form of waves, especially electromagnetic waves. Radio waves, X-rays and visible light are all forms of radiant energy.

radiation 1a. Energy in the form of electromagnetic waves or streams of particles, such as photons or electrons. Radiation is given off by nuclear reactions (as in fission) and by radioactive decay. **b.** The emission or movement of such energy through space or a medium, such as air. *See panels at* **conduction, electro-magnetic radiation. 2.** The use of such energy, especially X-rays, in medical diagnosis and treat-ment.

radiative zone The layer of a star, especially the sun, that lies just outside the core, where energy is transferred by means of radiation. In this layer, photons travel around in random movements until they enter the convection zone.

radical 1. *Mathematics.* A root, especially as indicated by a radical sign, such as $\sqrt{2}$. **2.** A group of atoms that behaves as a unit in chemical reactions and is often not stable except as part of a molecule. The hydroxyl, ethyl and phenyl radicals are examples. Radicals are unchanged by chemical reactions.

radio *noun* The equipment used to generate, alter, transmit and receive radio waves so that they carry information. —*adjective.* Involving the emission of radio waves: *radio frequency.*

■ **radial symmetry**
red horned starfish

radioactive decay The spontaneous breakdown of an unstable nucleus into a lighter nucleus. Radioactive decay causes the release of radiation in the form of alpha particles, beta particles or gamma rays. The end result of radioactive decay is the creation of a more stable atomic nucleus.

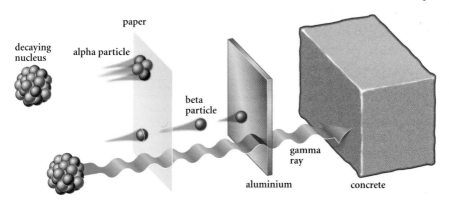

■ radiation

As the nucleus of a radioactive element decays, it releases alpha particles, beta particles or gamma rays. Alpha rays (a stream of alpha particles) are the weakest form of radiation and can be stopped by paper. Beta rays (a stream of beta particles) are able to pass through paper but not through aluminium. Gamma rays (a form of electromagnetic radiation) are the strongest. They are able to pass through paper and aluminium, but not through a block of lead or concrete.

---

radioactivity The emission of radiation by unstable atomic nuclei undergoing radioactive decay.

radio astronomy The branch of astronomy dealing with the detection of objects in space by means of the radio waves emitted by these objects.

radiocarbon A radioactive isotope of carbon, especially carbon-14.

radiocarbon dating A technique for measuring the age of organic remains based on the rate of decay of carbon-14. The carbon-14 present in an organism at the time of its death decays at a steady rate, and so the age of the remains can be calculated from the amount of carbon-14 that is left. *See panel on page 284.*

radio frequency A frequency at which radio waves can be transmitted, ranging from extremely

Did You Know?

radioactivity

Within the nuclei of stable atoms, such as those of lead, the force binding the protons and neutrons to each other individually is great enough to hold the nuclei together as a whole. However, the nuclei of other atoms are not stable and can rearrange themselves by emitting particles and energy in a process known as *radioactivity*. When enough particles and energy have been given off to create a new, stable nucleus (often the nucleus of an entirely different element), the radioactivity ceases. For example, uranium-238, a very unstable element, goes through 18 different stages of decay before finally turning into a stable isotope of lead, lead-206. (Some of the intermediate stages include the heavier elements thorium, radium, radon and polonium.) All known elements with an atomic number greater than 83 (bismuth) are radioactive, and many isotopes of elements with lower atomic numbers are radioactive too.

Did You Know?

radiocarbon dating

The cells of all living things contain carbon atoms that they take in from their environment. Back in the 1940s, the American chemist Willard Libby used this fact to determine the ages of organisms long dead. Most carbon atoms have six protons and six neutrons in their nuclei and are called carbon-12. Carbon-12 is very stable. However, a tiny percentage of carbon is made of carbon-14, or *radiocarbon*, which has six protons and eight neutrons and is not stable: half of any sample of it decays into other atoms after 5700 years. Carbon-14 is continually being created in the Earth's atmosphere by the interaction of nitrogen and gamma rays from outer space. Since atmospheric carbon-14 arises at about the same rate that the atom decays, the Earth's levels of carbon-14 have remained constant. In living organisms, which are always taking in carbon, the levels of carbon-14 also stay constant. But in a dead organism, no new carbon is coming in, and its carbon-14 gradually begins to decay. So by measuring carbon-14 levels in an organism that died long ago, researchers can calculate the year of its death. The procedure of radiocarbon dating can be used for remains that are up to 50,000 years old.

low frequency (no lower than 3000 hertz) to extremely high frequency (between 30 and 300 gigahertz).

radioisotope A radioactive isotope of a chemical element.

radiology The branch of medicine that deals with the use of X-rays and other forms of radiation in diagnosis and treatment.

radiometer A device used to detect and measure radiation. Radiometers consist of a glass bulb containing a partial vacuum in which four diamond-shaped paddles are mounted on a central axis. Each paddle is black on one side and silvery on the other. When radiation, such as sunlight, strikes them, the black side absorbs radiation and the silvery side reflects it, resulting in a temperature difference between the two sides that causes the paddles to spin. The stronger the radiation, the faster the paddles spin.

radiometric dating A method for determining the age of an object based on the concentration of a particular radioactive isotope contained within it. The amount of the isotope in the object is compared to the amount of the isotope's decay products. The object's approximate age can then be worked out using the known rate of decay of the isotope. Radiocarbon dating is one kind of radiometric dating, used for determining the age of organic remains that are less than 50,000 years old. For inorganic matter and for older materials, isotopes of other elements, such as potassium, uranium and strontium, are used.

radiosonde An instrument that is carried into the atmosphere, usually by balloon, to gather and transmit information about the weather.

radio wave An electromagnetic wave having a low frequency and long wavelength. Radio waves are used for the transmission of both radio and television broadcasts. They also include the microwaves used for cooking. Some celestial objects, such as pulsars, also emit radio waves. *See more at* **electromagnetic spectrum.**

radium A rare, bright-white, highly radioactive element that is an alkaline-earth metal and gives off its own light. It occurs naturally in very small amounts in ores and minerals containing uranium. Radium is used as a source of radon gas for the treatment of disease and as a neutron source for scientific research. The most common of its several isotopes has a half-life of 1622 years. It was discovered by Marie and Pierre Curie. *Symbol* **Ra.** *Atomic number* 88. *See* **Periodic Table,** pages 260–261.

radius (*plural* **radii**) **1.** A line segment that joins the centre of a circle or sphere with any point on the circumference of the circle or the surface of the sphere. It is half the length of the diameter. **2.** The shorter and thicker of the two bones of the forearm or the lower portion of the foreleg. *See more at* **skeleton.**

radon A colourless, odourless, radioactive element that is a noble gas. It is produced by the radioactive decay of radium and occurs in minute amounts in soil, rocks and the air near the ground. Radon is used as a source of radiation for the treatment of cancer and other diseases. Its most stable isotope has a half-life of about four days. *Symbol* **Rn**. *Atomic number* 86. *See* **Periodic Table,** pages 260–261.

rain Water that condenses from vapour in the atmosphere and falls to earth as separate drops from clouds.

rainbow An arc-shaped spectrum of colour seen in the sky opposite the sun, especially after rain, caused by the refraction and reflection of sunlight by droplets of water suspended in the air.

rainforest A dense evergreen forest with an annual rainfall of at least 406.4 centimetres.

RAM Short for *random access memory.* The main memory of a computer, in which data can be accessed by the central processing unit in any order without having to go through other data first. The random access of data greatly increases processing speed and efficiency.

Ramsay, Sir William 1852–1916. British chemist who discovered the inert gases argon, helium, neon, xenon and krypton.

Did You Know?

rainforest

Rainforests are, not surprisingly, forests where it rains a lot – between 406.4 and 1016 centimetres a year. Most of the world's rainforests lie near the equator and have tropical climates with temperatures that remain around 26.6°C all year long. However, there are also cooler rainforests, such as the one in the Pacific Northwest region of the United States and Canada. The largest rainforest in the world is the one located in the Amazon River basin in South America. Rainforests are extremely important because they help regulate the world's climate and because they host such extraordinary diversity of life. Scientists believe that as many as half of the Earth's different species of plants and animals are found only in the rainforests, which take up a mere 7 per cent of the world's landmass. Among other benefits, this biodiversity supports important biological research. For example, many of the natural chemicals used in medicines are found in plants that grow only in rainforests. Unfortunately, the demand for agriculture is causing many people to turn rainforests into farms and grazing land, and by some estimates more than half of the Earth's original rainforests have already been burned or cut down.

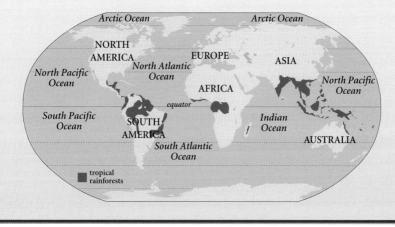

random access memory *See* **RAM.**

range 1. The set of all values that a given function may have. *Compare* **domain. 2.** The difference between the smallest and largest values in a set of data. If the lowest test score of a group of students is 54 and the highest is 94, the range is 40.

rapid eye movement *See* **REM.**

raptor 1. A bird of prey, such as a hawk, eagle or owl. **2.** Any of various mostly small, slender, meat-eating dinosaurs of the Cretaceous Period. Raptors had hind legs that were adapted for leaping and large, curved claws used for grasping and tearing at prey. Raptors were probably related to birds, and some even had feathers.

rare-earth element *See* **lanthanide.**

ratio A relationship between two quantities, normally expressed as the quotient of one divided by the other. For example, if a box contains six red marbles and four blue marbles, the ratio of red marbles to blue marbles is 6 to 4, also written 6:4. A ratio can also be expressed as a decimal or percentage.

rational number A number that can be expressed as an integer or a quotient of integers. For example, 2, –5 and $\frac{1}{2}$ are rational numbers. *Compare* **irrational number.**

ray 1. *Physics.* A thin line or narrow beam of light or other radiation. **2.** *Mathematics.* A geometric figure consisting of the part of a line that is on one side of a point on the line. **3.** *Botany.* A narrow flower resembling a petal, such as one of those surrounding the disc-shaped flower cluster of a daisy or sunflower.

Rb The symbol for **rubidium.**

Re The symbol for **rhenium.**

reactant A substance participating in a chemical reaction, especially one present at the start of the reaction.

reaction 1. A rearrangement of the atoms or molecules of two or more substances that come into contact with each other, resulting in the formation of one or more new substances. Chemical reactions are caused by electrons of one substance interacting with those of another. The reaction of an acid with a base, for example, results in the creation of a salt and water. Some, but not all, reactions can be reversed. **2.** A change to the structure of an atomic nucleus; a nuclear reaction. **3.** An action that results directly from or counteracts another action, especially the change in a body's motion as a result of a force applied to it. Some reactions counteract forces and are not readily apparent. When an object rests on a surface, for example a table, the downward force it applies to the surface is counteracted by an equal but upward force, or reaction, applied by the surface. *See more at* **Newton's laws of motion.**

read-only memory *See* **ROM.**

reagent Any substance involved in a chemical reaction, especially one used to detect, measure or produce another substance. *Compare* **agent.**

real number A number that is rational or irrational and not imaginary. The numbers 2, –12.5, $\frac{3}{7}$ and pi are all real numbers.

receiver A device, as in a radio or telephone, that converts incoming radio or microwave signals to a form, such as sound or light, that can be perceived by humans.

Recent *See* **Holocene.**

receptacle The enlarged upper end of a flower stalk that bears the flower or group of flowers. *See more at* **flower.**

receptor 1. A nerve ending specialized to sense or receive stimuli. Skin receptors respond to stimuli such as touch and pressure and signal to the brain by activating portions of the nervous system. Receptors in the nose detect odours. **2.** A cell structure or site that is capable of combining with a hormone, antigen or other chemical substance.

recessive Relating to the form of a gene that is not expressed as a trait in an individual unless two such genes are inherited, one from each parent. In an organism having two different genes for a trait, the recessive form is suppressed by its counterpart, or dominant, form located on the other of a pair of chromosomes. *See more at* **inheritance.** *Compare* **dominant.**

reciprocal Either of a pair of numbers whose product is 1. For example, the number 3 is the reciprocal of $\frac{1}{3}$.

recombinant DNA A form of DNA produced by combining genetic material from two different

length (*l*)

width
(*w*)

■ **rectangle**

To calculate the area of a rectangle, multiply the length by the width. A rectangle with a length of 10 metres and a width of 5 metres has an area of 50 square metres.

sources by means of genetic engineering. Recombinant DNA can be used to change the genetic make-up of a cell, as in adding a gene to make a bacterial cell produce insulin.

rectangle A four-sided plane figure with four right angles. A rectangle whose sides are equal is a square.

rectilinear Relating to, consisting of or moving in a straight line or lines: *a rectilinear path.*

rectum The lower end of the digestive tract, extending from the colon to the anus.

recurring decimal A decimal fraction in which a digit or group of digits would recur infinitely. For example, $\frac{1}{3}$ gives the recurring decimal 0.333333..., written as $0.\dot{3}$.

recycle To collect and usually reprocess discarded materials for reuse, often in another form. For example, newspaper and other paper waste can be reprocessed to make cardboard or insulation, and plastics can be melted down and moulded into new products. Recycling helps reduce pollution and conserve natural resources.

red blood cell Any of the disc-shaped cells that circulate in the blood of vertebrate animals, contain haemoglobin and give blood its red colour. The haemoglobin binds to oxygen, which is then transported by the cells to all of the tissues of the body. The red blood cells of mammals have no nucleus. Red blood cells are formed in the bone marrow. Also called *erythrocyte. See more at* **cell.**

red dwarf A star that is cool, small and very faint. Red dwarfs burn very slowly and live for about 100 billion years. Although they are difficult to see, they are probably the most abundant type of star. Proxima Centauri is a red dwarf star.

Did You Know?

red blood cells

Blood contains many cell types, but the distinctive red colour comes from the aptly named *red blood cells* (RBCs). RBCs have their rich red colour because of a vitally important iron-containing protein called haemoglobin. The protein picks up oxygen molecules as the blood exchanges gases in the lungs. The RBCs then carry oxygen to the far reaches of the body, where it is released for use by other cells, such as those of the brain and muscles. Just as importantly, after the RBC drops off its load of oxygen, its haemoglobin picks up carbon dioxide, the waste product of those brain and muscle cells, and brings it back to the lungs to be breathed out. All animals have some oxygen distribution system, but only vertebrate animals use RBCs. In some invertebrate animals, such as the earthworm, oxygen is transported using haemoglobin that is freely dissolved in the blood. Other invertebrates don't use haemoglobin at all. The horseshoe crab, for instance, uses copper instead of iron, making its blood blue instead of red.

■ **red blood cell**

red giant A star of great size and brightness that has a relatively low surface temperature, making it appear red. It is predicted that the sun will become a red giant in several billion years' time. *See more at* **star**. *See panel at* **dwarf star**.

red shift An increase in the wavelength of radiation emitted by a receding celestial body as a result of the Doppler effect. Objects appear reddish because the longer wavelengths of light are at the red end of the visible spectrum. *Compare* **blue shift**. *See panel at* **Doppler effect**.

red tide A population explosion of certain species of dinoflagellates, a kind of protozoan found in plankton. The dinoflagellates colour the water red or reddish-brown and secrete a toxin that kills fish. Red tide usually occurs in warm coastal waters.

reduction 1. *Mathematics.* The changing of a fraction into a simpler form, especially by dividing the numerator and denominator by a common factor. For example, the fraction $\frac{8}{12}$ can be reduced to $\frac{4}{6}$, which can be further reduced to $\frac{2}{3}$, in each case by dividing both the numerator and denominator by 2. **2.** *Chemistry.* A chemical reaction in which an atom or ion gains electrons, thus undergoing a decrease in oxidation number. If an iron atom having an oxidation number of +3 gains an electron, the oxidation number decreases to +2. *Compare* **oxidation**.

reduction-oxidation *or* **redox** A chemical reaction in which an atom or ion loses electrons and another atom or ion gains electrons, so that reduction and oxidation are taking place at the same time.

redwood A very tall, cone-bearing evergreen tree native to the coastal areas of northwest California and southern Oregon. Redwoods can grow to a height of over 100 metres.

reef An irregular mass of rock or coral that rises up to or near the surface of a body of water. *See more at* **coral reef**.

refinery An industrial plant for purifying a substance, such as petroleum or sugar, or converting it into a form that is more useful. These processes are carried out by mechanical and chemical means.

reflecting telescope A telescope in which light from an object is gathered and focused by a concave mirror. *See more at* **telescope**. *See panel at* **mirror**.

reflection 1. The turning back of a wave, such as a light or sound wave, when it encounters a boundary. Reflected waves return immediately to their original medium instead of entering the medium they encounter. ❖ According to the **law of reflection**, the angle of reflection of a reflected wave is equal to its angle of incidence. *See more at* **wave**. *Compare* **refraction**. **2.** Something, such as sound, light or heat, that is reflected. **3.** *Mathematics.* A transformation that produces a mirror image on the other side of a line of symmetry.

reflex An automatic, involuntary response to a stimulus that misses out the conscious areas of the central nervous system. Some reflexes are used to control continuous actions that are vital for survival, such as breathing and gut activity. This frees up the brain for other activities, while ensuring that these vital functions are not forgotten. Other types of reflex actions help organisms avoid or escape from danger, such as withdrawing the hand quickly from something hot or sharp. Reflexes enable these actions to take place much more rapidly than when conscious thought is involved, and so are more effective at preventing harm.

reflex angle An angle measuring more than 180° and less than 360°.

refracting telescope A telescope in which light from an object is gathered and focused by lenses. *See more at* **telescope**.

refraction 1. The bending or turning of a wave, such as a light or sound wave, when it passes from one medium to another medium of different density. *See more at* **wave**. *Compare* **reflection**. **2.** The apparent change in position of a celestial body caused by the bending of light as it enters the Earth's atmosphere.

refrigerant A substance, such as ice or ammonia, used to cool something by absorbing heat from it. Refrigerants are usually substances that evaporate quickly. In the process of evaporation they draw heat from surrounding substances.

regeneration Regrowth of lost or destroyed

parts or organs. Certain lizards, for example, can regenerate their tails if they lose them to a predator, and a number of invertebrate animals, such as starfish, can be cut into several pieces that will each regenerate into a whole new organism. Regeneration is common in plants, where cuttings can grow into a new plant.

regolith The layer of soil and loose rock resting on bedrock, constituting the surface of most land.

regular Having all sides or faces equal. A square is a regular polygon, and a cube is a regular polyhedron.

Regulus The brightest star in the constellation Leo. Regulus is a binary star, which has a much fainter companion.

regurgitation 1. The return of undigested food from the stomach to the mouth. 2. The food so returned.

relative atomic mass The mass of an atom of a particular element with reference to the mass of an atom of carbon-12 (*see* **atomic mass unit**). It is calculated as the ratio of the mass of a carbon-

■ **refraction**
Light waves change direction as they pass from one substance to another. This pencil appears to be bent as light reflected from the lower part of it travels through water, while light reflected from the upper part does not.

Usage

refraction/reflection

The words *refraction* and *reflection* describe two different ways that a light wave, sound wave or other wave can change direction when it encounters a boundary between two media. The media can be two different substances, such as glass and air, or they can be regions of a single substance that are in different states, such as regions of air that are at different temperatures. Reflection occurs when a wave hits the boundary and returns immediately to its original medium. Refraction occurs when a wave passes from one medium to another and is bent; that is, the wave deviates from the straight-line path it would have otherwise followed. For example, light passing through a prism is bent when it enters the prism and again when it leaves the prism. The light is therefore *refracted*. Light striking a mirror bounces off the silver backing without entering it. The light is therefore *reflected*. The boundary between the media does not have to be abrupt for reflection or refraction to occur. On a hot day, the air over the surface of an asphalt road is warmer than the air above it. Because light travels at different speeds in these two regions, we see an image that shimmers because its light waves are refracted.

12 atom to the average mass of all the isotopes of an element, in the proportions in which they are usually found. For example, the element chlorine has isotopes with relative atomic masses of about 35 and 37. Chlorine-35 atoms are about 3 times more common than chlorine-37 atoms, so the relative atomic mass of chlorine is about 35.5.

relative formula mass The sum of the relative atomic masses of each of the atoms in a compound. For example, the compound sodium chloride has the formula NaCl. The relative atomic mass of sodium is 23, while that of chlorine is 35.5, so the relative formula mass of sodium chloride is 23 + 35.5, which equals 58.5.

In the same way, water (H_2O) has a relative formula mass of 18. This is the sum of the relative atomic masses of two hydrogen atoms (1 + 1 = 2) and one oxygen atom (16).

relative humidity The ratio of the actual amount of water vapour present in the air at a given temperature to the maximum amount that the air could hold at that temperature. Relative humidity is expressed as a percentage. *Compare* **absolute humidity.**

relativity The two-part theory of physical laws developed by Albert Einstein. The first part, called the **theory of special relativity,** states that the laws of physics apply equally to any body or system of bodies having unchanging motion, and that the speed of light is always constant. The second part, the **theory of general relativity,** extends the first part to bodies in accelerated motion, such as bodies in gravitational fields. Some of the many consequences of the theory are that measurements of speed and time depend on the motion of the observer, that mass and energy are equivalent, and that time and space form a continuum called space-time. *See panels at* **acceleration, Einstein, gravity, space-time.**

relay An electrical switch that is operated by an electromagnet, such as a solenoid. When a small current passes through the electromagnet's coiled wire, it causes a movable iron bar to pivot and so open or close the switch.

REM Short for *rapid eye movement.* A stage of sleep characterized by twitching movements of the muscles of the eyes and face, faster heartbeat and increased circulation to the brain. Dreaming takes place during REM sleep.

remainder *Mathematics.* In division, the difference between the dividend and the product of the quotient and divisor. If 9 is divided by 4, the quotient is 2 and the remainder is 1, because 4 x 2 = 8 and the difference between 9 and 8 is 1.

remission A lessening or disappearance of the symptoms of a disease, especially cancer.

remora Any of several fish having a sucking disc on their head with which they attach themselves to sharks and other larger fish. They feed mainly on scraps of food left over from the sharks' meals.

renal Relating to the kidneys: *renal disease.*

renewable Relating to a natural resource, such as solar energy or wood, that is never used up or that can be replaced by new growth. *Compare* **nonrenewable.**

reproduction The process by which cells and organisms produce other cells and organisms of the same kind. Cell reproduction usually involves division of a cell into two identical parts by means of mitosis, or into four different parts by meiosis. ❖ The reproduction of organisms by the union of male and female reproductive cells (gametes) is called **sexual reproduction.** Most multicellular animals reproduce sexually. ❖ Reproduction in which offspring are produced by a single parent, without the union of reproductive cells, is called **asexual reproduction.** The fission (splitting) of bacterial cells is a form of asexual reproduction. Many plants and fungi are capable of reproducing both sexually and asexually, as are some animals, such as sponges.

reproductive cell A cell whose nucleus unites with that of a cell of the opposite sex to form a

Did You Know?

relativity

Developed as part of the theory of special relativity, Einstein's formula $E=mc^2$ expresses the equivalence of energy and mass. Energy (E) equals mass (m) multiplied by the square of the speed of light (c). Since the speed of light is a large number (299,792,458 metres per second), the formula shows that even small amounts of mass contain enormous amounts of energy. A mass weighing one-thirtieth of a milligram, if converted into energy, would equal the heat and light put out by a 100-watt light bulb over an entire year! This energy is stored in the mass itself and in the energy that holds it together, such as the energy that keeps the protons and neutrons together in the atomic nucleus. Einstein's formula opened the way to the discovery of nuclear energy, the energy that is released when atomic nuclei break apart or fuse together.

new organism. A reproductive cell contains only a single (haploid) set of chromosomes. Animal egg and sperm cells, the nuclei in grains of pollen, and egg cells in plant ovules are all reproductive cells. Also called *gamete, sex cell. See panel at* mitosis/meiosis.

reproductive system The system of organs involved with the reproduction of an organism, especially sexual reproduction. In flowering plants, for example, the reproductive system consists of pistils and stamens. In mammals, it consists mainly of the ovaries, uterus and vagina in females, and the testes and penis in males.

reptile Any of various cold-blooded vertebrate animals that have skin covered with scales or horny plates, breathe air using lungs and usually have a three-chambered heart. Reptiles reproduce sexually and lay eggs, which often have a leathery shell and are laid and hatch on land. Crocodiles, snakes, turtles and lizards are all reptiles.

reservoir 1. A natural or artificial pond or lake used for the storage of water. 2. An underground mass of rock or sediment that is porous and permeable enough to allow oil or natural gas to accumulate in it.

resin 1. Any of numerous clear or translucent, yellowish or brownish substances that ooze from certain trees and plants. Resins are used in products such as varnishes, lacquers, adhesives, plastics and drugs. *See panel at* **amber.** 2. Any of various artificial substances, such as polyurethane, that have similar properties to natural resins and are used to make plastics.

resistance 1. A force, such as friction, that prevents or slows down motion: *a car shaped to lessen wind resistance.* 2. The ability of a material or object to slow down the free flow of electrons of an electric current. Good conductors, such as copper, have low resistance. Good insulators, such as rubber, have high resistance. Resistance results in a transfer of electric energy into heat. 3. The degree to which an organism can defend itself against a disease or withstand the effects of a toxic substance, such as an environmental pollutant.

resistor A device used to control current in an electric circuit by providing resistance.

resonance The phenomenon whereby an oscillating system, such as a swing, will oscillate more strongly when it is exposed to a periodic force that is applied with the same frequency as that of the oscillating system. For example, a swing will swing to greater heights if each consecutive push on it is timed to be in rhythm with the initial swing. A radio is tuned by adjusting the frequency of the receiver so that it matches that of the incoming radio waves.

respiration 1. The process by which food substances, usually glucose, are broken down to supply energy to the cells. This is known as **cellular respiration.** When the process takes place in the presence of oxygen, the glucose is completely broken down to release the maximum amount of energy. Carbon dioxide and water are formed as waste products. This process is also known as **aerobic respiration.** When glucose is broken down to release energy in the absence of oxygen, much less energy is released and lactic acid or ethanol as well as carbon dioxide are the resulting waste products. This process is known as **anaerobic respiration.** 2. The process by which organisms exchange gases, especially oxygen and carbon dioxide, with the environment. In air-breathing vertebrates, respiration takes place in the lungs. In fish and many invertebrates, respiration takes place through the gills. Respiration in green plants occurs during photosynthesis. This process is commonly called respiration, as in *artificial respiration*, but scientifically it is known as *gas* or *gaseous exchange.*

respiratory system The system of organs and structures in which gas exchange takes place, consisting of the lungs and airways in air-breathing vertebrates, gills in fish and many invertebrates, the outer covering of the body in worms and specialized air ducts in insects.

reticulate Resembling or forming a net or network: *reticulate veins of a leaf.*

reticulum The second division of the stomach in ruminant animals, which together with the rumen contains microorganisms that digest fibre. The reticulum's contents are regurgitated for further chewing as part of the cud. *See more at* **ruminant.**

retina The light-sensitive membrane that lines the inside of the back of the eyeball, connected to the brain by the optic nerve. The retina of

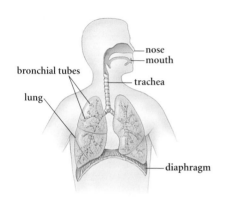

nose
mouth
bronchial tubes
trachea
lung
diaphragm

■ **respiratory system**

vertebrate animals contains specialized cells, called rods and cones, that absorb light of different wavelengths.

retinol *See* **vitamin A.**

retort A glass laboratory vessel in the shape of a bulb with a long, downward-pointing outlet tube. It is used for distillation or decomposition by heat.

retrograde Relating to the revolution in an orbit or rotation about an axis of a celestial body that moves clockwise from east to west, in the direction opposite to the movement of most celestial bodies.

retrovirus Any of a group of viruses containing RNA in which the RNA can convert to DNA inside a cell. Some retroviruses cause cancer in humans. HIV, the virus that causes AIDS, is a retrovirus.

reverse fault A geological fault in which the hanging wall has moved upwards relative to the footwall. Reverse faults occur where two blocks of rock are forced together by compression. *See more at* **fault.**

revolution 1. The motion of an object around a point, especially around another object or a centre of mass. 2. A single complete cycle of such motion.

Rf The symbol for **rutherfordium.**

Rh The symbol for **rhodium.**

rhenium A very rare, dense, silvery-white metallic element with a very high melting point. It is used to make catalysts and electrical contacts. *Symbol* **Re.** *Atomic number* 75. *See* **Periodic Table,** pages 260–261.

rheostat A resistor whose resistance can be continuously varied between two extremes so as to control the flow of current in an electric circuit.

rhesus monkey A small, yellowish-brown monkey of India, widely used in biological and medical research. The Rh (Rhesus) factor of the blood was first discovered in rhesus monkeys.

rheumatic fever A disorder that usually follows infection by certain bacteria and which has symptoms of inflammation of the joints, skin and heart. It occurs mainly in children and can cause permanent damage to the heart valves.

rheumatoid arthritis A chronic disease in which the joints, especially of the hands and feet, become inflamed, leading to stiffness, weakness and loss of movement.

Rh factor An antigen present in red blood cells, used in the classification of human blood. The

Usage

revolution/rotation

We use the words revolution and rotation – or the verbs revolve and rotate – to indicate cyclic patterns. We talk of crop rotation to refer to the successive planting of different crops on the same land, or of a revolving door to refer to a door turning about a central pivot. In everyday speech revolution and rotation are often used as synonyms, but in science they are not synonyms and have distinct meanings. The difference between the two terms lies in the location of the central axis that the object turns about. If the axis is outside the body itself – that is, if the object is orbiting about another object – then one complete orbit is called a revolution. But if the object is turning about an axis that passes through itself, then one complete cycle is called a rotation. This difference is often summed up in the statement: "Earth rotates on its axis and revolves around the sun."

blood cells of most people contain an Rh factor. For a blood transfusion to be successful, the blood of the donor must match that of the recipient, ie both must have or must be missing the Rh factor.

rhinoceros Any of several large African or Asian mammals having tough, mostly hairless skin, short legs with broad hooves and one or two upright horns on the snout. Rhinoceroses are plant-eating animals.

rhizoid A slender, root-like filament by which mosses, liverworts, fungi and the reproductive generation of ferns attach themselves to the material in which they grow and absorb nourishment.

rhizome A plant stem that grows horizontally under or along the ground and often sends out roots and shoots. New plants develop from the shoots. Ginger, iris and violets have rhizomes. Also called *rootstock. Compare* **bulb, corm, runner, tuber.**

rhodium A rare, silvery-white metallic element that is hard, durable and resistant to acids. It is used as a permanent plating for jewellery and is added to platinum to make hard alloys that can withstand high temperatures. *Symbol* **Rh**. *Atomic number* 45. *See* **Periodic Table,** pages 260–261.

rhombohedral *See* **trigonal.**

■ **rhizome**

rhombus A parallelogram having four equal sides. A square is a rhombus with angles of 90°.

rib 1. Any of a series of long, curved bones extending from the spine and enclosing the chest cavity. In mammals, reptiles and birds, the ribs curve towards the centre of the chest and in most cases attach to the sternum (breastbone). There are 12 pairs of ribs in humans. *See more at* **skeleton. 2.** One of the main veins of a leaf.

rib cage The bony structure in the chest formed by the ribs and sternum (breastbone) that encloses and protects the heart and lungs.

riboflavin A vitamin belonging to the B complex (B_2) that is important in carbohydrate metabolism and the maintenance of mucous membranes. It is found in milk, leafy vegetables, meat and egg yolks. *See also* **vitamin B complex.**

ribonucleic acid *See* **RNA.**

ribosome A sphere-shaped structure within the cytoplasm of a cell that is composed of RNA and protein and is the site of synthesis. Ribosomes are often attached to the membrane of the endoplasmic reticulum. *See more at* **cell.**

Richter scale A scale used to rate the strength

Word History

rhinoceros and hippopotamus

Two of the largest land mammals, the rhinoceros and hippopotamus, also have rather large names. These names, in fact, tell us something about the animals if we know how to work it out. The rhinoceros's name comes from Greek and is formed from *rhino–*, meaning "nose", and *keros*, meaning "horn". A rhinoceros is thus a "nose-horn". Hippopotamus also comes from Greek and is made of the words *hippos*, "horse", and *potamos*, "river". A hippopotamus is therefore a "river horse". The name was invented because hippos spend most of their lives in rivers or other shallow bodies of water (although they are not horses).

■ **rhombus**

or total energy of earthquakes. The scale has no upper limit but usually ranges from 1 to 9. Each increase in whole number represents a tenfold increase in magnitude, so that an earthquake rated as 5 is ten times as powerful as one rated as 4. An earthquake with a magnitude of 1 is detectable only by instruments (seismographs); one with a magnitude of 7 is a major earthquake. *See panel at* **earthquake.**

rickets A bone disorder in children that is caused by lack of vitamin D, either in the diet or from lack of exposure to sunlight. In a child with rickets, the bones do not grow properly and become soft and misshapen.

ridge *Meteorology.* A long, narrow area of high atmospheric pressure, often associated with fine weather and strong breezes. *Compare* **trough.**

rift 1. A fault along the border of a rift valley. **2.** A narrow break, crack or other opening in a rock, usually made by cracking or splitting.

rift valley 1. A long, narrow valley having normal geological faults on either side. Rift valleys usually form where the Earth's outer layer (the lithosphere) has become thin because of plate-tectonic processes. *See more at* **tectonic boundary. 2.** The deep undersea valley located along the centre of the mid-ocean ridge.

rift zone An area of the Earth's crust in which there are numerous rifts and rift valleys. *See more at* **tectonic boundary.**

Rigel A very bright, bluish-white giant star in the constellation Orion.

right angle An angle measuring 90°.

right-angled triangle A triangle having a right angle.

right ascension The position of a celestial object east of the vernal equinox along the celestial equator, measured as a horizontal angle and expressed in degrees or hours. Right ascension and declination are the measurements used to map objects on the celestial sphere. *See more at* **celestial sphere.**

rigor mortis Stiffening of the muscles after death. It occurs because the energy needed to interrupt the contraction of muscle fibres is no longer being produced.

ringworm Any of a number of contagious skin diseases caused by a fungus and resulting in ring-shaped, scaly, itching patches on the skin.

rip current A strong, narrow surface current that flows rapidly away from the shore. Rip currents form when water that has piled up along a shore due to wind and waves suddenly returns to deeper waters. Also called *rip tide.*

river A large, natural stream of fresh water that flows into the sea, a lake or another body of water. A river is usually fed by smaller streams that flow into it.

Rn The symbol for **radon.**

RNA Short for *ribonucleic acid.* The nucleic acid that determines protein synthesis in all living cells and the genetic make-up of many viruses. RNA consists of a single strand of nucleotides in a variety of lengths and shapes and is mainly produced in the cell nucleus. ❖ **Messenger RNA** is RNA that carries genetic information from the cell nucleus to the structures in the cytoplasm (known as ribosomes) where protein synthesis takes place. ❖ **Transfer RNA** is RNA that delivers the amino acids necessary for protein synthesis to the ribosomes. *Compare* **DNA.**

Word History

Rigel and star names

The history of astronomy owes much to Arabic scientists of the Middle Ages, who preserved the astronomical learning of ancient Greece and made improvements on it. The English names of many of the brightest stars in the heavens are Arabic in origin. The name of the supergiant star *Rigel,* for example, comes from the Arabic word for "foot" (the foot of the constellation Orion, that is). Some other important stars whose names are Arabic include *Aldebaran,* "the one following (the Pleiades)"; *Betelgeuse,* "hand of Orion"; *Deneb,* "tail" (of the constellation Cygnus, the swan); and *Altair,* "the flying eagle" (in the constellation Aquila, the eagle). The names of other stars are usually Greek or Latin, such as Antares or Sirius, as are the names of the constellations.

■ **RNA**

A: *adenine*   U: *uracil*
C: *cytosine*   G: *guanine*

robot A machine that can perform a variety of tasks either on command or by being programmed in advance.

rock 1. A relatively hard, naturally occurring mineral material. Rock can consist of a single mineral or of several minerals that are either tightly compacted or held together by a cement-like mineral matrix. The three main types of rock are igneous, sedimentary and metamorphic. 2. A large piece of such material; a boulder. *See table,* page 296.

rocket A vehicle or device propelled by one or more rocket engines, especially such a vehicle designed to travel through space.

rocket engine An engine that contains all the substances necessary for its operation and is propelled by a jet of hot gases produced by burning fuel. Since they do not rely on the oxygen in the atmosphere, rocket engines can operate in space.

rod One of the rod-shaped cells in the retina of the eye of many vertebrate animals. Rods are responsible for the ability to see in dim light. *Compare* **cone.**

rodent Any of various very numerous, mostly small mammals having large front teeth used for gnawing. The teeth grow throughout the animal's life, and gnawing keeps them from getting too long. Rodents make up about half the living species of mammals, and include rats, mice, beavers, squirrels, shrews and hamsters.

roe The eggs of a fish, often together with the membrane of the ovary in which they are held.

Roentgen, Wilhelm Konrad 1845–1923. German physicist who discovered X-rays and developed X-ray photography, revolutionizing medical diagnosis.

ROM Short for *read-only memory.* Computer hardware that holds permanently stored data. After the data is installed in ROM, it cannot be added to, modified or deleted. ROM usually contains instructions that enable the computer's operating system to communicate with other hardware.

rookery A place where certain birds or animals, such as crows, penguins and seals, gather to breed.

root 1. The part of a plant that usually grows underground, secures the plant in place, absorbs minerals and water, and stores food manufactured by leaves and other plant parts. In certain plants, additional roots grow out from the stem above ground, bending down into the soil, to provide more support. 2. Any of various other plant parts that grow underground, especially an underground stem such as a corm, rhizome or tuber. 3. The part of a tooth that is embedded in the jaw and not covered by enamel. 4. *Mathematics.* **a.** A number that, when multiplied by itself a given number of times, produces a specified number. For example, since $2 \times 2 \times 2 \times 2 = 16$, 2 is a fourth root of 16. **b.** A solution to an equation. For example, a root of the equation $x^2 - 4 = 0$ is 2, since $2^2 - 4 = 0$.

root hair A hair-like outgrowth of a plant root cell that absorbs water and minerals from the soil.

rootstock *See* **rhizome.**

rotation 1. The motion of an object around its own axis: *the daily rotation of the Earth.* 2. A single complete cycle of such motion. *See panel at* **revolution.**

rotational symmetry The characteristic of a shape that can be rotated so that it fits exactly onto itself in different positions.

rotator cuff A group of muscles and tendons attaching the shoulder to the scapula (shoulder blade) that provide stability to the shoulder joint and act to rotate the arm. Injuries to the rotator cuff often happen when the arm is repeatedly moved over the head with great force, as when bowling in cricket.

Rock Types

IGNEOUS ROCKS	METAMORPHIC ROCKS	SEDIMENTARY ROCKS

HOW THEY FORM

Igneous rocks form from cooling of magma (underground) or lava (at the Earth's surface). Many of the rocks that we see on the surface today actually formed deep down in the Earth and were later pushed to the surface by the processes of plate tectonics. Lava forms when magma from deep within the Earth comes up to the surface.

Metamorphic rocks form when igneous, sedimentary or other metamorphic rocks are subjected to great pressure and high temperatures deep within the Earth. This can happen on a very small scale where only the rocks in direct contact with a source of heat and pressure become metamorphosed, or it can happen on a regional scale, as along a mountain chain.

Sedimentary rocks form at the surface of the Earth, through the transport and deposition of sediments by water, wind or ice. The sediments can be fragments of fossils or sea shells, or small pieces of igneous, metamorphic or other sedimentary rocks. Some sedimentary rocks form as precipitation of crystals, such as salt, during the evaporation of water.

EXAMPLES

granite	basalt	slate	schist	sandstone	limestone
gabbro	pahoehoe	gneiss	marble	shale	conglomerate

CHARACTERISTICS

The crystals of the minerals that make up igneous rocks are tightly locked together because they form close to each other when the magma or lava becomes solid. Individual crystals often have sharp edges and geometric forms reflecting crystal shapes. Because new magma can form underground and move through fractures in rock, igneous rocks often have fractures filled with different types of igneous rock; these magma-filled fractures are called veins or pegmatites.

The crystals of minerals in metamorphic rocks have been stretched, folded or changed by the pressure and high temperature to which they have been exposed. Often the crystals have been reorganized into layers. Sometimes, if a mass of rock becomes very hot, partial melting of the original rock occurs and new minerals form. These minerals are often of gem quality.

Sediment grains are often rounded because they have been eroded by water, wind or ice. But they can also be sharp, especially in high mountainous areas, where rocks are mechanically broken down into sediments by the forces exerted by the formation and melting of ice. Sediment grains can be small, like sand, or they can consist of large cobbles and boulders. Often sedimentary rocks are layered, because their sediments were deposited over a long course of time. Sedimentary rocks often contain fossils.

rotifer Any of various tiny multicellular animals living in water and having a wheel-like ring of cilia at their front ends.

Roux, Pierre Paul Émile 1853–1933. French bacteriologist who assisted Louis Pasteur on most of his major discoveries. Roux carried out early work on the rabies vaccine and directed the first tests of the diphtheria antitoxin.

Ru The symbol for **ruthenium**.

rubber 1. An elastic material prepared from the milky sap of certain tropical plants, especially the rubber tree, and used after processing in a great variety of products, including electric insulation and tyres. **2.** Any of various synthetic materials having properties that are similar to those of this substance.

rubella *See* **German measles.**

rubidium A soft, silvery-white element that is an alkali metal. It ignites spontaneously in air and reacts violently with water. Rubidium is used in photoelectric cells and in making vacuum tubes. *Symbol* **Rb.** *Atomic number* 37. *See* **Periodic Table,** pages 260–261.

ruby A deep-red, translucent form of the mineral corundum that is valued as a precious stone.

rumen The first and largest division of the stomach in ruminant animals, in which the food is fermented by microorganisms. These microorganisms produce the enzyme cellulase, which enables them to digest the cellulose cell walls of the plant cells. Mammals such as cows and sheep cannot produce cellulase themselves. *See more at* **ruminant.**

ruminant Any of various hoofed, usually horned mammals, such as cattle, sheep and goats, that have an even number of toes. Ruminants have a stomach divided into four compartments (called the rumen, reticulum, omasum and abomasum). Microorganisms act on the cellulose in the rumen, and the partly digested food (the cud) is regurgitated into the mouth for further chewing to completely break down any remaining cellulose

cell walls. The cud is finally swallowed into the abomasum, the true stomach, and from there onwards digestion proceeds as normal. This process allows the animals to extract the maximum food value from plant material.

runner A slender stem that grows horizontally and puts down roots to form new plants. Strawberries are spread by runners. *Compare* **bulb, corm, rhizome, stolon, tuber.**

run-off Rainwater that runs over the surface and into streams when the ground is saturated.

Russell, Henry 1877–1957. American astronomer who studied binary stars and developed methods to calculate their mass and distances. He also demonstrated the relationship between types of stars and their brightness.

rust *noun* **1.** Any of the various reddish-brown oxides of iron that form on iron and many of its alloys when they are exposed to oxygen in the presence of moisture. *See panel at* **oxidation. 2.** Any of various plant diseases caused by parasitic fungi that produce reddish or brownish spots on leaves. —*verb* To become corroded or oxidized.

ruthenium A rare, silvery-grey metallic element that is hard, brittle and very resistant to corrosion. It is used to harden alloys of platinum and palladium for jewellery and electrical contacts. *Symbol* **Ru.** *Atomic number* 44. *See* **Periodic Table,** pages 260–261.

Rutherford, Ernest 1871–1937. New Zealand-born British physicist who was a pioneer of subatomic physics. He discovered the atomic nucleus and named the proton. Rutherford demonstrated that radioactive elements give off three types of rays, which he named alpha, beta and gamma. He also invented the term *half-life* to measure the rate of radioactive decay.

rutherfordium A synthetic, radioactive element that is produced by bombarding plutonium with carbon or neon ions. Its most stable isotope has a half-life of 65 seconds. *Symbol* **Rf.** *Atomic number* 104. *See* **Periodic Table,** pages 260–261.

S The symbol for **sulphur**.

sabre-toothed tiger Any of various large extinct cats of the Oligocene to Pleistocene Epochs having very long upper-canine teeth.

Sabin, Albert Bruce 1906–1993. American microbiologist and physician who developed a live-virus vaccine against polio that contained an active form of the polio virus (1957). This replaced the vaccine, invented by Jonas Salk, that contained an inactivated (and less effective) form of the virus.

sac A bag-like part in an animal or plant, often containing liquids. The human bladder is a sac.

saccharin A white, crystalline powder used as a calorie-free sweetener. It tastes about 500 times sweeter than sugar.

sacrum A triangular bone at the base of the spine, above the coccyx (tailbone), that forms the rear section of the pelvis. In humans it is made up of five vertebrae that have fused together by the onset of adulthood. *See more at* **skeleton**.

Sagittarius A constellation in the Southern Hemisphere near Scorpius and Capricornus.

salicylic acid A white, crystalline acid used to make aspirin, to treat certain skin conditions, and to preserve and flavour foods. Its systematic name is *2-hydroxybenzoic acid.*

saline Relating to or containing salt; salty. —*noun* **salinity.**

saliva The watery fluid that is secreted into the mouth by glands known as salivary glands. In many animals, including humans, it contains enzymes that help in the digestion of carbohydrates. Saliva also contains mucus, which lubricates food for swallowing.

salivary gland A gland that secretes saliva, especially any of three pairs of large glands in humans that secrete saliva into the mouth.

Salk, Jonas Edward 1914–1995. American microbiologist who developed the first effective vaccine against polio (1954).

salmon Any of various large food fish of northern waters, having pinkish flesh. Salmon swim from salt to fresh water to spawn, often climbing short waterfalls by leaping, and swimming against the currents of rapids.

salmonella A rod-shaped bacterium that causes food poisoning in humans.

salt 1. A colourless or white crystalline solid, NaCl, found naturally in all animal fluids, seawater, and in underground deposits. It is used widely as a food seasoning and preservative. Also called *sodium chloride.* **2.** Any of a large class of chemical compounds formed when one or more hydrogen ions of an acid are replaced by metallic ions. Salts have an electric charge, conduct electricity and dissolve completely in water.

saltpetre *See* **potassium nitrate.**

saltwater Consisting of or living in salty water, especially seawater: *saltwater fish.*

samarium A silvery-white metallic element of the lanthanide series that exists in several forms and has seven naturally occurring isotopes. It is used to make glass that absorbs infrared light and to absorb neutrons in nuclear reactors. *Symbol* Sm. *Atomic number* 62. *See* **Periodic Table,** pages 260–261.

sand 1. Small, often rounded grains or particles of disintegrated rock, larger than particles of silt. Although sand often consists of quartz, it can consist of any other mineral or rock fragment as well. Coral sand, for example, consists of limestone fragments. **2.** A loose collection or deposit of sand grains.

sandbar A long mass or low ridge of sand built up in the water along a shore or beach by the action of waves or currents.

sandstone A sedimentary rock formed of fine to coarse sand-sized grains that have been either compacted or cemented together. Although sandstone usually consists primarily of quartz, it can also consist of other minerals. Sandstone

■ sandbar
sandbar at Cape Cod, Massachusetts, USA

varies in colour from yellow or red to grey or brown. *See table at* **rock.**

Sanger, Frederick Born 1918. English biochemist. During the 1940s, Sanger devised methods of deducing the sequence of amino acids in the chains of the protein hormone insulin. For this he was awarded the Nobel Prize for chemistry in 1958. He then turned to the structure of nucleic acids, working on RNA and DNA; eventually he was able to deduce the full sequence of bases in the DNA of the virus Phi X 174 and mitochondrial DNA. Such methods led to the full base sequence of the Epstein-Barr virus by 1984. For this work Sanger shared (with Walter Gilbert and Paul Berg) the 1980 Nobel Prize for chemistry, thereby becoming the first scientist to win two Nobel Prizes in this field.

sap The watery fluid that circulates through a plant with vascular tissues. Sap moving up the xylem carries water and minerals, while sap moving down the phloem carries water and food.

sapphire Any of several fairly pure forms of the mineral corundum, especially a blue form valued as a gem.

saprophyte An organism, especially a fungus or bacterium, that lives on and gets its nourishment from dead organisms or decaying organic material. —*adjective* **saprophytic.**

sarcoma A usually malignant tumour arising in connective tissue.

satellite 1. A celestial body that orbits a planet; a moon. *See panel at* **moon. 2.** An object launched to orbit the Earth or another celestial body. Satellites are used for research, communications, weather information and navigation.

saturated 1. Relating to an organic compound in which all the carbon atoms are joined by single bonds and therefore cannot be combined with any additional atoms or radicals. Propane and saturated fatty acids are examples of saturated hydrocarbons. *Compare* **unsaturated. 2.** Relating to a solution that is unable to dissolve more of a solute. **3.** Containing as much water vapour as is possible at a given temperature. Air that is saturated has a relative humidity of 100 per cent.

saturated fat A fat whose triglyceride molecule contains three saturated fatty acids. Most fats derived from animal sources are saturated fats. Eating foods high in saturated fats can lead to cholesterol levels in the blood that are higher than normal. *Compare* **unsaturated fat.**

■ satellite
Communications satellites receive, amplify and transmit radio signals between dish antennas that may be hundreds of miles apart.

■ **saturated**
the ring chain of carbon atoms of a cyclopenta-ne molecule

saturation The vividness of a colour's hue. Saturation measures the degree to which a colour differs from a grey of the same brightness or lightness. *See more at* **colour.**

saturation point The point at which no further substance can be dissolved in a solution.

Saturn The sixth planet from the sun and the second largest, with a diameter about ten times that of the Earth. Saturn is encircled by a large, flat system of rings that are made up mostly of tiny particles of ice. *See table at* **solar system,** pages 314–315. *See panel at* **planet.**

saurian A lizard or similar reptile.

saurischian One of the two main types of dinosaurs. Saurischians have a pelvis similar to

■ **Saturn**

that of modern reptiles, and include the meat-eating theropods and the plant-eating sauropods. *Compare* **ornithischian.**

sauropod One of the two types of saurischian dinosaurs, widespread during the Jurassic and Cretaceous Periods. Sauropods were plant-eaters and often grew to tremendous size, having a stout body with thick legs, long slender necks with a small head, and long tails. Sauropods included the apatosaurus (brontosaurus) and brachiosaurus. *Compare* **theropod.**

savanna *or* **savannah** A flat, treeless grassland in warm regions.

Sb The symbol for **antimony.**

Sc The symbol for **scandium.**

scalar A quantity, such as mass, length or speed, whose only property is magnitude; a number. *Compare* **vector.**

scale[1] **1.** One of the small thin plates forming the outer covering of fish, reptiles and certain other animals. **2.** A similar part, such as one of the minute structures overlapping to form the covering on the wings of butterflies and moths. **3.** A small, thin, usually dry plant part, such as one of the protective leaves that cover a tree bud or one of the structures that contain the reproductive organs on the cones of a conifer. **4.** A plant disease caused by scale insects.

scale[2] **1.** An ordered system of numbering or indexing that is used as a reference standard in measurement, in which each number corresponds to some physical quantity. Some scales, such as temperature scales, have equal intervals; other scales, such as the Richter scale, are arranged as a geometric progression. **2.** An instrument or a machine for weighing.

scale insect Any of various small insects related to the aphids. The young suck juices from plants, and the adult females live under waxy, scale-like shells that they secrete on plant tissue. Scale insects can be very destructive to plants.

scalene Having three unequal sides, as a triangle that is neither equilateral nor isosceles.

scandium A soft, silvery, very lightweight metallic element that is found in various rare minerals and is a byproduct in the processing of certain uranium ores. It has a high melting point

■ **scalene triangle**

and is used to make high-intensity lights. *Symbol* Sc. *Atomic number* 21. *See* **Periodic Table,** pages 260–261.

scanning electron microscope An electron microscope that moves a beam of electrons across an object and creates a three-dimensional image from both the electrons scattered by the object and the electrons knocked loose from the object.

scanning tunnelling microscope A microscope used to make images of individual atoms on the surface of a material. The microscope has a probe ending in a tiny sharp tip that moves along the material's surface while emitting a stream of electrons. The flow of electrons is constant as long as the distance between the tip and the material's surface atoms is held constant. An image is formed based on the continual adjustments made to the height of the tip to keep the electron flow constant over the "bumps" that are the atoms.

scapula Either of two flat, triangular bones forming part of the shoulder. In humans and other primates, they lie on the upper part of the back on either side of the spine. Also called *shoulder blade. See more at* **skeleton.**

scarab Any of several often large beetles with broad black bodies that feed off the dung in which they also lay their eggs.

scarlet fever A severe contagious bacterial disease that is characterized by a high temperature and a scarlet rash on the skin. It mainly occurs in children.

scattering The spreading of a stream of particles or a beam of rays, as of light, over a range of directions as a result of collisions with other particles. Scattering is responsible for the colour of the sky. On a clear day, the sky is blue, because blue light from the sun is scattered by the atmosphere's particles to a greater degree than other colours of light. At sunset and sunrise, the sky appears red and yellow, because the light from the sun has passed a longer distance through air and some of the blue light has been scattered away, leaving yellow and red light which is less easily scattered.

scavenger An animal that feeds on dead organisms, especially a meat-eating animal that eats dead animals rather than hunting live prey. Vultures, hyenas and wolves are scavengers.

schist A metamorphic rock characterized by a very fine alignment of its minerals, which allows it to be easily split into flakes or slabs. Because schist often contains abundant mica, it usually has a shiny, grey appearance. *See table at* **rock.**

schistosomiasis Any of a group of diseases caused by flatworm parasites that infest the blood of humans and other mammals. Symptoms of the disease include severe diarrhoea and eventual damage to vital organs. Schistosomiasis is seen in rural areas of Africa, Latin America and Asia and is transmitted through contact with contaminated water.

schizophrenia Any of a group of severe mental disorders in which a person loses touch with reality. People with schizophrenia also experience abnormal thinking that usually interferes with their ability to work and communicate with others. The biological causes of schizophrenia are not well understood. It is associated with an imbalance of chemical substances in the brain and often runs in families.

Schrödinger, Erwin 1887–1961. Austrian physicist who was a founder of the study of wave mechanics. He developed a mathematical equation that describes the wave-like behaviour of subatomic particles. Schrödinger's equation was fundamental to the development of quantum mechanics.

Schwann, Theodor 1810–1882. German physiologist. He began studying digestion and isolating the enzyme pepsin from the stomach lining before moving on to look at the role of yeast cells in producing fermentation. Schwann also discovered the "Schwann cells" which compose the sheath around peripheral nerve axons, and he showed an egg to be a single cell which, once fertilized, evolves into a complex organism. His most renowned work, however, was on cell theory. In a major book of 1839 he contended that the entire plant or animal was comprised of cells, and that cells carry out independently the reactions of life, but that the life of the cells is also adapted to benefit and make possible the whole organism.

sciatic nerve A thick nerve that arises in the lower part of the spine and passes through the pelvis on its way to the back of the leg. It carries sensory information from the leg to the spine and controls the action of many muscles. The sciatic nerve is the largest nerve in the body.

science The investigation of natural phenomena through observation, experimentation and theoretical explanation. Although scientists and philosophers are not in general agreement about whether it is possible to describe the methods by which scientists work, many people would argue that the methods used by scientists include the careful observation of natural phenomena, the formulation of a hypothesis, the conducting of one or more experiments to test the hypothesis and the drawing of a conclusion that confirms or modifies the hypothesis. *See panel at* **hypothesis.**

scientific name A name used by scientists, especially the taxonomic name of an organism that consists of the genus and species. Scientific names usually come from Latin or Greek. An example is *Homo sapiens,* the scientific name for humans.

scientific notation A method of expressing numbers in terms of a decimal number between 1 and 10 multiplied by a power of 10. The scientific notation for 10,492, for example, is 1.0492×10^4.

sclera The tough, white fibrous tissue that covers all of the eyeball except the cornea.

scoliosis Abnormal sideways curvature of the spine.

scoria Rough, crusty solidified lava containing numerous cavities that originated as gas bubbles in the lava while it was still molten.

Scorpius A constellation in the Southern Hemisphere near Libra and Sagittarius.

scree Eroded and weathered rocks collected at the bottom of slopes.

scrotum The external sac of skin that encloses the testes in most male mammals.

scurvy A disease caused by lack of vitamin C in

■ **sea anemone**

the diet. It is characterized by bleeding of the gums, rupture of capillaries under the skin, loose teeth and weakness of the body.

Se The symbol for **selenium.**

sea 1. The continuous body of salt water that covers most of the Earth's surface. 2. A region of water within an ocean and partly enclosed by land, such as the North Sea. 3. A large body of either fresh or salt water that is completely enclosed by land, such as the Caspian Sea. 4. A mare of the moon.

sea anemone Any of numerous often brightly coloured sea-dwelling animals that resemble flowers and are related to the jellyfish and corals. Anemones are cnidarians and have a flexible cylindrical body with tentacles surrounding a central mouth.

seaborgium A synthetic, radioactive element that is produced by bombarding californium with oxygen ions or bombarding lead with chromium ions. Its most stable isotope has a half-life of about 20 seconds. *Symbol* **Sg.** *Atomic number* 106. *See* **Periodic Table,** pages 260–261.

sea cucumber Any of various invertebrate sea animals related to starfish and sea urchins, having a rough cucumber-shaped body and a mouth surrounded by tentacles. To distract an attacking predator, a sea cucumber can expel some of its internal organs, which later grow back.

sea horse Any of several small saltwater fish having a head resembling that of a horse, a body covered with bony plates, and a tail that can be curled around a supporting object. The male stores eggs in a pouch on its belly until they hatch.

seal Any of various meat-eating sea mammals having a streamlined body, thick fur or hair, and limbs in the form of flippers. Seals are related to but smaller than walruses.

sea level The level of the surface of the sea, used as a standard in determining land elevation or sea depths.

sea lion Any of several large seals, mostly of Pacific waters, having a sleek body with visible ears and brownish fur.

seam *Geology.* A thin layer or stratum, as of coal or rock.

sea slug Any of various colourful sea molluscs that lack a shell and gills but have fringe-like projections that serve as respiratory organs. Also called *nudibranch.*

season 1. One of four natural divisions of the year – spring, summer, autumn and winter – in the North or South Temperate Zones. Each season begins as the sun passes through a solstice or an equinox. 2. In some tropical climates, either of the two parts – rainy and dry – into which the year is divided. 3. A term for the fertile stage of the reproductive cycle of some mammals: *dogs chase after a bitch in season.*

sea squirt Any of various primitive sea animals having a transparent, sac-shaped body with two syphons. Sea squirts pump water through the syphons and filter it with gill-like structures to catch food particles. Sea squirts belong to the group known as tunicates.

sea urchin Any of various invertebrate sea animals having a round body covered by a shell with movable spines. Sea urchins are related to starfish.

seaweed Any of various algae or plants that live in the sea. Some species are free-floating, while others are attached to the seafloor. Seaweed range from the size of a pinhead to large fronds extending up to 30 metres in length.

sebaceous gland Any of the glands in the skin that secrete an oily material (called sebum) into the hair follicles.

sebum The fatty substance secreted by the sebaceous glands in the skin of mammals. It protects and lubricates the skin and hair.

sec Abbreviation of **secant.**

secant 1. A straight line or ray that intersects a curve, especially a circle, at two or more points. 2. The ratio of the length of the hypotenuse in a right-angled triangle to the side adjacent to an acute angle; the inverse of the cosine.

second 1. A unit of time equal to $\frac{1}{60}$ of a minute. 2. A unit of angular measurement equal to $\frac{1}{60}$ of a minute of an arc.

secondary 1. Relating to a secondary colour. 2. *Botany.* Relating to the cambium layer of tissue in plants, whose cells divide to create new vascular tissue and cause the plant to become wider and thicker.

secondary colour A colour produced by mixing two primary colours in equal proportions. *See more at* **colour.**

secondary sex characteristic Any of the physical traits in a sexually mature animal that are not directly involved in the act of reproducing. They include breast development in female primates, facial-hair growth in young men, the growth of antlers in antelopes, and colourful plumage in male birds. The appearance of secondary sex characteristics is determined by the sex hormones.

secondary wave An earthquake wave in which rock particles vibrate at right angles to the direction of wave travel. Secondary waves can travel through solids but not through liquids. Also called *S wave. See panel at* **earthquake.**

secrete To produce and discharge a substance, especially from the cells of specialized glands. For example, the endocrine glands secrete hormones.

sector The part of a circle bounded by two radii and the arc between them.

sedative A drug having a calming or quieting effect, often given to reduce anxiety.

sediment 1. *Geology.* Silt, sand, rocks, fossils and other matter carried and deposited by water, wind or ice. 2. *Chemistry.* Particles of solid matter that settle out of a suspension to the bottom of the liquid.

sedimentary Relating to rocks formed when sediment, such as sand or mud, is deposited and becomes tightly compacted. Sandstone, conglomerate and limestone are examples of sedimentary rocks. *See table at* **rock.**

seed *noun* A part of a flowering plant that contains an embryo and the food it will need to grow into a new plant. A seed is a mature fertilized ovule. —*verb* **1.** To plant seeds in soil. **2.** To attempt to produce rain by cloud seeding. *See more at* **cloud seeding.**

seed coat The outer protective covering of a seed. Also called *testa.*

seed leaf *See* cotyledon.

seedling A young plant that is grown from a seed, rather than from a cutting or bulb, for example.

segment **1.** The portion of a line between any two of its points. **2.** The region bounded by an arc of a circle and the chord that connects the endpoints of the arc. **3.** The portion of a sphere included between a pair of parallel planes that intersect it or are at a tangent to it.

seismic Relating to an earthquake or to other tremors of the Earth, such as those caused by large explosions: *a seismic disturbance.*

seismograph An instrument that detects and records vibrations and movements in the Earth, especially during an earthquake. By comparing the records produced by seismographs located in three or more locations across the Earth, geologists can determine the location and strength of an earthquake. ❖ The record produced by a seismograph is called a **seismogram.**

seismology The scientific study of earthquakes, including their origin, geographic distribution and effects, as well as the prediction of possible occurrences of earthquakes.

selenium A nonmetallic element that can exist as a grey crystal, a red powder or a black glassy material. It can convert light directly into electricity, and its ability to conduct electricity increases as light striking it becomes more intense. Because of this, selenium is used in photocopiers, photography and solar cells. *Symbol* **Se.** *Atomic number* 34. *See* **Periodic Table,** pages 260–261.

semen A whitish fluid that is produced by the reproductive organs of male mammals and carries sperm cells.

semi– **1.** A prefix that means "half", as in *semicircle,* half a circle. **2.** A prefix that means "partly", "somewhat" or "less than fully", as in *semiconscious,* partly conscious.

semiarid Having low rainfall but able to support grassland and scrubby vegetation; not completely arid.

semicircular canal Any of the three looped tubes of the inner ear that together work to maintain the sense of balance of the body.

semiconductor Any of various solid substances, such as silicon or germanium, that conduct electricity more easily than insulators but less easily than conductors. Semiconductors are able to do this because they have a small number of electrons that have escaped from the bonds between the atoms, leaving open spaces. Both the electrons and the open spaces can carry an electric current.

semipalmate Having partially webbed feet or toes, like many wading and shore birds.

Semmelweis, Ignaz Phillipp 1818–1865. Hungarian physician who was a pioneer of sterile surgical practices. He proved that infectious disease and death in the obstetric clinic where he worked were caused by medical students going directly from working on autopsies to treating patients. Semmelweis instituted strict rules governing hygiene that dramatically reduced the death rate.

sense organ In animals, an organ or part that is sensitive to a stimulus, such as sound, touch or light. Examples of sense organs include the eye, ear and nose, as well as the taste buds on the tongue.

sensor A device that responds to a physical stimulus and converts the stimulus into a signal conveyed to another device. For example, a sensor in a printer detects that the paper tray is empty and sends a signal to the digital display that the tray is out of paper.

sensory Involving the sense organs or the nerves that relay messages from them: *sensory receptors; a sensory nerve. Compare* **motor.**

sepal One of the separate, usually green parts extending from the base of a flower. Sepals look like small leaves, though in some plants they are coloured like petals. As a group, they form the

calyx, which surrounds and protects the flower bud. In some flowers, such as poppies, the sepals fall off after the flower bud opens. *See more at* **flower.**

sepsis Infection of the blood by disease-causing microorganisms, especially bacteria. —*adjective* **septic.**

septum (*plural* **septa**) A thin wall or membrane that separates two parts, structures or individual organisms. The chambers of the heart are separated by septa.

sequence 1. *Mathematics.* A set of quantities ordered in the same manner as the positive integers. A sequence can be finite, such as $\{1, 3, 5, 7, 9\}$, or it can be infinite, such as $\{1, \frac{1}{2}, \frac{1}{3}, \frac{1}{4}, \ldots \frac{1}{n}\}$. **2.** *Chemistry.* The order of molecules that make up the subunits of a chemical compound, especially the order of nucleotides in a nucleic acid or of the amino acids in a protein.

series *Mathematics.* The sum of a sequence of terms, for example $2 + 2^2 + 2^3 + 2^4 + 2^5 \ldots$

series circuit *See under* **circuit.**

serine A nonessential amino acid. *See more at* **amino acid.**

serum (*plural* **serums** *or* **sera**) **1.** *See* **blood serum. 2.** Blood serum extracted from an animal that has immunity to a particular disease. The serum contains antibodies to specific antigens and can transfer immunity to humans or other animals when injected.

server A computer that controls a central storage area of data that can be downloaded or manipulated by another computer.

■ **sessile**
coral

sessile 1. *Zoology.* Permanently attached or fixed; not free-moving: *Corals and mussels are sessile animals.* **2.** *Botany.* Stalkless and attached directly at the base: *sessile leaves; sessile fruit.*

set A collection of distinct elements that have something in common. In mathematics, sets are commonly represented by enclosing the members of a set in curly brackets, eg $\{1, 2, 3, 4, 5\}$, the set of all positive integers from 1 to 5.

sex 1. Either of two divisions, male and female, into which most organisms are grouped. Sex is usually determined by anatomy, the make-up of the chromosomes, and the type and amount of hormones produced. **2.** Sexual intercourse. —*adjective* **sexual.**

sex cell *See* **reproductive cell.**

sex chromosome Either of a pair of chromosomes, usually called X and Y, that in combination determine the sex of an individual in many animals and in some plants. In human beings, XX results in a female and XY results in a male but this varies from species to species. The sex chromosomes carry the genes that control the development of the reproductive organs. The Y chromosome in humans is very small and carries few genes beyond those needed for male reproductive development. However, the X chromosome carries a lot of extra information about a whole range of functions, including aspects of the clotting of the blood and colour vision.

sex hormone A steroid hormone that regulates the sexual development of an organism and is needed for reproduction. Testosterone and oestrogen are sex hormones.

sex-linked Carried on or transmitted by a sex chromosome. Sex-linked inheritance concerns the genes located on the sex chromosomes. Colour blindness in humans is a sex-linked trait.

sexual intercourse The process by which sperm from the male is deposited in the female during sexual reproduction.

sexually transmitted disease Any of various diseases, such as chlamydia, gonorrhoea and syphilis, that are transmitted through sexual intercourse or other intimate sexual contact. Formerly called *venereal disease.*

sexual reproduction *See under* **reproduction.**

Sg The symbol for **seaborgium.**

shale A fine-grained sedimentary rock consisting of compacted and hardened clay, silt or mud. Shale forms in many distinct layers and splits easily into thin sheets or slabs. It varies in colour from black or grey to brown or red. *See table at* **rock.**

shelf *See* **continental shelf.**

shell 1a. The usually hard outer covering of certain animals, such as molluscs, insects and turtles. **b.** The hard outer covering of a bird's egg. **c.** The leathery covering of a reptilian egg. **d.** The hard outer covering of a seed, nut or fruit. **2.** Any of the regions in which electrons are concentrated around the nucleus of an atom. Depending on the number of protons in the nucleus, atoms can have up to seven shells. Electrons in the outer shells have greater energy than those in shells closer to the nucleus. An electron in an inner shell can gain energy and move to an outer shell while, if there is space available, an electron can give off energy and drop from an outer shell to an inner shell. The energy is usually given off in the form of light. The innermost shell can hold two electrons, while others can hold different amounts, with the greatest amount being 32 electrons. *See more at* **atom.** *See panel at* **metal.**

shinbone *See* **tibia.**

shoal 1. A sandy elevation of the bottom of a body of water; a sandbar. **2.** A group of fish swimming together.

shock 1. A life-threatening condition marked by a severe drop in blood pressure, resulting from serious injury or illness. **2.** An instance of the passage of an electric current through the body. The amount of injury caused by electric shock depends on the type and strength of the current, the length of time the current is applied, and the route the current takes once it enters the body.

Shockley, William Bradford 1910–1989. American physicist who co-developed the transistor.

shock wave A large-amplitude wave formed by the sudden compression of the medium through which the wave moves. Shock waves can be caused by explosions or by objects moving through a fluid at a speed greater than the speed of sound. Because the waves generated in the fluid by the rapid movement cannot move at a speed greater than the speed of sound (thereby keeping pace with the object that caused them to form), they pile up and become compressed together.

shoot A new growth on a plant, such as a young branch or a sprout from a seed.

shooting star *See* **meteor** (sense 1).

short circuit A path that allows most of the current in an electric circuit to flow around or away from the principal elements or devices in the circuit. Short circuits can cause too much current to flow through one part of the circuit, often causing the circuit to break.

shortsightedness The ability to see objects at close range better than distant objects. Shortsightedness is caused by the eye focusing light in front of the retina instead of directly on it, usually as a result of an elongated eyeball or a misshapen cornea. Also called *myopia* and *nearsightedness. Compare* **longsightedness.**

■ **shale**
shale cliffs along Dempster Highway, Yukon Territory, Canada

■ shortsightedness

top: *A normal eye focuses light on the retina*
bottom: *An elongated eyeball causes light to focus in front of the retina*

---

shoulder blade *See* **scapula.**

shrub A woody plant that is smaller than a tree, usually having several stems rather than a single trunk; a bush.

Si The symbol for **silicon.**

sickle cell anaemia A hereditary disease characterized by red blood cells that are sickle-shaped instead of round because of an abnormality in the haemoglobin, the protein that carries oxygen in the blood. Because of their shape, the cells can cause blockage of small blood vessels in the organs and bones, reducing the amount of oxygen available to those tissues.

sidereal 1. Relating to the stars or constellations. 2. Measured by means of the apparent daily motion of the stars: *sidereal time.*

sievert A unit used to measure the amount of radiation necessary to produce the same effect on living tissue as one gray of high-penetration X-rays.

significant figures The digits in a decimal number that are warranted by the accuracy of the means of measurement. Significant figures are all the numbers beginning with the leftmost non-zero digit, or beginning with the first digit after the decimal point if there are no non-zero digits to the left of the decimal point, and extending to the

right. For example, 302, 3.20 and 0.023 all have three significant figures. Abbreviated to **s.f.**

silica Silicon dioxide, SiO_2, a compound that occurs widely in rocks and mineral forms, such as quartz, sand and flint, and is used to make glass, concrete and other materials. —*adjective* **siliceous.**

silicate 1. Any of a large class of chemical compounds composed of silicon, oxygen and at least one metal. Most rocks and minerals are silicates. Silicates are also one of the main components of bricks. 2. Any mineral containing the group SiO_4 in its crystal lattice. Micas and feldspars are silicate minerals.

silicon A nonmetallic element that occurs in both

Did You Know?

sickle cell anaemia

Genetic mutations can be good or bad, and sometimes they can even be both. The mutation that causes *sickle cell anaemia* is one example. It is harmful if a person inherits two copies of the mutated gene (one from each parent). The defective gene causes red blood cells to be distorted into a sickle shape, which makes it hard for them to pass through the tiny blood vessels where they give oxygen to body tissues. If a person's chromosomes have two copies of the mutated gene, serious sickle cell anaemia results, causing illness. However, there is actually some benefit if only one copy of the gene is inherited, since only very mild sickling of the cells occurs. It so happens that this mild sickling is harmful to the parasite that causes malaria, and can protect a person from that disease. In a region like tropical Africa where malaria is common, people who have the mutation in one gene are more likely to ward off a malarial infection and to live long enough to have children, who then inherit the gene in turn. And because inheriting two copies of the gene is much less likely than inheriting just one, the benefits of the gene outweigh its risks for most people in these regions.

grey crystalline and brown noncrystalline forms. It is the second most abundant element in the Earth's crust and can be found only in silica and silicates. Silicon is used in glass, semiconductors, concrete and ceramics. *Symbol* **Si**. *Atomic number* 14. *See* **Periodic Table,** pages 260–261.

silicone Any of a class of chemical compounds consisting of long chains of organic radicals that are each attached to silicon and oxygen atoms. Silicones are used to make adhesives, lubricants and synthetic rubber.

silk 1. A fibre produced by silkworms to form cocoons. Silk is strong, flexible and fibrous, and is essentially a long continuous strand of protein. It is widely used to make thread and fabric. **2.** A substance similar to the silk of the silkworm but produced by other insect larvae and by spiders to spin webs.

silkworm Any of various caterpillars that produce silk cocoons, especially the larva of a moth native to Asia. The fibre of silkworm cocoons is the source of commercial silk.

sill An approximately horizontal sheet of igneous rock located between layers of older rock.

silt Small grains or particles of disintegrated rock, smaller than sand and larger than clay. Silt is often found at the bottom of bodies of water, such as lakes, where it accumulates slowly by settling through the water.

siltstone A fine-grained sedimentary rock consisting primarily of compacted and hardened silt. It varies in colour from black or grey to brown or red. *See table at* **rock.**

Silurian The third period of the Palaeozoic Era, from about 439 to 408 million years ago, characterized by the appearance of jawed fish and the rise of the first land plants and invertebrate land animals. *See chart at* **geological time,** pages 148–149.

silver A soft, shiny, white metallic element that is found in many ores, especially together with copper, lead and zinc. It conducts heat and electricity better than any other metal. Silver is used in photography and in making electrical circuits and conductors. *Symbol* **Ag**. *Atomic number* 47. *See* **Periodic Table,** pages 260–261. *See panel at* **element.** ❖ An alloy of silver that contains up to 7.5 per cent copper or another

metal is called **sterling silver,** from which jewellery and silverware are made.

silver iodide A pale-yellow, odourless powder, AgI, that darkens when it is exposed to light. It is used in photography, as an antiseptic in medicine, and in cloud seeding.

silver nitrate A poisonous, clear, crystalline compound, $AgNO_3$, that darkens when exposed to light. It is used in photography and silver plating, and as an external antiseptic.

simian An ape or monkey.

simple fraction A fraction in which both the numerator and denominator are whole numbers, such as $\frac{5}{7}$.

simultaneous equations Two or more equations whose variables have the same values in both or all of the equations.

sin Abbreviation of **sine.**

sine The ratio of the length of the side opposite an acute angle in a right-angled triangle to the length of the hypotenuse.

sinus 1. A cavity or hollow space in a bone of the skull, especially one that connects with the nose. **2.** A channel for the passage of a body fluid, such as blood.

sinusoidal projection A method of making a flat map of the Earth so that the parallels and the prime meridian are straight lines and the other meridians are curved outward from the prime meridian. *Compare* **conic projection, homolosine projection, Mercator projection.**

Sirius The brightest star seen in the night sky. It is in the constellation Canis Major.

skeleton 1. The internal structure of vertebrate

■ **sinusoidal projection**

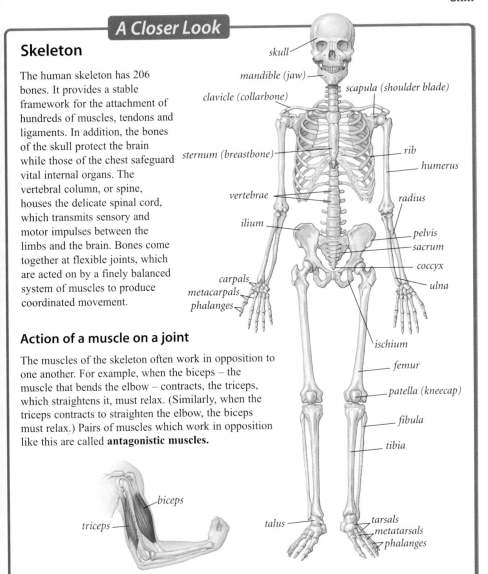

A Closer Look

Skeleton

The human skeleton has 206 bones. It provides a stable framework for the attachment of hundreds of muscles, tendons and ligaments. In addition, the bones of the skull protect the brain while those of the chest safeguard vital internal organs. The vertebral column, or spine, houses the delicate spinal cord, which transmits sensory and motor impulses between the limbs and the brain. Bones come together at flexible joints, which are acted on by a finely balanced system of muscles to produce coordinated movement.

Action of a muscle on a joint

The muscles of the skeleton often work in opposition to one another. For example, when the biceps – the muscle that bends the elbow – contracts, the triceps, which straightens it, must relax. (Similarly, when the triceps contracts to straighten the elbow, the biceps must relax.) Pairs of muscles which work in opposition like this are called **antagonistic muscles.**

skull
mandible (jaw)
clavicle (collarbone)
scapula (shoulder blade)
sternum (breastbone)
rib
humerus
vertebrae
radius
ilium
pelvis
sacrum
coccyx
ulna
carpals
metacarpals
phalanges
ischium
femur
patella (kneecap)
fibula
tibia
biceps
triceps
talus
tarsals
metatarsals
phalanges

animals, composed of bone or cartilage, that supports the body, serves as a framework for the attachment of muscles and protects the vital organs and associated structures. **2.** A hard protective covering or supporting structure of invertebrate animals. *See also* **endoskeleton, exoskeleton.** *—adjective* **skeletal.**

skin The outer covering of a vertebrate animal, consisting of two layers of cells, a thick inner layer (called the dermis) and a thin outer layer (called the epidermis). Structures such as hair, scales or feathers are contained in the skin, as are fat cells, sweat glands and sense organs (called skin receptors). Skin provides a protective barrier against disease-causing microorganisms and against the sun's ultraviolet rays. In warm-blooded animals, it helps maintain stable body temperatures by providing insulation or by increasing blood flow to the surface, which rids the body of excess heat.

Skinner, Burrhus Frederic 1904–1990. US psychologist famous for his work on animal behaviour. He invented the "Skinner Box", a chamber containing mechanisms for an animal to operate and an automatic device for presenting rewards, as a contribution to the study of animal behaviour. In education, his ideas led to the development of "programmed learning", a technique which tries to direct teaching to the needs of each individual and to reinforce learning by regular and immediate feedback.

skull The part of the skeleton that forms the framework of the head, consisting of the bones that protect the brain and the bones of the face. *See more at* **skeleton.**

sky The atmosphere, as seen from a given point on the Earth's surface.

slate A fine-grained metamorphic rock that forms when shale undergoes metamorphosis. Slate splits into thin layers with smooth surfaces. It ranges in colour from grey to black or from red to green, depending on the minerals contained in the shale from which it formed. *See table at* **rock.**

sleep A natural state of rest, occurring at regular intervals, in which the eyes usually close, the muscles relax, and responsiveness to external events decreases. Growth and repair of the tissues of the body are thought to occur during sleep, and energy is conserved and stored. In humans and some other animals, scientists have identified one phase of sleep (called Rapid Eye Movement or REM sleep) as the phase in which dreams occur. See also **REM.**

sleeping sickness An often fatal disease of humans and animals in tropical Africa, causing fever and extreme sluggishness. It is caused by infection with protozoans that are spread by the bite of the tsetse fly.

sleet Water that falls to earth in the form of frozen or partially frozen raindrops.

slide A thin, usually rectangular, glass plate on which something, such as a sample of rock or a

microorganism, is placed for examination under a microscope.

slime A slippery or sticky mucous substance secreted by certain animals, such as slugs or snails.

slime mould Any of various primitive organisms that exist in both unicellular and multicellular stages and are found on decaying plant matter. Slime moulds are classified as protists. ❖ **Cellular slime moulds** live as single, amoeba-like cells that move about feeding on bacteria. When food becomes scarce, they combine into large colonies that develop into multicellular, spore-producing structures. ❖ **Plasmodial slime moulds** exist as a mass of amoeba-like protoplasm (called a plasmodium) that contains many nuclei within a single cell membrane. The slimy masses move along ingesting bacteria and yeast. When food grows scarce, they stop moving and grow multicellular, spore-producing stalks.

slough *noun* The dead outer skin shed by a

Did You Know?

sleep

Shakespeare got it right. He said that *sleep* was the "balm of hurt minds" and that sleep "knits up the ravel'd sleeve of care". In other words, sleep helps overcome the stress of everyday life. So the third of your life you spend asleep is not a waste of time. All warm-blooded animals need to sleep. Studies have shown that animals that are not allowed to sleep for a long enough time can actually die. Babies, of both humans and animals, sleep even more than adults do. Researchers think that babies may sleep so much because it helps the young body continue to develop quickly. Not only are babies' bodies growing, but their brains are, too, and sleep is very important for the brain. During sleep, the brain sorts through experiences and stores important new information for later use. This processing of experiences, in fact, is thought to be a major source of dreams.

reptile or an amphibian. —*verb* To shed an outer layer of skin.

Sm The symbol for **samarium**.

small intestine The long, narrow, coiled section of the intestine that extends from the stomach to the beginning of the large intestine and in mammals is made up of the duodenum, jejunum and ileum. It contains digestive juices full of enzymes and most of the digestion of the food that is eaten takes place in the small intestine. The digested food molecules are also absorbed into the bloodstream in the small intestine. The lining is arranged in many microscopic folds known as villi which greatly increase the surface area both for enzyme action and for the absorption of the digested food molecules.

smallpox A highly infectious and often fatal disease caused by a virus and characterized by a high temperature, headache and pus-filled blisters that result in terrible scarring if the patient survives. Smallpox was dreaded for many centuries, killing millions of people all over the world. Following a worldwide vaccination campaign, smallpox was declared eradicated in 1980, although samples have been preserved in laboratories in the United States and Russia. *See panel at* **Jenner**.

smelt To melt ores in order to extract the metals they contain.

smog 1. A form of air pollution produced when sunlight reacts with hydrocarbons and nitrogen compounds released into the atmosphere, especially from traffic exhaust. Smog is common

■ **smog**
a cloud of smog over Santiago, Chile

in many large cities, especially during hot, sunny weather. It appears as a brownish haze and can irritate the eyes and lungs. **2.** Fog that has become polluted with smoke, especially smoke from burning coal.

smoke Liquid or solid particles dispersed through a gaseous medium.

smut Any of various plant diseases caused by parasitic fungi that form black, powdery masses of spores on the affected parts. Smut chiefly affects cereal grasses like corn and wheat.

Sn The symbol for **tin**.

snake Any of numerous meat-eating reptiles having a long narrow body with no legs, often just one lung, and a forked tongue. The jaws of a snake come apart and the body can expand to swallow prey that is much thicker than the snake itself. Some snakes have venom glands and sharp fangs that can give a poisonous bite.

snout The projecting nose, jaws or front part of the head of an animal.

snow Crystals of ice that form from water vapour in the atmosphere and fall to the ground.

snow line 1. The boundary marking the lowest altitude at which a given area, such as the top of a mountain, is always covered with snow. **2.** The boundary marking the furthest extent around the polar regions at which there is snow cover. The polar snow lines vary with the seasons.

soap A substance used for washing or cleaning, consisting of a mixture of sodium or potassium salts of naturally occurring fatty acids. Like detergents, soaps work by surrounding particles of grease or dirt with their molecules, thereby allowing them to be carried away. Unlike detergents, soap reacts with the minerals common in most water, forming an insoluble film known as scum that remains on fabrics. For this reason soap is not as efficient a cleaner as most detergents. This layer of scum is what causes the rings that are left around the bath when the water drains away. *Compare* **detergent**.

soapstone A soft metamorphic rock composed mostly of the mineral talc.

social science 1. The study of human society and of individual relationships within society. **2.** Any of various academic or scientific disciplines

sociology

relating to such study, including sociology, psychology, anthropology, economics, political science and history.

sociology The scientific study of human social behaviour and its origins, development, organizations and institutions.

Soddy, Frederick 1877–1956. British chemist who was a pioneer in the study of radioactivity. With Ernest Rutherford, he explained the atomic disintegration of radioactive elements. Soddy also coined the word *isotope* to describe elements that were chemically identical but had different atomic weights.

sodium A soft, lightweight, silvery-white metallic element that reacts explosively with water. It is the most abundant alkali metal on Earth, occurring especially in common salt. Sodium is very easily shaped, and its compounds have many important uses in industry. *Symbol* **Na**. *Atomic number* 11. *See* **Periodic Table**, pages 260–261.

sodium bicarbonate *See* **bicarbonate of soda**.

sodium chloride *See* **salt** (sense 1).

sodium fluoride A colourless, crystalline salt, NaF, used to fluoridate water and treat tooth decay. It is also used as an insecticide and a disinfectant.

sodium hydrogen carbonate A soluble carbonate often found in water. Used as an aid to raising in baking and sold as bicarbonate of soda.

sodium hydroxide A strongly alkaline compound, NaOH, used in making chemicals and soaps, in refining petroleum, and as a cleansing agent.

sodium nitrate A poisonous, white, crystalline compound, $NaNO_3$, used in solid rocket propellants, as a fertilizer, and in curing meat.

soft palate *See under* **palate**.

software The programs, programming languages, and data that direct the operations of a computer system. Word processing programs and Internet browsers are examples of software. *Compare* **hardware**.

Did You Know?

solar cell

How can light make electricity? By exciting electrons to break free from their atoms. A *solar cell* has an upper layer of negatively charged silicon, with free-flowing electrons, and a lower layer of positively charged silicon, with atoms that are missing some electrons. The placing of these two charged layers next to each other creates a weak electric field. When light penetrates the solar cell and reaches the positively charged layer, its energy is absorbed by some of the electrons which, in their extra-excited state, break away from their atoms. The electric field along the surface where the two layers meet then pushes these electrons into the negative layer. Meanwhile, other electrons in the positive layer move upwards into the space the first electrons left behind. In the negatively charged silicon layer, the electrons pile up, increasing the electric charge. When the two layers of a solar cell are connected to a circuit, the electrons flow out of the negative layer through the circuit and back to the positive layer, where they are attracted by the spaces left by the missing electrons. Along the way, the electrons power the inner workings of devices like calculators and spacecraft.

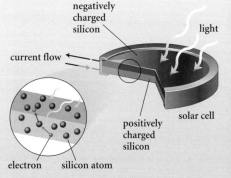

negatively charged silicon

light

current flow

positively charged silicon

solar cell

electron   silicon atom

Did You Know?

solar system

Usually, we think of the *solar system* as simply including the sun and the nine planets. We may even remember the moons that revolve around several planets. But actually, the solar system contains billions of other objects as well and extends far beyond the orbit of Pluto, the outermost planet. Several hundred thousand asteroids have been discovered, and countless smaller asteroids, including the chunks of debris formed during the collision of larger bodies, are out there as well. These smaller particles may come near the Earth – as many as a billion meteors, most the size of a speck of dust, cross through our planet's atmosphere each day. Astronomers have recorded more than 800 comets passing through the inner part of the solar system. Billions more, however, lie in the area surrounding the solar system, in the far reaches of the swarm of comets known as the Oort cloud or in the disc of debris known as the Kuiper belt. All of these objects travel around the sun at high speeds in paths called orbits. Some of these orbits, like those of the planets near the sun, are almost circular. Other orbits, like those of comets that make their way in among the planets, are stretched out into long ellipses.

soil The loose top layer of the Earth's surface, consisting of rock and mineral particles mixed with decayed organic matter (known as humus). Soil provides the support and nutrients that many plants need to grow.

solar 1. Relating to the sun: *solar radiation.* **2.** Using or operated by energy from the sun: *a solar heating system.* **3.** Measured with reference to the sun: *solar time.*

solar cell An electric cell that converts visible light into electrical energy. Solar cells are used as power supplies in calculators, satellites and other devices, and as a prime source of electricity in remote locations. Also called *photovoltaic cell.*

solar eclipse *See under* **eclipse.**

solar energy 1. The energy produced or radiated by the sun. **2.** Energy derived from the sun's radiation. Solar energy is used on Earth in various ways. It is used as a passive source of energy, for example, in the form of sunlight that comes through a window and heats up a room, or as an active source, as in the conversion of sunlight to electrical energy in solar cells.

solar flare A sudden eruption of hydrogen gas on the surface of the sun, usually associated with sunspots.

solar system 1. *Often* **Solar System.** The sun together with the nine planets and all other bodies that orbit the sun, including moons, asteroids and comets. *See more at* **nebular hypothesis.** *See Table,* pages 314–315. **2.** A system of planets or other bodies orbiting another star.

solar wind A stream of high-speed, charged atomic particles flowing outward from the sun's corona.

soldier A sexually undeveloped form of certain ants and termites, having a large head and powerful jaws that serve as fighting weapons.

solenoid A coil of wire that acts as a magnet when an electric current passes through it.

solid 1. *Physics.* One of the three basic forms of matter, composed of molecules that have little or no ability to exchange places. Unlike gases and liquids, a solid has a fixed shape, and unlike

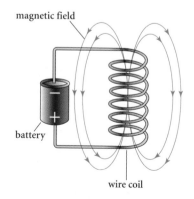

magnetic field

battery

wire coil

■ **solenoid**

The Solar System

Physical Properties of the Planets

Listed below are the nine planets that have been identified in our solar system. The **sidereal period** is the amount of time it takes for a planet to make one complete revolution around the sun. This is measured in relation to the fixed stars, in order to observe the orbit from a place outside our solar system. The sidereal period of Earth is exactly one year. The **rotational period** is the amount of time it takes for a body to make one complete rotation about its own axis. Earth rotates about its axis in

PLANET	EQUATORIAL DIAMETER *kilometres*	MASS $\times 10^{24}$ *kilograms*	SIDEREAL PERIOD *days*
Mercury	4880	0.33	87.97
Venus	12,104	4.87	224.7
Earth	12,756	5.97	365.26
Mars	6794	0.642	696.98
Jupiter	142,984	1900	4332.71
Saturn	120,536	568	10,759.5
Uranus	51,118	86.8	30,685
Neptune	49,532	102	60,190
Pluto	2274	0.0127	90,800

Physical Properties of the Sun

The **corona,** an irregular envelope of gas that surrounds the sun, extends about 13,000,000 kilometres past the sun's visible surface. The low-density gas in the corona ranges in temperature from 1 to 2 million degrees Celsius. In small, dark areas that appear on the surface, known as **sunspots,** the temperature drops by about 1000 to 2000 degrees Celsius. The sun is more than 330,000 times more massive than Earth and contains more than

DIAMETER *kilometres*	MASS $\times 10^{24}$ *kilograms*
1,390,000	1,989,100

slightly less than one sidereal day. Earth rotates from west to east, anticlockwise when seen from above the North Pole. If one of the other planets rotates on its axis clockwise from east to west (the manner opposite to that of Earth), the rotation is called **retrograde** and a minus sign (–) appears in front of the number of days in the planet's rotational period.

ROTATIONAL PERIOD *days*	AVERAGE SURFACE TEMPERATURE *degrees Celsius*	MEAN DISTANCE FROM SUN *(in millions) kilometres*
58.6	176	57.91
–243	457	108.2
0.99	14	149.6
1.03	–55	227.9
0.41	–153	778.3
0.45	–185	1429.4
–0.72	–214	2871.0
0.67	–225	4504.3
–6.39	–236	5913.5

99.8 per cent of the mass of the entire solar system. Because the sun is not a solid body like Earth, its rotational period is not the same everywhere on its surface. Its outer layers rotate at different rates in different places, taking a longer time at the poles. The sun's core, on the other hand, does rotate as a solid body.

TEMPERATURE *degrees Celsius*		ROTATIONAL PERIOD (OUTER LAYERS) *days*	
Surface:	6051	Equator:	25.4
Core:	16,000,000	Poles:	36

gases, a solid also has a fixed volume. **2.** *Mathematics.* A geometric figure that has three dimensions.

solid solution A uniform mixture of substances in solid form. Solid solutions often consist of two or more types of atoms or molecules that share a crystal lattice, as in certain metal alloys. Much of the steel used in construction, for example, is actually a solid solution of iron and carbon. The carbon atoms, which fit neatly within the iron's crystal lattice, add strength to its structure.

solid-state physics The branch of physics that specializes in the study of solids, especially in the electric and magnetic properties of solid crystalline materials, such as semiconductors.

solstice 1. Either of the two moments of the year when the sun is furthest north or south of the celestial equator. In the Northern Hemisphere, the summer solstice occurs on 20 or 21 June and the winter solstice occurs on 21 or 22 December. **2.**

Did You Know?

solution

A *solution* is a homogeneous mixture of two substances, that is, it has the same distribution of particles throughout. Technically speaking, a solution consists of a mixture of one or more *solutes* dissolved in a *solvent*. The particles of solute and solvent are molecules or ions, with one or more solvent molecules bound to each solute particle. Both the solvent and the solute can be solid, liquid or gas, but the solvent is usually liquid. We use solutions every day without realizing it. Sparkling mineral water is a solution of carbon dioxide gas in water. The vinegar we sometimes put in salad dressing or on chips is a solution of ethanoic acid (a liquid) in water. And seawater is a solution of sodium chloride (a solid) and water. Other common solutions are petrol and metal alloys, including the solution of copper and nickel that gets minted as pound coins and other non-paper money.

Either of the two points on the celestial sphere where the apparent path of the sun (known as the ecliptic) reaches its greatest distance from the celestial equator. *Compare* **equinox.**

soluble Capable of being dissolved. Salt, for example, is soluble in water.

solute A substance that is dissolved in another substance, forming a solution.

solution 1. *Chemistry.* A mixture in which particles of one or more substances are distributed uniformly throughout another substance, so that the mixture is homogeneous at the molecular or ionic level. The particles in a solution are smaller than those in either a colloid or a suspension. *Compare* **colloid, suspension. 2.** *Mathematics.* A value or values which, when substituted for a variable in an equation, make the equation true. For example, the solutions to the equation $x^2 = 4$ are 2 and –2.

solvent A substance that can dissolve another substance, or in which another substance is dissolved, forming a solution.

somatic Relating to the body. ❖ The cells of the body with the exception of the reproductive cells (gametes) are known as **somatic cells.** *See panel at* **mitosis.**

Somerville, Mary Fairfax Greig 1780–1872. Scottish astronomer and mathematician whose writings, particularly on astronomy, helped make science understandable to the general public.

sonar 1. A method of detecting and locating underwater objects, such as submarines or schools of fish, through the use of reflected sound waves. Because the speed of sound in water is constant (about 1500 metres per second), the time it takes for a transmitted signal to reach an object and return can be used to calculate the object's distance. **2.** The equipment used in doing this.

sonic barrier *See* **sound barrier.**

sonic boom The shock wave of compressed air caused by any object travelling faster than the speed of sound. The sonic boom of an aeroplane is often audible as a loud, explosive sound, and it sometimes causes damage to structures on the ground.

soot A black, powdery compound consisting mainly of carbon. Soot forms through the

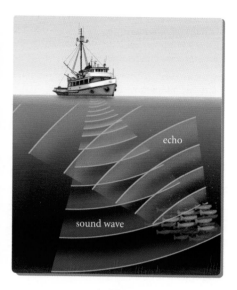

■ sonar

An electrical impulse is converted into sound waves that are transmitted underwater. The sound waves are reflected off objects in their paths, creating echoes that return to the vessel and are picked up by the sonar equipment.

incomplete combustion of wood, coal, oil or other materials.

sorption The taking up and holding of one substance by another. Sorption is used especially as a general term for absorption and adsorption.

sound[1] 1. A type of wave motion that originates as the vibration of a medium (such as a person's vocal cords or a guitar string) and travels through gases, liquids and elastic solids as variations of pressure and density. The loudness of a sound depends on the amplitude of the sound wave. The pitch depends on its frequency. **2.** The sensation produced in the organs of hearing by waves of this type. *See panel at* **ultrasound.**

sound[2] 1. A long body of water, wider than a strait, that connects larger bodies of water. **2.** A long, wide inlet of the sea, often parallel to the coast. The Sound dividing Sweden and Denmark is an example.

sound barrier The sudden, sharp increase in drag experienced by aircraft approaching the speed of sound. Also called *sonic barrier.*

Southern Cross A constellation in the polar region of the Southern Hemisphere near Centaurus.

Southern Hemisphere 1. The half of the Earth south of the equator. **2.** *Astronomy.* The half of the celestial sphere south of the celestial equator.

Did You Know?

sound

The form of energy called *sound* is produced when matter moves or vibrates. The vibrations are transferred to another medium, usually the air, and travel through it as sound waves. You hear a sound when its vibrations reach your eardrum, causing it to vibrate. The pitch of a sound is directly related to the frequency of the vibrations of its waves. People with excellent hearing can hear very low sounds, vibrating about 20 times per second, all the way up to high pitches with frequencies of 20,000 vibrations per second. Other animals can hear sounds at higher vibrations. Bats, for instance, can hear sounds with vibrations as high as 100,000 times a second. The loudness, or intensity, of sound is measured in decibels. The decibel scale is a logarithmic one, which means that an increase of 10 decibels corresponds to an increase in intensity by a factor of 10. Whispering has an intensity of about 10 decibels, while rustling leaves have an intensity of about 20 decibels – this means that rustling leaves are about 10 times louder than whispering. The softest sound humans can hear, at the very threshold of hearing, has a loudness of 0 decibels. A moderate conversation has a loudness of about 60 decibels, and thunder at very close range has a loudness of about 140 decibels. Sound with intensity greater than 85 decibels can cause ear damage, and sound with intensity above 120 decibels causes pain.

■ **South Pole**

southern lights *See* **aurora australis.**

South Pole The southern end of the Earth's axis of rotation, a point in Antarctica.

space 1. A set of points that satisfies some set of geometric rules: *a space of five dimensions.* **2.** The familiar three-dimensional region or field of everyday experience. **3a.** The expanse in which the solar system, stars and galaxies exist; the universe. **b.** The part of this expanse beyond the Earth's atmosphere.

space-time The four dimensions in which all objects are located and all events occur, viewed as a single and continuous framework for existence. Space-time consists of length, width and depth, plus the dimension of time. *See more at* **relativity.**

spawn *noun* **1.** The eggs of water animals such as fish, amphibians and molluscs. **2.** Offspring produced in large numbers. —*verb* To lay eggs; produce spawn.

speciation The formation of new biological species by the development or branching of one species into two or more genetically distinct ones. According to the theory of evolution, all life on Earth has resulted from the speciation of earlier organisms.

species A group of organisms having many characteristics in common and ranking below a genus. Organisms that reproduce sexually and belong to the same species interbreed and produce fertile offspring. *See table at* **taxonomy.**

specific heat capacity The amount of energy required to raise the temperature of unit mass of a substance by unit temperature. The SI unit of specific heat capacity is joules per kilogram per °C.

spectrograph A spectroscope able to photograph or otherwise record spectra. ❖ The photograph of a spectrum produced by a spectrograph is called a **spectrogram.**

spectrometer A spectroscope equipped with devices for measuring the wavelengths of the radiation observed by it.

spectroscope Any of various instruments used to measure the wavelengths and intensity of radiation by splitting the radiation up into a spectrum. In a light spectroscope, light enters a narrow slit, is focused into a thin beam of parallel rays by a lens, and passes through a prism that

Did You Know?

space-time

Before Albert Einstein's theory of relativity, people thought they lived in a three-dimensional world. Time was considered to be a completely separate entity. But Einstein realized that a more correct view put time and the three space dimensions on equal footing. Physicists call the four-dimensional framework within which they interpret nature *space-time.* In space-time two events that appear to happen at exactly the same time to one person in one place can appear to happen at different times to someone else in a different place. In other words, whether or not the events occur at the same time depends on the position and movement of the observers. How is this possible? Think of thunder and lightning. Lightning reaches the eye at the speed of light, while thunder reaches the ear at the much slower speed of sound. To an observer at the precise spot where lightning strikes, the thunder seems to come at the same moment. Several kilometres away, however, the lightning appears well before the thunder is heard. Similarly, if one observer were moving faster than the other towards or away from the lightning strike, each observer would experience the events at different time intervals. As Einstein's theory proved, everything in space-time is relative.

separates it into a spectrum. Other types of spectroscopes, such as the mass spectroscope, use magnetic fields to separate the incoming radiation.

spectrum (*plural* **spectra** *or* **spectrums**) 1. An arrangement of electromagnetic radiation by frequency and wavelength. As a whole, the electromagnetic spectrum ranges from radio waves to gamma rays. The visible spectrum is a band of colours seen when white light is broken up according to wavelengths, as when passing through a prism or striking water drops and producing a rainbow. 2. A distribution of charged atomic or subatomic particles arranged in order of masses, especially when arranged by a mass spectroscope.

speed *See panel at* **velocity.**

speleology The exploration and scientific study of caves.

sperm 1. In male animals, the reproductive cell whose nucleus is capable of fusing with the nucleus of an egg cell to form a new organism; a spermatozoon. A sperm has half as many chromosomes as the other cells of the body and moves to unite with the egg. 2. In plants, algae and certain fungi, the reproductive cell whose nucleus is capable of fusing with the nucleus of a female reproductive cell to form a new organism. A sperm has half as many chromosomes as the other cells of the organism and moves to unite with the egg.

spermaceti A white, waxy substance obtained from the head of the sperm whale and sometimes other whales, porpoises and dolphins, and used to make candles, ointments and cosmetics.

spermatophyte A plant that produces seeds, such as a conifer or flowering plant.

spermatozoon (*plural* **spermatozoa**) The mature reproductive cell of male animals. It is produced by the testis and is capable of fertilizing a female reproductive cell. A single spermatozoon carries only half as many chromosomes as the other cells of the body.

sphagnum Any of various greyish mosses that grow in swamps and bogs and decompose to form peat.

sphere A three-dimensional geometric surface having all of its points the same distance from a given point.

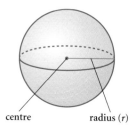

■ **sphere**
The volume (V) of a sphere can be calculated using the following equation:
$V = \frac{4}{3}\pi r^3$.

centre   radius (r)

spheroid A three-dimensional geometric surface generated by rotating an ellipse on or about one of its axes.

sphincter A ring-shaped muscle that encircles an opening or passage in the body. Contraction and relaxation of a sphincter closes and opens the passage.

Spica A bright binary star in the constellation Virgo.

spicule A needle-like structure or part, such as one of the mineral structures supporting the soft tissue of certain invertebrates, especially sponges.

spike 1. An ear of grain, such as wheat. 2. A long cluster of stalkless flowers, as in gladioli.

spina bifida A congenital defect in which the vertebral column is not fully closed, causing part of the spinal cord to bulge out. Spina bifida often results in damage to the spinal cord.

spinal column *See* **vertebral column.**

spinal cord The long, cord-like part of the central nervous system that is enclosed within the vertebral column (the backbone) and descends from the base of the brain. It branches to form the nerves that convey impulses to and from the tissues of the body.

spindle A network of cell fibres that forms in the nucleus during cell division. Duplicate strands of chromosomes attach along the centre of the spindle before separating and moving to opposite ends of the cell. *See more at* **meiosis, mitosis.**

spine 1. *See* **vertebral column.** 2. A sharp-pointed projection on a plant, especially a hard, narrow modified leaf, as on a cactus. *See more at* leaf. *See panels at* **cactus, thorn.**

spinneret One of the small openings in the back part of a spider or silk-producing insect larva,

spiracle

white matter grey matter

spinal nerve

inner and outer membranes

■ **spinal cord**

left: *section of vertebral column showing the spinal cord within the column*

right: *segment of spinal cord with nerve fibres arising from it*

---

through which the sticky fluid that dries into silk is released.

spiracle An opening through which certain animals breathe, such as the breathing holes of the stingray or one of the openings in the exoskeleton of an insect.

spirillum (*plural* **spirilla**) Any of various bacteria that are shaped like a spiral.

spirochaete Any of various bacteria that are shaped like a spiral, some of which can cause disease in humans.

spirogyra Any of various freshwater green algae having spiral-shaped bands of chloroplasts.

spleen An organ in vertebrate animals that in humans is located on the left side near the stomach. Mainly composed of lymph nodes and blood vessels, the spleen filters the blood, stores red blood cells, destroys old red blood cells, and produces white blood cells called lymphocytes.

splice To join together genes or gene fragments or to insert them into a cell or other structure, such as a virus. In genetic engineering, scientists splice together genetic material to produce new genes or to alter a genetic structure.

sponge 1. Any of various primitive invertebrate animals that live in the sea and are attached to

rocks or other objects. Unlike other animals, sponges have bodies with only one type of tissue and no organs. The bodies have many passages and chambers that water flows through so that food can be filtered out. **2.** The soft, porous, absorbent skeleton of certain of these animals, used for bathing, cleaning and other purposes.

spongy mesophyll A leaf tissue consisting of loosely arranged, irregularly shaped cells that have chloroplasts. The spongy parenchyma has many spaces between cells to facilitate the circulation of air and the exchange of gases. It lies just below the palisade layer. Also called *spongy parenchyma*. See more at **photosynthesis**.

spontaneous combustion The bursting into flame of a mass of material as a result of chemical reactions within the substance, without the addition of heat from an external source. Oily rags and damp hay, for example, are subject to spontaneous combustion.

sporangium (*plural* **sporangia**) A plant cell or structure in which spores are produced. Ferns, fungi, mosses and algae release spores from sporangia.

spore 1. A usually one-celled reproductive body

■ **sponge**
tube sponges

320

that can grow into a new organism without uniting with another cell. Spores have only a single set of chromosomes. Fungi, algae, plants that do not bear seeds, and certain protozoans reproduce asexually by spores. **2.** A similar one-celled body in seed-bearing plants that develops into either the embryo sac or a pollen grain. **3.** A rounded, inactive form that certain bacteria assume under conditions of extreme temperature, dryness or lack of food. The bacterium develops a waterproof cell wall that protects it from being dried out or damaged.

sporophyte In plants, fungi and certain algae, the individual organism or generation of organisms that produces spores. A sporophyte is formed from the union of the nuclei of male and female reproductive cells, and each of its cells has two sets of chromosomes. In non-vascular plants, such as mosses and liverworts, the sporophyte is a small plant or a part that grows on top of the gametophyte. In vascular plants, such as ferns, grasses, conifers and flowering plants, the sporophyte is the main form of the plant. *Compare* **gametophyte.**

spreading zone *See* **divergent plate boundary.**

spring 1. A device, such as a coil of wire, that returns to its original shape after being compressed or stretched. Because of their ability to return to their original shape, springs are used to store energy, as in mechanical clocks, and to absorb or lessen energy, as in the suspension system of vehicles. **2.** A small stream of water flowing naturally from the ground. **3.** The season of the year between winter and summer, during which the weather becomes warmer and plants revive. In the Northern Hemisphere, it extends from the vernal equinox to the summer solstice.

spring tide A tide in which the difference between high and low tide is the greatest. Spring tides occur when the moon is either new or full, and the sun and the moon are aligned with the Earth. When this is the case, their collective gravitational pull on the Earth's water is strengthened. *Compare* **neap tide.** *See more at* **tide.**

spruce Any of various evergreen trees or shrubs that have short, four-sided needles and hanging or drooping cones. Spruces are found chiefly in cooler temperate regions in the Northern Hemisphere.

spur A ridge of high land projecting into a valley as a result of glaciation.

squall A brief, sudden and violent windstorm, often accompanied by rain or snow.

square *noun* **1.** A rectangle having four equal sides. **2.** The product that results when a number or quantity is multiplied by itself. The square of 8, for example, is 64. —*adjective* Of, being or using units that express the measure of area: *square kilometres.* —*verb* To multiply a number, quantity or expression by itself.

square number An integer, such as 4 or 9, that is the square of another integer.

square root A number that, when squared, yields a given number. For example, since $5 \times 5 = 25$, the square root of 25 is 5. The written symbol is $\sqrt{\ }$.

Sr The symbol for **strontium.**

stable 1. A physical system is stable if it is unlikely to undergo a change of state by virtue of the energy stored in it. For example, a ruler lying flat on a table is stable, while a ruler standing on end is unstable, since the ruler standing on end has more gravitational potential energy which can be decreased if the ruler topples. **2.** Relating to a chemical substance that does not easily decompose or react with other substances. Water is an example of a stable compound, while argon is a stable element. By contrast, nitroglycerine is an unstable substance, liable to decompose violently under the slightest shock.

stainless steel Any of various steel alloys that are resistant to rusting and corrosion because they contain chromium and nickel.

stalactite A cylindrical or conical mineral deposit projecting downwards from the roof of a cave or cavern, formed by dripping water saturated with minerals. Stalactites form gradually as the minerals precipitate out of the saturated water. They usually consist of calcite, but can also consist of other minerals. *See panel on* page 322.

stalagmite A cylindrical or conical mineral deposit, similar to a stalactite, but built up from the floor of a cave or cavern. *See panel on* page 322.

stalk 1. *Botany.* **a.** The main stem of a plant. **b.**

Usage

stalactite/stalagmite

If you find it hard to remember the difference between stalagmites and stalactites, you are not alone. Both words refer to mineral deposits that form in caves. The source of each word is the Greek word *stalassein,* which means "to drip". This is appropriate, since each kind of deposit is formed by the dripping of mineral-rich water within caves. The difference is in position and orientation. A *stalactite* is an icicle-shaped deposit that hangs from the roof of a cavern, and a *stalagmite* is a conical mineral deposit that extends up from the floor of a cavern. And what do you call it when a stalagmite and stalactite meet and form a column? What else but a *stalacto-stalagmite!*

A slender structure that supports a plant part, such as a flower or leaf. **2.** A slender supporting or connecting part of an animal, such as the eyestalk of a lobster.

stamen The male reproductive organ of a flower, consisting of a filament and a pollen-bearing anther at its tip. *See more at* **flower.**

staminate 1. Having one or more stamens. **2.**

■ **stalactite/stalagmite**
Squoyah Caverns, Alabama, USA

Having stamens but no pistils. Male flowers are staminate.

standard time The time in any of the 24 time zones into which the Earth's surface is divided. Within each time zone, all clocks are set to the same time. The reference point on the Earth's surface is the zero meridian of longitude, which passes through the former site of the Royal Observatory at Greenwich in London. Time zones are described by their distance east or west of Greenwich.

standing wave A wave that does not appear to move. Standing waves occur when two similar waves travel in opposite directions between two fixed points, called nodes, at which there is no movement. Standing waves can be transverse waves, like waves in the sea, or longitudinal waves, like sound waves. Also called *stationary wave.*

stapes The innermost of the three small bones, called ossicles, of the middle ear. The stapes is also called the stirrup.

staphylococcus (*plural* **staphylococci**) Any of various bacteria that are normally found on the skin and mucous membranes of warm-blooded animals. *Staphylococcus* bacteria can cause a number of infections in humans, especially in open wounds. They can be fatal, particularly as some forms of *Staphylococcus* have developed resistance to most antibiotics.

star A celestial body that produces its own light and consists of a mass of gas held together by its own gravity. Nuclear fusion in the core of a star is the source of its energy.

starch 1. A carbohydrate that is the chief form of stored energy in plants, especially wheat, maize, rice and potatoes. Starch is a kind of polysaccharide and forms a white, tasteless powder when purified. It is an important source of nutrition and is also used to make adhesives, paper and textiles. **2.** Any of various substances, including natural starch, used to stiffen fabrics.

starfish Any of various invertebrate sea animals having a star-shaped body usually with five arms. The arms have rows of little suckers on the undersides, called tube feet, with which the animal moves around and grasps prey. Starfish are echinoderms, related to the sea urchins.

state of matter One of the principal conditions

A Closer Look

Star

A star is a giant sphere of gas that produces its own light by making its own energy. It generates this energy through nuclear fusion in its core, using as fuel the elements that make it up. Fusion in a star combines atoms of lighter elements, such as hydrogen, into different, heavier elements, such as helium. A massive star can burn its fuel into elements as heavy as iron. Nuclear fusion begins when a star is fully formed out of a nebula and ends when a smaller star burns out and becomes a white dwarf or when a massive star's iron core collapses in a supernova. Because a star's composition changes as it burns its fuel, it goes through a series of stages during the course of its life, hundreds of millions or billions of years long.

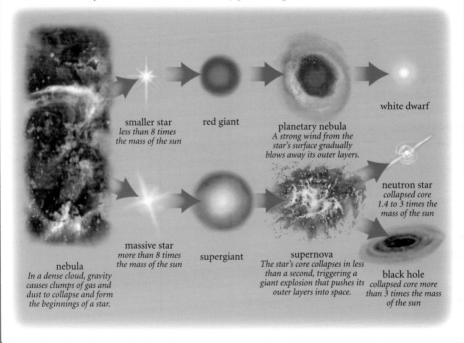

smaller star
less than 8 times the mass of the sun

red giant

planetary nebula
A strong wind from the star's surface gradually blows away its outer layers.

white dwarf

neutron star
collapsed core 1.4 to 3 times the mass of the sun

nebula
In a dense cloud, gravity causes clumps of gas and dust to collapse and form the beginnings of a star.

massive star
more than 8 times the mass of the sun

supergiant

supernova
The star's core collapses in less than a second, triggering a giant explosion that pushes its outer layers into space.

black hole
collapsed core more than 3 times the mass of the sun

in which matter exists. Matter is traditionally divided into three states – solid, liquid and gas. Ice, liquid water and steam, for example, are three states of matter of the same substance. The electrically neutral condition known as plasma is often considered a fourth state of matter.

static *adjective* **1.** Having no motion; being at rest. *Compare* **dynamic. 2.** Relating to or producing static electricity. —*noun* Distortion or interruption of a broadcast signal, such as crackling in a receiver or specks on a television screen, produced when static electricity or electricity in the atmosphere disturbs signal reception.

static electricity 1. Electric charge that accumulates on an object rather than flowing through it as a current. Static electricity forms especially when two objects that are not good electrical conductors are rubbed together, so that electrons from one of the objects rub off onto the other. This happens, for example, when combing one's hair or taking off a jumper. *See panel at*

charge. 2. An electric discharge, such as lightning, resulting from the accumulation of such a charge.

statics The branch of physics that deals with objects that are not in motion and with forces that are offset or counterbalanced by each other.

stationary wave *See* **standing wave.**

statistics 1. *Used with a singular verb.* The branch of mathematics that deals with the collection, organization, analysis and interpretation of numerical data. Statistics is especially useful in drawing general conclusions about a set of data from a sample of it. **2.** *Used with a plural verb.* Numerical data used in drawing general conclusions from a sample of it.

STD Abbreviation of **sexually transmitted disease.**

steady state A stable condition that does not change over time or in which any one change is continually balanced by another.

steady state universe A model of the universe in which the ratio of the amount of matter to volume remains the same as the universe continually gets larger. This model requires the unending creation of matter to allow for the unending expansion of the universe. It is generally believed to be discredited by the discovery of radiation remaining from the big bang. *Compare* **big bang.**

steam Water in its gaseous state, especially at a temperature above the boiling point of water (above 100°C at sea level). *See panel at* **vapour.**

steam engine An engine in which the energy of hot steam is converted into mechanical power, especially an engine in which the steam expands in a closed cylinder and drives a piston.

steel Any of various hard, strong and flexible alloys of iron and carbon. Often, other metals are added to give the steel a particular property. Chromium and nickel, for example, are added to steel to make it stainless. Steel is widely used in many kinds of tools and as a structural material in building.

stegosaurus *or* **stegosaur** Any of several plant-eating dinosaurs of the Jurassic and Cretaceous Periods. Stegosaurus had a spiked tail and an arched back with a double row of large, triangular, upright and bony plates. Although stegosaurs grew to around 6 metres in length, they had tiny heads with brains the size of a walnut.

stellar Relating to or consisting of stars: *stellar life cycles.*

stem 1. The main, often long or slender part of a plant that usually grows upward above the ground and supports other parts, such as branches and leaves. Some underground plant structures, such as rhizomes and corms, are stems rather than roots. **2.** A slender stalk supporting or connecting another plant part, such as a leaf or flower.

stem cell A cell that has the potential to develop into any of a number of different types of cells. Embryos have stem cells that can develop into almost any kind of body cell. Certain tissues in adults also produce stem cells, although the range of cells that they can develop into is limited.

steppe A vast, semi-arid, grassy plain, as found in southeast Europe, Siberia and central North America.

Steptoe, Patrick Christopher 1913–1988. English gynaecologist and reproduction biologist who pioneered in vitro fertilization. He had long been interested in laparoscopy (a technique of viewing the abdominal cavity through a small incision in the umbilicus) and in problems of fertility. He met Robert Edwards in 1968, and together they worked on the problem of in vitro fertilization of human embryos, which 10 years later resulted in the birth of a baby (Louise Brown) after in vitro fertilization and implantation in her mother's uterus. He continued to refine and develop infertility treatments from then onwards.

stereochemistry The branch of chemistry that is concerned with the spatial arrangements of atoms in molecules and with the chemical and physical effects of these arrangements.

stereoscope An optical instrument through which two slightly different views of the same scene are presented, one to each eye, giving an illusion of three dimensions.

sterile 1. Not able to produce offspring, seeds or fruit; unable to reproduce. **2.** Producing little or no plant life; barren: *a desolate, sterile region.* **3.** Free from disease-causing microorganisms: *a sterile bandage.* *—noun* **sterility.**

Did You Know?

stem cell

In 1998 there was a scientific breakthrough – two different teams in America managed to grow stem cells from human embryos in cultures in the laboratory, and keep them alive for several months. Why was this so exciting? Because embryonic stem cells can potentially grow into almost any type of tissue in the body. The hope is that eventually they can be used to grow new organs to be used for transplants – so that people will never again die waiting for a new heart, liver or kidneys. However, there is a big problem. The embryos used to provide the stem cells were either spare embryos produced during infertility treatment, or embryos which had been aborted. Some people have very strong objections to this use of human embryos. Others feel that the possible benefits are enormous and that, if the parents give permission, there is no reason why embryo tissue should not be used. There may be two possible solutions to this dilemma. Embryonic stem cells can be retrieved from the umbilical cord of babies immediately after birth, and if they can be cultured they would provide a ready source of cells. Secondly, it seems increasingly likely that stem cells from adults, although more specialized, may be able to be cultured and stimulated to form different tissues in the laboratory. Whatever happens, stem cells look set to play an important role in the medicine of the future.

sterling silver *See under* **silver.**

sternum A long, flat bone located in the centre of the chest, serving as a support for the collarbone and ribs. Also called *breastbone. See more at* **skeleton.**

steroid 1. Any of a class of organic compounds having as a basis 17 carbon atoms arranged in four rings. Steroids include the sex hormones, such as testosterone, and hormones produced by the adrenal glands. They also include sterols, such as cholesterol, and certain forms of vitamins. **2.** Any of various hormones having the structure of a steroid that are made synthetically, especially for use in medicine.

sterol Any of various alcohols having the structure of a steroid, including cholesterol. Sterols are found in the tissues of animals, plants, fungi and yeasts.

Stevens, Nettie Marie 1861–1912. American biologist who identified the role of X and Y chromosomes in determining the sex of an organism. Stevens studied the chromosomes of mealworm beetles, first establishing that chromosomes are inherited in pairs. She later showed that eggs fertilized by X-carrying sperm produced female offspring, while Y-carrying sperm produced a male. She extended this work to studies of sex determination in various plants and insects.

stigma The sticky tip of a flower pistil, on which pollen is deposited at the beginning of pollination. *See more at* **flower.**

stimulant A drug or other substance, such as caffeine, that speeds up or excites a body system, especially the nervous system.

stimulus (*plural* **stimuli**) Something that causes a response in a body part or organism. A stimulus may be internal or external. Sense organs, such as the ear, and sensory receptors, such as those in the skin, are sensitive to external stimuli such as sound and touch.

stipule One of the usually small, paired parts resembling leaves at the base of a leafstalk in certain plants, such as roses and beans.

stolon A form of asexual reproduction in plants. A stem grows down, touches the ground and then grows up again. Roots form at the point where the stem touches the ground, followed by shoots to form a new independent plant. Blackberries (brambles) reproduce using stolons.

stoma (*plural* **stomata**) **1.** *Botany.* One of the tiny openings in the outer surface of a plant leaf or stem, through which gases and water vapour pass. Most stomata are on the underside of leaves. **2.** *Zoology.* A mouth-like opening, such as the oral cavity of a nematode.

stomach 1. A sac-like, muscular organ in vertebrate animals that stores food and is a main organ of digestion. It is located between the oesophagus and the small intestine. **2.** A similar digestive structure of many invertebrates. **3.** Any of the four compartments into which the stomach of a ruminant is divided; the rumen, reticulum, omasum or abomasum.

stone **1.** *Geology.* A general term for rock, especially as used in construction. **2.** *Botany.* The hard seed of certain fruits, such as plums and cherries. **3.** *Medicine.* A hard mass of minerals or other substance, such as cholesterol, that forms in a body part or organ: *kidney stones.*

Stone Age The earliest known period of human culture, marked by the use of stone tools. *See* **Mesolithic, Neolithic, Palaeolithic.**

Stoney, George Johnstone 1826–1911. Irish physicist who in 1874 calculated an approximate value for the charge on the electron, a term he himself introduced, and made important contributions to the theory of gases and spectroscopy.

straight angle An angle having a measure of 180°.

strain **1.** A group of organisms of the same species, sharing certain characteristics not typical of the entire species but minor enough not to warrant classification as a separate breed or variety: *a drug-resistant strain of bacteria.* **2.** The extent to which a body is distorted when it is subjected to a deforming force, such as stress. The distortion can involve both a change in shape and in size. For example, linear strain (whether tensile or compressive) is defined as the change in length of the object divided by its original length. Strain is often expressed as a percentage, positive if the length or volume has increased, negative if it has decreased. ❖ In **elastic strain** the distorted body returns to its original shape and size when the force is removed. ❖ In **plastic strain** the distorted body does not return to its original shape and size even after the force has been removed. *Compare* **stress.** *See more at* **Hooke's law.**

strait A narrow waterway joining two larger bodies of water. The Strait of Gibraltar, for example, connects the Mediterranean Sea to the Atlantic Ocean.

stratification Formation or deposition of layers, as of rock or sediments.

stratocumulus A low-lying, often patchy cloud formation occurring in extensive horizontal layers with distinct, rounded tops.

stratosphere The layer of the Earth's atmosphere lying above the troposphere and below the mesosphere, from the tropopause to about 50 kilometres above the Earth's surface. In the stratosphere, temperatures rise slightly with altitude.

stratum (*plural* **strata** *or* **stratums**) **1.** A layer of rock whose composition is more or less the same throughout. A particular rock stratum is visibly different from the rock strata above and below it. **2.** A layer of tissue, as of the skin or another organ.

stratus (*plural* **strati**) A low-lying, greyish cloud layer that sometimes produces drizzle. A stratus cloud that is close to the ground or water is called fog.

streak The characteristic colour of a mineral after it has been ground into a powder. Because the streak of a mineral is not always the same as

■ **stratification**
limestone and sandstone strata near Sedona, Arizona, USA

its natural colour, it is a useful tool in mineral identification.

streamline To design or construct something so that it offers the least resistance to the flow of a fluid, especially air or water.

streptococcus (*plural* **streptococci**) Any of various bacteria that are normally found on the skin and mucous membranes and in the digestive tract of mammals. Different types of *Streptococcus* cause a variety of infections in humans, including sore throats, scarlet fever, pneumonia and blood infections.

stress 1. The force per unit cross-sectional area that tends to distort or deform something by compressing or stretching it. The unit of stress is the pascal. *Compare* **strain**. *See more at* **Hooke's law. 2.** A reaction by an organism to a disturbing or dangerous situation. In humans and other animals, the body's initial response to stress includes a rise in heart rate and blood pressure and a heightened state of alertness. A certain amount of stress may be necessary for an organism to survive, but too much stress can lead to ill health.

striation One of a number of parallel lines or grooves on the surface of a rock. Striations form when pieces of rock frozen into the base of a glacier move across the rock and scratch it, or when two blocks of rock along opposite sides of a fault plane slide past each other, scratching the outer surfaces of the rocks.

strike-slip fault A geological fault in which the blocks of rock on either side of the fault slide horizontally in opposite directions along the line of the fault plane. *See more at* **fault.**

string theory A theory in physics that views subatomic particles as string-like objects floating in space-time rather than as point-like objects. Space-time in string theory can have up to nine dimensions of space, plus the dimension of time. *See also* **superstring theory.**

strip mine An open mine, especially a coal mine, whose seams or outcrops run close to ground level and are exposed by the removal of overlying soil.

strobe light A lamp that produces very short, intense flashes of light by means of an electric discharge in a gas. The ability of strobe lights to

■ **strip mine**

"freeze" the motion of rapidly moving objects makes them very useful in photography and in making measurements of vibration or other types of high-speed motion.

stroke A sudden interruption in the normal functioning of the brain, often resulting in slurred speech and loss of muscle control and feeling on one side of the body. Strokes are usually caused by a reduction in blood flow to a part of the brain as a result of a blood clot forming or a blood vessel bursting in the brain.

strong nuclear force A force between elementary or subatomic particles that holds quarks together to form protons and neutrons, and also binds protons and neutrons together in the atomic nucleus. The strong nuclear force is one of the four basic forces in nature, along with gravity, the electromagnetic force and the weak nuclear force. Also called *strong interaction.*

strontium A soft, silvery metallic element that is an alkaline-earth metal and occurs naturally only as a sulphate or carbonate. One of its isotopes is used in the radiometric dating of rocks. Because strontium salts burn with a red flame, they are used to make fireworks and signal flares. *Symbol* **Sr**. *Atomic number* 38. *See* **Periodic Table,** pages 260–261.

strontium-90 A radioactive isotope of strontium having a mass number of 90 and a half-life of 28 years. Strontium-90 is the most dangerous component of the fallout from nuclear explosions because it can be absorbed by the body. It is also used in medicine to treat cancer.

structural formula A chemical formula that shows how the atoms making up a compound are arranged within the molecule. For example, the structural formula of aspirin is $CH_3COOC_6H_4COOH$, indicating that it is an acetate (CH_3COO) of a phenyl (C_6H_4) organic acid ($COOH$). Since structural formulae can get quite long, molecular formulae are sometimes used instead. *Compare* **molecular formula.**

strychnine An extremely poisonous, white crystalline compound derived from certain plants. It is used as a rat poison and was formerly used in medicine to stimulate the nervous system.

sturgeon Any of various large, primitive freshwater or saltwater fish having bony plates rather than true scales on its body. It is widely used for food, and its roe is a source of caviar.

style The slender part of a flower pistil, extending from the ovary to the stigma. *See more at* **flower.**

sub– A prefix that means: **1.** Underneath or lower, as in *subsoil.* **2.** A subordinate or secondary part of something else, as in *subphylum.* **3.** Less than completely, as in *subtropical.*

subatomic particle One of the basic units of which atoms and all matter are made. Protons, neutrons and electrons are subatomic particles.

subclass A subdivision of a class of organisms. A subclass contains one or more orders.

subcutaneous Located or placed just beneath the skin.

subduction zone A convergent plate boundary where one plate sinks (subducts) beneath the other, usually because it is denser. *See more at* **tectonic boundary.**

subkingdom A subdivision of a kingdom of organisms. A subkingdom contains one or more phyla.

sublimation The process of changing from a solid to a gas, or from a gas to a solid, without passing through an intermediate liquid phase.

suborder A subdivision of an order of organisms. A suborder contains one or more families.

subphylum (*plural* **subphyla**) A subdivision of a phylum of organisms. A subphylum contains one or more classes.

subset A set whose members are all contained in

Did You Know?

subatomic particles

At the beginning of the 20th century, scientists thought that atoms were the smallest units of matter. This view started to change following some experiments in the late 1800s involving electrical discharges. By the early 1900s it was clear that these discharges were composed of a new kind of particle, one that was much lighter than an atom of the lightest chemical element, hydrogen. These particles were named *electrons.* Furthermore, it was discovered that atoms themselves contained electrons; the electron thus became the first known *subatomic particle.* Since electrons have negative electrical charge, but the atoms containing them are neutral in charge, researchers believed that atoms must also contain positively charged particles that balanced the negatively charged electrons. This idea, together with research into radioactivity, led Ernest Rutherford to the discovery of the atomic nucleus in 1911. Rutherford saw the nucleus as the home of these positively charged particles (now called *protons*). Further experiments on radioactivity showed, by 1932, that the nucleus also contained a third kind of particle, the *neutron.* While electrons, protons and neutrons are the most familiar subatomic particles, they are not the only ones: dozens more have since been identified. Scientists now know that many subatomic particles are themselves made up of smaller units called *elementary particles,* such as neutrinos and quarks.

another set. The set of positive integers, for example, is a subset of the set of integers.

subsoil The layer of earth below the surface soil.

subspecies A subdivision of a species of organisms, usually based on geographical distribution.

substrate 1. The material or substance on which an enzyme acts. *See panel at* **enzyme. 2.** The surface on which plants, algae or certain animals, such as barnacles, live or grow. A substrate may serve as a source of food for an organism or simply provide support.

subtraction The act, process or operation of subtracting one number or quantity from another to compute their difference.

subtractive 1. Being any of the primary colours cyan, magenta or yellow, which can be combined using overlapping filters to produce all other colours. The filters absorb certain wavelengths and allow others to pass through. *See more at* **colour. 2.** *Mathematics.* Marked by or involving subtraction.

subtrahend A number subtracted from another. For example, in the expression 4 – 3, 3 is the subtrahend.

subtropical Relating to the regions of the Earth bordering on the tropics, just north of the Tropic of Cancer or just south of the Tropic of Capricorn. Subtropical regions are the warmest parts of the two Temperate Zones.

succession The gradual replacement of one type of ecological community by another, involving a series of changes especially in the dominant vegetation. For example, if a meadow is left unmowed, its grasses might be replaced first by fast-growing bushes and conifers, which after some years might be replaced in turn by slower-growing hardwoods. *See more at* **climax community.**

succulent A plant having fleshy leaves or stems that store water. Cacti are succulents.

sucker 1. *Zoology.* A part by which an animal sucks blood from or uses suction to cling to another animal. Leeches and remoras have suckers. **2.** *Botany.* A shoot growing from the base or root of a tree or shrub and giving rise to a new plant.

sucrose A crystalline sugar having the formula

Did You Know?

sublimation

We've all seen a solid heated to a liquid and a liquid heated to a gas. Ice, for instance, melts to become liquid water, and liquid water can be boiled away as steam. However, under the right conditions of pressure and temperature, something else can happen: the solid can turn directly into a gas. This strange process is called *sublimation.* The word also refers to the reverse situation, when a gas solidifies without becoming liquid first. The most familiar example of a solid turning into a gas is probably that of dry ice. Solid carbon dioxide – dry ice – seems to give off smoke at room temperature. This "smoke" is actually the solid carbon dioxide turning directly into a gas. Dry ice is useful for packing certain materials that need to stay cold, since it doesn't melt and get everything wet. A common example of a gas turning directly into a solid is the formation of frost from the extremely rapid cooling of water vapour.

$C_{12}H_{22}O_{11}$, found in many plants, especially sugar cane and sugar beet. Sucrose is used widely as a sweetener.

suction An act or force that reduces the pressure in a space, causing a fluid or solid to flow into it from a region of greater pressure.

Suess, Eduard 1831–1914. Austrian geologist who was the first to propose the existence of the early supercontinent Gondwanaland. He also investigated the origin of the Alps.

sugar 1. Any of a class of crystalline carbohydrates, such as sucrose, glucose or lactose, that dissolve in water and have a characteristic sweet taste. **2.** Sucrose.

sulphate A chemical compound made from sulphuric acid and containing the group SO_4.

sulphide A chemical compound of sulphur and another element or radical, such as hydrogen sulphide.

sulphur A pale-yellow, brittle nonmetallic element that occurs widely in nature, especially in volcanic deposits, many common minerals, natural gas and petroleum. It is used to make gunpowder and fertilizer, to vulcanize rubber and to produce sulphuric acid. *Symbol* **S**. *Atomic number* 16. *See* **Periodic Table**, pages 260–261.

sulphur dioxide A colourless, poisonous gas or liquid, SO_2, that has a strong odour. It is formed naturally by volcanic activity, and is a waste gas produced by burning coal and oil and by many industrial processes, such as smelting. It is also a hazardous air pollutant and a major contributor to acid rain.

sulphuric acid A strong corrosive acid, H_2SO_4. It combines very easily with water, making it a good drying agent, and is the most widely used acid in industry.

sum The result of adding numbers or quantities. The sum of 6 and 9, for example, is 15, and the sum of $4x$ and $5x$ is $9x$.

summer The usually warmest season of the year, occurring between spring and autumn. In the Northern Hemisphere, it extends from the summer solstice to the autumnal equinox.

summer solstice In the Northern Hemisphere, the solstice that occurs on 20 or 21 June, marking the beginning of summer and the day of the year with the longest period of sunlight. *Compare* **winter solstice**.

sun 1. Often **Sun**. The star that is orbited by all of the planets and other bodies of our solar system and that supplies the heat and light that sustain life on Earth. It has a diameter of about 1,390,000 kilometres, an average distance from Earth of about 150 million kilometres, and a mass about 330,000 times that of Earth. *See table at* **solar system**, pages 314–315. *See panel at* **dwarf star**. **2.** A star that is the centre of a system of planets.

sunspot Any of the relatively cool dark spots that appear in groups on the surface of the sun. Sunspots are associated with strong magnetic fields.

superconductor A metal or an alloy that at a very low temperature (close to absolute zero) conducts electric current with almost no resistance. Most superconductors work only at temperatures approaching –273.15°C, but a few alloys become superconductors around –129°C. Scientists hope to find materials that become superconductors closer to room temperature.

supercontinent A large continent that, according to the theory of plate tectonics, is thought to have split into smaller continents in the geological past. Pangaea and Gondwanaland are supercontinents. *See panel at* **Gondwanaland**.

supergiant A star that is larger, brighter and more massive than a giant star. Supergiants, such as Betelgeuse or Rigel, are thousands of times brighter than the sun. *See more at* **star**.

supergravity The part of supersymmetry theory that combines the theory of gravity with the theories of other fundamental forces (such as the strong force and the electromagnetic force) by assuming the existence of an exchange particle for gravitational force, known as the graviton.

supernova (*plural* **supernovae** *or* **supernovas**) A massive star that undergoes a sudden, extreme increase in brightness and releases an enormous burst of energy. This occurs as a result of the violent explosion of most of the material of the star, triggered by the collapse of its core. *See more at* **star**. *Compare* **nova**. *See panel at* **pulsar**.

supersonic Relating to or travelling at a speed greater than the speed of sound in a given medium, especially air.

superstring theory A type of string theory in which both the particles that transmit forces (such

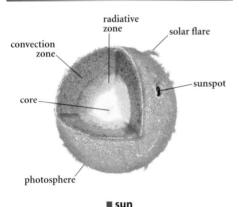

radiative zone
solar flare
convection zone
sunspot
core
photosphere

■ **sun**
cutaway diagram of the sun

as the photon, which carries the electromagnetic force) and the particles that make up matter (such as the proton) are viewed as string-like objects floating in space-time rather than point-like objects.

supersymmetry A theory in physics that states that for each subatomic particle that carries a force (such as the photon, which carries the electromagnetic force) there is a partner subatomic particle of matter. For example, the corresponding particle of the photon is called the photino, even though it has not yet been discovered.

supplementary angles Two angles whose sum is 180°.

surface tension A property of liquids whereby their surfaces behave as if they were covered by a thin, elastic film. Surface tension is caused by the uneven attraction that molecules at or near the surface of a liquid have for each other. Because of surface tension, small objects can be supported by the surface of a liquid without sinking. Insects, for example, can walk across the surface of a pond because of the surface tension of water. Surface tension also causes drops of a liquid to be shaped like spheres, since spheres have the least amount of surface area possible.

surface wave An earthquake wave in which rock particles vibrate at right angles to the direction of wave travel. Surface waves travel only on the Earth's surface, and not through it. Also called *L wave. See panel at* **earthquake.**

surfactant 1. A substance, such as detergent, that is added to a liquid to increase its ability to spread. **2.** A substance produced by the tiny air-filled sacs of the lung that reduces the surface tension of the fluids coating the lung. Surfactant helps keep the tiny air sacs from collapsing during normal breathing.

suspension A mixture in which small particles of a substance are dispersed throughout a gas or liquid. If left undisturbed, the particles are likely to settle to the bottom. The particles in a suspension are larger than those in either a colloid or a solution. Muddy water is an example of a suspension. *Compare* **colloid, solution.**

swallow Any of various small, fast-flying birds that have narrow pointed wings, a forked or notched tail, and a large mouth for catching flying insects in the air. Swallows migrate over thousands of kilometres each year.

swamp An area of low-lying wet or seasonally flooded land, often having trees and dense shrubs or thickets.

S wave *See* **secondary wave.** *See panel at* **earthquake.**

sweat The salty liquid given off by glands in the skin of mammals. As sweat evaporates, the skin cools, resulting in a reduction of body heat. ❖ The glands in the skin that secrete sweat are called **sweat glands.**

swim bladder *See* **air bladder** (sense 1).

symbiosis The close association between two or more different organisms of different species, often but not necessarily benefiting each member. —*adjective* **symbiotic.**

symmetry An exact matching of form and arrangement of parts on opposite sides of a boundary, such as a plane or line, or around a central point or axis.

sympathetic nervous system The part of the autonomic nervous system that tends to act in

Did You Know?

symbiosis

Two organisms that live together in *symbiosis* may have one of three kinds of relationships: mutualism, commensalism or parasitism. The *mutualism* shown by the rhinoceros and the tickbird benefits both. Riding on the rhino's back, the tickbird eats its fill of the ticks that bother the rhino while the rhino gets warning calls from the bird when it senses danger. In *commensalism,* one member benefits and the other is unaffected. Certain barnacles attach themselves to whales, gaining a safe home and transportation to food-rich waters. But the whales are generally unaffected by the barnacles' presence. In *parasitism,* though, one species generally gets hurt, as when fleas infest a dog's coat and feed on the animal's blood.

opposition to the parasympathetic nervous system, as by speeding up the heart and contracting the blood vessels. It also regulates the function of glands, particularly the sweat glands. The sympathetic nervous system is activated especially under conditions of stress.

symptom A sign or an indication of a disorder or disease, usually a noticeable change in how a person feels or looks. Sore throat, headache and higher than normal counts of white blood cells in the blood are symptoms of certain infections.

synapse The gap across which a nerve impulse passes from one nerve cell to another nerve cell, a muscle cell or a gland cell.

synchrotron A device that accelerates charged subatomic particles, such as protons and electrons, in a circular path, greatly increasing their energies. Unlike cyclotrons that consist of a continuous spiral through which particles are accelerated, synchrotrons consist of a single tube in the shape of a large ring. The particles rotate over and over again through this tube at increasing speeds. Synchrotrons are used to study subatomic structures. *See more at* **cyclotron.**

syncline A fold of rock layers that slope upwards on both sides of a common low point. Synclines form when rocks are compressed by plate-tectonic forces. They can be as small as the side of a cliff or as large as an entire valley. *Compare* **anticline.**

syndrome An abnormal condition or disease that is identified by a set group of physical signs and symptoms.

synthesis The formation of a chemical compound by combining simpler compounds or elements. —*verb* **synthesize.**

synthetic Produced by chemical synthesis, especially in a laboratory or other artificial environment.

syphilis A sexually transmitted disease caused by a bacterial infection that is characterized in its early stages by sores on the genitals. If untreated, skin ulcers develop, followed by often fatal infection of major organs of the body.

syphon **1.** A pipe or tube in the form of an upside-down U, filled with liquid and arranged so that the pressure of the atmosphere forces liquid to flow upwards from a container through the tube, over a barrier and into a lower container. **2.** A tubular animal part, as of a clam, through which water is taken in or expelled.

syringe A medical instrument used to inject fluids into the body or draw them from it.

system A group of elements or parts that function together to form a complex whole. For example, the bones, joints and other structures making up the skeleton of an animal form its *skeletal system.* A *weather system* is made up of the different masses of warmer and cooler air that are present in a region, along with any winds, clouds, rain or snow that they produce.

systole The period during the normal beating of the heart in which contraction of the ventricles occurs, forcing blood into the aorta and the arteries that lead to the lungs. *Compare* **diastole.**

Szilard, Leo 1898–1964. Hungarian-born American physicist who introduced the concept of the nuclear chain reaction. With Enrico Fermi, he built the world's first nuclear reactor. Szilard was instrumental in the development of the atomic bomb.

T_t

Ta The symbol for **tantalum**.

tactile Used for or sensitive to touch: *tactile organs.*

tactile hair A hair or hair-like structure that is highly sensitive to pressure or touch. Tactile hairs cover the bodies of most insects and are found in many mammals, especially as whiskers.

tadpole The larval stage of a frog or toad. A tadpole lives in the water, and has a tail and gills but no limbs. The tail and gills disappear as the legs and lungs develop and the tadpole approaches the adult stage.

taiga A forest located in the Earth's far northern regions, consisting mainly of cone-bearing evergreens, such as firs, pines and spruces, and some deciduous trees, such as larches, birches and aspens. The taiga is found just south of the tundra.

tail 1. The rear, elongated part of many animals, extending beyond the trunk or main part of the body. **2.** The long, bright stream of gas and dust forced from the head of a comet when it is close to the sun.

■ **tadpole**
development of a frog from a fertilized egg through several tadpole stages

Did You Know?

tails

The *tails* of cats and dogs are hard to miss. Sometimes they seem to be there only to be caught under chairs or get stepped on. But as a body feature, tails have many uses throughout the animal kingdom. Cheetahs use their tail for balance while running (as do cats and dogs), and the kangaroo balances with its tail while hopping. The Komodo dragon uses its heavy, powerful tail in combat with other dragons over food and mates. Birds in flight can make quick changes of direction by adjusting their tail positions. Wolves communicate to other wolves by positioning their tails in different ways. And as tadpoles change into frogs, they absorb their tails back into their bodies and make use of the nutrients stored in the tails. Monkeys sometimes hang from their tails, a talent apes gave up during evolution for reasons probably related to their more upright stance.

tailbone *See* **coccyx**.

talc A white, greenish or grey mineral that is a silicate of magnesium, usually occurring as massive mica-like flakes. It has a soft, soapy texture, and is used in face powder and talcum powder, for coating paper, and as a filler in paints and plastics. Talc is the mineral used to represent a hardness of 1 on the Mohs scale.

talon A sharp, curved claw on the foot of a bird or other animal such as a lizard, used for seizing and tearing prey.

talus[1] The bone that forms a joint with the tibia and fibula, making up the main bone of the ankle. *See more at* **skeleton**.

talus

talus[2] A sloping mass of rock fragments at the base of a cliff.

tan Abbreviation of **tangent**.

tangent 1. A line, curve or surface touching but not intersecting another. **2.** The ratio of the length of the side opposite an angle in a right-angled triangle to that of the side adjacent to the angle.

tantalum A hard, heavy, grey metallic element that is highly resistant to corrosion at lower temperatures. It is used to make light-bulb filaments, surgical instruments and glass for camera lenses. *Symbol* **Ta**. *Atomic number* 73. *See* **Periodic Table**, pages 260–261.

tapeworm Any of various long flatworms that live as parasites in the intestines of many animals, including humans.

tar 1. A thick, oily, dark substance consisting mainly of hydrocarbons, made by heating wood, coal or peat in the absence of air. **2.** *See* **coal tar**. **3.** A solid, sticky substance that remains when tobacco is burned. It accumulates in the lungs of smokers and contains a number of cancer-inducing chemicals (carcinogens).

tarantula Any of various large, hairy, mostly tropical spiders that have a painful but not dangerous bite. They do not spin webs, but live in burrows in the ground and hunt small frogs, toads, rodents and birds.

tar pit An accumulation of natural tar or asphalt at the Earth's surface, especially one that traps animals and preserves their bones after death.

tarsal Any of the bones of the foot lying between the ankle and metatarsals. *See more at* **skeleton**.

taste bud Any of numerous sense organs on the tongues of most vertebrate animals that are sensitive to five types of taste: sweet, sour, salty, bitter and monosodium glutamate. Evidence for receptors of this fifth taste, known by the Japanese word umami, was only recently discovered.

Taurus A constellation in the Northern Hemisphere near Orion and Aries.

taxonomy The scientific classification of organisms into specially named groups based on shared characteristics and natural relationships. *See table on* page 335.

Tay-Sachs disease A hereditary disease in which the products of fat metabolism accumulate

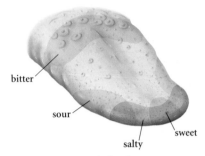

bitter

sour

salty

sweet

■ **taste bud**
This illustration shows the traditional description of where taste buds associated with the four main tastes are located. However, any taste bud is capable of detecting all the different tastes, although some are more sensitive to a particular taste than others.

in the nervous system, causing retardation, paralysis and death by the age of 3 or 4. It mostly affects children of eastern European Jewish descent.

Tb The symbol for **terbium**.

TB Abbreviation of **tuberculosis**.

Tc The symbol for **technetium**.

T cell Any of the lymphocytes which are activated by the thymus gland. They have receptors on the cell membrane which recognize foreign antigens. Once recognized, the antigen is bound to the T cell membrane and the cell then undergoes a rapid series of divisions. This produces clones of killer T cells which are all capable of recognizing and destroying the same antigen.

Te The symbol for **tellurium**.

tear A drop of the clear salty liquid secreted by glands (lacrimal glands) in the eyes. Tears wet the membrane covering the eye and help rid the eye of substances that cause irritation.

teat A projection near the centre of the mammary gland of most female mammals that contains the outlets of the milk ducts.

technetium A silvery-grey, radioactive metallic element. It was the first element to be artificially made, and it is produced naturally in extremely

Taxonomy

Taxonomy is the scientific classification of life. The system was originally developed in the 18th century by the Swedish botanist Carolus Linnaeus, who divided all forms of life into two large groups: the animal and plant kingdoms. Modern biologists have expanded Linnaeus's system and now recognize five separate kingdoms, as shown in the following table:

Kingdom	Type of Organisms
Prokaryota *or* **Monera**	bacteria and blue-green algae
Protista *or* **Protoctista**	single-celled organisms such as the amoeba, euglena and paramecium; also dinoflagellates, slime moulds and most algae
Fungi	mushrooms, yeasts, moulds and lichens
Plantae	plants
Animalia	multicellular animals

Kingdoms are the highest level of classification. Below the level of kingdom are six major lower levels arranged hierarchically. From highest to lowest these are: **phylum (or division,** in the plant kingdom), **class, order, family, genus,** and **species.** These can be further subdivided into subkingdom, subphylum, subclass, and so forth. These categories indicate how closely or distantly organisms are related to each other, based on structural and genetic similarities.

By convention, all taxonomic categories are written with a capital letter, except for species and subspecies names. Genus and species names are written in italic, as in *Tyrannosaurus rex* or *Homo sapiens.* The chart below compares the taxonomy of three organisms: a human, a dog and a goldfish. As the table shows, although the three species are different in many ways, they also share certain important taxonomic characteristics.

small amounts during the radioactive decay of uranium. Technetium is used to remove corrosion from steel. *Symbol* **Tc**. *Atomic number* 43. *See* **Periodic Table**, pages 260–261.

technology 1. The use of scientific and other technical knowledge to solve practical problems, especially in industry and commerce. **2.** The specific methods, materials and devices used to solve practical problems: *aerospace technology.*

tectonic boundary In the theory of plate tectonics, a boundary between two or more plates. The plates can be moving towards each other (at convergent plate boundaries), away from each other (at divergent plate boundaries) or past each

other (at transform faults). Maps of seismic and volcanic activity across the Earth indicate that most earthquakes and volcanic eruptions occur along or near tectonic boundaries. Scientists believe this is due to the scraping, pushing, pulling and melting of the Earth's outer layer (the lithosphere) along these boundaries.

tektite Any of numerous dark-brown to green glassy objects, usually small and round, composed of silica and various oxides and found in several parts of the world. They are thought to have come from the moon or to have resulted from impacts of large meteorites with the Earth's surface.

A Closer Look

Tectonic Boundaries

Subduction Zones

Two tectonic plates collide. The denser plate sinks below the other, and a deep trench forms where the two plates meet. The down-going plate heats up with depth and begins to melt. A chain of volcanoes forms in the overriding plate, creating an island arc in the sea or a mountain range along the edge of a continent. The Aleutian Islands and the Andes were formed in this way.

Hot Spots

A volcano forms over a hot spot – an area within the Earth that gives off a lot of heat from radioactive decay. The Hawaiian Islands were formed in this way.

Spreading Zones

As plates spread apart, new lava rises to the surface from deep within the Earth and cools to form new rock. The island of Iceland was formed in this way.

Before plates actually break apart, a rift valley forms. Sometimes seawater flows into it. This is how the Red Sea was formed.

Collision Zones

Two equally dense plates collide. Neither plate sinks below the other, and as the two push against each other a mountain chain forms. The Himalayas were formed in this way.

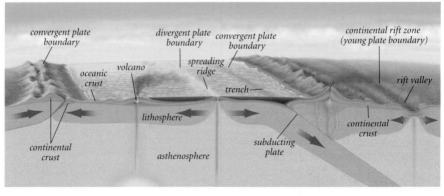

COLLISION ZONE   **HOT SPOT**   **SPREADING ZONE**   **SUBDUCTION ZONE**   **SPREADING ZONE**

tele– A prefix that means "at a distance", as in *telemetry.*

telecommunication The science and technology of sending messages over long distances by electronic transmission of impulses, as by telegraph, telephone, radio or television.

telegraph A communications system in which a message is sent in the form of electric impulses, either by wire or radio, to a receiving station.

telemetry The automatic measurement and transmission of data from a distant source to a receiving station. Telemetry is used, for example, to track the movements of wild animals that have had radio transmitters attached to them.

telescope 1. An arrangement of lenses, mirrors or both that collects visible light, allowing direct observation or photographic recording of distant objects. **2.** Any of various devices, such as a radio telescope, used to detect and observe distant objects by collecting radiation other than visible light.

telluride A chemical compound of tellurium and another element.

tellurium A nonmetallic element that occurs as either a brittle, shiny, silvery-white crystal or a grey or brown powder. Small amounts of tellurium are used to improve the alloys of various metals. *Symbol* **Te**. *Atomic number* 52. *See* **Periodic Table**, pages 260–261.

telophase The final stage of cell division, in which membranes form around the two groups of chromosomes, each at opposite ends of the cell, to produce the two nuclei of the daughter cells. In mitosis, telophase is preceded by anaphase. *See more at* **meiosis, mitosis.**

temperate Marked by moderate temperatures, weather or climate; neither hot nor cold.

Temperate Zone Either of two zones of the Earth between the tropics and the polar circles: the **North Temperate Zone**, between the Arctic Circle and the Tropic of Cancer, and the **South Temperate Zone**, between the Antarctic Circle and the Tropic of Capricorn.

temperature 1. A measure of the average kinetic energy of atoms or molecules in a system. **2.** A numerical measure of hotness or coldness on a standard scale, such as the Kelvin scale. *See panel at* **Celsius. 3.** An abnormally high body temperature. *See panel on* page 338.

temporal lobe The portion of each cerebral hemisphere lying to the side and rear of the frontal lobe, containing the main speech and language centres of the brain.

tendon A band of tough fibrous tissue that connects a muscle to a bone.

tendril A slender, coiling plant part, often a modified leaf or leaf part, that helps support the stem of climbing plants by clinging to or winding around an object. Pea plants and grape vines produce tendrils.

tensile strength The ability of a material to resist a force that tends to pull it apart. It is also

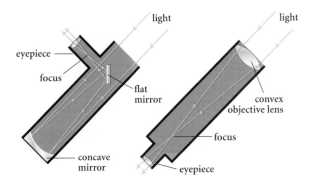

■ **telescope**
In a reflecting telescope (left), light is gathered by reflecting it off a concave mirror. It is then reflected off an angled flat mirror towards the eyepiece. In a refracting telescope (right), light is gathered by being refracted through a convex objective lens. It then exits in a direct line through the eyepiece.

Usage

temperature/heat

The molecules of all substances are in motion, and the energy associated with this motion is called kinetic energy. Temperature and heat are both ways of measuring this energy, but they do not mean the same thing. A substance's *temperature* is the average kinetic energy of the substance's molecules. By contrast, the total amount of heat energy in a substance is the sum of the kinetic energy of all the particles in it. Thus, the water in two different pans, one four times as large as the other, might be at the same temperature, but the water in the larger pan would contain four times as much heat, since it requires four times as much energy to raise the temperature to the temperature of the water in the smaller pan.

used to define the maximum tensile stress (the force per unit of cross-sectional area) that a material can withstand before it breaks apart.

tension 1. *Physics.* A force that tends to stretch or elongate something. **2.** *Electricity.* A difference of electrical potential; voltage: *high-tension wires.*

tentacle A narrow, flexible, unjointed part extending from the body of certain animals, such as an octopus, jellyfish and sea anemone. Tentacles are used for feeling, grasping or moving.

tephra Solid matter, such as ash, dust and cinders, that is ejected into the air by an erupting volcano.

tera– A prefix that means: **1.** One trillion (10^{12}), as in *terahertz,* one trillion hertz. **2.** 2^{40} (that is, 1,099,511,627,776), which is the power of two closest to a trillion, as in *terabyte.*

terabyte 1. A unit of computer memory or data storage capacity equal to 1024 gigabytes (2^{40} bytes). **2.** One trillion bytes. *See panel at* **megabyte.**

terbium A soft, easily shaped, silvery-grey metallic element of the lanthanide series. It is used in colour television tubes, X-ray machines and

lasers. *Symbol* **Tb.** *Atomic number* 65. *See* **Periodic Table,** pages 260–261.

term *Mathematics.* **1.** Each of the quantities or expressions that form the parts of a ratio or the numerator and denominator of a fraction. **2.** Any of the quantities in an equation that are connected to other quantities by a plus sign or minus sign.

terminal 1. *Electricity.* A position in a circuit or device at which a connection can be made or broken. *See panel at* **battery. 2.** *Computer Science.* A device, often equipped with a keyboard and a video display, by which one can read, enter or manipulate information in a computer system.

termite Any of numerous pale-coloured insects that live in large colonies and that feed on and destroy wood. Termites resemble ants in their appearance, manner of living and social organization, but they belong to a different order of insects.

terrestrial 1. Relating to the Earth or its inhabitants. **2.** Relating to, consisting of, living on or growing on land.

territory A geographical area occupied by a single animal, mating pair or group. Animals usually defend their territory vigorously against intruders. Different animals mark off territory in different ways, for example by leaving traces of their scent along the boundaries or, in the case of birds, modifying their calls to keep out intruders.

Tertiary The first period of the Cainozoic Era, from about 65 to 1.6 million years ago, characterized by the appearance of most modern classes of plants and mammals. *See chart at* **geological time,** pages 148–149.

Tesla, Nikola 1856–1943. Serbian-born American electrical engineer and physicist. He discovered the principles of alternating current (1881) and invented numerous devices and procedures that were essential to the harnessing of electricity and the development of radio.

testa *See* seed coat.

testicle Either of the testes of a male mammal, usually contained within a scrotum.

testis (*plural* **testes**) The reproductive organ of male animals, in which sperm and the sex hormones (androgens) are produced. Vertebrates have two testes, which in most animals are contained inside the body. However, in many

Biography

Nikola Tesla

In 1886, when Nikola Tesla went to work for George Westinghouse's electrical company, most commercially generated electricity was distributed over a direct current (DC) system. Such a system was very expensive to maintain, partly because much of the electricity was lost to resistance and wasted as heat in the wires. The alternating current (AC) system which Tesla invented could be transmitted over very long distances through the use of transformers, and was cheaper and easier to maintain than the DC system. Tesla gave public demonstrations of electricity to ease people's fears about the safety of the system (including having currents passed through his body to ignite flames). Tesla's invention of motors and generators to use with the AC system helped ensure that it would rapidly replace direct current throughout most of the world.

---

mammals they lie outside the body and are enclosed by the scrotum. This is because the testes seem to function at their best one or two degrees below the internal body temperature of most mammals.

testosterone A steroid hormone that regulates the development of the male reproductive system and male secondary sex characteristics. The main sources of testosterone in the body are the testes. Testosterone is the most important of the hormones known as androgens.

test tube A cylindrical tube of clear glass, usually open at one end and rounded at the other, used as a container for small amounts of a substance in laboratory tests and experiments.

tetanus A serious disease caused by bacteria that usually enter the body through a wound. Tetanus is characterized by painful contractions of the muscles, especially of the jaw, and can be fatal if untreated.

tetragonal Relating to a crystal having three axes, two of which are of the same length and are at right angles to each other. The third axis is perpendicular to these. The mineral zircon has tetragonal crystals. *See more at* **crystal.**

tetrahedron A three-dimensional geometric figure with four triangular faces.

texture *Geology.* The spatial relationships between the mineral grains making up a rock.

Th The symbol for **thorium.**

thalamus The part of the brain in vertebrate animals that lies at the rear of the forebrain. It relays sensory information to the cerebral cortex and regulates the perception of touch, pain and temperature.

Thales 624?–546? BC. Greek philosopher who was a founder of geometry and abstract astronomy.

thallium A soft, easily shaped, very poisonous metallic element that has a low melting point. It is used in photography, in making low-melting and highly refractive glass and in treating skin infections. *Symbol* **Tl.** *Atomic number* 81. *See* **Periodic Table,** pages 260–261.

thallus (*plural* **thalli**) A part of certain plants and plant-like organisms that is a single cell or a mass of cells and has not differentiated into a leaf, stem or root. Fungi, lichens, liverworts and most algae have thalli.

theorem A mathematical statement whose truth can be proved on the basis of a given set of axioms or assumptions.

theory A set of statements or principles devised to explain a group of facts or phenomena. Most theories that are accepted by scientists have been repeatedly tested by experiments and can be used to make predictions about natural phenomena. *See panel at* **hypothesis.**

thermal *adjective* Relating to heat. —*noun* A current of warm air that rises because it is less dense than the air around it.

thermal vent An opening in the Earth,

especially on the seafloor, that emits hot water and dissolved minerals.

thermion An electrically charged particle or ion that is emitted by a conducting material when heated by an electric current.

thermo– *or* **therm–** A prefix that means "heat", as in *thermometer.*

thermocouple A thermoelectric device used to make accurate measurements of temperatures, especially high temperatures. It usually consists of a circuit containing two junctions between wires of different metals. When one of the junctions is heated, and the other left cold, the difference in temperature causes an electric current to flow through the circuit. Because the size of the electromotive force (emf) generated depends on the temperature difference between the two junctions, a measurement of the emf can be used to calculate the temperature difference between the two junctions. Thermocouples are also used in the generation of electricity and in refrigeration devices.

thermodynamics The branch of physics that deals with the relationships between heat and other forms of energy.

thermoelectric Relating to electric energy produced by heat or to heat produced by electric energy. The thermoelectric energy of a nuclear power plant is produced by the heat generated from nuclear fission. Thermoelectric energy in cars is generated by a thermocouple, which makes use of differences in temperature to generate electricity.

thermometer An instrument used to measure temperature. There are many types of thermometers, each of which makes use of a physical effect of temperature to indicate the temperature of the medium being measured. The most common thermometer consists of a closed, graduated glass tube in which a liquid expands or contracts as the temperature increases or decreases. Other types of thermometers work by detecting changes in the volume of an enclosed gas or by registering changes in the electrical resistance of a conducting material at different temperatures.

thermonuclear 1. Derived from the fusion of atomic nuclei at high temperatures or the energy produced in this way. **2.** Relating to weapons based on nuclear fusion, especially as distinguished from those based on nuclear fission.

thermosphere The outermost layer of the Earth's atmosphere, lying above the mesosphere and extending hundreds of kilometres into outer space. In the thermosphere, which includes the exosphere and most of the ionosphere, temperatures increase steadily with altitude.

thermostat A device that automatically controls heating or cooling equipment in such a way as to keep the temperature nearly constant.

theropod One of the two main types of saurischian dinosaurs, widespread during the Mesozoic Era. Theropods were meat-eaters, walked on two legs, and had small forelimbs and a large skull with long jaws and sharp teeth. Most theropods were of small or medium size, but some grew very large, like the tyrannosaurs. *Compare* **sauropod.**

thiamine A vitamin belonging to the B complex (B_1) that is important in carbohydrate metabolism and normal activity of the nervous system. It is found in bran, yeast and meat. *See also* **vitamin B complex.**

Thompson, Benjamin. Count Rumford 1753–1814. American-born British physicist who conducted numerous experiments on heat and friction, which led him to discover that heat is produced by moving particles.

Thomson, Sir Joseph John 1856–1940. British physicist who discovered the electron. While experimenting with cathode rays, he deduced that the particles he observed were smaller than an atom. Thomson went on to study the ability of gases to conduct electricity.

thoracic Relating to or located in or near the thorax: *thoracic vertebrae.*

thorax 1. The upper part of the trunk in vertebrate animals. The thorax includes the rib cage, which encloses the heart and lungs. In humans and other mammals, the thorax lies above the abdomen. **2.** The middle division of the body of an insect, to which the wings and legs are attached. The thorax lies between the head and the abdomen. *Compare* **abdomen.**

thorium A silvery-white, radioactive metallic element of the actinide series. It is used for fuel in

Did You Know?

thermodynamics

Imagine watching two videos, each one lasting only a few seconds. The first shows a pendulum swinging, the second shows someone jumping from the top diving board into a swimming pool. Now run the videos backwards – which would look strange? The film of the swinging pendulum would look the same whether run forwards or backwards. The gravitational potential energy stored in the pendulum at the top of its swing is transferred to kinetic energy as it falls, and then back again to gravitational potential energy as it rises again. This situation is covered by the first law of thermodynamics (sometimes referred to as the *law of conservation of energy*) which states that energy cannot be created or destroyed, only transferred from one form to another – as we've just seen in the example of the pendulum.

Now think about the video of the person jumping into the swimming pool. It's funny to watch this video backwards because we just *know* that we're never going to see anyone doing this – but why? To understand, look at the energy transfers for this example, which go something like this:

| gravitational potential energy of person | » | kinetic energy of person as they enter the pool | » | kinetic energy of water displaced by person | » | kinetic energy of water molecules in pool ("heat") |

The energy that started out stored in the person as gravitational potential energy ends up raising the temperature of the water in the pool just a little bit. Although it's possible that this energy could find its way back to the swimmer, it's very unlikely – in just the same way as it's unlikely that a load of marbles dropped on the floor all end up in the same place. (And, even if the energy did find its way back to the person, all it would do is increase the random kinetic energy of the molecules making up their body, in other words increase their temperature. To make them leap back up onto the diving board the energy would have to make all the molecules in the person's body move with the same speed in the same direction at the same time – now that really is unlikely!)

The second law of thermodynamics tells us that energy tends to spread out from a place where it is very "concentrated" to one where it is less "concentrated". Hot things contain a lot of "concentrated" energy – so they tend to cool down as the energy spreads out and away from them, becoming less "concentrated". Cold things never become hotter just left to themselves – not because energy can't flow into them (the first law says that's OK) but because it is very unlikely that the energy will flow into them from their surroundings, becoming more "concentrated" (which is what the second law tells us). Since the second law tells us that you can only cool something down if there is nothing warmer around, it is impossible ever to reach absolute zero – which is the third law of thermodynamics!

some nuclear reactors and for improving the high-temperature strength of magnesium alloys. The only naturally occurring isotope of thorium is also its most stable, having a half-life of 14 billion years. *Symbol* **Th**. *Atomic number* 90. *See* **Periodic Table**, pages 260–261.

threonine An essential amino acid. *See more at* **amino acid.**

thrust The force that causes an object to move forward. Thrust in a jet or rocket engine develops as a reaction to the ejection of exhaust gases from the rear of the engine. Thrust in a propeller results from the spinning of the propeller blades that pushes air or water in a certain direction.

thulium A soft, easily shaped, silver-grey metallic element of the lanthanide series. An artificial radioactive isotope of thulium is used as a radiation source in small, portable X-ray machines. *Symbol* **Tm**. *Atomic number* 69. *See Periodic Table, pages 260–261.*

thunder The explosive noise that accompanies a stroke of lightning. Thunder is a series of sound waves produced by the rapid expansion of the air through which the lightning passes. *See panel at* lightning.

thunderstorm A storm of heavy rain accompanied by lightning and thunder and sometimes hail.

thymine A base that is a component of DNA. It forms a base pair with adenine.

thymus An organ in vertebrate animals located behind the top of the sternum (breastbone) where lymphocytes called T cells develop. In humans, the thymus stops growing in early childhood and gradually shrinks in size through adulthood.

thyroid gland A two-lobed gland located at the base of the neck in vertebrate animals. It secretes many hormones that are important for cell metabolism and normal growth and development.

Ti The symbol for **titanium.**

tibia The larger of the two bones of the lower leg or lower portion of the hind leg. Also called *shinbone. See more at* **skeleton.**

tick 1. Any of numerous small animals related to spiders and mites. Ticks attach themselves to the skin of humans and animals, and suck their blood. They often carry microorganisms that cause disease. 2. Any of various small bloodsucking insects resembling lice that are parasites on sheep, goats and other animals.

tidal pool A pool of water remaining after a tide has retreated. Also called *tide pool.*

tidal wave 1. The swell or crest of surface seawater created by the tides. 2. An unusual rise in the level of water along a coastline, as from a storm or a combination of wind and tide. 3. A tsunami.

tide The regular rise and fall in the surface level of the sea, caused by the gravitational attraction of the moon and to a lesser extent the sun. *See also* **ebb tide, flood tide, neap tide, spring tide.**

till A mass of boulders, pebbles, sand and mud scraped up by a moving glacier and deposited either by the glacier's movement or by its melting. Also called *boulder clay.*

timberline The highest elevation at which dense concentrations of trees exist.

time 1. A continuous, measurable quantity in which events occur in a sequence proceeding from

larynx
thyroid gland
trachea

■ **thyroid gland**
front view of a human thyroid gland

Usage

tidal wave/tsunami

In everyday speech, we use the word *tidal wave* to refer to a gigantic and enormously destructive wave caused by an underwater earthquake or volcanic eruption – what scientists would properly call a *tsunami.* When scientists use the word *tidal wave,* they normally are referring to an unusually large wave or bulge of water that sometimes occurs around a high tide. These tidal waves are certainly big and powerful, but they are tiny in comparison with tsunamis.

342

the past through the present to the future. *See panel at* **space-time.** **2a.** An interval separating two points of this quantity; a duration. **b.** A system by which such intervals are measured or such numbers are calculated: *standard time; daylight-saving time.*

time zone *See* **standard time.**

tin An easily shaped, silvery metallic element that occurs in igneous rocks. It has a crystalline structure and crackles when it is bent as its crystals break. Tin is used to coat other metals to prevent corrosion and is a part of numerous alloys, including bronze. *Symbol* **Sn.** *Atomic number* 50. *See* **Periodic Table,** pages 260–261. *See panel at* **element.**

tissue A large collection of similar cells that together perform a specific function in an organism. The organs of the body and the parts of a plant are composed of many different kinds of tissues, such as connective tissue or muscle.

titanium A shiny, white metallic element that occurs widely in all kinds of rocks and soils. It is lightweight, strong and highly resistant to corrosion. Titanium alloys are used especially to make parts for aircraft and ships. *Symbol* **Ti.** *Atomic number* 22. *See* **Periodic Table,** pages 260–261.

Tl The symbol for **thallium.**

Tm The symbol for **thulium.**

TNT Short for *trinitrotoluene.* A yellow, crystalline compound used mainly as an explosive.

toad Any of numerous amphibians related to frogs. Toads usually have broader bodies and shorter legs than frogs, and their feet have only a little webbing. Their skin is thick, rough, and often bumpy, and sometimes secretes toxic substances. Toads usually do not live in water as adults but prefer cool, moist places on the ground. However, they have to return to water to reproduce. *Compare* **frog.**

toluene A colourless liquid hydrocarbon, C_7H_8, that is poisonous and burns easily. It is used in fuels, explosives, dyes, medicines and many

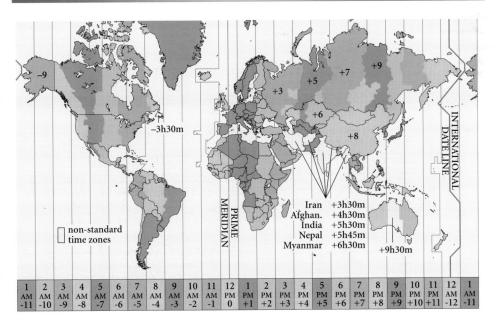

■ **time zone**

industrial chemicals. Also called *methylbenzene*.

ton 1. A unit of weight equal to 2000 pounds. Also called *short ton*. 2. A unit of weight equal to 2240 pounds. Also called *long ton*. 3. *See* **tonne.**

tongue 1. A muscular organ in most vertebrate animals that is usually attached to the bottom of the mouth. In some reptiles, such as snakes, the tongue is mainly used as a sense organ, while in some other animals, such as frogs, chameleons and anteaters, it is used to capture prey. The tongue is the main organ of taste in mammals and it is used to aid chewing and swallowing. In humans, it is also used to produce speech sounds. 2. A similar organ in certain invertebrate animals.

tonne A unit of mass or weight equal to 1000 kilograms. *See table at* **measurement.**

tonsils The two oval-shaped tissues at the back of the throat in mammals that lie between the mouth and the pharynx. The tonsils are thought to prevent infections of the breathing passages but often become infected themselves. ❖ Inflammation of the tonsils is called **tonsillitis.** ❖ Surgical removal of the tonsils is called a **tonsillectomy.**

tooth (*plural* **teeth**) 1. Any of the hard bony

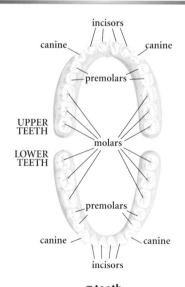

incisors
canine
canine
premolars
UPPER TEETH
molars
LOWER TEETH
premolars
canine
canine
incisors

■ **tooth**
a full set of adult human teeth

structures in the mouth used to grasp and chew food and as weapons of attack and defence. In mammals and many other vertebrates, the teeth are set in sockets in the jaw. In fish and amphibians, they grow in and around the palate. *See also* **dentition.** 2. A similar structure in certain invertebrate animals.

topaz 1. A colourless, blue, yellow, brown or pink mineral consisting largely of aluminium silicate and valued as a gem. Topaz is often found in pegmatites and is the mineral used to represent a hardness of 8 on the Mohs scale. 2. Any of various yellow gemstones, especially a yellow variety of sapphire or corundum.

topography 1. The shape, height and depth of the land surface in a place or region. Physical features that make up the topography of an area include mountains, valleys, plains and bodies of water. Man-made features such as roads, railways, and ports are also often considered part of a region's topography: *the mountainous topography of Switzerland.* 2. The detailed description or drawing of the physical features of a place or region, especially in the form of contour maps. *See more at* **gradient.**

topology The mathematical study of the geometric properties that are not normally affected by changes in the size or shape of geometric figures. In topology, a doughnut and a cup with a handle are equivalent shapes, because each has a single hole.

tornado A violently rotating column of air ranging from a few metres to nearly two kilometres in width and whirling at speeds estimated at around 500 kilometres an hour or higher. A tornado usually takes the form of a funnel-shaped cloud extending downwards out of a cumulonimbus cloud. Where the funnel reaches the ground, it can cause enormous destruction.

torque The tendency of a force applied to an object to make it rotate about an axis. Torque is equal to the amount of the force acting on the object multiplied by the distance between its point of application and the axis around which the object rotates (or would rotate if it were not fixed in place).

Torricelli, Evangelista 1608–1647. Italian mathematician and physicist who discovered that the atmosphere exerts pressure. He demonstrated

■ **tornado**

toxicology The scientific study of poisons, of their effects and detection, and of the treatment of poisoning.

toxin A poisonous substance produced by a living organism. Toxins can be products of ordinary metabolism (such as lactic acid), can be produced to kill or immobilize prey (such as the toxins in snake venom) or can be produced for self-defence (such as the cyanide produced by several plants). Toxins produced by bacteria cause disease.

trace element An element present in an organism in only very small amounts but essential for normal metabolism. Iodine and cobalt, for example, are trace elements required by humans.

tracer An identifiable substance, such as a dye or radioactive isotope, that can be followed through the course of a mechanical, chemical or biological process. Tracers are used to provide information about details of the process or about the distribution of the substances involved in it.

trachea 1. The tube-shaped structure in vertebrate animals that leads from the larynx to the bronchi and carries air to the lungs. In mammals, the trachea is strengthened by rings of cartilage. Also called *windpipe.* 2. A similar structure in insects and other arthropods.

that this pressure affects the level of mercury in a tube, thereby inventing the mercury barometer.

Torrid Zone The zone of the Earth between the Tropic of Cancer and the Tropic of Capricorn.

torsion The stress that an object undergoes when one of its ends is twisted out of line with the other end.

tortoise Any of various turtles that live on land.

tourmaline A silicate mineral consisting of aluminium, boron and other elements. Tourmaline occurs in many different translucent colours, usually in crystals shaped like 3-, 6- or 9-sided prisms. It is especially common in pegmatites.

Townes, Charles Hard Born 1915. American physicist who invented the maser, a device that amplifies and focuses short electromagnetic waves into intense beams. Townes's work laid the foundation for the development of laser technology.

toxic Poisonous.

tract A system of connected body organs and parts that work together to perform a specialized function, such as digestion in the digestive tract.

trade winds Winds that blow steadily from east to west and towards the equator over most of the Torrid Zone. The trade winds blow from the northeast in the Northern Hemisphere and from the southeast in the Southern Hemisphere, converging in the doldrums. *See more at* **wind.**

trait A characteristic or condition that is determined by one's genes. The colour of an animal's coat and the shape of a plant's leaves are physical traits. Nesting in birds and burrowing in rodents are examples of behavioural traits.

trajectory 1. *Physics.* The curve described by a projectile moving through space. 2. *Geometry.* A curve or surface that passes through a given set of points, or that intersects a given series of curves or surfaces at a constant angle.

transcription The process in a cell by which genetic material is copied from a strand of DNA to a complementary strand of RNA (called messenger RNA). Transcription takes place in the nucleus before messenger RNA is transported to the ribosomes, the places in the cell where proteins are made.

transducer A device that converts one type of energy into another. For example, the transducer in a microphone converts sound waves into electrical impulses, while the transducer in a loudspeaker converts electrical impulses into sound waves.

transfer RNA *See under* **RNA.**

transformation *Mathematics.* A change of size or position in a figure.

transformer A device used to change the voltage of an alternating current in one circuit into a different voltage in a second circuit. Transformers consist of a frame-like iron core that has a wire wound around each end. As a current enters the transformer through one of the coils, the magnetic field it produces causes the other coil to pick up the current. ❖ If there are more turns on the second coil than on the first coil, the outgoing

■ **transformer**

The increase or decrease in voltage is directly related to the number of turns of the wire. In the top transformer, the outgoing voltage is doubled because the secondary coil has twice as many turns as the first. In the bottom transformer, the voltage is halved.

current will have a higher voltage than the incoming current. This is called a **step-up transformer.** ❖ If there are fewer turns on the second coil than on the first, the outgoing current will have a lower voltage. This is called a **step-down transformer.**

transform fault A type of strike-slip fault that is common along the edges of tectonic plates in mid-ocean ridge regions. *See more at* **fault.**

transfusion The transfer of blood from one person to another. *See more at* **Rh factor.** *See panel at* **blood group.**

transistor An electronic device that controls the flow of an electric current and is used as an amplifier or switch. Transistors consist of three layers of semiconductor material connected to an electric circuit. In some transistors, the outer layers have an excess of electrons; in others, the middle layer has more electrons. Transistors work like gates, allowing or closing off the flow of electrons when an electric current or voltage is applied to a particular layer. Because of their tiny size and increased efficiency, transistors have replaced electron tubes in most electronic devices.

transition element Any of the metallic elements within Groups 3 to 12 in the Periodic Table. As atoms they all have two electrons in their outermost shell, and an incompletely filled inner subshell just beneath this outer shell. The transition elements within these groups are usually defined as those which form at least one ion in which the inner subshell is only partially full. Transition elements form alloys easily, have high melting points, and have more than one oxidation number because of their incomplete inner shells. *See* **Periodic Table,** pages 260–261. *See panel at* **metal.**

translation 1. The process in a cell by which a strand of messenger RNA (mRNA) directs the assembly of a sequence of amino acids to make a protein. Translation takes place in the ribosomes, which are the places in the cell where proteins are made. 2. *Mathematics.* A transformation with a sliding movement but no turning, using a vector.

translucent Transmitting light, but not clearly enough to be transparent. A translucent object causes enough diffusion of light for an object or image on the other side of it to be seen only

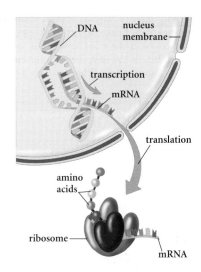

DNA nucleus
membrane—

transcription

mRNA

translation

amino
acids

ribosome—

mRNA

■ translation

indistinctly. Frosted glass is translucent. *Compare* **transparent.**

transmitter A device that generates radio or microwave signals, changes their amplitude or frequency so that they can carry information (such as spoken words) and finally radiates the resulting wave by means of an antenna.

transmutation The changing of one chemical element into another. Transmutations occur naturally through radioactive decay, or artificially by bombarding the nucleus of a substance with subatomic particles.

transparent Transmitting light so as to be seen through clearly. The glass in windows is usually transparent. *Compare* **translucent.** *See panel at* **glass.**

transpiration The process by which water moves from the roots of a plant up to the uppermost leaves. The water evaporates out through the stomata, found mainly on the underside of the leaves. The movement of water through the plant is known as the transpiration stream. Raised light intensity and increased temperatures speed up the rate of transpiration in plants.

transplant *noun* **1.** A plant that has been

uprooted and replanted. **2.** An organ or tissue of the body that has been transferred from one person or body part to another. —*verb* **1.** To uproot and replant a growing plant. **2.** To transfer tissue or an organ from one body or body part to another.

transpose To move a term or quantity from one side of an algebraic equation to the other by adding or subtracting that term to or from both sides. By subtracting 2 from both sides of the equation $2 + x = 4$, one can transpose the 2 to the other side, yielding $x = 4 - 2$, and thus determine that x equals 2. —*noun* **transposition.**

transversal *Mathematics.* A line that cuts a set of other lines.

transverse wave A wave in which the

Did You Know?

transpiration

Plants need much more water than animals do. But why? Plants use water not only to carry nutrients throughout their tissues, but also to exchange gases with the air in the process known as *transpiration*. Air, which contains the carbon dioxide that plant cells need for photosynthesis, enters the plant mainly through the stomata (tiny holes under its leaves). The air travels through tiny spaces in the leaf tissue to the cells that conduct photosynthesis. These cells are coated with a thin layer of water. The cell walls do not permit gases to pass through them, but the carbon dioxide can move across the cell walls by dissolving in the water on their surface. The cells remove the carbon dioxide from the water and use the same water to carry oxygen, the main waste product of photosynthesis, out of the cells. However, all this mixing of water and air in transpiration has one drawback: more than 90 per cent of the water sucked up by a plant's roots is lost by evaporation through the stomata. This is why a plant always needs water and why plants that live in dry climates, such as cacti, have reduced leaf surfaces from which less water can escape.

Did You Know?

transplant

When vital organs of the body fail, sometimes the only way doctors can save the life of their patients is to give them an organ *transplant*. The diseased organ – for example the kidneys, heart or liver – is removed from the body and replaced by a healthy organ from a donor. Usually the donor is someone who has died suddenly in an accident or from an unexpected event like a brain haemorrhage, although occasionally it is a living person. The big problem is that the tissue type of the donor must match that of the recipient as closely as possible, because otherwise the immune system of the body rejects the new organ and destroys it. Even when the donor organ is a good match, anyone who receives an organ transplant must take special drugs for the rest of their lives to suppress their immune system and prevent rejection.

There are never enough donor organs to supply everyone who needs them – thousands of people die every year waiting for a new organ. There are two ways in which research is trying to overcome this problem. In *xenotransplantation,* animals such as pigs could be genetically modified to grow hearts and other organs that are then recognized by the human body as human. This avoids any shortages of organs, but the technology is proving very difficult and there are many worries both about animal welfare and about animal diseases passing into people.

The alternative is stem cell research. This is work on special stem cells obtained from human embryos that can be kept almost indefinitely in the laboratory and have the potential to grow into almost any type of tissue. They are also free from the cell markers that trigger the immune response. Some people object to the use of material from embryos, but scientists are working hard on obtaining stem cells from umbilical cord blood taken after birth, and even on stem cells found in adults. Eventually they hope to use them to grow entire new organs. In the future, it is hoped that no one will have to die waiting for a transplant.

oscillations are perpendicular to the direction in which the wave is moving. For instance, in a wave in the sea, the molecules of water move up and down as the wave passes on its way towards the shore. *See more at* **wave.** *Compare* **longitudinal wave.**

trapezium (*plural* **trapezia**) A four-sided figure having two parallel sides.

trapezoid A four-sided figure having no parallel sides.

tree A perennial plant that typically has a single woody stem, and usually has branches and leaves.

tree line The highest elevation at which trees exist.

tremor A shaking or vibrating movement, as from a small earthquake.

triangle A closed geometric figure consisting of three sides. *See* **isosceles, right-angled triangle, scalene.**

triangulation 1. A method used to determine distances and directions of a region of land. The region is divided into a set of triangles based on a line of known length. The triangles are then measured using trigonometry. **2.** A method of determining the location of a boat or aircraft by means of trigonometry.

■ **trapezium**

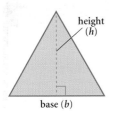

■ triangle

The area (A) of a triangle can be calculated using the following formula:

$$A = \frac{1}{2}bh.$$

Triassic The earliest period of the Mesozoic Era, from about 245 to 208 million years ago. During the Triassic Period, land life diversified, dinosaurs arose, and the earliest mammals appeared. *See chart at* **geological time,** pages 148–149.

tributary A stream that flows into a river or larger stream.

triceps The muscle at the back of the upper arm that straightens the elbow. The triceps has three points of attachment to bone at one end.

triceratops A large, plant-eating dinosaur of the late Cretaceous Period, measuring up to 7.5 metres in length. The triceratops had a beak-like mouth with a short horn over it and a long horn

over each eye. The back of its neck was covered with a wide, bony plate.

triclinic Relating to a crystal having three axes of different lengths intersecting at oblique angles. The mineral microcline (a type of feldspar) has triclinic crystals. *See more at* **crystal.**

tricuspid 1. A tooth having three points or cusps, especially a molar. 2. A heart valve consisting of three flaps between the right atrium and the right ventricle. It prevents a backflow of blood through the right side of the heart when the ventricles contract. *Compare* **bicuspid.**

triglyceride A compound consisting of three fatty acids and glycerol that is the chief constituent of fats and oils.

trigonal Relating to a crystal having three axes of equal length intersecting at oblique angles. This crystal system is considered a subset of the hexagonal system. The mineral quartz has trigonal crystals. Also called *rhombohedral. See more at* **crystal.**

trigonometric function A function of an angle, eg the sine, cosine or tangent, whose value is expressed as a ratio of two of the sides of the right-angled triangle that contains the angle.

trigonometry The study of the properties and uses of trigonometric functions.

trilobite Any of numerous extinct and mostly small arthropods that lived during the Palaeozoic Era. Trilobites had a hard outer covering divided into three lengthwise and three widthwise sections. Horseshoe crabs are considered to be their closest living relatives.

trinitrotoluene *See* **TNT.**

tritium A radioactive isotope of hydrogen whose nucleus has one proton and two neutrons and whose atomic mass is about 3. Tritium is rare in nature but can be made artificially in nuclear reactions. It is used in thermonuclear weapons and sometimes as a tracer. *See more at* **hydrogen.**

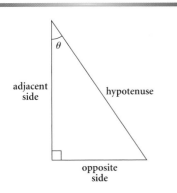

■ trigonometric function

In a right-angled triangle, the trigonometric functions are:

$$sine\ \theta = \frac{opposite}{hypotenuse} \qquad cosine\ \theta = \frac{adjacent}{hypotenuse}$$

$$tangent\ \theta = \frac{opposite}{adjacent}$$

trophic Relating to the feeding habits of different organisms in a food chain or web: *the trophic interactions between insects and mammals.* ❖ A group of organisms occupying the same position in a food chain is called a **trophic level.**

tropic 1. Either of the two parallels of latitude

■ **trilobite**

representing the points furthest north and south at which the sun can shine directly overhead. The northern tropic is the Tropic of Cancer, and the southern one is the Tropic of Capricorn. **2. tropics.** The region of the Earth lying between these latitudes and corresponding to the Torrid Zone. The tropics are generally the warmest and most humid region of the Earth. —*adjective* **tropical.**

Tropic of Cancer The parallel of latitude 23°27′ north of the equator. It forms the boundary between the Torrid Zone and the North Temperate Zone.

Tropic of Capricorn The parallel of latitude 23°27′ south of the equator. It forms the boundary between the Torrid Zone and the South Temperate Zone.

tropism Growth or movement of a plant or animal towards or away from an external stimulus, such as light, heat or gravity.

tropopause The boundary between the upper troposphere and the lower stratosphere, varying in altitude from about 8 kilometres at the poles to 18 kilometres at the equator.

troposphere The lowest region of the atmosphere, bounded by the Earth's surface and the tropopause and characterized by temperatures that decrease with increasing altitude. Weather and most cloud formations occur in the troposphere.

trough 1. A long narrow area of low atmospheric pressure. *Compare* **ridge. 2.** The lowest part of a wave. *See more at* **wave.**

true bug A wingless or four-winged insect having mouthparts adapted for piercing or sucking. Bedbugs and lice are examples of true bugs. *See panel at* **bug.**

true north *See* **geographic north.**

trypanosome Any of various parasitic protozoans that can cause serious diseases, such as sleeping sickness. They are transmitted by the bite of certain insects, such as tsetse flies.

trypsin An enzyme that aids digestion by

volcanic eruption   sea   land

■ **tsunami**
Waves created by a powerful underwater disturbance lose speed as they reach shallower water, but they gain height and get closer together.

speeding up the breakdown of proteins. It is produced by the pancreas and secreted into the small intestine.

tryptophan An essential amino acid. *See more at* **amino acid.**

tsetse fly Any of several bloodsucking African flies that often carry and transmit the protozoans that cause sleeping sickness.

tsunami A very large wave occurring in the sea that is caused by an underwater earthquake or volcanic eruption and often causes extreme destruction when it strikes land. *See panel at* **tidal wave.**

tuber The thickened part of an underground stem of a plant, such as the potato, bearing buds from which new plant shoots arise. *Compare* **bulb, corm, rhizome, runner.**

tubercle A small rounded projection or swelling, as on the roots of legumes or on skin or a bone.

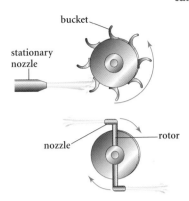

■ **turbine**

An impulse turbine (top) *rotates when the force of a stream of water hits cup-shaped buckets that are mounted around the perimeter of a rotor. In a reaction turbine* (bottom), *the pressure of the water being discharged from the nozzle forces the turbine to rotate in the direction opposite to the water's motion.*

tuberculosis A contagious disease caused by a bacterium and characterized by abnormal growths in the lungs or other body tissues. It is most often transmitted by breathing contaminated air and is most commonly found in areas where there is much overcrowding and poor social conditions. In the UK tuberculosis has been largely eradicated over the last century because of a major vaccination programme and greatly improved housing and working conditions.

tufa A rock formed of sediments deposited during the evaporation of lake water, spring water or groundwater. Tufa is usually composed of calcium carbonate.

tuff A rock made up of particles of volcanic ash, varying in size from fine sand to coarse gravel.

tumour An abnormal growth of tissue resulting from uncontrolled growth of cells and serving no function within the body; a cancerous growth. Tumours can be benign (unlikely to spread to other body parts) or malignant (likely to spread). *See panel at* **cancer.**

tundra A cold, treeless, usually lowland area of far northern regions. The subsoil of tundra is

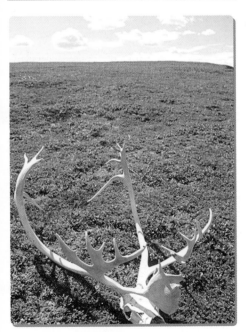

■ **tundra**
tundra in Northern Canada

permanently frozen, but in summer the top layer of soil thaws and can support low-growing mosses, lichens, grasses and small shrubs.

tungsten A hard, grey to white metallic element that is very resistant to corrosion. It has the highest melting point of all elements. Tungsten remains very strong at high temperatures and is used to make light-bulb filaments and to increase the hardness and strength of steel. Also called *wolfram. Symbol* **W**. *Atomic number* 74. *See* **Periodic Table**, pages 260–261.

tunicate Any of various primitive marine chordate animals having a rounded or cylindrical body that is enclosed in a tough outer covering. Tunicates start out life as free-swimming tadpole-like animals with a notochord (a primitive backbone). Many, such as the sea squirts, then lose the notochord and most of their nervous system as adults and become fixed to rocks or other objects.

turbine Any of various machines in which the kinetic energy of a moving fluid, such as water, steam, or gas is converted to rotary motion.

turbojet 1. A jet engine in which exhaust gas operates a turbine that in turn drives a compressor which forces air into the intake of the engine. **2.** An aircraft powered by an engine or engines of this type.

turbulent flow Movement of a fluid in which the individual particles of the fluid move in irregular patterns even though the overall flow is in one direction. Turbulent flow is common in nonviscous fluids which are moving at high velocities. *Compare* **laminar flow.**

turf A surface layer of earth containing a dense growth of grass and its matted roots.

Turing, Alan Mathison 1912–1954. British mathematician. In 1937 he formulated a precise mathematical concept for a theoretical computing machine, a key step in the development of the first computer. During World War II, Turing did important work on breaking German codes.

turpentine 1. A thin, easily vapourized oil, $C_{10}H_{16}$, that is distilled from the wood or resin of certain pine trees. It is used as a paint thinner and solvent. **2.** The sticky mixture of resin and oil from which this oil is distilled.

turtle Any of various reptiles living either in

Did You Know?

turbojet

Fully loaded, a jumbo-sized airliner weighs about 360,000 kilograms. Yet its *turbojet engines* are so powerful that it hurtles down the runway fast enough to lift it into air and climb to 35,000 feet. Where does this power come from? The answer is that it actually comes from the movement of air itself. Every turbojet has a compressor, a series of small rotating fan blades. These blades draw in air and pressurize it, driving it back into a combustion chamber where a fuel (such as kerosene) is injected and ignited. The burning of the fuel causes the air to expand, adding to the already high pressure and causing the mixture of hot air and gas to rush over turbines with enormous speed. This causes the turbine blades to turn, and they spin a drive shaft that rotates the compressor fans.

The hot pressurized air then blasts out the rear opening of the engine, forcing the plane forward. Most turbojet engines today are *turbofans* and have a large fan at the front that is turned by one of the turbines. Every second, the fan sucks in enough air to empty an average-sized house, adding to the volume and pressure of the air rotating the turbines and providing forward thrust.

water or on land and having a bony or leathery shell into which the head, legs and tail can be retracted for protection.

tusk A long, pointed tooth, usually one of a pair, projecting from the mouth of certain animals, such as elephants, walruses and wild pigs.

tympanic membrane *See* **eardrum.**

typhoid fever A life-threatening disease caused by bacteria and characterized by a high fever, intestinal bleeding and pink spots on the skin. It is transmitted through contaminated food and water.

typhoon A hurricane occurring in the western Pacific Ocean. *See panel at* **cyclone.**

typhus Any of several diseases transmitted by lice, fleas or mites and characterized by a fever and skin rash. The typhus which is carried by lice can cause epidemics of the disease and may be fatal in people with weakened immune systems.

tyrannosaurus *or* **tyrannosaur** A very large meat-eating dinosaur of the Cretaceous Period that had very small forelimbs and a large head with sharp teeth. It walked on two legs, probably bent forward with its long tail stretched out as a counterbalance. Tyrannosauruses grew to lengths of 14 metres or more.

tyrosine A nonessential amino acid. *See more at* **amino acid.**

U u

U The symbol for **uranium**.

udder A bag-shaped mammary gland of a cow and the females of related mammals, in which milk is formed and stored and from which it is taken in suckling or milking.

ulcer An inflamed sore on the skin or on a mucous membrane, for example in the mouth or stomach.

ulna The larger of the two bones of the forearm or lower portion of the foreleg. *See more at* **skeleton**.

ultrasound 1. Sound whose wave frequency is too high (over 20,000 hertz) to be heard by humans. 2. The medical use of ultrasound waves, especially to produce images of the inside of the body or to observe a developing fetus. — *adjective* **ultrasonic**.

ultraviolet *adjective* Relating to electromagnetic radiation having wavelengths shorter than those of visible light but longer than those of X-rays. *See more at* **electromagnetic spectrum**. —*noun* Ultraviolet light or the ultraviolet part of the spectrum. *See panel at* **infrared**.

umbel A flat or rounded flower cluster in which the individual flower stalks arise from about the same point on the stem. The geranium, milkweed and onion have umbels.

umbilical cord The flexible cord-like structure connecting a fetus at the abdomen to the placenta. It contains blood vessels that supply nourishment to the fetus and remove waste.

umbra 1. The darkest part of a shadow, especially the completely dark portion of the shadow cast by Earth, the moon or another body during an eclipse. 2. The darkest region of a sunspot. *Compare* **penumbra**.

uncertainty principle A principle in quantum mechanics stating that it is impossible to measure both the position and the momentum of very small particles (such as electrons) at the same time with accuracy. According to this principle, the more accurately the position of a small particle is known, the less accurately its mass and velocity can be known, and the more accurately its mass and velocity are known, the less accurately its position can be known. The uncertainty principle and the theory of relativity form the basis of modern physics.

undergrowth Low-growing plants, shrubs and young trees that grow alongside and beneath taller trees in a forest.

undertow An underwater current flowing strongly away from shore. Undertows are

Did You Know?

ultrasound

Many people own and use simple ultrasound generators: dog whistles that produce tones that dogs can hear but are too high to be heard by humans. Any sound whose frequency is higher than the upper end of the normal range of human hearing (higher than 20,000 hertz – that is, 20,000 sound waves per second) is called *ultrasound*. (Sound at frequencies too low to be audible – about 20 hertz or lower – is called *infrasound*.) The familiar medical ultrasound images (of a fetus in the womb, for example) are made by directing ultrasonic waves into the body, where they bounce off internal organs and other objects and are reflected back to a detector. Ultrasonic waves have very short wavelengths, and so they can create images of very small objects. Ultrasound can also be used to focus large amounts of energy into very small spaces, making it possible, for example, to break up kidney stones without making any surgical incisions.

generally caused by the seaward return of water from waves that have broken against the shore.

ungulate A hoofed mammal. There are two kinds of ungulates: those having an even number of toes (artiodactyls) and those having an odd number of toes (perissodactyls).

unicellular Having or consisting of a single cell; one-celled: *unicellular organisms. Compare* **multicellular.**

unified field theory A theory that combines the theories of the four basic forces of nature (electromagnetism, gravity, strong nuclear force and weak nuclear force) by establishing basic principles that apply to all of them and by determining how they are related to one another. No unified field theory that has been proposed so far has gained broad acceptance. Also called *grand unified theory.*

union A set whose members belong to at least one of a group of two or more given sets. The union of the sets {1,2,3} and {3,4,5} is the set {1,2,3,4,5}, and the union of the sets {6,7} and {11,12,13} is the set {6,7,11,12,13}.

univalve A mollusc, such as a snail, having a single shell. All univalves are gastropods. *Compare* **bivalve.**

universal time The mean time for the meridian at Greenwich in London (0° longitude), which runs through the former site of the Royal Observatory. It is used as a basis for calculating time throughout most of the world. Also called *Greenwich Mean Time.*

universe All matter and energy, including the Earth, the galaxies, and the contents of the space between the galaxies, regarded as a whole.

unsaturated **1.** Relating to an organic compound in which two or more of the carbon atoms are joined by a double or triple bond and therefore can be combined with additional atoms or radicals. Ethene, benzene and unsaturated fatty acids are examples of unsaturated compounds. *Compare* **saturated.** *See also* **monounsaturated, polyunsaturated. 2.** Relating to a solution that is capable of dissolving more solute than it already contains.

unsaturated fat A fat with a triglyceride molecule containing at least one unsaturated fatty acid. Fats derived from plants are often

■ **unsaturated**

unsaturated fats. Eating foods high in unsaturated fats can reduce the amount of cholesterol in the blood. *Compare* **saturated fat.**

unstable Opposite of **stable.** *See* **stable.**

uracil A base that is a component of RNA, forming a base pair with adenine during transcription.

uranium A heavy, silvery-white, highly toxic and radioactive metallic element of the actinide series. It occurs in several minerals and ores, such as pitchblende. Uranium is used as a fuel for nuclear reactors to generate electricity. *Symbol* **U.** *Atomic number* 92. *See* **Periodic Table,** pages 260–261.

Uranus The seventh planet from the sun and the third largest, with a diameter about four times that of the Earth. Uranus is composed mainly of hydrogen and helium gases and is encircled by a thin system of rings. *See table at* **solar system,** pages 314–315. *See panel at* **planet.**

urea The chief nitrogen-containing waste product excreted in the urine of mammals and some fish. It is produced by the breakdown of amino acids in the liver and is also made artificially for use in fertilizers and medicine.

ureter Either of two long, narrow ducts that carry urine from the kidney to the urinary bladder.

urethra The duct through which urine passes from the bladder to the outside of the body in most mammals and some fish and birds. In most male mammals, semen also passes through the urethra during ejaculation. It is impossible for urine and semen to pass through the urethra at the same time.

Urey

Urey, Harold Clayton 1893–1981. American chemist who discovered deuterium (1932). He also developed theories on the formation of the planets and on the synthesis of elements in the Earth's primitive atmosphere.

uric acid The chief nitrogen-containing waste product excreted in the urine of birds, insects and most reptiles. It is produced by the breakdown of amino acids in the liver.

urinary tract The system of organs of the body involved in the formation and excretion of urine. In most vertebrate animals, the urinary tract consists mainly of the kidneys, ureters and bladder. In most mammals, and some fish and birds, urine is discharged from the bladder through the urethra.

urine A liquid or semisolid substance containing waste products of metabolism that are filtered from the blood by the kidneys. In most mammals and some fish and birds, urine is stored in the urinary bladder and discharged from the body through the urethra.

Ursa Major Also known as the Great Bear, this constellation is found in the polar region of the Northern Hemisphere near Draco and Leo. The seven brightest stars of the constellation form an easily identified shape, resembling a giant ladle or saucepan. In the UK this pattern is known as the Plough, while in the United States it is called the Big Dipper, and among Hindus it represents the seven rishis, or holy sages of ancient times.

Ursa Minor Also known as the Little Bear, this constellation is also found near the north celestial pole. It contains an arrangement of stars known in the United States as the Little Dipper. More importantly, the brightest star in the constellation is the North or Pole star, Polaris, which is found at the end of the Bear's tail.

U-shaped valley A valley with a flat bottom and steep sides, formed by a glacier.

uterus The hollow muscular organ found in female mammals where the young develop inside

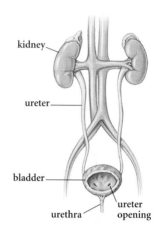

■ **urinary tract**
human urinary tract

the mother's body. A fertilized egg attaches to the lining of the uterus and develops into an embryo and then a fetus. The uterus provides a safe, cushioned environment with a plentiful supply of nutrients and oxygen that enables the developing fetus to thrive. In most mammals the uterus is divided into two parts, but in humans it is a single structure. It lies between the bladder and the rectum. The fallopian tubes open into the top part of the uterus, while the cervix opens into the vagina. The uterine muscles are capable of immensely strong contractions that are used to push the fully developed embryo out of the uterus through the cervix and vagina during birth. *See more at* **menstrual cycle.**

UV index A scale ranging from zero to ten, used to estimate the risk of sunburn in midday sunlight. The UV index takes into account conditions such as the amount of cloud cover and ozone in the atmosphere.

uvula The small cone-shaped mass of fleshy tissue that hangs from the end of the soft palate above the tongue in the back of the mouth.

V 1. The symbol for **vanadium. 2.** Abbreviation of **volume.**

vaccine A substance that stimulates cells in the immune system to recognize and attack disease-causing agents, especially through the production of antibodies. Most vaccines are given by injection or are swallowed as liquids. Vaccines may contain a weakened or dead form of a disease-causing microorganism such as a virus or bacterium. On the other hand, they may contain a DNA fragment or some of the antigenic markers that trigger the immune response. Whatever is used, it is important that the original disease cannot be caught from the vaccine. *See panel at* **Jenner.**

vacuole A space in a cell's cytoplasm that is surrounded by a membrane and filled with a watery fluid. The fluid stores food prior to digestion or waste products prior to excretion. *See more at* **cell.**

vacuum 1. A condition in which there is no matter or very little matter. **2.** An enclosed space, such as the space inside a container, in which there are far fewer gas molecules than in an equal volume of the air outside it. A vacuum has a much lower gas pressure than that of the atmosphere at sea level.

vacuum flask A small container with a double wall and a partial vacuum in the space between the two walls. Vacuum flasks are used to minimize the transfer of heat between the inside and the outside and thus keep the contents at a desired temperature.

vacuum tube An electron tube from which nearly all air has been removed so that the moving electrons don't collide with any gas particles and can move more efficiently from one electrode to the other. Cathode-ray tubes, which include television picture tubes and other video display tubes, are the most widely used vacuum tubes. *Compare* **electron tube.**

vagina The part of the reproductive tract in female mammals that is connected to the uterus at one end and opens to the outside of the body at the other end. Offspring pass through the vagina during birth.

vagus nerve A long nerve that passes from the brain to the face, trunk and abdomen. It controls the muscles of the larynx (voice box), stimulates digestion and regulates the heartbeat. The vagus nerve is a cranial nerve.

Did You Know?

vaccine

In the 1950s, polio epidemics left thousands of children with permanent physical disabilities. Today, young children are routinely offered a polio vaccine to protect them from the virus. This *vaccine,* like most others, works by stimulating the body's immune system to produce antibodies – substances that defend the body against infection by recognizing and destroying disease-causing agents like viruses and bacteria. Scientists usually prepare vaccines by taking a sample of the disease-causing agent and weakening it with heat or chemicals. That way, the agent loses its ability to cause serious illness but is still able to stimulate the body to produce antibodies and provide immunity. But finding safe vaccines that are also effective is a challenge. Today, scientists are able to change the structure of viruses and bacteria at the level of their DNA. They remove the most harmful fragments of DNA and then use what is left in vaccines. New vaccines containing harmless bits of DNA from disease-causing germs have also been developed, all to make diseases like polio a thing of the past.

valine An essential amino acid. *See more at* **amino acid.**

valley A long, narrow region of low land between ranges of mountains, hills or other high areas, often having a river or stream running along the bottom. Valleys are most commonly formed through the erosion of land by rivers or glaciers. They also form where large regions of land are lowered because of geological faults.

value 1. *Mathematics.* An assigned or calculated numerical quantity. **2.** The relative darkness or lightness of a colour. *See more at* **colour.**

valve 1a. Any of various mechanical devices that control the flow of liquids, gases or loose material through pipes or channels by blocking and uncovering openings. **b.** The movable part or element of such a device. **2.** Any of various structures that prevent the backwards flow of a body fluid. Examples include the valves between the chambers of the heart and the valves of the veins. **3.** One of the paired hinged shells of certain molluscs, such as clams and oysters.

vanadium A soft, bright-white metallic element that occurs naturally in several minerals. It has good structural strength and is used especially to make strong varieties of steel. *Symbol* **V.** *Atomic number* 23. *See* **Periodic Table,** pages 260–261.

Van Allen belt Either of two zones of high-intensity radiation surrounding the Earth. In these zones, a large number of atomic particles with high energies are trapped by the Earth's magnetic field.

Van de Graaff, Robert Jemison 1901–1967. American physicist. In 1929, he invented an electrical generator (later called the Van de Graaff generator) that was adapted for use as a particle accelerator and became an important research tool for atomic physicists. The generator was also used to produce a type of X-ray helpful in treating cancer.

Van de Graaff generator A device used to build up an electric charge by transferring charged particles from a moving belt to a spherical electrode. When an object, such as a person, touches the electrode, the generator transfers to the object the charge that has built up on the electrode. This means that a person's hair will stand on end if they touch the electrode as the positively charged particles race to the hair tips and then repel each other.

van der Waals force A weak force of attraction between two non-polar molecules. The weak force of attraction arises because of uneven charge distributions that exist momentarily in the electron clouds surrounding the molecule. This uneven charge distribution affects any other molecules close by, producing a corresponding uneven charge distribution in these too. The interactions between these molecules result in a net attractive force between them – although these forces are very small. The van der Waals force between atoms is what causes the noble gases to condense into a liquid as they are cooled.

vapour 1. The gaseous state of a substance that is liquid at room temperature. Because the carbon dioxide gas associated with dry ice is often referred to as a vapour, some scientists classify the gaseous state of substances that are solids at room temperature as vapours as well. **2.** A faintly visible suspension of fine particles of matter in the air, such as mist, fumes or smoke. **3.** A mixture of fine droplets of a substance and air, such as the fuel mixture of an internal-combustion engine. — *verb* **vaporize.**

vapour pressure 1. The pressure exerted by water vapour in the atmosphere. **2.** The pressure exerted by a vapour on the solid or liquid phase

electrode
collecting comb
conveyor belt
charged comb

■ **Van de Graaff generator**
Charge is transferred to the moving belt as it rubs on the lower pulley. This charge is carried up the belt and is transferred onto the upper electrode via the collecting comb.

with which it is in equilibrium. At pressures lower than the vapour pressure, atoms or molecules of the liquid or solid being vaporized can escape from the surface of the liquid or solid. At the vapour pressure, they cannot escape because the two phases are in equilibrium.

variable 1. A mathematical quantity capable of assuming any of a set of values, such as *x* in the expression 3*x* + 2. **2.** A factor or condition that is subject to change, especially one that is allowed to change in a scientific experiment to test a hypothesis. *See more at* **control.**

variable star A star whose brightness changes periodically. The variation can occur because of internal changes in a single star or because a darker star periodically eclipses a brighter star in a binary star system.

varicella *See* **chickenpox.**

vascular 1. *Zoology.* Relating to the vessels of the body, especially the arteries and veins, that carry blood and lymph: *the vascular system.* **2.** *Botany.* Relating to or having tissues that carry water and dissolved nutrients and food from one part of a plant to another. All seed-bearing plants and ferns have vascular tissues; bryophytes, such as mosses, do not. *See more at* **phloem, photosynthesis, xylem.**

vascular cambium The cambium that produces the vascular tissues xylem and phloem in woody plants. *See more at* **cambium.**

vas deferens Either of two ducts through which sperm passes from a testis to the urethra.

vector 1. A quantity, such as velocity or change of position, that has both magnitude and direction. *Compare* **scalar. 2.** An organism, such as a mosquito or tick, that spreads disease-causing microorganisms from one host to another without harm to itself.

Vega A star in the constellation Lyra. It is the fifth brightest star in the night sky.

vegetable 1. A plant that is cultivated for an edible part, such as the leaf of spinach. **2.** An edible part of one of these plants. *See panel at* **fruit.**

vegetable kingdom *See* **plant kingdom.**

vein 1. Any of the blood vessels that carry blood towards the heart. Veins are thin-walled and contain valves that prevent the backflow of blood.

Usage

vapour/steam

When we use the words *vapour* and *steam,* we usually think of a fine mist or other visible suspension of particles in the air. We speak of the steam that fills the bathroom after we take a shower or the vapour in the jet of water droplets that appears a short distance from the end of a boiling kettle. But to a scientist, these expressions are inaccurate. The word *vapour* refers to a gaseous state of a substance, and not to a mist of liquid droplets or fine solid particles. For instance, the fumes that arise when volatile substances such as alcohol and petrol evaporate are (not surprisingly) a vapour. Similarly, the visible stream of water droplets that rush out of the spout of the kettle is not steam. As the gaseous state of water heated past its boiling point, steam is invisible. Usually, there is a clear space of a couple of centimetres between the spout and the beginning of the visible stream of droplets. This space contains steam. The steam loses its heat to the surrounding air, then falls below the boiling point and condenses in the air as water droplets. It is not, scientifically speaking, water vapour.

All veins except the pulmonary vein (which returns to the heart from the lungs) carry blood having low levels of oxygen. **2.** One of the narrow, usually branching tubes or supporting parts forming the framework of a leaf or an insect's wing. *See more at* **leaf. 3.** A long, narrow deposit of mineral or rock found in another type of rock. Veins usually form when magma fills a fracture in a rock. —*adjective* **venous.**

veldt *also* **veld** An extensive, treeless grassland of southern Africa.

velociraptor A small but fast-running, meat-eating dinosaur of the Cretaceous Period about 2 metres in length. It had long curved claws, walked on two legs that were adapted for leaping and had a long stiff tail used as a counterweight. Velociraptors were a kind of raptor.

velocity The rate of change of distance with time in a specified direction.

vena cava Either of two large veins that carry blood with low levels of oxygen to the right atrium of the heart. The lower one, called the inferior vena cava, is the largest vein in the body. The upper one drains the blood from the head and top part of the body, and is called the superior vena cava.

venation 1. The distribution or arrangement of a system of veins, for example a leaf blade. **2.** The veins of such a system considered as a group.

venereal disease *See* **sexually transmitted disease.**

Venn diagram A diagram that uses circles to represent sets. Relations between the sets can be indicated by the arrangement of the circles, for example by drawing one circle within another to indicate that the first set is a subset of a second set.

venom A poisonous substance that is secreted by

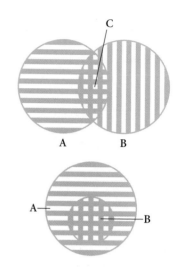

■ **Venn diagram**

top: *Sets* A *and* B *intersect to form set* C. *All members of* C *are common to* A *and* B.

bottom: *Set* B *is a subset of set* A. *All members of* B *are also members of* A.

certain snakes, spiders, scorpions and insects. It can be transmitted to a victim by a bite or sting.

ventral Of or on the front or lower surface of an animal.

ventricle 1. A chamber of the heart that receives blood from one or more atria and pumps it into the arteries. Mammals, birds and reptiles have two ventricles; amphibians and fish have one. **2.** Any of four fluid-filled cavities in the brain of vertebrate animals. —*adjective* **ventricular.**

Venus The second planet from the sun and the fourth smallest, with a diameter about 650 kilometres less than that of the Earth. Venus comes nearer to the Earth than any other planet and is the brightest object in the night sky aside from Earth's moon. It is the hottest planet in the solar system, with an average surface temperature of 457°C. *See table at* **solar system,** pages 314–315. *See panel at* **planet.**

Venus flytrap A type of carnivorous plant, usually found on poor, boggy soil, which has leaf blades edged with spines. The leaves form a trap and contain sensitive hairs. When a fly or other

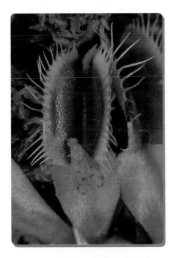

■ **Venus flytrap**

insect brushes against several of these hairs, the leaf trap closes and the spines overlap so the insect cannot get out. The plant then secretes digestive enzymes that break down the body of the insect, and the products of digestion are absorbed to provide mineral nutrition for the plant.

vernal equinox The moment of the year when the sun crosses the celestial equator while moving from south to north. It occurs on 20 or 21 March, marking the beginning of spring in the Northern Hemisphere. *Compare* **autumnal equinox.**

Vernier, Pierre 1580–1637. French mathematician and maker of scientific instruments, known especially for his invention of a highly exact scale.

vertebra (*plural* **vertebrae** *or* **vertebras**) Any of the bones that make up the vertebral column. Each vertebra contains a hollow section through which the spinal cord passes. *See more at* **skeleton.**

vertebral column The series of vertebrae extending from the base of the skull to the coccyx (tailbone) that forms the supporting axis of the body in vertebrate animals. It encloses and protects the spinal cord and provides a stable attachment for the muscles of the trunk. Also called *backbone, spinal column, spine.*

vertebrate Any of a large group of animals having a backbone, including fish, amphibians, reptiles, birds and mammals. Vertebrates are bilaterally symmetrical and have an internal skeleton of bone or cartilage, a nervous system along the back that is divided into brain and spinal cord, and not more than two pairs of limbs.

vertex (*plural* **vertices** *or* **vertexes**) **1.** The point at which the sides of an angle intersect. **2.** The point of a triangle, cone or pyramid that is opposite to and furthest away from its base; the apex. **3.** A point of a polyhedron at which three or more of the edges intersect.

vertical angles Two angles formed by two intersecting lines and lying on opposite sides of the point of intersection.

Vesalius, Andreas 1514–1564. Flemish anatomist and surgeon who is considered the founder of modern anatomy. His major work, *On the Structure of the Human Body* (1543), was based on his detailed dissection of corpses. *See panel on* page 362.

vesicle A small fluid-filled sac in the body or in an individual cell.

vestigial Relating to a body part that has become small and lost its use because of evolutionary change. Whales, for example, have small bones located in the muscles of their body walls that are vestigial bones of hips and hind limbs, while the human appendix is a vestigial organ of the gut.

veterinary medicine The branch of medicine that deals with the diseases or injuries of animals and their treatment.

vibration A rapid motion of a particle or an elastic solid back and forth in a straight line on both sides of a central position. Vibrations consist of many oscillations. *Compare* **oscillation.**

villus (*plural* **villi**) A small projection on the surface of a mucous membrane, especially that of the small intestine.

vinyl Any of various chemical compounds that contain the group C_2H_3 and are used to make plastics, fabrics and paints.

Virgo A constellation in the region of the celestial equator near Leo and Libra.

virology The scientific study of viruses and viral diseases.

Biography

Andreas Vesalius

Vesalius followed his family's tradition and studied medicine. On being awarded his degree, he began teaching and overseeing demonstrations of anatomy to students. To improve his knowledge he also dissected corpses – something that was unusual for a man in his position, who would usually have left such work to an assistant. After a few years, he became convinced that the anatomical theories put forward by Galen, a Greek physician whose ideas had been accepted as authoritative for over 1000 years, were not based on the human body. Instead, Vesalius maintained that Galen's description of the human body was based on dissections of pigs, dogs and other animals. Vesalius did what no one had done before: he critically evaluated Galen's anatomical texts, comparing them with the observations that he made himself during his dissections. Vesalius compiled his findings in a book on anatomy. He had artists make illustrations for it, and he supervised their work. His *On the Structure of the Human Body* was the most extensive and accurate description of the human body that had ever been compiled. By relying on careful observation instead of received wisdom, Vesalius revolutionized the field of anatomy, and of medicine and biology as well.

virus **1.** Any of a large group of disease-causing agents consisting of a segment of RNA or DNA within a protein shell. All viruses are parasites because they can reproduce only inside the cells of plants, animals and bacteria. Viruses are usually not considered to be living organisms. **2.** *Computer Science.* A computer program that is meant to disable or damage the computer's memory or to cause another program to malfunction. Computer viruses usually copy themselves over and over again. —*adjective* **viral.**

viscosity The resistance of a substance to flow. A substance that can flow easily has a low viscosity. A substance that cannot flow easily has a high viscosity.

viscous Having relatively high resistance to flow. As the molecules of a viscous fluid, such as honey, slide past each other, the friction between them causes the fluid to flow slowly.

vitamin Any of various complex organic compounds that are needed in small amounts for normal growth and activity of the body and are found naturally in foods obtained from plants and animals.

vitamin A A vitamin important for normal vision, tissue growth and healthy skin. It is found in fish-liver oils, milk, green leafy vegetables and yellow vegetables and fruits. Also called *retinol.*

vitamin B complex Any of a group of related vitamins important for normal cell growth and metabolism. The vitamins of the vitamin B complex include thiamine (vitamin B_1), riboflavin (vitamin B_2), pantothenic acid, niacin, biotin and folic acid. ❖ The complex also includes **vitamin B_6** (also called *pyridoxine*), which is important in protein and fat metabolism and in healthy nerve function. It is found in liver, wholegrain foods, fish, yeast and many vegetables. ❖ Another vitamin in this complex, **vitamin B_{12}** (also called *cobalamin*), is important in maintaining the health of blood and nerves. It is found in meat, eggs, milk and milk products.

vitamin C A vitamin important for healthy skin, teeth, bones and blood vessels. It is found especially in citrus fruit, tomatoes, potatoes and green leafy vegetables. Also called *ascorbic acid.*

vitamin D Any of a group of vitamins necessary for normal bone growth. Vitamin D is found in milk, fish and eggs and can be produced in the skin on exposure to sunlight.

vitamin E A vitamin important for normal cell growth and function. It is found in vegetable oils, wheat germ, green leafy vegetables and egg yolks.

vitamin K Any of a group of vitamins important for normal clotting of the blood. Vitamin K is found in green leafy vegetables, pork, liver and vegetable oils.

vitreous Relating to or resembling glass; glassy.

vitreous humour The jelly-like substance that

Did You Know?

vitamins

To help the cells in our bodies work properly, it is essential that we get a daily supply of vitamins. This link between vitamins and good health was made in the early 1900s by the Polish biochemist Casimir Funk. Funk was studying beriberi, a disease that damages nerves, when he discovered an organic compound that prevented this illness. He named the compound vitamine, or "life amine", a name that stuck even though most vitamins do not include the type of chemical called an amine. Another important piece of research was carried out in Cambridge by Sir Frederick Gowlan Hopkins who took two groups of young rats and fed each on a diet containing all the carbohydrates, proteins, fats, minerals and water they needed. He gave one group an additional very small amount of milk. The other group got no milk. The group given milk grew well and thrived. Without the milk – and the vitamins it contained – the other young rats grew very little. As soon as milk (and so vitamins) was added to their diet, their growth rate shot up. Today we know that vitamins help keep our bodies strong and healthy, in addition to preventing a variety of illnesses. But because our bodies cannot produce these compounds, we must get them in the foods we eat as part of a well-balanced diet.

---

fills the area of the eyeball between the retina and the lens.

viviparous Giving birth to living young that develop within the mother's body rather than hatching from eggs. Most mammals are viviparous. *Compare* **oviparous, ovoviviparous.**

vivisection The practice of examining internal organs and tissues by cutting into or dissecting a living animal.

vocal cords The two folded pairs of membranes in the larynx (voice box) that vibrate when air that is exhaled passes through them, producing sound.

voice box *See* **larynx.**

volatile Changing easily from liquid to vapour at normal temperatures and pressures.

volcanic arc *See* **island arc.**

volcano 1. An opening in the Earth's crust from which lava, ash and hot gases flow or are thrown out during an eruption. **2.** A usually cone-shaped mountain formed by the materials that flowed or were thrown out from such an opening. *See more at* **tectonic boundary.**

volt A unit used to measure electromotive force or potential difference. A potential difference of one volt exists between two points when one joule of work must be done to move one coulomb of charge between them.

Volta, Count **Alessandro** 1745–1827. Italian physicist who invented the electric battery (1800). Called the voltaic pile, it was the first device to produce a steady stream of electric current. The volt unit of electromotive force is named after him.

voltage Electromotive force or potential difference expressed in volts. A current of high voltage is used to transmit electric power over long distances.

voltaic cell A device that produces an electric current by means of a chemical reaction that causes ions to form at one electrode and flow towards another electrode. The electrodes are made of different metals and are immersed in a reactive solution of electrolytes. Car batteries are voltaic cells. *Compare* **electrolytic cell.**

voltmeter An instrument, such as a galvanometer, used for measuring the difference in voltage between two points in an electric circuit.

volume 1. The amount of space occupied by a three-dimensional object or region of space, measured in cubic units, eg mm^3, cm^3 etc. **2.** A measure of the loudness or intensity of a sound.

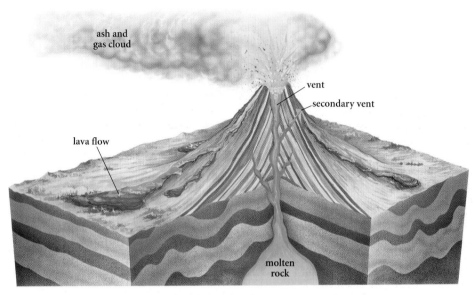

ash and
gas cloud

vent

secondary vent

lava flow

molten
rock

■ **volcano**

volumetric Relating to measurement by volume or to a unit that is used to measure volume.

voluntary Under conscious control. The muscles attached to the skeleton are voluntary muscles because they can be moved at will.

vortex (*plural* **vortexes** *or* **vortices**) A spiral motion of a fluid, especially a whirling mass of water or air that sucks everything near it towards its centre. Eddies and whirlpools are examples of vortexes.

vulcanize To harden rubber by heating it and combining it with sulphur. Vulcanization gives rubber more strength and elasticity.

vulgar fraction A fraction in which the numerator is smaller than the denominator, for example $\frac{7}{8}$. Also called **proper fraction.**

vulva The external genital organs of female mammals.

■ **vortex**

W The symbol for **tungsten**.

wadi A gully or streambed in northern Africa and southwest Asia that remains dry except during the local rainy season.

Waksman, Selman Abraham 1888–1973. American microbiologist who pioneered the development of antibiotics. His discoveries included streptomycin (1944), the first drug effective against tuberculosis.

Wallace, Alfred Russel 1823–1913. British naturalist who formulated a theory of evolution by natural selection independently of Charles Darwin. Wallace spent eight years (1854–1862) travelling in Malaysia and assembling evidence for his theories, which he sent to Darwin in England. Their findings were presented to the public in 1858.

Walton, Ernest Thomas Sinton 1903–1995. Irish physicist who developed the particle accelerator with John Cockcroft. Their experiments with it led to the first successful splitting of an atom, in 1932.

warm-blooded Having a relatively warm body temperature that stays about the same regardless of changes in the temperature of the surroundings. Birds and mammals are warm-blooded.

warm front The forward edge of an advancing mass of warm air that rises over a mass of cold air. A warm front is often accompanied by a prolonged period of steady rain. *See more at* **front.**

warren An area where a colony of rabbits lives in burrows.

wart 1. A small growth on the skin caused by a virus, occurring typically on the hands or feet. **2.** A similar growth, as on a plant.

wasp Any of numerous insects having two pairs of wings, mouths adapted for biting or sucking and, in the females, an egg-laying tube (called an ovipositor) that is often modified as a sting.

Wasps are related to ants and bees and can be solitary or live in colonies.

water A clear, liquid compound of hydrogen and oxygen, H_2O. Water covers about three-quarters of the Earth's surface and also occurs in solid form as ice and in gaseous form as vapour. It is an essential component of all organisms, and it is necessary for most biological processes. Water freezes at 0°C and boils at 100°C.

water cycle The continuous process by which water is distributed throughout the Earth and its atmosphere. Energy from the sun causes water to evaporate from the sea and other bodies of water and from soil surfaces. Plants and animals also add water vapour to the air by transpiration. As it rises into the atmosphere, the water vapour condenses to form clouds. Rain and other forms of precipitation return water to the Earth, where it flows into bodies of water and into the ground, beginning the cycle over again. Also called *hydrologic cycle.*

water flea Any of various small aquatic crustaceans, mostly of microscopic size, having especially long antennae that are used for

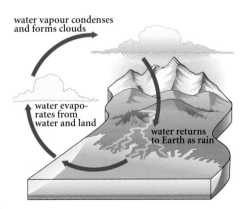

water vapour condenses and forms clouds

water evaporates from water and land

water returns to Earth as rain

■ **water cycle**

swimming. Water fleas are an important source of food for many fish.

watershed 1. The entire region that is drained by a river system. 2. A ridge forming a boundary between two different river systems.

water table The level at which the ground beneath the surface is saturated with water. The water table usually rises after heavy rainfall and the melting of snow and falls during drier periods.

water vapour Water in its gaseous state, especially in the atmosphere and at a temperature below the boiling point.

Watson, James Dewey Born 1928. American biologist who with Francis Crick identified the structure of DNA. By analysing the patterns cast by X-rays striking DNA molecules, they discovered that DNA has the structure of a double helix, two spirals linked together by bases in ladder-like rungs. Their discovery formed the basis of molecular genetics.

Watson-Watt, Robert Alexander 1892–1973. British physicist who pioneered the development of radar. In 1919 he produced a system for locating thunderstorms by tracking their radio emissions. In the 1930s Watson-Watt led the team that developed radar into a practical system for locating aircraft.

watt A unit used to measure power, equal to one joule of work per second.

Watt, James 1736–1819. British engineer, inventor and scientist. He invented the steam engine (1769) and devised the unit of horsepower. The watt unit of power is named after him.

wattage An amount of power, especially electrical power, expressed in watts or kilowatts.

watt-hour A unit of power, especially electrical power, equal to the work done by one watt acting for one hour. It is equivalent to 3600 joules.

wave A disturbance or vibration that transfers energy from one place to another. *See also* **longitudinal wave, transverse wave.** *See panel at* **refraction.**

wavelength The distance between one point on the disturbance of a wave and a similar point on the next disturbance.

wave mechanics A theory that explains the behaviour of subatomic particles as wave motion.

Certain physical phenomena, such as the movement of an electron from one atomic shell to another, can be accurately described using this theory.

wax Any of various solid, usually yellow substances that melt or soften easily when heated. Waxes are produced in nature by various animals and plants, or are made artificially. They are similar to fats, but are less greasy and more brittle.

weak nuclear force A force that causes subatomic particles within the nuclei of atoms to decay or break up into smaller particles and to give off energy as radiation. The weak nuclear force is one of the four basic forces in nature, being weaker than the strong nuclear force and the electromagnetic force but stronger than gravity. Also called *weak interaction.*

weather The state of the atmosphere at a particular time and place. Weather is described by variable conditions such as temperature, humidity, wind velocity, precipitation and barometric pressure.

weathering The breakdown of rock. Weathering can be caused by freeze-thaw (water freezes in cracks, causing splitting), hydration (absorption of water), oxidation (reaction with oxygen) and solution (rainwater dissolves the rock).

web 1. A structure of fine silky strands woven by spiders or by certain insect larvae. The web of a spider is used to catch insect prey. 2. A fold of skin or thin tissue connecting the toes of certain animals, especially ones that swim, such as water birds and otters. The web improves the ability of the foot to push against water. 3. *See also* **Web, World Wide Web.**

Wegener, Alfred Lothar 1880–1930. German physicist, meteorologist and explorer who introduced the theory of continental drift in 1915. His hypothesis was controversial and remained so until the 1960s, when new scientific understanding of the structure of seafloors provided evidence that his theory was correct. *See more at* **plate tectonics.**

weight 1. The force with which an object near the Earth or another celestial body is attracted towards the centre of the body by gravity. An object's weight depends on its mass (the amount

Waves

Sound, light, X-rays and other types of energy spread outwards in the form of waves. Mechanical waves travel through what is known as a medium: the medium of a sound wave consists of the atoms making up any form of matter, for example, and the medium of a wave in the sea is the seawater. Waves have a characteristic structure and fall into two basic types: longitudinal and transverse. They also have other properties that are illustrated below.

Structure of a Wave

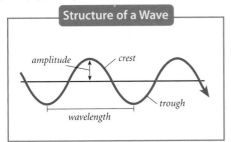

amplitude   *crest*

trough

wavelength

Wave Frequency

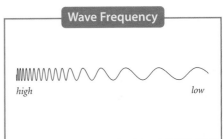

high   *low*

Types of Waves (as illustrated by a coil)

Longitudinal (medium is compressed)

Transverse (medium disturbed at right angles to direction of wave)

Interference

wave 1 – – –
+ wave 2 – – –
= wave 3 ——

Constructive (waves 1 and 2 in phase)   *Destructive* (waves 1 and 2 out of phase)

Reflection, Refraction and Diffraction

Reflection
The two angles are equal.

angle of incidence   *angle of reflection*

light ray

mirror

Refraction
The two angles are not equal.

angle of incidence

AIR

WATER

angle of refraction

light ray

Diffraction

light waves

Usage

weight/mass

No matter where it is, an object always has the same mass, which we measure in kilograms. The mass of an object is a measure of how much matter there is in it, and tells us about that object's tendency to resist changes to the way in which it is moving (which we call its inertia). On the other hand, an object's weight tells us the size of the force exerted on that object in a gravitational field – so weight is measured in newtons. If you were walking on the Moon, for example, your mass would be the same as it is here on Earth. Your weight, however, would be one sixth of what it is here on Earth, because of the smaller gravitational field around the Moon.

of matter it consists of) and the strength of the gravitational field. On Earth, for example, an object weighs less at the top of a very high mountain than it does at sea level, simply because the gravitational pull at the top of the mountain is weaker than it is at sea level. **2.** A unit used as a measure of gravitational force: *a table of weights and measures.* **3.** A system of such measures: *avoirdupois weight; troy weight.*

Weinberg, Steven Born 1933. American nuclear physicist who helped develop important theories explaining the relationship between the electromagnetic force and the weak nuclear force, two of the four basic forces of nature.

Western Hemisphere The half of the Earth that includes North America, Central America and South America.

Westinghouse, George 1846–1914. American engineer and manufacturer who introduced the high-voltage alternating current system for the transmission of electricity in the United States. A prolific inventor, Westinghouse received 361 patents in his lifetime, including the air brake, automated train-switching signals and devices for the transmission of natural gas. His inventions made an important contribution to the expansion of the railways.

wet cell An electric cell in which the chemicals producing the current are in the form of a liquid rather than in the form of a paste (as in a dry cell). Car batteries consist of a series of wet cells.

wetland A low-lying area of land that is saturated with moisture, especially when regarded as the natural habitat of wildlife. Marshes, swamps and bogs are examples of wetlands.

Did You Know?

wetland

The idea of a *wetland* may strike you as strange, because we usually think of the world as either wet (rivers, lakes, seas) or dry (mountains, plains, coasts). But wetlands are both. They're soggy enough that you wouldn't want to go camping in them, but there's enough soil for plants like reeds, bushes and even trees to take root and grow. In the past, many wetlands were filled in to make farmland or to develop the area for housing. Today, however, scientists have discovered that wetlands can act like huge filters, removing pollutants from the waters of an area before those substances can do harm. They can serve as reservoirs, and they may help in flood control by absorbing excess water. Wetlands are also home to many different plant and animal species that have evolved to live in the wetland's unique conditions.

wetlands in Kakadu National Park, Australia

whale Any of various, often large sea mammals that have a streamlined body resembling that of a fish, forelimbs shaped like flippers, a tail with horizontal flukes and one or two blowholes for breathing. The mouths of whales may contain teeth, or they may be filled wth baleen sheets that are used to filter plankton from the water.

whalebone *See* baleen.

whirlpool A rapidly rotating current of water or other liquid, such as one produced by the meeting of two tides.

white blood cell Any of various white or colourless cells in the blood of vertebrate animals, many of which act to protect the body against infection and to repair tissues after injury. White blood cells have a nucleus, unlike red blood cells, and are formed mainly in the bone marrow. The major types of white blood cells are granulocytes, lymphocytes and monocytes. Also called *leukocyte.*

white dwarf A whitish star that is very dense and very small, about the size of the Earth. A white dwarf is what remains after the central star of a planetary nebula burns out and becomes cool and dim. *See more at* star. *See panel at* dwarf star.

white matter The whitish tissue of the brain and spinal cord in vertebrate animals, made up chiefly of nerve fibres covered in myelin sheaths. *Compare* grey matter.

Whittle, Sir Frank 1907–1996. British aeronautical engineer and inventor who developed the first aircraft engine powered by jet propulsion (1937).

whole number A positive integer or zero.

whooping cough A bacterial infection of the airways and lungs that causes spasms of coughing ending in loud gasps. It occurs mostly in children and can lead to serious complications and even death. The incidence of whooping cough has fallen dramatically in countries such as the UK as a result of vaccination programmes. Also called *pertussis.*

Wilkins, Maurice Hugh Frederick Born 1916. British biophysicist who contributed to the discovery of the structure of DNA. He worked with Rosalind Franklin to produce X-ray studies of DNA that helped to establish its structure as a double helix.

Did You Know?

whale

In a submarine, you can travel down thousands of metres underwater. But if you swam outside it, the water pressure would crush you as if you were an empty drinks can. Amazingly, there are many animals that happily exist in such conditions. The sperm whale, for instance, may dive as deep as two miles with no ill effects. A male sperm whale has the same dimensions as a huge lorry, up to 18 metres long and 57 tonnes in weight. Many adaptations allow the huge creature, and other deep-sea organisms, to function normally at great depths. One important strength is actually a weakness: unlike our rigid ribs, the whale's flexible ribcage allows its chest cavity to collapse in a controlled way as the pressure increases. Other adaptations control the way gases are stored in the blood. Unlike people, whales do not have to return to the surface gradually to avoid getting the *bends* – the sometimes deadly formation of nitrogen bubbles caused by expanding gas in the blood. Because of this adaptation, whales can swim up and down as fast as they like, undergoing tremendous variation in pressure, with no ill effects.

Wilson, Charles Thomson Rees 1869–1959. British physicist noted for his research on atmospheric electricity. He developed the Wilson cloud chamber, a device that makes it possible to study and photograph the movement and interaction of electrically charged particles. *See more at* cloud chamber.

Wilson, Edmund Beecher 1856–1939. American zoologist who was one of the founders of modern genetics. He researched the structure and organization of cells, emphasizing the importance of cells as the building blocks of life. Wilson demonstrated the function of the cell and the significance of chromosomes, especially sex chromosomes, in heredity.

Wimshurst machine A machine used to

wind

generate static electricity and consisting of mica or glass discs that rotate in opposite directions. The discs have metal carriers, often made of tinfoil, on which charges are produced by induction. Wimshurst machines are used to demonstrate how electric charge works.

wind A current of air, especially a natural one that moves along or parallel to the ground.

wind-chill factor The temperature of motionless air that would make a person feel as cold as a particular combination of wind speed and air temperature. As the wind blows faster, heat is lost more quickly from exposed skin, making a person feel colder even though the air temperature remains the same.

windpipe *See* **trachea** (sense 1).

wind tunnel A chamber through which air can be forced at controlled speeds so its effect on an object, such as an aircraft, can be studied.

wing 1. One of a pair of specialized parts used for flying, as in birds, bats or insects. 2. A thin projection on certain plant seeds that are dispersed by the wind, such as the seeds of ash, elm and maple trees. 3. A part extending from the side of an aircraft, such as an aeroplane, having a curved upper surface that causes the pressure of air rushing over it to decrease, thereby providing lift.

winter The usually coldest season of the year, occurring between autumn and spring. In the Northern Hemisphere, it extends from the winter solstice to the vernal equinox.

winter solstice In the Northern Hemisphere, the solstice that occurs on 21 or 22 December, marking the beginning of winter and the day of the year with the shortest period of sunlight. *Compare* **summer solstice.**

wisdom tooth One of four molars, the last on each side of both jaws in humans, usually appearing in early adulthood.

wishbone The forked bone in front of the breastbone in most birds, consisting of the two collarbones partly fused together. It serves as a spring, capturing some of the energy during the downward stroke of the wings for release on the upward stroke.

wolfram *See* **tungsten.**

Wollaston, William Hyde 1766–1828. British chemist and physicist who discovered the elements palladium (1803) and rhodium (1804).

womb *See* **uterus.**

wood The tough, fibrous substance lying beneath the bark of trees and shrubs, consisting of the vascular tissue known as xylem. The main components of wood are cellulose and lignin.

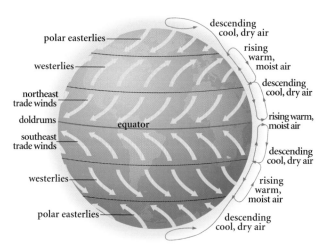

■ **wind**
Global wind patterns are determined by differences in atmospheric pressure resulting from the uneven heating of the Earth's surface by the sun. As warm, moist air rises along the equator, surface air moves in to take its place, creating the trade winds. Some of the air that descends at the two tropics moves away from the equator, creating the westerlies. The eastward and westward movement of these wind patterns is caused by the Earth's clockwise rotation.

Did You Know?

worms

Although there are many kinds of *worms,* both flat and round, we usually think of earthworms when someone mentions worms. Earthworms do not get a lot of respect these days, but Charles Darwin wrote an entire book explaining how important they are. "Long before [the plough] existed", he said, "the land was in fact regularly ploughed and still continues to be thus ploughed by earthworms. It may be doubted whether there are many other animals which have played so important a part in the history of the world". As they tunnel through the soil, earthworms open channels that allow in air and water. These channels improve drainage and make it easier for plants to send down roots. Earthworms eat and digest soil and the organic wastes it contains, and their own wastes provide nourishment for plants and other organisms. The tunnelling of earthworms brings up nutrients from deep soils to the surface. It is estimated that each year, earthworms in one acre of land move 18 or more tons of soil. We enjoy the fruits of this labour in the form of rich soil and healthy vegetation.

work The transfer of energy from one object to another, especially in order to make the second object move in a certain direction. Work is equal to the amount of force multiplied by the distance over which it is applied. If a force of 10 newtons, for example, is applied over a distance of 3 metres, the work done is equal to 30 newton metres (or 30 joules). *Compare* **energy, power.**

worker A member of a colony of social insects, such as ants or bees, that performs specialized work such as building the nest. Workers are usually sterile females.

World Wide Web The complete set of electronic documents stored on computers that are connected over the Internet and are made available by the process known as HTTP (Hypertext Transfer Protocol). The World Wide Web makes up a large part of the Internet. *See more at* **Internet.**

worm 1. Any of various invertebrate animals having a soft, long body that is round or flattened and usually lacks limbs. **2.** *Computer Science.* A destructive computer program that copies itself over and over again until it fills all of the storage space on a computer's hard drive or on a network.

Wu, Chien-Shiung 1912–1997. Chinese-born American physicist. Her research on electron emission in the decay of radioactive elements led her to disprove a long-held law of physics, called the law of symmetry, which held that the laws of nature are always symmetrical.

x-axis 1. The horizontal axis of a two-dimensional Cartesian coordinate system. 2. One of the three axes of a three-dimensional Cartesian coordinate system.

X-chromosome The sex chromosome that in human females is paired with another X-chromosome and in human males is paired with a Y-chromosome.

Xe The symbol for **xenon**.

xenon A colourless, odourless element that is a noble gas and occurs in extremely small amounts in the atmosphere. It was the first noble gas found to form compounds with other elements. Xenon is used to make lamps that make intense flashes, such as strobe lights and flashbulbs for photography. *Symbol* **Xe**. *Atomic number* 54. *See* **Periodic Table**, pages 260–261.

xenotransplantation Transplanting an organ from one species of animal into another completely different species. For example, scientists have tried to produce genetically engineered pigs that have human antigens on their heart cells. The idea is that these "human" pig hearts might be transplanted into humans who need a heart transplant. There are many problems with the technique.

xerophyte A plant that grows in an arid habitat; a desert plant. Cacti are xerophytes.

X-linked Relating to an inherited trait controlled by a gene on an X-chromosome.

X-ray 1. A high-energy stream of electromagnetic radiation having a wavelength shorter than that of ultraviolet light but longer than that of a gamma ray. X-rays are absorbed by many forms of matter, including body tissues, and are used in medicine and industry to produce images of internal structures. *See more at* **electromagnetic spectrum**. 2. An image of an internal structure, such as a body part, taken with X-rays.

X-ray astronomy The branch of astronomy dealing with the detection of objects in space by means of the X-rays they emit.

xylem A tissue in vascular plants that carries water and dissolved minerals up from the roots through the stem to the leaves and provides support for the softer tissues. Xylem consists of various elongated cells that function as tubes. In a tree trunk, the innermost part of the wood is dead but structurally strong xylem, while the outer part consists of living xylem, and beyond it, layers of cambium and phloem. *See more at* **cambium**, **photosynthesis**. *Compare* **phloem**.

■ **X-ray**
X-ray of a broken human leg

Y The symbol for **yttrium**.

Yalow, Rosalyn Sussman Born 1921. American physicist who developed the radioimmunoassay (RIA), an extremely sensitive technique for measuring very small quantities of substances such as hormones, enzymes and drugs in the blood.

yard A unit of length equal to 3 feet or 36 inches. *See table at* **measurement**.

y-axis 1. The vertical axis of a two-dimensional Cartesian coordinate system. 2. One of the three

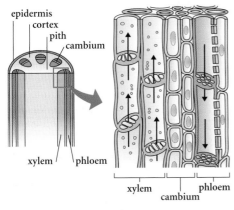

epidermis
cortex
pith
cambium

xylem | phloem

xylem | phloem
cambium

■ **xylem**

Xylem cells in the stem carry water from a plant's roots to its leaves. The phloem distributes food that is made in the plant's leaves to other parts of the plant. The cambium cells divide into either xylem or phloem cells. The cortex and pith, seen in the stem cross section, provide structural support.

axes of a three-dimensional Cartesian coordinate system.

Yb The symbol for **ytterbium.**

Y-chromosome The sex chromosome that is paired with an X-chromosome in human males.

yeast 1. Any of various one-celled fungi that can cause the fermentation of carbohydrates, producing carbon dioxide and alcohol. **2.** A commercial preparation in either compressed or powdered form that contains yeast cells. It is used to make bread dough rise.

yellow fever A life-threatening disease caused by a virus and characterized by a high temperature, jaundice and internal bleeding. Yellow fever occurs mainly in tropical regions of Africa and Latin America and is transmitted by mosquitoes.

Yersin, Alexandre Émile John 1863–1943. French bacteriologist. With Émile Roux, he isolated the toxin that causes the symptoms of diphtheria. Yersin later discovered the bacillus that causes bubonic plague and developed a serum to protect against it.

yew Any of various evergreen trees or shrubs that have short, flat needles and solitary seeds contained in a red, berry-like covering instead of a cone.

–yl A suffix used to form the chemical names of organic compounds when they are radicals (parts of larger compounds), such as *ethyl* and *phenyl.*

yolk The yellow internal part of the egg of a bird or reptile. The yolk is surrounded by the albumen and supplies food to the developing young.

yolk sac A sac attached to the gut of an embryo that encloses the yolk in bony fish, sharks, reptiles, mammals and birds. In most mammals, the yolk sac functions as part of the embryo's circulatory system before the placenta develops.

ytterbium A soft, silvery-white, easily shaped metallic element of the lanthanide series that occurs as seven stable isotopes. It is used as a radiation source for portable X-ray machines. *Symbol* **Yb.** *Atomic number* 70. *See* **Periodic Table,** pages 260–261.

yttrium A silvery, easily shaped metallic element that is found in the same ores as elements of the lanthanide series. Yttrium is used to strengthen magnesium and aluminium alloys, to provide the red colour in colour televisions, and as a component of various optical and electronic devices. *Symbol* **Y.** *Atomic number* 39. *See* **Periodic Table,** pages 260–261.

z-axis One of the three axes of a three-dimensional Cartesian coordinate system.

zebra mussel A small freshwater mussel, usually having a striped shell, that is native to Europe and Asia. Zebra mussels often clog water-supply pipes and reduce levels of plankton on which other water-dwelling life depend.

zenith The point on the celestial sphere that is directly above the observer.

zero The numerical symbol 0, representing a number that when added to another number leaves the original number unchanged. *See panel on* page 374.

zero gravity The condition under which a body appears to be weightless. This may occur in deep space, far from any other masses. It may also arise when an object like an aeroplane is in freefall, when the passengers inside it, accelerating zinc

downwards at the same rate as the aeroplane, no longer feel the floor pushing up on them, and so experience weightlessness. Since a spacecraft in orbit around the Earth is also in freefall, its occupants also experience weightlessness.

zinc A shiny, bluish-white metallic element that is brittle at room temperature but is easily shaped when heated. It is widely used in alloys such as brass and bronze, as a coating for iron and steel, and in various household objects. Zinc is essential to the growth of humans and animals. *Symbol* **Zn**. *Atomic number* 30. *See* **Periodic Table**, pages 260–261.

zincate A chemical compound containing the group ZnO_2.

zinc oxide A white or yellowish powdery compound, ZnO, used in paints and in various medicines and skin cosmetics.

zircon A brown, reddish to bluish, grey, green or colourless mineral that is a silicate of zirconium and occurs in igneous, metamorphic and sedimentary rocks, and especially in sand. The colourless varieties are valued as gems.

zirconium A shiny, greyish-white metallic element that occurs primarily in the mineral zircon. It is used to build nuclear reactors because it is not damaged from bombardment by neutrons and remains strong at high temperatures. Zirconium is also highly resistant to corrosion, making it a useful component of pumps, valves and alloys. *Symbol* **Zr**. *Atomic number* 40. *See* **Periodic Table**, pages 260–261.

Zn The symbol for **zinc**.

zodiac A band of the celestial sphere that extends about eight degrees both north and south of the ecliptic. It represents the path of the planets, the sun and the moon.

Did You Know?

zero

Zero is not nothing! It is a number that stands for nothing, and this is an important distinction. In many ways, zero is the most important of all numbers. When zero is added to or subtracted from a number, it leaves the number at its original value. Zero thus makes negative numbers possible. A negative number added to its positive counterpart always equals zero. Zero is also essential to representing many numbers, such as 203 and 1024. In these numbers zero serves as a placeholder in the system known as *positional notation*. Thus in 203, there are two hundreds, zero tens, and three ones. In other words, zero indicates that the value of the tens place is zero. In 1024, zero indicates that the value of the hundreds place is zero. When you think about it, if we didn't have zero, we wouldn't have hundreds, thousands or millions in our number system.

zoology The scientific study of animals, including their growth and structure.

zooplankton Plankton that consists of tiny animals, such as rotifers, copepods, krill and of microorganisms once classified as animals, such as dinoflagellates and other protozoans.

Zr The symbol for **zirconium**.

zygote The cell formed by the union of the nuclei of two reproductive cells (called gametes), especially a fertilized egg cell.

STUDY *Supplement*

Experiment Reports

The rules for scientific writing style (see section on **Science Essays**) apply for experiment reports, too.

Experiment reports use the following format: **Title – Abstract – Introduction – Materials and Methods – Results – Discussion – References**. Each section should be preceded by the appropriate heading which is emphasized in some way (bold, underlined or capitalized), apart from the title, which is itself emphasized.

Title

The title should be clear, informative and as specific as possible, so that the reader can see at a glance what the report is about. Make sure you include:

- the name of the substance, organism, situation etc being studied
- the aim of the experiment

Abstract

An abstract is an at-a-glance summary for people who may not wish to read the whole report. It is usually only required at university level and beyond. As it is a summary, it is written last of all. The abstract should be short (no more than one paragraph) and not go into detail. The reader must be able to understand it without having to refer to anything else. It usually includes:

- a description of the topic
- a summary of the methods used
- a summary of the results
- and most importantly, a summary of the main conclusion

Introduction

In the introduction you should include:

- how the experiment is relevant to your broad topic of study
- what the aim of the experiment is. If the aim is to test a hypothesis, then state the hypothesis, the thinking behind it and the predictions that you are testing.
- any relevant assumptions you are making. For example, *In investigating the acceleration due to gravity of a falling ball, I shall assume that air resistance is negligible.*
- any relevant background information on the topic. Cite and briefly discuss any important experiments carried out by others.

Materials and Methods

In this section you should describe what you actually did in the experiment without referring to the results. You need to write clearly and in detail. It should be possible for someone else to repeat the experiment simply from reading your description. Be sure to include information on:

- the materials and equipment you used
- how you used the materials
- sizes, measurements, concentrations etc

- any special reasons why you chose particular materials or methods
- any statistical methods you used to analyse the data
- the location and date, if it is a field study

Take care to:

- give only necessary details. For example, do not give the size of a beaker unless it is absolutely vital to an understanding of the experiment.
- avoid mentioning irrelevant matters such as how to clean up after the experiment or details specific to your circumstances such as "the assignment that our class was given".
- explain the reasons why you carried out a particular action. For example, you might write: *In order to test whether..., I...*
- show how you made the experiment as accurate as possible. For example, an unexpected result may have prompted you to take extra readings.
- use the first person (*I, we*) or the third person (*he, she, it, they*). Using the second person (*you*) sounds as though you are giving instructions to the reader. You can also use the passive, eg *a sample was taken* instead of *we took a sample*.
- write in the past tense. A report describes what you have actually done.

Results

In this section you should give the results of the experiment without referring to their significance regarding the aim of the experiment. Bear in mind the following:

- You must describe the main trends of your results. Refer in your description to the appropriate figures (diagrams, graphs, charts etc) and/or tables in the order in which they appear in the report.
- Figures and tables must be given a number followed by a title. They should be numbered separately; so, for example, if you had two figures and one table, they would be presented as: *Figure 1, Figure 2*, and *Table 1*. Make sure that the title is clear and informative, enabling the reader to understand the figure or table on its own without having to read through the report. Position the number and title at the bottom of a figure and at the top of a table. Remember to give a scale for each figure, if appropriate. Each graph axis must be labelled with the measured variable and its unit (for example, *length/m*).
- Do not repeat data in the text that you have already given in a figure or table. Instead refer in the text to the figure or table by its number; for example, either *Figure 1 shows that...* or *...as shown in Figure 1* or *...is shown to fluctuate (fig.1)*.
- If you are able to quantify the errors associated with the collection of your data, then this information should appear on your graphs as error bars, and in your tables as, for example, *length = 25cm (± 0.5)*.
- If you are making a statistical analysis, you must mention the level at which the trends were statistically significant.

Discussion

This section splits into two distinct elements – **Analysis** and **Evaluation**.

Analysis

Here you need to consider the evidence and analyse the results with regard to the aim of the experiment as stated in the Introduction. You should:

● explain the patterns and relationships exhibited by your results.

● explain to what extent the results support your hypothesis and/or predictions.

You may wish to:

● produce further figures, resulting from your analysis, that show the relationship between variables more clearly.

Evaluation

In this section you need to evaluate your experiment and discuss the soundness of the conclusions you have reached. You need to:

● discuss how your assumptions and analysis of errors might have an effect on your interpretation of the results.

● identify any anomalous results and give reasons for accepting or rejecting them.

● take into account alternative interpretations of your results which might be equally valid. What hypothesis or hypotheses other than your own might account for the results you obtained?

● explain to what extent the results have contributed towards an understanding of your broad topic of study.

● make recommendations, if any, for improved methods or further experiments which might help to resolve remaining difficulties in achieving the aim of the experiment or testing the hypothesis.

Science Essays

The basic principles of writing English essays apply to science essays too. Information and tips on good essay writing is provided in *Chambers Study Dictionary*.

In addition, scientific writing style has some rules of its own:

- Be particularly clear and concise.
- If you are writing about an organism, give the scientific name of that organism. If it also has a widely used common name, give both the scientific and the common names the first time you mention the organism, and afterwards give just the common name. Scientific names should be given in italics. The genus name begins with a capital letter and the species element begins with a small letter; for example, *Homo sapiens*. Once the scientific name has been given in this way, you may then abbreviate the genus name; for example, *H. sapiens*. Remember that scientific names behave like proper nouns: they are not preceded by the articles *the* or *a*; for example, *It has long been thought that Homo sapiens...*
- Make sure that any figures or tables you give follow the guidelines set out under **Results** in **Experiment Reports**, above.
- If you refer to a published work in the main body of your essay, give a paraphrase of the relevant information rather than an exact quotation. The precise words do not matter (as they might do in a literature essay); what matters is that you show you understand the material by presenting it in your own words.
- Use metric measurements always, and give the appropriate units in the standard abbreviations.
- Numbers below ten should be written out in words unless they are part of a measurement (for example, *4g* or *5cm*)
- Avoid starting sentences with a number. Either write out the number in words or restructure the sentence. So, for example, a sentence beginning *25 of those questioned said that...* could be rewritten as *Twenty-five of those questioned said that...* or *Of those questioned, 25 said that...*
- Take care to distinguish between singular and plural forms of nouns. Scientific terminology relies heavily on Latin-based words, in which the singular form is often shown by the ending *-us, -a, -um* or *-is* and the plural form by the ending *-i, -ae, -a* or *-es*. For example, *datum* is singular and *data* is plural. Sometimes the same form is used for both singular and plural; for example, *species*.

Theories

Big Bang Theory

A theory for the evolution of the universe which postulates that all matter and energy were once concentrated into an unimaginably dense state, from which it has been expanding after a gigantic explosion between 13 and 20 billion years ago. This explains why galaxies are seen to be moving away from each other. The main evidence in support of the theory is the cosmic background radiation (a relic of the early hot phase in the Big Bang universe) and the redshift of galaxies (in which the wavelength of light from galaxies is shifted closer to the red end of the spectrum the further away the galaxies are).

Chaos Theory

The theory that some systems, though governed by simple laws, are highly sensitive to starting conditions, which makes their behaviour extremely difficult to predict. Examples of chaotic systems are the weather and economics.

Collision Theory

A theory which explains how chemical reactions occur and which predicts the rate of reaction. For a reaction to take place the atoms in the reactants have to collide, which leads to the breaking and formation of bonds and thus to the creation of the product of the reaction. However, not all collisions lead to chemical change. If the reactants are made more concentrated and the temperature is raised, more collisions are brought about, increasing the rate of reaction.

Continental Drift

A theory put forward in 1912 to explain the distribution of the continents and oceans and the structural, geological and physical similarities between continents. The continents were believed to have been formed by the break-up of a single land mass hundreds of millions of years ago and to have then drifted apart. However, such movements could only be explained when plate tectonics began to be studied in the 1960s.

Darwinian Theory, Darwinism

See **Natural Selection**

Gaia Hypothesis

The theory that the Earth functions as a self-regulating living entity within the solar system. According to James Lovelock, who put forward the hypothesis in 1972, the Earth's living matter, air, oceans, and land surface form a complex system which can be seen as a single organism and which has the capacity to keep our planet a fit place for life.

Kinetic Theory

A theory which attempts to account for the physical properties of matter, especially gases, in terms of the movement of the atoms or molecules of which they are composed. In the simplest form of the theory, gas molecules are conceived as elastic spheres whose bombardment of the walls of the containing vessel causes the pressure exerted by the gas.

Lamarckism

One of the earliest theories of evolution, now discredited, which proposed that characteristics acquired during the lifetime of an organism could be transmitted from parent to offspring.

Theories

Natural Selection

Evolutionary theory, first proposed by Charles Darwin and Alfred Russel Wallace in 1858, which postulates the survival of those organisms that are best adapted to their environment. The characteristics which favour survival arise as random variations due to mutation and are then inherited.

Neo-Darwinism

The modern version of Darwin's theory of evolution by natural selection, incorporating the discoveries of modern genetics and laying particular emphasis on genetic mutations leading to variations in population.

Plate Tectonics

A geological theory, formulated in the 1960s, according to which the Earth's crust is composed of a small number of large plates of solid rock whose movements in relation to each other are responsible for continental drift, earthquake zones and volcanoes.

Quantum Mechanics

A theory that developed from the quantum theory and which is used in the interpretation of the behaviour of particles, especially subatomic ones.

Quantum Theory

A theory developed by Max Planck (1858–1947) and based on the principle that there is a minimum indivisible amount (a quantum) of certain physical properties, such as momentum, energy and electromagnetic radiation, that can exist. In particular, the theory postulates that the frequency of electromagnetic radiation is proportional to the energy associated with these quanta.

Relativity

Two theories of motion – Special Theory of Relativity (1905) and General Theory of Relativity (1916) – developed by Albert Einstein. They postulate that the speed of light in vacuo, c, is a fundamental constant, and go on to suggest that measurement of space, time and other physical properties is affected by the presence of mass and the position and motion of the observer.

Steady-State Theory

The theory that the universe has always existed and that it is constantly expanding and creating matter. The steady-state theory is now generally discredited and the Big Bang theory preferred.

String Theory

A theory in fundamental physics that attempts to construct a model of elementary particles from one-dimensional entities rather than the zero-dimensional "points" of conventional particle physics.

Unified Field Theory or Grand Unified Theory

The physicist's holy grail: a theory which simultaneously describes the four forces of nature (strong nuclear, weak nuclear, electromagnetic, and gravitational) as one. No such theory has yet been found.

General Prefixes and Suffixes

a-	without, opposite	hetero-	different
ab-	away from, opposite	hist(o)-	tissue
ad-	at, near	homo-	same
aer(o)-	air	hydr(o)-	water; hydrogen
anti-	against	hyper-	over; excessive
arthr(o)-	joint	hypo-	below; deficient
atmo-	vapour	inter-	between
auto-	self	intra-	within
bacteri(o)-	bacteria	iso-	equal; isomer
bi-	two	kary(o)-	nucleus
bi(o)-	life	leuc(o)-, leuk(o)-	white
cary(o)-	nucleus	-logy	study
chlor(o)-	green; chlorine	-lysis	loosening
chrom(o)-	colour; chromium	macr(o)-	large
chromat(o)-	colour; chromatin	mes(o)-	middle
-cide	killer	meta-	change; after
com-, con-	together, with	-meter	measuring device
-cyte	cell	micr(o)-	small
cyto-	cell	mon(o)-	one, single
-derm	skin	morph(o)-	form
di-	double	multi-	many
ecto-	outside, outer	myc(o)-	fungus
end(o)-	inside, inner	necr(o)-	death, corpse
entomo-	insect	neur(o)-	nerve
epi-	on, over	ocul(o)-	eye
-escent	becoming	olig(o)-	few
eu-	good, pleasant	-oma	tumour
exo-	outside, outer	omni-	all
gastr(o)-	stomach	oo-	egg, ovum
-gen	producing	oste(o)-	bone
geo-	earth	ovi-, ovo-	egg, ovum
-graphy	description	p(a)ed(o)-	child
gymno-	bare, naked	pal(a)e(o)-	old, ancient
hal(o)-	salt; halogen	peri-	around
h(a)em(o)-, h(a)ema-,		phag(o)-,	
h(a)emat(o)-	blood	-phage	eating, eater
hemi-	half	-phore	bearer

General Prefixes and Suffixes

photo-	light	sub-	under
-phyl(l)	leaf	syn-	together
phyt(o)-, -phyte	plant	-taxis, -taxy	movement to or from
pleur(o)-	side; pleura	tel(e)-	distant
-pod	feet	tel(o)-	end
poly-	many	therm(o)-	heat
pseudo-	false	trans-	across
pro-	before	tri-	three
rhiz(o)-	root	trich(o)-	hair
-scope	viewing instrument	troph(o)-, -trophy	nourishment
-scopy	viewing	-tropism, -tropy	turning to
-sperm	seed	uni-	one
sperm(o)-,		xer(o)-	dry
spermat(o)-	sperm; seed	zo(o)-	animal
-stat	device maintaining constancy		

SI Prefixes

Factor	Prefix	Symbol	Factor	Prefix	Symbol
10^{18}	exa-	E	10^{-1}	deci-	d
10^{15}	peta-	P	10^{-2}	centi-	c
10^{12}	tera-	T	10^{-3}	milli-	m
10^{9}	giga-	G	10^{-6}	micro-	μ
10^{6}	mega-	M	10^{-9}	nano-	n
10^{3}	kilo-	k	10^{-12}	pico-	p
10^{2}	hecto-	h	10^{-15}	femto-	f
10^{1}	deca-	da	10^{-18}	atto-	a

Using the Internet for Research

Where to Search

To begin your search through the Web, you have to decide which of the various search tools will best suit your purpose. There are three basic types of tool:

Search engine

A search engine will search its database of Web pages for a specific word and display a list of websites containing it. The database is compiled by a program which trawls the Web on the lookout for new sites. A search engine is therefore very comprehensive and useful for finding something specific and/or obscure.

Here are the addresses of some popular search engines:

- AltaVista – www.av.com
- Go – www.go.com
- Fast Search – www.alltheweb.com
- Google – www.google.com
- Lycos – www.lycos.com

These are just a few of the many available. You might want to try out some others as well (see **Recommended Websites** on page 15) and discover which you prefer.

Some search engines (for example, AltaVista and Google) also offer the facilities of a directory.

Directory

A directory is a selection of websites arranged according to subject. Unlike a search engine, the database of a directory is created by people not programs; consequently, you will find fewer sites featured. However, they will have been selected by the directory provider for their relevance and often a review of each site will help you to make your choice.

The sites in a directory are listed according to a branching system, starting with a general subject and branching into specific categories which then sub-branch into even more specific categories. This means that you can quickly find sites on a topic that interests you as well as seeing related sites on similar topics. You can also save time by first narrowing down your search to a particular category and then using the search engine within that category alone.

Here are the addresses of some directories:

- Yahoo – www.yahoo.com
- About.com – www.about.com
- Open Directory – http://dmoz.org

There are also more specialized directories which focus on particular subjects, some of them obscure. You can find these directories by looking in one of the following specialized directory guides:

- Directory Guide – www.directoryguide.com
- Gogettem – www.gogettem.com

Some specialized directories are called libraries. These are good for finding in-depth research material on specific subjects. Online libraries are generally compiled by academics, and so are often reliable and authoritative. Try:

- WWW Virtual Library – www.vlib.org

Bot

A bot (short for robot) collects and compares up-to-date information from a number of search engines and directories, carrying out so-called metasearches.

- MetaCrawler – www.metacrawler.com
- Search.com – www.search.com

Tip

The type of organization that maintains a website can be seen from the sequence of letters in its address. For example, *ac* or *edu* indicates that the site belongs to a university or college; *com* or *co* indicates a commercial enterprise; *gov* indicates a government department; *net* indicates a network provider; and *org* indicates a non-commercial organization.

How to Search

You might want to try searching first of all by using none of the above tools, but by simply guessing an address. This often works if you want general information about a company, organization or individual. Suppose you wanted information on a company named Huggle Helicopters plc. You could try typing www.hugglehelicopters.com (or www.hugglehelicopters.co.uk if it is a UK firm) or simply www.huggle.com into the address bar (called the location field in Netscape Navigator). If this does not produce a satisfactory result – perhaps because the company has an address that is nothing like its name or because it does not actually have a website – you will have to use a search tool.

Whether you are using a search engine, a directory or a bot, the searching process is similar. You type a keyword or keywords into the box provided and press return. You can also type in various signs and symbols which will help you to narrow down your search. The most important of these are:

- **AND** type this between two words and the search is restricted to sites containing both words
- **OR** type this between two words and the search is restricted to sites that contain either one word or the other, or both
- **NOT** type this in front of a word and the search is restricted to sites that do not contain that word
- **NEAR** type this between two words and the search is restricted to sites where the two words are fairly close (say within 20 words of each other)
- **+** use this in the same way as AND; it can also be used in front of a so-called stop word (a common word like "the", "of", "how" etc that is normally ignored in the search, or a single letter such as the initial in a name) and the stop word will then be included in the search
- **–** (minus sign) use this in the same way as NOT
- **" "** put quotation marks around a phrase and the search is restricted to sites containing exactly that phrase rather than the individual words
- **( )** use brackets instead of quotation marks in some search tools

So, for example, typing in **Issac Newton AND biography OR discoveries** will bring up sites about Issac Newton's life and sites about his discoveries, whereas typing in **Issac Newton AND biography AND discoveries** will only yield sites mentioning his life and his discoveries. However, the exact method of searching as well as the devices used can vary from search tool to search tool (for example, some use the signs **+** and **–** and some do not; some automatically include every word in the search, making **AND** and **NOT** redundant) so it is worth spending a few a minutes reading the instructions given in each site under *Help* or *Search tips* or *Refine your search* or similar. You will usually also be given the option of an advanced search, which will allow you to restrict your search even more.

Tips on Searching

- Speed up your search by restricting your search to the UK Web (this is usually an option in search engines). On the other hand, if you cannot find what you want it may be because you are restricting your search to the UK Web instead of taking advantage of the whole Web.

- Speed up your search by restricting it, if appropriate, to one language.

- If you are unsuccessful with one search engine, try a different one. Some engines search more Web pages than others or have a different database.

- If one keyword doesn't yield the result you want, try a different one related to the same subject.

- If the links are slow, either be patient or try later when the system will hopefully not be so busy. It is a good idea to avoid the peak times in the USA. Mornings are a good time for UK users.

- If you do not want pictures on websites, then switch to text only. It will make it faster to download pages. To switch off pictures in Microsoft Internet Explorer, click on Tools, then Internet Options, then Advanced, then Show Pictures.

- Add sites that you like to your favourites menu (in Internet Explorer) or bookmark them (in Netscape Navigator), so that you can easily return to them by clicking on them.

- Save time and money by collecting Web pages so that you can read them later. Allow each page to download fully. It will then be saved as a temporary file which you can access via the History menu when offline.

- Print out or save to disk any Web pages you are really interested in.

A few points to remember:

- If you have a lot of searching to do you need to be patient. The slowness of some sites to download can sometimes test your patience.

- If you need information that is up to date, you are more likely to find it online than in a library of books that were printed years ago. However, not all websites are regularly updated, so some caution is required.

- There is no guarantee that the information in a site is correct. Of course, errors occur in printed works, too, but are less likely because the works go through an editing and proofreading process. It is therefore advisable to use reliable sites provided by those who have reputations to maintain: organizations, companies, universities and academics.

- Depending on the contract you have with your Internet service provider and telephone company, using the Web can cost money every time you log on, particularly if you use it during the daytime.

Recommended Websites

Some Useful ICT Websites

www.searchengineguide.com – a guide to search engines
http://foldoc.doc.ic.ac.uk/foldoc – dictionary of computing
www.whatis.com – IT encyclopedia
www.pceverything.co.uk – all about PCs
www.computerhistory.org – the Computer Museum History Center

Some Useful Science Websites

www.nature.com – advanced but very interesting site of the science magazine
www.sciseek.com – a science search engine with many links
www.newscientist.com – the science magazine online
www.chemicalelements.com – facts about all the elements
www.msim.org.uk – the Museum of Science and Industry in Manchester
www.nhm.ac.uk – the Natural History Museum
www.gsc.org.uk – the Glasgow Science Centre
www.exploratorium.edu/science-explorer/ – fun science activities from a San Francisco museum
www.star.le.ac.uk/edu/index.html – lots of information about space and astronomy
http://seds.lpl.arizona.edu/billa/tnp – detailed information on the solar system

Some Useful Geography Websites

www.georesources.co.uk – links geared towards school work
www.bbc.co.uk/education/gcsebitesize/geography
www.internetgeography.co.uk
www.pavilion.co.uk/dwakefield – resources for the curriculum, plus links
www.cia.gov/cia/publications/factbook – World Factbook: information on all countries
www.geographical.co.uk – Geographical Magazine site
www.nationalgeographic.com – National Geographic magazine site
www.rgs.org – Royal Geographic Society

Some Useful Mathematics Websites

www.bbc.co.uk/education/gcsebitesize/maths – revision tips and links
www.mathforum.org – US site with lots of information, including a "Dr Math" section

Arttoday.com: **ammonite, amphibian (frog), amphibian (axolotl), antenna (beetle), Archimedes, badlands, barnacle, bee, blowhole, burl, camouflage, CAT scan, chrysalis, colony, comet, compound eye, Copernicus, coral reef (aerial view), coral reef (undersea view), corrosion, crater (Earth), crater (moon), Darwin, desert, drought, dune (live), dune (fossilized), Einstein, epiphyte, erosion, fossil, Franklin, galaxy, Galileo, geodesic dome, geothermal, glacier, graft, Herschel, iceberg, iguana, isomer, jellyfish, Jenner, Jupiter, Komodo dragon, lagoon, larva, leaf (broad leaf), leaf (grass), leaf (needle), leaf (spine), lichen, mammoth, manatee, Mars, Mendel, mesa, mimicry, moult, nebula, newt, Newton, octopus, pahoehoe, Pasteur, peninsula, Petri dish, platypus, pollen, Priestley, pterodactyl, pyrite, quartz, radial symmetry, rock types (igneous), rock types (metamorphic), rock types (sedimentary), sandbar, Saturn, sea anemone, sessile, shale, smog, solar system (sun), solar system (Mercury), solar system (Earth), solar system (Mars), solar system (Jupiter), solar system (Saturn), sponge, stalactite, stratification, strip mine, tornado, tundra, Venus flytrap, vortex, wetland, X-ray**

Chambers Harrap Publishers: **aerosol, cartilage, corona, DNA, lightning, trilobite**

Artwork sourced via Houghton Mifflin Company:

Academy Artworks **abscissa, acute angle, aerodynamic, aphelion, asymptote (both diagrams), atmosphere, atoll, complementary angles, conic projection, exterior angle, hypotenuse, interior angle, Klein bottle, nerve cell, perihelion, solenoid, sun, turbine (both diagrams), Van de Graaff generator**

Carlyn Iverson **adrenal gland, antibody, bone, brain, circulatory system, digestive tract, ear, eye, hair, heart, intestine, joint, kidney, meiosis, mitosis, pancreas,** **respiratory system, RNA, shortsightedness, skeleton (all diagrams), spinal cord, taste bud, thyroid gland, translation, urinary tract**

Cathy Hawkes **Periodic Table of the Elements**

Corbis **neon**/John Bartholomew

David Mackay Ballard **moon, pollution**

Elizabeth Morales **abdomen, artiodactyl, carbon cycle, coelacanth, constellation, elytron, enzyme, euglena, evaporation, Fahrenheit, fin, food chain, gill, inflorescence, metamorphosis, mitochondrion, nitrogen cycle, rhizome, tadpole, water cycle, xylem**

Fundamental Photographs **dispersion**/Richard Megna

Jerry Malone **celestial sphere, equator, homolosine projection, International Date Line, longitude, Mercator projection, periscope, refraction, sinusoidal projection, tooth, tsunami**

Matthew Pippin **piston**

Patrice Rossi Calkin **volcano**

Photo Researchers, Inc. **ozone**/NOAA/SPL

Precision Graphics **aneroid barometer, anticline, atherosclerosis, atom (all diagrams), bell curve, cathode-ray tube, cell (animal cell), cell (plant cell), centripetal force, circuit, cloud, colour (all diagrams), cone (eye), convection, cyclotron, desalinization, diode, eclipse, electromagnetic spectrum, fission (both diagrams), fluorescent lamp, flower (all diagrams), fulcrum, geological time, greenhouse effect (both diagrams), incandescent lamp, induction, internal combustion engine, laser, leaf (sorghum), leaf (sweetgum), manometer, Möbius strip, nuclear reactor, oscillation, parallax, photosynthesis (both diagrams), radiation, solar cell, sonar, star,** **taxonomy, tectonic boundaries, telescope (both diagrams), turbojet, wind**

Robin Storesund **aliphatic, aromatic, artesian well, benzene ring, bond (all diagrams), circle, cone (maths), continental shelf, covalent bond, crystal (all diagrams), cylinder, earthquake, ellipse, equilateral, equinox, fault (all diagrams), hexagon, hyperbola, isosceles, octagon, organic compounds (all diagrams), osmosis, parabola, parallelogram, pentagon, Ptolemaic system, rectangle, rhombus, saturated, scalene, sphere, time zone, transformer, trapezium, triangle, trigonometric function, unsaturated, Venn diagram, wave (all diagrams)**

Rolin Graphics, Inc **germination**

School Division, Houghton Mifflin Company **abacus, amber, geode**

Thom Gillis **Earth, North Pole, South Pole**

UG/GGS Information Services **acoustics, battery, biome, capacitor, Doppler effect, front, gear (all diagrams), graph, holography, hurricane, hydroelectric, inheritance, microwave, rainforest, satellite**

Wendy Smith **fir**

Science Photo Library: **acid rain**/Adam Hart-Davis, **amoeba**/Astrid and Hanns-Frieder Michler, **annelid**/Kjell B. Sandved, **aurora borealis**/Pekka Parviainen, **bacterium (sphere)**/Francis Leroy, Biocosmos, **bacterium (rod)**/Dr Gary Gaugler, **bacterium (spiral)**/Eye of Science, **cell (guard cell)**/Eye of Science, **cell (nerve cell)**/David Becker, **cell (red blood cell)**/Andrew Syred, **fractal**/Alfred Pasieka, **hydra**/Science Pictures Limited, **meniscus**/Sinclair Stammers, **Milky Way**/Allan Morton/Dennis Milon, **paramecium**/Dr David Patterson, **solar system (Neptune)**/Space Telescope Science Institute/NASA, **solar system (Pluto)**/NASA, **solar system (Uranus)**/NASA, **solar system (Venus)**/NASA